DICTIONARY
OF
AMERICAN
MILITARY
BIOGRAPHY

DICTIONARY
OF
AMERICAN
MILITARY
BIOGRAPHY

Volume III
Q–Z

ROGER J. SPILLER
Editor
JOSEPH G. DAWSON III
Associate Editor
T. HARRY WILLIAMS
Consulting Editor

Greenwood Press
Westport, Connecticut • London, England

Library of Congress Cataloging in Publication Data

Main entry under title:

Dictionary of American military biography.

   Includes index.
   Contents: v. 1. Creighton W. Abrams—Leslie R.
Groves—v. 2. Henry W. Halleck—Israel Putnam—
v. 3. John A. Quitman—Elmo R. Zumwalt, Jr.
   1. United States—Armed Forces—Biography. 2. United
States—Biography.   I. Spiller, Roger J.   II. Dawson,
Joseph G., 1945-   .
U52.D53   1984   355'.0092'2 [B]   83-12674
ISBN 0-313-21433-6 (lib. bdg. : set)
ISBN 0-313-24161-9 (lib. bdg. : v. 1)
ISBN 0-313-24162-7 (lib. bdg. : v. 2)
ISBN 0-313-24399-9 (lib. bdg. : v. 3)

Library of Congress Catalog Card Number: 83-12674
ISBN 0-313-21433-6 (lib. bdg. : set)

First published in 1984

Greenwood Press
A division of Congressional Information Service, Inc.
88 Post Road West, Westport, Connecticut 06881

Printed in the United States of America

10 9 8 7 6 5 4 3 2 1

Contents

Q

QUITMAN, John Anthony (b. Rhinebeck, N.Y., September 1, 1798; d. Natchez, Miss., July 17, 1858), general in the Mexican War. Quitman has long been regarded as one of the most gallant and flamboyant commanders in that war.

John Anthony Quitman was the third son of Frederick Henry and Anna Elizabeth (Hueck) Quitman. His father was a Lutheran minister who educated his son with the help of private tutors and intended for him to enter the ministry. But the young Quitman decided to go into teaching, being hired in 1816 by Hartwick Academy in Otsego County, New York, and two years later by Mount Airy College in Germantown, Pennsylvania, where he taught English. It was also while there that he decided to study for a career in law. So in the autumn of 1819 he went to Ohio, settling first in Chillicothe and later in the little town of Delaware. While in Ohio, he began his legal studies and was admitted to the bar. Quitman was soon thinking about another move, however, this time to the South. Leaving in November 1821, he traveled down to Natchez, Mississippi.

In Natchez he rose rapidly in the legal profession and quickly became prominent there. In December 1824 he married Eliza Turner, the only daughter of a very wealthy planter. Through this marriage, Quitman acquired a large estate, as well as status, power, and prestige. Quitman became infatuated with his new life-style; he greatly admired the planter aristocrats and believed that the slaves were the "happiest people I have ever seen." Likewise, Quitman engaged in an active political life. In 1827 he won a seat in the state legislature, and while serving there helped to bring about many reforms in the judicial system. He also did an outstanding job in preparing a militia system for the state. In addition, he was chancellor of the superior court from 1828 to 1834, a delegate to the constitutional convention of 1832, and in 1835 was elected president of the State Senate. As to political philosophy during this period, Quitman was known to be a strong advocate of states' rights.

Always interested in military affairs, Quitman got involved in the struggle for

Texas independence. He recruited and commanded a company known as the "Fencibles," and in 1836, after the fall of the Alamo, they headed for Texas. Although his outfit took no real part in the fighting, they probably did render some beneficial service in helping to protect some of the refugees fleeing from the Mexican leader Santa Anna. After returning from Texas, Quitman was commissioned by the governor as a brigadier general of the Mississippi militia. He took this appointment very seriously and worked hard at forming volunteer companies and instilling a high degree of discipline in his men. These efforts were rewarded when, in 1841, he was elected major general of the state's militia. Later, in 1845, he was an unsuccessful candidate for the U.S. Senate. Being quite bitter over this defeat, as well as deeply saddened by the death of four of his children, he retired more into private life for a time.

When war was declared against Mexico in 1846, Quitman offered his services to the president. However, President James K. Polk took no action on the matter because he did not especially like Quitman. But many prominent politicians, including John Caldwell Calhoun,* interceded in his behalf, and finally he was commissioned as brigadier general of volunteers. He then proceeded down to Camargo in northern Mexico to join the army of General Zachary Taylor.* Quitman first gained distinction at the Battle of Monterrey during September 1846. In that fiercely contested three-day battle, Taylor had decided to divide his force. He ordered the units under General William Jenkins Worth to attack to the north and west of the town, while other units, including Quitman's, attacked the eastern edge. Quitman's brigade played a prominent role in capturing an important enemy stronghold called Fort Teneria. The general and his men displayed extraordinary gallantry; the assault had been very costly, and Quitman even had his horse killed under him. Following the fort's capture, Quitman took an active part in entering the city itself, an effort that resulted in furious street-to-street and house-to-house fighting. Soon after the city's surrender, Quitman was one of those officers who was removed from Taylor and sent to serve under General Winfield Scott.*

After joining Scott and seeing some action at Vera Cruz and Alvarado, Quitman played a very conspicuous role during the war's final campaign in the battles around Mexico City. For example, Quitman won great fame at Chapultepec on September 13, 1847. His division charged its way up the side of a steep hill and took the castle fortress on its summit by assault, thus opening the way to the city of Mexico. Later that same day, in a bold bid for glory and renown, Quitman decided to send his forces down the causeway leading to the Belen Gate. Although General Scott repeatedly sent orders urging him to be cautious and informing him that the Belen causeway was intended only as a feint, Quitman and his staff later said they never received the orders. Whatever the case, in one of the most brilliant achievements of the war, Quitman led his troops down the causeway and into desperate fighting. At one point, to urge his men onward, the always flamboyant Quitman seized a rifle, tied a red handkerchief to it, and waved it over his head. By nightfall they had reached the Belen Gate, and when Scott suggested a temporary withdrawal, Quitman rejected the advice and declared: "The capital is mine, my brave fellows have conquered it, and by God, they shall have it!" At dawn, Quitman led his men into the city, raised the American flag, and thus became the first troops to enter the enemy capital. Although Scott was somewhat disgusted that the impetuous Quitman had grabbed most of the glory, he still appointed him to be the civil and military governor of the city. Upon his return to Mississippi shortly after the war, he was elected governor of that state, got involved in the filibustering expeditions that were attempting to liberate Cuba in order to annex it to the United States, and ended his career by serving in Congress from 1855 until his death three years later.

John Quitman's military career is of significance for several reasons. First of all, he played a big part in the conquest of Mexico City, which was the decisive military campaign of the war. Quitman performed brilliantly in this first successful invasion of a foreign country by the American Army. In spite of great obstacles and handicaps, Quitman and several other generals had fought superbly.

Second, Quitman was a good representative of the great enthusiasm found in the South for the Mexican War. Although Northern by birth, Quitman loved his adopted region and soon became Southern to the core. His tremendous enthusiasm for military things exemplifies what a number of historians have described as a "Southern military tradition." For instance, in a letter written just before he left for Mexico, Quitman states: "I have been an active officer in the militia more than twenty years, and I feel a deep interest in preserving the military reputation Mississippi acquired in former wars."

Likewise, Quitman also very well represents the often bitter hostility between regulars and volunteers. Officers of the Regular Army were often very critical of civilian and "political generals" like Quitman. On the other hand, Quitman and other volunteer officers often were very contemptuous of the West Pointers. They disliked all the frontline positions being given to regulars. For example, it was Quitman's firm opinion that the volunteers never got enough credit for what they did. And it is significant that just before Monterrey, Quitman said to his troops: "The eyes of the veteran officers of the army and the whole of the regulars will be fixed upon you.... Prove to them... that American volunteers are as admirable for their discipline and self-restraint as for their courage."

In regard to Quitman's own military abilities, the opinions vary. General Taylor thought Quitman was "unreliable, of mediocre ability, and afflicted with vanity." Scott was also somewhat critical of him at Mexico City for his insistence upon pushing an attack that was designed only as a feint, and in the process perhaps costing his division many unnecessary casualties in a thirst for glory. Another officer once commented that Quitman was a "weak, vain, ignorant, ambitious" man who was held in "supreme contempt" by practically all the officers in his command. But this rather negative appraisal of Quitman is more than balanced by the opinions of various other observers. Although at times he was too much the "Mississippi Hotspur," he was still probably the best of the volunteer generals. A fellow officer once wrote this about Quitman: "I never witnessed so much chivalrous heroism, united with so much concern for his men, and with so much cool intellectual battle wisdom." And finally, perhaps the best summation of all was given in 1860 by Major General William O. Butler when he said of John Quitman: "He was a military man by nature."

BIBLIOGRAPHY

Bauer, K. Jack. *The Mexican War, 1846–1848*. New York: Macmillan Company, 1974.
Claiborne, J.F.H. *Life and Correspondence of John A. Quitman*. 2 vols. New York: Harper and Brothers, 1860.
Elliott, Charles Winslow. *Winfield Scott: The Soldier and the Man*. New York: Macmillan Company, 1937.
Hamilton, Holman. *Zachary Taylor: Soldier of the Republic*. Indianapolis, Ind.: Bobbs-Merrill, 1941.
Singletary, Otis A. *The Mexican War*. Chicago: University of Chicago Press, 1960.

J. MICHAEL QUILL

R

RADFORD, Arthur William (b. Chicago, Ill., February 27, 1896; d. Bethesda Naval Hospital, Bethesda, Md., August 17, 1973), naval officer. Radford was associated with the "admirals' lobby" in 1949 but later served as chairman of the Joint Chiefs of Staff (1953–1957).

Arthur William Radford served as a commissioned officer in the U.S. Navy for forty-one years, from 1916 to 1957. His career spanned a dynamic period in American history during which time the United States fought three major wars and grew to be the strongest nation in the world politically, industrially, and militarily. Radford was graduated from the U.S. Naval Academy in 1916 and commissioned ensign. He served in the battleship *South Carolina* until the end of World War I.

A lieutenant in 1920, Radford became a naval aviator, and for three years (1921–1923) he was assigned to the newly created Bureau of Aeronautics in the Navy Department. Subsequently, he served with aviation units in the battleships *Colorado* and *Pennsylvania*. Radford's career as an air officer progressed swiftly as the naval air arm started to receive more attention and support in the 1920s. In 1923 he first qualified for carrier landings in the *Langley*, and in November 1929 he joined the carrier *Saratoga* where he commanded Fighter Squadron One from July 1930 to May 1931. By that time he had risen in rank to lieutenant commander. Radford was executive officer of the carrier *Yorktown* for a year starting in May 1940.

During World War II Radford served mostly in the United States and Hawaii, although he did command ships in the Pacific. With the rank of captain, he was director of aviation training (1942–1943) at the Bureau of Aeronautics where he made assignments for the Navy's pilots. In 1943 he was promoted to rear admiral and took charge of training on light carriers in Hawaii. In late 1943 he commanded the *Lexington* off Wake Island, and later he commanded the *Enterprise* in an operation in the Gilbert Islands. Back in Washington during 1944, Radford served as assistant chief of naval operations for air. Radford closed out the war in the

Pacific, commanding a carrier task group in the campaigns to capture Iwo Jima and Okinawa, with his flag in the new carrier *Yorktown*.

After World War II Radford was promoted to vice admiral and returned to Washington as deputy chief of naval operations (CNO) for air. In the capital he became embroiled in the arguments over defense unification and joined the controversial "revolt of the admirals." However, this controversy did not prevent the admiral from serving as councilor to two presidents. Radford was present in his position as commander in chief of the U.S. Pacific Fleet at the famous meeting of President Harry S Truman and General Douglas MacArthur* on Wake Island on October 15, 1950. Later, he consulted with President-elect Dwight David Eisenhower* in Korea after the election of 1952. Apparently, his demeanor and advice made a great impression on Eisenhower, who singled Radford out as the future chairman of the Joint Chiefs of Staff.

Radford's reputation as a distinguished naval officer was established before he became chairman of the Joint Chiefs of Staff in 1953. Thereafter, as the citation to the Gold Star in lieu of his Fourth Distinguished Service Medal read, "his keen thinking and considered military advice to the President, the National Security Council, and the Secretary of Defense had great influence on the military posture of our country and of our allies." Admiral Radford's long career and successful record in war and peace earned him an eminent voice as chairman of the Joint Chiefs. No other American professional military man had a bigger influence on presidential decisions during Eisenhower's first term in office. Radford wrote in his memoirs regarding his tenure as chairman: "The fact that the President had ordered me to consult with him whenever I thought it necessary or advisable was known by members of his cabinet; consequently, I had no difficulty communicating with key men in the whole administration." Soon Eisenhower asked Radford to meet with him every Monday morning when they were both in Washington, D.C. If Radford did not have anything in particular to take up with the president, Eisenhower "could just talk with me." Radford explained Eisenhower's request for company: "it would be relaxing for him in the midst of a heavy schedule of appointments with individuals who generally wanted something." Such access to the president was extremely unusual.

From his retirement in 1957 until his death in 1973, Arthur W. Radford was a consultant and held several directorships in business. His experience, integrity, sound judgment, and knowledge of world affairs made him as valuable in these business associations as he had been during a distinguished career of over forty years in the Navy.

Arthur Radford played a major role in the so-called admirals' lobby or admirals' revolt. The "revolt of the admirals" was a manifestation of the Navy's dissatisfaction over the prospect of reduced funding for Navy programs and the move toward unification of the services after World War II. In 1949 Radford and other talented naval officers, including Captain Arleigh Albert Burke* and Admirals Forrest Sherman (later CNO, 1949–1951), Robert B. Carney (CNO,

1953–1955), and Thomas H. Robbins, Jr. (later president of the Naval War College), actively opposed any reduced place for the U.S. Navy in the nation's defense establishment. The admirals especially opposed the possibility that the Navy's air arm, so laboriously built up during the past forty years, would be merged into or come under the control of the U.S. Air Force. Radford and the other admirals in the "lobby" believed that the United States must maintain a balanced defense capability then and in the future. The nation, the admirals argued, should not rely too much on one military branch or one type of weapon— that is, the Air Force and its strategic intercontinental bomber, the B–36, which Radford called a "billion dollar blunder."

In the battle over appropriations (at stake was a new sixty thousand-ton super aircraft carrier) and unification, the Navy appeared to be outgunned by the likes of General Omar Nelson Bradley* and Secretary of Defense Louis A. Johnson, whose statements and actions at the time indicated that the Army might try to absorb the Marine Corps. Obviously, if such action were taken it would further lessen the importance of the Navy. The admirals appeared to be further undercut when Secretary of the Navy Francis P. Matthews demanded that Admiral Louis E. Denfeld step down as chief of naval operations. Not surprisingly, Denfeld had been an ardent advocate of maintaining the Navy's strength vis-à-vis the other services.

Subsequently, however, Radford's efforts to bolster the Navy appeared to be vindicated. A congressional report issued in 1950, following special hearings conducted by Congressman Carl Vinson's House Armed Services Committee, leaned favorably toward the admiral's ideas of a balanced defense and proposed support for the new aircraft carrier. The Korean War demonstrated the need for closer interservice cooperation and the necessity of better coordination by civilians and military leaders in the new Department of Defense. Radford went on to serve as chairman of the Joint Chiefs of Staff (1953–1957) and supported coordinated use of Air Force and Navy air power.

BIBLIOGRAPHY

Coletta, Paolo E. *The United States Navy and Defense Unification, 1947–1953*. Newark: University of Delaware Press, 1980.

Davis, Vincent. *The Admirals Lobby*. Chapel Hill: University of North Carolina Press, 1967.

———. *Postwar Defense Policy and the U.S. Navy, 1943–1946*. Chapel Hill: University of North Carolina Press, 1966.

Eisenhower, Dwight D. *The White House Years*. Vol 1: *Mandate for Change, 1953–1956*. New York: Doubleday, 1963.

Jurika, Stephen, Jr., ed. *From Pearl Harbor to Vietnam: The Memoirs of Admiral Arthur W. Radford*. Stanford, Calif.: Hoover Institution Press, 1980.

Morison, Samuel E. *History of United States Naval Operations in World War II*. 15 vols. Boston: Atlantic, Little, Brown, 1947–1962.

CARL BOYD

RED CLOUD (b. at the forks of the Platte River, 1822; d. on Pine Ridge Reservation on December 10, 1909), Oglala Sioux war leader-diplomat.

Red Cloud was born near the site of present North Platte, Nebraska, during an era when Oglalas had very little contact with non-Indians except for occasional dealings with traders from St. Louis. Scattered information about his early years suggests that he was a volatile youngster who grew up in a traditional Indian environment incensed about his ineligibility for position as a civilian chief in his tribe because he was the son of an Oglala mother but a Brule father. Soon, however, he achieved distinction for military prowess and rose to the office of leading soldier (shirt-wearer) in the important military lodge of "Bad Faces." From appearances, his initial recognition came through his participation in the assassination of the domineering Oglala war leader Bull Bear in November 1841, but he earned his way to military prominence thereafter waging territorial wars against several neighboring tribes—Pawnees, Crows, Utes, and Shoshones—in order to assure the southern Oglala bands of ample supplies of meat, wild fruits and vegetables, and other natural materials.

In the 1850s and early 1860s he concentrated mainly upon the defense of the plains surrounding the upper Platte from encroachments by other Indians. But after receiving word of the expulsion of eastern Sioux from Minnesota in 1862–1863, following their defeat during the Minnesota Sioux War, he became increasingly dedicated to the defense of the land and culture of all Teton people from intrusions by non-Indians. Through the mid–1860s his anxiety and resentment grew steadily as whites crowded in around Oglala country to farm and raise livestock on the prairies and plains, and to mine gold and silver in the northern Rockies. Extreme tension finally erupted into "The Red Cloud War" in 1866–1867, after the U.S. Army appeared to erect several forts and to defend the construction of the Bozeman Trail across the aboriginal territory of the Oglalas in order to establish direct communication between the Missouri River and the gold mines of Montana. After several skirmishes, Red Cloud's forces challenged a column of eighty men led by Lieutenant Colonel W. J. Fetterman and destroyed the entire unit with ease.

The "Fetterman Massacre" suggested the superiority of Red Cloud's army in the region. Nevertheless, he fought only once more—in the "Wagon Box Fight" nearby, where Captain James Powell formed a corral of wagons and with the aid of rapid fire rifles stood off an Oglala attack at a loss of no more than five killed and two wounded. This show of intelligent tactics and superior weapons by an army officer in 1867 was followed by conciliatory talk on the part of federal negotiators in 1868. At Fort Laramie, they promised to meet the major demands of Red Cloud and other Indian leaders in the surrounding area: the abandonment of forts in Oglala country; the closing of the Bozeman Trail; and a guarantee that an area of some 60 million acres surrounding the Black Hills, set aside as the Great Sioux Reservation, would remain inviolate until a change in its status received the approval of three-fourths of the adult males in the signatory tribes.

Attempts by federal officials to honor these commitments, or to keep frontiersmen out of Oglala country, proved futile. First, the Union Pacific Railroad was completed up the Platte River route. Then, substantial groups of fortune-seekers appeared around the new agencies founded on the west bank of the Missouri River. Finally, a stream of gold-seekers filed into the Black Hills. Sitting Bull,* Crazy Horse,* and other war leaders took up arms in resistance and were to die violent deaths for their efforts. Perhaps sensing the possibility of a similar fate for himself, Red Cloud declared he would offer no further military resistance but would instead accept the offer of federal officials to "make him a chief." He would use that Indian Office-given position to offer peaceful opposition to all attacks on the traditional life-style and culture of the Oglalas, employing all obstructionist devices available short of armed rebellion. For a decade following the 1868 Fort Laramie Treaty, he acted as a leading diplomat from the Black Hills region (together with Brule chief Spotted Tail and others) for the purpose of demanding the equitable distribution of annuities, the honest administration of agency affairs, the placement of trans-Missouri agency head-quarters at points acceptable to the several Teton tribes, and the defense of the Black Hills region against intrusions either by the further negotiations of federal representatives or the illegal encroachments of white pioneers.

Red Cloud's diplomatic efforts doubtless made life easier for all Tetons who refrained from participation in the Great Sioux War of the mid–1870s, but they prevented neither the revision of the terms of the 1868 treaty following the dispersion of Sitting Bull's forces at the war's end, nor the immediate concen-tration of Tetons around agencies west of the Missouri under threat of military action on the part of the United States. By 1878 the Oglalas were forced to settle near their fourth and permanent agency, on the White River, which was named Pine Ridge rather than Red Cloud Agency to detract from the chief's importance. From that time until his death, Red Cloud sought to defend Oglala treaty rights and tribal legacies in every way possible short of military action. First, he vied with Valentine T. McGillycuddy for influence over reservation affairs until he won temporary victory by forcing the replacement of the strong-willed agent at Pine Ridge. Then, he resisted federal negotiations for the creation of several reservations, and the sale of surplus land, in the Black Hills region until they succeeded over his protests in the congressional "Sioux Agreement of 1889." Subsequently, he gave quiet approval to the Ghost Dance, until it led to the assassination of Sitting Bull and the massacre of his fellow tribesmen at Wounded Knee. He encouraged the perpetuation of traditional government by chiefs and headmen, resisted the lease of tribal lands to non-Indian cattlemen, and opposed the allotment of land and the sale of surplus acres on Pine Ridge Reservation. In virtually all of these efforts he failed, but he remained intransigent until 1904, when finally he gave way and accepted patent to an allotment of his own. There he lived out his remaining five years—blind, feeble, and disdained by white officials at the agency as well as by Oglala mixed-bloods who by then were striving to wrest power from traditionalists in voting districts all across the reservation.

Even though Red Cloud lived to witness defeat in most of the causes he tried to defend—the nomadic existence of a hunting-gathering society, the aboriginal claims of his tribe to a large part of the Black Hills region, and the traditional life-style of all of the Teton Sioux people—he enjoyed the satisfaction of major accomplishments before he died. From his origin as the product of an intertribal Sioux marriage, he rose to gain recognition as foremost military leader of Tetons in the southern Black Hills region during the 1860s. Working in that capacity, he forced the United States to give up vital interests in the Fort Laramie Treaty of 1868. After that, he gained recognition as a leading "chief" by federal officials, and through the influence of that office he worked to defend his tribe's interests through the critical years of settlement and adaptation to reservation life. Most important of all, he created—through half a century of public service—a legacy of uncompromising commitment to traditional Indian social practices and beliefs. This bequest, born of both military and diplomatic service, has been the contribution for which he has been best remembered from the time he was put to rest respectfully in consecrated burial ground at Holy Rosary Mission in 1909 to the present.

BIBLIOGRAPHY

Hyde, George E. *Red Cloud's Folk: A History of the Oglala Sioux Indians*. Norman: University of Oklahoma Press, 1937, 1957, 1967, 1976.
———. *A Sioux Chronicle*. Norman: University of Oklahoma Press, 1956.
Johnston, Sister Mary Antonio. *Federal Relations with the Great Sioux Indians of South Dakota, 1887–1933, with Particular Reference to Land Policy under the Dawes Act*. Washington, D.C.: Catholic University of America Press, 1948.
Nadeau, Remi A. *Fort Laramie and the Sioux Indian*. Englewood Cliffs, N.J.: Prentice-Hall, 1967.
Olson, James C. *Red Cloud and the Sioux Problem*. Lincoln: University of Nebraska Press, 1965.
Utley, Robert M. *The Last Days of the Sioux Nation*. New Haven, Conn.: Yale University Press, 1963.

HERBERT T. HOOVER

REED, Walter (b. Belroi, Va., September 13, 1851; d. Washington, D.C., November 22, 1902), U.S. Army bacteriologist. Reed is considered the key figure in the conquest of yellow fever.

Walter Reed was the descendant of Christopher Reed, an Englishman who settled in North Carolina in 1661. His formal education was interrupted by the Civil War but continued in 1867 with his admission to the University of Virginia. By 1869 he had completed his medical degree (M.D.), earning a second M.D. the following year at Bellevue Hospital Medical College in New York. From 1870 to 1875 he served as an intern in Kings County Hospital, Brooklyn; as an inspector for the boards of health in Brooklyn and New York City; and as a physician in Charity Hospital, Randall's Island, New York.

By 1874 Reed decided to try for an appointment in the Medical Corps of the

U.S. Army; in January 1875 he was commissioned a first lieutenant (assistant surgeon). In 1876 he was ordered from Willet's Point, New York, to Fort Lowell, Arizona Territory. He continued to serve at various posts until 1890, when he was reassigned to Baltimore, Maryland. While in Baltimore he continued his graduate study in bacteriology and pathology at Johns Hopkins Hospital. In 1893 Major Reed became the curator of the U.S. Army Medical Museum in Washington, D.C., and professor of bacteriology and clinical microscopy at the newly organized Army Medical School. Two years later, in 1895, he also chaired the Department of Bacteriology and Pathology at Columbian (George Washington) University Medical School.

Prior to the beginning of the Spanish-American War, Reed worked in the areas of erysipelas, an acute disease associated with the inflammation of the skin, and diptheria (he advocated treatment by antitoxin). In 1898 he chaired a committee investigating the causes and transmission of typhoid fever, a disease particularly prevalent in the military camps of the U.S. Volunteers. Published in 1904, his committee's "Report on the Origin and Spread of Typhoid Fever in U.S. Military Camps during the Spanish War of 1898" showed the importance of typhoid transmission by flies, dust, and contact, rather than the previously held theory of water transmission. Reed's work in diptheria and typhoid was only the beginning. By 1897 his interest in yellow fever had been spurred by the announcement of an Italian scientist, Dr. Giuseppi Sanarelli, that the bacillus *icteriodes* was the cause of the disease. At the direction of the surgeon general of the Army, Dr. George Miller Sternberg,* Reed and Dr. James Carroll investigated the bacillus, but it had no relationship to the disease.

At the turn of the century, yellow fever had made its appearance among U.S. Army personnel stationed in Havana, Cuba. A commission of U.S. Army medical officers was appointed to study the situation; Reed was chosen to head the team. The theory of mosquito transmission of yellow fever had been advanced as early as 1854 and in May 1900 was again set forth in an article by Dr. Henry Rose Carter. Pursuing this theory, Reed's commission decided to investigate the possibility of yellow fever being spread by the *Stegomyia* mosquito.

An experimental station was established near Havana, and during the seven months that experiments were conducted (June 25, 1900–February 4, 1901), the commission conclusively proved that yellow fever was transmitted by the mosquito *Stegomyia fasciata* (later reclassified *Aëdes Aegypti*). With this knowledge, U.S. Army medical personnel and sanitary engineers in Havana began at once to control the disease. The attack upon the mosquito population began in February 1901, reducing the number of cases of yellow fever from fourteen hundred in Havana in 1900 to thirty-seven for the entire island in 1901. By 1902 there was not a single case.

Upon Reed's return to Washington in February 1901, he resumed his work at the Army Medical School and Columbian. During the summer of 1902 he was awarded the honorary degree of A.M. by Harvard University and an L.L.D.

degree by the University of Michigan. He died on November 22, 1902, as the result of an appendicitis attack and was buried at Arlington National Cemetery. The U.S. Army's medical center in Washington is named in his honor.

Reed's work in yellow fever research assured his reputation. In the years prior to 1900, it had become almost a professional necessity for a physician to advance a theory on the causes of yellow fever. In the early experiments conducted by Reed's staff, soldiers slept with the clothing and bedding of yellow fever patients, but this did not prove to be the cause of the disease. It was two cases produced by the bites of mosquitoes that convinced Reed and his staff. On the basis of this knowledge he wrote a paper for the American Health Association in which he stated that the mosquito acted as an intermediate host for the transmission of the disease. The successful transmission of the disease to a human volunteer, Private John Moran, proved Reed's theory beyond a doubt. Since yellow fever could also be produced by injections of blood from a fresh case, a serum could be produced to prevent the spread of the disease.

Although the detailed work was conducted by Reed's staff, he planned and supervised the project. As a result of the discovery, yellow fever, which had once decimated as many as one-third of the Army's troops in Cuba, was brought under control. General Leonard Wood,* the military governor of Cuba, lauded Reed stating: "I know of no other man on this side of the world who has done so much for humanity as Dr. Reed. His discovery results in saving more lives than were lost in the Cuban war." Reed's work in yellow fever research ended the controversy over its causes and freed the Southern United States and Cuba from the dangers of this pestilence.

BIBLIOGRAPHY

Andrews, Peter. *In Honored Glory.* New York: G. P. Putnam's Sons, 1966.
Fox, Ruth. *Milestones of Medicine.* New York: Random House, 1950.
Wood, L. N. *Walter Reed, Doctor in Uniform.* New York: Julian Messner, 1943.

                                                                    JOHN NORVELL

RICKOVER, Hyman George (b. Maków, Russian Poland, January 27, 1900), naval officer. Rickover directed the program to develop the world's first atomic submarine.

Hyman G. Rickover was born in Russian-occupied Poland in 1900. Several years later his father Abraham joined the thousands of Jewish immigrants who left Eastern Europe for the United States. The elder Rickover settled in New York, set up a tailor shop, and sent for his family. In 1910 the Rickovers moved to Chicago where young Hyman tried to keep pace with his studies while supplementing the meager family income through a variety of part-time jobs. Unable to afford a college education, he received the support of a local congressman in 1918 for appointment to the U.S. Naval Academy at Annapolis.

Rickover's life at the Naval Academy forecast later experiences as a naval officer. He remained isolated from his more athletic and boisterous classmates, spending his time alone in his room. Each year Rickover fell near the bottom of his class in the subject of military character, and only strong performances in several academic subjects permitted him to graduate 107th out of 540 midshipmen in 1922. For the next five years Rickover served on board the destroyer *La Vallette* and the battleship *Nevada*. On both warships he continued to stay away from his comrades, preferring to study engineering in his quarters. This dedication was not entirely futile since he won the recognition of his superiors for improving the *Nevada*'s wiring and communication systems.

Rickover returned to the Naval Academy in 1927 for additional study and then enrolled at Columbia University where he received his master's degree in electrical engineering in 1929. From Columbia he went to submarine school at New London, Connecticut, and then into the submarine service. Rickover liked duty on the quiet undersea craft and worked tirelessly to upgrade the still primitive and dangerous machinery on the fragile warships. Nevertheless, the Navy Department neglected him for submarine command and in 1934 sent him first to the battleship *New Mexico* and then three years later to command the *Finch*, a dilapidated minesweeper used to tow gunnery targets. Dissatisfaction with the latter assignment probably convinced Rickover in 1937 to apply for permanent shore duty as an "Engineering Duty Only" officer.

Throughout most of World War II Rickover headed the Electrical Section of the Bureau of Ships in Washington where he directed improvements in the design of obsolete electrical equipment and overcame critical wartime supply shortages by extensive contracts with private industry. His aggressive management of the Electrical Section between 1941 and 1945 prompted deputy chief of the Bureau of Ships, Rear Admiral Earle W. Mills, to select Rickover for special assignment in 1946. Mills ordered Rickover to direct a team of naval officers dispatched to the Manhattan District laboratories at Oak Ridge, Tennessee to study developments in the new field of nuclear technology. Rickover enthusiastically visited those labs instrumental in the creation of the atomic bomb. He discussed the latest technology with engineers and read extensively about nuclear physics and engineering. He became convinced that the Navy could at once develop a nuclear reactor to power warships.

Unfortunately for Rickover, few naval officers shared his conviction about the immediacy of nuclear power. Although Chief of Naval Operations Chester William Nimitz* and others agreed that the Navy must develop an atomic submarine, their recommendations in 1947 were for long-term study and development rather than for a crash program. Consequently, Rickover launched a crusade to force reactor development and nuclear propulsion on a cautious naval establishment. Appointment as Navy liaison to the Atomic Energy Commission in 1948 and as head of the newly formed Nuclear Power Branch of the Bureau of Ships in 1949 gave Rickover the platforms to press his plans. Cleverly, he used each agency to prod the other into moving ahead rapidly on nuclear propulsion.

Moreover, he reestablished earlier contacts with civilian industrial contractors and developed valuable relations with congressional committees.

It was the growing fear of Russian nuclear power and the tensions of the Cold War rather than Rickover's agitation, however, which provided the final catalyst for construction of an atomic submarine. In August 1950 the Truman administration authorized development of such a weapon. This decision mobilized Rickover's team of naval and civilian engineers to design a water-cooled nuclear reactor for a submarine. Rickover determined to skip intermediate test stages and build the reactor and submarine hull concurrently. These steps facilitated early completion in 1954 of the world's first nuclear-powered submarine, the *Nautilus*.

While Rickover labored on the *Nautilus* project, he battled a naval establishment intent upon forcing his early retirement from the service. Finally, political and public pressure convinced the Navy to promote him to rear admiral in 1953, while at the same time successful sea trials of the *Nautilus* in 1955 strengthened his hold over the nuclear propulsion program. Now, subsequent changes in reactor design and in personnel selection would require Rickover's personal approval, and characteristically the admiral scrutinized every technical detail and examined every potential candidate for the nuclear navy. Moreover, triumph with the *Nautilus* led to his designation as head of a program to construct the first nuclear power plant in the United States at Shippingport, Pennsylvania. Rickover's nuclear network turned to the civilian project and grafted its rigorous safety standards and technical precision on to private industry. By December 1957 the generating station became operational.

The Shippingport project gave Rickover a reputation as one of the nation's leading nuclear engineers. At the same time he received additional national attention for a crusade to improve American education. Rickover had long stressed the necessity of thorough educational preparation for his engineers and naval officers and had formed nuclear power schools at New London in 1956 and Mare Island in 1958. But it was a trip to Russia in 1959 with Vice-President Richard M. Nixon which prompted Rickover to speak out on the apparent weakness of American education in comparison to that of the Soviet Union. In speeches, essays, and several books, the admiral lashed out at the deficiencies in the entire U.S. school system.

Public recognition brought new stature within the Navy. During the following years Rickover assumed more control over the Navy's nuclear program, observing sea trials of each new atomic warship and screening every officer for command of the expanding nuclear fleet. Yet he still confronted old animosities which surfaced from time to time, such as exclusion from the planning stages of the *Polaris* program to develop nuclear missile submarines. However, Rickover had become something of an institution, and when he reached mandatory retirement age in the early 1960s, he was retained through the next two decades as director of the Division of Naval Reactors.

Rickover's place in American military history will remain subject to heated debate. Interpretations of his contributions seem to generate strong differences of opinion, while uncertainty about the safety of nuclear power adds to the ongoing controversy about Rickover. Admirers call him the father of the nuclear navy, while critics claim that others were equally capable of developing the nuclear navy and with far less friction and high-handed measures. In fact, a number of naval officers did recognize the potential of nuclear powered warships after World War II, and many worked to develop such a program. Only Rickover, however, risked his career and battled the bureaucracy to ram through an immediate and practical program. The early stages of nuclear power development required a gadfly to keep the issue burning as postwar America tried to define its military requirements and priorities.

Rickover was more than a promoter and publicist. He was the force behind the entire naval nuclear program. His dogged perseverance, incessant badgering, and engineering know-how contributed substantially to the successful harnessing of nuclear energy for military purposes. Rickover's reactor program revolutionized naval warfare. Now warships could remain at sea indefinitely without refueling and submarines could circle the globe without surfacing to replenish batteries. Whether less abrasive officers might have eased some of the growing pains of the nuclear navy seems less important than the effective leadership Rickover supplied in the birth of a nuclear fleet.

BIBLIOGRAPHY

Blair, Clay, Jr. *The Atomic Submarine and Admiral Rickover*. New York: Henry Holt, 1954.

David, Heather M. *Admiral Rickover and the Nuclear Navy*. New York: G. P. Putnam's Sons, 1970.

Hewlett, Richard G., and Francis Duncan. *Nuclear Navy. 1946–1962*. Chicago: University of Chicago Press, 1974.

Polmar, Norman. *The Atomic Submarine*. Princeton, N.J.: Van Nostrand Reinhold Company, 1963.

Rickover, Hyman G. *Education and Freedom*. New York: Dutton and Company, 1959.

JEFFERY M. DORWART

RIDGWAY, Matthew Bunker (b. Fortress Monroe, Va., March 3, 1895), Army officer. Ridgway commanded the 82d Airborne Division in World War II and Allied ground forces during the Korean War.

Ridgway was born into the Army, at Fortress Monroe, where his father, a colonel of artillery, was then stationed. The "Army brat" was graduated from West Point in 1917 (along with Mark Wayne Clark* and Joseph Lawton Collins*). Lieutenant Ridgway's first duty assignment was a 3d Infantry border post, Camp Eagle Pass, in Texas. Ridgway spent all of the months of World War I at this fortification, where he eventually rose to command of the regimental headquarters company.

In the fall of 1918 Ridgway returned to West Point as an instructor of French and Spanish and director of athletics. Six years as a teacher at the Military Academy were followed by two years as a student in the Infantry School, Fort Benning, Georgia. The remainder of the 1920s and 1930s were consumed in the peripatetic manner common to peacetime service in the officer corps: constantly changing duty assignments, ranging from northern China (with George Catlett Marshall*), through Texas, Nicaragua, Bolivia, Georgia, Panama, the Philippines, Kansas (Command and General Staff School), Illinois, Washington, D.C. (Army War College), San Francisco (the Presidio), and Brazil (again with Marshall). Finally, as the two-decade journey ended, he was assigned to the War Plans Division of the General Staff in Washington.

Early in 1942, shortly after America entered World War II, Ridgway, by then a two-star general, assumed command of the 82d Infantry Division from Omar Nelson Bradley.* The 82d, which had a distinguished record in World War I, had been reactivated because of the war. Within a few months of his assumption of command, he was asked to convert his division into an airborne unit. The airborne concept of inserting units into combat behind enemy lines—utilizing gliders and paratroopers—was then new to warfare. The first large-scale application was in the German assault on Crete (May 1941), a costly experiment the Nazis never repeated.

Ridgway created one of the Army's first airborne units. He and his command were ordered to North Africa in the spring of 1943. He continued the preparation of his troops in Morocco until July, when part of the 82d made the first large-scale night jump in history as part of the assault on Sicily. Poor ground-air coordination and other factors caused the troopers to be dropped, not in the designated area near the town of Gela, but in small groups dispersed over hundreds of square miles of Sicilian terrain. The error worked out for the best, however, because the reports of American forces coming from so many locales at once threw the German and Italian commanders into a state of confusion. General Karl Student, Germany's authority on airborne operations, said (in 1945) that the troopers of the 82d brought success to the Allied invasion of Sicily, particularly since they blocked the Hermann Goering Armored Division from reaching the beaches being invaded by General George Smith Patton, Jr.* One wag described the Sicilian drop as "the best-executed snafu in the history of military operations." The airborne drop on Sicily did demonstrate that a new tactical tool was available: vertical envelopment.

For a time after Sicily, the high command of the Army was skeptical about the validity of airborne operations, but Ridgway and other advocates persistently supported the concept, and three airborne divisions (the 82d, 101st, and the British 6th) participated in the Normandy D-Day invasion. Ridgway jumped with the 2d Battalion of his 505th Parachute Regiment during the night of June 5, 1944. It was the objective of the 82d to hold the causeways that criss-crossed the flooded areas just beyond Utah Beach. Following the landing of his gliders the next morning, Ridgway's division captured Ste. Mère-Église, the first French city to be liberated. The 82d achieved its primary objective but sustained 46 percent casualties, not uncommon in such operations.

The success of the airborne mission convinced General Dwight David Eisenhower* of the utility of vertical envelopment, and he created the First Allied Airborne Army and named Ridgway to head the XVIII Corps. Command of the 82d was transferred to James Maurice Gavin.* The 101st was led by Maxwell Davenport Taylor.* These two divisions were promptly loaned to the British for Operation MARKET-GARDEN, a scheme by Field Marshall Bernard Montgomery to trap a German army in Holland. A British general (Frederick Browning) was made commander of the operation. The American airborne forces achieved their objectives, but the operation was a failure. Ridgway, who had no command responsibilities in this campaign, believed that it failed because the British high command was much too timid in moving up armor and ground forces in support of the American and British airborne units.

The forces commanded by General Ridgway participated in the bitter six weeks of fighting in the Ardennes, crossed the Rhine at Wesel, fought their way through the Ruhr pocket, crossed the Elbe, and finally made contact with Soviet forces (May 2, 1945), just as the war in Europe ended. In all these operations, Ridgway's forces performed gallantly and well; their commander was always in the forward positions when the going got rough.

Following the war, Ridgway assumed command of the Mediterranean Theater of Operations. In January 1946, however, he was transferred to London as Eisenhower's representative on the Military Staff Committee of the United Nations, an advisory body to the Security Council. Other assignments followed in the pre-Korean War period: chairman, Inter-American Defense Board (1946–1948); commander in chief, Caribbean Command (1948–1949); and, in October 1949, deputy chief of staff for administration and training.

General Walton Harris Walker,* commander of the Eighth Army fighting in Korea, was killed in an accident on December 23, 1950. Ridgway was designated as his replacement and immediately left Washington for Korea. General Douglas MacArthur,* who had been trying to direct the war from Tokyo prior to Walker's death, turned over complete control of all ground forces to Ridgway. The Eighth Army had been seriously demoralized and physically chewed up by a surprise Chinese Communist offensive that would eventually drive the Eighth well below the 38th parallel. Ridgway began by countermanding a standing order to hold current positions at all costs. He told his commanders to fall back in good order on predetermined phase lines.

A new Communist offensive in January 1951 drove Ridgway's forces some seventy-five miles south of Seoul where the line finally held. Two months earlier, MacArthur had informed the Pentagon that he would need four more divisions to stabilize his line: Ridgway did it with the available forces. Some four weeks after assuming command of an army in retreat against vastly superior forces, he launched a counteroffensive (January 25, 1951). His force—some 365,000 soldiers—surged forward against the 484,000 troops of Lin Piao, falling back briefly in the face of heavy counteroffensives, but always recovering and pressing onward throughout February. By the end of the month Ridgway had regained the 38th parallel and gone beyond it. That line would ebb and flow with the tide of offensives and counters, but the war was to end many months later with the South Korean border essentially *status quo ante bellum.*

President Truman ended a long struggle with the intractable MacArthur on April 11, 1951 by relieving him of all his commands, including commander in chief, Far East, and United Nations commander, and turning them over to Ridgway. Two months later the truce negotiations began that were to drag on interminably, and the major operational phase of the Korean War ended.

In May 1952, President Truman selected Ridgway, by then a four star general, to replace Eisenhower as the head of the North Atlantic Treaty Organization (Supreme Commander, Allied Powers in Europe). In the thirteen months Ridgway directed NATO, he enlarged it from twelve divisions to almost eighty (including active and reserve divisions). He instilled in the NATO forces his conviction that all of free Europe should be defended, not just those areas that were readily defensible.

Ridgway returned to Washington in October 1953 to assume the highest of Army posts, that of chief of staff. His two-year tenure was a time of great conflict. Senator Joseph McCarthy was at the peak of his demagoguery and freely abused Secretary of the Army Robert T. Stevens and many ranking officers. One of Ridgway's achievements during his two-year tenure was to prop up the flagging morale of the officer corps against McCarthy's virulent and largely unwarranted attacks.

The chief of staff also had considerable difficulty in his dealings with Secretary of Defense Charles Wilson. Wilson espoused a reduction of conventional ground forces in favor of the doctrine of massive retaliation. Ridgway repeatedly challenged this so-called New Look for the American military in the belief that it was a serious error to place so much reliance on nuclear weaponry. In 1955, at the age of sixty, he completed his two year tour as chief of staff and resigned from active service.

Matthew Ridgway was a pioneer in airborne warfare. He organized the 82d Airborne into an effective fighting machine. Later, as commander of the XVIII Corps in the First Airborne Army, he devised techniques for the utilization of such forces that were of immeasurable consequence in the conduct of the European Campaign. He trained most of the other senior airborne commanders in World War II. The tactical employment of vertical envelopments as an important weapon in a commander's arsenal owes much to Ridgway's innovative approach.

In Korea he demonstrated that troops properly employed and motivated can triumph over superior numbers and adverse conditions. Furthermore, Ridgway demonstrated that as an off-site tactician, MacArthur was not all that legend made him out to be.

Ridgway's tenure as chief of staff is of profound significance in the history of the American military for three reasons. First, he fought brilliantly and effectively against the doctrine of massive retaliation. He argued that a primary reliance on atomic devices would render America impotent in dealing with conventional wars that did not call for either the strategic or tactical application of nuclear weaponry. He also argued that massive retaliation was morally wrong and could never lead to a durable peace. Second, he developed (along with Gavin and Taylor) the concept of the flexible response in brushfire conflicts. This was a carefully measured and articulated response that would minimize the possibility of escalation into a nuclear Armageddon.

Lastly, as the French were losing their grip on Indochina and President Eisenhower was considering the possibility of American intervention, Ridgway produced what later came to be called the Ridgway Report. The report laid out in specific, documented language the terrible price in men, money, and material which the United States would have to expend if it became involved in Vietnam. Ridgway's report was a prime determinant in Eisenhower's decision not to join the conflict. There is some paradox in a professional soldier arguing against a military solution, but it speaks of Ridgway's character that he considered this to be the most important contribution of his entire career.

Ridgway embodied all the virtues this nation needs in its military leadership. He was brilliant, highly principled, nonpolitical, and courageous. In the pantheon of twentieth-century American soldiers four figures will always stand out from the shadows: George Marshall, Dwight Eisenhower, Douglas MacArthur, and Matthew Ridgway.

BIBLIOGRAPHY

Alberts, Robert C. "Profile of a Soldier: Matthew B. Ridgway." *American Heritage* 27 (February 1976): 4–7, 73–82.
Eisenhower, John. *The Bitter Woods*. New York: Putnam's, 1969.
Halberstam, David. *The Best and the Brightest*. New York: Random House, 1969.
Manchester, William. *American Caesar: Douglas MacArthur, 1880–1964*. Boston: Little, Brown and Company, 1978.
Ridgway, Matthew B. *The Korean War*. Garden City, N.Y.: Doubleday, 1967.
———. *Soldier: The Memoirs of Matthew B. Ridgway*. New York: Harper, 1956.

RICHARD F. HAYNES

RINGGOLD, Samuel (b. Front Park, near Hagerstown, in Washington County, Md., 1800; d. Point Isabel, Tex., May 11, 1846), father of the "flying artillery."

Samuel Ringgold was the eldest son of Samuel and Maria Ringgold. His father was a large landowner and Maryland state senator and Democratic congressman (1810–1821); his maternal grandfather was John Cadwalader, a Philadelphia-born Revolutionary general and Maryland state legislator. Educated at the U.S. Military Academy at West Point (1814–1818), Ringgold graduated fifth in a class of twenty-three cadets. He entered the Army as a lieutenant, and from then on his career was one of steady promotion and active duty: second lieutenant (2d Artillery, 1818); first lieutenant (3d Artillery, 1822); brevet captain for

"Faithful Service Ten Years One Grade" (1832); captain (3d Artillery, 1836); and brevet major for "Meritorious Conduct in the War Against the Florida Indians" (1838).

Assigned to duty at Fort Mifflin, Pennsylvania (1818), he later served as acting aide de camp to Winfield Scott* (December 1818–July 1821). He was on topographical duty from July to December 1821 when he became aide de camp to Scott (December 1821–July 1822). After a brief tour of duty at Fort Severn, Maryland, in 1824, he went to the Artillery School for Practice at Fortress Monroe, Virginia (1824–1826). On ordnance duty from 1826 until 1831, he then transferred to garrison duty at Fort Macon, North Carolina (1832–1835). After a tour on ordnance duty (1835–1836), Ringgold served in the Seminole War (1836–1837). While in Florida he became ill from "exposure" and never fully recovered his health. Ringgold went north on sick leave and then traveled to Europe where he studied briefly at the *École Polytechnique* in Paris and the Military Institution (forerunner of Sandhurst, the Royal Military College) in Woolwich, England. When Ringgold returned to America, Secretary of War Joel R. Poinsett (on November 5, 1838) ordered him to establish a horse artillery company at Carlisle Barracks.

There Ringgold set about organizing, equipping, and training Company C of the 3d Artillery as "horse artillery." (The men were now mounted and no longer rode on the limbers or caissons.) He also concerned himself with improving the technical features of the guns (including the design of the elevating screw and the firing mechanism, the length of the sponge, and the arrangement of the gun crew). Eventually, Ringgold's battery, the first horse artillery unit in the country, consisted of six guns, six caissons, two battery wagons, and two forges, pulled by six teams of six horses each. Twelve mounted cannoneers followed each gun. Finely honed and drilled to a state of near perfection, the unit could, within minutes, advance at a full gallop, unlimber, fire, remount, and move to another position on the field, repeating the maneuver. "The whole scene appeared like some wild and inexplicable phantasmagoria," one amazed spectator reported.

> On one occasion we beheld this corps drilling. The scene was two hills, nearly half a mile apart, with a gently sloping vale between. Now the batteries could be discerned on the brow of the furthest hill, half concealed in the white vapor that floated back after the explosion; now they would be seen, for an instant's transit, . . . then they were visible swinging around and unlimbering on the neighboring crest; and next, after another stunning explosion, and before we could recover sight of the guns, the whole corps would go thundering back to its first position, a confused mass of horsemen, caissons, and artillery vanishing through clouds of dust, and amid a shaking of the ground, as if an earthquake was passing.

Schooled according to tenets laid out for the British light artillery, Ringgold's company became the pride of the Army and was often used for parade-ground demonstrations at Fort McHenry and other places to attract recruits. Ringgold led his new unit to Camp Washington, a camp of instruction near Trenton, New Jersey, in 1839.

In 1840 the War Department adopted the manual of instruction used by the French field artillery. The designs and modifications developed over the years by the French, British, and American artillery were all intended to improve the flexibility, mobility, and cohesion of the batteries in order to reduce the turning radius of the gun carriages and caissons and the time required to unlimber the cannons and get them into action. The various systems also sought to improve the method for carrying ammunition and for mounting the gun crews. Ringgold, however, preferred the English system. Because of Ringgold's objections, the War Department suspended those sections of the "Instructions for Field Artillery, Horse and Foot" applicable to the light horse artillery. Assigned to an artillery review board in 1843, he worked for a new scheme that would incorporate the best of both the British and French systems. The War Department adopted the Ringgold system (an "English-Americanized" revision of the French instructions) on March 6, 1845. Following his work on the artillery board, Ringgold returned to garrison duty at Fort McHenry (1843–1846).

In addition to perfecting the horse artillery, the innovative artillery officer also introduced a new dragoon and light artillery saddle and bridle arrangement. After field tests in 1841, the Quartermaster Department issued the "Ringgold saddle" (patented in 1844) in limited numbers. The Army replaced it with an improved model, the "Grimsley saddle," in 1847. The bridle remained in use until 1885.

Despite the disapproval of his physician, who believed that Ringgold was too weak to go through another arduous campaign, the artillery major joined the "Army of Occupation" in Texas in 1846. Severely injured by Mexican artillery fire at the Battle of Palo Alto (May 8, 1846), Ringgold died three days later. He was forty-six years old, the first West Point graduate to be killed in the Mexican War.

An officer of inventiveness, imagination, industry, and steady competence, Samuel Ringgold moved the art of light artillery tactics significantly forward—thus earning the appellation "father of the flying artillery." During the years between the War of 1812 and the Mexican War, the War Department strove to improve and systematize the artillery. Through this effort, and the constant diligence of Ringgold, the American light artillery became highly mobile and deadly accurate.

At Palo Alto the Mexican Army under the command of General Mariano Arista received a lethal demonstration of the new horse artillery when Ringgold's battery, positioned within a hundred yards of the enemy lines, helped repel the Mexican attacks. The fire from Ringgold's guns, eyewitnesses noted, seemed to mow down whole platoons of the enemy at a time. Meanwhile, a detachment (consisting of two guns from Ringgold's battery) under Lieutenant Randolph Ridgely moved to the American right rear where the guns, along with infantry formed into a square, repulsed a charge of enemy lancers. Out of a force of 3,709 men, the Mexicans lost 257 killed, wounded, or missing. Perhaps no more than twelve Mexicans died as a result of musket fire. The vast majority of the casualties were caused by Ringgold's light horse artillery—brutal testimony to the effectiveness of the American cannoneers. Although strategically indecisive, Palo Alto was a tactical victory for the American Army. Modern and contemporary authorities agree that the artillery won the day.

Before the battle, Zachary Taylor,* the American commander, had been skeptical of the usefulness of the light artillery and had planned to drive the Mexicans from the field by means of a massed bayonet attack. Ringgold, however, convinced him to give the artillery a chance to prove itself. Now even Taylor was impressed.

Unfortunately, Ringgold was mortally wounded while directing the fire of his pieces. A romantic, contemporary drawing shows Ringgold sliding gracefully from his horse—two neat holes through both thighs. The injuries were far more traumatic. Hit by a six-pound cannon ball, the major suffered massive wounds; anterior muscle and tissue were torn away at right angles. Transported to Point Isabel, Taylor's supply base, Ringgold lived another sixty hours. The attending naval physician reported that Ringgold was coherent and seemed to be experiencing relatively little pain despite the enormity of his wounds:

> During the night he gave many incidents of the battle, and spoke with much pride of the execution of his shot. He directed his shot not only to groups and masses of the enemy, but to particular men in their line; he saw them fall, their places occupied by others, who in their turn were shot down...and he felt as confident of hitting his mark as though he had been using a rifle.

A certain irony attended his passing. The man who more than any other single officer worked to make the horse artillery an instrument of precise execution was himself mutilated by fire from an enemy whose copper cannon balls were so light and ineffective that soldiers could usually step easily out of the way as the Mexican shots bounced and ricocheted through the grass.

BIBLIOGRAPHY

Bauer, K. Jack. *The Mexican War, 1846–1848*. New York: Macmillan Company, 1974.
Dillon, Lester R., Jr. *American Artillery in the Mexican War, 1846–1847*. Austin, Tex.: Presidial Press, 1975.
Nichols, Edward J. *Zach Taylor's Little Army*. New York: Doubleday, 1963.
Smith, Justin H. *The War with Mexico*. Vol. 1. Gloucester, Mass.: Peter Smith, 1963. (Originally published, 1919.)
Steffen, Randy. *The Horse Soldier, 1776–1943: The United States Cavalryman: His Uniforms, Arms, Accoutrements, and Equipments*. Vol. 1. Norman: University of Oklahoma Press, 1977.

FRANK J. WETTA

RIPLEY, Eleazer Wheelock (b. Hanover, N.H., April 15, 1782; d. West Feliciana, La., March 2, 1839), general in the War of 1812. Ripley was a controversial commander in the War of 1812 and has generally been regarded unfavorably by modern historians.

Eleazer Ripley was the son of Sylvanus and Abigail (Wheelock) Ripley. He came from a distinguished background; his father was professor of divinity at Dartmouth for many years, and his maternal grandfather, Eleazer Wheelock, had been the original founder of that college. Ripley graduated from Dartmouth in 1800, studied law in the offices of several of his relatives, and was admitted to the bar. Soon afterwards he went to live in Maine, which was then a province of Massachusetts. He did well in the practice of law, became very interested in politics, and became an active member of the Democratic party. In 1807 Ripley was elected to the Massachusetts legislature and was selected as speaker of that body in 1811. In 1812 he won election to the State Senate and soon became known as a strong supporter of war with England.

When war did break out in 1812, Ripley entered the Army and was commissioned a lieutenant colonel. He worked hard at getting his district into a condition of readiness, supervised recruiting, and immersed himself in military studies. Between June and September 1812 his recruits were formed into the 21st Infantry. Ripley used the winter months to instill discipline into his men, and it became one of the model regiments of the Army and was ready for action in the spring.

Upon leaving winter quarters in 1813, he was promoted to the rank of colonel. Ripley saw his first battle action at the attack on York, now Toronto, in April 1813 and also took part in the assault on Fort George in May. Then, in October, Ripley's regiment went with James Wilkinson* on the ill-fated expedition to Montreal and Quebec. Ripley's men performed especially well at Chrysler's Farm, and in the report of the battle, Ripley was among those officers mentioned with distinction. Hoping in 1814 to provide better leadership and more fighting effectiveness, the Madison administration began retiring some of the more elderly commanders and gave assignments to some promising young officers. Ripley was one of those singled out for promotion and was appointed brigadier general on April 15, 1814.

Ripley's next assignment was to be part of the Niagara Campaign of 1814. Jacob Jennings Brown's* army was to cross into Canada; Winfield Scott* commanded the first brigade while Ripley commanded the second. Although Ripley was dubious about the invasion, he still performed rather ably and courageously. On July 3, 1814, the American Army crossed over from Buffalo and took Fort Erie. One day later a British army was encountered at Chippewa, and the Americans won a stunning victory. Although Ripley's brigade had not seen much action in the battle, three weeks later on July 25 another major encounter occurred at Lundy's Lane near Niagara Falls, and there Ripley would play a very conspicuous role. Late at night, Ripley was in charge of the unit that was finally able to capture the heights upon which the British had their artillery. With their guns captured, Ripley, in a brilliant action, broke the enemy's left and forced them back. He was also able to repulse three subsequent furious efforts by the British to retake their guns. By midnight, with both Brown and Scott seriously wounded, Ripley was placed in command. Following Brown's last order to him, Ripley withdrew his exhausted men from the field. Although the circumstances regarding Ripley's retreat are disputed, the fact is that the British guns were left on the hill and were soon recovered by the enemy. As a result, Brown ordered Ripley to go out the next morning to resume the battle and retake the artillery. Seeing that the British force was about twice his numbers, Ripley turned around and went back to Fort Erie. Brown was always highly critical of Ripley for his decisions at Lundy's Lane. In fact, completely disgusted with Ripley, he appointed General Edmund Pendleton Gaines* to command Fort Erie.

At Fort Erie, Ripley worked with the greatest zeal to strengthen its defenses and kept an unceasing watchfulness. On August 14, he discovered indications of an assault and warned Gaines. When the British attacked, Ripley superbly handled the defense of his section of the fort. After the enemy was pushed back, General Gaines praised Ripley for the "judicious disposition" of his force and for his "steady disciplined courage." Later, in a successful American sortie outside the fort on September 17, Ripley was seriously wounded in the neck. Congress later voted him a gold medal in recognition of his service at Chippewa, Lundy's Lane, and Fort Erie.

After the war, Ripley was made a major general by brevet, but he resigned from the Army in 1820 and went to New Orleans to resume the practice of law. Also resuming his interest in politics, he was elected to Congress in 1834 and again in 1836. Soon after going to Congress, Ripley was greatly stunned by the death of his only son in the Fanning massacre in Texas. After several years of declining health, he died at his plantation in Louisiana.

Eleazer Ripley's military career is significant for several reasons. First, Ripley was part of the move toward youth that was instituted by the government to give the American forces better leadership and more vigor. This can be clearly seen in the fact that the generals of the Regular Army in 1812 averaged sixty years of age. But two years later, the newly appointed commanders had an average age of only thirty-six. For example, Ripley was just thirty-two when he was promoted in 1814.

Ripley has significance, too, because of his important part in the famous Niagara Campaign of 1814. This invasion of Canada demonstrated that American troops could fight with bravery, steadiness, and determination on foreign soil. As a soldier, Ripley was noted for being a good disciplinarian and a stubborn fighter. These same traits were evidenced by the young American army in Canada during 1814 when it participated in some of the toughest and most punishing actions of the war. The discipline and determination instilled into those men by commanders like Ripley were even noticed by the British general at Chippewa, Phineas Riall, when he declared: "Those are Regulars, by God."

Ironically, however, this same Niagara Campaign that had made the reputation of Jacob Brown and Winfield Scott also damaged that of Ripley. There was much criticism of his conduct during the entire campaign. For instance, he objected to the attempt to capture Fort Erie, was slow in leaving the American shore, was dilatory after Chippewa, favored returning to American soil right after Lundy's Lane, and opposed the sorties that had been launched from Fort Erie during the British siege. However, most of the criticism of Ripley centered around his behavior at Lundy's Lane. General Brown, of course, was angry that Ripley had not removed the captured British artillery from the heights and was exasperated when Ripley would not renew the fight the morning after. Brown wrote a letter to the secretary of war saying that the troops "under able direction. . . might have done more and better." And the militia commander, General Peter Porter, was always critical of Ripley, maintaining that the battlefield should never have been abandoned.

But in all fairness, it must be remembered that Ripley abandoned the field upon the direct orders of the wounded Brown. And while he certainly should have spiked the captured cannon, it was also true that there were no drag ropes or horses available to effect a removal of the guns. More than one fellow officer testified to Ripley's calm and courageous conduct during the battle. For instance, Captain William McDonald, at a special court of inquiry, complimented Ripley's behavior, stating that he had "made every possible exertion to inspire and encourage his troops, exposed his person during the hottest fire of the enemy. . . gave his orders with perfect coolness and deliberation." Similarly, in regard to the incidents on the morning following the battle, when the enemy's overwhelming superiority in size is considered, it would seem that Ripley made the correct decision. Several other officers later agreed that it would have been consummate folly to attempt to regain possession of the battlefield.

In conclusion, while Ripley was certainly too cautious on many occasions, and while he lacked the dash and aggressiveness of Scott and Brown and hence suffered by comparison, he definitely did not lack courage and he often performed very well indeed when on the defensive. All things considered, it would seem that General Ripley's military reputation has been unduly maligned and censured, and he has been denied some of the credit that is his due.

BIBLIOGRAPHY

Baylies, Nicholas. *Eleazer Wheelock Ripley*. Des Moines, Iowa: Brewster and Company, 1890.
Coles, Harry L. *The War of 1812*. Chicago: University of Chicago Press, 1965.
Cruikshank, Ernest, ed. *The Documentary History of the Campaign on the Niagara Frontier, 1814*. Vol. 4. New York: Arno Press, 1971.
Mahon, John K. *The War of 1812*. Gainesville: University of Florida Press, 1972.

J. MICHAEL QUILL

ROCKENBACH, Samuel Dickerson (b. Lynchburg, Va., January 27, 1869; d. Washington, D.C., May 16, 1952), father of the American Tank Corps.

Samuel Dickerson Rockenbach was the son of Jeanie Nicolson and Francis Joseph Rockenbach. The mother traced her roots to colonial Virginia. The father, a French immigrant, was a lieutenant in Robert Edward Lee's* Army of Northern

Virginia. Samuel D. Rockenbach, raised on romantic stories of the Civil War, desired a military career.

After attending Lynchburg grammar and high schools, he enrolled in the Virginia Military Institute (VMI) in 1885. Rockenbach was the cadet first captain, stood third in his class, and was an honor graduate with a degree in civil engineering in the class of 1889. After graduation, he declined VMI's offer of an adjunct professorship in the Department of Mathematics. He became the commandant of Kemper Military School in Booneville, Missouri. There, he was appointed a captain in the Missouri militia; for four months in the summer of 1890, he worked as a civil engineer for the C and U Railroad in Colorado.

Still wanting a military career, he took and passed the competitive examination for a commission. In June 1891 he was appointed a second lieutenant of cavalry and was assigned to the 10th Cavalry Regiment, although he was temporarily detailed to Troop C, 9th Cavalry, at Fort Leavenworth, Kansas. He joined his parent regiment at Fort Grant, Arizona Territory, in January 1892 but was temporarily assigned to the Indian Company, 11th Infantry Regiment. In April 1892 he was given command of Troop H, 10th Cavalry Regiment, which was en route to Fort Buford, North Dakota. He commanded both the troop and the post until August 1893, when he attended the Cavalry Troop Officers School at Fort Leavenworth, Kansas, graduating in 1894.

In 1894 VMI, with approval of the secretary of war, invited Rockenbach to become the commandant of cadets and professor of applied mathematics. In February 1895 VMI, again with the secretary of war's consent, secured a congressional resolution to enable him to remain at the school. At the end of the year, he received a vote of approval from the Board of Visitors, was elected to the position, and was asked to resign from the Army to accept. He refused and in July 1895 rejoined his regiment at Fort Assinniboine, Montana, where for the next three years he was engaged in surveying and mapping. He served and formed a lasting professional friendship with John Joseph Pershing* during the Cree Campaign. At various other times he was the regimental and post quartermaster and adjutant.

As regimental quartermaster, he moved the 10th Cavalry Regiment to Chickamauga Park, Georgia, at the outbreak of the Spanish-American War. He was selected to be the aide de camp to Brigadier General Guy V. Henry. During the actual campaign, he conducted a reconnaissance under fire to select artillery sites to shell Santiago. At other times he carried messages between Major General William Rufus Shafter* and Rear Admiral William Thomas Sampson,* including the surrender proposal. During the Puerto Rican Campaign, he landed at Guanico and conducted the reconnaissance for General Henry's advance on Arecibo and Otuadi where notice of the surrender Protocol was received. After the war, he resigned from Henry's staff and returned to the United States to marry Emma Baldwin.

He rejoined his regiment in December 1898, serving as regimental adjutant and quartermaster. After its transfer to Fort Sam Houston, Texas, he also became the post adjutant until Congress passed a law requiring that a regimental adjutant be a captain. At that point he became a squadron adjutant but retained his post adjutant assignment until the 10th Cavalry Regiment was transferred to Manzanilla, Cuba, in May 1899. In addition to his regimental duties, he was the engineering officer for the Santiago Military District until 1902. He returned to the United States and was assigned to the Engineer Department in Washington, D.C. He helped to select the site for Fort Oglethorpe, Georgia, and designed its water and sewage systems. It was the first bacterial sewage plant in the Army.

Rockenbach was restive in his assignment since it was rumored that his regiment was to be transferred to the Philippines. Rockenbach secured a transfer to the 12th Cavalry Regiment in 1903 and was assigned to the Philippines late the next year. He held various assignments, including command of a battalion of Philippine Scouts, chief scout for his commander, and civil governor of the Cotabato District on the island of Mindanao. During his tour of duty, he was promoted to captain.

In 1911 he returned to the United States after a tour through Siberia, Russia, Germany, France, Italy, Japan, China, and England where he studied the organization of the various European and Asian military powers. On his return he was assigned to the Army War College at Fort Leavenworth, Kansas, graduating in 1912. After graduation he was assigned to the 11th Cavalry Regiment and saw strike duty in Colorado during 1914.

World War I erupted in Europe. Since he was familiar with many German officers and spoke fluent German, Rockenbach was assigned to be an observer with the German Army. He held that assignment until the spring of 1915 when failing diplomatic relations forced his recall.

On his return from Europe, he was promoted to major, detailed to the Quartermaster Corps, and assigned to Brigadier General John J. Pershing's staff. He was the quartermaster for the Punitive Expedition. Following the Pancho Villa affair, he continued on Pershing's staff and was selected to be the quartermaster for the American Expeditionary Force. Rockenbach organized and prepared Base Section 1 so that when the first American troops arrived in France, the supply facilities were operational and functional.

In 1917, Pershing was seeking a qualified officer to head the American Tank Corps. He chose Rockenbach because of his personal knowledge of the man, his administrative talents, his ability to improvise, his ability to cooperate with the Allies, and his experience with motor vehicles from the Punitive Expedition. While Rockenbach fought the administrative battles, he turned to Major George Smith Patton, Jr.* to train the proposed twenty light tank battalions. In addition to the responsibility he carried as commander of the Tank Corps, Rockenbach was the U.S. representative to the Inter-Allied Tank Committee and Pershing's principal tank advisor. In August 1918 he became the chief of the Tank Corps, First American Army. He now had a tactical command. His tankers fought brilliantly in the battles of St.-Mihiel and the Meuse-Argonne, winning admiration and praise from many senior officers.

After the war, in addition to still commanding the Tank Corps, he again commanded Base Section 1 until his return to the United States in June 1919. Reverting to his permanant rank of colonel, he retained his position as chief of the Tanks Corps until June 1920, when Congress merged the tanks with the Infantry Branch. At that time, he transferred to infantry and assumed command of the Tank School, Fort Meade, Maryland, until he was promoted to brigadier general in January 1924. He commanded the Military District of Washington until July 1927, when he was transferred to command the 2d Cavalry Brigade. In September 1928 he assumed command of the 2d Artillery Brigade at Fort Sam Houston, Texas. The next year he became the commanding general of the 2d Division and Fort Sam Houston. He held the latter post until his retirement in 1933.

Samuel D. Rockenbach's fame was his administrative genius. As a boy he dreamed of a military career. His early life romanticism faded under the Virginia Military Institute's demanding discipline and curriculum. He graduated self-confident, self-disciplined, and thoroughly grounded in mathematics, science, and engineering. During his career, some confused his personal traits with aloofness or rigidity.

His early military career was the same as that of most junior officers. His attention to minute details and his customary thoroughness became known to his superiors. As a consequence, instead of troop duty, he often served as squadron, regimental, post adjutant, or quartermaster. Often he held several of the assignments at the same time. Other times he was a general's aide, served on a general's staff, or held engineering assignments.

When he was assigned to General John J. Pershing's staff as quartermaster officer, he complained bitterly to the quartermaster general that the assignment had the effect to "suspend me from rank and command, sentence me to hard labor, and to pay an annual fine of $2,000," the amount of bond he was required to post. Having made his protest, he accomplished his assignment in his customary thorough manner. He organized and commanded the first motorized supply system used in a military campaign. After the Punitive Expedition, he continued on Pershing's staff. It was an unforeseen blessing, for when Pershing was named to command the American Expeditionary Force, he named Rockenbach his quartermaster officer. Again with his usual manner, his ability to improvise, and his diplomacy, Base Section 1 was ready when the first American troops arrived in France.

Pershing was seeking a qualified officer to head the American Tank Corps. Familiar with the Virginian's qualities and knowing that Rockenbach coveted a combat command, Pershing gave him the assignment. He faced the challenge of his career. He had to create a battle-ready force which some Americans thought unnecessary. His skills were severely tested, but in the battles of St.-Mihiel and the Meuse-Argonne, the Tank Corps more than justified its existence. Many of his thoughts on training, tactics, logistics, and maintenance are now Army doctrine.

Rockenbach returned to the United States hoping that the Tank Corps would remain a separate army integral to the Army, and he labored to that end. But American historical tradition, an economy-minded Congress, neo-isolationism, international disarmament sentiment, and the National Defense Act of 1920 worked against him. That law gave the tanks to the infantry. In his final report as chief of the Tank Corps he wrote, "the successful development and value of the arm (tanks) in the future depends upon the sympathy and support it is given." Infantry gave it very little of either during the next two decades. Even more disheartening, many of his officers returned to their branches, fearing that being in infantry tanks would lessen their own opportunities for advancement.

A few officers heard Rockenbach's message and risked their careers to continue his advocacy. His dream was fulfilled in 1940 with the creation of the Armored Force. For his efforts he is known as the father of the Tank Corps—perhaps we can add the Great-Grandfather of the Armored Force—or today, Armor.

BIBLIOGRAPHY

Blumenson, Martin, ed. *The Patton Papers, 1885–1940*. Boston: Houghton Mifflin Company, 1972.
Gunsburg, Jeffery A. "Samuel Dickerson Rockenbach: Father of the Tank Corps." *Virginia Cavalcade* 26, No. 1 (Summer 1976): 39–47.
Houston, Donald E. *Hell on Wheels: The Second Armored Division*. San Rafael, Calif.: Presidio Press, 1977.

DONALD E. HOUSTON

RODGERS, John (b. near Havre de Grace, Md., ca. 1771–1773; d. Philadelphia, Pa., August 1, 1838), naval officer. Rodgers was the senior American naval officer during the War of 1812, and he proposed a strategy of fleet action rather than single-ship cruises.

John Rodgers' parents, "Colonel" John Rodgers and Elizabeth Reynolds Rodgers, founded the United States' premier naval family, with flag rank descendants into the twentieth century. "Colonel" Rodgers had emigrated from Scotland in 1760 and had settled in Harford County, Maryland. By 1775 he owned and operated a tavern near modern Havre de Grace. He raised a company of Maryland militiamen for the patriot cause and in 1778 was commissioned a captain. Although he never held a higher rank, he was always known as "Colonel" Rodgers.

John Rodgers was one of the earliest of eight children. Fascinated by the sea, but disliking school and farming, the young man attempted to run away to Baltimore to join a merchantman. Seeing the boy's ardor, his father agreed to sign him up as an apprentice if the youth promised to abstain from alcohol. John took the oath and abstained from alcohol for the rest of his life. Service aboard the merchantman was good for the young man who soon was made a ship's officer. By the time he was twenty Rodgers had his own ship which engaged in general European trade out of Baltimore. Rodgers spent eleven years in the merchant marine where he, like so many other Americans, learned well the practical skills of sailing, navigation, and seamanship.

When the Quasi-War with France began in 1798, Rodgers accepted a commission as second lieutenant aboard the 38–gun frigate *Constellation* under Thomas Truxton.* The first lieutenant resigned shortly after, and Rodgers became the executive officer of the frigate. He was serving in that capacity when the American vessel captured the French frigate *Insurgente* (36 guns) on February 9, 1799. Rodgers was honored for the victory along with the rest of the crew of the *Constellation*, and as a further recognition of his abilities, he was promoted to the rank of captain—the first American officer to be promoted to that rank under the new government. He was given the captured vessel to command. Later Rodgers transferred to the 20–gun corvette *Maryland* in which he sailed to the West Indies. At the end of the war, Rodgers bore the American minister and a new treaty to France.

Unsure of his future with the Navy, Rodgers returned to merchant service for several months. Returning to Baltimore in May 1802, he was recalled to service in the Navy and sailed to the Mediterranean where he participated in the actions against the Barbary pirates until the summer of 1806. As captain of the 28–gun frigate *John Adams*, Rodgers along with Lieutenant Andrew Sterrett commanding the 12–gun schooner *Enterprise* captured and destroyed the largest vessel in the Tripolitan fleet. During his North African service, Rodgers was at times commander of the U.S. fleet in those waters and hence was entitled to be called "commodore." By 1806 Rodgers had succeeded Commodore Edward Preble* as the U.S. commander and negotiated peace terms with Tripoli along with the civilan U.S. minister, Tobias Lear. Rodgers took a hard line in the negotiations, for he never believed that the lives or comfort of the American prisoners in the Tripolitan jails were worth trading for a dishonorable peace backed by tribute. During this period Rodgers took umbrage at the remarks of Captain James Barron and challenged the captain to a duel. Barron declined the challenge.

Returning to the United States in 1806, Rodgers married Minerva Denison of Sion Hill, Maryland. She bore him eleven children, one of whom was Rear Admiral John Rodgers, Jr.*

Back in the United States, Rodgers was one of the members of the naval board which found Captain James Barron guilty of failure to do his duty as senior officer aboard the *Chesapeake* when it submitted to the *Leopard* (July 1807). Barron was suspended without pay for five years. From 1807 to 1809 Rodgers enforced the Jefferson administration's embargo north of the Delaware River.

In 1810 Rodgers, as captain of the 44–gun frigate *President*, commanded a fleet in charge of protecting the northern portion of the American coast. On May 16, 1811, the *President* severely damaged the British 20–gun sloop, *Little Belt*. The British captain claimed that Rodgers had used unfair methods, but an American court of inquiry upheld Rodgers' account. Rodgers was hailed as a hero by President Thomas Jefferson and the secretary of the Navy. Rodgers' success was seen as just revenge for the *Leopard*'s earlier humiliation of the *Chesapeake*.

Rodgers was the senior, active duty, naval officer in the War of 1812. On hearing of the outbreak of the war, Rodgers ordered his fleet of three frigates and two lesser ships to sea. He feared that if he delayed, the British would blockade the American coast and prevent his departure. Rodgers was the only American naval captain in the war to recommend concentration and fleet action. He understood that an American fleet's presence would force the British Navy to concentrate its own ships. If the strategy was successful, it meant that the Royal Navy would do less damage to American merchantmen than would more scattered enemy vessels on single-ship cruises.

While the *President* was engaged in a fight with the British frigate *Belvidera* (36–guns), a gun burst and Rodgers suffered a broken leg. His small fleet sailed east to Spain and then north to the British Isles where he failed to sail into the Channel and the Irish Sea, an omission which later strategists have frequently criticized. On this cruise the American fleet took only eight enemy merchantmen. This lack of success, in contrast to the more colorful single-ship duels of other American captains, convinced the administration that fleet cruises were not only unprofitable but dangerous as well since a large portion of the American Navy could be lost in one unsuccessful battle. Rodgers' two other cruises, with smaller fleets, were equally unsuccessful.

In June 1814 Rodgers accepted command of the new 44–gun frigate *Guerriere* which was then being finished in Philadelphia. He never was able to get this vessel to sea during the war. In August 1814 he and his sailors were ordered to Washington and later to Baltimore to defend these cities. During the battle for the cities, his sailors' efforts were decisive in protecting the inner harbor.

After the war Rodgers was appointed head of a Board of Navy Commissioners which Secretary of the Navy William Jones had suggested was necessary for better naval administration. The commissioners ran all the nonpolitical aspects of the Navy from supplies and strategy to personnel and contracts. In 1823 Rodgers served a short time as interim secretary of the Navy. The next year he resumed active command as commodore of the Mediterranean Squadron. His flagship was the 74–gun *North Carolina*, a ship-of-the-line. Rodgers returned to Washington in 1827 where he once again headed the Board of Navy Commissioners. He resigned due to ill-health on May 1, 1837, and died on August 1, 1838, at the Naval Asylum in Philadelphia. He is buried in the Congressional Cemetery in Washington.

Several modern historians consider Rodgers the premier American naval strategist of the War of 1812. His idea to maintain fleet cohesion during the War of 1812 was far ahead of his time and would only be recognized two generations later by the great naval theorist Alfred Thayer Mahan.* Rodgers' fleet, although unsuccessful by contemporary standards, did force the British to concentrate their forces. This permitted American merchantmen to return home safely. Rodgers was disappointed that his own contemporaries failed to recognize the importance of his novel strategic ideas.

He always was more a theorist than a fighter. Several times during the war, Rodgers had the opportunity to place himself near the jugular of British trade but failed to take the necessary risks. He was a methodical leader, disciplined and stern. Never a lovable or colorful sailor, Rodgers nonetheless provided the early American Navy with a worthy heritage of naval strategy and an example of competent leadership.

BIBLIOGRAPHY

Eckert, Edward K. *The Navy Department in the War of 1812*. Gainesville: University of Florida Press, 1973.
Forester, Cecil S. *The Age of Fighting Sail, The Story of the Naval War of 1812*. Garden City, N.Y.: Doubleday and Company, 1956.
Guttridge, Leonard F., and Jay D. Smith. *The Commodores, The U.S. Navy in the Age of Sail*. New York: Harper and Row, 1969.
Mahon, John J. *The War of 1812*. Gainesville: University of Florida Press, 1972.
Paullin, Charles O. *Commodore John Rodgers, Captain, Commodore, and Senior Officer of the American Navy, 1773–1838, a Biography*. Cleveland: Arthur H. Clark Company, 1910.

EDWARD K. ECKERT

RODGERS, John, Jr. (b. Havre de Grace, Md., August 12, 1812; d. Washington, D.C., May 5, 1882), naval officer.

John Rodgers, Jr., was the fourth child of Commodore John Rodgers* and Minerva Denison Rodgers. His early education took place in Washington, D.C., where his father served two long terms as the president of the Board of Navy Commissioners. An appointment as an acting midshipman was obtained for him in April 1828, and the following February he was sworn into the Navy. Between 1829 and 1832 he served in the Mediterranean Squadron in the 44–gun frigate *Constitution* and the 18–gun sloop-of-war *Concord*. In March 1833 he attended a school for midshipmen on the 44–gun frigate *Java* in the Norfolk Navy Yard, and a year later he passed his examination for lieutenant. Unfortunately, there were no vacancies in that rank, so he remained a passed midshipman for nearly six years. In the fall of 1834 he took a leave of absence to attend the University of Virginia, where he studied mathematics and natural philosophy. The spring of 1836 found him back on active duty doing survey work in New York Bay, followed by an assignment to the brigantine *Dolphin* in the fall. The *Dolphin* and one other ship became the Brazil Squadron. Rodgers gained valuable experience as acting lieutenant and acting master of the *Dolphin*.

In 1839 he got his first command, the 1–gun schooner *Wave*, and service in the Second Seminole War. While in Florida he later commanded the 18–gun brig *Jefferson* and led a land patrol into the Everglades against the Seminole Indians. In 1840 he finally made lieutenant.

Subsequent assignments included duty with the Home Squadron (1842–1844), superintending shipbuilding in Pittsburgh (1844–1846), and serving with the Africa and Mediterranean Squadrons (1846–1849), the Coast Survey (1849–

1852), and the North Pacific Surveying Expedition (1852–1856). When the leader of the expedition, Commander Cadwalader Ringgold, became ill in 1854, Rodgers was placed in charge. Rodgers was promoted to commander in 1855. For most of the period from July 1856 to the outbreak of the Civil War, Rodgers was in Washington preparing reports on the expedition. On November 25, 1857, he married Ann Elizabeth Hodge of Washington, who subsequently bore him one son and two daughters.

For Rodgers the Civil War began with an unsuccessful attempt to destroy the dry dock at Norfolk before it fell into Confederate hands. He was captured, paroled, and returned to Washington. After a brief assignment to Cincinnati, where he supervised the building of a gunboat flotilla, he was given command of the screw gunboat *Flag* and joined the blockading force off Charleston, South Carolina. He helped to plan the assault on Port Royal, participated in a demonstration against the defenses of Savannah, and led forces in the seizure of Fernandina, Amelia Island, and St. Mary's, in Georgia. In the Peninsula Campaign he commanded the ironclad gunboat *Galena* which bombarded the Confederate fort at Drewry's Bluff on the James River. *Galena* was hit more than forty times and had its armor pierced thirteen times, but the battle did not end until it ran out of ammunition. In July 1862 Rodgers was promoted to captain.

Four months later Rodgers was given command of the monitor *Weehawken*. While en route from New York to Port Royal, he brought this ship through a heavy gale, thereby demonstrating the seagoing qualities of monitors. In the *Weehawken* Rodgers led the attacking forces of Admiral Samuel Francis Du Pont* against Fort Sumter. The *Weehawken* was hit fifty-three times, but only one shot penetrated its armor. Du Pont accepted the recommendation of Rodgers and his fellow officers not to renew the attack. For this decision Du Pont came under severe criticism and was relieved. While awaiting Du Pont's successor, Rodgers in the *Weehawken* fought and won a battle with the Confederate ironclad ram *Atlanta*. For this he received the thanks of the Congress and was promoted to commodore in March 1863. The last phase of the war found Rodgers in command of the new monitor *Dictator*, a ship with many problems, so many that he did not participate in the final battles of war.

Postwar service was highlighted by the cruise of the monitor *Monadnock* and three other ships around the horn to San Francisco; by Rodgers' command of the Boston Navy Yard (1866–1869); and by his promotion to rear admiral and his assignment to lead the Asiatic Fleet (1870–1872). While Rodgers' men were surveying a river in Korea they were fired upon by forts. Rodgers responded by landing a large force, capturing the forts, and demolishing them. After this duty came the command of the Mare Island Navy Yard (1873–1877) and the post of superintendent of the Naval Observatory, which he held from 1877 until his death. In addition, between July and November 1881 Rodgers served as the president of a nine-member Naval Advisory Board which made recommendations to the secretary of the Navy on the number and type of vessels to be built. The board urged that thirty-eight unarmored cruisers be built, including eighteen steel vessels, and thereby helped to set the stage for a naval renaissance that took place after Rodgers' death. Bright's disease conquered John Rodgers, and he died in Washington in 1882 at the age of seventy.

John Rodgers was a lucky man. He began his career when his father was the most prominent officer in the service. His first two superiors had close ties with his father. Young Rodgers had the best possible environment for nurturing his nautical inclinations and for insuring that every achievement was noticed. When his father died in 1838, Rodgers was an acting lieutenant, but he still had influential friends and family connections who undoubtedly helped his career along. Unlike many officers who had long periods ashore on half-pay status while awaiting orders, Rodgers had almost constant employment, which made for a variety of experiences and a diverse background. In a naval career that lasted over forty-seven years, he spent more than twenty-six at sea.

But if family and friends helped him to get professional opportunities, it was up to Rodgers to make the most of them. This he did. He had intellectual curiosity, and a single-minded dedication to whatever he was engaged in at the time. If he was not brilliant, he was conscientious and thorough. He was a perpetual optimist. This quality reinforced his personal bravery. Rodgers had an excellent reputation as a commander. He did not have the arrogance, pomposity, and sense of self-importance that characterized many of his contemporaries. Instead, he was calm, steady, patient, and understanding. He projected a sense of maturity, reasonableness, and moral courage. He seems to have been a loving and devoted husband and father as well. To some of his friends, his success was simply the triumph of the pure in heart. For the military man, he epitomized the slogan: fortune favors the bold.

Yet Rodgers himself recognized his limitations. In 1865, when he had a chance to become the head of a Navy bureau, Rodgers indicated a lack of desire for such an administrative job. He said that if he had one talent, it was in commanding ships and men. His record tends to bear that out. He was the happiest on small ships where there was less formality. His reputation rests mainly on the scientific work he directed in the North Pacific Surveying Expedition and his fighting record in the Civil War, including his work with monitors and ironclads.

BIBLIOGRAPHY

Anderson, Bern. *By Sea and by River: The Naval History of the Civil War.* New York: Alfred A. Knopf, 1962.

Cole, Allan B., ed. *Yankee Surveyors in the Shogun's Seas: Records of the U.S. Surveying Expedition to the North Pacific Ocean, 1853–1856.* Princeton, N.J.: Princeton University Press, 1947.

Johnson, Robert E. *Rear Admiral John Rodgers, 1812–1882*. Annapolis, Md.: Naval Institute Press, 1967.
Reed, Rowena. *Combined Operations in the Civil War*. Annapolis, Md.: Naval Institute Press, 1978.

HAROLD D. LANGLEY

ROGERS, Robert (b. Methuen, Mass., November 7, 1731; d. London, England, May 18, 1795), founder and leader of Rogers' Rangers in the Great War for the Empire. Rogers was a pioneer in the early development of ranger training and tactics.

Robert Rogers was the son of a pioneering New England farmer who removed with his family from Massachusetts to the New Hampshire frontier in 1739, settling at the Great Meadow not far from the present Concord. There young Rogers grew up in close familiarity with the forest and developed for himself the skills needed for survival therein. During King George's War (1744–1748), while still a boy, he gained his first experience in wilderness warfare by participating as a volunteer in an expedition against hostile Indians. By the time he reached his majority he was tall, strong, and wise in the ways of the wilderness. A fighter by instinct, Rogers unfortunately was less well endowed with certain other attributes, such as prudence, sophistication, and self-control, that might have helped him build a more successful career in the civil community. For the remainder of his life, whenever he was out of active military service, Rogers tended to flounder.

In 1755, as the last of the great colonial wars was getting underway, Rogers found himself on the wrong side of the law and joined the New Hampshire provincial forces to escape prosecution. Gaining a captain's commission, he led his command to Lake George as part of the provincial army under the command of Major General William Johnson* of New York. There Rogers served with conspicuous success as leader of scouting parties sent northward down the lakes to reconnoiter the French positions at Ticonderoga and Crown Point. Johnson called Rogers, admiringly, "the most active Man in our Army." During the ensuing winter Rogers continued this grueling and hazardous kind of service, all the while gaining additional experience and skill in the wilderness tactics for which he soon would be famous.

The following year Rogers was given command of an independent company of rangers, men specially enlisted for scouting activity in the contested wilderness. Soon, under his dynamic leadership, the rangers developed into an elite, if rough and ready, corps of fighting woodsmen trained by methods which Rogers himself had devised as a result of his own experience. During the campaigning of 1756 they operated in the area of Lake George and Lake Champlain, sometimes employing whaleboats in the warmer season and skates or snowshoes in wintertime. They were especially effective in scouting enemy positions, cutting off small parties from fortified bases, and taking prisoners for interrogation. So impressive were Rogers' achievements that British regular officers began doing short tours of duty with his units in order to gain similar skills. The British generals James Abercromby, John Campbell Loudoun,* and Jeffery Amherst* all came to appreciate the value of Rogers' Rangers. It was for Loudoun's benefit in particular that Rogers drew up a set of instructions for ranger operations, later incorporated and published in his *Journals*. The kind of activity in which he specialized was extremely dangerous and not invariably successful. For example, in January 1757 he was ambushed by the French near Ticonderoga and took heavy losses. A little over a year later, also near Ticonderoga, Rogers' command suffered a casualty rate of nearly 70 percent in the disastrous "Battle on Snow-shoes," but Rogers never faltered and managed to lead the survivors safely back to their base.

Promoted to the rank of major, Rogers participated in Abercromby's futile campaign against Ticonderoga in 1758 and Amherst's successful advance to Crown Point the following year. On October 6, 1759, he surprised and ravaged the Indian town of St. Francis near the junction of the river of that name and the St. Lawrence, but the victorious rangers suffered severely during the long, difficult withdrawal through two hundred miles of wilderness. The following spring Rogers again operated out of Crown Point. Commanding a detachment of rangers and light infantry, he surprised and largely destroyed the village of Ste. Thérèse on the Richelieu River. Later he was in the forefront of Colonel William Haviland's advance toward Montreal and was present at the capitulation of that last important center of French power on September 8, 1760. Rogers then was dispatched to the area of the Great Lakes to inform Detroit of the British success and accept the surrender of that post, which he accomplished before the end of November.

By this time Rogers' exploits had made his name known throughout the colonies, and his fame had crossed the ocean to England itself. In 1761, with the Cherokee War underway, Amherst gave Rogers a regular commission as captain of one of the Independent Companies stationed in South Carolina, but the New Englander arrived in that colony too late to see action. Returning to the North, he took command of an Independent Company in New York. During Pontiac's* Uprising Rogers was a member of the expedition led by Captain James Dalyell for the relief of Detroit. When Dalyell was killed in action near Detroit on July 31, 1763, Rogers helped cover the retreat to the fort; it was his last fight against Indians.

In 1765 Rogers journeyed to England in search of preferment. His fame as a Ranger gained him an audience with King George III. Designated commander of Fort Michilimackinac at the western end of Lake Huron, he returned to America and proceeded to his new post. There, wrestling with problems of Indian relations and the fur trade, he came under suspicion of treason and was placed under close arrest. Rogers subsequently was tried at Montreal, and although acquitted, his reputation had been seriously damaged. For years he had been heavily in debt, largely as a consequence of his failure to keep adequate records while in military command. His creditors dogged him during much of the remainder of his life, and he once spent nearly twenty-two months as a debtor under confinement in London's Fleet Prison.

At the outset of the American Revolution the patriots suspected Rogers of being pro-British and rejected his offer to take up arms in their cause. Later, he offered himself to the British commander, General Robert Howe, who gave him command of a battalion of American rangers. Rogers saw some action in New York, without notable success, and was retired in 1777. His days of glory now were long in the past. In 1778 the long-suffering woman he had married in 1761, and by whom he had his son Arthur, divorced him. Rogers again went to England, where his addiction to alcohol became an increasing problem. Finally, after years of debt and near-poverty, he died in London on May 18, 1795, and was interred at St. Mary's, Newington.

Robert Rogers was, in the main, a failure in civil life and is remembered only as the daring commander of rangers. A modern biographer, John Cuneo, has said that, although Rogers himself was not formally trained as a military officer, he "successfully compressed the shapeless mass of backwoods fighting experiences into a simple exposition of small unit tactics soundly based on timeless principles: mobility, security, and surprise" (p. 59). The effectiveness of Rogers' Rangers inspired the formation of a special regiment of British regulars (eventually the 80th) specifically trained and equipped for wilderness warfare, an important early step in the establishment of "light infantry" in the British Army.

Surprisingly, for a rough frontiersman, Rogers left two publications of his own as monuments to his career, both produced in England when he was visiting that country in 1765. The first, titled *Journals of Major Robert Rogers*, constitutes his personal account of his exploits during the Great War for the Empire. The second, titled *A Concise Account of North America*, was intended to stimulate British exploitation of the continent's vast interior, recently wrested from the French. Rogers' contribution to the composition of the play *Ponteach, or the Savage of America*, published anonymously but sometimes attributed to him, was probably minimal.

Rogers clearly belongs in the line of innovative colonial soldiers such as Benjamin Church,* who successfully adapted European military practices to American wilderness conditions, borrowing heavily from the Indians. He is perhaps best recognized as an exemplar of the cherished, if not fully justified, American tradition that the homespun American citizen-soldier, because of his frontier expertise, was superior on his own ground to the formally trained European regular.

BIBLIOGRAPHY

Armour, David A., ed. *Treason? At Michilimackinac: The Proceedings of a General Court Martial Held at Montreal in October 1768 for the Trial of Major Robert Rogers*. Mackinac Island, Mich.: Mackinac Island State Park Commission, 1967.

Cuneo, John R. *Robert Rogers of the Rangers*. New York: Oxford University Press, 1959.

Gipson, Lawrence Henry. *The Great War for the Empire: The Victorious Years, 1758–1760* [The British Empire Before the American Revolution, Vol. 7]. New York: Alfred A. Knopf, 1949.

Rogers, Robert. *Journals of Major Robert Rogers*. Introd. by Howard H. Peckham. New York: Corinth Books, 1961.

DOUGLAS EDWARD LEACH

ROOSEVELT, Theodore (b. New York City, N.Y., October 27, 1858; d. Long Island, N.Y., January 6, 1919), assistant secretary of the Navy, volunteer Army officer, president of the United States. During his presidency, Roosevelt devoted unusual attention to modernizing the American armed forces, especially the Navy.

Prompted by the actions of his father, a rich New York glass importer, an asthmatic and sickly young Theodore Roosevelt made room in a scholastic schedule devoted to such subjects as ornithology, philately, and biology, adding strenuous physical exercises. By his teenage years, Roosevelt began living the "strenuous life," performing rituals of exercise which included wrestling, boxing, hiking, shooting, swimming, and horseback riding. T.R. studiously sampled the curricula in history and natural science at Harvard College. He began the research that resulted in the first of many books, *The Naval War of 1812* (1882). Graduating Phi Beta Kappa from Harvard in 1880, Roosevelt entered Columbia Law School but left in 1881 after being elected as a Republican to the lower house of the New York state legislature.

Grief-stricken at the death of his young wife, Roosevelt abandoned the familiar environs of New York in 1884 to become a "cowboy," operating a ranch in Dakota Territory. The change of scene did him good, and, energetically as usual, in 1886 he bustled back to politics, campaigning for the office of mayor of New York City. He lost. Sitting out of politics temporarily, T.R. plunged into writing and produced essays and books, including *Ranch Life and the Hunting Trail* (1888) and the first two volumes of his four-volume opus *The Winning of the West* (1889).

In 1889 Roosevelt returned to politics, taking the appointment of President Benjamin Harrison to a seat on the U.S. Civil Service Commission. After serving enthusiastically for six years on what had been a rather drab panel, T.R. sought the appointive position as president of New York City's Board of Police Commissioners. A crimefighting commissioner, Roosevelt stalked the streets for two years. The Navy had been one of his special interests ever since he heard his uncles Bulloch (James and Irvine) talk about their days in service to the Confederacy. T.R. and friends (including U.S. Senator Henry Cabot Lodge) pressed President-elect William McKinley to make him assistant secretary of the Navy in 1897. Roosevelt made the assistant secretary's traditionally mundane billet into one of influence. Taking an interest in everything in the Navy Department,

T.R. interrogated officers, inspected ships and ordnance, and investigated plans at the Office of Naval Intelligence. He naturally joined other scholars, businessmen, politicians, and military officers (including his friend Captain Alfred Thayer Mahan*) who wanted to lead America into the race for colonies. Sensing that war with Spain was in the offing over the matter of Cuba's revolution, T.R. helped to put the Navy on a war footing. Soon after the mysterious destruction of the U.S. battleship *Maine* in Havana, Cuba, America and Spain were at war. Recognizing that the old Spanish Pacific colony of the Philippines was vulnerable to attack, Roosevelt sent a war-warning message to Commodore George Dewey* commanding the U.S. Asiatic Squadron. Dewey took his squadron and struck the Spanish at Manila Bay, winning a great victory.

Meantime, Roosevelt, at age forty and with poor eyesight, used his political connections to obtain a lieutenant colonelcy of volunteers. Resigning as assistant secretary, he dashed around recruiting men into the 1st U.S. Volunteer Cavalry Regiment, popularly known as the "Rough Riders." The regiment's commanding officer, Colonel Leonard Wood,* was later promoted, allowing Roosevelt to gain the colonelcy. Roosevelt's Rough Riders, a handpicked one thousand out of twenty-three thousand applicants, hailed from Texas and Harvard, Dakota and Yale, Arizona and Princeton. Cowboys and polo players, businessmen, and Indians volunteered to serve with T.R., who packed twenty pairs of spectacles to take to Cuba. He won no friends in the Army by criticizing his superiors and the War Department's bad rations. The Rough Riders acquitted themselves well, making a national hero out of their colonel. Victory at the battle on San Juan Heights led logically to high political office.

In his Brooks Brothers khaki uniform, Roosevelt returned to New York and was elected governor in 1898. Charging into the governorship as he had up San Juan Hill, he vetoed bills of the legislature, advocated new taxes on businesses, and promoted "Progressive" reforms. Such actions alienated T.R. from the conservative New York Republican machine, which arranged to slide him out of the governorship and into the moribund national vice-presidency. The McKinley-Roosevelt ticket won the election in 1900. On September 6, 1901, President William McKinley was wounded by an assassin at the Pan American Exposition in Buffalo, New York. He died eight days later.

Roosevelt took the oath of office and soothingly pledged to hold to McKinley's policies. Within a few months, however, he began displaying the same political flair that had antagonized conservative New York Republicans. T.R. arbitrated the Coal Strike of 1902, instigated "trust-busting" cases against big corporations, called for Progressive agencies to regulate business, and popularized national parks and environmental conservation, all of which could be seen as departures from McKinley's policies.

Roosevelt was one of America's most active presidents in foreign affairs. Angered that Colombia would not accept a treaty allowing the United States to build a canal through the Colombian province of Panama, T.R struck a bargain with the Panamanians just hours after they revolted against Colombia's government. (Begun in 1904, the Panama Canal was completed in 1914.) In 1904 Roosevelt added to the Monroe Doctrine a controversial corollary which stated that the United States would not let European countries use force to collect debts owed them from Latin American nations. Instead, America would supervise the collection of such debts and police the hemisphere. In 1906 Roosevelt won the Nobel Peace Prize for bringing an end to the Russo-Japanese War. He pushed for an international conference to discuss various claims and disputes in Morocco.

Knowing that diplomacy was ineffective without a strong military force to back it up, Roosevelt devoted much of his time to military matters. Relying on Secretary of War Elihu Root* to look after the Army, T.R. focused his attention on the Navy. Under Roosevelt, the U.S. Navy added new ships, increased the number of sailors, and stressed modernized gunnery. He made provisions for concentrating scattered battleships into a fleet. In late 1907 the president sent the U.S. battlefleet around the world on a fourteen-month cruise. By the end of the administration, T.R. had boosted the United States to rank third in naval strength behind Britain and Germany.

Leaving the presidency in 1909, Roosevelt still followed the "strenuous life." His big game hunt to Africa was a grand adventure. Returning to America, he argued with his chosen successor, William Howard Taft, over antitrust and conservation policies. Failing to gain the Republican nomination for president, Roosevelt ran as a third party candidate in 1912, heading the Progressive or "Bull Moose" ticket and promising increased government regulations in his "New Nationalism" platform. The split among the Republicans gave the election to the Democratic candidate, Woodrow Wilson. Following the election, T.R. pursued his multifaceted interests. He went on a hazardous trip to the Amazon River Basin. He had presented historical lectures at England's Oxford University in 1910 and was president of the American Historical Association in 1913. During the Great War, T.R. criticized the lack of preparedness in Wilson's defense policy. After a German submarine sank the *Lusitania* in 1915, Roosevelt promoted a program called the Plattsburgh Training Camp Movement, designed to give military training to college students. When the United States declared war on Germany in 1917, Roosevelt offered to raise a new Rough Rider-style infantry division, but Secretary of War Newton Diehl Baker* declined his services.

While considering the possibility of running for the 1920 Republican presidential nomination, Roosevelt suffered a coronary embolism and died on January 6, 1919, at Sagamore Hill, his home on Long Island.

Theodore Roosevelt serves as an important figure in America's transition from the nineteenth to the twentieth century. He was very knowledgeable in many fields but an expert in none. Whether it was as a legislator or police commissioner, cowboy or big-game hunter, naval secretary (albeit assistant) or volunteer soldier, historian or naturalist, amateur athlete or trust-buster, governor or president— he did well in all his chosen roles, enjoying himself, building his reputation as a man of action and accomplishment.

For the Army, the service in which he spent his hectic Rough Rider days and three quiet years (1882–1884) as a New York National Guard officer, Roosevelt had no great affection or particular interest, beyond modernization. But when Congress declared war on Spain he jumped ship from the Navy Department to become a volunteer Army officer for practical considerations. As a naval observer or supernumerary, he would be unlikely to get the recognition that would come from a battlefield victory. T.R. was like many nineteenth-century volunteer Army officers, expecting that he could quickly pick up the essentials of soldiering, providing inspired leadership but lacking discipline, regarding most Army regulations as mumbo-jumbo, and not getting along well with regimented regulars. In fact, Roosevelt's relations with the Army were stormy, a natural consequence of his criticism of General William Rufus Shafter,* commander of U.S. forces in Cuba, and his assumption that the War Department mishandled supplies and medical services during the Spanish War. (Evidently, T.R.'s public complaints cost him a recommendation for the Medal of Honor, which would have perfectly crowned his active service.) As president, Roosevelt took the side of Secretary of War Elihu Root in the dispute with Commanding General Nelson Appleton Miles* over staff organization. The president relied on Root to carry out the plan of reorganization. (The resulting changes were called the "Root Reforms," not the "Roosevelt Reforms.") Like most nineteenth-century American presidents, T.R. thought that a small Army was capable of winning the battles it might have to fight. Mustering about seventy-seven thousand officers and men in 1908, the Army contained eight thousand fewer soldiers than when he inherited the presidency from McKinley.

When Roosevelt was first inaugurated, he possessed a better understanding of naval matters than any president before or since. His understanding was not as thorough as professionals in such fields as ordnance, for example, but his breadth of knowledge about the Navy was remarkable. As assistant secretary of the Navy, T.R. thought that airplanes might have military utility. He went for a test dive in a submarine prototype. Possessing good strategic sense, Roosevelt conjured up for the Naval War College a theoretical problem of simultaneous crises over Hawaii (involving Japan) and Cuba (involving Spain): T.R. saw the need for a two-ocean navy. However, in the early 1900s the concept of a two-ocean navy had not gained favor among most politicians. In fact, he was president in an era when mammoth military budgets were not politically acceptable.

Roosevelt wanted a large, modern navy with offensive capabilities to shield America's commerce, enforce the Monroe Doctrine, guard the Panama Canal, and protect new island colonies. He envisioned that a navy with such capabilities would actually act as a deterrent to war. Thus, Roosevelt set out to build new ships and replace old ones; reorganize the fleet; increase the number and quality of naval officers and enlisted men; and reform naval administration, training, and gunnery. He tried to resolve a debate over the location of the main U.S. military base in the Pacific. Meanwhile, there was the continuing confusion and concern over strategy: was Britain a future friend or foe? And what of Japan,

Britain's ally in the Pacific? To what extent would the German Empire become a rival to the United States in the Pacific and the Caribbean? Roosevelt was not successful in reaching all his goals. Six secretaries of the Navy served in T.R.'s cabinet, indicating that the president was actually his own naval secretary.

T.R. had no doubt how the strength of an early twentieth-century navy was measured—by the number of modern battleships it possessed. The American Navy enjoyed an inflated reputation among its citizenry and in Congress: the defeat of Spain's inadequate navy had seemed so easy. But none of America's battleships in service in 1901 displaced more than 11,500 tons or had a top speed of more than sixteen knots. Most of America's battleships were deemed suitable for "coastal defense" and were designed with less armor, speed, ordnance, and cruising range than the best British, German, and French battleships. T.R. intended to replace the coastal defense ships with ocean-going battleships. Accordingly, during his first years in office, the president obtained appropriations for ten battleships, as well as four armored cruisers, and seventeen miscellaneous vessels. In 1904 T.R. examined the plans of the proposed battleship *New Hampshire* and recommended to the Naval Board of Construction that the ship's battery be changed to all 11– or 12–inch guns rather than the hodgepodge of guns in the design. By making this recommendation (which the board did not adopt), Roosevelt was anticipating the revolutionary *Dreadnought* a year before the British began its construction. With these new ships built or building, T.R thought he had the basis for his modern battlefleet. Then in 1906 Britain launched the *Dreadnought*, which displaced eighteen thousand tons, was capable of twenty-one knots, and mounted ten 12–inch guns. *Dreadnought*'s size, speed, and revolutionary all big-gun battery outclassed America's battleships afloat and under construction. U.S. battleships were obsolete, except for use against a lesser naval power, such as Spain. To keep up technologically with Britain (but not in numbers of ships), Germany, and France, America would have to engage in a construction program more expensive and advanced than that which T.R. had just put through Congress. Between 1906 and 1909, Roosevelt asked Congress to provide for ten more battleships, during years when he had anticipated that one per year would be satisfactory. Congress approved funding for six of the ships.

In 1901 the ships of the U.S. Navy were scattered in small squadrons at several stations around the world. Following general guidelines on fleet concentration laid down by Alfred Thayer Mahan, T.R. began his reorganization plan, withdrawing ships from the European and South Atlantic Stations and combining them with the North Atlantic Squadron to form the Atlantic Fleet. Additional cruisers reinforced the Asiatic Squadron, which was redesignated the Asiatic Fleet. Plans were made to form a Pacific Fleet. Thus, the battleships would be concentrated in the Atlantic ready to oppose the fleet of any potential enemy. When T.R.'s Panama Canal was completed, battleships could pass through from one ocean to another.

During his seven and one-half years in office, T.R. pursued a policy that led

Congress to more than double the number of enlisted men in the Navy. The enlisted strength went from 18,800 in 1901 to 44,100 in 1909. Roosevelt obtained better food and higher pay for sailors. The number of officers also increased, going from 1,700 in 1901 to more than 2,500 in 1909. Many of these new officers came from the expanded classes at the U.S. Naval Academy at Annapolis, but T.R.'s plan to involuntarily retire older line officers to create faster promotions for younger officers was less than a complete success. Increasing the number of modern ships in service was encouraging to energetic junior and midlevel officers, including Roosevelt's naval aide, William Sowden Sims.*

In December 1907 the Great White Fleet started on its 'round-the-world-voyage under the command of Robley Dunglison Evans.* Roosevelt ranked this controversial martial display as one of the most important acts of his presidency, saying that the voyage was intended to give the sixteen white-painted battleships experience at fleet training, call Congress' attention to the need for additional naval appropriations, and impress the Japanese government. Japanese officials had been making bellicose remarks because of the mistreatment of Japanese immigrants in California. Relations with Japan were eased by the "Gentlemen's Agreement" (1907), in which T.R. promised that Japanese settlers would receive fair treatment, and the Root-Takahira Agreement (1908), in which both nations agreed to continue the Open-Door Policy in China and respect the integrity of each other's territory in the Pacific. On the other hand, some Japanese leaders may have been inspired by the Great White Fleet to push plans for a stronger Japanese Navy. The voyage of the battlefleet was a typical showmanlike gesture on Roosevelt's part, but the cruise was more than a bravura performance. Men and machines were tested. More Americans saw the need for having a two-ocean navy. A big Pacific base and new naval facilities on the West Coast were obviously necessary.

Politics played a major part in the location of American naval yards and bases. Twenty installations were located on the Atlantic Coast, two on the Gulf of Mexico, and only two on the Pacific. In 1903 T.R. arranged for a ninety-nine year lease for Guantanamo Bay, Cuba. But would the location of a primary American military base in the Pacific be in the Philippines or Hawaii? In 1908 T.R. finally chose Pearl Harbor, Hawaii, and Congress appropriated funds for the base. This decision left the Philippines—which T.R. called "America's Achilles heel in the Pacific"—without adequate defenses.

During his presidency, Roosevelt had significantly increased the size and efficiency of the U.S. Navy. The fleet was top-heavy with battleships at the expense of cruisers and other ships, but T.R.'s objective was to get the big ships on line first. By 1909 America had become the world's number three naval power, behind Britain and Germany.

Many men who met Roosevelt or who wrote about him later mistook his unquenchable enthusiasm for immaturity. (Sir Cecil Spring Rice, a British diplomat, once remarked, "You must always remember that the President is about six.") T.R. was militaristic; he said that "a thousand rich bankers cannot leave such a heritage as Farragut left.'' Probably he was the most belligerent man ever to receive the Nobel Peace Prize. But in T.R.'s view a militarily unprepared nation was weak and thus tempted an attack by stronger nations. During the seven and one-half years of his administration, the United States was not involved in a general war.

Born in the Victorian era, Teddy Roosevelt became a man of the technological twentieth century. He was a multitalented, dynamic leader. Through the steps he took to enlarge and modernize the Navy, Roosevelt made his mark on American military developments. More than most presidents, he understood the close connection between military power and statecraft.

BIBLIOGRAPHY

Beale, Howard K. *Theodore Roosevelt and the Rise of America to World Power*. Baltimore: Johns Hopkins University Press, 1956.
Braisted, William R. *The United States Navy in the Pacific, 1897–1909*. Austin: University of Texas Press, 1958.
Harbaugh, William H. *The Life and Times of Theodore Roosevelt*. New York: Oxford University Press, 1975.
Jones, Virgil C. *Roosevelt's Rough Riders*. New York: Doubleday, 1971.
Marks, Frederick W., III. *Velvet on Iron: The Diplomacy of Theodore Roosevelt*. Lincoln: University of Nebraska Press, 1979.
Morison, Elting E. *Admiral Sims and the Modern American Navy*. Boston: Houghton Mifflin Company, 1942
O'Gara, Gordon G. *Theodore Roosevelt and the Rise of the Modern Navy*. Princeton, N.J.: Princeton University Press, 1943.

JOSEPH G. DAWSON III

ROOT, Elihu (b. Clinton, N.Y., February 15, 1845; d. New York City, N.Y., February 7, 1937), lawyer, statesman. As secretary of war, 1899–1904, Root sponsored the ''Root reforms'' that laid the organizational foundation for the modern U.S. Army.

Root's paternal and maternal ancestors were prosperous, sometimes distinguished New Englanders; his maternal great-grandfather John Buttrick commanded the Massachusetts troops at Concord Bridge and gave the order for the ''shot heard 'round the world.'' Moving to the Utica area of New York, both families produced educators and became associated with Hamilton College, where in November 1849 Root's father, Oren Root, hitherto teaching in various academies, became professor of mathematics, astronomy, mineralogy, conchology, botany, geology, and civil engineering. The third of four sons, Elihu attended Hamilton College and graduated in 1864. He attempted to enlist in the Union Army but was rejected because of frail health. Earning his way through New York University Law School by teaching, he graduated in 1867.

Root practiced law in New York City in various partnerships and developed four main legal specialties: banking cases, railroad cases, suits over wills and estates, and municipal government cases. As a trial lawyer, he early distinguished himself for his commanding presence and mastery of detail. His early municipal cases included service as counsel to James H. Ingersoll, a relative of Root's partner and co-defendant with William Marcy "Boss" Tweed in the prosecutions that attended the breaking of the Tweed Ring. In the sequel, Root became assistant counsel to Tweed himself, one of a numerous and often distinguished group, but liable to guilt by association, particularly in later years in the pages of the Hearst press. Rising rapidly to the summit of the New York bar during the final quarter of the century, Root also became counsel to various prominent business firms and figures, such as the Havemeyer Sugar Refining Company and Peter A.B. Widener. He first pleaded before the U.S. Supreme Court in 1884, representing the restaurateur "Charlie" Delmonico, who had been defrauded in mining litigation.

Root's attitudes and associations were conservative and conventional for a man of his station. Joining the Union League Club of New York, he met there Salem H. Wales, retired managing editor of *Scientific American*. Invitations to Wales' home led to Root's marriage to Wales' daughter, Clara Francis Wales on January 8, 1872.

Root felt that "the office of being a leading lawyer in New York City was the only one I ever cared about," but gradually he was drawn into Republican politics. As a member of the Executive Committee of the Union League Club, he came to know Chester A. Arthur, who persuaded him to accept a nomination for judge of the court of common pleas in 1879. Root lost the election, but in 1883 Arthur, now president, appointed him U.S. attorney for the Southern District of New York. In 1883–1884 Root was also a member of the Republican Central Committee of New York, and he helped in the reorganization that created the new County Committee in 1884, of which he became an original member and, in 1886, chairman. Never a "Stalwart" despite his association with Arthur, Root moved increasingly toward the moderate reformist, good government wing of the Republicans. In the New York State Constitutional Convention of 1894, he was acting chairman of the Rules Committee and chairman of the Judiciary Committee, the latter post making him majority floor leader. He worked effectively for a revised state judiciary and toward some separation of municipal from state and national politics.

Root persuaded a close friend, Cornelius Bliss, to accept President William McKinley's appointment as secretary of the interior and thus early gained McKinley's favorable attention. In July 1899 McKinley called on Root to become secretary of war. The president believed an experienced lawyer was needed to frame the government of the island possessions newly acquired from Spain. Protesting that he knew nothing about the Army, Root accepted the post on the ground that he was qualified to make "colonial business a specialty."

Root's distinction as secretary of war rests in no small way on his achievements in the colonial business. He made an inspired choice when on December 13, 1899, he appointed Major General Leonard Wood* military governor of Cuba. Wood employed peculiarly autocratic methods to pursue Root's stated goal of redeeming the American pledge of Cuban self-government; but the autocracy was combined with efficiency, and the effects included major accomplishments in public works, public health, and education. If progress toward Cuban independence was much more ambiguous, probably little more was possible given pervasive American skepticism, including that of Wood and Root, about Cuban capacity for self-government. In the Philippines, Root similarly maintained an ostensible policy of advancing self-government; was similarly supported by an able lieutenant on the scene, William Howard Taft, as chairman of the Second Philippine Commission and then civil governor under the Philippine Government Act of 1902, prepared largely by Root; and again achieved uncertain results in the ostensible aim but tangible improvements in administration. Furthermore, Root presided over the Army's suppression of the main forces of the Filipino Insurrection, an achievement that, if also incomplete, appears nevertheless as a remarkably swift triumph over an irregular, insurrectionary force in light of later American experiences. In Puerto Rico, Root also helped establish efficient administration and substantially, though not completely, achieved his aim of incorporating the island into the U.S. tariff system.

Root's stature in military history rests to a greater extent on the organizational reforms in the War Department that he felt obliged to undertake despite his lack of military experience. He early concluded that the Army needed a general staff to direct its "intellectual exercise" and to plan for war. The chief of staff could replace the commanding general as senior professional officer and solve long-standing problems in the chain of command. Root also concluded that the Army needed a senior professional school, a war college, to educate officers in preparation for war. The similar recommendations of a board headed by Brigadier General William Ludlow, appointed by Root in 1900, led to Root's appointment of the War College Board in 1901, both to act as an embryo General Staff and to advance Army education. Over the opposition of Commanding General Nelson Appleton Miles* and other Army and congressional conservatives, Root at length secured the General Staff Act of 1903, which created the General Staff Corps and the office of Chief of Staff and permitted the War College Board to give way to an Army War College. Meanwhile, through sponsorship of the Militia Act of 1903, also called the Dick Act, Root transformed the historic state militia into essentially the modern National Guard, with the beginnings of effective federal control over militia training and efficiency.

Root resigned his secretaryship late in 1903 so that he could resume family life in New York, and he returned to his law practice on February 1, 1904. But as he said of entering the War Department, "I took the United States for my client," and he proved to have bound himself too closely to the client to stay away. After working diligently in 1904 for the reelection of President Theodore Roosevelt,* he accepted Roosevelt's call to become secretary of state on July 19, 1905. Roosevelt was mainly his own secretary of state, and he initiated the American plunge into European diplomacy in the Algeciras Conference over Root's misgivings. Root could act effectively, however, in areas in which Roosevelt took a lesser interest, softening the effects of the Roosevelt Corollary and improving relations with Latin America in a tour of the southern continent in connection with the Third Conference of the American Republics at Rio de Janeiro in 1906, and pursuing his hope for the arbitration of international disputes through securing a voluntary arbitration pledge at the Second Hague Conference in 1907 and through negotiation of twenty-seven bilateral arbitration treaties. In the Japanese war scare that grew out of San Francisco school segregation, Root remained calmer than Roosevelt, and in general his influence was exerted toward good relations with Japan, notably in the Root-Takahira Agreement of 1908.

Root resigned from the State Department in January 1909 to accept a U.S. Senate seat from New York and entered upon a more overtly political career. Here his legal knowledge and administrative talents proved of less value than in the executive departments, and he was soon injured further by the growing split between Roosevelt and President Taft. Despite his friendship for Roosevelt, Root remained faithful to his party and was temporary chairman of the Republican National Convention in 1912. After the election of 1912 he strove to reunite the Republican party, and his election as president of the New York State Constitutional Convention was a measure of partial success in binding up the wounds.

Root left the Senate in 1915. While he was critical of President Woodrow Wilson's neutrality policy, when the United States entered World War I he urged his party to cooperate with the Democratic administration's war measures. In 1917 Wilson appointed him to head a mission to Russia to seek ways of bolstering the regime created by the March Revolution. The sweep of Russian events condemned the Root mission to frustration, though Wilson's lack of responsiveness to its reports did not help matters. Root continued in his moderate stance during the League of Nations debate, opposing Article X but favoring acceptance of the Treaty of Versailles with reservations.

As an extension of his dedication to international arbitration, Root served on the Committee of Jurists that created the Permanent Court of International Justice. He campaigned tirelessly for American membership in the court. He was a delegate to the Washington Conference of 1920–1921. Long a friend of Andrew Carnegie, he was president of the Carnegie Endowment for International Peace from 1910 to 1925, chairman of the board of the Carnegie Institution from 1913 to 1937, and president of the Carnegie Corporation in 1919–1920 and its chairman of the board from 1920 until his death. He died of complications following bronchitis and pneumonia.

Lord Haldane, preparing after the Boer War to fit the British Army for the demands of twentieth-century world power, said: "Really, you know, I do not need to know anything about armies and their organization, for the five reports of Elihu Root, made as Secretary of War in the United States, are the very last word concerning the organization and place of an army in a democracy." Such praise is not only substantially merited but also familiar enough that it scarcely requires elaboration.

The limitations of the Root reforms are less often clearly stated. Root was realistic in accepting the National Guard as the only politically feasible principal reserve for the U.S. Army, but he acquiesced in serious imperfections in the Dick Act, such as ambiguity about whether the Guard could be required to serve outside the United States, and in the long run such temporizing nourished delusions about readiness that still plague the reserve forces. Root's conception of the Army War College blurred the functions of a higher professional school with those of an adjunct of the General Staff so confusingly that the War College was long delayed in establishing itself as an educational institution. Root's conception of the General Staff was probably based less on the German model, called to his attention along with the writings of Emory Upton* by Lieutenant Colonel W. H. Carter, than on his aim of bringing to the Army the principles of business management developed in the corporate world. This purpose linked his War Department reforms to one of the principal themes of the Progressive Movement. But like his idea of the War College, his conception of the General Staff was less than clearly thought out. He hoped simultaneously to give the Army effective management and to free the General Staff from day-to-day administration so that it could plan. The effect was to lift the General Staff into an ivory tower, leave the real control of the Army in the traditional War Department bureaus, and delay the assured ascendancy of the General Staff at least until Leonard Wood's tenure as chief of staff and probably until World War I.

For all that, Root, the civilian without military experience, focused steadily on the mission of the peacetime army as preparation for war. Few soldiers have had a vision so uncluttered by nonessentials. To permit the Army in its new role as an instrument of world power to prepare effectively for war was the goal and, however imperfectly, the achievement of the Root reforms.

BIBLIOGRAPHY

Bacon, Robert, and James B. Scott, eds. *The Military and Colonial Policy of the United States: Addresses and Reports by Elihu Root.* Cambridge, Mass.: Harvard University Press, 1924.
Hammond, Paul Y. *Organizing for Defense: The American Military Establishment in the Twentieth Century.* Princeton, N.J.: Princeton University Press, 1961.
Hewes, James E., Jr. *From Root to McNamara: Army Organization and Administration, 1900–1963.* Washington, D.C.: Center of Military History, 1975.
Jessup, Philip C. *Elihu Root.* 2 vols. New York: Dodd, Mead, 1938.
Leopold, Richard. *Elihu Root and the Conservative Tradition.* Boston: Little, Brown, 1954.

RUSSELL A. WEIGLEY

ROSECRANS, William Starke (b. Delaware County, Ohio, September 6, 1819; d. near Los Angeles, Calif., March 11, 1898), Army officer, public official. Rosecrans was a senior Union officer in the Western Theatre during the Civil War.

William S. Rosecrans came from one of the pioneer families that settled in

Ohio. His father was a farmer-merchant of modest means, and Rosecrans received only a sporadic education in public schools. He was a voracious reader, however, and was able to educate himself. He secured an appointment to the U.S. Military Academy at West Point, New York, in 1838. Rosecrans performed well while at the Academy, graduating number five in a class of fifty-one. Because of his academic performance, he was rewarded with a commission as brevet second lieutenant, Corps of Engineers, as of July 1, 1842. An assignment to the Engineers was usually given only to the best Academy graduates. After working for a year on fortifications at Hampton Roads, Virginia, Rosecrans returned to West Point for the next four years as an assistant professor of engineering.

For the next several years Rosecrans was engaged in a number of different Army engineering projects until he resigned as of April 1, 1854, to enter business as an architect and civil engineer in Cincinnati, Ohio. He then moved to western Virginia to serve briefly as president of the New Coal River-Slack Water Navigation Company, resigning in 1857 to refine kerosene in Cincinnati. That year, he was severely burned by an explosion of a "safety" kerosene lamp on which he was working, taking many months to recover. In early 1861 his company was just beginning to be profitable.

On the outbreak of the Civil War, Rosecrans served as a volunteer aide to Major General George Brinton McClellan,* organizing and training new troops from April 19 until June 10, when he was appointed colonel of the 23d Ohio Volunteer Infantry Regiment. As a promising officer and a Catholic and a Democrat, Rosecrans was an ideal choice for a Republican administration seeking broad support. President Abraham Lincoln* approved his commission as a brigadier general in the Regular Army, ranking from May 16. He commanded a brigade in McClellan's operations in western Virginia, and he won the Battle of Rich Mountain, July 11. Rosecrans succeeded McClellan in command of the Department of the Ohio before being assigned to command the Department of Western Virginia from September 21 to April 7, 1862.

Rosecrans was transferred west to command a division of the Army of the Mississippi and participated in the siege of Corinth, Mississippi, May 22–30. He commanded the Army of the Mississippi from June 11 until October 20. Rosecrans, under the command of Major General Ulysses Simpson Grant,* fought in the Battle of Iuka, Mississippi, September 19, but failed to trap the retreating Confederate forces as Grant had planned. This was the beginning of the friction that developed between the two men. The following day, Rosecrans learned that he had been promoted to major general to rank from March 21. In the Battle of Corinth, October 3–4, Rosecrans was attacked, and after a brief penetration by the Confederate forces into Corinth, he repulsed them while inflicting heavy losses. Rosecrans, however, delayed pursuing the disorganized Confederates for a day, allowing them to escape with most of their equipment which further annoyed Grant. Even so, Rosecrans had demonstrated considerable skill in his handling of the troops during the actual engagement.

With these two partial successes to his credit, Rosecrans was placed in command of the Army of the Cumberland in middle Tennessee on October 27 to face the Confederate Army of the Tennessee under Braxton Bragg.* Late in December, after building up his supplies in Nashville, Rosecrans advanced on Bragg, meeting him in the Battle of Murfreesboro (Stone's River), December 31. Bragg's aggressive attack was a tactical success, and his army inflicted more than thirteen thousand Union casualties while suffering only nine thousand of their own. Rosecrans was in a vulnerable position, but Bragg did not renew the assault. The Confederate force withdrew toward Tullahoma, Tennessee, on January 3, allowing Rosecrans to claim victory by virtue of having possession of the battlefield.

Rosecrans spent the next six months planning, organizing, and equipping his army. While his army grew stronger, Bragg's was shrinking. This fact was obvious to Rosecrans' superiors who constantly urged him to act while he had the advantage. Finally, on June 24, Rosecrans opened a brilliant campaign, and, by September 9, he had maneuvered Bragg out of Chattanooga without a fight. But help was on the way for Bragg's depleted army in the form of reinforcements from Mississippi and a corps from the Army of Northern Virginia under James Longstreet.* In the Battle of Chickamauga, Georgia, September 19–20, Rosecrans made a serious error by moving a division and leaving a gap in his line which the attacking Confederates exploited with disastrous effects. Apparently defeated by Bragg, he left the battlefield before the battle was over. The heroic stand of Major General George Henry Thomas* saved the army from complete annihilation. Rosecrans retreated to Chattanooga with his disorganized forces and was besieged, inexplicably allowing Bragg to occupy the high ground around the city. Cut off from significant resupply, Rosecrans faced a grim situation. He began planning for the reopening of his supply lines but had not acted when Thomas relieved him by Grant's orders on October 19.

Rosecrans' last active command was the Department of the Missouri from January 28 to December 9, 1864. He became alarmed about an alleged conspiracy uncovered in the state. Predicting an uprising, he constantly called for reinforcements for a relatively inactive military theater at a time when Union armies elsewhere needed every available soldier. These constant calls dismayed Grant, leading him to observe that Rosecrans would make similar calls if he were "stationed in Maine." After his removal from command in Missouri, Rosecrans was either awaiting orders or on leave of absence, until his resignation as of March 28, 1867.

After his resignation, Rosecrans served briefly as the U.S. minister to Mexico until Grant was elected president. He then pursued various mining, manufacturing, and railroad interests in California and Mexico, and served in the U.S. House of Representatives as a Democrat (1881–1885). As chairman of the House Committee on Military Affairs, Rosecrans was one of the few people in the country to oppose Grant's restoration to general after he had suffered severe financial reverses and was dying from cancer.

Rosecrans' reputation as a military commander is mixed. An intelligent man, an excellent planner and organizer, he sometimes lacked aggressiveness in executing his plans. His early successes in western Virginia demonstrated his organizational abilities and a marked ability to work with volunteer troops—an essential ingredient for success during the Civil War. He was personally brave under fire, but he had a tendency to get excited and give too many orders which were confusing to his commanders during the heat of battle. And, at times, he demonstrated flashes of strategic genius as he did during the summer of 1863.

Rosecrans bitterly denounced Grant's version of the battles of Iuka and Corinth, but the record indicates that Rosecrans was slow to move at crucial moments. This slowness was costly, allowing Confederate forces to escape from precarious situations without further molestation. And this slowness to move was even more costly after the Battle of Murfreesboro. Rosecrans evidently believed that it was unwise for the country to fight more than one major battle at a time, which may explain his delay in attacking Bragg when the Confederate Army of Tennessee was vulnerable. Had Rosecrans moved on Bragg earlier when Confederate forces were occupied at Vicksburg and in Pennsylvania, he might have been able to inflict a fatal blow to the Confederacy. Rosecrans' campaign of maneuver in the summer of 1863 was brilliantly executed. But it occurred at a time when Bragg could not afford to fight until help could arrive from the east and west after July 1863. Without this help, there would not have been a Battle of Chickamauga. During this battle Rosecrans lost his head and fled from the battlefield in despair at a time when he should have been doing all in his power to reorganize his shattered army.

Embittered by his relief at Chattanooga, Rosecrans developed a life-long hatred for Grant, blaming him for many of the things that had befallen him. It is true that Grant developed a healthy dislike for Rosecrans and refused to consider him for any important field command. But no amount of hatred, or making of excuses, could undo the consequences of that day at Chickamauga.

BIBLIOGRAPHY

Bearss, Edwin. *Decision in Mississippi.* Jackson, Miss.: Mississippi Commission on the War between the States, 1962.
Catton, Bruce. *Grant Moves South.* Boston: Little, Brown and Company, 1960.
Lamers, William M. *The Edge of Glory: A Biography of General William S. Rosecrans.* New York: Harcourt, Brace and World, 1961.
McDonough, James L. *Stone's River.* Knoxville: University of Tennessee Press, 1980.
Tucker, Glenn. *Chickamauga.* Indianapolis, Ind.: Bobbs-Merrill, 1961.

DAVID L. WILSON

S

ST. CLAIR, Arthur (b. Thurso, Caithness, Scotland, 1736 or 1743 [sources differ]; d. Westmoreland County, Pa., August 31, 1818), soldier and politician of the Revolutionary era.

Very little is known of St. Clair's youth, and even his ancestry is unclear. He was well educated and may have attended the University of Edinburgh. On May 13, 1757, he purchased a commission as ensign in the 60th Regiment of Foot, the Royal Americans. He first saw action at Louisbourg in 1758, and at Quebec in 1759 Lieutenant St. Clair climbed the cliffs with Colonel William Howe's advance force.

St. Clair was sent to Boston with dispatches, and he returned there in May 1760 to marry Phoebe Bayard, a niece of Governor James Bowdoin. After further service in Canada he resigned from the Army in April 1762, and nothing is known of his life for the next few years. St. Clair appeared in the late 1760s as a large landowner in the Ligonier Valley of Pennsylvania, near Pittsburgh. He supported the proprietary government in its disputes with Virginia but played no part in the controversies with the mother country. In the summer of 1775 he was elected colonel of the Westmoreland County militia, and on January 3, 1776, the Continental Congress named him colonel in the Continental service. He recruited his regiment rapidly and marched to Canada in time to cover the retreat from Quebec and Montreal.

Congress promoted St. Clair to brigadier general on August 9, 1776, and in November he was ordered to march his brigade south to join General George Washington.* He led his troops across the Delaware River and into Trenton during Washington's daring attack of December 26. St. Clair was credited by his friends with suggesting the flanking movement which was the key to Washington's victory at Princeton on January 3, 1777. In recognition of his achievements, St. Clair was promoted by Congress on February 19, becoming the only Pennsylvanian to win the rank of major general.

Early in June St. Clair was ordered to Ticonderoga, the only fortress in the path of the expected British advance from Canada. When he assumed command on June 12 he found the fort in disrepair, with a garrison of twenty-two hundred to defend works designed for a force of ten thousand. He acted energetically to rebuild the fortifications before the enemy reached Ticonderoga. John Burgoyne's army appeared on July 1, but instead of assaulting the American works, the British pulled their artillery up the supposedly impossible slopes of nearby Sugar Loaf (renamed Mount Defiance by the British). Faced by a bombardment to which he could make no reply, St. Clair decided to save his troops and abandon Ticonderoga. The evacuation was successfully achieved on the night of July 5–6, but St. Clair was relieved of command while Congress investigated. After many delays and political disputes, he was tried by court-martial in August 1778 and completely exonerated.

St. Clair had a horse killed under him while at Brandywine, endured the winter at Valley Forge, and fought at Monmouth, as a staff officer. Upon his vindication by the court-martial, St. Clair was given command of a division of the Pennsylvania Line, and he took charge briefly at West Point when Benedict Arnold's* treason was discovered. In 1781 he brought additional Pennsylvania troops to Yorktown for the final days of the siege. He was later sent southward with six regiments to reinforce General Nathanael Greene,* but he saw no further combat. St. Clair's last service was in calming a mutiny of Pennsylvania troops who threatened Congress in June 1783.

The war and his long absence from home had greatly injured St. Clair's finances, and he settled in Philadelphia as a merchant and city auctioneer. He was elected to the Continental Congress on November 11, 1785. As president of Congress for the year 1787, he presided during the adoption of the Northwest Ordinance, and on October 5, 1787, Congress named him as the first governor of the new Northwest Territory.

As governor St. Clair also had charge of negotiations with the Indians, but he was unable to persuade them to make way for the advance of settlement. After Josiah Harmar was defeated by the Indians in 1790, the new federal government determined upon stronger measures. On March 4, 1791, President Washington appointed St. Clair major general, but St. Clair retained his civil office as governor while serving as the highest ranking officer of the Army. Secretary of War Henry Knox* directed St. Clair to march through Indian Country to the forks of the Maumee River (Fort Wayne, Indiana), where he was to build a fort. Next he was to seek out the Indians and "strike them with great severity." His force of regulars, six-month levies, and Kentucky militia gathered slowly at Fort Washington in Cincinnati, while the War Department and its contractors mismanaged the supply, food, and transport arrangements. St. Clair's men, far fewer than the intended three thousand, ill-equipped and only partly trained, moved north on October 4, almost three months behind schedule. At sunrise on November 4, along the banks of the upper Wabash River (at Fort Recovery, Ohio), about one hundred miles north of Cincinnati, his camp was surprised by the confederated tribes of the Northwest. After several hours of bloody fighting, with the soldiers in the open and the Indians well concealed, St. Clair ordered a withdrawal. At this point his troops broke and ran the twenty-nine miles back to Fort Jefferson before nightfall. Of some fourteen hundred soldiers on the battlefield, St. Clair lost more than six hundred killed and nearly three hundred wounded, the greatest losses ever suffered by the U.S. Army in an engagement with the Indians.

Because St. Clair was the only major general in the Army, it was impossible to convene the court-martial he requested. His campaign was investigated by a committee of the House of Representatives, and St. Clair was absolved from blame. The War and Treasury departments, the contractors, and the quartermaster were severely criticized by the committee. Arthur St. Clair left the Army forever but continued as governor, stubbornly resisting the growing demand for statehood in Ohio until he was removed from office on November 22, 1802. He returned to the Ligonier Valley and spent his declining years trying to vindicate his reputation and settle his Revolutionary War accounts. He died poor and almost forgotten in 1818.

Arthur St. Clair was a competent but unimaginative officer who was very unlucky in his two opportunities for independent command. Although he came to America as a British Army officer, he remained as a permanent settler and never visited his native Britain. A true patriot, he was a reluctant rebel who remained deeply conservative in his politics, a firm Federalist among increasingly hostile frontiersmen.

His wife inherited a fortune of £14,000, but St. Clair failed both in trade and as a landowner. As an officer and as governor, his career was marked by strict honesty, and he made no profit from his long service in the Northwest. He openly denounced land speculation by holders of public office, an exceptional opinion for the 1790s. His long service in both military and civil appointments between 1776 and 1802 came not only from a firm sense of duty but also from his need for a steady salary.

Most scholars agree with the court-martial that his evacuation of Ticonderoga was entirely justified, although Samuel Adams and General Philip Schuyler* insisted that the fort could have been defended. Ticonderoga was popularly believed to be impregnable, and St. Clair was widely criticized for its loss. Yet had he delayed one day longer he would have been cut off by both land and water and subjected to continuous plunging artillery fire. The fact that Washington found him worthy of trust demonstrates the approval of a most demanding military critic.

It would be easy to say that St. Clair's 1791 campaign was doomed from the beginning, but this is untrue. His appointment and the plan for the campaign came so late in the season that he lacked time to prepare properly. Nevertheless, despite age, generally poor health, and recurring attacks of the gout, St. Clair exerted himself to raise the Western militia and prod the delinquent recruiters and the quartermaster appointed by Secretary Knox. He was compelled to do most of his own staff work, and he did it well. He was troubled by desertion, inadequate food, unfit equipment, and early frosts which destroyed the forage, but still he moved his column forward. He must be blamed, however, for continued arguments with his officers, for his slow advance, and for his total lack of intelligence. St. Clair had no idea which Indian nations or how many fighting men were gathered to oppose him, or where they were concentrated. St. Clair had little understanding of frontier warfare despite his long military career, and he made no use of his experienced Kentucky militiamen as scouts. Despite all of his problems and errors, there still would have been no disaster had he simply ordered out patrols when his troops were called to arms before dawn on November 4. Instead, they were dismissed at sunrise, and then the Indians attacked through the mists. St. Clair conducted an energetic defense for several hours and then led the remainder of his men in breaking through the enemy surrounding his camp. Only then did his troops panic and run. St. Clair showed his strong character in his report to Knox, making no effort to hide his terrible losses or evade responsibility. The House committee, the first congressional investigation under the new Constitution, found that he was not to blame for the failure of his expedition, and in the strict sense this was true. Arthur St. Clair was a stubborn and unfortunate general, never a popular commander, but he was always a brave and honest man.

BIBLIOGRAPHY

Freeman, Douglas Southall. *George Washington*. 7 vols. New York: Scribner's, 1948–1957.
Furlong, Patrick J. "The Investigation of General Arthur St. Clair, 1792–1793." *Capitol Studies* 5 (Fall 1977): 65–86.
Jacobs, James R. *The Beginning of the U.S. Army, 1783–1812*. Princeton, N.J.: Princeton University Press, 1947.
Kohn, Richard H. *Eagle and Sword: The Federalists and the Creation of the Military Establishment in America, 1783–1802*. New York: Free Press, 1975.
St. Clair, Arthur. *A Narrative...the Campaign Against the Indians...Under the Command of Major General St. Clair*. Philadelphia: Jane Aitken, 1812. Reprinted, New York: Arno Press, 1971.
Smith, William H. *The St. Clair Papers. The Life and Public Services of Arthur St. Clair...with His Correspondence and Other papers*. 2 vols. Cincinnati: Robert Clarke and Company, 1882. Reprinted, New York: Da Capo Press, 1971.

PATRICK J. FURLONG

SAMPSON, William Thomas (b. Palmyra, N.Y., February 9, 1840; d. Washington, D.C., May 6, 1902), naval officer. Sampson was commander in chief of the North Atlantic Squadron at the time of the defeat of Admiral Pascual Cervera's squadron in the Spanish-American War.

William T. Sampson was the oldest child of Presbyterian Scotch-Irish immigrant parents who settled in Palmyra, New York. An excellent student, young Sampson won an appointment to the U.S. Naval Academy in 1857. He was an outstanding student at the Naval Academy and was especially interested in ordnance. He was first in his class in his last three years and earned a reputation at the Academy for modesty and scholarship.

As a graduate in the spring of 1861, Sampson helped to defend the Naval Academy grounds against unfriendly local citizens while the underclassmen were transferred to Newport, Rhode Island. At the end of April he reported to Commander John Adolphus Bernard Dahlgren,* the famous gun inventor, at the Washington Navy Yard. The capital was in a state of tension in those early weeks of the Civil War, and Sampson found himself concerned with cut telegraph lines, damaged or destroyed rail bridges, and attacks on Potomac steamers. In May Sampson served a brief stint aboard the sloop *Pocahontas*, and in June he reported to the *Potomac*, now an acting master, for nine months' duty in the Gulf of Mexico.

In 1862 Sampson was promoted to lieutenant and began his first assignment as an instructor at the Naval Academy, temporarily established at Newport. His great interest in armor, steam engines, and ordnance led him to accept the wartime teaching post without protest. In 1863 he served on a practice cruise to England and France aboard the frigate *Macedonia*. Sampson's midshipmen included most of his future captains and the leading naval officers of the Spanish-American War.

In 1864 Sampson was ordered to the South Atlantic Blockading Squadron as executive officer in the new monitor, *Patapsco*. He won praise for his coolness and composure when the *Patapsco* was sunk by a Confederate torpedo. In July 1866, amidst sharp cuts and economies in the Navy, he was promoted to lieutenant commander.

After the Civil War, Sampson's assignments were varied. He served for two years as a watch officer aboard the screw frigate *Colorado* of the European Squadron. In 1868 he began three energetic years of service as head of the new Department of Physics and Chemistry at the Naval Academy. He was then assigned as executive officer in the frigate *Congress* on European Station from 1871 to 1874. In was a time of embarrassment for U.S. naval officers as they witnessed a dramatic decline in every area of their nation's naval establishment. Sampson returned to the Naval Academy in 1874 where he introduced advanced scientific studies in several areas. Sampson's first command was aboard the screw gunboat *Swatara* in 1882. His next assignment was as assistant to the superintendent of the Naval Observatory in Washington for two years under four different superintendents; in effect, he headed the observatory. From 1884 to 1886 Sampson was inspector of ordnance and head of the Torpedo Station in Newport, where, with Commodore Stephen Bleeker Luce,* he urged the creation of the Naval War College. Commander Sampson returned to Annapolis in September 1886 for three years as superintendent of the Naval Academy. As superintendent he presided over meetings of the U.S. Naval Institute during a period of vigorous technical activity. Sampson was promoted to captain in March 1889.

Captain Sampson left the Academy in the summer of 1890 to supervise the final technical installations aboard the new cruiser, *San Francisco*. On March 31, 1891, with Rear Admiral George Brown aboard, the *San Francisco*, commanded by Sampson, left for observation patrol off strife-torn Chile. In June 1892 Sampson became superintendent of the naval gun foundry in Washington and then served as chief of the Bureau of Ordnance, 1893–1897. Placed in command of the new battleship *Iowa* in June 1897, Sampson impressed Assistant Secretary of the Navy Theodore Roosevelt* as talented, level-headed, and dependable during fleet drills off the Virginia capes.

Sampson presided over the board of inquiry on the *Maine* disaster in Havana and, in recognition of his outstanding record, was appointed commander in chief of the North Atlantic Squadron on the eve of war with Spain. On April 21, 1898, he hoisted the pennant of rear admiral aboard his flagship, *New York*, and began to move his forces to a blockade of northern Cuba. He unsuccessfully sought from the Navy Department a clarification of operations between himself and Commodore Winfield Scott Schley* of the Flying Squadron. Schley, though two numbers senior to Sampson, was finally placed under Sampson's orders on May 24 by Secretary of the Navy John D. Long.

After an eastward cruise to Puerto Rico in search of Admiral Pascual Cervera's fleet, Sampson returned first to Key West and a meeting with Schley (May 18) and then to a blockade of Cuban waters. Sampson established that Cervera was in Santiago and ordered Schley (May 25) to proceed there at once and blockade the harbor. He returned to Key West to convoy Army units and learned that Schley had not moved directly into blockade position. He went there himself and arrived on June 1 and met with Schley. Sampson established an effective month-long close blockade of Santiago with searchlights fixed at night on the narrow harbor entrance. He seized Guantanamo Bay, supervised operations in support of the Army, directed all minor operations, bombardments, and reconnaissance, and was in command of more than one hundred vessels.

On the morning of July 3 Sampson had sailed seven miles to the east for a conference with General William Rufus Shafter* when Cervera's squadron came out of Santiago and under the guns of the blockading force. Every Spanish vessel was captured or destroyed, with only minimal U.S. casualties. However, the press deserted Sampson and made Schley the hero of the successful action against the Spanish, though Sampson was defended by the service and the Navy Department.

Although in poor health, Sampson continued in command of the North Atlantic Station for one more year. He became commandant of the Boston Navy Yard at the end of 1899, but his health continued to decline. On May 6, 1902, he died in Washington.

Sampson was a distinguished naval leader whose reputation has suffered from controversies inspired by sensational newspaper stories in an age noted for journalistic excesses. His meticulousness at every stage of his service at the Naval

Academy helped the institution make a difficult transition into the age of advanced technology and scientific education. His thorough knowledge of armor plate metallurgy was of considerable value in the advancement of the American steel industry and the design and construction of modern naval vessels.

In the Spanish-American War Sampson successfully bore primary responsibility for preventing attacks on American coastal cities by locating and confining the Spanish Squadron. He provided the Army with transportation and supplies under difficult circumstances, and carried on effective reconnaissance and communications operations over an extensive range with limited equipment. His knowledge of armor and gunnery, and his experience with the men and ships under his command enabled him to construct an effective blockade which ultimately forced the enemy into a desperate attempt to escape. His effective gunnery drills, fleet exercises, and blockade plans prior to the battle all contributed to the American victory off Santiago. With pride he reported to Washington: ''The fleet under my command offers the nation as a Fourth of July present the whole of Cervera's fleet.''

At first, all the acclaim and admiration for the victory in Cuba went to Sampson; then within a few days the brilliance of his fame faded. He was criticized for minimizing Schley's accomplishments, for stealing a victory that was not his. Circumstances had drawn him off the battleline that morning and had delayed his return to action. The press divided into pro-Schley and pro-Sampson factions, and the Congress fueled the controversy by refusing to confirm the Navy Department's August 10, 1898, recommendation that Sampson be advanced eight numbers and Schley six. Finally, both men were made rear admirals by the Personnel Act of 1899, but Sampson never properly gained the recognition from his countrymen which he so properly deserved for his exemplary service and achievements.

BIBLIOGRAPHY

Azoy, A.C.M. *Signal 250! The Sea Fight Off Santiago*. New York: David McKay Company, 1964.
Herrick, Walter R., Jr. *The American Naval Revolution*. Baton Rouge: Louisiana State University Press, 1966.
Karsten, Peter. *The Naval Aristocracy: The Golden Age of Annapolis and the Emergence of Modern American Navalism*. New York: Free Press, 1972.
West, Richard S. *Admirals of American Empire*. New York: Bobbs-Merrill Company, 1948.

PHILIP Y. NICHOLSON

SCHLEY, Winfield Scott (b. Frederick County, Md., October 9, 1839; d. New York City, N.Y., October 2, 1909), naval officer. Schley is known for his command of the Flying Squadron at the victorious Battle of Santiago, July 3, 1898, in the Spanish-American War.

Winfield Scott Schley was born in his father's manor house, ''Richfields,'' in Frederick County, Maryland. He won appointment to the U.S. Naval Academy in 1856 through the assistance of Representative H. W. Hoffman. Though not known for his scholarship, he loved the work and the camaraderie of his two practice cruises.

His first post was aboard the steam frigate *Niagra* in June 1860. At the outset of the Civil War the *Niagara* was placed on blockade duty off Charleston. Schley's first command was the delivery of the captured prize *General Parkhill* to the admiralty court in Philadelphia. Subsequently, Schley twice won distinction for hazardous volunteer duty under fire in small boats during a year's blockade duty off Mobile Bay. Promoted to lieutenant in 1862, he was made executive officer of the steam gunboat *Winona* in the squadron of Admiral David Glasgow Farragut* at Mobile Bay. He was navigator in the steam sloop *Richmond* and acted in command of the large ship on the occasional absences of the captain and executive officer. He was in command during the May 26, 1863, bombardment of Port Hudson, Louisiana, and won praise from Farragut for his fighting spirit. After his marriage to Annie Rebecca Franklin in September 1863, he was assigned to the Bureau of Ordnance. Later, Schley became executive officer in the double-ender *Wateree* for a futile search mission in the Pacific for the Confederate raider *Shenandoah*.

Twenty years of stagnation and decline characterized the U.S. Navy after the Civil War, but Schley remained popular with his associates and was on the fringes of that group of officers who gained the best assignments. He was acting assistant professor of Spanish at the Naval Academy from 1867 to 1869, and became friendly with George Dewey* who, along with William Thomas Sampson,* came to Annapolis at the same time. As executive officer aboard the screw cruiser *Benicia* (1869–1873), Schley saw action in a punitive expedition in Korea in June 1871. He added four more years at Annapolis as chairman of the Modern Languages Department, and from 1876 to 1879 Commander Schley was skipper of the frigate *Essex* in the South Atlantic. Next he was posted to Boston for four years as an inspector in the Lighthouse Service. Schley worked closely with Secretary William E. Chandler as chief of the apprentice system in the Bureau of Equipment and Recruiting in 1883. Schley gained national attention in 1884 for his successful and hazardous command of the *Thetis* and *Bear* in the rescue expedition that returned Army Lieutenant Adolphus W. Greely* and six other survivors from near death in the Arctic Ocean north of Greenland. In recognition of his achievement, Schley, though a commander, was made chief of the Bureau of Equipment and Recruiting, where he served from 1884 to 1889.

Schley was promoted to captain in 1887 and was given command of the new cruiser *Baltimore* in July 1889. In 1891 he persuaded Secretary Benjamin F. Tracy to send him to Chile with the *Baltimore* during the diplomatic crisis there. Schley's action in cutting the telegraph cable from the rebel-held city of Iquique increased the Chileans' hostility toward the United States and focused that hostility most sharply on the *Baltimore* and her crew. A fight in the True Blue Saloon in Valparaiso resulted in the death of two of Schley's sailors; others were injured and thirty-six arrested. These troubles provoked sharp diplomatic reaction and the threat of war for several months. After his return from Chile, Schley moved to New York where he served as inspector for the Third Lighthouse District from 1892 to 1895.

In October 1895, after brief service on the Board of Inspection and Survey, Schley took command of the armored cruiser *New York*, the flagship of Admiral F. M. Bunce's Atlantic Squadron. He was named commodore in March 1898 and placed in command of the fast cruiser *Brooklyn*, the flagship of the Flying Squadron. His orders were to protect the coastal cities of the United States, an assignment, wrote Secretary of the Navy, John Long, that "was especially desirable, and one to which any one of his seniors might have felt entitled."

The declaration of war with Spain in April 1898 and the discovery of Admiral Pascual Cervera's squadron near Martinique sent Schley and his squadron to join Admiral Sampson and the Atlantic Squadron. Their object was to blockade the Spaniards in Cuba. Schley was indirectly placed under Sampson's command and sent to blockade the southern railroad port of Cienfuegos where Cervera was believed to have gone. Schley seemed to hesitate there, remaining in place from May 22 to 24 in spite of urgings to go to Santiago. His slow journey to Santiago where he first failed to establish a close blockade, then his peculiar retrograde movement toward Key West, and finally his leisurely return at about seven knots to Santiago earned him sharp criticism. (After the war President Theodore Roosevelt* convened a special naval court of inquiry to investigate the charges raised about his conduct. Admiral George Dewey presided, and in late 1901 the court of inquiry found Schley's actions prior to June 1, 1898, to be characterized by "vacillation, dilatoriness, and lack of enterprise.")

From June 1 to July 3, 1898, Schley's squadron joined Sampson's forces in a carefully controlled blockade of Santiago. When Cervera's ships made an attempt to escape, Schley's *Brooklyn* led in the attack which resulted in a complete victory over the Spanish. Sampson had withdrawn aboard the *New York* to confer with General William Rufus Shafter* seven miles east of the battle, and by the time Sampson had returned, the Spanish had been beaten. This prompted some public resentment over crediting the victory to Sampson. A subsequent Sampson-Schley controversy was carried on in the press and by their staffs, though Schley publicly acknowledged Sampson's right to the victory as the commander of U.S. naval forces at the time of the battle.

Schley was welcomed as a hero in New York and Washington in August 1898. He was promoted to rear admiral in 1899, and in November of that year was named commander in chief of the South Atlantic Station where he served until shortly before his retirement on October 9, 1901, at the statutory age limit of sixty-two. He traveled widely, speaking frequently as an honored and popular figure, and in 1904 he published his autobiography, *Forty-Five Years under the Flag*.

Undoubtedly, Schley was a controversial officer. In the Chilean crisis of 1891, he vigorously defended his sailors and won their warmest praise in return. He maintained that they had not been drunk or provocative; rather, they had been victims of premeditated attacks by Valparaiso's populace, aided by officials and police.

As chief of the Bureau of Equipment, Schley instigated important changes beneficial to sailors. On his urging the Navy adopted the practice of issuing standardized clothing to sailors. He established the first school to train Navy cooks and urged the use of a pension system for sailors comparable to that avialable to soldiers of the U.S. Army.

Schley's caution during the uncertain period prior to the exact location of Cervera's squadron in Santiago was said to have been due to a "passion for full bunkers." (Apparently, his rescue of Lieutenant Greely in the Arctic Ocean strongly impressed upon Schley the need for proper coal reserves.) Schley was known to regularly subtract from his coal reserves the amount needed to return to Key West, a possible contingency, though never really a necessity.

The court of inquiry that criticized his cautious actions before June 1, 1898, praised Schley for his coolness in battle. He was said to have "encouraged in his own person, his subordinate officers and men to fight courageously." His old friend, Admiral Dewey, dissented from the criticism of the majority. Dewey believed that Schley had been "in absolute command, and is entitled to the credit due to such a commanding officer for the glorious victory which resulted in the total destruction of the Spanish ships." In spite of controversy, Schley's reputation rests on his outstanding capabilities and achievements as a naval commander.

BIBLIOGRAPHY

Azoy, A.C.M. *Signal 250! The Sea Fight off Santiago*. New York: David McKay Company, 1964.
Herrick, Walter R., Jr. *The American Naval Revolution*. Baton Rouge: Louisiana State University Press, 1966.
Schley, Winfield Scott. *Forty-Five Years under the Flag*. New York: D. Appleton and Company, 1904.
West, Richard S., Jr. *Admirals of American Empire*. New York: Bobbs-Merrill, 1948.

                                                                    PHILIP Y. NICHOLSON

SCHOFIELD, John McAllister (b. Gerry, N.Y., September 29, 1831; d. St. Augustine, Fla., March 4, 1906), Army officer. Schofield was a Union corps commander and commanding general of the U.S. Army, 1888–1895, perhaps the most effective peacetime occupant of that office.

Son of a Baptist minister, John M. Schofield passed his childhood in Chautauqua County, New York, and his adolescence in Freeport, Illinois. An outgoing congressman's search for a replacement appointee to the U.S. Military Academy diverted the Illinois youth from his contemplated law studies; he finished seventh of fifty-two in the class of 1853. Schofield's early duties as an artillery officer took him to Florida and then, after a bout with malaria, to Professor W.H.C.

Bartlett's Philosophy Department at West Point. In 1857 he married Bartlett's daughter, Harriet. Three years later, the young first lieutenant, discouraged about promotion prospects, obtained leave from the Army to accept a physics professorship at St. Louis's Washington University.

This civilian position placed Schofield at the heart of the Missouri secession controversy, and by the end of November 1861, he was a brigadier general of both the U.S. Volunteers and the state militia. Except for a month's respite heading a division, John Schofield passed the first three years of the Civil War in military commands within the Missouri-Kansas political cauldron.

In January 1864 General Schofield's Missouri ordeal terminated with an appointment to his cherished field command over the Department and Army of the Ohio. With essentially a corps-size unit, he led the smallest of the three grand divisions in the army of William Tecumseh Sherman* in the drive upon Atlanta. Following that city's fall, Schofield and his army assisted George Henry Thomas,* whom Sherman had left to manage further operations against Confederates under John Bell Hood.* Thomas assigned Schofield to hinder Hood's invasion of Tennessee sufficiently to permit the concentration of the main Federal force at Nashville. Accomplishing this objective, General Schofield escaped an entrapment and seriously weakened the army of his aggressive opponent, a West Point classmate, in two battles. At Spring Hill, Tennessee, on November 29, 1864, Hood failed to defeat an entrenched Union division under David S. Stanley, and the next day at Franklin, repeated Confederate assaults upon Schofield's entire army could not break his lines. As a result of the Franklin victory, John M. Schofield added a Regular Army brigadier general's commission to the two stars he then held in the U.S. Volunteers. Schofield reinforced Thomas in Nashville, but the superior's cautious deliberation before finally moving against the vastly outnumbered Hood frustrated the subordinate.

Transferred east with his command by his own request in early 1865, Schofield directed the operations capturing Wilmington, Kinston, and Goldsboro, North Carolina. There, presently reunited with Sherman, he concluded the war as commander of the Department of North Carolina.

In June he turned his attention to foreign affairs at the invitation of General Ulysses Simpson Grant* who proposed that Schofield organize, under the auspices of the Mexican Republic, an army of Americans to drive the French out of that country. Favoring less bellicose means, Secretary of State William H. Seward deflected development of Grant's audacious plan, yet increased pressure upon the French by dispatching John Schofield under State Department authority to Paris in November 1865.

After a half-year's sojourn in Europe, General Schofield became commander of the Department of the Potomac in August 1866. The imposition of congressional Reconstruction in March 1867 put him over the first of the newly drawn military districts, the state of Virginia. Personally sympathetic to conservative whites and dubious of black suffrage, Schofield, in his government of Virginia, steered an extraordinarily delicate course which met the requirements of the

Reconstruction Acts, heeded interests of native whites, and preserved his own nonpartisan military identity. This Reconstruction record augmented by excellent personal relations with General Grant made John M. Schofield a compromise choice for secretary of war during the impeachment crisis of 1868. Upon the condition that the War Department act entirely within existing law and through regular military channels, the young general consented to his nomination before the conclusion of President Andrew Johnson's trial, and he joined the cabinet shortly after.

Promoted to major general in the Regular Army upon Grant's inauguration, Schofield, over the next nineteen years, held a series of departmental and divisional commands—Department of the Missouri, 1869–1870; Division of the Pacific, 1870–1876, including a reconnaissance mission to Hawaii in 1872–1873; Department of West Point, 1876–1880, where he was superintendent of the Military Academy; the short-lived Division of the Gulf, 1881; a second tour at the Division of the Pacific, 1882–1883; Division of the Missouri, 1883–1886; and Division of the Atlantic, 1886–1888.

The year 1888 impressed itself upon John Schofield's professional and personal life. In August, according to the custom of elevating the ranking officer, President Grover Cleveland named him to command the Army. In December he suffered the death of his wife; two and one-half years later, he married Georgia Kilbourne, a much younger woman who survived him.

Commanding General Schofield, having observed the failure of his two predecessor's bold assertions of control over staff as well as line, fashioned an ostensibly modest solution to the conduct of his grandly titled office. He turned the practical impossibility of dividing military and administrative functions between himself and the secretary of war into a declaration of complete subordination as the secretary's military advisor. Disclaiming the prerogative of commanding the bureau chiefs, Schofield steadily sought out the substance rather than appearance of power in a bureaucracy—ready access to information. With these novel approaches, he enjoyed largely cordial and effective relations with the four war secretaries under whom he served.

General Schofield's leadership of the Army coincided with dynamic institutional reform in which he could claim a prominent role. Within the officer corps, examinations for promotion, lineal instead of regimental advancement, post lyceums, and vigorous support of the existing service schools fostered professionalism. To reduce the high desertion rate, the War Department ameliorated conditions for enlisted men through an improved ration, more attractive enlistment terms, and the establishment of post exchanges, schools, and gymnasiums. A streamlined departmental organization of the line replaced the awkward mix of divisions and departments, and the Army accelerated its previously set policy of concentration at larger posts connected to the railway network. Throughout Schofield's seven years as general in chief, the U.S. Army operated primarily as a constabulary. In an era of federal inaction and impotence, the military decisively confirmed the distribution of wealth and power by its intervention in labor disputes in 1892 and, more importantly, in 1894.

Above all, military power precisely clarified the locus of sovereignty as white settlement pushed aside the Indians—the land's original inhabitants. The Army's historic mission of Indian control assumed two new distinctions under General Schofield. First, Indian Wars actually ended with the engagements at Wounded Knee and White Clay Creeks in December 1890; second, to hasten the termination of all Indian duty, Schofield, after initial reluctance, pressed the radical internal program of enlisting Indians as regular soldiers.

In theory, the Army existed for war. Military thinkers, including John M. Schofield, eliminated the necessity of specific defensive contingencies by conceiving a world of unspecified predatory great powers responsive to national weakness. During Schofield's tenure as commanding general, application of these martial doctrines was partially revealed in the report of the Endicott Board in 1886. General Schofield, as president of the Board of Ordnance and Fortification, was in the best position to see to the implementation of the Endicott Board's report. Always keenly interested in the artillery, Schofield eagerly promoted the central assignment of that branch in modern "scientific" war.

Retiring in September 1895, with a long-coveted third star which Congress had given him in February, Schofield maintained his public interest in military and veterans affairs. He devoted the first two years of his retirement to writing his memoirs, and during the war with Spain, he briefly and unhappily served as informal personal military advisor to President William McKinley. Most enduringly, John Schofield advocated a general staff system, an idea he had endorsed while still in command of the Army, and his appearance in 1902 before the Senate Military Committee helped counter the adverse testimony by Commanding General Nelson Appleton Miles* regarding the general staff bill proposed by Secretary of War Elihu Root.*

Like other officers, John M. Schofield proved his military prowess at the corps level in the Civil War, but through his lengthy, unusually diverse career spanning sensitive positions and even extending abroad, he developed a singular genius for administration which his somewhat thin-skinned temperament made more remarkable. Conservative in viewpoint, he found most of his duties congenial, especially those which served to maintain or strengthen established social and economic arrangements. Yet, his abiding soldierly identity permitted a perceptible, though slight, detachment from the real holders of this power.

In the latter part of the nineteenth century, as Robert Wiebe has shown, the lag of beliefs and institutions behind rapid alteration of the nation's material base precipitated a pervasive sense of crisis uneasily resolved in a new order. By this light, the U.S. Army with its cohesive professional officer corps, its burgeoning technology, and its assigned employment formed a vanguard of the emerging national perspective. Framed accordingly, Schofield's experience, values, and considerable intellect uniquely prepared him to command the Army at a time of active institutional innovation that logically led to the Root reforms.

BIBLIOGRAPHY

Cosmas, Graham A. *An Army for Empire: The United States Army in the Spanish-American War*. Columbia: University of Missouri Press, 1971.
McDonough, James L. *Schofield, Union General in the Civil War and Reconstruction*. Tallahassee: Florida State University Press, 1972.
Schofield, John M. *Forty-Six Years in the Army*. New York: Century Company, 1897.
Utley, Robert M. *Frontier Regulars: The United States Army and The Indian, 1866–1891*. New York: Macmillan Company, 1973.
Weigley, Russell F. "The Military Thought of John M. Schofield." *Military Affairs* 28 (Summer 1959): 77–84.
Wiebe, Robert H. *The Search for Order, 1877–1920*. New York: Hill and Wang, 1967.

J. THOMAS CROUCH

SCHRIEVER, Bernard A. (b. Bremen, Germany, September 14, 1910). Air Force officer, developer of intercontinental ballistic missiles (Atlas, Thor, Titan, and Minuteman) and strategic bombers (B–58).

A native of imperial Germany, Ben Schriever migrated to the United States in 1918 when he was only eight years old. He came with his mother and brother to the small German-American community of New Braunfels, Texas, where he was reunited with his father, Adolph Schriever. As an engineer for the North German Lloyd Steamship Line, Adolph had been interned in the United States in 1917 when his ship was seized in port. Once reunited, the family was suddenly struck by tragedy as Adolph was killed in an industrial accident in September 1918.

Forced by circumstances to relocate several times, the family settled in San Antonio. There Schriever became a U.S. citizen in 1923 and attended public schools, excelling in mathematics and receiving national awards for achievement. Enrolling in Texas A&M College, he received both a degree in engineering and a reserve appointment in the U.S. Army field artillery in 1931.

A yen for flying, however, led him to enroll in the Army Air Corps Flight School in San Antonio. Surviving the rigorous academic requirements and hazardous flight training (an average of one crash every thirty hours of flying time per aircraft), he became a military pilot in 1932. The 1930s were lean for both the conservative Army Air Corps and reserve officer Schriever. Between 1932 and 1938 he had several service breaks, and during those times he worked as a commercial pilot and for a short period directed a Civilian Conservation Corps camp in New Mexico. During one tour on active duty Schriever was stationed in Panama where he met and married Dora Brett, daughter of Brigadier General George H. Brett.

In 1938 he received a Regular Army commission and was assigned to Wright Field in Dayton, Ohio, as a test pilot. More than any of his previous experiences, this assignment caused him to focus on the intricacies of aircraft research and development. This became his life-long interest as he pursued an advanced aeronautical engineering degree at the Wright Field Air Corps Engineering School

(1939–1941), and still another engineering degree at Stanford University (1942). Graduating in the early summer of 1942, he left immediately for the Pacific Theater.

Between June 1942 and September 1945 Schriever flew sixty-three combat missions, most of them as a B–17 pilot. Rising rapidly in rank as well as responsibility, he progressed from captain to colonel and from pilot to chief of staff of the Fifth Air Force. He participated in campaigns for the Bismarck Archipelago, Leyte, Luzon, Papua, North Solomons, South Philippines, and the Ryukyu Islands.

When the war ended, many Army airmen left the service; Schriever remained, choosing to pursue his interests in research and development. He became chief of scientific liaison for material at Headquarters Army Air Forces. Subsequently, he worked in key staff positions in planning, developing, and evaluating new aircraft and weapons. An advocate of small, high-density, supersonic bombers, he was instrumental in developing the B–58 strategic bomber. After eight years at Headquarters USAF, he became assistant commander of the Air Research and Development Command in June 1954.

For the next five years Schriever directed the Air Force's intercontinental ballistic missile efforts. In quick succession he and his team of Air Force specialists and their counterparts in industry designed, procured, tested, produced, and deployed the Atlas, Thor, Titan, and Minuteman missiles. All became operational, and all required extensive and costly construction of new facilities. This, too, was Schriever's responsibility.

So successful were these missile programs that Schriever became commander of the Air Force Research and Development Command in April 1959. Two years later he conceived and effected the consolidation of all Air Force technical and logistical efforts into one organization, the Air Force Systems Command. More significantly, he changed the concept of material development and acquisition from a functional to a systems approach. As recognition for his leadership, he was promoted successively to brigadier general in 1953, major general in 1955, lieutenant general in 1959, and general in 1961.

During the final five years of his military career, General Schriever led the Air Force Systems Command. He fostered research in aerospace medicine, implemented new systems management policies, and introduced new procedures for long-range forecasting of technological changes. A strong advocate of placing the military into space operations, he became the director of the Manned Orbital Laboratory in 1965, a position he held jointly with that of commander of the Air Force Systems Command. In September 1966 he retired from active duty, completing thirty-three years of service.

When Ben Schriever entered the Army Air Corps in 1932, the process of acquiring new aircraft centered on private airframe contractors delivering airplanes to the military services for competition, inspection, and purchase. When he retired in 1966, the Air Force, utilizing a systems management approach, had become the focal point for virtually all new weapon systems. The acquisition of new weapons, such as strategic bombers, fighters, and intercontinental ballistic missiles, had markedly changed through the insistence on technologically superior performance standards, adherence to preestablished production schedules, and reliance on cost-control measures. Schriever's role in this transformation was pivotal.

Following World War II he favored and fostered new methods of managing research, development, and acquisition of aircraft and ballistic missiles. He helped formulate design and performance standards for many of the Air Force's fighters and bombers. The B–58 bomber can be attributed to his insistence on high altitude supersonic performance in a high-density, delta wing airframe.

Unquestionably, his greatest achievement occurred when he served as Air Force project manager for ballistic missiles, 1954–1959. At a time when intelligence estimates revealed that the Soviet Union was developing and deploying intercontinental ballistic missiles, Schriever led the U.S. effort to design, procure, test, produce, and deploy the Atlas, Thor, Titan, and Minuteman missiles. Of these, the solid-fuel Minuteman missiles deployed in underground, hardened silos and dispersed throughout the western part of the United States represented a technological breakthrough. Throughout the 1960s and 1970s the Minuteman was the bulwark of the United States' strategic nuclear forces.

General Schriever's leadership in developing ballistic missiles led to his advocacy of using space for manned military operations. As director of the Manned Oribital Laboratory Program in the mid-1960s he tried to get Secretary of Defense Robert Strange McNamara* and Congress to approve his extensive plans. He failed, largely because of Secretary McNamara's opposition.

Both Schriever and McNamara were strong-willed, technically oriented leaders. Schriever believed in exploiting technology in order to develop and use superior weapons; McNamara insisted on realistic programs and adherence to cost-effective criteria prior to program approval. Often at an impasse, the two clashed frequently during the 1960s.

So too did Generals Schriever and Curtis Emerson LeMay,* commander of the Strategic Air Command (1948–1957) and chief of staff of the Air Force (1961–1965). The issue was the proper design and performance characteristics for the Air Force's future strategic bomber. Schriever put forth the B–58; LeMay countered with an improved B–52 and the B–70. The debate was sustained, lasting almost fifteen years, and neither man was vindicated. LeMay saw the B–70 canceled by Secretary McNamara in 1963, while Schriever retired from active duty in 1966, never having been chief of staff of the Air Force.

BIBLIOGRAPHY

Beard, Edmund. *Developing the ICBM: A Study in Bureaucratic Politics.* New York: Columbia University Press, 1976.
Kanter, Arnold. *Defense Politics: A Budgetary Perspective.* Chicago: University of Chicago Press, 1979.

Peck, Milton J., and Frederic M. Sherer. *The Weapons Acquisition Process, An Economic Analysis*. Boston: Harvard University, 1962.
Schriever, Bernard M. "The USAF Ballistic Missile Program." In *The United States Air Force Report on the Ballistic Missile Program: Its Technology, Logistics, and Strategy*. Edited by K. F. Gantz. New York: Doubleday, 1954.
Schwiebert, Ernest G. *A History of U.S. Air Force Ballistic Missiles*. New York: Frederick A. Praeger, 1964.

JOSEPH P. HARAHAN

SCHUYLER, Peter (b. Albany, N.Y., September 17, 1657; d. The Flatts, now known as Watervliet, February 19, 1724), soldier, landowner, official of colonial New York. Schuyler's constant contact with the Iroquois made him indispensable to the colonial governors of New York during the first two French and Indian Wars.

Peter Schuyler was the second son born to Philip Pieterse Schuyler, a recent immigrant from Amsterdam, and Margaret Van Slichtenhorst, whose father was of the local aristocracy. Philip held official and military offices under both the Dutch and English administrations. Peter attended a newly established common school, but his real education came from his early and constant involvement in military and public affairs. In 1685, Schuyler at age twenty-seven was appointed a lieutenant of calvary in the Albany militia by Governor General Thomas Dongan.

On July 22, 1686, Albany became a city after being granted a charter by Governor Thomas Dongan who also appointed Peter Schuyler as the first mayor. He remained mayor of Albany from 1686 to 1694. One of his duties as mayor was to serve as president of the Board of Indian Commissioners.

In 1689, as a result of William of Orange's ascending the throne of England, Jacob Leisler* seized control of New York and declared himself governor of the colony. Leisler's rule was disputed only in Albany, as Schuyler, Robert Livingston, and others refused to acknowledge his authority. There is no way to predict how long Schuyler and his allies could have successfully resisted Leisler's power had it not been for the ensuing developments in Europe.

Europe, France, and England became embroiled in the War of the League of Augsburg, and it was only a matter of time before the repercussions of that conflict were felt in North America. Early in 1690 Count Louis de Frontenac, governor general of French Canada, devised a plan calling for three simultaneous raids that would cripple the English frontier of New York and New England. Frontenac unleashed his French and Indian forces on the frontier of New York and New England. In New York, the settlement at Schenectady was destroyed. At least 194 white settlers were killed and 83 captured across the northern frontier. On the very edge of the frontier, Albany was helpless and sought aid from New England, but when they vacillated, Schuyler reluctantly sought aid from Leisler. Schuyler, although anti-Leisler, had no choice but to accept the aid readily offered by Leisler, who wasted no time in placing pro-Leislerians in the Albany government with the exception of Schuyler who was retained as mayor.

At an intercolonial congress convened in New York by Leisler, Peter Schuyler proposed a plan for the invasion of Canada. The plan called the "Glorious Enterprise" envisioned an overland force attacking Montreal while a naval expedition attacked Quebec. Schuyler's plan was adopted, but both phases of the "Glorious Enterprise" were failures. The overland force, led by Connecticut's Major Fitz-John Winthrop,* got no further than Lake Champlain due to the lack of promised canoes and Indian forces. The naval expedition reached Quebec but found it too well defended and after a perfunctory bombardment withdrew.

Upon his return to Albany in October 1690, Schuyler was relieved of his duties as mayor by Leisler. This suspension of duties lasted until the arrival of Governor Henry Sloughter and the subsequent imprisonment of Leisler in March 1691. Schuyler then resumed his duties as mayor and commander of the Albany militia.

In May 1691 Schuyler led a combined force of 250 English, Dutch, and Indians on a raid into Canada. Their target was the French farming community of La Prairie, which Schuyler's brother, John, had successfully raided in 1690. The French were prepared for Schuyler, and his force fought several sharp engagements before they could regain their canoes and head for Albany. Upon his return to Albany, Schuyler was made a judge of common pleas, and in March 1692 he was appointed to the Provincial Council by Governor Benjamin Fletcher.

In the winter of 1693 the French and their Indian allies attacked the Mohawk villages that lay along the Mohawk River. The English military commander, Major Ingoldsby, hesitated and the French would have escaped (a move that would have damaged Anglo-Iroquois relations) had it not been for Schuyler, who engaged the French in a running battle in which many of the Mohawk captives escaped. For this action the Mohawk Nation was grateful to Schuyler, and his bravery did not go unnoticed. From that point on, when French envoys attempted to gain influence among the Iroquois, Schuyler and his reputation kept that influence to a minimum. In 1696 Governor Fletcher took the handling of Indian affairs away from the magistrates of Albany and appointed a board of four commissioners, of which Schuyler was one. In 1697 Governor Fletcher gave a large grant of land to Schuyler, who was already a large landowner, and to the other members of the commission. The new governor, Richard Coote, the earl of Bellmont and a Leislerian, disliked Schuyler and his influence on the colony's affairs. He forced Schuyler to renounce his gift of land from Governor Fletcher. As much as Governor Bellmont disliked Schuyler, he needed him for his knowledge of the Iroquois. In 1698 Governor Bellmont sent Schuyler to Canada to inform Frontenac of the Treaty of Ryswick and for the release of English prisoners.

During Queen Anne's War, 1701–1713, Schuyler was active in his post, acting as liaison between the British and the Iroquois. In 1709 Schuyler took part in an abortive expedition to Canada which halted at Wood Creek on Lake Champlain due to the lack of naval support. In 1710, in order to secure additional aid from England, Schuyler and five Mohawk Sachems went to the court of Queen Anne. Schuyler not only wanted increased aid and support for his Canadian invasion, but also to impress the Mohawks with the might of England. It is said that at Queen Anne's court he refused the honor of knighthood. In 1711 Schuyler accompanied the abortive Walker Expedition to Canada, as well as realigning the Onondaga Indians back into the English camp by debunking French claims of English hunger for Iroquois lands.

After the close of Queen Anne's War, Schuyler remained dedicated to the needs of the Iroquois. As president of the Provincial Council, he was designated acting governor from July 1719 to September 1720. A few of his appointments prior to the arrival of Governor William Burnet angered Schuyler's political opponents. Governor Burnet saw in Schuyler the potential to be a leader of an opposition faction and took steps to remove Schuyler from the council, which he did in 1722. After his removal from the council, Schuyler retired to his estate, "The Flatts," where he died on February 19, 1724.

Peter Schuyler spent nearly fifty years of his life trying to solidify the English presence on the Albany frontier. He was active in all sectors of civil government. Besides his commission as a colonel in the militia, Schuyler served with distinction on numerous committees and on such posts as governor of the colony of New York, mayor of Albany, president of the Provincial Council, and president of the commissioners on Indian affairs.

His primary concern for most of his military and political life was the final removal of the French presence in Canada. To this end, he planned and executed a number of raids into Canada and planned or helped to plan three invasions of French Canada. He also stressed military preparedness for the northern frontier, and he cited the 1690 massacre at Schenectady as an example of what would happen if Albany slackened its defenses.

Schuyler was indefatigable with his dealings with the Iroquois nations. He imitated the example of the French emissaries who traveled from Iroquois village to village attempting to persuade the Iroquois to side against the English. Schuyler saw the loyalty of the Iroquois as essential for the survival, both economically with the fur trade and literally of Albany and the entire northern frontier. To that end, Schuyler worked to improve the English image among the Iroquois and succeeded. Throughout his long tenure as a colonial statesman, soldier, and landowner, he commanded public respect by virtue of his physical courage and personal integrity.

BIBLIOGRAPHY

Kim, Sung Bok. *Landlord and Tenant in Colonial New York, Manorial Society, 1664–1775*. Chapel Hill, N.C.: University of North Carolina Press for the Institute of Early American History and Culture, Williamsburg, Virginia, 1978.

Leach, Douglas Edward. *Arms for Empire—A Military History of the British Colonies in North America, 1607–1763*. New York: Macmillan Company, 1973.

Osgood, Herbert L. *The American Colonies in the Eighteenth Century*. Vols. 1 and 2. New York: Columbia University Press, 1924.
Peckham, Howard Henry. *The Colonial Wars 1689–1762*. Chicago: University of Chicago Press, 1964.
Reynolds, Cuyler. *Albany Chronicles. A History of the City Arranged Chronologically.* Albany, N.Y.: J. B. Lyon Company, 1906.
Trelease, Allen W. *Indian Affairs in Colonial New York*. Ithaca, N.Y.: Cornell University Press, 1960.

CHARLES LEON GORDON

SCHUYLER, Philip (b. Albany, N.Y., November 10, 1733; d. Albany, N.Y., November 18, 1804), Revolutionary War general. Schuyler was commander of the Northern Department of the Continental Army, 1775–1777.

Born into a prominent New York family with Dutch antecedents, Philip Schuyler was raised in the aristocratic environment of the Hudson Valley squirearchy. Tutored at home and in Albany schools, young Schuyler received a classical education at a Huguenot academy in New Rochelle. As a youth, he joined trading expeditions into the Indian Country where he learned the Mohawk tongue and where he befriended chiefs of the Six Nations. His marriage in 1755 to Catherine Van Rensselaer linked him to influential landlords, and his visits to England in 1761–1762 sharpened his business acumen.

Schuyler served as a militia captain during the French and Indian War under prominent British officers—Colonels William Johnson,* John Bradstreet, James Abercromby, and General Sir Jeffery Amherst.* Although Schuyler witnessed combat at Forts Oswego and Ticonderoga, he specialized in quartermaster duties. Ranked as a colonel by 1759, Schuyler participated in four campaigns, and he mastered the techniques of feeding, housing, and transporting troops in the forests. He also understood the Indian and the strategy of defending the northern frontier.

As a wilderness entrepreneur, Schuyler inherited a vast agricultural and commercial empire which he expanded by speculating in land, by colonizing fertile tracts, and by developing a rudimentary manufacturing center at his Saratoga estate. Schuyler was also active politically. After a brief apprenticeship in local government, Schuyler was elected to the Provincial Assembly in 1768. He was a cautious but consistent critic of British imperialistic policies toward the colonies. But he refrained from proclaiming the radical rhetoric of resistance to constitutional authority, for he at first was a reluctant rebel, hoping for reconciliation with the Crown. In January 1775, Schuyler led the Assembly's opposition to coercive British legislation, and soon after, he was elected a delegate to the Second Continental Congress. There he impressed George Washington,* his Virginia counterpart, defended the unauthorized seizure of Ticonderoga by Ethan Allen* and Benedict Arnold,* and helped to procure supplies for the patriot army at Boston.

Appointed a major general in June 1775, Schuyler, as commander of the

Northern Department (New York), prepared for an invasion of Canada. He supervised the mobilization of troops, the acquisition of provisions, and the manufacture of weapons. He directed the construction of roads, docks, wharves, boats, foundries, fortresses, hospitals, as well as sawmills, grist mills, and powder mills. Schuyler likewise negotiated with the Iroquois in order to blunt Tory efforts to foment Indian warfare. Because of Schuyler, the Six Nations remained neutral until 1777.

Schuyler planned to lead the expedition northward by capturing St. John's on Lake Champlain, by advancing along the Sorel River that flowed to the St. Lawrence River, and by capturing Montreal. Then, in conjunction with a smaller force under Arnold advancing through Maine, Schuyler expected to capture Quebec before winter. But involved in Indian affairs at Albany, Schuyler ordered Brigadier General Richard Montgomery* in August to attack St. John's. Schuyler followed in September and directed the siege. Debilitated by chronic sickness, however, Schuyler returned to Ticonderoga, to direct the provisioning of Montgomery's force. St. John's fell to the Americans in October, and Montreal in November. In late December Montgomery and Arnold led a valiant but aborted assault on Quebec. During the winter of 1775–1776 Schuyler remained in New York funneling supplies to the pathetic American army that invested Quebec. In early May 1776, plagued with smallpox and overwhelmed by newly arrived troops from Britain, the Northern army, now under General John Thomas, retreated to Sorel. Reinforced with regiments led by General John Sullivan* in late May, the Americans attempted but failed to halt the British offensive at Three Rivers. Sullivan's battered army retreated to Lake Champlain to await evacuation. Toiling to extricate the nearly trapped American command, Schuyler acquired enough boats and canoes to convoy the troops to Ticonderoga.

During the summer of 1776 Schuyler, assisted by General Horatio Gates,* his rival for command in the North, supervised the defense of Ticonderoga and the construction of a navy at Skenesboro. Although the enemy fleet defeated the ramshackle squadron at Valcour Island in October, Sir Guy Carleton, the British commander, hesitated to attack sturdy Ticonderoga and to campaign in the winter. Consequently, his army retired to Canada for the season. Schuyler's delaying tactics thus provided the patriots with another precious year to retain northern New York.

Schuyler was frequently castigated in Congress, particularly by New England delegates, for alleged failures in the Canadian operations. Sensitive to criticism, the haughty Schuyler bitterly contested the charges. So acerbic was the dispute that in March 1777 Congress reprimanded Schuyler for his intemperate remarks, and he was relieved of his position. Yet in May, when the nation needed him in the North to ward off another enemy offensive from Canada, Schuyler was reinstated in command.

Schuyler remained at Albany during the early summer of 1777 as General John Burgoyne's redcoats sailed unopposed to Ticonderoga. In July Schuyler ordered General Arthur St. Clair* to evacuate the fortress in order to save the army. Unprepared for the loss of the so-called Gibraltar of the North, Congress was infuriated with the surrender of the bastion and the threat to the Hudson River. Plunged again into controversy, Schuyler meanwhile removed his troops to safety, lured Burgoyne down the waterways, and devised such tactics—wrecking roads and bridges, toppling trees over trails, destroying foodstuffs—that Burgoyne found his march from Skenesboro to the Hudson a logistical nightmare. Schuyler cannot be credited with the American victory under General John Stark over the British at Bennington, Vermont, in August, but he ordered a defense on the Mohawk that led to Arnold's victory at Fort Stanwix. Yet Schuyler hesitated to confront the British in pitched battle, he procrastinated about a defense north of Albany, and he increased the demoralization of his troops. In August Schuyler was replaced by Gates. Hence, while Gates was properly praised for triumphs over Burgoyne at Bemis Heights in September and at Freeman's Farm in October, it was Schuyler who had saved the Northern army for the great victories.

The acrimonious debates about Schuyler continued. Accused of negligence that led to the fall of Ticonderoga, Schuyler was tried by a congressional court of inquiry in the autumn of 1778, but he was exonerated. Yet Schuyler's reputation was marred, he was intensely disliked by the troops, he bickered constantly with ranking officers and with prominent politicians, and he symbolized a string of disasters. After additional disputes, Schuyler resigned his commission in 1779.

Schuyler kept his interest in Indian and military affairs. Elected to Congress in 1779, he advised Washington about General John Sullivan's expedition to the Iroquois country, and he assisted in the reorganization of Army staff departments. Still an influential figure in the postwar era, Schuyler, one of New York's first senators, championed the ratification of the federal Constitution. Due to ill-health, he retired from public life in 1798 and lived out his remaining years in Albany.

Schuyler's military career was quite controversial. Although experienced in wilderness warfare, he never held an independent command before the Revolution. His qualifications for a generalship in 1775 were questionable, but the political necessity of placating his supporters determined his appointment.

Schuyler demonstrated energy and foresight in organizing the Northern army. On his first field command at St. John's, however, he selected difficult terrain to initiate the siege, he overestimated British strength, and he left the fighting to Montgomery. It was Montgomery, ably assisted by Arnold, and not Schuyler—who remained at Saratoga—who nearly conquered Canada. Schuyler acted vigorously in the spring of 1776 to save the Northern army from disaster during its retreat, but he was invariably blamed for the fiasco. Schuyler's arrogance, his indecisiveness, his contentious nature, and his intolerance of spirited New England soldiery increased his unpopularity and diminished his prestige with the military. In 1777 he neglected to appraise adequately the strength and movements

of Burgoyne's army, and, consequently, he justly shared in the blame for Ticonderoga's loss. Castigated for repeated failures, for the dismal state of army
morale on the Hudson, and for irregularities in the commissary, Schuyler epitomized two years of frustration for the Northern army.

Yet in fairness to Schuyler, it should be noted that he suffered acutely from
gout and pleurisy and that these ailments may have hampered his efficiency. He
correctly visualized his role as a pacifier of the Indians, and as the coordinator
of equipment and provisions for his army. Schuyler grasped the strategic significance of Lake Champlain, and he undertook the construction of a fleet.
Unfortunately for him, Congress failed to determine the scope of his authority,
neglected to consult him about appointments to his staff, and delayed in for-
warding him men and material. His decision to rescue Sullivan's army was
sound, his plan to forestall Carleton at Ticonderoga was correct, and his advice
to evacuate Ticonderoga in 1777 was likewise sensible. Yet, the haughty patroon
had a stormy military career, and he symbolized failure, for he never had the
luck, or the qualities, that could inspire troops. The congressional decision to
replace him with Gates at Saratoga was necessary to regenerate a dispirited
Northern army.

Schuyler, the only high-ranking officer of the Revolution who never participated in a single major battle, merits attention for his knowledge of Indian affairs,
for his strategic vision, and for his mastery of logistics. He made a distinct
contribution to the war effort, not as a colorful leader on the battlefield, but as
the tireless administrator behind the lines who prepared the Northern army for
eventual victory.

BIBLIOGRAPHY

Bird, Harrison. *March to Saratoga*. New York: Oxford University Press, 1963.
Bush, Martin A. *Revolutionary Enigma. A Re-appraisal of General Philip Schuyler of
    New York*. Port Washington, N.Y.: Ira J. Friedman, 1967.
Gerlach, Don R. *Philip Schuyler and the American Revolution in New York, 1733–1777*.
    Lincoln: University of Nebraska Press, 1964.
Lossing, Benson J. *The Life and Times of Philip Schuyler*. 2 vols. New York: Sheldon
    and Company, 1860.
Rossie, Jonathan Gregory. *The Politics of Command in the American Revolution*. Syr-
    acuse, N.Y.: Syracuse University Press, 1975.
Tuckerman, Bayard. *Life of General Philip Schuyler, 1733–1804*. New York: Dodd,
    Mead, and Company, 1903.

                                                              RICHARD BLANCO

SCOTT, Hugh Lenox (b. Danville, Ky., September 22, 1853; d. Washington,
D.C., April 30, 1934), soldier, diplomat, Indian authority.

Hugh Scott was the scion of a respected New Jersey family with links to
Benjamin Franklin. Although he was born in Kentucky, Scott was raised in the
home of his maternal grandfather, the prominent theologian, Dr. Charles Hodge,

in Princeton, New Jersey. After attending Edgehill and Lawrenceville academies, Scott matriculated at the U.S. Military Academy, graduating on June 19, 1876.

From 1876 to 1898 Scott spent most of his time in the American West serving in Army posts from the Dakotas to Oklahoma. In the West he acquired a vast knowledge of Indian life and became an authority on the sign language of the Plains tribes. His study of Indian culture made him an adept negotiator with the Indian. He worked effectively to quell the outbreak of the Ghost Dance disturbances in Oklahoma and served as the guardian for Geronimo* and his Apaches when they were relocated in Oklahoma in the 1890s. Scott retained a major interest in Indian affairs throughout his life.

With the outbreak of the Spanish-American War, Scott's career took on an international dimension. After sitting out the war with training units in the South and missing out on any fighting, Scott participated in the military occupation of Cuba (1899–1902) and served as governor of the Sulu Archipelago in the Philippines. He showed himself as a competent administrator and skilled negotiator and gained the friendship and support of the influential General Leonard Wood.*

Following his work as a colonial agent, Scott spent six relatively quiet years in which he served as superintendent of West Point and performed a variety of other military duties. This period coincided with the growing modernist-traditionalist debate within the U.S. Army, and during this time Scott began to interest himself in the question of modernizing the Army.

Scott rose to national attention after 1912 when the Mexican Revolution spilled over the border to affect U.S. diplomacy. First as a commander of American forces on the Mexican border and later as a special diplomatic envoy, Scott became deeply involved in diplomacy with Mexico. He quickly became the foremost backer of the mercurial Pancho Villa in Villa's bid for power in Mexico, and he frequently served as a contact between Villa and the Wilson administration. In addition, Scott conducted a variety of important diplomatic missions to resolve local crises on the border. In 1914–1915 he negotiated an end to an attack on the border hamlet of Naco, Sonora, which had resulted in loss of life and property on the American side of the border in Naco, Arizona, and had raised the spectre of American military retaliation. In August 1915 Scott obtained relief for American cattlemen and mineowners whose interests had been threatened with expropriation.

In 1916 after Villa's bid for power had failed and he had turned against the United States provoking the Pershing Expedition, Scott again served as a diplomat. When the Punitive Expedition's penetration into Mexico threatened war between the United States and the Mexican government of Venustiano Carranza, Scott held an important negotiation with Mexico's Minister of War Alvaro Obregón. This conference delayed the final confrontation with Mexico until after the *Sussex* crisis with Germany had eased.

Concurrently with his Mexican involvements, Scott rose to the position of chief of staff of the U.S. Army in 1914. His rise was aided by the fact that his brother, William, had served as a faculty colleague of Woodrow Wilson at

Princeton. As chief of staff Scott chose to work quietly within the system for preparedness and army reform. Scott cooperated with Secretaries of War Linley Garrison and Newton Diehl Baker* to resist narrow, partisan congressional attacks on the staff system. The experience of the Punitive Expedition convinced Scott of the chronic need for an improved system of raising manpower, and he became an open advocate of universal military service in December 1916. He remained active as chief of staff through the early days of American entry into World War I.

Mandatory retirement and old age prevented Scott from making major contributions to the American effort in World War I, but he remained quite active, serving as a member of the Root Mission to Russia in 1917 and commanding the training of certain units in the United States. Following the war, Scott spent an active retirement serving on the Board of Indian Commissioners and the New Jersey Highway Commission. He devoted much of his time to writing his memoirs and to correspondence and study concerning the Indian.

Born too late for the Indian Wars and too early for active duty in World War I, Hugh Scott was a soldier who negotiated more than he fought. Yet, his career criss-crossed many of the important events and issues of the period when the United States became a world power and the American Army changed from a frontier fighting force into a modern military establishment. Ambitious, able, and many-faceted, Scott was not given to public pronouncements or to working out of channels. An administrator and conciliator rather than an original thinker or rebel, Scott made important if secondary contributions to American military and diplomatic history.

Most at home with the Indian, Scott became a respected student of Indian life and a scholar on the Indian sign language. His own views on the Indian represented a balanced perspective that the modernization of the Indian should not be at the expense of destroying all Indian culture. Scott's willingness to accept Indians as equals carried over to his treatment of Cubans, Mexicans, and American blacks.

In diplomacy Scott was an adept personal negotiator at his best in one-on-one confrontations with his opposite number. His major involvements were with the Mexican Revolution where he was one of many Americans seeking to influence the Wilson administration in a desired course of action. His own advocacy of Villa sheds light on American policymaking during the period, and his own negotiations on the border attest to his bargaining skills.

As chief of staff of the Army Scott encountered the most criticism from contemporaries and later historians. A career soldier committed to routine and the bureaucracy, Scott has been faulted for his naivete, his overattention to detail, and his lack of commitment to reform. However, these criticisms ignore Soctt's preference for working within the system and his significant accomplishments therein. Scott was not a seminal thinker, but he could effectively implement the ideas of others as his work for conscription attested. Nor was Scott a publicity-seeking political soldier like his mentor Leonard Wood. In the Wilson administration with its hostility to anything that smacked of militarism, Scott believed the only way to proceed was gradually within channels. To be sure, his age and his preoccupation with other issues did impede his efforts at army reform, but they should not obliterate his real contributions.

BIBLIOGRAPHY

Clendenen, Clarence C. *The United States and Pancho Villa*. Ithaca, N.Y.: Cornell University Press, 1961.
Link, Arthur S. *Wilson: Confusions and Crises*. Princeton, N.J.: Princeton University Press, 1964.
Harper, James W. "Hugh Lenox Scott: Soldier Diplomat, 1876–1917." Ph.D. dissertation, University of Virginia, 1968.
Scott, Hugh L. *Some Memories of a Soldier*. New York: Appleton-Century, 1928.
Vandiver, Frank E. *Black Jack, The Life and Times of John J. Pershing*. 2 vols. College Station, Tex.: Texas A&M University Press, 1977.

JAMES W. HARPER

SCOTT, Winfield (b. Laurel Branch, Va., near Petersburg, Dinwiddie County, June 13, 1786; d. West Point, N. Y., May 29, 1866), general, military theorist, diplomat, candidate for the American presidency.

Winfield Scott was sprung from a warrior clan. His grandfather, James Scott, fled to America after surviving the massacre at Culloden in 1746, and his father, William Scott, served in the American Revolution as a captain. His elder brother, James, was a regimental commander in the War of 1812. When Winfield was six years old, his father died, and his mother, Ann Mason Scott, followed her husband eleven years later. Ann Scott's grandfather was John Winfield, a very wealthy colonial planter. From this source, young Winfield was the recipient of an adequate, if somewhat limited, patrimony.

The U.S. Military Academy at West Point came into existence in 1802, but inasmuch as that school was in its infancy, and also because he had not yet determined to become a soldier, Scott entered William and Mary College in 1805. He disliked the college, in part because of a campus religious controversy, and he left it the same term as he entered, whereupon he traveled to Petersburg and read law in David Robinson's office.

Shortly following the *Chesapeake-Leopard* affair in 1807, Scott enlisted in the cavalry, and he immediately distinguished himself by seizing a British boat and its eight occupants, among whom were two officers. By May 1808, Scott was designated a captain of light artillery. His next duty assignment was in 1809 in New Orleans. He was so unimpressed by the quality of the officers there that he determined to quit the service and to reenter the law. At this time, in his youthful exuberance, he had somewhat less than privately censured his departmental commander, General James Wilkinson,* as a traitor and an accomplice in the Burr Conspiracy. Wilkinson proffered charges against Scott, who, in turn, was relieved of his commission for a year. In the face of this brazen assault,

Scott's mind again turned to the law, but with Congress' declaration of war in 1812, he received the rank of lieutenant colonel. In October Scott distinguished himself at the Battle of Queenston Heights, where he was captured. Paroled, he next found action at Fort George, where he was wounded. He was then attached to the command of his old enemy, Wilkinson. Despite his unhappy situation, he busied himself with the training of the soldiery, and his successes gained the attentions of President James Madison and Secretary of War James Monroe.

By March 1819 Scott was raised to brigadier general, and the following July he distinguished himself at the spectacular Battle of Chippewa. He also fought at Lundy's Lane, where, once again, he was badly wounded. This time his brilliant service merited his superiors' attentions, and he was given medals by both Virginia and Congress and brevetted to the rank of major general.

At the war's conclusion, Scott wrote the new U.S. Infantry drill manual and then went to Europe, where he continued his military studies with which he had become fascinated. Upon his return to America in 1817, he married Maria D. Mayo of Richmond, Virginia. He made practical use of his knowledge through his office as the repeated president of the Army's Board of Tactics, and in 1834–1835, after yet one more trip to Europe, he expanded and honed the three-volume *Infantry Tactics*, which was published in 1835.

When Major General Jacob Jennings Brown* died in 1828, Major General Alexander Macomb* was elevated to the position of commanding general of the Army. Miffed at what he considered to be a slight, Scott tendered his resignation which was refused. In 1832 he was again commanding troops in the Black Hawk War, but his participation in that conflict was limited when he fell victim to cholera. Recovering, in 1835 he was sent to carry on a war against the Indians in Florida. While on a campaign against the Creeks, Andrew Jackson,* who had a distrust of Scott, first relieved him for dilatoriness and then had the conduct of his campaign examined by a court of inquiry, which in turn dismissed the charges, and in fact commended Scott's efforts. In 1838 he was actively engaged in various efforts in diplomacy with the British, Canadians, and Cherokees.

When General Macomb died in 1841, Scott rose to the command of the U.S. Army. He was a particularly active commander, and his reforms in uniform dress, temperance, military prisons, and education were widely noted. During this period, he made a serious blunder and an even greater indiscretion. He publically endorsed Henry Clay for the presidency. This ineptness earned deserved difficulties with the Democratic administration of President James K. Polk (1845–1849).

Upon the outbreak of the Mexican War, General Zachary Taylor* performed creditably against the Mexicans in northern Mexico, but it was strategically infeasible to win in that theater alone. With some reluctance, Polk sent Scott on an expedition into Mexico's interior via the Gulf coast and Vera Cruz. It is in this role that Scott's reputation as a major military captain rests. In a brilliant campaign, the likes of which has never before or since been witnessed in American military annals, Scott, despite great weaknesses in logistics and troops, overcame a more numerous enemy, who enjoyed the advantage of interior lines. Throughout, his campaign was conducted with intelligence and humanity, and even managed to earn the admiration of the Mexicans themselves. It was also in Mexico that Scott's temperament again ran afoul of civilian leadership, and he was the victim of another court of inquiry, this one seeded with his political and professional enemies. Nevertheless, his signal achievements could not be denied, and he was saved by a grateful Congress and once more rewarded with another gold medal struck in that body's name. Ultimately, he was elevated to the rank of lieutenant general, the first American to hold that exalted rank since George Washington.* In 1852 Scott was nominated to the presidency by the Whig party, but he was overwhelmingly defeated by Franklin Pierce of New Hampshire, a former subordinate of his in the late war.

In 1860, on the eve of the American Civil War, Scott urged President James Buchanan to aid Fort Sumter and other important Federal military installations in the South. Buchanan ignored his advice. When Abraham Lincoln* became president, the situation had so badly deteriorated that success in such a venture was virtually impossible. Though aged and infirm, Scott still proposed a plan, which with variations, was to be the general strategic concept of the United States in the Civil War. The Anaconda Plan, as it was known, called for seizure of the Mississippi River and blockade of southern ports. He hoped that this effort would strangle the Confederacy and diminish the use of invading Federal troops. As it was perceived by President Abraham Lincoln and General Ulysses Simpson Grant,* however, the employment of attacking columns was necessary.

Scott retired from the army on All Hallow's Eve in 1861. Although a Virginian, he supported the Union, and his resignation prompted the strongest praise from Lincoln. He was nearly eighty when he died, and he was buried at West Point amidst honors and kudos.

Winfield Scott was one of the greatest field commanders in modern military history. His praises are recorded by numerous military figures, including both Arthur Wellesley, the duke of Wellington, and the Baron Antoine Henri Jomini. He was a commander who often fought under severe handicaps, but whose genius overcame the most imposing obstacles. In this respect, he resembles John Churchill, the duke of Marlborough: neither ever lost a battle, and Scott's relations with Polk and Congress are reminiscent of the duke's with Queen Anne and Parliament. In addition, by force of his personality, integrity, and ability, he molded American military thought into the best European examples and advanced theories. In recent times, it has become fashionable to deny the influences of Jomini on American military development and to denigrate Scott's personal influence. Such is the whim of historical writing and the pervasive influence of the age of twentieth-century total war on the historical community. But to the end, Jomini's influence on Scott was unmistakable, and Scott's influence on the American Army profound. *Vis fortisimme in aetate tractabile erat.*

BIBLIOGRAPHY

Bauer, K. Jack. *The Mexican War, 1846–1848*. New York: Macmillan Company, 1974.
Elliott, Charles Winslow. *Winfield Scott: The Soldier and the Man*. New York: Macmillan
　　Company, 1937.
Johnston, Robert Matteson. *Leading American Soldiers*. New York: Henry Holt, 1907.
Mansfield, Edward Deering. *The Life and Military Services of Lieut.-General Winfield
　　Scott*. New York: N. C. Miller, 1862.
Sabin, Edwin Legrand. *Into Mexico with General Scott*. Philadelphia: J. B. Lippincott,
　　1920.
Scott, Winfield. *Memoirs of Lieut.-General Scott*. 2 vols. New York: Sheldon, 1864.
Smith, Arthur D. Howden. *Old Fuss and Feathers: The Life and Exploits of Winfield
　　Scott*. New York: Greystone Press, 1937.
Smith, Justin H. *The War with Mexico*. New York: Macmillan Company, 1919.
Wright, Marcus Joseph. *General Scott*. New York: D. Appleton, 1894.

JAMES W. POHL

SEMMES, Raphael (b. Charles County, Md., September 27, 1809; d. Mobile, Ala., August 30, 1877), naval officer. Semmes is noted for his command of the Confederate commerce raider *Alabama* during the Civil War.

Raphael Semmes was the eldest son of Richard Thompson Semmes and his wife Catherine (Middleton) of French ancestry. His parents died early in his childhood, and he was raised by an uncle in Georgetown, District of Columbia. In April 1826 he was appointed a midshipman in the U.S. Navy by President John Quincy Adams, probably through the influence of another uncle, Benedict J. Semmes, an influential Maryland planter.

Eleven years passed before Semmes was promoted to lieutenant. This was not because of a poor record; he stood second in his class in 1832 at a naval school, and according to scattered references his performance at sea was satisfactory. The problem was that throughout the period promotion was extremely slow. During these years he served successively in the naval sloops *Lexington* and *Erie*, the frigate *Brandywine,* the schooner *Porpoise*, and the frigate *Constellation* on the Mediterranean, West India, and the South Atlantic Stations, and along the Florida coast during the Seminole War. Between tours of sea duty Semmes spent lengthy periods on shore. In 1832 he was placed in charge of the Navy's chronometers and became so fascinated by them that they became a lifetime hobby. He also spent some time on hydrographic surveys, studied and practiced law, and married Anne Elizabeth Spencer in May 1837. His marriage occurred three months after he was promoted to lieutenant.

During the next decade his professional career followed a normal peacetime routine of sea and shore duty. When the Mexican War broke out, Semmes was assigned to command the brig *Somers* deployed on blockade duty along the eastern coast of Mexico. Semmes was in command of this unlucky ship when she foundered during a sudden squall with the loss of more than half of her crew. The court of inquiry exonerated him of blame. He continued in active service during the war as flag-lieutenant to Commodore David Conner,* with the shore-based naval artillery at the bombardment of Vera Cruz and the expedition against Tuxpan, and accompanied the army of General Winfield Scott* to Mexico on special duty.

The war ended in 1848, and Semmes, like many others, discovered that there were more officers than ships available. During his final years as a U.S. naval officer, he was on awaiting-orders status much of the time. While on active service, he commanded two small vessels, the schooner *Flirt* and the storeship *Electra*; was inspector of clothing and provisions at the Pensacola Naval Station in Florida; and served on court-martial and lighthouse duty. He was promoted to commander in 1855. Semmes resigned his commission in the U.S. Navy on February 15, 1861. At that time he was stationed in Washington, D.C., as chairman of the Lighthouse Board.

In 1841 Semmes had established legal residence in Alabama and considered Mobile his home. His resignation followed his state's secession and the creation of the Confederacy. In March he was appointed a commander in the Confederate States Navy. Even before this date Semmes had performed his first service for the new government by purchasing munitions, ordnance, machinery, and vessels in the North. After that he was made chief of the Lighthouse Bureau, but in April 1861 he was appointed to command the *Sumter*, the first Confederate commerce raider.

Semmes commanded the *Sumter* approximately a year—from her fitting out in New Orleans until she was blockaded by Union warships at Gibraltar and subsequently sold. Although the *Sumter* was too small and slow to be an effective commerce raider, she nevertheless captured eighteen prizes. Perhaps most important was the experience Semmes gained and the reputation he began to acquire as the beau ideal of a commerce destroyer.

At Nassau on the way home Semmes received orders to take command of the *Alabama* or *Enrica*, as she was christened at her launching in Liverpool. The vessel left England under British papers, and near the Azores took on her armament and was commissioned as a Confederate man-of-war. After a brief shakedown cruise, the *Alabama* captured and burned several whaling vessels in mid-Atlantic, took a number of vessels off the Newfoundland Banks, sailed for the Caribbean where coal and provisions were taken on board ship, and then sank the Union steamer *Hatteras* in a short and brisk action off Galveston, Texas. News of his promotion to captain as well as the thanks of Congress reached Semmes during his sortie in the Gulf of Mexico. After drifting down the coast of Brazil, the *Alabama* spent the summer months of 1863 cruising in the South Atlantic. Two months were spent in the vicinity of Capetown, South Africa, with negligible results (one vessel captured) before proceeding on an extended cruise through the Indian Ocean into the China Sea, reaching Singapore just before Christmas 1863. The ship then returned to European waters via the Indian Ocean and the South Atlantic, arriving at Cherbourg, France, on June 11, 1864. Since commissioning, the *Alabama* had sailed approximately seventy-five thousand miles and had taken sixty-four prizes. Three days after the Confederate warship anchored in the French harbor, the Union screw sloop *Kearsarge* took up station off the port.

Despite the *Alabama*'s poor condition, Semmes decided to fight the Union vessel. On Sunday, June 19, with thousands of people watching from the cliffs, the two warships engaged each other outside French waters, beyond the three-mile limit. The action lasted just over an hour with the two protagonists firing broadsides as they steamed in slowly narrowing circles. At the beginning of the eighth circle, when the warships were approximately four-hundred yards apart, the *Alabama* sank. Semmes along with a large number of his crew were picked up by the English yacht *Deerhound* and carried to England.

After a period of rest and relaxation in England and on the Continent, Semmes returned to the Confederacy by way of Mexico. He was promoted to rear admiral and in January 1865 was given command of the James River Squadron. This final naval command lasted less than three months. On April 2, General Robert Edward Lee* informed President Jefferson Davis* that Richmond must be abandoned. That night the ironclads and wooden vessels of the James River Squadron were set afire and scuttled or blown up. The squadron's personnel were evacuated by train, and in Danville, Virginia, they were formed into a naval brigade under Semmes' command as brigadier general. The brigade retreated to Greensboro, North Carolina, where as a part of the army of General Joseph Eggleston Johnston,* it surrendered. Semmes was paroled, went to his home in Mobile, but was later arrested. After being held for three months, charges were dropped and he returned home.

During the postwar years Semmes served as a probate judge for a brief period, as a professor at Louisiana State Seminary (now Louisiana State University), and as editor of a newspaper. He also practiced law. In 1869 he published *Memoirs of Service Afloat During the War Between the States*. This was the second of his autobiographical works. The first, *Service Afloat and Ashore During the Mexican War*, was published in 1852. He died in 1877 and was buried in Mobile.

Semmes was a competent and respected naval officer, but something of a loner and a maverick. He was unpopular with both superiors and subordinates. According to Rear Admiral Charles Wilkes* in his autobiography, these traits were apparent even as a midshipman. Because of his martial bearing, waxed mustaches, and imperial-style chin whiskers, sailors nicknamed him "Old Beeswax," "Old Bim," and "Marshall Pomp."

Semmes unquestionably was the ablest and most successful of the Confederate commerce raiders. As commander of the *Sumter* and the *Alabama*, he took eighty-two prizes (by far more than any other raider commander) and caused considerable damage to the American merchant marine. Because of these exploits he is the best known of the Confederate naval officers.

BIBLIOGRAPHY

Boykin, E. C. *Ghost Ship of the Confederacy: The Story of the Alabama and Her Captain, Raphael Semmes*. New York: Funk and Wagnalls, 1957.

Dalzell, George W. *The Flight from the Flag: The Continuing Effect of the Civil War upon the American Carrying Trade*. Chapel Hill: University of North Carolina Press, 1940.

Delaney, Norman C. *John McIntosh Kell of the Raider Alabama*. University: University of Alabama Press, 1973.

Roberts, W. Adolphe. *Semmes of the Alabama*. Indianapolis, Ind.: Bobbs-Merrill Company, 1938.

Summersell, Charles G. *The Cruise of C.S.S. Sumter*. Tuscaloosa, Ala.: Confederate Publishing Company, 1965.

WILLIAM N. STILL

SHAFTER, William Rufus (b. Kalamazoo County, Mich., October 16, 1835; d. Bakersfield, Calif., November 13, 1906), Army officer. Shafter commanded the U.S. Army in Cuba during the Spanish-American War.

Shafter's parents moved from Vermont to Michigan where his father, Hugh, engaged in farming. Young Shafter attended school in Galesburg, Michigan, and later taught school and worked on his father's farm. Shafter sought further education and was attending Prairie Seminary in Richland County when the Civil War came.

Shafter enlisted as a first lieutenant in the 7th Michigan Volunteer Infantry Regiment and saw his first action of the Civil War in the Federal disaster at Ball's Bluff on the Potomac River (October 1861). He participated in the Peninsula Campaign of General George Brinton McClellan* during May-July 1862. Shafter was wounded and refused to leave the field at Seven Pines (Fair Oaks) on May 31-June 1, 1862, and was brevetted lieutenant colonel for gallantry in action. (Subsequently, on June 12, 1895, he was awarded the Congressional Medal of Honor for his role in this engagement.) On September 5, 1862, he was promoted to major, 19th Michigan Volunteer Infantry. (During a brief leave of absence, he married Harriet Amelia Grimes of Athens, Michigan. One daughter graced this long and happy union.) In June 1863 he was promoted to lieutenant colonel and one year later was named colonel, 17th U.S. Colored Infantry. This marked the beginning of a long association with black troops and provided invaluable experience in the post-Civil War period. Shafter was prominent in the action at Nashville, December 15–16, 1864, won the respect of General George Henry Thomas,* and on March 13, 1865, was promoted to brevet brigadier general of volunteers.

The end of the Civil War brought a drastic reduction in the armed forces, but Shafter wished to remain in the service. With the enthusiastic support of General Thomas, he was assigned to the 24th Infantry. This was a new regular regiment, one of four, composed of black troops with white officers and was regarded as an experiment in the use of blacks as regular troops. All four regiments, the

24th and 25th Infantry and the 9th and 10th Cavalry, were assigned to the turbulent Texas frontier.

For a decade Shafter served along the Rio Grande and in West Texas where conditions bordered on anarchy. His campaigns against hostile Indians—including Kiowas, Comanches, Apaches, and Kickapoos, the Kickapoos residing in Mexico—were all characterized by swift, aggressive, and effective action. In the summer of 1875 Shafter was ordered to explore, map, and evaluate the flora, fauna, water, and fuel resources of the Staked Plains of Texas, as well as to drive from that mysterious region any Indians found there. With a command composed of units of his own regiment and six troops of the black 10th Cavalry ("Buffalo soldiers"), he made a dogged and thorough sweep of this North American "Sahara." The command covered more than twenty-five hundred miles under the most trying conditions and provided the first reliable information about this vast tableland for oncoming settlers. Shafter earned a reputation in the frontier army as an able and imaginative officer, although he was often volatile and abusive with his troops. His staff found him warm and humorous when relaxed and totally dedicated to the Army.

Shafter's service in the Southwest came to an end in 1879 when he was promoted to colonel, 1st Infantry Regiment, and transferred to the Department of the Columbia. For nineteen years Shafter served in the Departments of the Columbia and California. These were times of comparative quiet with little opportunity for distinction or promotion.

With the outbreak of the war with Spain in April 1898, however, Shafter was promoted to major general of volunteers and was given command of the expeditionary force to Cuba with headquarters at Tampa, Florida. The nation was eager but ill-prepared for war, and the task of assembling, organizing, equipping, and supplying the army at Tampa proved an almost overwhelming one. Shafter, now nearing sixty-three years of age, weighed more than three hundred pounds and suffered intensely in the humid heat of a Florida summer. Nevertheless, he managed to bring some order out of chaos and to embark about sixteen thousand soldiers on thirty-two transports and to sail for Cuba on June 14, 1898.

The expeditionary force landed at Daiquiri on June 22, took Siboney the next day, and defeated the Spanish at Las Guasimas on June 24. Shafter then launched his main attack on the port city of Santiago de Cuba. Heights surrounding the city on its land side were stormed and taken without heavy loss, but Shafter hesitated to assault the formidable fortifications guarding the entrances to Santiago. His hesitancy brought a barrage of criticism from many of his officers and men and a tidal wave of complaint in the United States. Shafter's cause was made infinitely worse by his poor relations with numerous war correspondents who had flocked to the fighting front. Never sensitive about public relations, Shafter had alienated the correspondents by his gruff manner, corpulence, and untidy dress. The end result was a steady stream of uncomplimentary articles that were published in the newspapers and became, particularly in the Hearst and Pulitzer newspapers, little short of venomous.

Shafter ignored his critics and focused his attention on his army. His soldiers were falling victim to malaria, yellow fever, and dysentery. Shafter needed reinforcements, and an attack on the city would certainly produce heavy casualties; he had never believed in a large "butcher bill." Therefore, with considerable skill, he undertook negotiations leading to the surrender of the Spanish forces under General Jose Velasquez Toral. After the Spanish fleet had fled the harbor of Santiago and been destroyed by the American blockading fleet (under the command of Winfield Scott Schley*), Shafter was able to conclude terms of surrender with Toral on July 17, 1898. Shafter's invasion of Cuba had accomplished its objective with a minimum loss of life, but he did not emerge from the war as a popular hero. The savage attacks on him had done much to destroy his reputation and shunted him into relative obscurity.

With the war at an end, he was assigned to command the Department of California with headquarters at San Francisco. On October 16, 1899, he retired as a brigadier general, but remained in command of the department under his volunteer rank of major general until June 30, 1901. The next day he was advanced to the grade of major general on the retired list.

Shafter's place in American military history has suffered primarily because of criticism of his conduct of the Cuban Campaign, and much of this was unfair. Never one to court publicity and contemptuous of his critics, Shafter never attempted to answer the attacks made on him. Actually, many of the problems that arose during the Spanish-American War were not of his making. Given the state of unpreparedness coupled with unrealistic expectations, Shafter had done well by any standard. Nevertheless, the campaign remains one of the most criticized in U.S. military history.

His Civil War record was outstanding and appreciated by his superiors, but he never attracted public attention to the degree of other young officers such as George Armstrong Custer,* Ranald Slidell Mackenzie,* Wesley Merritt,* or George Crook.* It is equally true that Shafter never received appropriate recognition for his service in the Southwest. His dedication, energy, and aggressiveness contributed materially to peace along that tortured frontier, and his campaign on and exploration of the Staked Plains spurred settlement of that region.

Shafter's forty years of service were marked by unswerving loyalty and devotion to his country, and he performed ably in his assigned tasks. He merits a more prominent place in our military history than he has received.

BIBLIOGRAPHY

Holbrook, Stewart H. *Lost Men of American History*. New York: Macmillan Company, 1946.
Leckie, William H. *The Buffalo Soldiers: A Narrative of the Negro Cavalry in the West*. Norman: University of Oklahoma Press, 1967.

Millis, Walter. *The Martial Spirit*. New York: Houghton Mifflin Company, 1931.
Trask, David F. *The War with Spain in 1898*. New York: Macmillan Company, 1981.

WILLIAM H. LECKIE

SHARPE, Henry Granville (b. Kingston, N.Y., April 30, 1858; d. Providence, R.I., July 13, 1947), Army officer, logistician, commissary general of subsistence, 1905–1912; quartermaster general, 1916–1918.

Henry Granville Sharpe's paternal ancestors immigrated from the Palatinate to Kingston, New York, in 1712, and soon established the family as substantial members of the community. His father, George Henry Sharpe, rose to the rank of brevet major general in the Civil War and later served as a member of the New York state legislature and as collector of the port of New York. Through his mother, Caroline Hone (Hasbrouck) Sharpe, he was related to the prominent Hasbrouck family of New Jersey. Young Henry attended Phillips-Andover Academy and matriculated at Rutgers College from which he later (1917) received an honorary Master of Science degree. He entered the U.S. Military Academy in June 1876, having received an unexpected appointment from President Ulysses Simpson Grant,* a friend of his father.

For two years following his graduation from West Point in 1880, Sharpe served as a second lieutenant in the 4th U.S. Infantry Regiment at Fort Laramie, Wyoming. In June 1882 he resigned his commission and was occupied for a short time with railroad construction work. He reentered the Army in September 1883 with a commission as captain and commissary in the Subsistence Department. Between 1883 and 1898 he served variously as a depot, post, and purchasing commissary of subsistence at New York City, West Point, Omaha, Vancouver Barracks, Portland (Oregon), St. Louis, and Boston, gaining experience in all aspects of subsistence operations and being promoted to major and commissary in November 1895.

At the outbreak of the Spanish-American War Sharpe sought field service but was assigned as chief commissary at Camp George H. Thomas, Chickamauga Park, Georgia. Amidst a multitude of logistical problems his management of the camp's food supply was the one bright spot, and he was specially commended for his work. He was promoted to lieutenant colonel and deputy commissary general in June 1898 and accompanied General John R. Brooke and the I Army Corps to Puerto Rico in July 1898. There he served in a number of key subsistence postions. He returned to the United States in December 1898 for a brief assignment as purchasing commissary at Chicago.

In July 1899 Sharpe was reassigned to Washington as a special assistant to the commissary general. He was promoted to colonel and assistant commissary general in 1901 and served as acting commissary general during the absence of General J. F. Weston in the summer of 1901. In 1902 he was assigned as chief commissary of the Division of the Philippines in which position he served with great effectiveness. He returned home on sick leave in June 1904 and was once again detailed as a special assistant to the commissary general.

Upon the retirement of Commissary General Weston in October 1905 Sharpe, with the active support of former Secretary of War Elihu Root* and many of the Army's highest ranking line and staff officers, was appointed commissary general. As commissary general he worked actively to improve the ration and to introduce better methods of food preparation for an army globally deployed and larger in size than at any time since the Civil War. A school for cooks and bakers at Fort Riley, Kansas, in 1905 was established through his persistent agitation.

In 1912 the Subsistence, Quartermaster, and Pay Departments were consolidated into a single Supply Department. Although Sharpe had been the leader of the drive for consolidation and was the senior of the three bureau chiefs involved, he was passed over as head of the new Quartermaster Corps in favor of his West Point classmate, James B. Aleshire. Recognized publicly by Aleshire as the "father of consolidation," Sharpe accepted appointment as a brigadier general in the new corps in August 1912 and continued to serve in the Washington headquarters.

When General Aleshire was retired by reason of ill-health in September 1916 Sharpe, having again garnered the active support of leading Army and political figures, including Secretary of War Newton Diehl Baker,* was promoted to quartermaster general. His appointment came in the midst of active operations of the Army on the Mexican border which had depleted the perpetually short stocks of reserve supplies and stretched the thin manpower resources of the Quartermaster Corps to their limit. Faced with the probability of American involvement in the world war then raging in Europe, Sharpe attempted to prepare the Army's supply system for the immense demands that loomed ahead. He met both the indifference and fiscal restraint of the Congress and a decided lack of cooperation from the War Department General Staff which had been created in 1903 to coordinate just such Army planning and preparations.

Even after the United States entered the war in April 1917, Sharpe was not properly informed of planned operations or of proposed troop strengths by the General Staff to which he had to look for all planning information. Despite growing confusion in the procurement and transportation areas, the Quartermaster Corps erected the necessary training camps, moved the new recruits to them, fed the troops well, and clothed and equipped over 1.5 million men by January 1, 1918. At the same time Sharpe had to cope with a massive expansion of the corps itself which ballooned from its prewar strength of 8,100 officers and men to 5,080 officers and 134,000 enlisted men by the end of 1917.

In December 1917, just as the Quartermaster Corps was beginning to overcome many of the problems of supporting a mass army, Sharpe was abruptly removed from his position as quartermaster general and was detailed to serve on the ineffectual and short-lived War Council. His duties as quartermaster general were assumed by another of his West Point classmates, Major General George Washington Goethals,* an engineer. In June 1918 Sharpe was reassigned as a major general of the line to command the Southeastern Department with headquarters at Charleston, South Carolina, where he remained, except for a five-month inspection tour in Europe in 1919, until May 1, 1920, when he was retired at his own request after forty-three years of service.

Following his retirement Sharpe traveled widely, spending several years in Europe observing conditions following the war. In 1921 he published an *apologia* entitled *The Quartermaster Corps in the Year 1917 in the World War* in which he cited the achievements and tribulations of the Corps during the period of his direction. In the calmer atmosphere that followed the successful conclusion of the war effort, Secretary of War Baker attempted to rectify the summary dismissal of Sharpe as quartermaster general and to recognize Sharpe's substantial contribution to the war effort, especially his efficient management of the Army's food supply. In January 1923 Sharpe was awarded the Distinguished Service Medal. He refused to accept the award, however, since it officially covered only his service in the Southeastern Department. Sharpe retained a lively interest in the Quartermaster Corps and the professional development of its officers until his death at the age of eighty-nine at Providence, Rhode Island, on July 13, 1947. He was buried in Arlington National Cemetery.

Henry Granville Sharpe embodied in one person the characteristic virtues of both the small, conservative nineteenth-century army with its powerful, bureaucratic staff system and the new, dynamic army of the twentieth century with its growing sense of professionalism and "rational" organization. Sharpe obtained his initial appointment to the Subsistence Department in the customary political manner, quickly mastered the bureaucratic intricacies of the old staff system as well as its technical details, and rose to become the very model of the traditional bureau chief.

The relief of Sharpe as quartermaster general in December 1917, for it was nothing less, cast him in the role of scapegoat for the tremendous logistical problems encountered in mobilizing and deploying the U.S. Army in World War I. That most of the problems faced in 1917 stemmed not so much from the internal inefficiencies of the supply departments as from the traditional American reluctance to prepare in peacetime for future conflict, the hesitancy of President Woodrow Wilson and Secretary of War Baker to exert direct and positive control over the war effort, and the ineptitude of the fledgling General Staff in focusing on a policy that emphasized rapid, massive mobilization of personnel without due consideration of the capabilities of the existing logistical system to support them, was not apparent in the decision to replace Sharpe with Goethals, the vigorous promoter of new management techniques derived from the business world. What was so ignominiously attacked in 1917 was not so much Sharpe's management of supply preparations for the war as the old bureau system he represented.

Despite his position as a "traditional" bureau chief, Sharpe himself had a good claim to sit among the "new men" who transformed the U.S. Army at the turn of the century with a fresh enthusiasm for the serious study of their profession. Indeed, he was the first of the Army's modern logisticians, concerned not merely with one fuctional aspect of supplying forces in the field, but with the entire scope of the systematic support of Army operations and with the interrelated nature of strategy, tactics, and logistics.

In 1893 Sharpe published one of the few comprehensive works on military logistics to originate in the United States up to that time, *The Art of Subsisting Armies in War*, in which he drew upon military history and contemporary foreign subsistence theory and practice to suggest several innovative ideas in military supply. He pointed to the logistical constraints on strategy and tactics and suggested that supply was the controlling factor, which indeed it has proven to be in modern war. Here, too, twenty years before the event, is found his recommendation for consolidation of the existing commodity-oriented supply bureaus into one functionally organized department. In 1895 Sharpe received the Gold Medal Prize of the U.S. Military Service Institution for his essay on "The Art of Supplying Armies in the Field as Exemplified during the Civil War." His essay is still one of the most comprehensive and useful descriptions of Civil War logistical organization and practice.

In *The Provisioning of the Modern Army in the Field*, published in 1905, Sharpe outlined the novel idea, apparently adopted by him from Armand Furse, a British officer and logistician, that the theater of operations should be divided into a combat zone and a communications zone and that the supply services and line of communications of an army in the field should be entrusted to a "General of Communications," thus leaving the Army commander free to conduct the tactical battle. Both concepts were soon incorporated into U.S. Army doctrine and remain a part of it today.

Henry G. Sharpe's active military service fell almost equally on either side of the Spanish-American War of 1898, often considered the watershed between the "Old Army" and the "Modern Army." Although his role as the last of the powerful bureau chiefs brought him notoriety and humiliation, Sharpe's active contribution to the professional revolution that transformed the U.S. Army at the beginning of the twentieth century through the systematic study of the military art in all its aspects has been overlooked almost entirely. His dual career suggests that scholars may well have drawn too sharply the line between the "traditional" bureaucrats of the supply departments and the "rational" young professionals of the General Staff.

BIBLIOGRAPHY

Risch, Erna. *Quartermaster Support of the Army: A History of the Corps, 1775–1939.* Washington, D.C.: Quartermaster Historian's Office, Office of the Quartermaster General, 1962.

Sharpe, Henry G. *The Art of Subsisting Armies in War.* New York: John Wiley and Sons, 1893.

———. "The Art of Supplying Armies in the Field as Exemplified During the Civil War." (1895 Gold Medal Prize Essay.) *Journal of the Military Service Institution* 18, No. 79 (January 1896): 45–95.

———. *The Provisioning of the Modern Army in the Field.* Kansas City, Mo.: Franklin-Hudson Publishing Company, 1905.

———. *The Quartermaster Corps in the Year 1917 in the World War.* New York: Century Company, 1921.

CHARLES R. SHRADER

SHAYS, Daniel (b. probably, Hopkinton, Mass., 1747; d. Sparta, N.Y., September 29, 1825), soldier and partisan leader.

Daniel Shays had little education and probably grew up in what might be termed "rural poverty." In his early twenties he worked as a hired man in Brookfield and in July 1772 married Abigail Gilbert. His only claim to prominence before 1775 seems to have been that he served unofficially as drill sergeant at musters of the local militia. With the news of the British march against Lexington and Concord, Shays reported for active duty and served until the end of April. Sometime in the next six weeks, perhaps with a body of local militia, he joined the patriot army gathering around Boston. At Bunker Hill he fought gallantly, was cited for bravery, and was promoted for gallantry in action.

Shays appears to have then served continuously until the fall of 1780. He saw action at Saratoga and at Stony Point, and perhaps in other engagements as well. There is a report that he was once wounded in battle, but there is no record of it. In 1779 he was promoted to the rank of captain in the 5th Massachusetts Regiment, retroactively to the start of the year 1777. James Truslow Adams wrote that he was popular with his men and had the "reputation of a brave and efficient officer." It is thought by some that he served at least briefly under the command of the Marquis de Lafayette*; at least we know that Lafayette gave him an expensive sword and that Shays sold it because of his poverty.

Shays resigned from the Army in October 1780 and settled on a farm in Pelham, Massachusetts, where he was both elected and appointed to numerous positions of local leadership and responsibility. After the Revolution, Shays found himself caught up in the economic collapse that was so widespread and was embroiled in the protests that followed. In the summer of 1786 debt-ridden farmers prevented the sitting of the court of common pleas and general sessions, probably intending merely to prevent additional imprisonment for debt. Then fearful of possible punishment, the leaders planned to prevent the sitting of the supreme court in Springfield at the end of September. About eight hundred militia prepared to defend the court. The protestors mustered about the same number of men, but they were inadequately armed and lacked any effective organization. A compromise was reached and violence avoided. Shays was chairman of a committee that drafted a series of resolutions, and his name was given wide circulation as a leader of the insurgents.

In January 1787 Massachusetts political leaders, and the conservative eastern portion of the state in general, feared open revolution. General Benjamin Lincoln,* in command of a hastily mustered force of militia, was ordered to march to the Connecticut River Valley and to suppress any organized rebellion. Shays became the accepted leader of one group of insurgents, and Luke Day of another group. Poorly equipped, Shays and Day planned to unite their forces and attack the arsenal at Springfield. Communication between the two leaders was inadequate; Shays' force attacked General Shepard without waiting for Day. Apparently, Shepard ordered his men to fire over the heads of Shays' advancing men and then ordered Shays to halt. The insurgents continued to advance. Shepard then had his men fire directly at Shays' force. A few men were killed and wounded, and Shays' men retreated in disarray, perhaps without firing any shots.

General Lincoln arrived with his force and attempted negotiation with Shays. Although a letter from Rufus Putnam implies that Shays was anxious to call off all resistance, the negotiations met with failure. Lincoln attacked Shays' force at Petersham, in a blinding snowstorm. Shays' men were routed and dispersed, and Shays sought refuge over the state line in Vermont. Condemned to death, Shays petitioned for a pardon. It was granted, on June 13, 1787, with the provision that Shays would never again seek or accept either military or civil office.

Shays removed to western New York soon afterwards. He lived simply and inconspicuously for more than thirty years, dying in Sparta, New York, in 1825.

Other than his service as a militia drill sergeant in the period 1770–1775 and his gallant conduct at Bunker Hill, there is little in the record to indicate military leadership on the part of Daniel Shays. It seems probable, as Marion L. Starkey and Rufus Putnam have suggested, that Shays was forced into a position of leadership and that he simply became a symbol of the very real grievances of an impoverished rural population. Nothing in the record of his brief engagement with General Shepard or his utter rout by General Lincoln suggests a military officer of great courage or able leadership. Apparently, he was a simple man of strong and honest convictions who found himself in an untenable position and was loyal to his point of view.

BIBLIOGRAPHY

Adams, James Truslow. *New England in the Republic*. Boston, 1926.
Egleston, John. *The Life of John Paterson*. New York, 1898.
Starkey, Marion L. *A Little Rebellion*. New York, 1955.
Taylor, Robert J. *Western Massachusetts in the Revolution*. Providence, R. I., 1954.

RALPH ADAMS BROWN

SHELBY, Isaac (b. Maiden's Choice farm [near Hagerstown], Md., December 11, 1750; d. Traveler's Rest [near Danville], Ky., July 18, 1826), militia leader in the War of Independence and the War of of 1812, twice governor of Kentucky.

Isaac Shelby was the son of Evan and Letitia Cox Shelby. The elder Shelby had come to America at the age of twelve from his native Wales. Although the family prospered, accumulating substantial frontier acreage in Maryland and later in southwestern Virginia, Isaac received only a rudimentary education.

Business reverses during the 1760s in the always unpredictable Indian trade prompted the family to move in 1770 to the valley of the Holston River, near present-day Bristol in Virginia and Tennessee. In the 1770s it lay on the main path of the Wilderness Road to Kentucky. Both Evan and Isaac Shelby became officers of the Fincastle County, Virginia, militia, and Isaac's younger brother served as a private.

The outbreak of Lord Dunmore's War in 1774 pitted the Virginia militia under the last of the colony's royal governors against the Shawnee Indians of the upper Ohio Valley. Under dispute were irreconcilable claims to trans-Allegheny lands by Virginia planter-speculators and Indian tribesmen. The Shelbys were among eleven hundred men mustered from Botetourt, Augusta, and Fincastle counties under the command of Andrew Lewis, lieutenant of Botetourt. Lewis had orders from Governor Lord Dunmore to rendezvous on the Ohio with a comparable force under the personal direction of the governor. Following a swift, exhausting march across the mountains of western Virginia, Lewis' frontier militiamen reached Point Pleasant at the mouth of the Kanawha. There, at dawn on October 10, 1774, they were assailed by a large war party of Shawnee led by Cornstalk. Hours passed of fierce, costly battling quite uncharacteristic of the skirmishing common to the American frontier. At the head of seventy-five men, Isaac Shelby took a decisive part in the Battle of Point Pleasant by winning and holding high ground on the Indians' flank. Eventually, the Indians broke off the struggle and recrossed the Ohio. For some months after the disbandment of Lewis' militia army, Shelby remained at Point Pleasant as second-in-command of the small garrison left there. Although inconclusive, the 1774 campaign had prepared the way for the beginnings of settlement in Kentucky, a frontier visited by Shelby in 1775 and again in 1776 to survey lands for himself and for Richard Henderson's Transylvania Company.

Shelby's career as a pioneer was interrupted by the Revolution, however, and in 1776 he was named a militia captain by the Virginia Committee of Safety and a year later was designated commissary by Governor Patrick Henry. From 1777 to 1779 he gathered supplies (often using his own credit) and built boats for both Continental and militia use. Among other activities, Shelby furnished support for George Rogers Clark's* Illinois Expedition of 1779 and for the defeat of Dragging Canoe's Chickamaugas on the Tennessee River that same year. As a boundary surveyor Shelby was surprised to discover in 1779 that his Holston lands actually lay inside North Carolina (now Tennessee). Very soon he was named colonel of the militia of the new North Carolina county of Sullivan and elected to that state's legislature; he had previously served a term in the Virginia Assembly.

The summer of 1780 found Shelby visiting Kentucky, where he learned of the fall of Charles Town, South Carolina, weeks earlier. Hastening back to Sullivan County, he raised a short-term volunteer militia regiment which he led in several successful late-summer actions in South Carolina. Shortly after the disbandment of his command, Shelby heard of threats by Major Patrick Ferguson and his large force of Loyalists to attack the backwoods region. With other North Carolina and Virginia militia county colonels—John Sevier, Charles McDowell, William Campbell, and Benjamin Cleveland—Shelby called for a rendezvous of mounted militiamen at Sycamore Shoals (Elizabethton, Tennessee) on September 25, 1780. Over a thousand men came forward and crossed the mountains to attack Ferguson on October 7 at King's Mountain—just beyond the South Carolina line. Using the sharpshooting and infiltration tactics of the Western frontier, the "over-mountain men" overwhelmed the Loyalists, killing some three hundred and capturing an additional seven hundred. It was the first major reverse suffered by the British since making the South their main active theater, and it was followed by other American strategic successes the next year.

After participating in the closing phases of the War of Independence in South Carolina, Shelby settled permanently in Kentucky where in 1783 he married Susannah Hart. Already well-known throughout the Western County, Shelby quickly became a Kentuckian of prominence: high sheriff of Lincoln County, a militia colonel, and a leader of the movement to separate Kentucky from Virginia. In 1792 he took office as the new state's first governor. Governor Shelby staked out a central position between Kentucky's nationalists and separatists. He never overtly promoted disunion, but his continuing anxiety over raids by the Indians of the Old Northwest and his desire that Kentucky agricultural commodities enjoy the right of deposit in Spanish-held New Orleans made Shelby a sharp critic of the cautious diplomacy of President George Washington.* To General Anthony Wayne's* Indian campaigns north of the Ohio he gave unstinting and effective support.

At sixty-one Shelby was recalled to the governorship in 1812. As wartime commander in chief of his state's militia, he labored so indefatigably to procure supplies and raise troops, both regular and militia, that Kentucky shouldered a disproportionate share of the war's burdens. At the end of August 1813, Shelby personally mustered and led some thirty-five hundred mounted Kentucky-militia volunteers to join the northwestern army of William Henry Harrison,* an augmentation of strength that made possible Harrison's pursuit of General Henry Proctor's and Tecumseh's* mixed British and Indian force into Upper Canada. The resultant American victory in the Battle of the Thames on October 5, 1813, would have been impossible without the large-scale participation of Kentucky's citizen-soldiery. It brought to a triumphant close America's generation-long struggle to gain effective control over its Great Lakes territories.

After the war Shelby declined President James Monroe's 1817 offer of the secretaryship of war. He did, however, agree to serve with Andrew Jackson* as a commissioner to purchase from the Indians the territory between the Tennessee and Mississippi rivers.

Over a thirty-nine-year span Isaac Shelby fought not only in the opening and closing battles for mastery of the Ohio Valley and the Old Northwest, but also in the Revolution's turning point in the South. Among frontiersmen of the early

American republic Shelby's calm, dignified, affable demeanor inspired general confidence and trust. If in action he lacked the fire and drive of a George Rogers Clark or an Andrew Jackson, Shelby was nevertheless courageous and dependable. And as a military manager he was quite exceptional among the militia leaders of the trans-Allegheny frontier. Lacking formal training as a soldier and never a Regular Army officer, Shelby was well prepared for frontier warfare by his own background and experience. His work as a surveyor had enhanced his understanding of the lay of the land on a very broad scale. As his gubernatorial correspondence demonstrates, the grand strategy of 1813 was Shelby's—not Harrison's or Secretary of War John Armstrong, Jr.'s. Moreover, Shelby's work as a frontier tradesman and militia commissary gave him at least a rudimentary grasp of the all-important logistical aspects of warfare. Too, Shelby's personality added to his military effectiveness. He grasped fully the strengths and limitations of frontier militiamen and tried to employ them intelligently. He was unselfish enough to function harmoniously and successfully in a divided command, as at King's Mountain, or to subordinate himself willingly to a younger man of lesser abilities, as with Harrison in 1813. Finally, Shelby's universal reputation for shrewdness and personal integrity served him well, remaining intact through several morale-shattering American defeats in 1812–1813 and leaving the governor with a reservoir of public confidence upon which to draw at the time of his decisive militia muster of August 1813. Neither a romantic figure of folklore nor a Man on Horseback, Shelby played a role of paramount importance in the conquest of the early frontier.

BIBLIOGRAPHY

Clark, Thomas D. "The Jackson Purchase." *The Filson Club History Quarterly* 50 (1976): 302–20.
"Correspondence Between Governor Isaac Shelby and General William Henry Harrison." *Register of the Kentucky Historical Society* 20 (1922): 130–44.
"Correspondence of Gov. Isaac Shelby." *Register of the Kentucky Historical Society* 8–9 (1910–1911), *passim*.
Draper, Lyman C. *King's Mountain and Its Heroes*. Cincinatti: 1881.
Hammack, James Wallace, Jr. *Kentucky and the Second American Revolution*. Lexington, Ky.: 1976.
Padgett, James A., ed. "Some Letters of Isaac Shelby." *Register of the Kentucky Historical Society* 37 (1939): 1–9.
Stone, Richard G., Jr. *A Brittle Sword: The Kentucky Militia, 1776–1912*. Lexington, Ky.: 1977.
Wrobel, Sylvia, and George Grider. *Isaac Shelby* Danville, Ky.: 1974.

RICHARD G. STONE, JR.

SHERIDAN, Philip Henry (b. Albany, N.Y., March 6, 1831; d. Nonquitt, Mass., August 5, 1888), Army officer. Sheridan commanded the Federal Army of the Shenandoah during the Civil War.

Sheridan sprang from Irish Catholic parents. Philip's father settled his family in Somerset, Ohio, where he toiled as a construction worker and raised a brood of six. Philip obtained an appointment to the U.S. Military Academy when the first appointee failed to qualify. He was graduated in 1853 finishing thirty-fourth in a class of fifty-two. Sheridan had not been a prize pupil; in fact, he had been suspended from the Academy for one year after he lunged at an upperclassman with a bayoneted rifle. When the Civil War began in 1861, Phil Sheridan was an obscure lieutenant of infantry serving in Oregon.

During the early months of the war, Captain Sheridan held administrative positions until he became quartermaster on the staff of Henry Wager Halleck* during the campaign against Corinth, Mississippi (April 1862). Sheridan wrangled the colonelcy of the 2d Michigan Cavalry Regiment. Next, he got command of a cavalry brigade and led it on a successful raid against Booneville, Mississippi. He was promoted to brigadier general of volunteers and given command of an infantry division. In a defensive role, Sheridan's division repulsed Confederate attacks ordered by Braxton Bragg* at the battles of Perryville, Kentucky (October 1862) and Stones River, Tennessee (December 31, 1862-January 3, 1863). William Starke Rosecrans* favorably cited Sheridan's tenacity, and "Little Phil" was promoted to major general of volunteers.

At the Battle of Chicamauga, Tennessee (September 19–20, 1863), Sheridan learned stern lessons in tactics. While his division was maneuvering, it took the brunt of an unexpected attack by troops under James Longstreet.* Sheridan's men broke, suffered heavy casualties, and shared the ignominy of the rest of the Federal right wing, which all but disintegrated.

Sheridan rebounded in the battles around Chattanooga. Under Ulysses Simpson Grant,* Union forces attacked Bragg's Confederates, who occupied defensive works on Missionary Ridge. In a concerted Union attack (November 25, 1863), Sheridan's soldiers were ordered to expel Confederates from positions at the foot of the ridge. This they did, but after taking fire from Confederates on the crest, the soldiers themselves began an unordered but unstoppable advance up Missionary Ridge. Sensing victory, Sheridan joined his men in routing the Confederates.

Five months later Grant was general in chief of all Union armies, traveling with General George Gordon Meade* and the Army of the Potomac. Grant wanted a new commander for the army's cavalry and picked Sheridan, who reorganized the corps. Over Meade's objections, Sheridan got Grant's permission to lead his horse soldiers on a raid. The Richmond Raid (May 9–24, 1864) was a controversial exploit. Taking his ten thousand troopers, Sheridan rode toward Richmond, drawing James Ewell Brown Stuart* with him, and engaged in several skirmishes. Then Sheridan's force collided with Stuart's five thousand cavalrymen and killed the South's cavalier-hero at Yellow Tavern. Despite criticisms that the Richmond Raid had accomplished little, Sheridan set out with his men again (June 7–28). At Trevilian Station Sheridan suffered a reverse, but his second raid gained him favorable publicity in the North, and the rampaging Federal cavalry was disconcerting to the Southern government.

In July 1864 Jubal Anderson Early* led his army of doughty Confederates out of the Shenandoah Valley, threatening Washington and distracting Grant as he grappled with the Army of Northern Virginia under Robert Edward Lee.* Consequently, Grant ordered Sheridan to take command of the army of the Shenandoah (about forty thousand men), destroy Early's army (about twenty thousand men), and lay waste to the Valley, Lee's supply source. In August Sheridan moved cautiously into the Valley where several Union generals had come to grief. Marching over Opequon Creek, Sheridan attacked Early on September 19 in his defensive positions outside Winchester. The assault was carried by Rutherford Hayes' brigade of the VIII Corps under George Crook.* Sheridan was victorious and sent Early "whirling through Winchester." Three days later Sheridan confronted Early again at Fisher's Hill, turning the Confederate left, with Hayes again in the van. Had Sheridan's cavalry blocked Early's retreat, the Confederate Army might have been annihilated. Sheridan was promoted to brigadier general in the Regular Army.

Believing that Early was defeated, Sheridan posted his army in poorly chosen positions along Cedar Creek and went to Washington to confer with Halleck. Meanwhile, Early received reinforcements and planned a surprise attack. Before dawn on October 19, 1864, in a well-executed assault, Early's Confederates, led by John Brown Gordon,* struck the poorly disposed Federals, routing Crook's VIII Corps. But Horatio Wright of the VI Corps was able to establish a defensive line. About midmorning Wright expected Early to deliver the *coup-de-grace*; it never came. Early hoped that his daybreak success would be enough to win the field. Then, Sheridan returned.

The sound of the guns had awakened Sheridan in Winchester, where he had stopped on his way from Washington. He gathered his staff and made haste to Cedar Creek. Stragglers lined the roads, and scattered squads and wayward companies had stopped to boil coffee. They evidenced no interest in returning to Cedar Creek. Sheridan called to his soldiers, promising that they would win the day yet. Incredibly, they responded to his call. Once-beaten soldiers and faltering officers turned around and followed their little general back into battle. Arriving at Wright's line, Sheridan planned a counterattack, which he sent in at 4:00 P.M. This stroke drove Early from the field and ruined his army, which suffered nearly three thousand casualties, lost twenty-five guns, and left most of its supply wagons behind. Sheridan was supreme in the Shenandoah.

During February and March of 1865, after his troops had ravaged the Valley, Sheridan launched the Northern Virginia Raid, with the objective of capturing the rail center at Lynchburg. The raid resulted in the destruction of several miles of railroad, but Sheridan turned away from Lynchburg when reports indicated that it might be too strongly held for his cavalry to take. After resting for less than a week, Sheridan, under Grant's orders, applied almost continual pressure on Lee's retreating army. At Five Forks (April 1), he won a victory that blocked Lee's escape. On April 9 Sheridan was present for Lee's surrender at Appomattox.

Sheridan assumed important commands after the Civil War. In charge of the

Division of the Gulf (1865–1866), he used demonstrations along the Rio Grande to persuade Napoleon III's French Army to end its occupation of Mexico in May 1866. Then Sheridan turned to Reconstruction, and President Andrew Johnson appointed him commander of the Fifth Military District (Texas and Louisiana). Sheridan sternly administered the district and supported the Radical Republicans, which prompted the conservative Johnson to order him to the Indian frontier. Promoted to lieutenant general in 1869, Sheridan commanded the Division of the Missouri, virtually the whole West between the Mississippi and the Rockies. Using the vainglorious George Armstrong Custer,* Sheridan saw to the defeat of all major Indian tribes in the region by 1878. He was commanding general of the Army from 1884 until his death in 1888. He had been promoted to full general just before he died.

Sheridan, like Grant, had the good fortune to serve in the West and to hold a series of increasingly responsible commands before being ordered to revitalize the Army of the Potomac's Cavalry Corps. During his career, Sheridan never fit any idealized picture of the professional Army officer—coincidentally, another trait he shared with Grant. Sheridan was short (he stood only five feet–five inches), swarthy, and long-armed. He had receding hair and a ragged mustache. But he was a skilled rider, and on the back of his horse, Sheridan's long torso and broad shoulders made him appear tall. Sheridan had a ferocious temper and wielded one of the most profane vocabularies in the Army. The most controversial display of Sheridan's temper occurred late in the war, at Five Forks, where he removed Gouverneur Warren for delivering a tardy and poorly directed attack.

Sheridan showed more restraint when he argued with his superior, General Meade, over how the Cavalry Corps should be used—as wagon guards or as mounted juggernaut. Sheridan's raiders sapped the spirit of Lee's cavalry, ripped up rail tracks, threatened Richmond, killed Jeb Stuart, disrupted supply lines, and caused doubts about Confederate defenses and capabilities.

In the Shenandoah, Sheridan had his greatest successes. Yet his command in the Valley, like the value of his raids, has been criticized. Supposedly, he won cheap victories against inferior Confederate forces. Actually, Sheridan was a winner where other Federal commanders had been losers. Nathaniel Banks, James Shields, and John Charles Frémont* had been baffled in the Valley by Thomas Jonathan ("Stonewall") Jackson,* though the Union generals led forces that were numerically superior to Jackson's. Jube Early was no Stonewall Jackson, but Federal victories were not predestined by virtue of numbers alone. Twice Sheridan struck Early hard and refused to be defeated at Cedar Creek where all signs seemed to point to a Union rout. Other Union commanders might have yielded the field to Early; instead, Sheridan counterattacked and crippled Early's army. In the process, Sheridan won a signal victory, became a Northern hero, and sparked the reelection of President Abraham Lincoln.*

Despite the fact that Sheridan refused to attack the rail center at Lynchburg, he demonstrated a consistent offensive spirit and repeatedly sought out the enemy army and brought it to combat. In the post-Civil War West, Sheridan showed the same offensive spirit, organizing an extraordinary winter campaign (1868–1869), and ruthlessly pushed his subordinates in the Red River War (1874–1875), the last major Indian war in Texas and Indian Territory. Eventually his subordinates, including Ranald Slidell Mackenzie,* followed Sheridan's example and devastated the Indians' supplies in campaigns reminiscent of his Shenandoah Valley campaign.

Sheridan was determined in defense and relentless in attack. He envisioned the Union victorious, and he helped to make that vision a reality. Sheridan deserves to be ranked as the third most important Union general (behind Grant and William Tecumseh Sherman*) and was among the best combat commanders of the U.S. Army in the nineteenth century.

BIBLIOGRAPHY

Catton, Bruce. *A Stillness at Appomattox.* Garden City: Doubleday and Company, 1953.
Dawson, Joseph G., III. *Army Generals and Reconstruction: Louisiana, 1862–1877.* Baton Rouge: Louisiana State University Press, 1982.
Fuller, J.F.C. *The Generalship of Ulysses S. Grant.* New York: Dodd, Mead, and Company, 1929.
O'Connor, Richard. *Sheridan the Inevitable.* Indianapolis, Ind.: Bobbs-Merrill, 1953.
Williams, T. Harry. *Hayes of the Twenty-third: The Civil War Volunteer Officer.* New York: Alfred A. Knopf, 1965.

JOSEPH G. DAWSON III

SHERMAN, William Tecumseh (b. Lancaster, Ohio, February 8, 1820; d. New York City, N.Y., February 14, 1891), Army officer. Sherman is especially noted for his Atlanta Campaign and is notorious for his devastating marches through Georgia and South Carolina in the Civil War.

The sixth of eleven children of Charles and Mary Sherman, "Cump" was named for Tecumseh,* the great Shawnee statesman and warrior whom his father particularly admired. When Judge Sherman died of a sudden fever in 1829, "Cump" was reared with the family of Thomas Ewing, his father's closest friend and a rising star in national politics. Senator Ewing appointed Sherman to the U.S. Military Academy in 1836, and he was graduated four years later sixth in a class of forty-three.

Commissioned second lieutenant in the artillery, Sherman spent eighteen months with the 3d Artillery in Florida during the final stages of the second Seminole War (1836–1842). In February 1842 his company was transferred to Fort Morgan near Mobile, and six months later it was sent to occupy Fort Moultrie, South Carolina, where it remained until the Mexican War. Sherman spent the war years on recruiting service and later on staff duty in California, where he observed the height of the Gold Rush in 1849. Returning to Washington the next year, he married Ellen Ewing, a daughter of his "second" father. The couple had eight children. After being promoted to captain, Sherman served briefly at St.

Louis and New Orleans before resigning his commission in 1853 to become a banker.

Lacking "sense enough to keep out of such disreputable business," Sherman's branch bank in California failed and he lost his own fortune repaying funds he had invested on behalf of Army friends. He was by his own admission "a dead cock in the pit" when he was named superintendent of a new military institution in Louisiana in 1859. An obvious success, he resigned one year after the school (now Louisiana State University) opened because Louisiana had voted to secede and Sherman was unconditional in his loyalty to the Constitution.

Commissioned colonel in June 1861, he commanded a brigade at the First Battle of Bull Run (July 21), where his men fought "disorganized but not scared." He next was assigned to the Department of the Cumberland where his ultimate reponsibility as commander was the defense of Kentucky. Sherman's private assertion that two hundred thousand troops would be needed for any offensive action (he had but twenty thousand) was publicized out of context and led to so much public ridicule that in November 1861 he asked to be relieved. Many officers and politicians at this time thought Sherman insane; he considered himself a failure.

The efforts of Thomas Ewing and his own brother, Senator John Sherman, saved him for the Army. From a training command in St. Louis he went to Paducah, Kentucky, where he forwarded the men and supplies needed by Ulysses Simpson Grant* in his Fort Donelson Campaign, and in March 1862 Sherman's newly organized division was with the expeditionary force moving up the Tennessee to sever Confederate railroad communications between Memphis and the East. He fought well at Shiloh (April 6–7), although Sherman had ignored all reports of approaching Confederates and did not order his men to intrench. Following the siege of Corinth, Sherman was given command of the District of West Tennessee, and in December 1862 he led an expedition of thirty-thousand men down the Mississippi to attack Vicksburg while Grant pressed overland along the Mississippi Central Railroad against the main Confederate forces. When a cavalry strike against his supply bases forced Grant to give up his first attempt to take Vicksburg, Sherman was left to his own devices near the city. On December 29 he suffered a severe repulse at the hands of Stephen Dill Lee* in attempting to storm Confederate fortifications at Chickasaw Bluffs. He subsequently served with John Alexander McClernand* in the capture of Arkansas Post.

Sherman's XV Corps played a prominent and often an independent role in Grant's repeated attempts to take Vicksburg, and his main responsibility during the siege was to hold off a relieving Confederate army under Joseph Eggleston Johnston.* Subsequently, when Grant was ordered to relieve Chattanooga, he intended to make his main attack with Sherman's corps against the Confederate right, but the terrain made progress difficult and the battle was won by a "simultaneous" attack against the Confederate center atop Missionary Ridge. Sherman later returned to Vicksburg to lead two divisions 150 miles into the interior to destroy the arsenal, supply depots, and intersecting railroads at Meridian.

After Grant went east in March 1864 to assume overall command of the Union armies, Sherman was given the Military Division of the Mississippi. His mission in Grant's strategy in 1864 was "to move against Johnston's army, to break it up, and to get into the interior of the enemy's country . . . inflicting all the damage [possible] . . . against their war resources." The first step was Atlanta, one hundred miles distant and protected by mountain ranges and rivers running at right angles to Sherman's obvious line of advance, the Western and Atlantic Railroad. Coordinating the three armies of the Tennessee, the Cumberland, and the Ohio, Sherman adroitly maneuvered Johnston out of successive defensive positions. Although repulsed at Kennesaw Mountain (June 27), two months from the day that Union armies everywhere began their advance Sherman was within sight of Atlanta. After John Bell Hood* replaced Johnston, Sherman's armies beat back a series of fierce counterattacks and the noose around Atlanta gradually tightened. Disdaining a regular siege, Sherman inched his way southward to cut off the only remaining railroad feeding Atlanta, and on September 2 he announced the capture of "the Gate City of the South."

Leaving his good friend George Henry Thomas* behind to defend Tennessee, Sherman destroyed Atlanta and then cut loose from his own supply line to march sixty thousand men through Georgia to the sea, destroying the war potential of the area and much private property in the process. His troops stormed Fort McAlister near Savannah on December 13, and Savannah was captured in time for Sherman to present the city to Abraham Lincoln* "as a Christmas gift."

Three weeks later he was on the move again, marching northward through the Carolinas and a possible juncture with Grant's army at Petersburg. A desperate Confederate attack against Sherman's left wing at Bentonville, North Carolina (March 19–21) failed to deter him, and after he was joined at Goldsboro by thirty thousand additional troops that had marched inland from the coast, Johnston, who had been returned to command, had no choice but to surrender. Sherman's initial terms were too widesweeping and generous to be palatable to the Radical Republicans in control after Lincoln's assassination, but the two generals finally came to reasonable terms on April 26, 1865, near Durham, North Carolina. The Civil War was virtually over.

After the war Sherman commanded one of three territorial divisions, embracing the lands between Ohio and the Rockies, in which capacity he directed small campaigns against the Indians and gave "continuous active aid" to the completion of the Union Pacific Railroad in 1869. When Grant was elected president, Sherman was promoted full general and was made general in chief of the Army. He tried to centralize the Army by bringing the bureau chiefs of the War Department under his direct control, but Grant supported his secretary of war in this bureaucratic battle. In disgust, Sherman moved Army headquarters to St. Louis. His continued interest in military lessons of the war, which he wrote about at length in his *Memoirs* originally published in 1875, prompted him to support the tactical reforms of Emory Upton.* Sherman also encouraged Upton to undertake his more celebrated studies of armies abroad and military policy at home. In 1881 Sherman founded the School of Application for Infantry and Cavalry at Fort Leavenworth (now the U.S. Army Command and General Staff College) so that the entire Army could "keep up with the rapid progress in the science and practice of war." Sherman's outspoken *Memoirs* continued to feed old controversies and contributed to the harsh view of him that was growing in the South. He retired from the Army in 1884 and died seven years later, one of the most venerated Union leaders in the war.

Sherman was an indispensable member of that team of Union generals that engineered the final Union victory. His Atlanta Campaign is the only Civil War campaign universally regarded as a masterpiece of *both* offensive and defensive maneuver, and his March to the Sea and subsequent sweep through the Carolinas, which he regarded as "by far" his "most important in conception and execution," contributed heavily to the material and psychological collapse of the Confederacy. A cautious tactician—"fighting is the least part of a general's work," he would insist—Sherman lacked the killer's instinct of striking for the jugular. But from the first he clearly understood the nature and scope of the conflict and the direction military operations must take. Never did he underestimate the will of the South to resist, but he was no less determined that the Union should control the Mississippi. Sherman fought the war with a single eye rare even for that generation. "Let every thought of the mind, every feeling of the heart, every movement of a human muscle, be directed to one sole object— successful war and consequent peace," and he never forgot that "the legitimate object of war is a more perfect peace." Grant's Vicksburg Campaign convinced Sherman that an army could free itself from its communications, and this knowledge, coupled with his conviction that the Civil War differed from European wars in that "we are not only fighting armies, but a hostile people," found its ultimate expression in his celebrated and controversial March to the Sea. A daring and imaginative strategist, Sherman excelled in logistics, and his skillful management of the railroads attracted the attention of soldiers abroad.

Defining strategy as "common sense applied to the art of war" in a day when most generals still obeyed the formal, time-honored maxims of Baron Antoine Henri Jomini, Sherman was as pragmatic as his Prussian contemporary Helmuth von Moltke, who similarly viewed strategy as "a system of expedients." B. H. Liddell Hart has elevated Sherman's system of expedients into a formal system called the "Strategy of Indirect Approach." More than any other general from history, Sherman contributed to the evolution of Liddell Hart's theories, which in turn directly influenced the concept of *blitzkrieg*. In European military circles no Civil War commander has had a greater following than Sherman.

BIBLIOGRAPHY

Barrett, John G. *Sherman's March Through the Carolinas*. Chapel Hill: University of North Carolina Press, 1956.

Lewis, Lloyd. *Sherman: Fighting Prophet*. New York: Harcourt, Brace and Company, 1932.

Liddell Hart, B. H. *Sherman: Soldier, Realist, American*. New York: Dodd, Mead and Company, 1929.

Merrill, James M. *William Tecumseh Sherman*. Chicago: Rand McNally and Company, 1971.

Sherman, William T. *Memoirs of Gen. W. T. Sherman*. 2 vols. New York: Charles L. Webster and Company, 1891.

Turner, George E. *Victory Rode the Rails: The Strategic Place of the Railroads in the Civil War*. Indianapolis, Ind.: Bobbs-Merrill, 1953.

JAY LUVAAS

SHIRLEY, William (b. Preston, Sussex, England, December 2, 1694; d. Roxbury, Mass., March 24, 1771), British colonial governor of Massachusetts and the Bahamas; organizer of the Louisbourg siege of 1745; Edward Braddock's* successor in the French and Indian Wars, 1755.

William Shirley was the son of a London merchant whose family can be traced for many generations in Sussex County, England, and who were related to families much more famous and wealthy than they were, the Onslows, Westerns, and Walsinghams. William attended the Merchant Taylors' School in London, Pembroke College, Cambridge, and Inner Temple. He held a clerkship in the London government (1717–1719) prior to his admission to the bar in 1720. About that time he married Frances Baker, the heiress of a London merchant, and practiced law. Inherited estates in Sussex helped him defray expenses as his family increased in size, and a colonial appointment eventually seemed a way of procuring English patronage and a better living. By 1731 he decided to test his luck in Boston, Massachusetts, where he soon became advocate general of the British admiralty court and a client of the important patronage distributor, the Duke of Newcastle.

Soon after the War of Jenkins' Ear broke out, Shirley managed in 1741 to win appointment as Massachusetts governor. He entered government at a time of political crisis, and he sought to draw the disaffected elements into a partnership in which he gained privileges for them from the British ministry in exchange for cooperation. War contracts for provisions became the greatest prize, but military commissions, civilian appointments, and favors in England were also important. The colony built up its defenses in the meantime, and many people were ready in 1744 when France became an enemy of England to attack Canada. In this imperialist drive Shirley was as much a follower as a leader, but in 1745 the major assault at Fort Louisbourg on Cape Breton Island was prepared by him and led by Sir William Pepperrell.* He and his supporters convinced the governors of the American colonies to raise men and materiel, with perhaps thirty-six hundred men recruited and well over one hundred vessels commissioned. At a critical point seven major warships of the British fleet joined the colonial armada, and the expedition besieged the fortress for nearly six weeks until its defenders capitulated.

The capture of Louisbourg inspired three colonial mobilizations in 1746, 1747, and 1748, but each failed, in turn, for want of British military and naval support. The peace of Aix-la-Chapelle of 1748 restored the fortress to France but set up a boundary commission of which Shirley became a member to determine the colonial territories of England and France. It met in France and was generally ineffective in reducing the tensions along the Quebec-British colonial border. By 1753 Shirley was convinced of the mounting crisis in America and returned to his Massachusetts post in mid-August.

No sooner was he back in office than he urged a restoration of frontier defenses and took steps to increase garrisons in Maine and western Massachusetts. He led an expedition up the Kennebec River in June and July 1754 but found no French to chase or fight, only good land for settlement. Meanwhile, colony representatives joined with others at Albany, New York, where they considered regional defense and colonial union. Although Shirley pressed the Massachusetts legislature to accept the plan for union, it was the only legislature to debate the question. The British government then turned to a military solution for the problem of colonial defense, and at about the same time Shirley joined neighboring governors in plans to remove the French from Nova Scotian borders.

Before their plans were carried out, the British government decided to send Edward Braddock to the colonies with an army and to commission Shirley a colonel of a British regiment to be newly raised in America. In anticipation of Braddock's arrival, Shirley and associates developed a plan to coordinate colonial attacks upon the French in Nova Scotia and northern New York. Braddock later approved this plan and authorized another attack against Fort Niagara on Lake Ontario. He put Shirley in charge of those forces and named him second-in-command. Shirley succeeded his commander when Indians and French ambushed the British in July 1755 near present-day Pittsburgh and killed Braddock.

Shirley had planned to meet Braddock before Fort Niagara where two armies would join in the siege and then return by way of Albany to help in the campaign against Fort Ticonderoga and Crown Point. He and the commander of that offensive, Sir William Johnson,* had already argued about manpower, Indian auxiliaries, and supplies. Braddock's death served only to aggravate conditions, and Shirley now limited his objective to the refortification of Fort Oswego in Lake Ontario. Johnson's campaign was even less a success than Shirley's, because he was attacked and wounded by the enemy and never reached his objective. Only the northern campaign that Shirley had organized recorded successes in Nova Scotia.

At the end of the fighting season, the military disappointments could be attributed to a faulty battle plan and Braddock's death. While the British reassessed the hostilities, Shirley was left without much guidance for 1756 and suffered hostility from friends of William Johnson who aroused politicians in New York. Without plans and without support, he developed his own campaign along the same lines as Braddock's in 1755, but he lacked the money and power to carry it off. He lost more precious time by being indecisive. When he was superseded by John Campbell,* the Earl of Loudoun, in July 1756, the French had taken Fort Oswego and had reinforced most frontier bases. Loudoun was equally indecisive but pressed charges of incompetence against Shirley who was recalled to England and removed also as governor of Massachusetts.

For the better part of two years Shirley fought these charges and succeeded finally in clearing his name. Plainly, the ministry was at fault for not advising him on a battle plan. He was advanced in 1759 to the dignity of lieutenant general and appointed governor of the Bahamas. By 1761 he was resident there and remained until 1769 when he retired to Boston. As governor he improved island defenses, discouraged smuggling, and reformed some institutions. His son Thomas succeeded him and carried the family tradition of able civilian leadership as governor of Dominica and the Leeward Islands. Shirley's daughters married into the Erving, Temple, and Hutchinson families, and his grandchildren divided in their opinions of the American Revolution.

Shirley's military career was the unnatural extension of his long service as a public official in which he sought to draw Englishmen on both sides of the Atlantic into common imperial bonds of cooperation. Shirley was an imperialist and hoped to extend the empire into Canada and to the Mississippi River. For him war was a means to use contracts and commissions to win support of an expansionist foreign policy.

As the principal organizer of New England defense in 1754, 1755, and 1756, Shirley popularized imperial expansion and won considerable support for his ideas and efforts. His lack of military training was his undoing, but he also became involved in doubtful military accounting procedures. Shortcuts circumventing red tape brought great criticism, but he was never accused formally (nor was there evidence) of personal corruption.

Shirley's reputation should rest upon his successful, energetic governorship of Massachusetts (1741–1749, 1753–1756). His legal training and political savvy in balancing political interests helped him contribute much to the development of a creative administration and strong ties with Great Britain.

BIBLIOGRAPHY

Lincoln, Charles Henry, ed. *Correspondence of William Shirley*. 2 vols. New York: Macmillan Company, 1912.
Rawlyk, G. A. *Yankees at Louisbourg*. Orono: University of Maine Press, 1967.

Schutz, John A. *William Shirley: King's Governor of Massachusetts*. Chapel Hill: University of North Carolina Press, 1961.
Wood, George Arthur. *William Shirley: Governor of Massachusetts 1741–1756*. New York: Columbia University Press, 1920.

JOHN A. SCHUTZ

SHORT, Walter Campbell (b. Fillmore, Ill., March 30, 1880; d. Dallas, Tex., September 3, 1949), soldier, business executive. Short was a principal figure in the Pearl Harbor controversy.

Walter Short, son of Scotch-Irish parents, Dr. Hiram Spait Short (a physician) and Sarah Mineriva Stokes Short, graduated with a Phi Beta Kappa key from the University of Illinois (B.A., 1901). Although appointed a second lieutenant in February 1901, he taught mathematics at Western Military Academy before accepting his commission in March 1902. There followed a successful, if largely unremarkable, military career: Short was stationed at the Presidio in San Francisco (April 1903) and then transferred to the 25th Infantry at Fort Reno, Oklahoma (1903–1907). Following a brief tour of duty in the Philippines (1907–1908), he joined the 6th Infantry in Nebraska. Other assignments took him to Alaska, California (1913), and Fort Sill, Oklahoma, where Short became the secretary of the School of Musketry and commander of the 12th Infantry. At this time (November 1914), he married Isabel Dean of Oklahoma City. They had one child, Walter Dean Short, a future colonel in the U.S. Army. His next tour of duty was with the 16th Infantry attached to General John Joseph Pershing's* expeditionary force in Mexico (March 1916). Four months later he was promoted to captain. During World War I, Short served as a small-arms training officer in Georgia. In June 1917 he went to France with the 1st Division. His administrative experience included staff positions with the I Corps automatic weapons school and the II Corps infantry weapons school. Now a lieutenant colonel (a temporary rank), he was attached to the training section of the General Staff (April-November 1918). His professionalism won him the Distinguished Service Medal for "conspicuous service in the inspecting and reporting upon frontline conditions" and for his efficiency in training machine gun crews.

Short saw combat during the battles of Aisne-Marne, St. Mihiel, and the Meuse-Argonne. During the occupation of Germany, he became the assistant chief of staff in charge of training for the Third Army. In 1919 he returned to the United States to serve as an instructor at the General Services Schools at Fort Leavenworth, Kansas. (Simultaneously, he attended the School of the Line, graduating in 1921.) In August 1919 Short reverted to the rank of captain and reported for duty with the 6th Division in Illinois as assistant chief of staff for operations and supply. Promoted to major in July 1920, Short was assigned to the War Department General Staff. For the next three years, he was with the Far Eastern Section of the Military Intelligence Division.

In 1922, Short published a textbook entitled *Employment of The Machine Gun*. His co-invention of an improved machine gun carrier also reflected his interest in automatic weapons. A lieutenant colonel in 1923, he attended the Army War College and then served with the 65th Infantry at San Juan, Puerto Rico. From August 1928 until September 1930 Short was an instructor at the Command and General Staff School at Fort Leavenworth, and the following years served as assistant to the chief of insular affairs and with the 6th Infantry at Jefferson Barracks, Missouri. He was then assigned to the Infantry School at Fort Benning, Georgia, as assistant commandant. In December 1936 he became a brigadier general and in February 1938 the commander of the 2d Infantry Brigade at Fort Ontario, New York. From there Short assumed command (June 1938) of the 1st Infantry Brigade at Fort Wadsworth, and in 1939 he became commander of the 1st Division at Fort Hamilton. Promoted to major general (1940), he was ordered to Columbia, South Carolina.

On February 8, 1941, General George Catlett Marshall* chose him to command the Hawaiian Department with the temporary rank of lieutenant general. The forty-three thousand air and ground forces under Short were assigned, in conjunction with the Navy, the defense of Oahu and the base at Pearl Harbor.

Following the Japanese attack on December 7, 1941, Short was demoted in rank to major general and was relieved of his command on December 17, 1941. Under pressure, Short applied for retirement. This became effective on February 28, 1942. He retired on three-quarters pay. The War Depatment never gave Short the opportunity to defend himself before a military court.

During his retirement, Short worked for the Ford Motor Company as a traffic manager in Dallas, Texas. He remained with Ford until 1946. He died in 1949 of a chronic heart ailment complicated by emphysema. He was buried at Arlington National Cemetery.

Was Walter Short guilty of dereliction of duty? Of bad judgment? Of errors in judgment? Had he failed as a commander? On the other hand, was Walter Short a scapegoat? Was he a good soldier thrown to the wolves to divert public attention from mistakes made in Washington? Was he a sacrificial victim in the coverup of some nefarious plot? An "American Dreyfus"?

No one should doubt that Short was a competent officer, industrious and conscientious. Possessing tactical skill, command and administrative experience, and an advanced military education, he was an assured military manager. It was not his career that came into question after December 7, 1941, but the decisions he made as the commander of the Hawaiian Department in the eleven months preceding the Japanese attack.

Eight separate investigations sought to find the reasons for the Pearl Harbor debacle. During these inquiries Short's role in the fiasco was of major concern. The first investigation (authorized by the president and headed by Supreme Court Justice Owen Roberts) issued a report in January 1942 that accused Short and his naval counterpart, Admiral Husband Edward Kimmel,* of bad judgment and dereliction of duty. The Army Pearl Harbor Board (which concluded its investigation in October 1944) also held Short responsible but concluded that the chief of staff, George C. Marshall, and his chief of War Plans Division, General L. T. Gerow, shared in the responsibility for the disaster. In an addendum to the report, Secretary of War Henry Lewis Stimson* insisted that Short had received adequate warning and that the circumstances of the attack did not excuse the Hawaiian commander's mistakes.

A joint congressional panel also conducted an inquiry into the attack. The majority report concluded that the Hawaiian commanders had failed to respond adequately to warnings from Washington, to prepare a unified defense system, to maintain an effective reconnaissance, to prepare to meet all possible attacks, and to employ their forces in such a way as to minimize damage in the event of an attack. The minority Republican report placed emphasis on the mistakes made in Washington.

A brief in Short's defense, however, would include the following points. First, the civilian and military leaders, including Short, expected the Japanese to attack somewhere in Southeast Asia—not at Pearl Harbor. Second, the chief of staff (on November 27, 1941) instructed Short to take measures to prevent sabotage but to avoid alarming the local civilian population. This Short did. Since neither Marshall nor Gerow responded to Short's report on his preparations (a report that indicated the base was not on full alert and that left out an effective defense against air attack), the War Department tacitly approved measures that inadvertently left Oahu vulnerable. Third, the authorities in Washington were in possession of vital information concerning a possible attack. The War Depatment withheld this information, acquired through the decoding of Japanese secret messages, from the local commanders. Fourth, the warnings sent to Hawaii were often incomplete, misleading, and confusing.

In addition, there is a Devil Theory of the Pearl Harbor debacle which, if it were true, would help exonerate Short: President Franklin Roosevelt withheld information from the local commanders, intentionally exposing the U.S. Pacific Fleet to attack. Since Hitler had given the United States no cause to enter the war on the Allied side, the president sought to entice the Japanese to strike, thus bringing America into the war through the back door. Afterwards, Roosevelt sought to cover up the affair by shifting the blame to the local commanders. The fleet and, incidentally, the career of an honorable soldier were sacrificed to further Roosevelt's political and diplomatic ambitions.

Yet, there is a less sinister interpretation of what went wrong: The American defeat at Pearl Harbor was a military defeat; the Army and Navy commanders in Washington and Pearl Harbor failed to gauge correctly the enemy's intentions and capabilites. It was not a unique failure; military history is replete with instances where the enemy surprised their opponents. Nor was it the result of evil designs or gross incompetence. Short, Kimmel, and the General Staff (as well as the civilian leaders) were looking the wrong way when the Japanese delivered a strategic left hook.

In the belief that the war would begin somewhere else, Short emphasized training and antisabotage precautions (the American planes were parked wing-tip to wing-tip in neat rows on the morning of the attack) over reconnaissance and constant radar surveillance. This was not carelessness but miscalculation. Nevertheless, it was not Short's duty to reason where the Japanese Imperial forces would strike, nor was it necessary for him to be privy to all the information possessed in Washington. He was an outpost commander, responsible locally for the defense of his men and equipment.

The eight battleships sunk or damaged, the 247 planes wrecked, and the 2,330 men killed and 1,145 wounded were violent testimony to these errors in judgment. To be fair, Short was not the only one to make mistakes to misread the enemy's intentions. But he and no one else commanded the Hawaiian Department. The Pearl Harbor defeat occurred because good men like Short made the wrong decisions. They believed an attack on Pearl Harbor improbable and, therefore, ignored, out of a mass of intelligence reports, those signals that in retrospect pointed to an impending attack. Pearl Harbor was a tragedy of errors. It was a tragedy for the men who died that awful Sunday morning in 1941 and for their commander, Walter Campbell Short.

BIBLIOGRAPHY

Beard, Charles A. *President Roosevelt and the Coming of the War, 1941*. New Haven, Conn.: Yale University Press, 1948.
Melosi, Martin V. *The Shadow of Pearl Harbor: Political Controversy Over the Surprise Attack, 1941–1946*. College Station, Tex.: Texas A&M University Press, 1977.
Prange, Gordon. *At Dawn We Slept*. New York: McGraw Hill, 1981.
Report of the Joint Committee on the Pearl Harbor Attack. Washington, D.C.: U.S. Government Printing Office, 1946.
Wohlstetter, Roberta. *Pearl Harbor: Warning and Decision*. Stanford, Calif.: Stanford University Press, 1962.

FRANK J. WETTA

SIMS, William Sowden (b. Port Hope, Canada, October 15, 1858; d. Boston, Mass., September 25, 1936), naval officer. Sims commanded U.S. naval forces in Europe during World War I.

Born in Canada and raised in Pennsylvania, William S. Sims received an appointment to the U.S. Naval Academy at Annapolis in 1876. Four years later the popular, enthusiastic Sims managed to graduate thirty-third in a class of sixty-two men, a tenuous ranking for a navy which in 1880 offered few opportunities for promotion in its tiny fleet. For nearly a decade Sims bounced from ship to ship, including the obsolete wooden steamers *Tennessee, Colorado, Swatara,* and *Yantic*. Bored, the tall, handsome American officer applied in 1888 for a year's leave to study the French language in Paris.

Return to the sea in 1889 rejuvenated Sims. First, he taught aboard the school ship *Saratoga* between 1889 and 1893 and then served on the China Station in the swift, steel cruisers *Philadelphia* and *Charleston*, early representatives of a modern "New American Navy." The latter assignment launched Sims on a life-long mission to reform the equipment, doctrine, and organization of the U.S.

Navy. As *Charleston*'s intelligence officer in Asian waters between 1894 and 1896, Sims not only observed the modern European warships on station but also studied at first hand the results of several exciting sea battles fought during the Sino-Japanese War of 1894–1895 between fleets of steel warships armed with rifled ordnance. His intelligence reports back to the U.S. Office of Naval Intelligence in Washington discussed the impact of modern guns upon armor plate, electrical wiring, and woodwork, as well as the effectiveness of battleships against smaller warships. Sims' thorough reports drew praise not only from his superior officers but also from Assistant Secretary of the Navy Theodore Roosevelt.*

Intelligence gathering continued to influence Sims' career. As a result of his work in Asia, the department appointed the dashing lieutenant as U.S. naval attaché to Paris and St. Petersburg in 1896. During the next three years, Sims collected volumes of notes on the latest foreign naval developments, ship designs, and tactics, all of which seemed more advanced than similar progress in the U.S. Navy. During the Spanish-American War, Sims purchased vital supplies for his navy from foreign sources, hired spies, and provided valuable intelligence on Spanish ship movements and war policies.

Sims returned to sea again in 1900, serving for the next three years in the Asiatic Squadron on board the battleship *Kentucky,* monitor *Monterey*, and armored cruiser *New York*. There on the distant China Station, Sims' years of repressed frustration over the inferiority of the Navy crystallized into ideas about specific reforms. It helped that during these critical years, Sims found likeminded officers with whom to exchange views. He discussed gunnery reform and continuous-aim firing techniques with British officer Percy Scott, the concept of an all-big-gun battleship with Homer Poundstone, and the necessity of a naval general staff system with Albert L. Key. At the same time, the new president Theodore Roosevelt, a Progressive reformer himself, assisted the growing group of naval progressives.

The Navy Department recalled Sims from the Far East in 1902, probably at Roosevelt's suggestion, to assume charge of the chaotic office of the inspector of target practice. For seven years Sims trained the fleet's officers and gun crews in his fire control system. This tour coincided with the most intense years of Roosevelt's Progressivism, and infused with the spirit of the era, Sims joined other officers such as Albert Key, Bradley Allen Fiske,* Frank K. Hill, and Richard Drace White to press for radical improvements in battleship design, gunnery, personnel promotion, and departmental planning and organizational structure. The departmental improvement most agitated those insurgents who demanded creation of an office of naval operations. Naturally, the more conservative officers and departmental bureaucrats resisted rapid change as too disruptive and thus battled to muzzle Sims and his fellows. Cliques formed, and professional arguments spilled over into politics and congressional hearings. Finally, President Roosevelt sided with the more moderate faction, which supported minor naval reforms such as Secretary of the Navy George von Lengerke Meyer's Aide System.

Disappointed but not subdued, Sims continued to agitate for more sweeping reforms while serving as the Navy's youngest battleship commanding officer in the *Minnesota* between 1909–1911, as instructor at the Naval War College at Newport during 1911–1913, and as comanding officer of the Atlantic Fleet's torpedo flotilla the next two years. Commanding the flotilla provided the most opportunities to put Progressive theories into practice. Sims developed tactical doctrine to coordinate his destroyers, and he gathered a new generation of youthful reformers around him, including Dudley W. Knox, John V. Babcock, William V. Pratt, and Hutchinson Cone. Then in 1915 Sims assumed command of the dreadnought *Nevada*. This assignment took him away from Washington during Bradley Fiske's crusade to create an office of the chief of naval operations, and when Secretary of the Navy Josephus Daniels* emasculated Fiske's plans, Sims momentarily escaped the ensuing controversy.

American entry into World War I in April 1917 found Sims en route to London on a secret mission to discuss possible Anglo-American operations against German submarines. Once appointed commander of the U.S. naval forces operating in Europe, characteristically Sims bombarded the Navy Department with recommendations to improve the convoy system, antisubmarine warfare doctrine, intelligence-gathering methods, and strategic war planning. His responsibilities ranged over a wide front from liaison with the British Admiralty to coordinating U.S. naval operations in the North Sea and the Mediterranean. To carry out these assignments, Sims organized his own naval planning section in London and manned this naval general staff with capable officers, including Babcock, Knox, Nathan C. Twining, Harry E. Yarnell, and Frank H. Schofield. Throughout the war, however, Sims worried about his ill-defined authority as force commander and was troubled over an apparent indifference to his personnel and equipment requirements.

When Sims returned to the United States after the war, he resolved to reveal what he believed was gross mismanagement of the Navy Department during the war by Secretary Daniels and Chief of Naval Operations William S. Benson. As a sign of protest, war hero Sims refused to accept any medals or honors from the department, and a number of other naval officers followed his lead. Having caught public and congressional interest with this gesture, Sims unleashed a series of accusations about the Navy's supposed inability to fight a strong enemy. Such criticisms led to a congressional investigation in 1920 which, while reaching no firm conclusions, succeeded in ripping the Navy apart and creating a bitter Sims-Daniels feud.

Finally, in 1922 Sims retired from his last post as president of the Naval War College, ending four decades of naval service. Retirement did not remove Sims' insurgent voice, however. Whether making speeches around the country or writing scathing essays from his home in Newport, Rhode Island, Sims stirred up controversial issues, such as citing the Navy's failure to recognize that air power had made the battleship obsolete. Indeed, the greying former officer continued his iconoclasm until his death in Boston on September 25, 1936.

Most military reformers create controversy within their establishment, and Sims was no exception. Witty, dynamic and restless, he displayed little patience with petty bureaucrats or mediocre fellows. Unfortunately, the Navy abounded with both. Several times Sims considered pursuing more exciting careers elsewhere, but loyalty to the service and love for the seafaring life always drew him back. Moreover, the turn-of-the-century Navy afforded just enough outlets to absorb the energies of a dynamic reformer such as Sims. Whether collecting intelligence in China, training naval gunners, indoctrinating young officers in destroyer tactics, or directing operations in London, Sims assumed that his contributions were instrumental in creating a more efficient and modern American navy.

In fact, Sims was one of the most effective proponents of U.S. naval expansion between 1894 and the early 1930s. Furthermore, he implemented many of his ideas into actual practice to improve the fleet. Yet, while early reforms pointed to concrete technical and organizational needs, leading to specific improvements, his later agitation aimed at broader, more ambiguous goals, proving less effective. At times, Sims lost sight of attainable objectives, seemingly pressing reform merely for the sake of reinforcing his insurgent image. This stubborn side of Sims' reformism cost valuable support from Progressive officers and politicians. In his final years of insurgency, Sims personalized opposition to his ideas, treating Daniels, Benson, and even life-long friend Albert P. Niblack as enemies rather than fellows working toward common advancement of the U.S. Navy.

BIBLIOGRAPHY

Daniels, Josephus. *The Wilson Era: Years of War and After, 1917–1923*. Chapel Hill: University of North Carolina Press, 1946.
Dorwart, Jeffery M. *The Office of Naval Intelligence: The Birth of America's First Intelligence Agency, 1865–1918*. Annapolis, Md.: Naval Institute Press, 1979.
Morison, Elting E. *Admiral Sims and the Modern American Navy*. Boston: Houghton Mifflin Company, 1942.
Sims, William S., and Burton J. Hendrick. *The Victory at Sea*. New York: Doubleday, Page, 1920.
Trask, David F. *Captains and Cabinets: Anglo-American Naval Relations, 1917–1918*. Columbia: University of Missouri Press, 1972.

JEFFERY M. DORWART

SITTING BULL (b. near Many-Caches, on Grand River in western South Dakota, early 1830s; d. Standing Rock Reservation, near his birthplace, December 15, 1890), Hunkpapa Sioux, soldier and medicine man. Sitting Bull is remembered best for the leadership he gave Teton people in resistance to Anglo-

American frontiersmen and federal Indian policies during the last half of the nineteenth century.

Sitting Bull was born near the site Many-Caches, where Hunkpapa people stored supplies along Grand River, and "became a man" according to the rules of tribal tradition. During his teen years, he demonstrated prowess as a hunter by killing buffalo, proved himself as a soldier by counting coup against enemies from neighboring tribes, and prepared himself for spiritual leadership by making vision quests. As he approached adulthood, he also achieved social status by earning membership in the Strong Heart Warrior Society of his Hunkpapa tribe. And in the mid-1850s he gained political influence by taking charge of the Strong Hearts, after demonstrating extraordinary valor in a battle during which he killed a Crow chief and suffered a gunshot wound that caused him to limp for the rest of his life.

Although the Hunkpapa leader never held the office of chief, he gained prestige which exceeded that of high-ranking political leaders in his tribe for his protracted effort to defend Hunkpapa territory and culture against all intrusions. For more than a decade, he worked mainly to protect the hunting and gathering lands of his tribe against invasions by other Indian groups from the West, waging intermittent war on the Crows, Arikaras, Mandans, Gros Ventres, Assiniboines, Blackfeet, Flatheads, Piegans, and Shoshones. In the late 1860s, he concentrated largely upon resistance to encroachments into the Hunkpapa sanctuary by non-Indians, who came up the Missouri Valley from the Southeast. For example, he led Indian forces in attacks on a settlement around Fort Buford, after it was founded in 1866 by the U.S. Army at the confluence of the Yellowstone and Missouri rivers. He also caused such difficulty for white military units and communications on the Northern Plains that veteran missionary Pierre-Jean DeSmet trekked up the Missouri as envoy extraordinary for the federal government, in the years 1867 and 1868, to make peace with him and heads of other warring societies who by then looked to him for leadership.

DeSmet recognized Sitting Bull's growing influence among western Sioux outside his own tribe by calling him "generalissimo" of dissidents beyond the Missouri. In the late 1860s, some twenty thousand Tetons who resisted federal efforts to draw them into camps around agencies, where they could be assigned small farms and be acculturated in preparation for incorporation into Anglo-American society, selected Sitting Bull as principal defender of Sioux nationalism. He had no occasion to exercise his new position for several years. The 1868 Fort Laramie Treaty, which forbade whites from entering the Black Hills region without permission from the Sioux, temporarily quieted interracial tension. But when in the early 1870s gold seekers entered Dakota Territory without regard for the treaty terms, Sitting Bull began to assemble his followers, and after it became clear that the Ulysses Simpson Grant* administration would do little to prevent this flagrant violation of the 1868 treaty, he joined forces with Cheyenne leader Two Moon. Then on June 25, 1876, he provided strategic leadership as tactical commanders in his army, such as Gall and Crazy Horse,* led approximately three thousand men to annihilate the 7th Cavalry of George Armstrong Custer* in the Battle of the Little Big Horn.

After savouring victory in this famous battle a short time, Sitting Bull suffered reverses that soon convinced him he could not win his war against the United States. So many Indian soldiers left his army to join their families in search of food that he could not muster a force large enough to save American Horse from siege by George Crook's* men at Slim Buttes. After former Indian Commissioner George Manypenny appeared to warn Tetons that the federal government would pay no more treaty benefits until they surrendered the Black Hills, many chiefs and headmen turned in their arms and ponies, affixed their signatures to Manypenny's agreement, and advised their constituents to accept confinement on reservations. By late fall in 1876, Sitting Bull retained a following of only a few chiefs and approximately one thousand determined traditionalists, who obviously were no match for the U.S. forces that combed the Northern Great Plains to track them down.

To protect this remnant, which stuck by him for fear of stern reprisals, if not death, the Hunkpapa leader now began an odyssey that exiled him from the Grand River area for nearly seven years. First, he withdrew into the High Plains of eastern Montana, where Colonel Nelson Appleton Miles* pursued him to demand his immediate surrender. From there he crossed the border, hoping officials in the new Dominion of Canada would offer him and his followers the same privileges of sanctuary and land assignment they had given earlier to Isanti refugees from the Minnesota Sioux War. The Canadians were not that accommodating, however. They were not indebted to the Tetons, as they were to the eastern Sioux people for their support against U.S. forces in the Northwest campaigns of the War of 1812. Dominion leaders told the Teton emigrés they could remain north of the border only as long as they demanded no material support and caused no trouble.

Sitting Bull imposed on the hospitality of his reluctant hosts until the spring of 1881, when his position in southern Saskatchewan became untenable. Buffalo herds dwindled. Canadian officials remained firm in their refusal to distribute rations. Bedraggled Tetons wandered in search of hides and furs to trade for food and ammunition at Wood Mountain. Finally, they began to break away in small groups to throw themselves on the mercy of U.S. officials. Sitting Bull realized his authority had deteriorated beyond repair, and on July 19, 1881, he presented himself and 187 followers for surrender at Fort Buford. Major D. A. Brotherford collected their arms and horses and placed the prisoners on the steamboat *General Sherman* for transfer to Fort Randall, where they were incarcerated for nearly two years.

When Sitting Bull finally returned to his birthplace near Standing Rock agency on May 10, 1883, his days as a military figure were over. Now he served mainly as spiritual leader at the grounds near his cabin on Grand River, where Teton traditionalists gathered to discuss means of resistance to forced acculturation. For several years, Agent James McLaughlin (who had been assigned at Standing

Rock in 1881 to integrate refugees into reservation society and promote their adaptation to the Anglo-American life-style) negated the Hunkpapa leader's influence by sending him off the reservation at every opportunity. In 1883 Sitting Bull left the reserve to welcome the first locomotive on the Northern Pacific Railroad into Bismarck. In 1884 he went with Colonel Alvaren Allen to parade before curious citizens in St. Paul. The following year, he accompanied Buffalo Bill Cody and his Wild West Show on a tour of the East. But in 1886 he rejected an invitation to go with Buffalo Bill to Europe. Instead, he remained at home to resist the acculturation of his people and to thwart federal efforts to bargain for the further reduction of the Great Sioux Reservation west of the Missouri.

Sitting Bull failed to prevent that transaction. The reduction of the reservation was accomplished in the Great Sioux Agreement of 1889. But he continued to defend Sioux nationalism and traditions amid gatherings of Peacepipe religionists and Ghost Dancers at his home. By the fall of 1890 federal officials were convinced that the only way to prevent his leading an armed rebellion was to again make him prisoner at some fort a long distance from his followers. On the eve of December 14, McLaughlin sent Indian Police Captain Bullhead with forty-three men, reinforced by an army unit under Captain Edmund Fechet from Fort Yates, to take him into custody. Early in the morning of December 15, Bullhead brought Sitting Bull to the front yard of his cabin, where angry traditionalists opened fire. When the shooting ended, seven policemen and eight Ghost Dancers lay on the ground around the body of the fallen leader.

Captain Fechet wrote an appropriate epitaph for Sitting Bull: "Since the days of Pontiac,* Tecumseh* and Red Jacket, no Indian has had the power of drawing to himself so large a following of his race and molding and wielding it against the authority of the United States." From years of combat service to protect Hunkpapa territory against encroachment by neighboring tribes, he emerged as a rallying point for all Tetons who were determined to defend the Black Hills region against invasions by Anglo-American frontiersmen and U.S. military units, and to preserve Sioux nationalism and culture in the face of determined efforts by federal officials to destroy them. That he did not triumph in the former contest with white society, or succeed completely in the latter, does not diminish his importance in history. He was at least the equal of any other leader who rose up to prevent the engulfment of western Indian societies by non-Indian forces during the last half of the nineteenth century.

BIBLIOGRAPHY

Burdick, Usher L. *The Last Days of Sitting Bull.* Baltimore: Wirth Brothers, 1941.
Fiske, Frank Bennett. *Life and Death of Sitting Bull.* Fort Yates, N.D.: Pioneer-Arrow Print, 1933.
Garst, Shannon. *Sitting Bull: Champion of His People.* New York: J. Messner, 1946.
MacEwan, John Walter Grant. *Sitting Bull: The Years in Canada.* Edmonton, Alb.: Hurtig Publishers, 1973.

Johnson, W. Fletcher. *The Red Record of the Sioux: Life of Sitting Bull and History of the Indian War of 1890–91.* Edgewood, S.D.: Edgewood Publishing Company, 1891.

Vestal, Stanley. *Sitting Bull: Champion of the Sioux.* Boston and New York: Houghton Mifflin Company, 1932.

                                                    HERBERT T. HOOVER

SMITH, Edmund Kirby (b. St. Augustine, Fla., May 16, 1824; d. Sewanee, Tenn., March 28, 1893), Army officer. Kirby Smith commanded the Confederate Trans-Mississippi Department during the Civil War.

Although born on the Florida frontier, where his father was serving as a federal district judge, Edmund Kirby Smith came from staunch Connecticut stock on both sides of his family. His maternal grandfather was Ephraim Kirby of Litchfield, who gained a considerable reputation by pioneering the field of legal reporting. Edmund's father, Joseph Lee Smith, had distinguished himself in the War of 1812 and opted briefly for a military career thereafter. Two uncles and an uncle-in-law on his mother's side made similar decisions to reinforce a strong military tradition for young Edmund and his older brother Ephraim. The father deliberately bestowed upon both his sons the maternal family name to reinforce their proud heritage.

Considerable discussion has centered around Edmund's later use of this family name. Throughout his early years he was known among family and friends as "Ted" or by his given name, while his brother Ephraim went by "Kirby." Following the brother's death in the Mexican War, Edmund began using the signature "E. Kirby Smith," a name which became synonymous with him, perhaps to distinguish him in part from the many other Smiths in Confederate service. So regular did the name's use become that following the war his family became known as the "Kirby Smith family," and after his death adapted it as "Kirby-Smith." By his son's testimony, however, Edmund considered himself a Smith until the day he died.

So strong was the family military tradition that Edmund was only slightly consulted about his future career. He was expected to follow in the footsteps of his father, uncles, and older brother (Ephraim graduated from West Point in 1826). To that end his father enrolled Edmund in Benjamin Hallowell's Preparatory school at Alexandria, Virginia, which had trained Robert Edward Lee* and others. By 1841 his instructors there considered him ready for West Point, and his appointment was secured without difficulty. He had a routine four years at the Military Academy (although coming close to losing his commission at the end because of nearsightedness) and graduated twenty-fifth of forty-one in the class of 1845.

Smith chose the infantry branch and was assigned to the 5th Infantry Regiment, which was about to embark for Texas to join Zachary Taylor* along the border. He was thus among the first to cross the Rio Grande in May 1846 as the Mexican War got underway. He fought at Palo Alto, Resaca de la Palma, and Monterrey before being transferred to the army led by General Winfield Scott* for the overland march to Mexico City. From the landing of the troops at Vera Cruz through the final assault on the fortress at Chapultepec, Smith fought bravely. He shared the campaign with his brother, Ephraim, who was killed at Chapultepec, and one of his uncles. Smith was brevetted first lieutenant for his gallantry at Cerro Gordo.

Following the war Kirby Smith spent a year at Jefferson Barracks before receiving assignment to West Point as assistant professor of mathematics in the fall of 1849. After a three-year tour at the Academy, he rejoined his regiment on the frontier where he commanded the military escort for the Mexican Boundary Commission designated to establish the border in the wake of the Gadsden Purchase. Smith also received appointment as botanist to the expedition and produced a report which the Smithsonian Institution subsequently published.

In the fall of 1855 Kirby Smith received his captaincy and orders to report to the newly formed 2d Cavalry from which would spring so many Union and Confederate generals, including Robert E. Lee and Albert Sidney Johnston.* For the next five years he saw service on the southwestern frontier, but took time out for a furlough in 1858 to make an extensive tour of Europe.

Kirby Smith resigned from the Federal Army on March 3, 1861, simultaneously with his promotion to major. After a brief visit home he reported to Montgomery, Alabama, where he received a commission as lieutenant colonel of cavalry through the intervention of his good friend Earl Van Dorn. Assigned to Lynchburg, Virginia, he organized and mustered into service various regiments as they arrived before joining Joseph Eggleston Johnston* at Harper's Ferry as his adjutant. Promoted to brigadier general in June, Kirby Smith fought at First Manassas (Bull Run) where he received a severe shoulder wound. He recuperated at Lynchburg and there he married Cassie Selden, daughter of a prominent family, whom he had met during his earlier stay.

After spending the winter with the army of Pierre Gustave Toutant Beauregard* at Manassas, Kirby Smith was ordered to Knoxville in late February 1862 to take command of the Department of East Tennessee. There he met a great deal of pro-Union hostility, especially after the instigation of the Confederate draft in April. The Federal Army nibbled away at his territory piecemeal, and he became convinced of the necessity of a Confederate strike into middle Tennessee and Kentucky in order to relieve the pressure on Chattanooga and recover the Cumberland Gap. He finally secured the assent of Braxton Bragg,* and the two of them launched their campaign in August.

Kirby Smith made his move first, fighting a sharp but successful battle at Richmond, Kentucky, on August 30 and moving on to occupy Lexington from where he could threaten Cincinnati. This forced the Federal evacuation of Cumberland Gap. With Confederate hopes high, Bragg, who had moved northward in Kirby Smith's wake, allowed himself to be diverted from potential success by an attempt to invest a Confederate governor at Frankfort. Kirby Smith missed the subsequent Battle of Perryville (October 8) but urged Bragg to make another stand at Harrodsburg. After much deliberation, Bragg instead ordered the evacuation of Kentucky and a retreat back to east Tennessee. For his part in the campaign Kirby Smith received promotion to lieutenant general and the commendation of the Confederate Congress, but it was small consolation for what he believed to have been a missed opportunity.

Early in 1863 Kirby Smith was called to Richmond for consultation and then was informed that he would be sent to the Trans-Mississippi to assume command there. His department consisted of all the territory west of the Mississippi River—a vast area held by scattered commands numbering only some thirty thousand troops. Following the fall of Vicksburg in July, the area became sufficiently isolated that he was required to exercise both civil and military authority over the region. In the two years that followed, he worked closely with the governors of the four states under his jurisdiction and sought to keep the authorities at Richmond informed, but the task was difficult. He thwarted the only major drive against him when he turned back General Nathaniel Banks' Red River Campaign in the spring of 1864 and a supporting move by General Frederick Steele down from Arkansas. That fall Smith sent General Sterling Price on an unsuccessful raid into Missouri in an effort to relieve the pressure on Atlanta. In February of that year Kirby Smith was commissioned a full general in recognition of his services in his difficult post. He became the last Confederate commander to surrender his force on June 2, 1865, at Galveston, Texas.

Hearing of Robert E. Lee's arrest shortly thereafter, Kirby Smith fled to Mexico, as had many others from his command, and then to Cuba. He returned to the United States in November 1865 and held various positions in the postwar era. From 1870 to 1875 he served as president of the University of Nashville, resigning this post to accept a professorship of mathematics at the University of the South in Sewanee, Tennessee, where he remained until his death.

Coming from a family with a strong military tradition, Edmund Kirby Smith had a career that reinforced the image established for him early in life. He distinguished himself in both the Mexican and Civil Wars while performing valuable service on the frontier in the interim. He stood in strong contrast to Braxton Bragg during their service together in the Western theater in 1862 with his decisive early campaign and his desire to make a final stand after the Battle of Perryville. It was his announced distaste for continued service under Bragg that led to his appointment to the Trans-Mississippi. Smith had also earned the strong admiration of Jefferson Davis* because of his aggressiveness.

Kirby Smith proved to be the strong hand that the Trans-Mississippi needed. He exercised effective control over a large, hitherto loosely organized region, working well with both the political leaders of the area and his military subordinates with the exception of General Richard Taylor who was angered by Kirby Smith's handling of the Red River Campaign. Given the difficulty of communication following the fall of Vicksburg, Smith became almost an authority unto himself although he never lost touch with the realities of either his situation or that of the Confederacy as a whole.

BIBLIOGRAPHY

Castel, Albert. *General Sterling Price and the Civil War in the West*. Baton Rouge: Louisiana State University Press, 1968.

Johnson, Ludwell H. *Red River Campaign: Politics and Cotton in the Civil War*. Baltimore: Johns Hopkins University Press, 1958.

Kerby, Robert L. *Kirby Smith's Confederacy: The Trans-Mississippi South, 1863–1865*. New York: Columbia University Press, 1972.

Parks, Joseph H. *General Edmund Kirby Smith, C.S.A*. Baton Rouge: Louisiana State University Press, 1954.

Winters, John D. *The Civil War in Louisiana*. Baton Rouge: Louisiana State University Press, 1963.

WILLIAM E. PARRISH

SMITH, Holland McTyeire (b. Hatchechubbee, Ala., April 20, 1882; d. San Diego, Calif., January 12, 1967), Marine Corps officer. Smith was a pioneer in amphibious warfare techniques before and during World War II.

Holland Smith, son of a prominent Alabama lawyer, was graduated in 1901 from Alabama Polytechnic Institute (now Auburn University) and from the University of Alabama Law School in 1903. He was admitted to the bar but disliked the practice of law and soon sought a commission in the Army. Finding no immediate opening in that service, he turned to the Marines, passed a competitive examination, and was commissioned a second lieutenant in the Marine Corps in March 1905. After training at the School of Application, Annapolis, he reported to the Marine Brigade in the Philippine Islands. Subsequently, he was assigned to various posts in the United States, returned to the Philippines, and served aboard a cruiser in the Far East. In 1909 he participated in an expedition to Nicaragua and, in 1916, in another to Santo Domingo, where he came under fire for the first time.

During World War I Smith was among the first Americans to sail for France. He attended the Army Staff College at Langres, joined the staff of the Marine Brigade, 2d Division, and was awarded the *Croix de Guerre* for courage displayed during the Battle of Belleau Wood. He was then specially chosen as a Marine officer to serve on the staff of the I Corps, First Army, where he participated in the Aisne-Marne, St. Mihiel, Oise, and Meuse-Argonne offensives.

In 1920–1921 Smith attended the Navy War College and was then appointed as the first marine to serve on the Joint Army-Navy Planning Committee, a small group that formulated long-range war plans. He spent an uneventful year in Haiti in 1925 and completed the Marine Corps Field Officers' Course in 1927. In 1937, after various assignments ashore and afloat, he was appointed to the staff of the commandant of the Marine Corps as director of operations and training and in 1939 became assistant commandant.

Late in 1939 Smith was promoted to brigadier general and was given command of the 1st Marine Brigade at Quantico, Virginia. He immediately moved the brigade to Cuba and directed a period of such demanding training that he acquired the nickname "Howlin' Mad." In 1941 the brigade was expanded into the 1st Marine Division which shortly afterward was combined with an Army division to form the I Corps (Provisional) Atlantic Fleet. Smith was promoted to major general and, as the choice of Admiral Ernest Joseph King,* was named to command the I Corps. Although originally intended as an expeditionary force, the I Corps became a training command and until June 1943, Smith directed the training of the Army and Marine divisions preparing for landings in both the Atlantic and Pacific theaters.

In June 1943 Smith was appointed to command the V Amphibious Corps, a joint Army-Marine expeditionary force to be used by Admiral Chester William Nimitz* in his drive across the Central Pacific. In November 1943 the V Corps opened the drive by seizing Makin and Tarawa atolls in the Gilbert Islands. Early in 1944 V Corps troops captured several atolls in the Marshalls, including Kwajalein and Eniwetok. In June they struck the Marianas, first securing Saipan and then seizing Tinian and Guam. In August 1944 Smith, now a lieutenant general, was named to command the newly formed Fleet Marine Force, Pacific, and early in 1945 commanded three Marine divisions in the assault on Iwo Jima—the most desperate battle in the Marine Corps history.

In July 1945 Smith returned to San Diego as commanding general, Marine Training and Replacement Command, and in August 1946 he retired with the rank of general. He settled in La Jolla, California, and in 1948 published his controversial autobiography, *Coral and Brass*, which was highly critical of the conduct of the Pacific War.

Although he was popularly known as "Howlin' Mad," Smith has more appropriately been called the Father of Amphibious Warfare. He was a leader in the development of the amphibious techniques that made possible the landings in both the Atlantic and Pacific during World War II. When he took command of the 1st Marine Brigade in 1939, little actual training in amphibious techniques had been done, but because of the outbreak of war in Europe, Smith received support that had been unavailable to his predecessors. During intense training in Cuba and the Caribbean, he and his staff developed methods and techniques for landing on a hostile shore.

An early and crucial problem encountered was the lack of special landing craft. The ordinary ship's boats then used were inadequate, and Smith demanded better. He experimented with a shallow-draft boat, originally developed for Prohibition-era rum-runners, which could run up on the beach, rapidly discharge its cargo, and pull back under its own power. He tested and improved an amphibian tractor, originally designed for rescue work in the Everglades, which could function either as a boat at sea or as a tractor ashore. Through his efforts, both of these vital craft were adopted and were available for wartime landing operations.

Other basic problems of amphibious warfare included: organizing and equipping troops for rapid debarkation; devising a method for the rapid transfer of troops from ship to landing craft; "combat loading" vessels to ensure that needed supplies were unloaded first; controlling landing craft during the movement from ship to shore; and providing naval gunfire and air support to the assault troops. By the time the United States entered the war, Smith had devised solutions to these problems, developed a doctrine of amphibious warfare, and established himself as the leading authority on amphibious operations. It was natural, then, for him to have been chosen to train, not only Marines, but a number of Army divisions as well. His work laid the foundation for the success of American landing operations during the war.

As a commander in the Central Pacific, Smith demanded hard-driving, relentless assaults that kept continual pressure on the enemy. He was not callous, but he believed that a swift assault shortened the battle and saved lives in the long run. Many believed that his fighting spirit, imparted to Marines at all levels, significantly shortened the island battles and may have provided the margin of victory on bitterly contested Iwo Jima. Smith considered himself a special spokesman for the Marines and was noted for his vehement arguments with his Navy colleagues about the proper conduct of amphibious operations. Prior to Tarawa, for example, he insisted upon the allotment of additional amphibious tractors, and at Tinian, he insisted that the landing be made across beaches which his naval superior considered unusable. In both instances his judgment was correct. The landing at Tarawa could easily have failed without the additional tractors, and the landing at Tinian was a nearly perfect operation. At Iwo Jima, Smith was unsuccessful in his argument for extending the length of the pre-invasion bombardment from three to ten days. Later, he and other Marines charged that the failure to lengthen the bombardment was a major reason for the heavy casualties suffered on Iwo Jima.

On Saipan, Smith relieved the unaggressive commander of an Army division. Such a relief of an Army general by a Marine was unprecedented, and it precipitated a controversy that seriously threatened interservice cooperation in the Pacific. The Army commander in the area charged that Smith was blindly prejudiced against Army units and urged that no Army troops ever again be placed under his command. Historians have generally agreed that the relief was justified, but Smith was embittered by the incident and its aftermath, in which he was portrayed as a butcher who recklessly threw away the lives of his men. In his autobiography, *Coral and Brass*, Smith attempted to vindicate himself, but the book was so marred by hindsight, second-guessing, and criticism of his colleagues that it actually harmed his reputation. Unfortunately, the relief incident and the allegations in *Coral and Brass* have come to overshadow Smith's pivotal role in the development of amphibious warfare and his contributions to victory in the Pacific.

BIBLIOGRAPHY

Dyer, George C. *The Amphibians Came to Conquer: The Story of Admiral Kelly Turner*. 2 vols. Washington, D.C.: U.S. Government Printing Office, 1972.

Heinl, Robert D., Jr. *Soldiers of the Sea: The United States Marine Corps, 1775–1962*. Annapolis, Md.: Naval Institute Press, 1962.

Hough, Frank O., et al. *History of U.S. Marine Corps Operations in World War II.* 5
  vols. Washington, D.C.: U.S. Government Printing Office, 1956–1971.
Isely, Jeter A., and Philip A. Crowl. *The U.S. Marines and Amphibious War.* Princeton,
  N.J.: Princeton University Press, 1951.
Morison, Samuel E. *History of U.S. Naval Operations in World War II.* 15 vols. Boston:
  Atlantic, Little, and Company, 1947–1962.

NORMAN V. COOPER

SMITH, John (b. Willoughby by Alford, Lincolnshire, England, late December 1579 or early January 1580; d. London, June 21, 1631), a founder of Virginia
and a leading promoter of British America.

Son of a yeoman farmer, John Smith spent his boyhood in a village near the
English Channel. After schooling until age fifteen, he was apprenticed to a
merchant but soon left to attend what a contemporary called "that university of
warre, the Low Countries." There Smith served for two or three years among
English volunteers aiding the Netherlands against Spain. Almost nothing is known
about his role, but it launched a long and often improbable military career. In
1599 he quit the Netherlands, perhaps because of a Dutch-Spanish truce; during
the next year he was employed briefly as a servant-companion to the sons of the
lord of Willoughby Manor and visited Scotland in vain search of a courtier's
position. According to Smith's later and often cryptic autobiography, he then
returned to Lincolnshire to sharpen his military skills. He studied military writings
(*"Machiavells* Art of Warre, and *Marcus Aurelius"*) and practiced horsemanship
under the earl of Lincoln's Italian riding master.

In 1600 Smith sought a more exotic theater of war. Disturbed by Western
Europe's fratricidal struggle among Christians, Smith headed east to the Balkans,
where the Holy Roman and Ottoman Empires still battled. En route Smith had
an incredible series of adventures, including his first sea battle.

In Austria-Hungary, Smith gained quick recognition for his imaginative tactics
and unusual fortitude. In his first campaign, he showed his superiors a system
of long-distance signaling by torches, and he convinced them to set off thousands
of small explosions in imitation of musketfire. Both schemes contributed to a
major victory, and Smith was promoted to captain. He earned further glory by
contriving "fiery Dragons"—a combination of gunpowder, pitch, brimstone,
turpentine, quartered musket balls, and other ingredients—to catapult at the
enemy.

In 1602 a realignment of Christian forces brought Smith into the service of
Zsigmond Bathori, prince of Transylvania. When Bathory's army reached a
temporary stalemate with its Turkish opponents, "the Lord *Turbashaw*" (in
Smith's account) challenged any Christian captain to individual combat. Smith
was chosen by lot to be his opponent. With pageantry and weaponry more
appropriate to an earlier century, Smith killed Turbashaw and two others in
individual combats before the cheering armies and from each contest brought
his opponent's head. Such heroism earned Smith a promotion to sergeant major

(that is, major of his regiment) and from Prince Zsigmond a pension and an armorial insignia (certified in 1625 by England's college of heraldry as a coat of arms) featuring three Turks' heads.

Smith had one more taste of military glory before his fortunes and his locale changed drastically. His "pretty stratagem" of arming his horsemen with flaming lances in a night attack brought another victory, but in a subsequent battle the Moslems routed the Christians. Smith was left wounded on the battlefield. Pillagers sold him for potential ransom to a Turkish Basha, who sent Smith as a slave to Constantinople and later as a field hand to Tartary, west of Crimea. Smith eventually killed his overseer, escaped to Russia, and in 1603 returned to England by way of Austria, where he secured his release from service to the prince, and Africa, where he survived another sea battle.

America next caught Smith's fancy. In 1606 he joined the London Company of Virginia's expedition to establish a colony near Chesapeake Bay. En route to Virginia, Smith was arrested and almost hanged by a faction that distrusted him, for reasons that are not altogether clear. Such internal dissension plagued his few years in America and the colony for decades.

Smith spent most of his first year at Jamestown exploring the Chesapeake area and negotiating with the Indians. In the fall of 1607 he was ambushed and captured when his small party ventured too far inland. After Pocahontas rescued him from execution, Smith returned to Jamestown (where his opponents again tried to hang him), with valuable information about the Indians and with their grudging respect for his courage and talent. Throughout his two and a half years in Virginia, Smith was more successful than most of the colony's early leaders in getting food from the Indians and in enlisting their cooperation.

In September 1608 the Virginia council, of which Smith was a member, elected him president. The colony was short on supplies and overstocked with incompetent colonists, many of them too lazy even to forage. Smith forced everyone to work. He also used a clearing outside the pallisaded fort for mandatory close-order drill and marksmanship, partly to strengthen the colony's defense, partly to impress the Indians. During his year in office, Smith kept the colonists relatively safe and well fed.

After a severe gunpowder wound sapped his strength and a new cabal ousted him from office, Smith returned to England in October 1609. The London Company refused to send him back to Virginia, despite his conviction that he alone could save the troubled colony—especially after Opechancanough's* massacre of nearly 350 colonists in 1622 led to full-scale military conflict. In 1614 Smith sailed to northern British America (which he named New England on his map of 1616), but in 1615 French privateers captured and kept him prisoner for several months when he tried to return to New England.

Smith devoted the last fifteen years of his life to colonial promotion, primarily through his prolific writing. His *True Relation* (1608) appeared while he was still in Virginia, and his *Map of Virginia, With a Description of the Countrey* (1612) came out a few years after his return. Beginning in 1616, with *A De-*

scription of New England, his books appeared with increasing frequency and with broader themes. *New Englands Trials* (1620; enlarged edition 1622) and *The Generall Historie of Virginia, New-England, and the Summer Isles* (1624) were probably his most influential works. All stress military preparedness. *Sea Grammar* (1627) became a standard manual on seafaring, both peaceful and belligerent. Smith died at the age of fifty-one, shortly after completing *Advertisements for the Unexperienced Planters of New-England, or any where* (1631).

Like so many of his contemporaries who established outposts along the Atlantic coast, Smith was a professional soldier. Such men were in wide demand, not only because the colonies expected trouble with the Indians (Spain's experience showed that to be likely) and from other European powers, but also because the colonists themselves needed discipline and firm leadership. Most of the early settlements, especially in Virginia, were frontier garrisons. Every able-bodied man was at least a part-time soldier; the leaders' authority was virtually absolute; most supplies and quarters were owned and distributed by the company; and the settlement itself was usually a pallisaded fort. Men with military backgrounds in the Low Countries or Ireland, therefore, took leading roles in the early stages of colonization, and in Virginia the president (later governor) was a veteran soldier throughout the first two decades. Smith's military counterparts outside Virginia included Miles Standish* in Plymouth, John Endecott and John Underhill in Massachusetts, John Mason and Lion Gardiner in Connecticut, and Thomas Cornwallis in Maryland. But only Endecott came close to matching Smith's combination of military and political involvement.

Smith stood out from his contemporaries in several respects. Certainly, his breadth and intensity of experience were unusual. So were the range of his vision and the depth of his commitment to British colonization in every region and by any sponsoring group. Whereas most of the soldier-settlers served a single colony, sometimes a single community, Smith was directly involved in Virginia and, more briefly, in New England, and his imperialism knew no geographical boundaries. As Smith urged in 1616, "So that the businesse [of colonization] prosper, I have my desire; be it done by Londoner, Scot, Welch, or English, and there is more then enough for all, if they could bee content but to proceed."

In Virginia, Smith's military responsibilities were threefold: to prepare adequate fortifications at Jamestown and its outposts; to train his men in the elements of soldiering; and to mislead the enemy into thinking that the colony was much stronger than it was. At the same time, he sought Indian food, information, guides, and safe passage through hostile territory while giving little in return except harmless trade goods. The firearms which the Indians craved were forbidden articles of commerce. Smith, in fact, spent much of his time recovering, by threat or force, guns that the Indians acquired by illicit trade, theft, or skirmishes. He was overwhelmingly successful, not only in keeping the Indians without firearms but also in convincing them that the colony possessed far more military power than it actually did. Powhatan could almost certainly have exterminated the Virginia outposts by denying them food and assaulting anyone who ventured out of the fort. That he chose not to oust the colony suggests that the chief saw either compensating advantages in the presence of a weak European trading post or that enough of his men truly feared English firearms and Smith's apparent invincibility to avoid a showdown—or both.

Long after he left Jamestown, Smith claimed that "The Warres in *Europe, Asia,* and *Africa* taught me how to subdue the wilde Salvages in *Virginia* and *New-England* in *America.*" In terms of his attitudes toward military foes of a drastically different culture and of his general military training, the boast was true. In terms of strategy and tactics, however, it was mostly metaphorical. In America Smith fought no sea battles, besieged no fortresses, lofted no "fiery Dragons," and led no cavalry charges. (There were almost no horses in Virginia during Smith's tenure.) Nor did Smith engage in individual combat to entertain rival armies. He did, however, singlehandedly subdue a chief who ambushed him, and on another occasion he challenged Opechancanough, Powhatan's half-brother and leader of two later Virginia massacres, to individual combat. Opechancanough refused to fight, but he did not forget.

Smith's many books, especially his *Generall Historie,* are crammed with advice about military preparations and about the best way to confront the Indians. Smith was never gentle about such matters. He was a rough-hewn soldier with little sympathy for his opponents, especially those from another culture. Even his employers in London Company thought him too impetuous. Smith countered that he was timid compared to the Spanish *conquistadors,* and on the whole he was. Despite his often brusque ways, his Indian policy depended more on craft than on brute strength. "To express all our quarrels, trecheries and incounters amongst those Salvages, I should be too tedious," one of the colonists reported, "but in breefe at all times we so encountered them, and curbed their insolencies, that they concluded with presents to purchase peace; yet we lost not a man: at our first meeting our Captaine ever observed this order, to demand their bowes and arrowes, swordes, manteles and furrs, with some childe or two for hostage, whereby we could quickly perceive, when they intended any villany." If such tactics did not work, Smith could be merciless. Once he had half a dozen Indians killed, their houses burned, and their canoes and fishing weirs confiscated for his use, all because the Indians resisted English encroachment on their territory. On another occasion he insisted that the Indians trade with him "or I mean to load [my ship] with your dead carcases." Smith could rightfully boast that however brusque his methods, his administration was more peaceful than that of most of his predecessors and immediate successors. Later he could also claim that his advice was widely read and often followed. From the hindsight of three and a half centuries, however, it is apparent that a belligerent and ethnocentric approach to Indian-European relations, so pronounced in Smith and most of his contemporaries in America, frequently turned the American frontier into a battleground.

Because the evidence for most of Smith's deeds comes largely from his own writings, and because those deeds often stretch credulity, his reputation has ranged from blatant liar to robust hero. Recent scholarship has come to Smith's defense, especially on his Hungarian exploits, and even the Pocahontas episode is now widely accepted. Smith is generally acknowledged to have made crucial contributions to the survival of England's first permanent American colony, and to have substantially advanced the ideas and techniques of British imperialism.

BIBLIOGRAPHY

Arber, Edward and A. G. Bradley, eds. *Travels and Works of Captain John Smith.* 2 vols. Edinburgh: John Grant, 1910.
Barbour, Philip L. *The Three Worlds of Captain John Smith.* Boston: Houghton Mifflin Company, 1964.
Morgan, Edmund S. *American Slavery, American Freedom: The Ordeal of Colonial Virginia.* New York: W. W. Norton Company, 1975.
Morton, Richard L. *Colonial Virginia.* Vol. 1. Chapel Hill: University of North Carolina Press, 1960.
Smith, Bradford. *Captain John Smith: His Life and Legend.* Philadelphia: J. B. Lippincott Company, 1953.
Vaughan, Alden T. *American Genesis: Captain John Smith and the Founding of Virginia.* Boston: Little, Brown and Company, 1975.

ALDEN T. VAUGHAN

SMITH, Oliver Prince (b. Menard, Tex., October 26, 1893; d. Los Altos, Calif., December 25, 1977), Marine Corps officer. Smith led the epic Marine Corps breakout from the Chosin Reservoir during the Korean War.

Oliver Prince Smith was born into a family that had settled in Virginia in 1740. His father died when Smith was young. His mother, a devout Christian Scientist, moved her family to Santa Cruz, California, in 1903. Smith remained a Christian Scientist all his life. He did not drink or swear, and he was considered to be a deeply religious person. He worked his way through the University of California at Berkeley, graduating in 1916. He was a member of the university Reserve Officer's Training Corps (ROTC). After graduation, Smith worked for the Standard Oil Company for a year. When the United States entered World War I in April 1917, he applied for a Marine Corps Reserve commission under a program for the direct commissioning of college graduates with ROTC experience. The Marine Corps accepted his application, and Smith was commissioned a second lieutenant in the reserves on May 4, 1917. He planned to stay in the Marine Corps only as long as the war lasted.

He was almost immediately ordered to the Marine Barracks on Guam to free a more experienced officer for duty in France. While sailing to Guam, Smith was one of a group of young lieutenants who invited Army Captain Benjamin Oliver Davis,* a Negro, to sit at the head of their table in the wardroom after Davis refused the ship's quartermaster's request that he eat in his stateroom. While on Guam, Smith transferred to the regular Marine Corps. His college girl friend, Esther King, came to Guam, and they were married on the island.

During the next two decades, Smith held a variety of assignments. In May 1919 he returned to the United States at Mare Island Marine Barracks, San Francisco. Ordered to sea duty in 1921, he served as commanding officer of the Marine detachment aboard the battleship *Texas* until 1924. Smith then began a four-year tour in the personnel section at Marine Corps Headquarters, Washington, D.C. In 1928 Smith went to Port-au-Prince, Haiti, to work as assistant chief of staff to the commandant of the *Garde d'Haiti* (formerly the *Gendarmerie d'Haiti*), a combined army and police force established by a Haitian treaty with the United States. Most of its officers were enlisted or commissioned U.S. Marines, while its enlisted personnel were Haitians. Smith held the rank of captain in the *Garde*, which was also his Marine Corps rank at that time. After three years in Haiti, Smith was ordered to the field officers' course at the Army Infantry School, Fort Benning, Georgia. Among the instructors at the school were George Catlett Marshall* and Omar Nelson Bradley,* and two of Smith's classmates were Walter Bedell Smith* and Terry de la Mesa Allen,* both of the Army. In June 1932, after graduation, Smith was sent to teach at the company officers' course at the Marine Corps facility at Quantico, Virginia. The next year he was assigned as assistant operations officer of the 7th Marine Regiment, also at Quantico. In 1934 Captain Smith and his family began a two and one-half year stay in France, where he took a course of study of the *Ecole Supérieure de Guerre* in Paris. In 1936 he returned to the schools at Quantico to teach amphibious operations. It might have been during this period that Smith received his nicknames of "the student general" and "the professor" from his contemporaries. Having been promoted to major while in France, Smith was promoted to lieutenant colonel in 1938. In July 1939 Smith was assigned as operations officer of the Fleet Marine Force, the combat arm of the Marine Corps, for duty at Marine Corps Base, San Diego.

In June 1940 he became commanding officer of the 1st Battalion, 6th Marine Regiment. In May 1941 he sailed with his regiment for Iceland where he remained for almost a year. Then Smith became executive officer of the Division of Plans and Policies at Marine Corps Headquarters.

Smith was ordered to join the 1st Marine Division in January 1944, while it was engaged in action on New Britain. On March 1 he took command of the 5th Marine Regiment. He had until March 6 to plan a landing on the Willaumez Peninsula behind Japanese lines and to capture what was believed to be their withdrawal center at Talasea. Smith received the Bronze Star with combat "V" for that operation. He was promoted to brigadier general and was made assistant division commander. The division was brought back to Pavuvu in the Russell Islands May 1944. Smith was in charge of planning the division's landing on Peleliu and related islands in the Palau Operation. Smith, operating from an antitank ditch, commanded the operations on shore during the first day of the Peleliu landing that September. In November he became the Marine deputy chief of staff to Army Lieutenant General Simon Bolivar Buckner, commanding the

Tenth Army for the Okinawa operation. He served on the Tenth Army staff throughout the Okinawa Campaign.

In July 1945 Smith returned to the United States to command the Marine Corps Schools at Quantico. The following year the commandant of the Marine Corps, General Alexander Archer Vandegrift,* appointed him to a board of three generals to study the influence of the new atomic weapons on the future of amphibious warfare. That board recommended development of the helicopter as the future solution to the twin problems of the need to disperse the naval force over a wide area while having to concentrate the landing force at the place of the assault. In late 1948 Smith, then a major general and assistant commandant of the Marine Corps and chief of staff, was asked by the commandant, General Clifton B. Cates, to head a second board to examine measures which the Marine Corps should take to meet its responsibilities for leadership in amphibious warfare. The Smith Board recommended (1) that until major advances were made in helicopter technology, few advanced tactics could be developed, and (2) that the time was rapidly approaching when helicopter squadrons should be organized to support the Fleet Marine Force. Smith could soon put into practice those observations on the use of the helicopter.

Shortly before the outbreak of the Korean War, in July 1950, Smith was ordered to Camp Pendleton, California, to command the 1st Marine Division. He had less than twenty days from receipt of the directive to prepare the bulk of the division to move out to the Far East. Smith did the planning for and then led his division in three of the most difficult campaigns of the war. That September, Smith's division led the surprise landing at Inchon, behind the enemy's lines, in a move designed to trap and destroy the invading North Korean forces. Smith's immediate superior, X Corps commander, Army Major General Edward Mallory Almond,* did not understand the specialized requirements of an assault landing in a narrow harbor with exceptionally high tides. Smith and Rear Admiral James H. Doyle, however, were able to successfully plan this complicated landing without too much interference from higher levels. *Time* magazine put Smith on the cover of its September 25, 1950, issue for this achievement.

Under pressure from Almond to capture Seoul exactly three months from the date of the North Korean invasion, Smith was able to secure the South Korean capital adequately for the ceremony General Douglas MacArthur* staged, with Smith present, turning the city back to the South Koreans. The 1st Marine Division then returned to Inchon and landed on the east coast of Korea for the attack north to the Yalu River to complete the conquest of North Korea.

Near the end of October 1950 the division began its march to the Chosin Reservoir. At one time, Smith's battalions were strung out over a two hundred mile line as they went north. He was careful not to divide his forces any more than he had to and to secure his main supply route. Throughout this period, as in the Inchon and Seoul campaigns, Smith used his helicopters for the purposes envisioned in the reports he had helped write earlier. They were used in reconnaissance, evacuations, resupply, and other capacities. Only the assault role was missing. On November 2 the Chinese Communist forces attacked units of the division in great strength. The northern advance of the Marines was over. On December 11 Smith was able to complete the fighting seventy-eight-mile withdrawal of his division to safety. In below-zero weather against eight Chinese Communist Army divisions, Smith first regrouped his forces and then organized the advance back to the sea, bringing his wounded and his equipment with him. Supported by Marine, Navy, and Air Force aircraft, the Marines reached the coast with forty-four hundred battle casualties and innumerable cases of frostbite and pneumonia. The Chinese Communists lost an estimated twenty-five thousand killed.

In early December, while Smith was planning his withdrawal, he gave an interview to a journalist which probably resulted in a famous quotation that is popularly attributed to him, but which Smith denied saying (he was famous in the Marine Corps for not drinking or swearing). Smith is alleged to have said upon being asked if the Marines were retreating under fire, "Retreat Hell, we're just attacking in another direction." In trying to explain that because the Marines, and their supporting forces, were surrounded and under attack from all sides and, thus, would have to fight no matter in which direction they moved, he might have said, as one obituary worded it, "We are not retreating—we are just attacking in a different direction." But his denials were unable to stop the circulation of the first version of that quotation.

After a period of rest and recuperation, Smith's division again was in combat. As part of the IX Corps, he was engaged in the February 1951 counteroffensive when Army Major General Bryant E. Moore suddenly died and Lieutenant General Matthew Bunker Ridgway* ordered Smith to take command of IX Corps. In one of the rare episodes when a Marine Corps general commanded a joint Army-Marine Corps division or corps, Smith commanded IX Corps from February 24 to March 5, 1951, when an Army general arrived to take over the corps.

In April 1951 Smith was assigned to command Camp Pendleton. He was promoted to lieutenant general in 1953 and took command of Fleet Marine Force, Atlantic, which consisted of the bulk of Marine Corps combat strength oriented towards the Atlantic Ocean. Subsequently, Smith headed another board to consider the requirements for small and medium helicopters in the Marine Corps. His board recommended extensive use of the medium helicopter. Smith retired on September 1, 1955, and was promoted to general at that time.

Smith was a student and teacher of military science. He participated in campaigns on New Britain, Peleliu, and Okinawa during World War II. After the war, he helped prepare the Marine Corps for potential nuclear warfare with his participation on study boards that developed the use of the helicopter by the Marine Corps. During the Korean War, he directed the 1st Marine Division in the difficult surprise landing at Inchon that changed the course of the war. His finest hour came when the Chinese Communists entered the war and eight of their divisions attacked his at Chosin Reservoir. His careful planning and refusal to spread out his regiments enabled the Marines to withstand the assault. His leadership and planning for the fighting withdrawal enabled the Marines to maintain their tactical integrity and to destroy the eight enemy divisions as combat forces. That in turn enabled X Corps to evacuate the North Korean coast and to stay in the war as a tactical formation. Smith's withdrawal against heavy odds (Almond had told him to abandon his equipment) sustained the morale of the American and other United Nations forces at a critical time in the Korean War.

Smith was a scholar of warfare, a planner of amphibious operations, and a combat leader, and he excelled at those aspects of twentieth-century military life.

BIBLIOGRAPHY

Heinl, Robert D., Jr. *Victory at High Tide: The Inchon-Seoul Campaign.* Philadelphia: J. B. Lippincott Company, 1968.
Montross, Lynn, et al. *U.S. Marine Operations in Korea.* 5 vols. Washington, D.C. : U.S. Government Printing Office, 1954–1972.
Rawlins, Eugene W. *Marines and Helicopters, 1942–1962.* Washington, D.C.: U.S. Government Printing Office, 1976.
Shaw, Henry I., et al. *History of U.S. Marine Corps Operations in World War II.* 5 vols. Washington, D.C.: U.S. Government Printing Office, 1958–1971.

MARTIN K. GORDON

SMITH, Walter Bedell (b. Indianapolis, Ind., October 5, 1895; d. Washington, D.C., August 9, 1961), staff officer and diplomat.

Known by the nickname "Beetle," Walter Bedell Smith was the son of William Long Smith—a merchant by profession—and Ida Frances Smith. He was raised in Indianapolis and studied briefly at Butler University before being forced to withdraw due to his father's illness.

In 1911 he joined the Indiana National Guard and rose to the rank of first sergeant in 1913. In 1917, he was commissioned a second lieutenant in the Reserve Army, having completed an officer's candidate course. (He joined the Regular Army in 1920.) During World War I, he saw action in Europe with the 4th Infantry Division—participating in the battles of the Marne and Aisne, where he was slightly wounded.

Transferred home, he worked in the newly formed Bureau of Military Intelligence in Washington, D.C., and served four years as assistant to the chief coordinator of the Bureau of the Budget. He also spent two years in the Philippines with the 45th Infantry, commanding native troops. In 1929 he was promoted to the rank of captain.

During the 1930s Smith acquired most of his formal military education. He studied at the Infantry School at Fort Benning, Georgia, the Command and General Staff School at Fort Leavenworth, Kansas, and finally at the Army War College in Washington, D.C. Between training assignments, he held the positions of secretary and then instructor at the Fort Benning School. There Lieutenant

Colonel George Catlett Marshall,* assistant commandant of the school, first made Smith's acquaintance.

Advancement in the peacetime army was slow, but Smith made major in 1939. In that same year, General Marshall became the Army Chief of Staff and brought Smith to Washington to fill the post of assistant secretary to the General Staff. He assumed the duties of secretary in 1941 and consequently became the first secretary to the Anglo-American chiefs of staff after the United States entered World War II. Added responsibilities brought promotions and honors—the rank of brigadier general in 1942 and the Distinguished Service Medal in 1943.

America's total unpreparedness at Pearl Harbor spurred controversy among politicians, historians, and others almost from the very day of the attack. In his capacity as secretary to the General Staff, Smith became embroiled in this dispute. The day before Pearl Harbor, he neglected to forward a pouch containing intelligence reports to General Marshall who was spending the weekend outside of Washington. The pouch contained intercepted Japanese messages pertaining to the impending attack, but Smith would later tell congressional investigators that he had been led to believe that it held only partially decoded Japanse cables which were not urgent. So he took it upon himself to hold the material until Marshall's return the following Monday. Some would later criticize Smith's role and motives here, but this episode apparently had no impact on the course of his career.

General Marshall respected Smith's competence as a staff officer, but General Dwight David Eisenhower* prevailed upon Marshall to transfer Smith to his staff in late 1942. Smith served as Eisenhower's chief of staff in the North African and Mediterranean theaters. On behalf of Eisenhower, he negotiated the surrender of Italy and signed the formal document in September 1943.

When Eisenhower took command of the Allied Expeditionary Forces, Prime Minister Winston Churchill wanted Smith to remain as chief of staff in the Mediterranean. But Eisenhower thought that Smith was indispensable, so now Lieutenant General Smith assumed the same position for Supreme Headquarters, Allied Expeditionary Forces (SHAEF). As Eisenhower's emissary, he participated in the 1945 Malta Conference and was a member of the Allied group that accepted Germany's surrender in May of that year.

The war's end provided little respite. President Harry S Truman nominated Smith to succeed W. Averell Harriman as ambassador to the Soviet Union only a few months after Smith's return from Europe. Now a major general, Smith received congressional approval to maintain his military rank while serving in this diplomatic post.

Smith's tenure in Moscow, which lasted until March 1949, was a stormy period for Soviet-American relations, during which time he gained valuable experience in dealing with the Russians. As ambassador, he was a member of the official delegations to the Paris Peace Conference in 1946 and all of the foreign ministers conferences between 1946 and 1949. He held up the Moscow end of the delicate diplomatic negotiations during the volatile Berlin crisis. He took the time at the end of his ambassadorship to record his experiences and impressions of these turbulent years. The memoir *My Three Years in Moscow* was published in 1950.

Upon his return to the United States, he served briefly as commander of the First Army before President Truman appointed him as the nation's second director of the Central Intelligence Agency (CIA). Truman gave him a mandate to reorganize that agency. While in that post, Smith became a general in 1951.

When Eisenhower became president, Smith moved from the CIA to the State Department. He resigned from active military service and accepted Eisenhower's nomination as undersecretary of state, a post second only to Secretary of State John Foster Dulles. Smith was one of the few men to hold critical positions in both the Truman and Eisenhower administrations. As undersecretary, he headed the U.S. delegation to the 1954 Geneva Conference which tried to settle the Vietnam dilemma.

At the end of that year, Smith resigned from government service to enter private industry. He died in Washington on August 9, 1961.

Walter Bedell Smith was not a typical Army officer. In a military where West Point graduates predominated, he was an exception. He had begun as a private in the National Guard—something some of his condescending colleagues never forgot—and rose slowly through the ranks. Like Marshall and Eisenhower, his military "patrons," his place in history hinges on governmental service beyond his years in the Army.

Descriptions by friends and associates reveal two distinct sides to Smith's personality. One side suggested the common touch. He liked the nickname "Beetle." He was an expert fly fisherman and had an obsession with meticulously fashioning fly rods from bamboo. He was as proud of this reputation as a sportsman as any of his other accomplishments. But another side dominated his professional life. He was a man of few words. Brusque and demanding, he commanded the respect of his subordinates and knew how to get things done. He had few close friends. In fact, one journalist lamented the paucity of humorous anecdotes about his life.

This suited the responsible roles he filled in the Army. Although he started out as an infantry officer, his true expertise surfaced when he assumed staff duties. He was a capable organizer. Eisenhower described him as "a master of detail with clear comprehension of main issues. Serious, hard-working, and loyal, he proved equally capable in difficult conference [sic] as he was in professional activity. Strong in character and abrupt by instinct, he could achieve harmony without appeasement."

Impressed by Smith's wartime reputation, Truman chose him as ambassador to the Soviet Union. The late 1940s was a time of growing distrust of the Russians. The containment policy was slowly taking shape. As the United States assumed its role as a world power, the Truman administration sought men with experience in dealing with the Russians and with unquestioned loyalty to their country.

During the war, Eisenhower had entrusted his chief of staff with responsibility for negotiating with the Russians on military matters. And the Russians came to respect Smith's fairness and evenhandedness. At the same time, Smith's political views were clearly consistent with the administration's. He opposed communism and had little sympathy for the Soviet totalitarian government. He was a cold warrior in an age of cold warriors.

His proven administrative ability coupled with his knowledge of the Soviet Union later made Smith a leading candidate for director of a CIA that badly needed his organizing hand. And finally, his success in the two previous positions combined with the respect Eisenhower personally had for him contributed to Smith's nomination as undersecretary of state. The nomination met little opposition in the Senate, even though Senator Joseph McCarthy was reaching the peak of his influence in 1953 and was attacking all who were in any way linked to the Roosevelt and Truman administrations.

Smith's career and hence his place in history transcended his generalship. Yet it was his qualities of leadership and administrative skills fostered while in the Army and the close relationships with Marshall and Eisenhower that led to his important roles in the postwar American government.

BIBLIOGRAPHY

Eisenhower, Dwight D. *Crusade in Europe*. Garden City, N.Y.: Doubleday and Company, 1948.
Pogue, Forrest C. *George C. Marshall: Ordeal and Hope, 1939–1942*. New York: Viking Press, 1965.
———. *George C. Marshall: Organizer of Victory, 1943–1945*. New York: Viking Press, 1973.
———. *The United States in World War II: The European Theater of Operations, the Supreme Command*. Washington, D.C.: U.S. Government Printing Office, 1954.
Smith, Walter Bedell. *My Three Years in Moscow*. Philadelphia: J. B. Lippincott Company, 1950.
U.S. Congress, Senate, Committee on Foreign Relations. *Hearings on the Nomination of Walter Bedell Smith to the Under Secretary of State*. February 4, 1953, 83d Cong., 1st sess. Washington, D.C.: U.S. Government Printing Office, 1953.

T. MICHAEL RUDDY

SOMERVELL, Brehon Burke (b. Little Rock, Ark., May 9, 1892; d. Ocala, Fla., February 13, 1955), Army engineer and logistician. Somervell was head of the Army Service Forces during World War II.

Brehon Somervell was born into a well-established and socially prominent family. His father was practicing medicine at the time of General Somervell's birth. In 1906 the family moved to Washington, D.C., where Somervell's mother, a former school teacher, established a fashionable girls' finishing school, Belcourt Seminary, where the general's father also taught. In 1910 Somervell received an appointment to the U.S. Military Academy, where he graduated four years later, sixth in a class of 160 cadets. He was commissioned a second lieutenant in the Corps of Engineers.

Somervell's first assignment was in France, where he served as assistant to the military attaché until September 1914. In that position, he helped expedite the transport of Americans back to the United States once World War I erupted. Upon his own return to the United States, he was assigned to duty in the Office of the Chief of Engineers, serving there until May 1915. He then served in various posts at Fort Belvoir, Virginia, and in New England until December 1915, when he was ordered to Fort Sam Houston, Texas. From March to September 1916 he accompanied General John Joseph Pershing* on the Punitive Expedition against Pancho Villa in Mexico. He attended the Engineer School in Washington, D.C., during the winter of 1916 and thereafter served for a short period of time in the district engineer's office in Pittsburgh. In May 1917 he was promoted to captain.

Somervell helped recruit and organize the 15th Engineer Regiment, the first engineer regiment sent abroad after the United States entered World War I. It arrived in England in July 1917 and left for France soon after, with Somervell as its adjutant. In France, the regiment worked on a number of large construction projects, and, for his efforts, Somervell received the Distinguished Service Medal. In October 1918 he joined the 89th Division with the temporary rank of lieutenant colonel and became assistant chief of staff, G–3, in charge of operations. After the Armistice, he was assistant chief of staff, G–4, in charge of both personnel and supply. When the division was shipped back to the United States in May 1919, Somervell remained overseas as G—4 of the Third Army, the force assigned to occupy the U.S. zone in Germany. In August 1919, while in Germany, he married Anna Purnell, a YMCA volunteer from Chicago; they had three daughters. Once the Army was reorganized on a peacetime basis, Somervell reverted to the permanent rank of major in July 1920.

During the next fifteen years, Somervell spent three tours in the Office of the Chief of Engineers and was also assigned to the New York, Memphis, and Washington engineer districts. He completed courses at the Engineer School, the Command and General Staff School, and the Army War College. Twice he went abroad for special missions conducted by Walker D. Hines, with whom he had a close friendship. The two men first met in 1919 in Germany. Hines had just become arbitrator of shipping on the Rhine River, and he turned to Somervell for assistance in preparing a report on transportation along the river. He called on Major Somervell again in the mid-1920s to help prepare surveys and reports for the League of Nations dealing with navigation conditions on the Rhine and Danube rivers. In 1933–1934 Somervell worked with Hines on an economic survey of Turkey that was to be used as the basis for a five-year plan of industrialization. In April 1934 he returned to the United States and reported for duty with the Office of the Chief of Engineers. Somervell was promoted to lieutenant colonel, his first promotion in fifteen years, on August 1, 1935. Shortly thereafter, he was sent to work on the Florida Ship Canal. This project, however, was aborted a year later because of a lack of congressional support and consequent shortage of funds.

From July 1936 to November 1940 Somervell, on detached service, served as chief of the Works Progress Administration in New York City, supervising more than two hundred thousand men on various construction projects, including La Guardia Airport. He gained a national reputation as a firm, though conciliatory, manager who got things done. Consequently, in December 1940, just after having been promoted to colonel, Somervell was transferred to Washington, where he was given the task of reorganizing the floundering Quartermaster Corps Construction Division in order to meet the demands of an expanding army. Within a year he had completely turned the program around; the new construction program (which included the building of the Pentagon) was months ahead of schedule. Somervell always emphasized speed rather than cost, claiming that time was more important than money. By February 1941 more than 485,000 persons were employed on Army construction projects. Meanwhile, Somervell had been promoted to brigadier general (temporary) on January 29, 1941. Ten months later, he was selected as the new assistant chief of staff, G–4 (logistics) in the War Department General Staff. He received his second star in January 1942, an occasion that was marred by the death of his wife that same month.

In March 1942 the Army chief of staff, General George Catlett Marshall,* personally selected Somervell to head a collection of technical and administrative agencies called the Services of Supply, renamed the Army Service Forces a year later. The organization was responsible for the centralized control of supply and administration for the entire Army within the United States. During World War II, it provided most of the logistics support for troops overseas. In the same month that the Services of Supply was organized, Somervell was promoted to lieutenant general (temporary). A year later, March 1943, he married Mrs. Louise Hampton Wartmann, a former student of his parents at Belcourt Seminary. On March 6, 1945, at the close of an illustrious Army career, Somervell was promoted to general (temporary).

General Somervell retired in January 1946 with the permanent rank of major general. He became president of the Koppers Company and, using some of his Army Service Forces veterans as assistants, imposed the same strong management control over the company that had been his trademark throughout his career. He established a Control Division to ensure quality in the company's products and received periodic reports which allowed him to anticipate trouble spots and to plan for the future. In 1948 Somervell was promoted to a four star general in the U.S. Army (retired). He died of a heart attack in 1955 and was buried beside his first wife in Arlington National Cemetery.

As a result of his unorthodox military career—a mixture of civilian and Army assignments—Somervell developed an unusually keen sense of management and organization. He rarely accepted an existing arrangement just because it happened to be the way things had always been done, particularly if he saw in such an arrangement an obstacle to his own plans. He had little use for procrastinators, bureaucratic red tape, and opposing authority. His commanders were instructed to make use of "judicious shortcuts in procedure to expedite operations." His dogged determination to succeed in his mission undoubtedly alienated some, but the general was also capable of instilling tremendous loyalty among those closely associated with him. Somervell drove himself at least as hard as he drove his subordinates, and he generally succeeded in meeting, if not surpassing, his own goals. Senator Harry Truman commented, "I will say this for General Somervell, he will get the stuff, but it is going to be hell for the taxpayer."

Few organizations have been more closely identified with the personality of a single man than the Army Service Forces. Hundreds of thousands of workers, both military and civilian, worked for the organization. Contractors and employees were asked to work long hours to turn out necessary supplies. Railroad managers and trainmen worked equally hard to transport the supplies to the seaports, where shipping companies, stevedores, and seamen labored to move the equipment overseas. Presiding over all of this was General Somervell, who was able to keep this far-flung bureaucracy going through his own will and efforts. His achievement was a critical contribution to the U.S. effort during World War II and helped determine the course of logistics operations for years to come.

BIBLIOGRAPHY

Coll, Blanche D., Jean E. Keith, and Herbert H. Rosenthal. The *Corps of Engineers: Troops and Equipment*. Washington, D.C.: U.S. Government Printing Office, 1958.

Fine, Lenore, and Jesse A. Remington. *The Corps of Engineers: Construction in the United States*. Washington, D.C.: U.S. Government Printing Office, 1972.

Leighton, Richard H., and Robert W. Coakley. *Global Logistics and Strategy*. 2 vols. Washington, D.C.: U.S. Government Printing Office, 1955, 1968.

Millet, John D. *The Organization and Role of the Army Service Forces*. Washington, D.C.: U.S. Government Printing Office, 1954.

Ruppenthal, Roland G. *Logistical Support of the Armies*. 2 vols. Washington D.C.: U.S. Government Printing Office, 1953, 1959.

Smith, R. Elberton. *The Army and Economic Mobilization*. Washington, D.C.: U.S. Government Printing Office, 1959.

MARTIN REUSS

SPAATZ, Carl Andrew (b. June 28, 1891, Boyerstown, Pa.; d. Washington, D.C., July 13, 1974), Army officer, Air Force officer. Spaatz was one of the main disciples of William ("Billy") Mitchell* and was the first chief of staff of the U.S. Air Force.

Spaatz was one of five children of a Pennsylvania Dutch family who added an extra "A" to their last name in 1937 to assure proper pronunciation. His father was a printer and a Democrat state senator. At West Point, Spaatz acquired the nickname "Tooey" because of his resemblance to an upperclassman, and graduated into the infantry in 1914. After service at Schofield Barracks, he learned to fly at San Diego and transferred to the Air Service of the Signal Corps. He served with the Punitive Expedition under John Joseph Pershing's* command that pursued Pancho Villa deep into Mexico. As a major with the American Expeditionary Force in France, Spaatz was assigned to training duties but went "AWOL to the front." He flew with a British unit while on leave and downed two German planes in a single action, narrowly escaping capture when he nearly ran out of gas. His extracurricular successes gained him a Distinguished Service Cross—and direct orders to return to his training duties.

In the 1920s and early 1930s Spaatz was a strong supporter of Billy Mitchell, and like many officers of that period spent a long time in grade, in his case fifteen years as a major. Taciturn and blunt, Spaatz served as a defense witness at the Mitchell court-martial. As a result of that symbolic defeat, air power enthusiasts in the Air Service/Air Corps undertook a series of publicity-making flights, inadvertently aided by Charles Lindbergh's dramatic transatlantic flight in 1927. Spaatz served as part of a "flying circus" demonstration team and won the Distinguished Flying Cross when he made an endurance refueling flight in the first week of January 1929, staying in the air almost 151 hours with Ira Clarence Eaker,* who was then a major, and Elwood Quesada, then a lieutenant, both of whom became major commanders in the U.S. Army Air Force in World War II.

Spaatz reluctantly attended the U.S. Army Command and General Staff College in 1935–1936, commenting that he had never seen a happy general. In that period, most Air Corps officers saw Leavenworth as less desirable an assignment than a flying command or attendance at the Tactical School at Maxwell Field.

In 1940, Spaatz went with an observer team to the United Kingdom and was chief of the Army Air Forces Materiel Division at the time of Pearl Harbor. In May 1942 he went to England to command the Eighth Air Force, which began operations against targets in Europe in August 1942. Three months later, Spaatz became Allied Air Forces commander under Dwight David Eisenhower,* during Operation TORCH, the invasion of North Africa, and remained in the Mediterranean until early 1944. In spite of his bluff manner, Spaatz got along well with the British and became an advocate of systematic analysis of weapons effects of the type carrried out by Sir Solly Zuckerman, when others were not at all interested. The Spaatz-Zuckerman relationship led to a bombing of the Island of Pantellaria along lines suggested by scientific analysis which led to surrender of the garrison before a scheduled landing took place.

In the spring of 1944, Spaatz returned to Britain to command the newly formed U.S. Strategic Air Forces in Europe, where he argued for a redirection of the air offensive against vulnerable points in the German war network, moving away from attacks on specific aircraft-related industries to key arteries and nodes, the transportation system, and synthetic oil production facilities. Spaatz faced not only resistance from the Royal Air Force's Sir Arthur "Bomber" Harris, who wanted area attacks, but also a diversion of the Allied Air Forces to supporting the ground forces before, during, and after Operation OVERLORD, the major invasion of France. In the early summer of 1944 the Allied air forces again struck at transportation and oil, a tactic that proved dramatically successful. The starvation of German air and tank forces of fuel and lubricant blunted their effectiveness in such cases as the Battle of the Bulge and the defense of Budapest, and blocked the Germans' ability to bring their jet fighter force into full play. Spaatz shared one article of faith with Harris, the belief that air power properly applied could have eliminated the need for the D-Day invasion, an assertion that continues to be a main item of debate in respect to air power in World War II.

In June 1945, a month after Germany's downfall, Spaatz went to Guam to command U.S. Strategic Air Forces in the Far East, presiding over Curtis Emerson LeMay's* program of area firebomb raids, as well as the dropping of atomic bombs on Hiroshima and Nagasaki.

In the postwar period, Spaatz, who had attended all the main surrender ceremonies, became a strong publicist of air power. In 1947 he succeeded General Henry Harley ("Hap") Arnold* as chief of the U.S. Army Air Forces and then became the first U.S. Air Force chief of staff, with the creation of an independent American air element resulting from the National Security Act of 1947. After retirement in 1948, Spaatz became national security affairs correspondent for *Newsweek* magazine. He also served as chairman of the Civil Air Patrol and the International Reserve Committee, as well as a member of the committee that chose Colorado Springs as the Air Force Academy site. He is buried there.

Spaatz remains a somewhat enigmatic figure, in spite of his role as the major American commander of strategic air power in World War II, and his extensive comments in the popular press during the Cold War. A biography of substance is overdue, particularly since he and George Churchill Kenney* showed the least tendency to get hung up on tactical method and dogma, to seek for success by alternatives within the general framework of air power, and not let too many chips ride on one number. In looking at Spaatz, one feels that, in spite of a certain amount of stylized bluster and pugnacity, he resembles Douglas MacArthur,* a first-class mind unchallenged in his environment by frequent contact with other first-class minds. In any event, his star has faded far out of proportion to his importance in the shaping of air power in World War II and the early Cold War.

BIBLIOGRAPHY

DuPre, Flint O. *U.S. Air Force Biographical Dictionary*. New York: Franklin Watts, 1965.
Craven, Wesley Frank, and James Lea Cate, eds. *The Army Air Forces in World War II*. 7 vols. 1948–1954.
Zuckerman, Sir Solly. *From Apes to Warlords*. London: Hamish Hamilton, 1978.

ROGER BEAUMONT

SPRUANCE, Raymond Ames (b. Baltimore, Md., July 3, 1886; d. Pebble Beach, Calif., December 13, 1969), naval officer. Spruance was the principal

American naval commander in the Central Pacific during World War II and victorious commander at Midway.

Before the war, Spruance seemed an unlikely candidate for a future fleet commander. He was reared by women—at times by a domineering mother and at times by three young and adoring maiden aunts. His father was a recluse whom he hardly knew. As a teenager he wrote and published poetry that displayed his sensitivity and imagination. Spruance attended the Naval Academy with the class of 1907 because he could not afford to pay for his own university education. He was unhappy there because of the discipline, the hazing, and the sterile curriculum. Yet he was an excellent student, but so inconspicuous that few of his classmates knew him well. He was described in his yearbook as a shy young man, open and innocent, who would hurt nothing and no one, except in the line of duty.

Shortly after graduation, Spruance sailed around the world with the Great White Fleet, which was initially under the command of Robley Dunglison Evans.* Spruance so enjoyed the experience that it was then that he decided to be a career naval officer. In 1909 he studied advanced electrical engineering for a year at the General Electric Company in Schenectady, New York, and became one of the Navy's finest technical experts. Consequently, Spruance received a number of engineering assignments and could have chosen to become a limited-duty specialist. He decided, however, to remain an unrestricted line officer.

He received his first of six commands in the Philippines, the primitive destroyer *Bainbridge*, in March 1913. He was promoted to lieutenant commander in August 1917 shortly after the United States entered World War I and began to mobilize the fleet. However, he never saw action owing to shipyard assignments in the United States. After the war his sea duty tours followed the normal peacetime routine, including command of the destroyers *Aaron Ward, Percival, Dale* and *Osborne*. His sixth—and major—command was the battleship *Mississippi* (1938). Spruance was regarded as a superb shiphandler and a quiet, conscientious, competent skipper.

Spruance supported not only his own family, but his mother and aunts as well. After World War I he became discouraged with his low pay and very nearly resigned his commission, but he remained in the service because his father-in-law told him he was too honest to be a successful businessman. Spruance believed that the only meaningful duty for promotion was at sea, and there he remained as long as he could. Even though he often became seasick, he was a stoic who would not admit to physical discomfort. Shore duty was for relaxation, and when he came ashore he sought comfortable quarters and pleasant surroundings; he neither worked overtime nor brought work home. He sought neither favors nor friends in high places nor duty in Washington to advance his career. He once told his close friend William Frederick Halsey, Jr.,* that he was simply trying to be a good naval officer. Spruance's last three tours of shore duty were at the Naval War College as a student and then as a staff officer. It was there that he learned the fundamentals of strategy and operational planning.

Selected for rear admiral in the fall of 1940, Spruance found that his assignment was to establish the Tenth Naval District Headquarters in San Juan, Puerto Rico. Spruance subsequently supervised the construction of numerous bases and airfields in the Caribbean as a result of the general mobilization for war. In September 1941 Spruance took command of Cruiser Division Five in Pearl Harbor and was surface screen commander for Halsey's carrier task force in the early months of World War II. After his ships protected the task force which carried the Army aircraft that flew in the famous attack on Tokyo led by James Harold Doolittle,* Spruance relieved Halsey, who was seriously ill. Spruance took command of the American carrier force that sank four Japanese carriers in the victory at the critical Battle of Midway (June 1942). Coupled with the Battle of the Coral Sea (May 1942, under Admiral Frank Jack Fletcher*), Midway blocked the expansion of the Japanese and actually put them on the defensive. Furthermore, the loss of four aircraft carriers, as well as losing the battle itself, was a tremendous psychological blow to the Japanese Navy. Spruance's ship disposition and use of available aircraft were brilliant. Midway was one of the most decisive battles of World War II.

Spruance then came ashore as chief of staff to Admiral Chester William Nimitz,* commander in chief, Pacific, at Pearl Harbor. A year later Spruance returned to sea as commander of the Fifth Fleet, leading American forces across the Pacific to the very shores of Japan. These campaigns included the seizures of major islands and island groups, including the Gilberts, Marshalls, Marianas, Iwo Jima, and Okinawa. Another of Spruance's famous fights was the Battle of the Philippine Sea; although Japan lost more than 450 aircraft in one day in the "Marianas Turkey Shoot," the Japanese fleet escaped. Afterwards Spruance was criticized for his passive defense off the shores of Saipan. Spruance claimed he had carried out his primary mission of protecting the troops ashore.

After the war Spruance ended his active duty as president of the Naval War College, although Fleet Admiral Ernest Joseph King* considered Spruance as well qualified to be the next chief of naval operations. Called out of retirement to become ambassador to the Philippines in 1952, Spruance and the Central Intelligence Agency worked together to ensure the election of Ramon Magsaysay as president under circumstances that seemed acceptable then under the threat of communision but that are subject to criticism today. Spruance retired again in 1955 and spent his remaining years at his home in Pebble Beach.

Because he abhorred publicity, Spruance was not well known by his fellow Americans. To his colleagues and subordinates he seemed rather an austere, remote, almost mysterious figure. In reality, he was a superb combination of fighter and intellectual. In Samuel Eliot Morison's* words, Spruance was "secure within, a modest and a great man who should have been given a fifth star."

His intellectualism was not the kind associated with philosophy, science, or advanced degrees, and he disliked writing and speeches. He had superior mental power and relied solely upon his intellect—and never his emotions—when he fought the Japanese. He respected the Japanese as fighters and did not allow hatred to distort his judgment. War to him was an intellectual challenge that stimulated his mind. Spruance pragmatically accepted the notion that war meant killing and that many people would have to die. But he did everything in his power to reduce American casualties, primarily through meticulous planning and use of violent, overwhelming force, swiftly applied. In his judgment it would have been proper to use poison gas on Iwo Jima; American lives would have been spared, and no civilians were on the island. Spruance pitied the civilians who suffered in war, and he deplored the B–29 fire raids against Japan.

Spruance encouraged initiative in combat by telling his subordinates what he wanted done, giving them the necessary resources and then leaving the tactical direction entirely to the commanders at the scene. His operations orders were famous for their precision and clarity. Once the fighting started, Spruance would neither interfere nor offer advice, but he would make major decisions and issue general directives when necessary. His mind was always fresh and rested because of his splendid health and aloofness from details. His avoidance of long working hours seemed like laziness to some, but it was Spruance's way of conserving his health through a long war.

His moral courage was manifested by his incorruptible integrity. He spoke the truth, and he did what was morally right regardless of the possible conse- quences to his own career. At the height of the war Spruance spoke in California and publicly criticized the unjustified imprisonment of Japanese-American citi- zens in concentration camps. Immediately after the war, he argued publicly against the punitive confiscation of Japanese territory and recommended a drastic reduction in the size of the postwar American Navy because there were no more enemy naval powers in the near future.

Spruance's physical courage was unbelievable, and he was apparently fatal- istic. Throughout the war his flagship was often attacked, yet he seemed oblivious to personal danger. He would gaze serenely at bombers diving upon him from above and was indifferent to projectiles from shore batteries bracketing his ship. Transcending his other virtues, however, was his fighting spirit: his eagerness and desire to come to grips with the enemy, to press on with vigor and deter- mination against all obstacles, and to keep fighting until the battle was won. A complex and fascinating man, he was an enigma to everyone. Above all, he was a master of the art of naval warfare.

Morison wrote the words that provide the best brief description of Raymond Spruance: "Power of decision and coolness in action were perhaps Spruance's leading characteristics. He envied no one, regarded no one as rival, won the respect of everyone with whom he came in contact, and went ahead in his quiet way, winning victories for his country."

BIBLIOGRAPHY

Buell, Thomas B. *The Quiet Warrior: A Biography of Admiral Raymond A. Spruance.* Boston: Little, Brown and Company, 1974.
Forrestel, Emmet P. *Admiral Raymond A. Spruance, USN: A Study in Command.* Wash- ington, D.C.: U.S. Government Printing Office, 1966.

Lord, Walter. *Incredible Victory*. New York: Harper and Row, 1967.
Morison, Samuel E. *History of U.S. Naval Operations in World War II*. 15 vols. Boston: Atlantic, Little, Brown and Company, 1947–1962.
Reynolds, Clark G. *The Fast Carriers: The Forging of an Air Navy*. New York: McGraw-Hill, 1968.

THOMAS B. BUELL

SQUIER, George Owen (b. Dryden, Mich., March 21, 1865; d. Washington, D.C., March 24, 1934), military scientist; inventor; chief signal officer of the Army, 1917–1923.

The importance of George Squier's career is inversely proportional to the attention it receives in both serious and popular works. Encompassing the fateful decades that opened with the Spanish-American War and closed with the senate's rejection of the Versailles Treaty, his career resulted in establishing new, important institutions of scientific research in the military and promoting the application of science to warfare.

After his mother died, George Squier was taken to his grandfather's Michigan farm at the early age of seven. His only sister, Mary, to whom he always remained closely attached throughout his bachelor life, lived with friends of the family. When old enough to be apprenticed to a local shopkeeper, Squier quietly wrote competitive examinations for entry into West Point. Surpassing thirty other young men, he won an appointment for entry in 1883. On graduation in 1887, he stood first on the order of merit in discipline and ranked seventh in general merit.

Squier's highly unusual career began in characteristic style; at Fort McHenry he applied for Ph.D. training at The Johns Hopkins University where he studied under some of the finest minds of his generation: Henry Rowland in physics, Joseph Ames in mechanics, and Ira Remsen in chemistry. He graduated in the summer of 1893, most likely the first Ph.D. in the U.S. Army. With this first-class preparation in electrical science and convinced of the importance of applying the new sciences to military problems, Squier set about institutionalizing scientific research in the Army. In the course of the next several years he helped found the *Artillery Journal*, established the first Army Electrical Engineering Laboratory at Fortress Monroe, and attended the Colombian Exposition of 1893 as the official Army representative. His own research led to a novel gun chronograph utilizing photography and electromagnetism and capable of measuring exterior and muzzle velocities of artillery shells. He pioneered the military application of radio in America in 1897 by ringing bells, lighting lamps, firing cannon, detonating mines, and starting machinery by remote radio control.

Squier's research also led him into fields with possible commercial application which he happily exploited, revealing the international inventor-entrepreneur side of his personality. The first of such inventions was the Synchronograph, a high-speed transmitter capable of attaining signaling speeds of between twelve hundred and three thousand words per minute, and tested abroad in the laboratory of the Government Post Office in Great Britain. With a civilian partner, Squier formed the Crehone-Squier Intelligence Transmission Company to develop and market their invention. Shortly afterward, and to his commercial detriment, Squier received orders to proceed to the newly won Philippines and take charge of laying submarine cables between the islands.

Two years after returning from the Pacific, Squier was designated to take charge of establishing the first Signal School at Fort Leavenworth in 1905. Squier initially espoused the use of aeronautics for military operations there. Ballooning and aviation became popular topics under Squier's tutelage. He included a formal requirement to instruct students in military aeronautics in the educational charter of the Army's first professional college.

After he came to Washington as assistant chief signal officer in 1907, his involvement in aviation intensified. He recommended formation of an Aeronautical Division (which was accepted), wrote the specifications for the world's first military aircraft, conducted acceptance trials of the Army's first Wright Flyer, promoted military aviation in engineering and flying circles, and recommended a National Aeronautical Research Laboratory—all before 1910.

During the lull of aviation activity in 1909–1910, Squier returned to his radio laboratory. In just over a year he applied for four fundamental patents in the art of multiplex telephony, dubbed "wired wireless." By this means, he could simultaneously transmit and receive several verbal messages over a single wire, which is the basis for modern telecommunications systems. With the registry of these patents, the work of government scientists revealed its potential for commercially lucrative applications and eventually caused a redirection of the law governing rewards for valuable inventions. His entrepreneurial instincts prevailed within two years when he found himself in London as U.S. military attachée. There he formed a partnership with Muirhead and Company, the world's largest manufacturer of cable terminal equipment. Also while in London, he formed an Empire-wide enterprise with Lee DeForest, the patent-holder of triode vacuum tubes.

At the personal invitation of Lord Horatio Herbert Kitchener, Squier secretly visited the battlefront in France in November 1914 where he observed, with fascination and a sense of history being formed, the uses of airplanes in battle. Shortly after another visit a year later, Squier was tapped to return to America to lead what would be called the biggest thing of the war—aviation.

Nine months after Squier set foot in New York, he was promoted to brigadier general from lieutenant colonel and appointed chief signal officer of the Army. Within his charge were the entire aviation and communications missions of the Army. His responsibilities spanned the military uses of radio, submarine cables, telegraphy, cryptography, photography, meteorology, rockets, guided missiles, airplanes, devices for clandestine signaling, and psychology. He oversaw an assemblage of operational, technical, and research duties which were beyond the ken or competence of any one man. The impossible magnitude and scope of the assignment dramatized the extent of the Army's failure in accommodating scientific research within the military. Despite Squier's prophetic insights and bottomless energy in building military aviation along pioneering industrial, scientific, engineering, and doctrinal dimensions, his reputation received a fearful bruising when responsibility for military aviation was removed from his control in May 1918. Expectations unconditioned by any comparable experiences led to bitter complaints and disappointments over progress of aircraft construction and delivery programs. He could nevertheless take rightful credit by the end of World War I, albeit still denied him, for founding two still great laboratories in aviation and communications—Langley Field, Virginia and Fort Monmouth, New Jersey; for institutionalizing scientific cooperation between governmental departments—particularly with the NACA, the National Research Council, and military aviation service; for advancing strategic military thinking in his strong personal sponsorship of the Liberty Eagle—the predecessor of the V1 and V2; for perfecting tactical (and civil) employment of aircraft by developing reliable, high-powered voice radio for airplanes; and incorporating modern industrial practices into the production of radios and aircraft.

By 1919 the Army succeeded in institutionalizing scientific research and development for military purposes. A new relationship between professional science and engineering and the Army emerged from World War I. The career-long efforts of Major General Squier were instrumental in shaping the new relationship. For twenty years he moved in the vanguard of those trying to bring science into the Army. His enthusiasm marked him for praise by progressive Army officers and criticism from conventional minds. His influence deeply touched the American military development of the two great technological revolutions of his time—radio and airplanes. But his scientific education and reputation tended to set him apart from other officers. Relationships with civilians were often more intimate and comfortable. Squier's position on the bridge between science and engineering on the one side and the military on the other facilitated passage of the latest industrial and scientific revolutions into the Army camp.

BIBLIOGRAPHY

Clark, Paul W. "Major General George Owen Squier: Military Scientist." Ph.D. dissertation, Case Western Reserve University, 1974.
Kennelly, A. B. "George Owen Squier." National Academy of Sciences Biographical Memoirs 20 (1934).

PAUL W. CLARK

STANDISH, Miles or Myles (b. England, ca. 1584; d. Duxbury, Plymouth Colony [now Massachusetts], October 3, 1656), military leader of the Pilgrims.

Little is known of Standish's life prior to the voyage of the *Mayflower* to New England in 1620. It is said that he was born in Chorley, Lancashire. In his youth he served as a soldier in the Netherlands, aiding the Dutch in their struggle against Spain. Coming to the notice of English Separatist leaders as a mature professional soldier, this short, sturdy, reddish-haired officer was retained by the Pilgrims to go with them to America and serve as their military advisor, helping them defend themselves against hostile Indians and other potential enemies.

As soon as the *Mayflower* arrived in Provincetown Harbor near the tip of Cape Cod in November 1620, Standish had an opportunity to demonstrate his qualities as a leader of armed men. He was given command of three successive exploring expeditions ashore. During the third of these excursions, while camped in the shelter of a hastily erected barricade of brush near the present Eastham, the little company suddenly was attacked by a band of Indians shooting arrows. Standish effectively rallied his amateur soldiers to such a resolute defense of their position that the Indians gave up the attack and fled. Had this ''First Encounter'' gone the other way, with the exploring party being massacred or taken captive, there probably would have been no Plymouth in American history.

Standish rendered an even more significant and lasting form of service after the Pilgrims had selected Plymouth as their place of settlement, in helping them make arrangements for defending the community. Initially, at the crest of the low hill overlooking the village, he had them construct a simple platform on which they mounted several pieces of artillery. Later, he designed and sited a more elaborate system of fortifications consisting of a wooden blockhouse on the hill, a palisade extending downward from the blockhouse in two directions to protect the village on its most vulnerable sides, and a small wooden redoubt at the intersection of the two village streets. Standish also provided the Pilgrim men with basic training in weaponry and tactics, and helped them begin the organization of a militia system based upon the principle of compulsory training for all adult males. Since February 17, 1621, Standish had been the officially designated commander of the little colony's armed force, a post he was to hold for the next thirty-two years.

During the earliest months of 1621, in dread wintertime, the Pilgrim community lay in the grip of debilitating disease which carried off nearly half their number, including Standish's wife Rose. The bluff soldier distinguished himself in this different kind of battle by his kindness and fidelity in tending to the needs of the sick, a service that later was memorialized by Governor William Bradford himself in his classic account *Of Plimoth Plantation*. With the arrival of spring there came to Plymouth the powerful Sachem of the Wampanoag tribe, Massasoit, to regularize relations between Indians and whites. Bradford, no doubt in close consultation with Standish, concluded with Massasoit a very satisfactory treaty which was honored by both peoples for many decades and went far to guarantee the security of the colony. After the year's harvest had proved good, the Pilgrims held the first Thanksgiving, a holiday in which Indians joined with the English settlers in feasting. On that memorable occasion Standish entertained the assemblage (and impressed the Indians) by putting his men through their military drill.

Standish's long service as Plymouth's chief soldier never led him into a real battle. His experiences of action were limited to the few occasions when the government of the colony, finding itself threatened by some small group of

Indians or non-Puritan traders, sent him out with a party of militia to deal with the problem. Thus, in 1621 Standish overawed a minor chief known as Corbitant, with little bloodshed. His most violent and least honorable act occurred in 1623 when he and a party of Plymouth men, using deception, entrapped and killed in cold blood several Massachusetts Indians who had been uttering threats against the safety of English colonists. Significantly, Bradford passed lightly over this deplorable act of preventive assassination when composing his annals. In 1628 Standish, at the head of an armed party, arrested Thomas Morton, leader of an undisciplined group of traders at Merrymount (now Quincy, Massachusetts), a serio-comic affair that gave birth to Morton's contemptuous title for his diminutive antagonist—Captain Shrimp. Only once during his military career in America did Standish confront a European foe, when Plymouth contracted with an armed merchant ship to attack the French post at Castine, Maine, in 1635. On that mission Standish went along in another vessel. Not having actual control over the handling of the merchant ship, he was unable to have the French position bombarded effectively, and the operation ended in failure. Standish's last military service in the field occurred in 1645 when, at a time of impending war with the powerful Narragansett tribe of Rhode Island, the aging but dauntless commander personally led Plymouth's forty-man company westward to stand on guard at the frontier.

In addition to his primary responsibility as military commander of the colony, Standish began accepting major civic responsibilities almost from the beginning. The colony government sent him back to England in 1625 for the purpose of making more favorable arrangements with the merchant capitalists who were providing financial backing for the Pilgrim venture. Two years later a small group of colony leaders, including Standish, undertook to shoulder Plymouth's total indebtedness in return for a six-year monopoly of trade. Standish also was one of the founders of the new settlement of Duxbury, across the harbor from the original Pilgrim village. He and his second wife, Barbara, established their residence there probably about 1632. By that time he was climbing the ladder of material success, accumulating land and cattle. He served for many years as an assistant in the colony government, possibly first assuming that responsibility as early as 1624 and certainly serving in that capacity in 1633–1635, 1637–1641, and 1645–1656. From 1652 to 1655 he also was the colony's treasurer. There can be no doubt that Standish, the professional soldier, had earned the abiding trust of his Pilgrim companions. In 1656 illness finally overtook him. He died on October 3 of that year and was buried at Duxbury. His survivors included his wife and four sons—Alexander, Miles, Josiah, and Charles.

As a military commander Standish may have been short-tempered and somewhat flamboyant, but his personal courage is beyond question. With Gaius Julius Caesar, whose *Commentaries on the Gallic War* was a cherished volume in his personal library, Standish believed that the commander must encourage his men by his own conspicuous bravery. He helped form early Puritan New England's basic Indian policy, which was to strive for Indian friendship with just treatment, but to move expeditiously and decisively against any Indian menace. Being the only original settler with expert knowledge of military affairs, Standish made his greatest contribution by providing the Pilgrims with basic military training, by making their settlement defensible, and by helping organize a practical system of militia for the colony. Without this contribution and Standish's active role as commander, the early colonists might have stumbled into an Indian war that could have meant the demise of Plymouth Colony.

BIBLIOGRAPHY

Bradford, William. *Of Plymouth Plantation, 1620–1647.* Edited by Samuel Eliot Morison. New York: Alfred A. Knopf, 1953.
Heath, Dwight B., ed. *A Journal of the Pilgrims at Plymouth* [Mourt's Relation]. New York: Corinth Books, 1963.
Langdon, George D., Jr. *Pilgrim Colony: A History of New Plymouth, 1620–1691.* New Haven and London: Yale University Press, 1966.
Shurtleff, Nathaniel B., and David Pulsifer, eds. *Records of the Colony of New Plymouth in New England.* 12 vols. Boston: 1855–1861.
Willison, George F. *Saints and Strangers, Being the Lives of the Pilgrim Fathers & Their Families, with Their Friends & Foes.* New York: Reynal and Hitchcock, 1945.

DOUGLAS EDWARD LEACH

STANTON, Edwin McMasters (b. Steubenville, Ohio, December 19, 1814; d. Washington, D.C., December 24, 1869), secretary of war.

Edwin Stanton, the eldest of four children, dated his American ancestry to early seventeenth-century New England. His father was David Stanton, a village doctor whose strong views on matters of theology and slavery caused ruptures first with the Quakers and then with the Methodists; his mother was Lucy Norman Stanton. His parents contributed financially, if modestly, to the abolitionist endeavors of Benjamin Lundy. Physically a rather delicate youth, Stanton contracted asthma at a young age and suffered from it the rest of his life. It did not sap his energy for education, however, and after attending private schools, he earned admission to Kenyon College in 1831. He did not graduate, but he did gain admission to the bar in 1835 and shortly went into partnership with Benjamin Tappan.

Stanton's professional standing steadily improved, and complex civil cases involving patent and contract law brought him national attention; in 1856 he ended a ten-year residence in Pittsburgh to move to Washington and appear more regularly before the Supreme Court. In 1859 he helped defend a personal friend, the future Civil War General Daniel Sickles, in a notorious murder triangle. The defense of temporary insanity, here asserted in a murder case for the first time in America, together with Stanton's adroitness in stressing for a Victorian jury the security of home and family, saved the day, and Stanton's reputation climbed higher.

At this time Stanton also represented the government as special counsel in a series of complex land title cases involving fraudulent claims and deeds stemming from the period of Mexican occupation of California. When in December 1860 the secession crisis occasioned a remaking of President James Buchanan's cabinet, Attorney General Jeremiah Sullivan Black, who had hired Stanton for the California cases, secured him the attorney generalship as Black himself became secretary of state. Stanton's reputation for integrity, hard work, and attention to detail, together with his outspoken Union sympathies and his prominence in Democratic political circles, strengthened his nomination. Patriotism, the desire to stiffen Buchanan's responses to secession, and the attractiveness of the position combined to secure his acceptance.

Out of the government after the inauguration of Abraham Lincoln,* Stanton publicly criticized the new president. In January 1862, however, Lincoln appointed him secretary of war in place of Simon Cameron, who along with Treasury Secretary Salmon Chase urged Lincoln to select him. A long-time Democratic regular and now a "War Democrat," Stanton at first seemed to some congressional Republicans a questionable choice, but after an interview Senator William Pitt Fessenden reported that Stanton espoused the Republican view of the secretary's job, the military conduct of the war, "the negro question, and everything else."

Stanton continued in the cabinet after Lincoln's assassination in April 1865, although an estrangement with Andrew Johnson over Reconstruction policy widened to the point that in August 1867 Johnson suspended him as secretary of war and appointed Ulysses Simpson Grant* as a temporary replacement. In January 1868 the Senate refused to sanction the suspension, Grant yielded the office, and Stanton resumed it, but without Johnson's approval. In February Johnson removed Stanton and appointed the adjutant general, Lorenzo Thomas, to replace him, thus precipitating impeachment. Even in the absence of verbal or written communication with the president, Stanton continued to function as secretary of war during the impeachment trial, and on May 26, 1868, when the trial ended in Johnson's favor, Stanton resigned. He resumed his private law practice and declined to seek public office, but he did accept President Grant's nomination to a seat on the Supreme Court. The Senate confirmed the nomination, but Stanton died four days later without having taken the oath.

A number of personal tragedies marred Stanton's life. The deaths of his daughter Lucy in 1841, his first wife Mary in 1844, and his brother Darwin (by suicide) in 1846 changed him from a warm, outgoing socializer to a brooding introvert. Those who had official dealings with him as secretary of war often found him brusque and irascible. He could be petulant, overbearing, and unalterably convinced of his own rectitude, qualities that Lincoln skillfully turned aside but that reacted in a simmering chemistry with Andrew Johnson's own volatile characteristics and contributed to Stanton's ouster from the cabinet.

Modern scholarship leaves little doubt regarding the quality of Stanton's performance as secretary of war under Lincoln; his performance in Johnson's cabinet is more controversial. According to his most recent biographers, Benjamin P.

Thomas and Harold M. Hyman, in January 1862 Stanton walked into a situation where "the corruption and confusion that develped in Cameron's lax regime had lessened the power and prestige of an office that had none to spare." Stanton found himself "secretary of a war" and set about a major renovation of the War Department's administrative structure and practices. He cut through unnecessary red tape and insisted on efficiency and accuracy from subordinates. Rather than fill up War Department jobs with office seekers, he gave preference to soldiers with minor ailments that disqualified them from field duty. He increased central control over the telegraph, a new military tool, and closely watched news releases. He strengthened internal security, a natural move in a civil war marked by suspension of the privilege of the writ of *habeas corpus* and by military trial of civilians. His close working relationship with the Joint Committee on the Conduct of the War, particularly its prominent Republican members, exemplified a mutual cooperation with the legislative branch that extended beyond Appomattox into Reconstruction and contributed to Stanton's difficulties with Johnson.

Stanton's harsh and uncompromising relations with many high-ranking officers showed that for him there was no excuse for incompetence and no substitute for victory. A friend of General George Brinton McClellan* in the early months of the war, he became convinced that McClellan was incapable of senior command and urged Lincoln to remove him. He viewed with suspicion a number of generals at the corps and division level in the Army of the Potomac who were McClellan's favorites, and he sanctioned the arrest without charges and the six-month incarceration without trial of Brigadier General Charles P. Stone following the 1861 fiasco at Ball's Bluff. Although Stanton's aversion to West Pointers changed as the war progressed, he never did care for Irvin McDowell,* Ambrose Everett Burnside,* or Joseph Hooker.* George Gordon Meade* he publicly supported in spite of his belief that Meade could have destroyed the army of Robert Edward Lee* following Gettysburg. Stanton's impetuosity sometimes interfered with his ability to distinguish between incompetence and well-intentioned error, as in the case of his public treatment of William Tecumseh Sherman* when the government had to renounce the politically unacceptable surrender terms Sherman had offered Joseph Eggleston Johnston* in mid-April 1865.

Perhaps Stanton's most serious wartime error of judgment—"one of the colossal blunders" of the war, according to Thomas and Hyman—was his two-month suspension of recruiting in April 1862, prompted by expectations of approaching victory and the desire to revamp recruiting policies. On the other hand, Thomas and Hyman have countered unfair criticism for actions connected with Lincoln's assassination. Charges that he became a virtual dictator in the hours and days after the event lose their force in the light of conditions and attitudes at the time. He certainly wished to see the conspirators punished, and he had no doubts about the propriety of a military trial, but it is unlikely that he conspired with Judge Advocate General Joseph Holt to prevent presidential clemency for Mrs. Anna Surratt. And certainly the recurring, nonscholarly assertion that he conspired in the assassination itself has no validity.

Stanton's contributions to the Union victory were major. His careful administration of the War Department not only supported armies in the field but also relieved Lincoln of a number of psychological and political burdens. His commitment to civilian control of military institutions led him to the position, as Thomas and Hyman have phrased it, that "No officer had the right to treat the President, the Secretary, or Republican congressmen with contempt."

During Reconstruction, however, Stanton's perception of his own relations with Andrew Johnson were quite different. Johnson showed a determination to procccd with his own lenient policy of restoration, in the face of congressional objection; by the time Congress enacted its own policy in the First Reconstruction Act of March 2, 1867, the extent of his disagreement with Stanton was evident. Stanton had begun helping to draft legislation that directly impinged upon the constitutional authority of the president as commander in chief, a practice that continued into the summer of 1867. Johnson's suspension of Stanton followed Stanton's refusal to resign.

Stanton's motives for this defiance were not primarily personal, for he had often expressed the desire to return to private life. The Army performed on-site supervision of Reconstruction and thus would have to enforce any plan, whether presidential or congressional. Stanton agreed with the goals of the congressional plan, believed that Johnson would do whatever was possible to subvert it, worried that the Army would have insufficient support to carry out its functions, and saw his own continuance in office as vital to the welfare of the nation. It was a patriotically motivated view of his functions as secretary of war, but such a view of acceptable relationships within the executive branch, if suffered to prevail, would have seriously eroded the constitutional control of the president over his highest subordinates.

BIBLIOGRAPHY

Beale, Howard K., ed. *The Diary of Gideon Welles*. 3 vols. New York: W. W. Norton, 1960.
Pratt, Fletcher. *Stanton: Lincoln's Secretary of War*. New York: W. W. Norton, 1953.
Randall, James G., and David Donald. *The Civil War and Reconstruction*. 2d ed., revised. Lexington, Mass.: D. C. Heath, 1969.
Sefton, James E. *The United States Army and Reconstruction, 1865–1877*. Baton Rouge: Louisiana State University Press, 1967.
Thomas, Benjamin P., and Harold M. Hyman. *Stanton: The Life and Times of Lincoln's Secretary of War*. New York: Alfred A. Knopf, 1962.

JAMES E. SEFTON

STARK, Harold Raynsford (b. Wilkes-Barre, Pa., November 12, 1880; d. Washington, D.C., August 20, 1972), naval officer. Stark served as chief of naval operations, 1939–1942, and commander of U.S. Naval Forces in Europe, 1942–1945.

Harold R. Stark was the fifth of five children born to Benjamin Franklin Stark and Mary Frances Warner. The roots of the Stark family have been traced to medieval Scotland. The first Stark arrived in Massachusetts in 1630, and the family moved first to Connecticut and then to northeastern Pennsylvania in the early nineteenth century. As a youth, Stark learned to sail on Lake Carey near Wilkes-Barre, where he kept a summer home in his later years.

Appointed by the secretary of the navy, Stark entered the U.S. Naval Academy in 1899, where he sailed and rowed in intercollegiate competition, and sang in the Naval Academy choir. In his first year there some historically minded upperclassmen inaccurately recalled the words of American General John Stark at the Battle of Bennington in 1775: "We will win today or Betty Stark will be a widow." (Her name was Molly.) Frequently, Midshipman Stark was required to come to attention and repeat the general's famous words. As a result, he acquired the nickname "Betty" which stuck with him for life. He graduated from the Naval Academy in 1903, ranking thirtieth in a class of fifty.

As a junior officer Stark served in a wide variety of ships, including the screw sloop *Hartford*, the last full-rigged sailing ship in the U.S. Navy. In 1904 he participated in the landing of U.S. Marines at Samana Bay, Dominican Republic. In 1907 he married his childhood sweetheart, Katharine Rhoads. Stark sailed around the world from 1907 to 1909 in the battleship *Minnesota* which was a part of the Great White Fleet, initially commanded by Admiral Robley Dunglison Evans.* Stark's first command came at the age of twenty-nine when he commanded a torpedoboat; between 1909 and 1915 he commanded four ships. During the latter part of this period his flotilla commander was Captain (later Admiral) William Sowden Sims,* and the two men established a long-lived and close relationship based on mutual respect and admiration. In 1914 Assistant Secretary of the Navy Franklin D. Roosevelt was a passenger in Stark's ship, and he offered to "take the conn" through a particularly difficult stretch of water along the Maine coast. Stark refused to relinquish his responsibility, telling Roosevelt that he doubted the latter's authority to relieve him. That voyage marked the start of a friendship that lasted until Roosevelt's death in 1945.

When the United States entered World War I in 1917, Stark was assigned to the Asiatic Fleet in Manila as commander of a flotilla of destroyers (then known as torpedoboats). The Navy Department soon ordered them transferred to the European war zone. After a hectic month in which necessary repairs were completed and complicated logistic arrangements were made, Stark sailed from Manila for Gibraltar with these five coal-burning ships. The route across the Indian Ocean at the height of the monsoon season brought them exceedingly foul weather for most of the eighty-one day, eleven thousand mile voyage. Despite adverse weather, the ships reached Gibraltar in good condition and were ready for escort duty. For this exploit, Stark received the first of three Distinguished Service Medals awarded to him during his career. By the end of 1917 he was assigned to the staff of Admiral Sims, then commander of U.S. Naval Forces Operating in European Waters. Serving on Sims' staff, Stark was exposed to the complexities of supporting large naval forces abroad and to the intricacies of collaborating with allies. This experience would be most useful to him during World War II.

During the years between the two world wars, Stark enhanced his reputation as a first-rate, seagoing naval officer. He also served as naval aide to two Secretaries of the Navy: Charles Francis Adams from 1930 to 1933 and then Claude A. Swanson in 1933. He achieved the pinnacle of ship command when he was ordered to the battleship *West Virginia* as her captain in late 1933.

Although Stark still held the rank of captain in 1934, he was assigned as chief of the Bureau of Ordnance, a position normally held by a rear admiral. Promotion to the ranks of the flag officers soon followed. In 1937 Stark returned to sea duty in command first of a division of cruisers and then of all the cruisers of the Battle Force of the U.S. Fleet. President Franklin Roosevelt appointed him chief of naval operations in 1939, a position he held until 1942 when he went to London to become commander of U.S. Naval Forces in Europe. Although he passed the statutory retirement age in 1944, he remained at his London post until August 1945. He retired from active duty in 1946, following the joint congressional investigation into the attack on Pearl Harbor. During his retirement he engaged in many philanthropic activities; among them were the Navy Relief Society and Wilkes College in his native Wilkes-Barre, Pennsylvania.

Stark had a multifaceted naval career. Early he established a reputation as a first-rate shiphandler and a strict but fair officer. The ships he commanded were taut, happy ships, and they performed well. Later, he became an ordnance specialist. As chief of naval operations under President Roosevelt, he had to deal with a president who fancied himself a naval expert. Stark recognized that the Navy was not ready for war, and with the president's approval he sought and obtained authorization and funds from Congress to commence a shipbuilding program that would make the United States supreme at sea. In addition, he supervised a dramatic expansion both of naval facilities and of the numbers of officers and men in the Navy. The U.S. Navy that fought World War II was largely his creation.

Stark prepared an analysis of the world situation for President Roosevelt in November 1940. He concluded that there were four possible courses of action open to the United States. He recommended alternative "D," and this memorandum became known as the "Plan Dog Memorandum." ("D" in military parlance was "Dog" at that time.) It articulated the basic American grand strategy in World War II: since Germany presented the greatest threat to the United States, Germany, therefore, must be defeated first. In furtherance of this Atlantic strategy, Stark invited the British to send a high-level delegation to Washington in early 1941. The resulting ABC–1 agreement was important strategic planning in advance, and it laid the foundation for future Anglo-American cooperation during World War II. Stark was convinced that the survival of Britain was necessary for the security of the United States, and for this reason during the summer of 1941 he constantly urged the president to do more to assist the British.

By early autumn 1941 the U.S. Navy was for all practical purposes at war against Germany in the Atlantic in support of Great Britain.

Because Germany posed the greater danger to the United States, Stark opposed any action, such as an oil embargo, that might provoke a Japanese military and naval response in the Pacific. Meanwhile, the Army and the Navy did what little was possible to repair years of neglect of American fortifications and military and naval strength in the Pacific and Far East. As the crisis with Japan developed, he sent a series of official dispatches and letters, as well as informal letters, to the commanders of the U.S. Pacific and Asiatic Fleets informing them of current developments and future prospects.

Once America entered the war, Stark assisted in the establishment of the Combined Chiefs of Staff, the committee that planned Anglo-American strategy for the war under the overall direction of President Roosevelt and British Prime Minister Winston Churchill. It soon became clear that a senior American naval officer would be needed in London as liaison between the Navy Department and the British Admiralty, headquarters of America's principal naval ally. Since Stark had been instrumental in preparing the basis for Anlgo-American cooperation, he was the ideal choice for the post of commander, U.S. Naval Forces, Europe, with headquarters in London. His duties there were complex and varied. Because the Royal Navy had primary responsibility for the naval war in Europe, his liaison duties between Washington and London were critically important. In addition, he was responsible for the construction, maintenance, and then disestablishment of U.S. naval bases first in the United Kingdom and later in France and Germany; and for the complex logistic support for all U.S. naval forces in Europe. Finally, he performed numerous delicate diplomatic tasks, such as acting as American representative to French General Charles de Gaulle. Stark's efforts contributed immeasurably to the smoothness of joint and combined military relations and operations during World War II.

BIBLIOGRAPHY

Buell, Thomas B. *Master of Sea Power: Admiral Ernest J. King*. Boston: Little, Brown and Company, 1980.

Herzog, James H. *Closing the Open Door*. Annapolis, Md.: Naval Institute Press, 1973.

Leutze, James R. *Bargaining for Supremacy: Anglo-American Naval Collaboration, 1937–1941*. Chapel Hill: University of North Carolina Press, 1977.

Morton, Louis. "Germany First: The Basic Concept of Allied Strategy in World War II." In *Command Decisions*. Edited by Kent R. Greenfield. Washington, D.C.: U.S. Government Printing Office, 1960.

Simpson, B. Mitchell, III. "Admiral Harold R. Stark, USN, Chief of Naval Operations, 1939–1942." In *The Chiefs of U.S. Naval Operations*. Edited by Robert W. Love. Annapolis, Md.: Naval Institute Press, 1980.

B. MITCHELL SIMPSON III

STERNBERG, George Miller (b. Otsego County, N.Y., June 8, 1838; d. Washington, D.C., November 3, 1915), surgeon general, author, scientist. Sternberg is known as the father of American bacteriology.

George Miller Sternberg grew up in the academic and religious environment of Hartwick Seminary, Otsego County, New York, where his father was principal and minister. The oldest of a large family, young Sternberg interrupted his studies at Hartwick to work in a bookstore for a year and teach in rural schools for another three years to help out financially. By the time he returned to the Seminary, where he taught his last year, Sternberg was determined to be a doctor and spent his free hours studying anatomy and physiology with Dr. Horace Lathrop of Cooperstown. He did his formal medical training at Columbia University's College of Physicians and Surgeons in New York City, graduating in 1860. Before joing the Army in 1861, he worked briefly on Long Island and had a small practice in Elizabeth, New Jersey.

Sternberg was appointed assistant surgeon of the U.S. Army on May 28, 1861, and his first command was with General George Sykes' battalion in the Army of the Potomac. After being captured at the Battle of Bull Run on July 21 of the same year, Sternberg rejoined his division in front of Washington, participated in the battles of Gaines' Mill and Malvern Hill, contracted typhoid fever, and was sent north. For the remainder of the war, he served in Army hospitals in Rhode Island, Ohio, with General Nathaniel P. Banks' expedition to New Orleans and in the Office of the Medical Director of the Gulf.

From the close of the war until 1879, he served in various posts in Kansas, the Atlantic seaboard, and the West; participated in Indian campaigns, notably the Nez Perce Campaign; and contracted yellow fever at Fort Barrancas, Pensacola, thereafter becoming immune. After his experiences at Fort Barrancas, his interest in yellow fever aroused, Sternberg published two articles on the disease (in 1875 and 1877) in the *New Orleans Medical and Surgical Journal*, the first of many scientific papers and texts. An interest in disinfection was kindled when he represented the Army Medical Department at the American Public Health Association Meeting in Richmond in November 1878. Three years earlier he had been promoted to major.

In 1879 Sternberg was given an excellent opportunity to develop his enthusiasm for research and exploration when he was sent to Havana with the Yellow Fever Commission of the National Board of Health. His handling of yellow fever epidemics in the past (in New York Harbor, Pensacola, Fort Barrancas, New Orleans) and his personal immunity led to his selection. For three months, Sternberg looked into the cause and nature of the disease using for the first time photomicrography to examine the blood and tissues of yellow fever patients, and associating with Dr. Carlos Juan Finlay, the proponent of the transmission of yellow fever by mosquito.

For more than a decade the Army doctor continued his research in bacteriology and the etiology of disease. In 1880 the National Board of Health sent Sternberg to New Orleans to investigate the cause of malaria by testing the soundness of other people's claims. While stationed at Fort Mann, California, in 1881, Sternberg demonstrated and photographed the tubercle *bacillus*. The same year he announced simultaneously with Louis Pasteur his discovery of the *pneumococcus*, though he did not associate it in his first publication with pneumonia. Sent to Baltimore in 1884 as attending surgeon and examiner of recruits, Sternberg continued his experiments under the auspices of the American Public Health Association at the laboratories of the Johns Hopkins Hospital and in Washington, D. C. A year later he published a prize-winning paper on disinfection and disinfectants. In 1885 Sternberg was the first American to demonstrate the *plasmodium* of malaria, and in 1886 the *cabilli* of tuberculosis and typhoid fever. After investigative visits to Brazil and Mexico the following year, he proved fallacious the claims of their scientists to have discovered the cause of yellow fever. The decade of research enabled Sternberg to publish in 1892 his *Manual of Bacteriology*, the first textbook on the subject. The year before he had been promoted to lieutenant colonel.

Sternberg was rewarded for these endeavours by being made surgeon general in May 1893 with the rank of brigadier general. During his nine years as surgeon general, he established the Army Medical School, the Army Dental Corps, the Army Nurse Corps, the Army's first tuberculosis hospital at Fort Bayard, New Mexico, and a surgical hospital (forerunner of Walter Reed General Hospital) at Washington Barracks. He also appointed and supported the Typhoid Fever Board and Yellow Fever Commission (both headed by Major Walter Reed*) and was sent to Cuba during the Spanish-American war.

After retirement in 1902, Sternberg pursued philanthropic and social welfare activities. On behalf of the working people of Washington, he labored for decent housing and for tuberculosis care, which led to the founding of the Washington Sanitary Housing Company and the Washington Sanitorium. He was on the boards and active in hospitals and health and relief associations.

Sternberg's colorful and useful career was full of high honors. He was a delegate to the International Sanitary Conferences in Rome and Moscow, an honorary member of the Royal Academy of Medicine of Rome, Rio de Janeiro, and Havana, a fellow of the Royal Microscopel Society of London, president of the American Public Health Association, the American Medical Association, and other scientific organizations, and a recipient of many honorary degrees.

As surgeon general Sternberg is given credit for originating the idea of the Reed Board to investigate yellow fever in Cuba, for selecting its members, and for outlining its procedures. His earlier experiments in etiology of yellow fever cleared the ground for the board's discovery of the vector—an outstanding contribution to humanity. Of less impact but also important were his creating new corps, founding hospitals, and establishing the first Army Medical School, "America's oldest school of preventive medicine," which Surgeon General William Alexander Hammond* had tried in vain to do thirty years before. But as a war surgeon general, his reputation suffered. Political passion and war fever led some to accuse Sternberg of poor administration and to blame him for many of the medical problems affecting American troops—criticism that the Dodge Commission of 1900 later refuted.

His monument in Arlington testifies to his scientific achievements: "Pioneer American Bacteriologist, distinguished by the causation and prevention of infectious diseases, by his discovery of the microorganism causing pneumonia, and scientific investigation of yellow fever, which paved the way for the experimental demonstration of the mode of transmission of the disease." Sternberg's indefatigable work in the United States and in Central and South America, investigating fallacious claims regarding the causes of disease, eliminated many erroneous ideas and facilitated the work of scientists who followed him investigating the same field. Sternberg also gave us some of the earliest works on immunology, developed photomicrography in this country with remarkable photographs of bacteria and microorganisms, and contributed to scientific literature no less than 150 books, reports, and articles.

BIBLIOGRAPHY

Ashburn, P. M. *A History of the Medical Department of the United States Army.* Boston and New York: Houghton Mifflin Company, Riverside Press, 1929.

Hume, Edgar Erskine. *Victories of Army Medicine. Scientific Accomplishments of the Medical Department of the United States Army.* Philadelphia, London, Montreal: J. B. Lippincott Company, 1943.

Gibson, John M. *Soldier in White: The Life of General George Miller Sternberg.* Durham, N.C.: Duke University Press, 1958.

Sternberg, Martha L. *George Miller Sternberg; A Biography.* Chicago: American Medical Association, 1920.

Stone, R. French, M.D. *Biography of Eminent American Physicians and Surgeons.* Indianapolis: Carlon and Hollenbeck, Publishers, 1894.

MARY E. CONDON

STEUBEN, Frederic Willliam Ludolf Gerhard Augustin, "Baron von," (b. Magdeburg, Prussia, September 17, 1730; d. near Remsen, N.Y., November 28, 1794), professional soldier and inspector general of the Army of the United States. Steuben's signal accomplishment was to train the Continental Army as regular infantry of the line capable of standing up to the British in the field.

Steuben's father was an officer of engineers in the Prussian and Russian armies, and from his first days at Magdeburg, a key Prussian fortress, the future baron was exposed to guns, parades, and military trappings. Frederick William entered the Prussian Army in 1746 as a lance corporal. By the time the Seven Years' War broke out in 1756, he was a first lieutenant in the crack Lestwitz Regiment. Determined that the war would see him "either in Hades, or at the head of a regiment," Steuben attained neither, although he was twice wounded at Prague (1757) and again at Kunersdorf (1759). He spent a year on detached duty with a Free Battalion, as light infantry was then called, and for a time served as a general staff officer. Captured by the Russians in 1761, it was Steuben, probably while on parole, who was among the first to inform Frederick the Great of the death of his sworn enemy, the Empress Elizabeth, in 1762, causing Russia to change sides and then to drop out of the war altogether. In 1763 Steuben was one of fifteen officers selected to be taught the art of war under the personal supervision of Frederick, but soon after the war, probably because he was not of the hereditary nobility, he was retired from the Army.

Steuben spent the next decade at the court of a petty and bankrupt German principality, meanwhile trying in vain to find employment in the armies of France, the Empire, Sardinia, and even the East India Company. Not until the outbreak of the American Revolution was there a need for his talents. Recruited initially as a technical advisor to help train the American soldiers to look after arms and equipment that the French were sending surreptitiously before openly concluding a formal alliance, Steuben reached George Washington's* encampment at Valley Forge in February 1778. The Americans desperately lacked food, clothing, shelter, training, and discipline, and Washington, who was painfully aware that he needed a competent professional to hammer his army into shape, named Steuben acting inspector general.

In this capacity Steuben, working through a special company formed from the different regiments, taught the shivering Continentals the simplified rudiments of Prussian drill. By spring Washington's men knew how to bear arms, to march, to quickly form from column into line, and to fire with precision and at command. Above all they had learned how to use the bayonet. At Monmouth (June 28, 1778) those who saw the regiments of Washington's left wing wheel systematically into line under fire with the poise and precision of veterans, beat back a furious British assault and then counterattack with the bayonet, were impressed with what had been accomplished. When Congress officially created the Inspector General's Department the following February, Steuben became responsible for training all American troops.

Writing from memory, he salvaged whatever seemed essential from the Prussian regulations that could be adapted to a system based upon British organization and in a situation where soldiers were motivated by devotion to the cause and their leader rather than the harsh discipline and fear that kept Frederick's troops in line. By March 1779 he had produced his own *Regulations for the Order and Discipline of the Troops of the United States*, which by act of Congress became official doctrine. Steuben's Blue Book, as it was called, was reprinted more than seventy times before it was replaced in 1812 by a manual based upon French drill.

Steuben's accomplishments as inspector general have obscured his other services. When West Point was threatened in June 1780, Washington sent him to give "advice and assistance" to the commanding officer. Steuben also sat as a member of the court-martial that sentenced Major John André for his role in the plot to deliver this strategic stronghold to the British. Later that year Steuben went to Virginia to raise and equip reinforcements for Nathanael Greene* in the Carolinas. After surviving temporary setbacks when the British seized Richmond and later his own depot, Steuben rejoined Washington to command one of his three divisions before Yorktown. His previous experience in Europe was indispensable in helping to guide the Continentals in the intricacies of eighteenth-century siegecraft. Steuben saw no further action before he retired from the Army in 1784.

Although he remained in the United States, his hopes for a generous settlement from Congress for his services were never realized. A good disciplinarian but a bad manager of funds, Steuben could not even realize profit from the sixteen thousand acres in the Mohawk Valley given him by the state of New York. "In this country," he complained, "the laborers are barons and the barons are beggers." He continued to write on military affairs, and in his recommendations for a Swiss militia system to supplement the small Regular Army, for the harbor defenses of New York, and for the establishment of a military academy, Steuben continued to contribute to the military needs of the young republic. And as one of the founders of the Society of the Cincinnati he helped to keep alive the ideals of the Revolution. A confirmed bachelor, Steuben died on his Mohawk Valley estate without ever having found Eldorado: but if he was still in debt, he left his adopted nation even more in his debt.

Steuben was not an aristocrat. The prefix *von* signifying nobility had been inserted by a grandfather anxious to do well by his descendants, and he awarded himself the title of baron shortly before the American Revolution. Probably to cultivate the support of Frederick the Great, he also changed his last three christened names to August Henry Ferdinand, which "happened" also to be the names of Frederick's brothers, and just before leaving for America Steuben promoted himself in rank from captain to lieutenant general!

The *ersatz* baron, however, quickly became a genuine patriot, and herein lies the secret of his accomplishments. Any Prussian drill sergeant might have instructed the troops at Valley Forge, but Frederick himself could not have adapted the Prussian system to new and such radically different conditions. This required a mental retooling of the basic assumptions that lay behind all military training, which is why Steuben stressed the need for officers to cultivate the affection of their troops by treating the men "with every possible kindness and humanity." Fear and discipline would not motivate the American volunteer. Steuben's *Regulations*, it has been said, ran second only to the Bible on the reading list of American officers.

Many have paid tribute to the memory of Steuben and to his distinctive contributions to the cause of American independence, but of all testimonials the old general probably would have most preferred the "Creed adopted by the Officers of the American Army at Verplanck's Point" in 1792, particularly that portion of the "Apostle's Creed" affirming:

> We believe that George Washington is the only fit man in the world to head the American Army . . . that Nathaniel Greene was born a general . . . (and) that Baron Steuben has made us soldiers, and that he is capable of forming the whole world into solid column, and deploying it from the center. We believe in his *Blue Book*. We believe in General Knox and his artillery. And we believe in our bayonets. Amen!

BIBLIOGRAPHY

Busch, Noel F. *Winter Quarters. George Washington and the Continental Army at Valley Forge*. New York: Liveright, 1974.

Cronau, Rudolf. *The Army of the American Revolution and Its Organizer*. New York: Rudolf Cronau, 1923.

Kapp, Friedrich. *Life of Frederick William von Steuben*. New York: Mason Brothers, 1859.

Palmer, John McAuley. *General von Steuben*. New Haven, Conn.: Yale University Press, 1937.

Riling, Joseph R. *Baron von Steuben and his Regulations. Including a Complete Facsimile of the Original Regulations for the Order and Discipline of the Troops of the United States*. Philadelphia: Ray Riling Arms Books Company, 1966.

JAY LUVAAS

STILWELL, Joseph Warren (b. Palatka, Fla., March 19, 1883; d. San Francisco, Calif., October 12, 1946). Commander of U.S. Forces in the China-Burma-India Theater in World War II.

Joseph W. Stilwell was the older son of the four children born to Benjamin and Mary (Peene) Stilwell. Although born in Florida, Joseph spent his early years in Great Barrington, Massachusetts, and Yonkers, New York. Believing that the youth needed more discipline, his father arranged for Joseph to enter the U.S. Military Academy in 1900. Joseph graduated four years later, ranking thirty-second in a class of 124.

The 12th Infantry in the Philippines provided Stilwell with his first assignment. He stayed there for fourteen months, engaging in anti-guerrilla activities, before returning to West Point as an instructor in the Department of Modern Languages. Before 1917 he would alternate one more tour with the 12th Infantry in the Philippines (1911–1913) and with the faculty at West Point (1913–1917). While on leave in 1911, he made his first visit to China.

With the American entry into World War I Stilwell received a temporary promotion to major and an assignment as brigade adjutant in the 80th Division at Fort Lee, Virginia. In December 1917 he left for France, where he served as chief intelligence officer for the IV Corps.

During the war, Stilwell also saw staff service with the British 58th Division and the French XVII Corps (at Verdun). He returned to the American intelligence staff in April 1918, in time to help prepare plans for the offensive against St.-Mihiel. The explosion of an ammunition dump near Belrupt almost cost Stilwell his eyesight and severely impaired his vision. After the Armistice, Stilwell took part in the occupation duties assigned to the IV Corps. His wartime experiences earned for him not only the Distinguished Service Medal but also temporary promotions to lieutenant colonel and colonel.

Having been returned to the United States and the rank of captain, Stilwell volunteered to become a language officer for China. This assignment took him first to the University of California to study the Chinese language and then, with the new rank of major, to Peking by August 1920. While studying in California, Stilwell purchased land at Carmel, where he and his family eventually built a home.

Before Pearl Harbor, Stilwell served three separate tours in China, totaling ten years. From 1920 to 1923 he performed general duties as a student at the North China Union Language School, as a road engineer, and as an intelligence agent. Prior to his second assignment in China, Stilwell attended Infantry School at Fort Benning, Georgia (1923–1924) and Command and General Staff School at Fort Leavenworth, Kansas (1925–1926). The second China tour (1926–1929) placed Stilwell as a battalion commander in the 15th Infantry at Tientsin. The executive officer, George Catlett Marshall,* was impressed by Stilwell's performance. Stilwell eventually became acting chief of staff, and, while in China, he also earned a promotion to lieutenant colonel. Stilwell left China in 1929, proudly holding the title of handball champion of the Far East.

From 1929 to 1932 Stilwell taught at the Fort Benning Infantry School. He acquired the nickname "Vinegar Joe" there. An unhappy student, who had suffered one of Stilwell's notorious tongue-lashings, drew a caricature of Stilwell's head atop a bottle of vinegar. After a two-year stint training the organized reserves in San Diego, Stilwell returned to China for the third time (1935–1939). Promoted to colonel, he received orders to be the military attaché in China.

In 1939 George C. Marshall, the new army chief of staff, recommended Stilwell for promotion to brigadier general. With his first star, Stilwell assumed command of the 3d Brigade of the 2d Division at Fort Sam Houston, Texas. He merited a certain measure of fame by telling an inquiring cavalry officer that the only role for a horse in the fighting in China was "good eating, if you're hungry." In July 1941 Stilwell was named commanding officer of the III Corps with headquarters at the Presidio of Monterey, California. By then he had earned a second star and had commanded the 2d Division at Ford Ord, California.

Soon after Pearl Harbor, Marshall summoned Stilwell to Washington. Although originally slated to command a proposed invasion of North Africa, Stilwell, now with three stars, was subsequently appointed chief of staff to Generalissimo Chiang Kai-shek on March 10, 1942. Concurrently, Stilwell received two other challenging assignments: commanding officer of all American forces in the China-Burma-India Theater (CBI) and selection by Chiang Kai-shek to command the 5th and 6th Chinese armies. Traveling throughout CBI, Stilwell immediately became entangled in the Allied loss of Burma. Only a courageous "walkout" to India in May 1942 by Stilwell and over one hundred people averted his own capture by the Japanese.

Following the Burma debacle, Stilwell set out to revitalize the CBI and, specifically, to train and equip Chinese troops so that they could play a key role in the defeat of Japan. In 1943 he took on yet another difficult responsibility, becoming deputy commander to Lord Louis Francis Mountbatten for the new South East Asia Command. During 1944 Stilwell participated in the Chinese military efforts that reclaimed northern Burma. Friction with Chiang Kai-shek and other influential Chinese leaders gradually led to a crisis later that year. The U.S. government proposed that Chiang appoint General Stilwell (he had received a fourth star on August 1, 1944) to command all Chinese forces. The ensuing political and military deadlock grew more intense, and, eventually, Washington had to acquiesce in Chiang's demand that Stilwell be recalled.

Stilwell departed for the United States on October 21, 1944, under strict orders to maintain silence about his situation. In January 1945 he received an assignment to supervise the training of American ground forces, and, in June, he became commanding officer of the Tenth Army in Okinawa. The Japanese surrender cut short plans to have the Tenth Army participate in the invasion of Japan. Ironically, Stilwell might have been involved with the liberation forces destined for China, but Chiang Kai-shek insisted that Stilwell not be allowed to go to China. Stilwell attended the surrender ceremony aboard the U.S.S. *Missouri*, and on September 7, he presided over the surrender ceremony at Okinawa.

In October 1945 Stilwell returned to the United States. He was assigned temporarily as president of the War Equipment Board. Three months later, he earned an appointment as commanding officer of the Sixth Army in charge of Western Defense Command with headquarters in San Francisco. During 1946 his serious medical condition, heretofore undiscovered, was diagnosed as cancer of the stomach with severe deterioration of the liver. Joseph W. Stilwell died on October 12, 1946, in San Francisco. He left his wife, Winifred (Smith), whom he married in 1910, and five children.

Despite a long and successful Army career prior to December 1941, Stilwell is best remembered for his role in World War II. Controversy surrounds his war record. Some critics believe that he was hopelessly out of his league, trying to contend with Chinese politics and coalition diplomacy, while others think that he performed heroic duty, trying to carry the fight against the Japanese in what was supposed to be a key theater of the war.

In fact, Stilwell was thrust into an impossible situation. President Franklin D. Roosevelt, Secretary of War Henry Lewis Stimson,* and Army Chief of Staff George C. Marshall expected Stilwell not only to command all American forces in the CBI but also to serve as chief of staff to the Generalissimo. These two major responsibilities carried several other demanding duties, such as the administration of Lend Lease in China, command of the Chinese forces in India, command of the Chinese armies in Burma, and supervision of the Chinese Training and Combat Command. Each, of course, was a full-time job. Moreover, with the creation of the South East Asia Command (SEAC) in 1943, a third major responsibility fell to Stilwell, who was appointed deputy commander of SEAC.

His superiors in Washington repeatedly voiced their confidence to Stilwell that he was the best man for these difficult missions. Stimson, and especially Marshall, assured him that they understood his complex situation. Yet, Stilwell suffered the consequences of an eccentric organizational structure. Lord Mountbatten, Supreme Allied commander of South East Asia Command (SACSEA), pointed out that Stilwell could not possibly fulfill his three chief responsibilities because "only the Trinity could carry out his duties which require him to be in Delphi, Chungking and the Ledo Front simultaneously." Like a circus performer, Stilwell tried to wear three hats and juggle the attendant responsibilities of each, all at the same time. Questions of priorities and allegiance had to be resolved. Mountbatten thought that Stilwell, despite his title as deputy SACSEA, did not pursue the best interests of SEAC. Similarly, Chiang Kai-shek criticized his chief of staff for not sufficiently championing the Chinese cause in the politics of coalition diplomacy.

Another obstacle in Stilwell's path stemmed from the low supply priority allocated to CBI. The lack of equipment and the general shortage of supplies nourished a deep sense of frustration in Stilwell. He complained bitterly, "Peanut [Chiang Kai-shek] and I are on a raft, with one sandwich between us, and the rescue ship is headed away from the scene." Paradoxically, it is impossible to analyze Stilwell's performance without keeping in mind the relatively high strategic value placed on China. Future plans called for China to provide the base of operations for the final assault on Japan.

Stilwell was, above all, an excellent soldier. He made the military his career, and he knew his profession. In addition, his long experience in China before the war rendered him uniquely qualified for combat service there. He combined his expertise with an unshakable conviction that the Chinese soldier, if properly trained and equipped, was the equal of any soldier in the world. His confidence earned a certain confirmation when Chinese forces under his command reclaimed much of northern Burma during the first half of 1944. He devoted himself to breaking down the Chinese "defensive" psychology, especially that of the Kuomintang leadership under Chiang. His efforts, however, brought him only frustration. In fact, Stilwell courted controversy by expressing a desire to lead the Chinese Communist forces, who, in his opinion, earnestly wanted to fight the enemy.

Upon leaving China, Stilwell candidly acknowledged his "glaring deficiencies as a diplomat." He seemed to know his own strengths and weaknesses far better than anyone else. To the extent that each party caught in a personality clash bears a measure of responsibility for the problem, Stilwell must, consequently, be accorded some blame for the deteriorating relationship with Chiang Kai-shek. Stilwell disparagingly called him "Peanut" and made little effort to hide his strong dislike for the Generalissimo and the Kuomintang leadership. And this unfolded in a country where "face" and style are all-important. It is of little solace that he upheld the image of "Vinegar Joe" at the cost of damaged relations within the coalition and detraction from the war effort.

Nevertheless, Stilwell did realize some success in his assignments. His leadership contributed to Chinese military victories in Burma, which restored some confidence and self-esteem for the Chinese. Moreover, despite dark days, China did stay in the war against Japan. In addition, Stilwell's plans for the reorganization of the Chinese Army seemed to hold promise, at least at the time of his recall, for a brighter, more stable future in China.

Much of the criticism of Stilwell really should be directed against the central direction of the war in Washington. Heaping one impossible task after another on Stilwell, the American leaders simply deluded themselves with confident assurances about his considerable capabilities. Stimson later explained, "We knowingly gave him the toughest task in this war and it proved even harder than we anticipated."

Ironically, the crisis leading to his recall sprang from an attempt to give Stilwell yet another difficult assignment, namely, commander of all Chinese forces. No one man could handle all those responsibilities. His integrity, courage, and expertise were the equal to those of any man; nonetheless, somehow more was required in this impossible situation. Laden with hopeless tasks and conflicting responsibilities, Stilwell performed individual efforts that must be admired as among the greatest in World War II. The evolution of coalition warfare, however, had come to stress corporate management and institutionalized effort over rugged individualism. Perhaps his own words most effectively sum up his style and his wartime experience in China: "I've done my best and stood up for American interests. To hell with them."

BIBLIOGRAPHY

Belden, Jack. *Retreat with Stilwell*. New York: Alfred A. Knopf, 1943.

Dorn, Frank. *Walkout with Stilwell in Burma*. New York: Thomas Y. Crowell Company, 1971.

Romanus, Charles F., and Riley Sunderland. *Stilwell's Command Problems*. Washington, D.C.: Office of the Chief of Military History for the Department of the Army, 1956.

————. *Stilwell's Mission to China*. Washington, D.C.: Office of the Chief of Military History for the Department of the Army, 1953.

Tuchman, Barbara W. *Stilwell and the American Experience in China, 1911–1945*. New York: Macmillan Company, 1970.

White, Theodore H., ed. *The Stilwell Papers*. New York: William Sloane Associates, 1948.

                                                                    JOHN J. SBREGA

STIMSON, Henry Lewis (b. New York City, N.Y., September 21, 1867; d. Huntington, Long Island, N.Y., October 20, 1950), statesman. Stimson was Secretary of War during World War II.

Born into a family with strong roots in seventeenth-century Massachusetts, Henry L. Stimson was the son of Lewis Atterbury Stimson and Candace Wheeler. Stimson's father was a Civil War veteran who had first taken a seat on the stock exchange before studying the medicine he began to practice in 1873. Some three years later, Mrs. Stimson died; consequently, the young Henry and his sister went to live with their grandparents while their father buried himself in his demanding medical practice.

Following local schooling in New York, Stimson began his formal education by attending Andover Academy (1880–1884), Yale (1884–1888), and Harvard Law School (1888–1890). As Stimson later explained in his autobiography, Yale provided him with a "corporate spirit and democratic energy," whereas at Harvard he experienced the work of "independent thinking unlike anything [he] had met before."

From Harvard, Stimson returned to New York City and soon began a clerkship with the firm of Root and Clarke (1891). Two years later he married Mabel White of New Haven, Connecticut. While with Root and Clarke, Stimson became a skilled trial lawyer as he confronted the bustling world of American finance and corporate enterprise. Although he did not withdraw from this world as his father had done, Stimson had little professional interest in big corporate cases and fees (what he called the "green goods business"). Instead, he channeled his energies into public service in the manner of his mentor and partner, Elihu Root,* who was one of the most prominent men in the New York bar and the Republican party. Soon Stimson, who was a friend of Theodore Roosevelt* and a moderate Progressive, was fully engaged in local politics where he observed at first hand the activities of political bosses in the city.

In 1906 President Roosevelt appointed Stimson U.S. attorney for the Southern District of New York. He vigorously recruited talented young men (such as Felix Frankfurter) for his staff and then initiated a series of very successful cases on what he called "the new front of great corporate transgression" in an effort to stop unregulated and uncontrolled corporate behavior.

Returning to private law practice in 1909, Stimson ran unsuccessfully for governor of New York in 1910 and then joined the Taft administration in 1911 as secretary of war. From 1911 to 1913 Stimson tried to upgrade the U.S. Army through tactical reorganization of troop units to ensure more effective training and to resolve the hobbling conflict between the Army's line and staff officers by supporting his chief of staff, General Leonard Wood,* and the General Staff Corps.

When the Taft administration left office, Stimson returned to private life but found he preferred politics to practicing law. Thus, he began to advocate preparedness in 1915, and following the entry of the United States into World War I, he earned a commission and went to France in early 1918 when as a lieutenant colonel in the field artillery, he saw action along the Chemin des Dames in Lorraine.

After the war Stimson supported, with reservations, Woodrow Wilson's League of Nations and the World Court, but he spent most of the 1920s working on three big corporate cases. In 1927 President Calvin Coolidge sent him to Nicaragua to see if he could settle the fighting there. In five weeks he worked out a peace treaty, but hostilities resumed shortly after he left the country. Later that year Coolidge appointed Stimson governor general of the Philippines. Although he held that post for only a year (March 1928–February 1929), Stimson worked hard to improve relations between the United States and its island possession by promoting Filipino economic development rather than independence.

President Herbert Hoover recalled Stimson in 1929 to serve as secretary of state. In that office, he worked hard to improve relations with Latin America, to reduce naval armaments at the London Conference (1930), and to cope with the problem of war debts and reparations through a debt moratorium.

After fighting broke out in Mukden, Manchuria, between the Japanese and Chinese in September 1931, Hoover and Stimson tried to rally world opinion against Japan. These efforts were to no avail; consequently, Stimson sought stronger measures in the form of economic sanctions, but Hoover rejected this idea outright. Frustrated and unable to move the Japanese to a conciliatory position, Stimson proposed that the United States should not recognize a treaty between China and Japan that had been reached by military means. He supported his position with moral and legal arguments based on the Kellogg-Briand Pact of 1927, the League of Nations Covenant, and the Nine-Power Treaty of 1922. Nonrecognition, however, had little effect on the Japanese and changed nothing in China.

Stimson left office in 1933 and spent the next seven years periodically speaking out in favor of causes such as trade reciprocity and tariff reform. In the late 1930s he was outspokenly critical of isolationism and the existing neutrality legislation. He feared the growing power of the fascist states, and, when war came in 1939, he called for moral and material support to the nations fighting Germany and Italy. These controversial views found favor with President Franklin Roosevelt who appointed Stimson, then seventy-two, secretary of war.

Once again Stimson surrounded himself with talented and capable men and began to bring order and purpose to the War Department. He vigorously supported Roosevelt in the destroyer-for-bases deal, the peacetime draft law, and Lend Lease legislation. In his own department, Stimson exercised strong leadership and energy at the top by establishing programs that provided for orderly training and material for the troops. He also made sure that his chief of staff, General George Catlett Marshall,* had genuine power as the Army's senior officer, as they dealt with the problems of industrial mobilization and the deficiencies of American organization for war.

As relations with the Japanese continued to deteriorate, Stimson called for a firm policy in dealing with them, but he, like too many other American leaders, was caught by surprise when they attacked Pearl Harbor. Subsequent investigations of the attack found that he was not responsible for the inadequate defenses there. Later, he supported the evacuation and relocation of Japanese-Americans on the West Coast of the United States for national security reasons.

In 1942–1943 Stimson spent much of his time trying to find a way to fight the German U-boat menace in the Atlantic and to persuade Roosevelt to open a second front in Europe through a cross channel attack. The development of radar and the availability of great numbers of patrol planes and naval craft eventually checked the U-boats, but the cross channel attack was delayed by Allied leaders until the Normandy invasion of June 1944.

Because reorganization of the Army in 1942 took the secretary of war out of the direct line between the president and the chief of staff on purely strategic matters, Stimson found that he was principally occupied with administrative matters such as policy planning for the treatment of postwar Germany. On this matter, he strongly opposed Treasury Secretary Henry Morgenthau's plan to deindustrialize Germany, and he helped to persuade Roosevelt to adopt a more moderate plan.

In late 1941 Stimson also began to supervise development of the atomic bomb. After Roosevelt's death in 1945, he informed the new president, Harry S. Truman, of the work on the bomb—about which Truman knew nothing—and he chaired the Interim Committee which recommended that the bomb be used against Japan. Stimson later wrote that he supported this recommendation because he wanted "to end the war in victory with the least possible cost in the lives of the men in the armies which [he] had helped to raise."

Always an internationalist, Stimson subsequently recommended that the United States share its scientific knowledge of atomic power with the Soviet Union and Great Britain as a first step toward a mutual halt in further bomb construction. This far-sighted proposal was soon forgotten, however, in the growing Cold War between the United States and the Soviets. Stimson retired (September 21, 1945) and returned to his beloved home on Long Island where he lived until his death.

As a statesman, Henry L. Stimson was more the prophet than the prince in his idealistic attitude, his moral righteousness, and his vision for the United States in international politics. Yet he tempered these qualities with a flexibility of mind and purpose that indicated he was a man who was fully committed to making a better world through public service.

While serving as a cabinet officer under Hoover and Roosevelt, Stimson helped to shape the postwar world. The Hoover-Stimson policy of nonrecognition of Japanese aggression in China and his subsequent advocacy of continued support for China in the early 1940s were important factors in the Japanese decision to attack the United States. Consequently, some observers have argued that Stimson sought a "backdoor to war," but the accumulated evidence indicates that he was not a party to any "conspiracy" to force the Japanese to attack Pearl Harbor.

Throughout his public service, Stimson was always considered by his contemporaries to be a man of great integrity and moral stature. Nevertheless, in 1942 he ordered the relocation of thousands of Japanese-Americans on the West Coast on the grounds of national security, even though he knew his order violated their civil rights.

Similarly, Stimson recommended that the atomic bomb be dropped on Japan, which has led some critics to claim that he wanted the United States to use the bomb to manipulate the Russians in the Far East or Eastern Europe. But paradoxically, he then argued that the United States should exchange scientific information about atomic power with the Soviets in an effort to prevent a nuclear arms race—which indicated that he had a profound understanding of the consequences of this new weapon for the future peace of the world.

BIBLIOGRAPHY

Current, Richard N. *Secretary Stimson: A Study in Statecraft*. New Brunswick, N.J.: Rutgers University Press, 1954.
Ferrell, Robert H. *Henry L. Stimson*. Vol. II of Robert H. Ferrell and Samuel Flagg Bemis, eds. *The American Secretaries of State and Their Diplomacy*. New York: Cooper Square Publishers, 1963.
Morison, Elting E. *Turmoil and Tradition: A Study of the Life and Times of Henry L. Stimson*. Boston: Houghton Mifflin Company, 1960.
Stimson, Henry L. *The Far Eastern Crisis: Recollections and Observations*. New York: Harper and Brothers, 1936.
————, and McGeorge Bundy. *On Active Service in Peace and War*. New York: Harper and Brothers, 1947, 1948.

                                                          JOHN M. LINDLEY

STOCKTON, Robert Field (b. Princeton, N.J., August 20, 1795; d. Princeton, N.J., October 7, 1866), naval officer, politician. Stockton is sometimes considered the conqueror of California.

Stockton was born into one of the socially and politically most eminent families in New Jersey. His grandfather Richard Stockton had been a signer of the Declaration of Independence; his father, also named Richard, was a distinguished lawyer who served in both houses of Congress. His mother, Mary Field Stockton, came from a closely related family. The fourth of nine children, young Robert was privately educated until he entered the College of New Jersey (Princeton) in 1808. Although he remained in college only a year and a half, Stockton gave promise as a student of mathematics, languages, and elocution. On September 5, 1811, for reasons that are not clear, he secured a warrant as midshipman.

He joined the frigate *President* under Commodore John Rodgers,* participating in the June 23, 1812, chase of the British frigate *Belvidera*. When Rodgers assumed charge of the frigate *Guerriere*, building at Philadelphia, Stockton accompanied him. During the British invasion of Chesapeake Bay in 1814, Rodgers commanded a body of sailors assisting in the defense of Baltimore and Washington. Stockton served as his aide. He took part in the defense of Fort McHenry and as an acting master's mate in operations against a British squadron in the Potomac River. Stockton received his promotion to lieutenant on December 9, 1814. The following year he sailed to the Mediterranean in the *Guerriere* but soon moved to the schooner *Spitfire* as first lieutenant. In the *Spitfire* he participated in the June 1815 capture of a pair of Algerian warships which brought peace with that Barbary power. Stockton returned to the Mediterranean the following year in the ship-of-the-line *Washington* and joined the sloop-of-war *Erie* as second lieutenant. His tour was marked by a series of duels and temporary command of the sloop.

At about this time Stockton developed an interest in the American Colonization Society which later caused him to organize and head its New Jersey branch. In 1821, after placing the schooner *Alligator* in commission, he carried Dr. Eli Ayers of the Society to Africa and assisted him in negotiating the acquisition of the site for the first settlement in Liberia. While off Africa, Stockton seized four French slavers and during the return voyage fought a successful engagement with the Portuguese ship *Marriana Flora*. The *Alligator* subsequently joined the antipiracy patrol in the West Indies. On May 1, 1822, Stockton comanded an expedition that destroyed three piratical craft and freed their prize. The young officer helped survey the Southern coast in 1823–1824 during which time he met and married Harriet Maria Potter of Charleston, South Carolina. He returned to survey duty in 1826–1828.

On the death of his father in 1828, Stockton inherited the family estate "Morven" in Princeton, as well as a substantial income. During the next decade he concentrated on his growing financial interests, especially the Delaware and Raritan Canal and the Camden and Amboy Railroad across New Jersey. On their behalf he made at least one trip to Europe. He also devoted much energy and money to horse breeding, developing a noted stable. No less important were his political activities. Stockton began as a supporter of John Quincy Adams but became disenchanted with what he considered the president's excessive partisanship and shifted to ardent support of Andrew Jackson.*

Although promoted to master commandant on May 27, 1830, Stockton did not resume his naval career until 1838 when he joined the ship-of-the-line *Ohio* as executive officer. Upon his promotion to captain on December 8, 1838, Stockton left the ship in the Mediterranean to visit England to study naval architecture and marine engineering. This brought him into contact with the Swedish engineer John Ericsson* who in 1839 built the 39-ton iron-hulled tug *Robert F. Stockton* for use on the Delaware and Raritan Canal. She was the first commercially successful screw steamer. Stockton's experience with her led him to promote screw propulsion within the U.S. Navy and to encourage Ericsson to move to America.

Following his return home Stockton threw himself into the 1840 elections, stumping New Jersey for the Whig ticket of William Henry Harrison* and John Tyler. From this effort developed a close and long-lasting personal friendship with Tyler. Stockton supported Tyler in his break with the Whigs in 1841. Later that year Tyler offered to appoint him Secretary of the Navy which Stockton refused, preferring to superintend the construction of his long-sought, and Ericsson-designed, screw warship, the *Princeton*. Upon completion of the pioneer vessel, Stockton made a demonstration voyage along the coast. Off Washington on February 28, 1844, while the vessel was thronged by distinguished visitors, the *Peacemaker*, a 12-inch wrought iron shell-gun designed by Stockton burst, killing the secretaries of state and Navy and a number of others. Stockton himself was among the injured. In April 1845 the James K. Polk administration diverted Stockton and a small squadron including the *Princeton* from a Mediterranean cruise to Texas waters to deter any Mexican action during the annexation negotiations. While in Texas Stockton, apparently on his own, participated in a scheme to provoke a Mexican attack as a means of hastening Texan acceptance of annexation.

In October 1845 he embarked in the frigate *Congress* to join the Pacific Squadron as vice commodore. Stockton reached California immediately following the seizure of Monterrey and San Francisco to find the excessively cautious and ailing Commodore John D. Sloat fearful that he had acted precipitously. Sloat hastily transferred command to Stockton and departed. Stockton then formed an alliance with the politically powerful John Charles Frémont;* took Frément's band of "Bear Flaggers" into service; issued a bombastic proclamation announcing his intention to seize the remainder of the state; and completed the conquest by the middle of August. Stockton's ill-conceived occupation policies provoked a revolt in Los Angeles in late September which rapidly spread throughout all of southern California. Not until late December 1846 could Stockton collect sufficient supplies at San Diego to start the reconquest. Stockton's sailor army, stiffened by a small detachment of regular soldiers who had escorted Brigadier General Stephen Watts Kearny* from Santa Fe, fought two skirmishes with the rebels and reoccupied Los Angeles on January 10, 1847. Three days later Frémont, marching south from Monterrey, unilaterally signed a convention with the remnants of the rebels to end the uprising.

After the capture of Los Angeles, a bitter dispute arose between Stockton and Kearny over control of the government. Stockton as conquerer claimed the right to create an occupation government, while Kearny relied on his orders from the president to govern the province. The deadlock lasted nearly two months and was resolved only by the arrival of Commodore W. Branford Shubrick who superseded Stockton in command.

Stockton returned home overland to receive a hero's welcome as the conqueror of California. At a banquet in his honor in Philadelphia on November 30, 1847, he advocated the occupation of all of Mexico as the only way to regenerate its inhabitants and prepare them for self-government. Despite the public welcome, Stockton's reputation within the service suffered badly from his California activities. He had shown himself too arrogant, inflexible, ethnocentric, and militarily incompetent to secure another command. On May 28, 1850, he resigned from the Navy.

As the leader of the New Jersey Democrats, Stockton secured election to the U. S. Senate, taking his seat on March 4, 1851. In the Senate he played a major role in abolishing flogging and a less vigorous one in the drive to stop the Navy's grog ration. Stockton resigned his seat on January 10, 1853, and accepted the presidency of the Delaware and Raritan Canal. Apparently related to his departure from the Senate was his growing interest in the Know Nothing movement. He did not again serve in public office except to attend the Washington Peace Conference promoted in 1861 by ex-President Tyler in an abortive effort to halt the slide into the Civil War.

Stockton exemplified the vigorous, self-assured, and often irritating leaders of midcentury America. A highly religious man, he strove to correct injustices and to use his position and wealth for the general good. Yet as his California activities demonstrated, he lacked balance and tolerance and demonstrated a weak grasp of military strategy, as well as a tendency to replace reason with bombast.

BIBLIOGRAPHY

Bancroft, Hubert Howe. *History of California*. Vol. 5. San Francisco: The History Company, 1888.
Bauer, K. Jack. *The Mexican War, 1846–1848*. New York: Macmillan Company, 1974.
————. *Surfboats and Horse Marines*. Annapolis, Md.: Naval Institute Press, 1969.
Langley, Harold D. *Social Reform in the United States Navy, 1798–1867*. Urbana: University of Illinois Press, 1967.
Price, Glenn W. *Origins of the War with Mexico*. Austin: University of Texas Press, 1967.
Seager, Robert, II. *And Tyler Too*. New York: McGraw-Hill Book Company, 1963.
Smith, Justin H. *The War with Mexico*. 2 vols. New York: Macmillan Company, 1919.

K. JACK BAUER

STODDERT, Benjamin (b. Charles County, Md., 1751; d. Georgetown, Md., December 13, 1813), first Secretary of the Navy. Stoddert is considered the architect of Federalist naval policy.

Stoddert, a descendant of an old Scotch family, was just completing his apprenticeship as a merchant when the American Revolution began. In 1777 he served as a captain, later major, in a Pennsylvania cavalry regiment, but he resigned in April 1779 when his regiment was united with another and he was outranked by all its officers. Twice wounded at the Battle of Brandywine, he was granted a physical discharge. He then served, however, as secretary of the Board of War from September 1, 1779, to February 6, 1781. With the war over, he turned to commerce. Moving with his bride to Georgetown, Maryland, he entered the mercantile firm of Forrest, Stoddert, and Murdock, which traded particularly with England and France. He not only acquired large tracts of land in what is now the District of Columbia, but he also served President George Washington* by quietly buying land for the government in the District. He also sired eight children.

A staunch Federalist and highly respected businessman, at the age of forty-six years Stoddert, after George Cabot declined, was asked by President John Adams to fill the newly created position of Secretary of the Navy. Stoddert agreed and on June 17, 1798, entered upon his duties, at $800 a year, at the capital, then in Philadelphia.

Stoddert assumed office when the foreign relations of the United States were exceedingly difficult. American ships were caught between the orders in council of the British and the decrees of the French issued during the war that had begun in 1793. The John Jay Treaty with Britain (1796) eased British spoliations and impressment; it also helped restore Anglo-American harmony to the point that the two navies cooperated against the French, particularly in the West Indies. It provoked France, however, to loose its privateers upon American commerce and to insult the United States in the XYZ Affair in 1797, thereby driving President Adams to break diplomatic relations; he would have declared war had not Stoddert and others objected. Nevertheless, the Navy had to be augmented if a war were to be fought at sea. Moreover, it was necessary to separate its administration, heretofore vested in the War Department. Therefore, a Navy Department was created on April 30, 1798.

The Navy Act of 1794, passed from a desire to chastise the Barbary pirates, established the U.S. Navy by providing that six frigates be acquired "by purchase or otherwise." If they were to be built, construction on them would stop if satisfactory terms were made with Algiers. Despite peace with Algiers in 1796, Federalists were able to overcome Republican opposition and call for the completion of at least three of the yet unfinished ships (the 44-gun frigates *Constitution* and *United States* and the 36-gun frigate *Constellation*).

On May 28, 1798, Congress authorized American warships to capture French warships and privateers, but no merchantmen, in American waters; on June 13, it suspended commerce with France; and on July 7 it abrogated its treaties with France and then authorized the capture of its armed ships on the high seas. The Quasi-War had begun. On July 11 Congress created the Marine Corps, and Stoddert drafted the rules for its administration.

When Stoddert took office, his Navy consisted of twenty-two ships carrying 456 guns and 3,484 men. In two years he augmented this force to thirty-five warships and fifteen lesser vessels, with 154 officers, six thousand enlisted men, and about one thousand marines. This force reduced French privateering to such negligble proportions that in 1799 Stoddert advocated showing the flag in European waters. Arguments over seniority in rank between the officers detailed to command the *Constitution* and the *United States* so delayed sailing that the venture was canceled.

Although Stoddert was authorized to control operations as well as personnel and logistics, he was granted only the aid of two officers, a chief clerk, various subordinate clerks, and a messenger. While he saw that ships were repaired and supplied through naval agents located in each major port, he took it upon himself to direct and handle his naval officers. Knowing that their record in the Quasi-War would establish important traditions, he sought officers eager to excel. Of his five leading captains—John Barry, Samuel Nicholson, Silas Talbot, Richard Dale, and Thomas Truxton*—he found in the last the ideal qualities he sought. In turn, he accepted many useful suggestions for improvement that Truxton offered. Among these was a description of the duties aboard ship that he used to revise *Navy Regulations*.

When President Adams sought peace with France beginning in 1799, the British became hostile again and increased their spoliations and impressment. Unlike the other cabinet members, Stoddert advised Adams that he should continue to seek peace. Adams did so, with the result that he split his party and suffered defeat in the election of 1800. He never held Stoddert culpable, and he believed his affirmation of loyalty.

With the war ended and the government having moved to Washington, Stoddert's Navy was at peak strength. The Navy had taken eighty-four French ships and recaptured about 150 American vessels. It had so protected American commerce during the Quasi-War that overseas trade had actually increased, thereby furnishing badly needed tax revenues. Fearing too drastic a demobilization, Stoddert asked Congress to keep thirteen frigates in the peacetime Navy and to authorize a permanent naval establishment of twelve 74-gun ships-of-the-line, twelve frigates, and twenty to thirty smaller ships, "sufficient to inspire respect for our neutrality in future European Wars." Were not such a force provided, the next European war would see American ships taken, American seamen impressed, and "our sea coast ports and harbors insulted and ultimately the weaker parts of the Union invaded." Congress ignored his argument; by 1801 most of his ships had been sold off or laid up, and he had only six left on active duty. Nor did Congress accept Stoddert's suggestion that a board of senior officers be established to advise the secretary on professional matters. Such a board was eventually created—in 1815. Congress left alone, however, the six navy yards he had created with funds he had switched from appropriations for building ships.

Stoddert retired on March 31, 1801, and returned to Georgetown and the world of commerce. His profits dwindled because of Jeffersonian restrictions on trade with England and France, the War of 1812, and the shift of trade from inland ports to large coastal harbors. He also was a good prophet in predicting that the incoming Jeffersonian-Republicans would fail to provide a navy adequate to protect the nation's interests.

Given an awfully broad span of control, Stoddert assumed responsibilities later divided among a secretary, bureau chiefs, and a chief of naval operations. Throughout his administration he had to overcome objections from the Republicans. These Francophiles held that the War Department sufficed to administer the Navy. They opposed a navy because it was expensive, increased the national debt, expanded presidential power, would involve the United States at war with Britain, would lead to the creation of a standing navy and an aristocratic officer corps, and would delay the development of the West. Furthermore, the Jeffersonians argued that it made no sense to have a large navy when no European power could send its entire fleet to America because of weather and the need to defend the homeland. Stoddert's answer was that a navy was necessary to support the nation's great maritime interests, thereby reducing insurance rates and, in the case of the Barbary corsairs, avoid the humiliation of paying tribute. A navy had economic and political as well as military importance: it had helped win our independence, protected the nation and its trade and fisheries, was useful in winning respect for a policy of neutrality, and could be used to hold the balance of power in America and gain respect from Europe by threatening the West Indies. Finally, a navy was beneficial economically to all sections, for the Southern states could provide ship timbers and naval stores; the Middle States, iron; and the North, shipbuilding and skilled seamen.

Stoddert was able to obtain the ships to fight the Quasi-War and, largely by drawing upon the merchant marine, to provide them with crews. With the British friendly, he concentrated upon the West Indies where the French were at a disadvantage, provided escort for numerous commercial convoys, and from the British he learned about signaling, tactics for maneuvering in formation, and the spirit that generates professionalism. He had supported Adams in seeking peace with France, in abrogating the possibly entangling French Alliance of 1778, and in clearing the way for the Louisiana Purchase. Although the ships he acquired were sold off and his men were demobilized, the navy yards and timber preserves he acquired remained for future use. Conscious that he was the first secretary of the Navy and thus responsible for creating a tradition of greatness, he carefully established sound precedents and was humble enough to accept advice in so doing, as from Joshua Humphreys* on shipbuilding and Truxton on naval rules and regulations and training methods. An exceedingly capable administrator, he was also well versed in the meaning and need of sea power.

BIBLIOGRAPHY

Allen, George W. *Our Naval War with France*. Boston: Houghton Mifflin Company, 1909.
———. *Our Navy and the Barbary Corsairs*. Boston: Houghton Mifflin Company, 1905.
Carigg, Joseph J. "Benjamin Stoddert." In *The American Secretaries of the Navy*. Edited by Paolo E. Coletta. 2 vols. Annapolis, Md.: Naval Institute Press, 1979.
Jones, Robert F. "The Naval Thought and Policy of Benjamin Stoddert, First Secretary of the Navy, 1798–1801." *American Neptune* 24 (January 1964): 61–69.

PAOLO E. COLETTA

STUART, James Ewell Brown ("Jeb"), (b. Laurel Hill Plantation, Patrick County, Va., February 6, 1833; d. Richmond, Va., May 12, 1864), Army officer. Stuart commanded the Cavalry Corps, Army of Northern Virginia, during the Civil War.

Stuart was the son of Archibald and Elizabeth Pannill Stuart; the family, of Scottish descent, settled in Virginia in 1738. After an early education at home and in Wytheville, Virginia, and two years at Emory and Henry College, he was appointed to the U.S. Military Academy and graduated thirteenth of forty-six in the class of 1854. Brevetted second lieutenant in the Regiment of Mounted Rifles, he was commissioned in that rank on October 31, 1854, and in March 1855 he was transferred to the 1st Cavalry Regiment. On November 14, 1855, at Fort Leavenworth, Kansas, he married Flora, daughter of Colonel Philip St. George Cooke.* Three children (one of whom died in infancy) were born of the marriage. In Stuart's five years with the 1st Cavalry, it kept the peace in "Bleeding Kansas'' and carried out expeditions, in one of which he was wounded, against hostile Indians. In October 1859, while on leave, Stuart volunteered as aide to Robert Edward Lee* and with him participated in the capture of John Brown at Harper's Ferry.

In January 1861 Stuart applied for "a position" in the Southern army which he expected to be formed; on May 3, following the secession of Virginia and his own promotion to captain, he resigned from the U.S. Army. Commissioned in the state forces of Virginia on May 6, 1861, he was assigned in June to the command of the 1st Virginia Cavalry, as colonel from July 16. While training his regiment, he also screened the army of Joseph Eggleston Johnston* at Winchester, Virginia, when the Federal army of Robert R. Paterson moved against it. Stuart distinguished himself in the Battle of Bull Run by the manner in which he protected the left flank of the brigade comanded by Thomas Jonathan ("Stonewall") Jackson.* On September 21 Stuart was promoted to brigadier general, Confederate States Army, and given command of a five-regiment cavalry brigade.

In the spring of 1862 Stuart attracted national attention. Sent by General Lee to locate the right flank of the Union Army on the Peninsula, he circled the army instead of returning the way he had come. This "brilliant exploit," as Lee called it, made Stuart the cavalryman par excellence of the Confederacy.

After the Seven Days' battles, in which Stuart covered Jackson's approach and protected his flanks, he was promoted to major general and given command of the cavalry of the Army of Northern Virginia, organized as a three-brigade division. In the Second Bull Run Campaign, he led a raid around the flank of the Union Army and captured papers belonging to General John Pope,* which led to Lee sending Jackson's corps on its epic march to Pope's rear and thus set the stage for the Battle of Second Bull Run. Occupied mainly in scouting and screening in the ensuing Maryland Campaign, in the Battle of Antietam Stuart's cavalry and artillery, in a flank position, assisted materially in checking the Federal assaults on Jackson. After the battle, and the retreat of the army to Winchester, Stuart led a raid (October 9–12) to Chambersburg, Pennsylvania; riding around the Union Army, he outdistanced pursuit and recrossed the Potomac with twelve hundred captured horses, and with the loss of one man wounded. As the Union and Confederate armies moved east toward Fredericksburg, Stuart clashed repeatedly with the Federal cavalry, notably at Barbee's Cross Roads (November 5). In the three months following the Battle of Fredericksburg, his cavalry engaged in constant harassment of the Federal lines of communication.

After reporting to General Lee the advance of the Union Army toward Chancellorsville, Stuart brought him word on the evening of May 1, 1863, that the Federal right flank was "in the air." This led to Jackson's flank march and successful attack on the XI Corps. When Jackson and Ambrose Powell Hill* were wounded on the evening of May 2, Stuart took command of the corps, and the next morning, in some of the heaviest fighting of the war, drove the Federal infantry out of Chancellorsville.

The cavalry subsequently was given a month's rest, but at dawn on June 9, at Brandy Station, it was attacked by General Alfred Pleasanton's Federal cavalry in full strength. Stuart was saved from a damaging defeat by his own determined leadership (lacking on the other side), the valor of his men, and a great deal of luck. He was severely criticized by Southern newspapers for having been taken by surprise; there is little doubt that the criticism influenced his actions in the ensuing campaign.

Following Brandy Station, Stuart had the task of keeping the Federal cavalry away from the gaps through the Blue Ridge, thus protecting the march of the Confederate infantry northward to Pennsylvania. On June 17, 19 and 21, the two cavalry forces fought at Aldie, Middleburg, and Upperville, respectively. Tactically defeated in the last two of these engagements, Stuart nevertheless prevented the Federals from reaching the gaps. General Lee's orders to Stuart (June 23) for his march into Maryland lacked precision; Stuart interpreted them as authorizing a circuit of the Union Army, and the crossing of the Potomac well to the east of the mountains. The intent of Lee's orders, and the validity of Stuart's interpretation, remain the subject of controversy. The result was that for seven days (June 25–July 1) Stuart and his three best brigades were out of touch with their army. Lee was to state that his movements were "much embarrassed" by their absence.

Stuart's march, slowed by the 125 supply wagons he captured on June 28 and by a fight with Judson Kilpatrick's cavalry at Hanover on June 30, took him north to Carlisle, Pennsylvania, where he learned that the army was at Gettysburg. He arrived there on July 2, with an exhausted command. The next day, at Cress's Ridge, he attacked the cavalry brigades of J. B. McIntosh and George Armstrong Custer,* with the evident objective (contrary to his claim) of breaking through to the rear of the Union position on Cemetery Ridge, as it was being charged frontally by George Edward Pickett.* The attack failed, and Stuart was himself driven back with loss. On the retreat to the Potomac, he protected the left flank and rear of the army, and in a series of combats with the Federal cavalry, kept it away from Lee's position at Williamsport until the army was able to recross the river.

In August Stuart's command was reorganized into a corps of two divisions, but he was not promoted to lieutenant general, the rank of officers commanding corps of infantry. In the Bristoe Campaign, at Liberty Mills (September 23), he was attacked front and rear by the divisions of Kilpatrick and John Buford, but extricated himself with a vigorous counterattack. At Brandy Station (October 11), the situation was reversed; he had Buford and Kilpatrick surrounded, but they were able to break through to safety. At Buckland Mills (October 19), Stuart routed Henry E. Davies, Jr.'s, cavalry brigade. Except for the brief interruption of the Mine Run Campaign (November 26–December 1), the winter was uneventful, Stuart's chief concern being the steady deterioration of the condition and numbers of his horses.

In March 1864 Philip Henry Sheridan* was given command of the Cavalry Corps of the Army of the Potomac. On the night of May 3 the Union Army advanced into the Wilderness. Until the arrival of Lee's infantry, Stuart harried the Federal advance, and on May 5 and 6, posted on the right of the army, he had a series of hard fights with Federal cavalry.

On May 9, authorized to cut loose from the army in order to "whip Stuart," Sheridan started toward Richmond with his corps of about ten thousand. Stuart started after him, but with only three of his six brigades, numbering about four thousand. Stuart's conduct of the operation was faulty in the extreme. On May 11, when he offered battle at Yellow Tavern, all the advantage lay with Sheridan's Federals, and Stuart was decisively defeated. In the thick of the fight, Stuart was mortally wounded; removed to Richmond, he died on the evening of the next day.

Stuart's place in the Confederate pantheon, beside Lee and Jackson, is secure; he owes it as much to his impact on the imagination as to his military achievements. Faced with the disciplinary problems that plagued all Confederate commanders, he created the Confederate cavalry in the East and made it in his own image, an extension of his high spirits and aggressiveness. He led by example, and had the trust and devotion of his men. Stuart had his faults; his boisterousness, flamboyance, vanity, and craving for admiration repelled many. He was only twenty-eight years old when he became a major general, however, and his faults were those of youth and of the high mettle which in a cavalryman was a virtue. Underlying them were a deep religious faith and an unquestioning dedication to the cause for which he fought. It was no common man who gained the affection and admiration of Jackson and Lee.

As a cavalryman, Stuart's greatest skill was that of an outpost officer, locating and identifying the enemy and ascertaining his intentions. When news of Stuart's death was brought to Lee, he said, "He never brought me a piece of false information." In a postwar conversation, Lee spoke of him as his "ideal of a soldier . . . always cheerful . . . always ready for any work, and always reliable."

Stuart's tactics were in the light cavalry tradition; he was devoted by instinct to the "cavalry spirit," the aggressive movement, the headlong charge with the saber. There were no subtleties, no novelties, in his battle tactics. Only when the character of the terrain inhibited mounted action did he resort to dismounted tactics. Commanding an auxiliary force, he did not make strategic decisions, nor did his talents lie in that direction. Stuart can be faulted for his addiction to showy raids, which, apart from their impact on morale, had minimal military value; he can be faulted also for the excessive demands he often made on the stamina of his men and animals. But, with all his weaknesses and strengths, human and military, he was unique. There was only one Jeb Stuart, and he had no successor.

BIBLIOGRAPHY

Blackford, William W. *War Years with Jeb Stuart*. New York: Charles Scribner's Sons, 1945.

Borcke, Heros von. *Memoirs of the Confederate War for Independence*. Edinburgh and London: W. Blackwood and Sons, 1866; reprinted, New York, 1938.

McClellan, Henry B. *I Rode with Jeb Stuart*. Bloomington: Indiana University Press, 1958 (original edition, 1885).

Starr, Stephen Z. *The Union Cavalry in the Civil War*. 2 vols. Baton Rouge: Louisiana State University Press, 1979–.

Thomason, John W., Jr. *Jeb Stuart*. New York: Charles Scribner's Sons, 1941.

STEPHEN Z. STARR

SULLIVAN, John (b. Somersworth, N.H., February 17, 1740; d. January 23, 1795, Durham, N.H.), Revolutionary War general. Sullivan commanded expeditions to Rhode Island and to the Iroquois Country.

The son of Irish indentured servants who settled in New Hampshire, John Sullivan was educated by his schoolteacher father. Young John read law in Portsmouth, and at nineteen, he opened his own practice. After marriage in 1760, he resided in Durham where he purchased land, built mills, and pursued a legal career. Sullivan was a militia major, a champion of American independence, and in November 1774 he led a raid on the British fortress in Portsmouth. Regarded as an ardent spokesman for freedom, he was elected to the Provincial Assembly and to the Continental Congress.

Appointed a brigadier general in June 1775, Sullivan led the New Hampshire brigade at the siege of Boston where his two raids on British outposts were repulsed. During the investment of the city, Sullivan was applauded for valor, but he frequently quarreled with the medical and commissary departments, and bickered with his Assembly over regimental appointments.

In April 1776 Sullivan was ordered to reinforce the Northern Army at Quebec. When he arrived on the scene, the patriot forces were retreating up the St. Lawrence River before an enemy offensive. Determined to cling to Canada, Sullivan devised an ill-fated attack at Three Rivers. Thereafter, his command retired up the Sorel River to Lake Champlain, and then to the safety of Fort Ticonderoga. Superseded by General Horatio Gates,* Sullivan threatened to resign, but soothed by George Washington* and by promotion to major general, he remained in the Army.

Sullivan next participated in the Long Island Campaign. His task in August 1776 was to guard roads leading to Brooklyn Heights which protected the East River. Sullivan failed to watch Jamaica Pass through which British troops poured at night to outflank the American regiments. Fighting bravely, the outwitted Sullivan was captured at Flatbush Pass. Washington managed to ferry his army to New York, and in October he extricated his men from Manhattan to White Plains.

As a prisoner of Lord William Howe, the British commander, Sullivan agreed to convey armistice terms to the rebels, and he was paroled to present these arrangements to Congress. Angry with Sullivan's battlefield blunders and with his unauthorized role in the peace overtures, delegates questioned his competence. By September Sullivan was exchanged, and soon after, he joined Washington's retreat through New Jersey to the Delaware.

Sullivan served skillfully under Washington at the battle of Trenton. Likewise at Princeton, his brigade played a key role in capturing the village. In these engagements, Sullivan demonstrated his tactical ability, but under Washington's close supervision. Yet Sullivan became increasingly embittered—he suffered from a stomach ulcer, he drank excessively, and he resented being denied the command of Ticonderoga. Even Washington, invariably patient with his erring generals, had to admonish Sullivan for his intemperate outbursts.

Anxious to demonstrate his military prowess, Sullivan in August 1777 planned a daring sortie on Staten Island. But because of faulty intelligence, insufficient boats, and poor troop discipline, the expedition fared so poorly that Sullivan underwent a court of inquiry. Even though he was exonerated, delegates continued to question his fitness for command, but Washington maintained his defense of the fiery Irishman. Another crucial test for Sullivan came at Brandywine in September 1777 when Washington assigned him the right wing. Sullivan neglected to study the terrain and to reconnoiter enemy movements, and like Washington, he overlooked a wide flanking movement by the enemy. Sullivan's subordinates were unable to reinforce him. His division was saved from destruction only by the timely arrival of Nathanael Greene's* troops and by Howe's lethargic pursuit after the British victory. Delegates again clamored for Sullivan's dismissal, but Washington assumed the blame for the disaster. Then came another test for Sullivan, for Washington entrusted him to lead the American right wing during the attack in October on Germantown. As a result of several mishaps—poor maps, complicated maneuvers performed in darkness, a stout British artillery defense—the assault was repulsed. Washington again rose to Sullivan's defense in Congress, but, this time somewhat belatedly.

Sullivan served at Valley Forge in the winter of 1777–1778 where his major contribution was to direct the construction of a bridge over the Schuylkill. During the encampment, Sullivan complained incessantly about the lack of proper rewards due him and about his right to an independent command. Washington finally relented and directed Sullivan to lead an expedition against the British naval base at Newport, Rhode Island, and to cooperate in the difficult amphibious operation with a French naval squadron.

Sullivan planned astutely for the venture, but, typically, he antagonized his subordinates and his superiors with endless complaints. He also angered the French over protocol, and he changed his tactics without consulting his allies. Close to success during the siege in August 1778, Sullivan suddenly had to terminate his attack, for the French ships, confronted unexpectedly by a British fleet, had to sail off during a storm to Boston. After fierce combat at Quaker Hill, Sullivan skillfully evacuated his troops from the island. But he tactlessly denounced the French for leaving the Americans stranded, and he thereby strained the Bourbon alliance.

Martial glory had again eluded Sullivan, but in March 1779 he had another opportunity. With some misgivings, Washington appointed him to lead an expedition to the Finger Lakes of New York in order to destroy the Iroquois war potential. Washington planned the undertaking, assigned mostly Continentals to the task, and made it one of the largest offensive operations of the war. With General James Clinton forging westward along the Mohawk, Colonel Daniel Broadhead boating up the Allegheny, and Sullivan's main force marching up the Susquehanna, the Americans planned to devastate the settlements of the Six Nations. Although Sullivan was ordered to invade in May, he procrastinated for weeks at Easton and then at Tioga Point, embittered about the lack of men and material. In August Sullivan led five thousand troops in the Indian Country, razing villages, destroying crops, and butchering cattle. At Newton (Elmira), a small Indian force retaliated, but Sullivan easily repulsed them. He continued westward, wrecking settlements on the Genesee River, but encountering supply shortages, he did not attack the British base at Fort Niagara. Sullivan temporarily broke the power of the Iroquois and received the thanks of Congress. Yet the contentious Sullivan provoked another controversy by charging the Board of War with inadequte support during his march to the interior. When Sullivan again offered to resign his commission, Congress accepted, and his military career was terminated.

Sullivan's fitness for high command was questionable, but he was named to please New Hampshire delegates. Brave to the point of folly and ambitious for national fame, Sullivan overestimated his abilities.

His forays on British lines at Boston in 1775 were poorly planned. His decision to attack at Three Rivers was strategically unsound, and his indecisiveness during the retreat from Canada almost cost the nation the Northern army. His selection of swampy Ile aux Noix at the tip of Lake Champlain to regroup his smallpox-ridden force was a serious blunder; he was saved only by General Philip Schuyler's* alacrity in evacuating him by boats. Although staff coordination at Long Island was faulty, Sullivan alone was responsible for guarding the American right flank, and his negligence here was inexcusable. His raid on Staten Island was another fiasco. Sullivan performed poorly at Brandywine, and he shared in the blame for Germantown. How he managed to retain Washington's confidence remains a puzzle.

When he was closely controlled in combat by Washington, as at Trenton and Princeton, Sullivan performed capably. His arrangements for the attack on Newport were astute, and his plan of attack sound; he missed a victory there only due to ill fortune. Sullivan's greatest military achievement was to destroy the Indian menace in western New York. Yet, he failed to strike at Fort Niagara, he left untouched dozens of Indian villages, and his so-called punitive expedition had only a temporary impact in staving off future raids, for the Iroquois returned with a vengeance to devastate the frontier until March 1782.

The epitome of the soldier patriot who seldom wavered in the fight for independence, Sullivan achieved only limited fame. Petulant and contentious, Sullivan was one of Washington's most controversial generals. Because of his own poor judgment, his temperamental outbursts, and his record of incredibly bad luck, Sullivan failed to achieve the martial glory he sought.

BIBLIOGRAPHY

Cook, Frederick. *Journals of the Military Expeditions of Major General John Sullivan Against the Six Nations of Indians in 1779 with Records of Centennial Celebrations*. Auburn, N.Y.: Knapp, Peck, and Thomson, 1887.
Flick, Alexander C. *The Sullivan-Clinton Campaign in 1779*. Albany: University of the State of New York, 1929.
Graymont, Barbara. *The Iroquois in the American Revolution*. Syracuse, N.Y.: Syracuse University Press, 1972.
Rossie, Jonathan Gregory. *The Politics of Command in the American Revolution*. Syracuse, N.Y.: Syracuse University Press, 1975.
Whittemore, Charles P. *A General of the Revolution. John Sullivan of New Hampshire*. New York: Columbia University Press, 1961.
————. "John Sullivan: Luckless Irishman." In *George Washington's Generals*. Edited by George Allan Billias. New York: William Morrow and Company, 1964.

                                                                RICHARD BLANCO

SULTAN, Daniel Isom (b. Oxford, Miss., December 9, 1885; d. Washington, D.C., January 14, 1947), Army officer; Deputy commander, China-India-Burma Theater during World War II; first soldier to receive three Distinguished Service Medals.

A native of Mississippi, Daniel Sultan began his formal college education in 1901, at his state's university. But in 1903, he fulfilled a personal and family dream by entering West Point where he played football and was chosen all-American center. Commissioned a second lieutenant of engineers, on January 14, 1907, the same day as his graduation, he had not attained scholastic heights, but he had attained a solid foundation in engineering that would propel his career for the next forty years.

After an initial assignment of a year with the 3d Battalion of Engineers, Fort Leavenworth, Kansas, he was reassigned to Washington Barracks (now Fort Belvoir, Virginia, and home of the Engineer Corps) where he remained until 1912. While there he completed the Engineer School, was promoted to first lieutenant, and soon after was reassigned as instructor in civil and military engineering at West Point. Although promoted to captain while at West Point (February 1914), there is much indication that he preferred an Army field role to his role as pedagogue.

Upon completing his tour at West Point, he began a series of choice command and staff positions. In September 1916 Sultan was assigned to the Philippines where he commanded engineer troops in charge of all fortifications on the islands, including the construction and maintenance of fortifications on Corregidor. As a result of his own superlative work (which would later be tested by the Japanese) and the American entrance into World War I, he received two promotions in quick succession—to major in May 1917 and lieutenant colonel in August of the same year.

Reassigned in March 1918 to the War Department General Staff, he was promoted to colonel in July and ordered to duty with John Joseph Pershing's* General Staff in France. He was there only a year when he returned to Washington to work on the staff of the Army chief of staff. His work with commissioned personnel and with demobilization earned him his first Distinguished Service Medal, the highest Army award for service.

Shortly after the end of World War I, Sultan reverted to his permanent grade of major, but he continued receiving the assignments and schooling that would ensure his peacetime advancement. He graduated from the Command and General Staff School at Fort Leavenworth in 1923 and was assigned as district engineer, Savannah, Georgia, supervising river and harbor improvements. He graduated from the Army War College in 1926 and remained in Washington as resident member of the Board of Engineers for Rivers and Harbors for three years. During this period his appearance before various congressional committees won him the confidence of Capitol Hill and a reputation as a presenter of cold facts untainted with political consideration.

In August 1929 he was assigned to Nicaragua as commander of U.S. Army troops and as a member of the Interoceanic Canal Board in charge of the survey for a second canal. He was personally convinced that the project was essential, holding with proven military logic that it would be more difficult for an enemy to stage a surprise attack against two canals than against one. Promoted to lieutenant colonel on October 1, 1930, he was still on station in Nicaragua when a devastating earthquake struck. For his professional handling of the Army's massive relief activities he received not only his second Distinguished Service Medal, but also the Medal of Merit and Medal of Distinction from the Nicaraguan president and Congress, respectively.

After a two-year tour as district engineer for Chicago, he was again reassigned as engineer-commissioner to Washington where he was promoted to colonel in October 1935. With more than thirty years of service, mostly as an engineering officer, he was destined to combine this talent with a field command.

In August 1938 he assumed command of the engineers at Fort Logan, Colorado, and then with promotion to brigadier general in December, he assumed command of the post. From Colorado, he moved to Hawaii as commander of the 22d Infantry Brigade, and later as commanding general of the Hawaiian Division. In April 1941 promotion to major general earned him command of the 38th Division, and he returned to his home state of Mississippi. He was a Regular Army officer replacing a National Guard commander of a Guard Division—seen by *Time* magazine as a "small but hopeful sign that the United States Army might be on its way to getting tough—tough enough to face modern military competition."

General Sultan had a major role in that competition, first as commanding general of the VIII Army Corps and then in late 1943, shortly after his promotion to lieutenant general, as deputy commander, China-Burma-India Theater, under General Joseph Warren Stilwell.* With a capable deputy, Stilwell was freed from numerous administrative burdens. In his own words, Stilwell declared that

Sultan "was the best thing that ever happened to CBI." A highly qualified engineer, a proven field commander, and an efficient administrator, Sultan's principal area of responsibility from the onset was India-Burma. He was to provide liaison between the theater headquarters in New Delhi and field headquarters in Burma and to supervise the total American war effort in India and Burma. Determining what that effort should be was not difficult. The Russo-Japanese nonaggression pact insured that China would get no help from Russia; the Japanese were in control of Indochina, so China could expect no help from the French; the Japanese also occupied all Chinese seaports and so there was no help for China from the sea. An overland route from India-Burma to China, he determined, was the best way to get critically needed supplies to China and to fight the Japanese at the same time. In this effort, Stilwell supported him implicitly—support that contributed to Stilwell's own command problems—with the Chinese over supplies and troop utilization and with the British who wanted to bypass Burma, leave China as a Sino-American action, and concentrate primarily on restoring British colonialism in Southeast Asia. Throughout this period, Sultan forwarded intelligence information from New Delhi and acted as Stilwell's safety valve, providing a sounding board and unswerving loyalty to his commander.

When Stilwell was recalled in October 1944, Sultan took over the "Jungle Half" of Stilwell's old command. As commander of the India-Burma Theater, Sultan continued with his administrative responsibilities but now commanded the India-based American and Chinese troop operations in Burma. The Joint Chiefs outlined his primary mission: to ensure an uninterrupted flow of supplies to the China Theater. To accomplish this mission he had an American force of 183,920 troops and five Chinese divisions which he committed to driving the Japanese from the jungles of Burma and securing the land and air routes to China. Sultan grasped the importance of that mission, for he realized that the Chinese armies had held up numerous Japanese divisions that could have been used and still could be used against the Allies in the Pacific.

Sultan further realized that the problem of breaking the blockade of China was more a problem of tactics than of engineering. Therefore, he hastily settled administrative details and flew to direct field activities in Burma. In joint operations with forces of the China Theater, within ten weeks he had pushed further than in the previous year. His adeptness as tactician and as engineer ensured victory at Myitchina, followed by the official opening of the land route to China on January 22, 1945. Renamed the Stilwell Road by Chiang Kai-shek, the Burma-Ledo Road, Sultan acknowledged, was really opened by Stilwell's own "indomitable will."

Victorious in Burma, Sultan was now called upon to provide his experienced troops as reinforcements for China. He accepted a dwindling command willingly for he knew it was for the good of China and the Allied effort. With the liberation of Rangoon in June 1945, the Allies achieved total victory in Burma, and General Sultan was called back to Washington to receive his third Distinguished Service Medal and a new assignment. George Catlett Marshall,* Army chief of staff, had appointed him inspector general of the Army, a fitting post for a career soldier, a man of unquestionable integrity and dedication to duty.

It was while in this post that Sultan died, leaving a wife of more than thirty years and a military career of forty years worthy of emulation.

To properly appreciate Dan Sultan's place in American military history, one might look at his accomplishments in fortifying the Philippines. The defenses of Corregidor, although eventually surrendered, were never breached—a major tribute to Sultan, the military engineer. One might also examine the interoceanic canal surveys that Sultan completed on site in Nicaragua. These same surveys have been used recently as more thought has been given to a second canal route—further testimony to Sultan's skill as engineer and as military strategist.

His appearances before various U.S. congressional committees as engineer commissioner for Washington, D.C., are also noteworthy. By sheer force of personality he won the support and confidence of critical politicians by hard facts unembellished with political considerations.

And for his role in the Orient during World War II, he should be remembered, indeed admired, for not only enduring the rigors of command, but also for drastically increasing supplies to a blockaded China through land, river, pipe, and air communications. His accomplishments in this area were acclaimed by the Army chief of staff as "astonishing," and three times during his career the Distinguished Service Medal was pinned to his uniform.

But stopping there, one would miss the quintessence of the man—Sultan's personal qualities, the qualities of a professional soldier in a democratic republic. He was not spectacular in the sense that Douglas MacArthur,* Dwight David Eisenhower,* or George Smith Patton, Jr.,* were spectacular, but Dan Sultan's accomplishments were mammoth and his methods were sound. His was a quiet competence, a dedication to duty and mission unencumbered by thoughts of personal gain. He was loyal to superiors, to subordinates, and to his nation. And he earned the confidence of his troops, the admiration of his colleagues, and the respect of his adversaries. Daniel Sultan lived and died a professional soldier—content.

BIBLIOGRAPHY

Anders, Leslie. *Ledo-Road: General Joseph W. Stilwell's Highway to China*. Norman: University of Oklahoma Press, 1976.

Romanus, Charles F., and Riley Sunderland. *Stilwell's Command Problems*. China-Burma-China Theater, U.S. Army in World War II, Office of Chief of Military History, U.S. Department of the Army, Washington, D.C., 1956.

Wedemeyer, Albert C. *Wedemeyer Reports*. New York: Henry Holt and Company, 1958.

White, Theodore H., ed. *The Stilwell Papers: General Joseph W. Stilwell's Iconoclastic Account of America's Adventures in China*. New York: Schocken Books, 1972.

JOHN R. MILLER

SUMMERALL, Charles Pelot (b. Blount's Ferry, Fla., March 4, 1867; d. Washington, D.C., May 14, 1955), Army officer, military educator.

Charles Summerall was the son of Elhanan Bryant Summerall and Margaret Pelot Summerall. The father, a former plantation owner impoverished by the Civil War, made a living as an artisan. Charles' mother was a former school teacher. Summerall attended Porter Military Academy in Charleston, South Carolina, from 1882 to 1885 and after graduating taught school in Florida until his appointment to the U.S. Military Academy at West Point in 1888. He reached the cadet rank of first captain before he was graduated in 1892.

Summerall was commissioned as a lieutenant in the infantry, but in March 1893 secured a transfer to the artillery. He served as an aide to Brigadier General Alexander Pennington, commander of the Department of the Gulf, during the Spanish-American War (1898). He then commanded an artillery battery in the Philippine Insurrection (1899–1900) and again in the China Relief Expedition at the time of the Boxer Rebellion (1900–1901). In the effort to relieve the besieged legations at Peking, Summerall's guns were instrumental in breaking down the gates leading to the Forbidden City.

After returning to the United States in 1901, Summerall married Laura Mordecai, daughter of Brigadier General Alfred Mordecai of the Ordnance Department, and was soon promoted to the rank of captain. He was promoted to the field grade ranks between 1901 and 1917 while serving variously as a battery commander, a fortress engineer in Alaska, senior instructor of artillery tactics at West Point, lecturer at the Army War College, and assistant to the chief of the Militia Bureau. He took special interest in the artillery instruction of National Guard troops and was instrumental in acquiring additional practice ranges for the Army and National Guard before 1917.

Soon after American entry into World War I, Summerall was promoted to the rank of colonel and assigned to the Baker Commission for the purpose of helping to draw up the organizational plans for the American Expeditionary Force (AEF) to be sent to France under General John Joseph Pershing.* Summerall was subsequently promoted to the rank of brigadier general and given command of the artillery brigade of the 42d Infantry ("Rainbow") Division, which he accompanied to Europe. Soon after his arrival in France, he was given command of the artillery brigade of the 1st Infantry Division. His guns played an important role in the division's capture of key ground near Cantigny in May 1918. When General Robert Lee Bullard* was promoted to command an army corps, Summerall succeeded him as commander of the 1st Division in July. Under Summerall's command the 1st Division saw heavy fighting at Soissons and in the St. Mihiel salient (July-September). After the 1st Division was assigned to Pershing's great offensive in the Meuse-Argonne sector in late September, Summerall was promoted to the rank of major general and given command of the V Corps. This unit was in the forefront of the fighting until the Armistice of November 11, 1918. Summerall was decorated with the Distinguished Service Cross and the French *Croix de Guerre*.

Following the Armistice, Summerall commanded various corps on occupation duty in the German Rhineland. He also attended the signing of the Treaty of

Versailles on June 28, 1919, at the close of the Paris Peace Conference. Upon his return to the United States, he reverted to the peacetime rank of brigadier general but was soon again promoted to major general and subsequently to lieutenant general. From 1921 to 1924 he commanded the Army's Hawaiian Department, and in 1925 he served for a time as a judge in the court-martial of Brigadier General William ("Billy") Mitchell.* On November 21, 1926, he assumed the duties of Army chief of staff and in 1929 was promoted to the rank of general. He retired from his post as chief of staff and from the Army on November 20, 1930, at age sixty-three.

After a brief retirement in Florida, Summerall assumed the duties of president of The Citadel, the Military College of South Carolina at Charleston, in September 1931. He held this post for nearly twenty-two years before retiring on June 30, 1953, when he was eighty-six years old. He lived in retirement at Aiken, South Carolina, until a terminal illness led to his admission to Walter Reed Army Hospital in August 1954. He died there on May 14, 1955, at age eighty-eight.

Summerall's reputation rests chiefly on his performance as an expert in artillery, and one historian has rated him as perhaps the most original American tactician in World War I. Certainly, the close coordination of artillery and infantry in his commands of World War I had much to do with the reputations of the 1st Division and the V Corps. Summerall perfected the so-called creeping barrage that preceded the advance of infantry, and he reintroduced direct fire by guns located in the frontlines. Summerall probably merits the reputation of being the finest American artilleryman of his generation.

His performance as Army chief of staff was more mixed in results. He did not take kindly to Billy Mitchell's air power ideas, and he even opposed spending more funds on the Army Air Corps. He authorized an experimental all-mechanized force, but only in response to an order by the secretary of war. The recommendations that flowed out of the experiment were accepted in principle, but only with painful slowness was anything done. Summerall worked to strengthen the traditional arms, getting the Army's budget increased by one-third while in office, but he opposed a recombination of the Field Artillery and Coast Artillery long after the technical reasons for their separation had been overcome. He left the army stronger than when he found it, but he was by nature a conservative rather than an innovator.

As president of The Citadel and as a military educator, he was predictably more successful in strengthening the old values than in developing new ones, but he took a keen interest in cadet instruction and managed to wrest enough of a budget from the South Carolina legislature to keep the state-supported school financially afloat during the difficult years of the Great Depression. By the end of his long tenure in office, he had managed to double both the size of the corps of cadets and the school's physical plant. His late-Victorian values and extreme age were less well suited for coping with the problems of the post-World War II world, but he passed on to his successor as president an institution with a reputation as one of the best of its type in the United States.

BIBLIOGRAPHY

Harbord, J. G. *The American Army in France, 1917–1919*. Boston: Little, Brown and Company, 1936.
MacCloskey, Monro. *Reilly's Battery: A Story of the Boxer Rebellion*. New York: Richards Rosen Press, 1969.
Pratt, Fletcher. *Eleven Generals: Studies in American Command*. New York: William Sloan Associates, 1949.
Vandiver, Frank E. *Black Jack: The Life and Times of John J. Pershing*. College Station: Texas A&M University Press, 1977.

                                                                    LARRY H. ADDINGTON

SWIFT, Eben (b. Fort Chadburne, Tex., May 11, 1854; d. Washington, D.C., April 25, 1938), soldier, military educator. As cavalryman, historian, teacher, and educational innovator, Swift exercised a pervasive and permanent influence on the U.S. Army as it developed in the early twentieth century.

Serving in every commissioned grade from second lieutenant to major general, from graduation in 1876 from the U.S. Military Academy to statutory retirement in 1918, Swift gave over half his long life to the Army. Throughout his life, he was motivated by two forces: love for the Army (especially the cavalry) and untiring determination to improve military education and training. Born into the Army on the pre-Civil War frontier, the son of Army Surgeon (and brevet Brigadier General) Ebenezer Swift and Sarah Edwards (Capers), he grew up on Army posts to win appointment to the Academy in 1872. There he met Arthur Lockwood Wagner,* class of 1875, who played a central role in organizing the U.S. Army Infantry and Cavalry School at Fort Leavenworth in the 1890s.

Following graduation and commissioning, only days before the Custer Massacre, young Swift served his apprenticeship in Indian campaigns in Colorado, Idaho, Montana, Nebraska, and Wyoming, riding against Bannocks, Cheyenne, Sioux, and Utes for a dozen years. Regimental adjutant in the 5th Cavalry from 1878 to 1887, he became Brigadier General Wesley Merritt's* aide for three years, and after three more years with the 5th in Indian Territory he went on to Leavenworth in 1893 as instructor in military art under Wagner. After five years at Leavenworth, Swift had various duties with the Illinois National Guard during the Spanish-American War, as well as special duty in Cuba and Puerto Rico, returning to Washington in 1903 for a year in the adjutant general's office. From 1904 to 1906 he served again at Leavenworth, as senior instructor in military art and assistant commandant. From there he went to the Army War College as director until 1910, with detached service in Manchuria in the summer of 1910 to study the Russo-Japanese War. His active service in the twentieth century included campaigning against the Moros in the Philippines, 1912–1913, as lieutenant colonel and colonel of the 8th Cavalry; chief of staff of the Western

Department; a third brief stint at Leavenworth as commandant until promotion to brigadier in September 1916; commander, Provisional Cavalry Division in Mexico to August 1917; and commander, Camp Gordon, where he organized and commanded the 82d Division, to December 1917. Then he went to France and on to Italy in February 1918 as chief of the American military mission and commander, U.S. forces. In June 1930 he was promoted to major general.

Swift found himself in the 5th Cavalry on the frontier; he also found a model in that regiment's baby-faced colonel, Wesley Merritt.* Although he was attached to five other cavalry regiments—the 1st, 4th, 8th, 9th, and 12th—Swift's heart belonged to the 5th, but not exclusively. While at West Point he had met Susanne Bonaparte Palmer, daughter of General Innis Newton Palmer. After a long courtship, interrupted by forays against the Indians, Swift married her at Merritt's Washington home in 1880. Their union produced seven children, five of whom grew to maturity. One of their four sons, Innis Palmer Swift, followed his father to the Academy, class of 1904, and served with distinction until retirement as a major general.

During his early years with the 5th Cavalry, Eben Swift became a seasoned professional officer, learning from harsh field experience and developing ideas and programs for enhancing the effectiveness of the Army. He worked zealously at improved marksmanship, with both pistol and rifle, and he began to write. His first efforts appeared in *The Army and Navy Journal* and *The Journal of the U.S. Cavalry Association*, in 1888, while he was serving as Merritt's aide. The *Cavalry Journal* article argued "Sabers or Revolvers?" and Swift came down eloquently on the side of the revolver. So began a long career as an essayist on cavalry tactics, weaponry, military history, troop training, and officer education. His history of the 5th Cavalry, in *The Journal of the Military Service Institution (JMSI)* in 1891, won praise from Merritt: "You write splendidly; you ought to write more." His short essay, part of *JMSI*'s series, "Historical Sketches of the Army," was indeed splendidly written; it is superb military history, warmed by his affection for his regiment, illuminated by brilliant descriptive passages, enriched by apt historical illustrations, and everywhere brightened by Swift's sharp perceptions and ever-ready wit. These became the hallmarks of everything Swift wrote thereafter: clear and concise statement, logical development of argument or exposition, abundant historical precedents, and always that Swiftian humor, his "saving sense of the ridiculous."

In part because of these publications, Swift went to Leavenworth in 1893 as assistant instructor in military art, working with Arthur Wagner who had joined the faculty of the Infantry and Cavalry School in 1886. The two made a natural team; their work, Timothy Nenninger asserts, "laid the basis for Leavenworth methods, course content, and overall objectives until World War I." Out of this collaboration came valuable innovations in American military education and problem-solving, some of which are still active Army doctrine and practice. They include the applicatory method of instruction, greater use of the German *Kriegspiel*, and most significant of all, the development of the five-paragraph field order. All bear the mark of their developer, Eben Swift. Fortunately, he explained all of them in one classic exposition, an article engagingly entitled "The Lyceum at Fort Agawam" (*JMSI*, March 1897). Its style is clear, crisp, and incisive, with now and then an Emersonian aphorism worth noting, like: "A habit of deciding what others should do instead of thinking about what you should be doing yourself has brought disaster to many a good man."

The heart of his lyceum lesson Swift called "The Art of Command Orders." His studies of military history had convinced him that many military failures had flowed from unclear, confused, defective, badly worded orders. His solution? An "invariable model" for all field orders, whether for a small command or a large. "The idea," Swift explained, "is to group all information in such a way that the eye will catch the same thing at the same place always, and thus you lessen the danger of leaving something unprovided for."

Swift began teaching his standard system of writing orders at Leavenworth in 1894, and it quickly beame the common language of the U.S. Army, with the happy result that "Leavenworth men" have been able to use that common language effectively, uniformly, and universally ever since. His "invariable model" became a basic tool, a military weapon with greater impact on modern military art than bayonet, saber, and revolver combined. Swift made his major contributions to American military history in the Leavenworth schools in the 1890s. Arthur Wagner "in 1894 attributed the success of the entire department[of military art] to Swift's 'able and zealous efforts'." Furthermore, Swift continued the work, improved his applicatory method, took the lead in refining and adapting *Kriegspiel* for American use (even translating Prussian *Kriegsakademie* sources), and popularized map maneuvers and tactical rides, not only in the Leavenworth schools when he returned in 1904 but after that at the War College as well. There he applied his Leavenworth experience, methods, and practices to improve that institution and through it the officers who would provide AEF leadership. And he continued to write.

Swift's articles, book reviews, essays, lectures, letters, notes and comments continued to appear in the *Cavalry Journal* and *JMSI* until the outbreak of World War I. His contributions range from "Peon or Soldier" in the *JMSI* (1902), drawn from his experience with a Puerto Rican provisional regiment, to a section for the *Centennial of the United States Military Academy* on "Services of Graduates of West Point in Indian Wars," from tributes to Wagner (*JMSI*, 1909) and Merritt (*Cavalry Journal*, 1911) to a potpourri of articles on cavalry and cavalry tactics, "Peace Training for Officers," and an occasional venture into Civil War history, in which he became a recognized authority. His writings continued even after his retirement: a lengthy essay on Thomas Jonathan ("Stonewall") Jackson's* leadership, for example, and a discursive and revealing folder of memoirs reviewing his entire career.

In his long life of service to his nation and its Army, Eben Swift gave unstintingly, selflessly, concerned always to achieve the best, to devise ways and means of making that army, and especially its officers, more alert and efficient, better educated, more intelligently effective in meeting its challenges. Swift's inquiring mind drove him to question, to examine, to devise and execute methods and techniques which left permanent marks on that Army as it developed professionally in the first decades of this century. It is entirely appropriate that Eben Swift should have been inducted into the Fort Leavenworth Hall of Fame on the one hundred and twenty-fifth anniversary of his birth, May 11, 1979.

BIBLIOGRAPHY

Cullum, George Washington, comp. *Biographical Register of Officers and Graduates of the United States Military Academy at West Point, New York, Since Its Establishment in 1802.* Supplement VI–A.

Nenninger, Timothy K. *The Leavenworth Schools and the Old Army: Education, Professionalism, and the Officer Corps of the United States Army, 1881–1918.* Westport, Conn.: Greenwood Press, 1978.

DUDLEY T. CORNISH

SWIFT, Joseph Gardner (b. Nantucket, Mass., December 31, 1783; d. July 23, 1865), military engineer. Swift is considered to be the first graduate of the U.S. Military Academy.

Descended from a family that had established itself in America as early as 1634, Joseph Swift was the son of a physician on the island of Nantucket. He moved to Taunton, Massachusetts, with his parents in 1792. The young man was thrilled by stories of the American Revolution told by David Cobb, a family friend who had been an aide de camp to George Washington.* When Swift showed an inclination toward a military career, Cobb persuaded President John Adams to appoint him a cadet in the Corps of Artillerists and Engineers. Reporting to Newport, Rhode Island, in June 1800, Swift served under the veteran engineer Lieutenant Colonel Louis de Tousard, who treated the precocious young man with great deference.

In October 1801 Swift was transferred to the military post at West Point, New York. Besides being a repository for Revolutionary War booty, West Point was also the site of a military school of rather indifferent quality. At the time of Swift's matriculation, West Point had neither an established curriculum nor a specified time for completion of a course of studies. Recognizing the need to improve the infant school, Congress formally established the U.S. Military Academy on March 16, 1802, and placed it under the Corps of Engineers. After being examined by the faculty in September, Swift and one other cadet were graduated on October 12, 1802, and commissioned as second lieutenants in the Corps of Engineers. Since Swift's name was listed first, he became the first graduate of West Point.

Initially assigned to the West Point garrison, Swift continued to take courses in addition to his regular duties until his departure in April 1804. He was then posted to North Carolina as superintending engineer of the defenses of the Cape Fear River. While there, in January 1805, he assumed command of Fort Johnson, becoming one of the first members of the Corps of Engineers to command troops from other branches of the Army. Before leaving North Carolina for West Point in March 1807, Swift married Louisa Walker of Wilmington and rose to the rank of captain.

Promoted to major in early 1808, Swift was placed in charge of the defenses of the Eastern Department. While there he met William Eustis of Boston, who became James Madison's secretary of war in March 1809. Eustis sought Swift's advice on military matters and in exchange helped the engineer to make important contacts in government circles. Assigned to the Cape Fear again in the fall of 1809, Swift had little to do for several years, since funding for fortifications had declined drastically. The monotony was broken only by court-martial duty in the fall of 1811 at the trial of Major General James Wilkinson.* Swift and the court found Wilkinson not guilty, a decision that seriously damaged his friendship with Secretary Eustis.

Swift was touring Southern coastal defenses when the War of 1812 broke out in June. Promoted lieutenant colonel of engineers in July, he joined the staff of Major General Thomas Pinckney as chief engineer of the Southern Department. Following the resignation of Colonel Jonathan Williams, chief engineer of the Army, Swift was nominated as his replacement. Although Secretary Eustis favored Robert Fulton for the position, Swift was confirmed by Congress in December 1812, with promotion to colonel dating from July 31. Not yet twenty-nine years of age, Swift as chief engineer of the U.S. Army was also superintendent of the U.S. Military Academy, although his engineering duties usually kept him absent from West Point.

Swift's first assignment as chief engineer was to command American defenses on Staten Island, but he soon sought a tranfer to a more active area of operations. In August 1813 he joined Major General James Wilkinson as chief engineer, Northern Army. Swift participated in Wilkinson's abortive expedition down the St. Lawrence River and was present at the Battle of Chrysler's Farm on November 11, 1813. Shortly thereafter he was sent to Washington to report to President Madison. A friend and occasional defender of Wilkinson, Swift apparently fell into disfavor with Secretary of War John Armstrong, Jr.,* because of his relationship with the general. Armstrong reluctantly approved Swift's promotion to brevet brigadier general in February 1814, but he denied Swift's request to join Jacob Jennings Brown's* forces on the Niagara frontier. Instead, Swift was chosen to strengthen the land defenses of New York City. Beginning in July 1814, he designed and constructed an elaborate defensive system for both New York City and Brooklyn. Completed in November 1814, the works were never tested by an enemy. Nevertheless, grateful New Yorkers voted Swift a "Benefactor to the City."

One of the obvious lessons of the War of 1812 was the extreme vulnerability of America's coastal cities to seaborne attack. In response, President Madison proposed and Congress funded what would ultimately become the Third System of American coastal fortification. Unfortunately, Secretary of War William Crawford believed that only a European engineer was qualified to supervise such an ambitious program. Accordingly, in April 1816 Congress authorized the hiring of an assistant to the Corps of Engineers with rank and pay equivalent to that of Chief Engineer Swift. To fill the position Crawford chose Simon Bernard,* formerly an officer on the staff of Napoleon Bonaparte. At the same time a Board of Fortifications was established, with Bernard at its head.

Insulted by Crawford's opinion that American engineers were incapable of designing and building American fortifications, Swift bitterly opposed Bernard's appointment. Aware of Swift's feelings, Madison and Crawford banished the chief engineer to West Point to assume personal direction of the Military Academy, leaving Bernard free to direct the fortification program. Nominally superintendent since 1812, Swift had long maintained a strong interest in the Military Academy. During his numerous absences, the school had been left in the hands of Captain Alden Partridge, an increasingly erratic educator.

After only two months at West Point, Swift returned to Washington to protest the War Department's practice of dealing directly with Bernard, and in Washington he remained. When the pressure for Partridge's removal became too great, Swift reluctantly replaced him with Sylvanus Thayer* in July 1817. Forced to resign from the service, Partridge lodged charges of maladministration against the chief engineer, but they were quickly dismissed. Resuming his engineering duties, Swift soon discovered that Simon Bernard had become the dominant figure on the Board of Fortifications. Unable to swallow his pride any longer, Swift resigned from the Army on November 12, 1818.

Immediately following his resignation, Swift was appointed surveyor of the port of New York. In 1825 he became vice-president of the Life and Trust Insurance Company. When the company failed in 1826, Swift was forced to liquidate his assets to satisfy the company's creditors, and John Quincy Adams removed him from the surveyorship. After an unhappy interlude as a farmer in Tennessee, Swift returned to New York City and resumed his career as a civil engineer. In 1829 Andrew Jackson* appointed him to supervise harbor improvements on the Great Lakes, a position he held for sixteen years. When work on the lakes languished due to lack of funds, Swift did engineering work for railroads in Louisiana and New York. Resigning from the Great Lakes project in 1845, he declined further government service and retired to Geneva, New York, living quietly there until his death on July 23, 1865.

Joseph Gardner Swift is most often remembered as being the first graduate of the U.S. Military Academy, but this was an accident of circumstances rather than a meritorious accomplishment. Swift's intellectual abilities, however, were not small, as his career demonstrated. Well attuned to the political realities of the day, he took great care to cultivate friends in positions of influence. Only once did he seriously falter in his relationship with the chief executive, and the election of 1828 quickly returned him to official favor.

Superintendent of West Point for six years, Swift left no great institutional changes behind to mark his presence. Indeed, his support of the troublesome Alden Partridge tended to erode the government's confidence in the school. Nevertheless, Swift kept the Military Academy alive and functioning so that others might have a foundation upon which to build. His greatest service to West Point undoubtedly was the selection of Sylvanus Thayer for training abroad, which prepared Thayer to become one of the Military Academy's greatest superintendents.

Swift's place in history rests most importantly upon his career as an engineer, both military and civil. Possibly the first military engineer to be trained solely within the United States, he became the symbol of the U.S. Army Corps of Engineers in its fight to escape foreign domination. As a civilian engineer, Swift was especially prominent in railroad construction; his New Orleans and Lake Pontchartrain Railroad was reputedly the first to utilize T-rails in the United States. Perhaps most important of all, Swift, as one of America's first native-born engineers, served as a model for young engineers to emulate in the decades to come.

BIBLIOGRAPHY

Ambrose, Stephen E. *Duty, Honor, Country: A History of West Point*. Baltimore: Johns Hopkins University Press, 1966.

Cullum, George Washington, comp. *Biographical Register of the Officers and Graduates of the U.S. Military Academy at West Point, N.Y., from its Establishment, March 16, 1802 to the Army Re-organization of 1866–67*. New York: D. Van Nostrand, 1868.

———. *Campaigns of the War of 1812–15, Against Great Britain, Sketched and Criticised; with Brief Biographies of the American Engineers*. New York: James Miller, Publisher, 1879.

Ellery, Harrison, ed. *The Memoirs of Gen. Joseph Gardner Swift, LL.D., U.S.A.* Worcester, Mass.: F. S. Blanchard and Company, 1890.

Moore, Jamie W. *The Fortifications Board, 1816–1828, and the Definition of National Security. The Citadel: Monograph Series: Number XVI*. Charleston, S.C.: 1981.

Stuart, Charles B. *Lives and Works of Civil and Military Engineers of America*. New York: D. Van Nostrand, Publisher, 1871.

WILLIAM GLENN ROBERTSON

T

TATTNALL, Josiah (b. "Bonaventure," near Savannah, Ga., November 9, 1795; d. Savannah, Ga., June 14, 1871), naval officer. Tattnall's half-century of distinguished service in the U.S. Navy was overshadowed by his decision during the Civil War to sink the Confederate ironclad ship, the *Virginia* (formerly the *Merrimack*), to prevent its capture by Union forces.

Josiah Tattnall was born at the family estate of his parents, Josiah and Harriet Fenwick Tattnall. His paternal great-grandfather, who settled in South Carolina in 1700, was of English and French stock. The family name evolved from the original de Taten to Tatenhall and subsequently Tattnall. At the age of ten, Tattnall was sent to England to be educated under the supervision of his maternal grandfather. He returned to Savannah six years later, and on January 1, 1812, he was appointed midshipman in the U.S. Navy. During the course of the War of 1812, Midshipman Tattnall served on the 38–gun frigate *Constellation* in the Chesapeake Bay and the 18–gun brig *Epervier* at Savannah, Georgia. After the war Tattnall participated in operations against the Barbary States.

Following his marriage on September 6, 1821, to Henriette Fenwick Jackson, Lieutenant Tattnall attended Partridge's Military School. Beginning in 1822 and continuing throughout the remainder of the decade, First Lieutenant Tattnall participated in the suppression of piracy in the West Indies. In 1831, shortly after he assumed command of the 10–gun schooner *Grampus*, Tattnall captured the Mexican pirate brig *Montezuma*, which had recently attacked the American schooner *William A. Turner*. In 1835, while commanding the barque *Pioneer*, Tattnall returned President Antonio Lopez de Santa Anna of Mexico to Vera Cruz following his capture by Texans during their war for independence. Contemporaries credited Tattnall's judicious handling of Santa Anna's return with saving the Mexican president from certain death at the hands of his political enemies. The consequent publicity made Tattnall a national figure.

Promoted to the rank of commander in 1838, Tattnall spent most of the 1840s and 1850s at the Boston Navy Yard, the Pensacola Navy Yard, and the Naval

Station at Sackets Harbor. Interspersed among the shore assignments, Tattnall commanded the 18–gun corvettes *Fairfield* and *Saratoga* in the Mediterranean and the gunboat *Spitfire* in the Gulf of Mexico. Commanding the *Spitfire* during the Mexican War, Tattnall won additional national acclaim during the siege of Vera Cruz. Severely wounded in his right arm, Tattnall returned to Georgia where the legislature received him as a war hero. He was promoted to captain on February 5, 1850, during lengthy assignments at the navy yards at Boston and Pensacola. In 1857 Captain Tattnall was ordered to the East Indies to command, with the rank of commodore, the naval forces in the East India Squadron. During that duty Tattnall again attracted public attention when he ignored his country's neutrality in Asian affairs and rushed to aid British ships trapped by Chinese guns on the Pei-ho River. Commodore Tattnall justified his actions with the exclamation that "Blood is thicker than Water!" The U.S. government later upheld such rationalization. When he returned to the United States in 1860, accompanying Japan's first ambassador to the United States, Tattnall was President James Buchanan's guest of honor at a White House dinner.

On the eve of the Civil War, Commodore Josiah Tattnall reluctantly resigned his commission in the U.S. Navy and became senior flag officer in the navy of Georgia. A month later he was commissioned a captain in the Confederate Navy. Always outspoken, the aging captain remarked that he would be in his grave long before the Confederacy had a fleet. With one river steamboat and three tugs improvised into men-of-war, Tattnall directed hit-and-run attacks on the Union's blockading vessels under Samuel Francis Du Pont* and John Rodgers.* Again with considerable reluctance Tattnall, on March 21, 1862, replaced the wounded Commander Franklin Buchanan* in command of the Confederate iron-clad *Virginia* (formerly the USS *Merrimack*). The command of this celebrated vessel was considered the most prestigious assignment in the Confederate Navy, but in spite of the *Virginia*'s recent and spectacular destruction of Union ships in Hampton Roads and the battle with its ironclad rival, the *Monitor*, Tattnall knew his ship's limitations. Its unwieldy bulk, its unreliable engines, and the stout appearance of the *Monitor* made his own ship something less than all Southerners claimed for it. Tattnall looked upon the indecisive four-hour battle between the two ironclads on March 9 as the real index of the *Virginia*'s future usefulness. Southern expectations would eventually evaporate, and with them Tattnall's reputation.

After forty-five days of fruitless effort to lure Union ships into deep water, Commodore Tattnall resigned himself to the use of his ship as a symbolic protection to Norfolk, the navy yard, and the James River approach to Richmond. Meanwhile, naval authorities and the Southern people clamored for something more. Upon the decision by General Joseph Eggleston Johnston* to evacuate the Norfolk area, Tattnall decided to move the *Virginia* into the James River, but Union troops marched into the area before the plan could be effected. Rather than surrender his ship and his three hundred crewmen, Tattnall gave the order to destroy "the pride of the Confederate Navy." Public shock and condemnation soon followed, but Tattnall's action was upheld by unanimous vote in general court-martial. He returned to Savannah and resumed command of the naval defense of Georgia and South Carolina, but was quickly relieved by the Confederate Secretary of the Navy Stephen Russell Mallory* who demanded that the Union blockade be broken. Tattnall was consequently limited to duty at the shore station at Savannah, where he directed the building of the ironclad *Savannah* and the *Milledgeville*, both of which Mallory later destroyed to prevent their capture by Union troops under General William Tecumseh Sherman.*

Commodore Josiah Tattnall and his family spent the four years following the Civil War in Nova Scotia. They returned to Savannah in 1869 when the city council created the office of Inspector of the Port. Tattnall held that office until his death seventeen months later. On the day of his funeral, June 16, 1871, Savannah's flags flew at half-mast, all places of business closed for the day, and all church bells tolled for ninety minutes.

Commodore Josiah Tattnall sacrificed the rewards of a half-century of service in the U.S. Navy to the Confederate cause. Forced to start at the bottom to build a Georgia-South Carolina squadron to attack enemy blockades, he lost any chance to prove his worth in that capacity when he was assigned to command the *Virginia*. He was well aware of the circumstances that preordained the disaster that awaited him on that assignment. Upon his return to Savannah, he was relieved of his full command at the time he seemed ready to challenge the Union blockade along the Georgia coast. His final effort to aid the Confederate States—the construction of two war vessels—was nullified when Sherman's approach forced their destruction. Commodore Josiah Tattnall is buried in the family cemetery at "Bonaventure." The USS *Tattnall*, a destroyer (No. 125), served in the Atlantic and Pacific during World War II, and to perpetuate the name, a second ship, the USS *Tattnall* (DDG–19), was launched in 1961.

BIBLIOGRAPHY

Davis, William C. *Duel Between the First Ironclads*. Garden City, N.Y.: Doubleday and Company, 1975.
Jones, Charles C., Jr. *The Life and Services of Commodore Josiah Tattnall*. Savannah, Ga.: Morning News Steam Printing House, 1878.
Melton, Maurice. *The Confederate Ironclads*. New York: Thomas Yoseloff, 1968.
Still, William N., Jr. *Iron Afloat: The Story of the Confederate Armorclads*. Nashville, Tenn.: Vanderbilt University Press, 1971.
Trexler, Harrison A. *The Confederate Ironclad Virginia (Merrimac)*. Chicago: University of Chicago Press, 1938.

VERNON GLADDEN SPENCE

TAYLOR, Maxwell Davenport (b. Keytesville, Mo., August 26, 1901), Army officer. Taylor commanded the 101st Airborne Division in World War II and helped to shape U.S. policy during the Vietnam War.

Taylor grew up in small-town Missouri, the only child of a railroad attorney.

Taylor's maternal grandfather, a Confederate veteran who had lost an arm in the Civil War, imbued the boy with the romance of military service. At the age of five, Taylor notified his parents that he intended to go to West Point.

World War I was ending as Taylor entered the U.S. Military Academy. At the time, the faculty contained several figures destined for prominence in World War II, including Joseph Lawton Collins,* Matthew Bunker Ridgway,* and Omar Nelson Bradley.* The superintendent was Douglas MacArthur,* then a brigadier general. Taylor had an enviable career at West Point: captain of cadets, captain of the tennis team, and fourth in his graduating class (1922).

During the 1920s Lieutenant Taylor served with engineering units in Maryland and Hawaii, and later he attended the Field Artillery School at Fort Sill, Oklahoma (1932–1933). Through his recognized facility with languages, Taylor drew several special assignments. To perfect his skill in French, the Army sent him to Paris in 1927. After teaching French and Spanish at West Point, he was assigned to the U.S. Embassy in Tokyo to learn Japanese (1935). He had attended the Command and General Staff School at Fort Leavenworth, Kansas (1933–1935), and later went to the Army War College (1939–1940). In 1940, because of his expertise in Spanish, Taylor was selected to participate in a mission to Latin America which determined the military equipment needs of eight hemispheric nations in view of the threat posed by Nazi Germany.

Taylor followed the Latin American mission with a one-year stint as commander of the 12th Field Artillery Battalion of the 2d Infantry Division, San Antonio, Texas. In July 1941 he was assigned to the military secretariat of the Army Chief of Staff, General George Catlett Marshall.* Taylor served in that post until the spring of 1942 when he was appointed chief of staff and artillery commander of General Ridgway's 82d Infantry Division, Camp Claiborne, Louisiana.

The fall of Crete to German parachute and glider forces caused the U.S. Army to take an immediate interest in creating airborne divisions. The 82d Infantry was ordered to Fort Bragg, North Carolina, where, supplemented by preexisting parachute elements, it was split into the 82d and 101st Airborne Divisions. Ridgway retained Taylor as artillery commander of the 82d. Following reorganization and training, the 82d was ordered to Morocco in 1943 to prepare for the assault on Sicily, which occurred in July. Taylor helped to plan but did not participate in the actual airborne operations in Sicily, which were calamitous to the point where the Army wavered on any future division-size airborne operations. Taylor conducted his artillery forces in the Sicilian Campaign with distinction.

Prior to the invasion of Italy, Taylor was chosen for a daring mission behind enemy lines. The Italians had overthrown Mussolini and replaced him with Marshall Pietro Badoglio as prime minister. Badoglio proposed an armistice, followed by Italy's switch to the Allied side in the war, with one condition: Allied troops must be provided immediately to defend Rome. The assault on Rome would divert German forces from the main invasion point at Salerno, and

General Dwight David Eisenhower* agreed to commit the 82d Airborne. But Taylor, Ridgway, and other officers had doubts about the Italians' ability to provide support for the division. To resolve the doubts, Taylor and an Air Corps colonel were sent on a secret mission to Rome. Traveling by British PT boat, Italian corvette, and ambulance, and clothed in regular American uniforms, Taylor and his companion determined that the landing would be a disaster and aborted it just as the first planes left the ground.

Taylor did not participate with the 82d in the assault on Salerno, for he was ordered to join an Allied mission to the Badoglio "government in exile." Taylor was selected because of his fluency in the language and his skill at diplomacy. At the end of 1943, the 82d was transferred to Northern Ireland to prepare for Operation OVERLORD, the Allied invasion of France, and Taylor was reassigned to the division. In February 1944 Taylor was selected as the new commander of the 101st Airborne "Screaming Eagle" Division.

In the darkness before dawn on D-Day (June 6, 1944), Major General Taylor parachuted with his men into Normandy, becoming the first American general to fight in France in World War II. His objective was to secure four elevated causeways which provided the only possible routes inland for the invasion forces from Utah Beach. Heavy German antiaircraft fire and poor visibility resulted in poor dispersion of the paratroopers. Nevertheless, Taylor rallied those of his troops he could find and captured the all-important causeways. Following the capture of Cherbourg, the 101st, having sustained casualties totaling one-third of the division, was withdrawn to England.

The division next saw action in the invasion of Holland (Operation MARKET-GARDEN), the largest airborne assault in history. Taylor jumped with his division on September 17, 1944, and succeeded in capturing several assigned bridges. But poor weather, bad planning, and unexpectedly heavy German resistance prevented the British 1st Division from securing the key bridge at Arnhem, dooming the operation to failure. Although MARKET-GARDEN failed in its prime objective of a Rhine crossing, it did create a major salient in the German line.

Early in December 1944 Taylor was ordered to Washington to discuss a reorganization of airborne divisions. While he was away, German forces surrounded the 101st at Bastogne in the famed Battle of the Bulge. Brigadier General Anthony McAuliffe, commanding in Taylor's absence, became a symbol of American tenacity by his refusal to surrender. Taylor rejoined his division on December 27. The 101st, along with other units, was able to eliminate the Bulge on January 17, 1945. This was the last major engagement of the war for the division.

As World War II ended, Taylor was named the fortieth superintendent of West Point. He revised and updated the course of study significantly. In particular, he increased the number of courses in the humanities and social studies. Furthermore, he initiated an intercollegiate student forum which brought in civilian participants. "The cadets," Taylor believed, "should not live in a mental cloister."

In 1949, after more than three years at West Point, Taylor was sent back to Germany, where he held important command positions. In 1951 he returned to Washington to serve as assistant chief of staff.

In 1953 Taylor was named commander of the Eighth Army in Korea. The war was winding down and ended a few months after he assumed command. In November 1954 Taylor, by now a four star general, was assigned to Japan to take charge of all U.S. Army forces in the Far East Command.

President Eisenhower made Taylor chief of staff, replacing General Ridgway, on June 30, 1955. For the next four years Taylor argued the Army's case against the "New Look" and massive retaliation doctrines which held sway during the Eisenhower administration. By his own admission, Taylor was not particularly successful. But his views on defense, particularly the doctrine of flexible response, were advocated by John F. Kennedy in his successful campaign for the presidency in 1960. Following his retirement in July 1959, Taylor served briefly as chairman of the board of a utilities company.

Kennedy called Taylor to Washington late in April 1961 to head the Cuba Study Group, charged with studying the Bay of Pigs debacle and making recommendations on policy relative to guerrilla warfare. Impressed with his efforts, Kennedy appointed Taylor to a new position, "Special Military Representative of the President." In this role Taylor led a mission to South Vietnam to recommend courses of action that the United States might take relative to the escalating activities of communist insurgents. In his report, Taylor recommended that a U.S. military presence in Vietnam should function primarily as a "logistical task force" and as an "emergency reserve in a military crisis."

At the request of President Kennedy, Taylor replaced General Lyman Lemnitzer as chairman of the Joint Chiefs of Staff (JCS) on October 1, 1962. The new chairman received a baptism of fire, for the Cuban missile crisis erupted just two weeks into his tenure. During the hectic thirteen days that followed, he opposed the eventual strategy (a naval "quarantine") in favor of strikes that would destroy the missile sites in Cuba.

Following Kennedy's assassination, Taylor stayed on as chairman under President Lyndon Johnson. Taylor took the lead in forming the JCS recommendation that American efforts in Vietnam be twofold: "an intensified counterinsurgency campaign in the south and selective air and naval attacks against targets in North Vietnam." When it became necessary in June 1964 to replace Henry Cabot Lodge, an aspirant for the Republican nomination, as ambassador to South Vietnam, Johnson chose Taylor. As ambassador, he continued to have influence on military policy, and the president also made him responsible for the entire military program in Vietnam. Consequently, Taylor was closely associated with the U.S. military commander, General William Childs Westmoreland.* Taylor resigned at the end of the year he had agreed to serve in Saigon. Johnson promptly appointed him as special counsel to the president, and he held this post until 1969. Taylor was also chairman of the President's Foreign Intelligence Advisory Board.

Maxwell Taylor was in the vanguard of those advocating the use of division-size airborne units in vertical envelopments. His (and Ridgway's) persistent arguments in favor of this technique, even after the poor initial showing in Sicily, helped make a success of the Normandy invasion. His decision to abort the airborne assault on Rome during the war was correct, in view of the paucity of Italian logistical support and the resistance Allied forces met in their drive toward Rome.

As superintendent of West Point, Taylor initiated reforms in the curriculum that are worthy of note. Academy graduates since his tenure have had a broader education that better prepares them for military leadership in a complex world.

As Army chief of staff, Taylor fought against the massive retaliation doctrine favored by the Eisenhower administration. He had (with contributions from Ridgway and James Maurice Gavin*) devised a sound rationale for the doctrine of flexible response. Although he was not successful with Eisenhower, his arguments were heard and accepted by John Kennedy and became the policy of that administration following the 1960 election.

President Kennedy followed Taylor's recommendation regarding a limited commitment of U.S. forces to South Vietnam for counterinsurgency purposes. That this strategy failed, as did every other strategy later pursued, was due to a complex of circumstances both military and political.

The belief that nuclear conflict was both unthinkable and unlikely was best expressed by Taylor in his book *The Uncertain Trumpet* (1959). Taylor was convinced that the conflicts with which America would most likely be confronted would be "wars of national liberation." Such unconventional warfare, he believed, would require forces-in-being trained in counterinsurgency. Subsequent events have served more to confirm than to repudiate his judgment.

BIBLIOGRAPHY

Halberstam, David. *The Best and the Brightest*. New York: Random House, 1969.
Ridgway, Matthew B. *Soldier*. New York: Harper, 1956.
Taylor, Maxwell D. *Swords and Plowshares*. New York: W. W. Norton and Company, 1972.
————. *The Uncertain Trumpet*. New York: Harper, 1960.

RICHARD F. HAYNES

TAYLOR, Zachary (b. Orange County, Va., November 24, 1784; d. Washington, D.C., July 9, 1850), major general, 12th president of the United States. Taylor was one of the two principal American commanders in the 1846–1848 War with Mexico.

Although he was born in Virginia and elected president from Louisiana, Zachary Taylor's most significant identification was with pioneer Kentucky. Brought to a farm on the edge of Louisville at the age of eight months, he literally grew up with the state, lived there constantly until he entered the Army at twenty-three, and frequently returned. As would be expected in a frontier and near-frontier environment, his formal education was slight.

Commissioned a first lieutenant of infantry in 1808, Taylor became a captain two years later. In September 1812, when things had been going badly for U.S. outposts in the Old Northwest, he gallantly defended Fort Harrison on the Wabash River in Indiana Territory. For this he received the brevet of major.

In 1814, at Credit Island in the Mississippi River, Major Taylor was less fortunate. Overmatched by British and Indian firepower, he retreated for the only time in his life. In 1832, during the Black Hawk War, Taylor—now a colonel—participated in the Battle of the Bad Axe in what is now Wisconsin. In 1837 he defeated Seminole and Mikasuki Indians on the north shore of Lake Okeechobee, Florida. Brevetted brigadier general in recognition of that achievement, he remained in Florida two and a half years in command of the peninsula.

Still not widely known, Taylor was sixty years old in mid–1845 when the annexation of Texas made warfare with Mexico possible. At issue were disputed stretches of land between the Nueces River and the Rio Grande, and President James K. Polk placed Taylor at the head of American Army units at Corpus Christi.

Taylor continued at that Gulf site until early 1846, when with his small force he was ordered to the Rio Grande's east bank opposite Matamoros. In April Mexican detachments crossed the river and inflicted casualties. Taylor then marched eastward to secure his supply base at Point Isabel. Returning, he found a Mexican army—led by Mariano Arista—confronting him.

Palo Alto on May 8, 1846, was the first battle of the Mexican War. Taylor limited it mainly to an artillery duel in which he had a decided advantage. The next day at Resaca de la Palma, infantry and cavalry were also committed. The result was undoubted: the Mexicans fled across the Rio Grande to Matamoros and beyond. Throughout the United States, overnight, Taylor was acclaimed a hero.

War having been declared in Washington, the first target in Mexico was Monterrey where Pedro de Ampudia awaited the Americans. The action took place on September 21–23, when Taylor split his force in two and made substantial advances into the strongly fortified city. Victory, however, eluded him. Being a long way from his base of supplies, he agreed to an armistice. This involved the departure of Ampudia's army, a temporaray cessation of hostilities, and Monterrey's occupation by Taylor's men.

While many Americans viewed the Monterrey development as a Taylor triumph, the unauthorized armistice displeased Polk. The president now assigned Winfield Scott* to land at Vera Cruz and thence push on to Mexico City, confining Taylor's activities to a holding operation in the north.

Taylor was irate upon learning that most of his seasoned soldiers, including virtually all his regulars, would immediately be transferred to Scott's column. General Antonio López de Santa Anna, getting wind of the depletions, launched a campaign against Taylor and attacked him on Buena Vista's rugged terrain where Taylor—again unauthorized—had recently advanced.

The Battle of Buena Vista occurred on February 21–23, 1847, a few miles south of Saltillo. Santa Anna had twenty thousand men and Taylor fewer than five thousand, many of them green and only 10 percent of them regulars. The outcome, long in doubt, was the most spectacular victory of Taylor's military career. It had more than anything else to do with his elevation to the White House.

At its national convention in June 1848, the Whig party made Taylor its presidential nominee. The number-one question before the country was whether slavery would be permitted in the vast area ceded to the United States by Mexico in the Treaty of Guadalupe Hidalgo.

Both Taylor and Lewis Cass, his Democratic opponent, dodged the issue. Not so Martin Van Buren, candidate of the fledgling Free Soil party. Van Buren's presence in the race enabled Taylor to win in pivotal New York. Taylor carried half the states, eight in the South, seven in the North. In the electoral college, he defeated Cass 163 to 127.

When one thinks of Taylor's brief presidency, the sectional abrasiveness of 1850 looms large. Would slavery be extended west and southwest, or would the institution be contained within the fifteen states where it was legal?

Democrats, Whigs, and Free Soilers in Congress debated the problem for nine months. A Senate committee proposed a compromise, based chiefly on California's admission as a free state and on applying the expedient of popular sovereignty to other Western areas.

No one in the House or Senate opposed such a compromise more adamantly than Taylor. Although Taylor welcomed the free-state California concept, he wanted New Mexico to be a free state too. He was incensed by threats that the slave state of Texas, claiming part of New Mexico, might dispatch a militia expedition against U.S. troops at Santa Fe.

The crisis in Washingon was acute. Charges and countercharges heated the blood. Congressmen went armed to Capitol Hill. There was danger of civil war. It was even reported that, in the event of overt challenges to federal authority, Taylor intended to take the field in person against any and all disunionists.

At the peak of the crisis, Taylor suddenly died. His successor, Millard Fillmore, favored an adjustment incorporating the popular sovereignty provision. With the prospect of a presidential veto no longer a factor affecting their procedures, congressmen in September enacted the Compromise of 1850.

Most of Taylor's military service, which lasted nearly forty years, occurred in periods of tranquility. Stationed mainly in the Northwest and Southwest, usually in command of frontier forts, he maintained peace with Indian tribes and guarded pioneer settlements.

When the hour of combat came, he demonstrated courage and resourcefulness. Prior to Mexico, these qualities were clearest in Florida Territory where he experienced greater success than any contemporary in connection with the Seminoles.

In the Mexican War, Taylor's personality for the first time was a subject of national scrutiny. Utterly natural, unpretentious, rarely wearing a uniform, he strongly appealed to the soldiers who served under him, though some West Pointers and other officers found him deficient in the science of arms.

Especially at Monterrey and Buena Vista, it was evident to all that Taylor gave no thought to his personal safety. Both before and after times of triumph, he was characterized by genuine modesty.

Taylor became a major general soon after Resaca de la Palma. This was his highest military grade. He saw no action after Buena Vista, returning in December 1847 to Louisiana where throughout the following year he commanded the Army's southern division.

Because Taylor planted cotton and owned over a hundred slaves, both Southerners and Northerners were surprised when in the presidential chair he so sternly opposed slavery's expansion. Taylor's resolution in this regard fundamentally reflected his Western background and the convictions he formed as an officer in the West. Growing to manhood in Kentucky, a state at least as much Western as Southern, he was deeply influenced by his Army years in the Northwest and Southwest alike. These reinforced the westernness of his youth and made him a nationalist through and through.

Understanding Taylor contributes importantly to clear comprehension of his times. Belying sectionalistic stereotypes and theories of economic determinists, "Old Rough and Ready" in his straightforward way was as undeviatingly devoted to the Union as Andrew Jackson* and Abraham Lincoln* were.

BIBLIOGRAPHY

Bauer, K. Jack. *The Mexican War, 1846-1848*. New York: Macmillan, 1974.
Dyer Brainerd. *Zachary Taylor*, Baton Rouge: Louisiana State University Press, 1946.
Hamilton, Holman. *The Three Kentucky Presidents: Lincoln, Taylor, Davis*. Lexington: University Press of Kentucky, 1978.
————. *Zachary Taylor*. 2 vols. Indianapolis, Ind.: Bobbs-Merrill, 1941, 1951. Reissued in Hamden, Conn.: Archon Books, 1966.
Henry, Robert S. *The Story of the Mexican War*. Indianapolis, Ind.: Bobbs-Merrill, 1950.
Singletary, Otis A. *The Mexican War*. Chicago: University of Chicago Press, 1960.
[Taylor, Zachary.] *Letters of Zachary Taylor, from the Battle-fields of the Mexican War*. Rochester, N.Y.: Genesee Press, 1908. Reissued in New York: Kraus Reprint Company, 1970.

HOLMAN HAMILTON

TECUMSEH (b. near Springfield, Ohio, March 1768; d. near Thames River, Canada, October 5, 1813), Indian war chief.

Tecumseh was born in March 1768 near the present site of Springfield, Ohio, to a Shawnee father and a Creek mother. The frontier of the Old Northwest where he grew up was then especially violent because of the American Revolution. In the main the Indians of the region, comprising many small tribes, sided with the British; thus, between them and the white American frontiersmen there was incessant conflict on a small but terrible scale. Of course, Tecumseh himself was too young to take part in the engagements of the Revolution but not too young to feel their impact. His father was killed in 1774 when he refused to act as guide to a white expedition against other Indians. Ever afterwards his mother instilled revenge in him. With the other tribespeople, he was embittered when in 1777 white men killed Cornstalk, the venerable head chief of the Shawnees, in irrational retaliation for the murder of a white man which Cornstalk could not have prevented and with which he had nothing whatever to do. Next, in 1780 George Rogers Clark* entered the Ohio area and laid waste the fields and towns of the Shawnee. Two years later, once more in senseless retaliation, white men massacred the unarmed Christian Indians who were clustered at Gnadenhutten in east-central Ohio. Indeed, almost every major event confirmed the boy, Tecumseh, in his deep hatred of white civilization.

One of Tecumseh's earliest biographers, Benjamin Drake, asserted that Tecumseh always had a passion for war. As a child he played at war and organized his playmates like a chief. Whether or not this is true, it is certain that the boy and then the youth learned from every scrap of fighting he witnessed. He was present, not as a participant, in the last actions of the Revolution on the frontier. One of these was an attack which the Indians made on Bryant's Station, Kentucky, on August 15, 1782. It failed. In contrast, four days later, on August 19, he witnessed the greatest victory that the Indians ever won against the Kentuckians at Blue Licks. His own first active participation in a fight took place in 1784 (he was sixteen) when the party he was with attacked white people in flatboats on the river. On this occasion his associates burned a prisoner to death; Tecumseh was so revolted by this horror that he prevented repetitions of it when he had the power. His passion for war was not built upon a thirst for blood. He would never take part in the abuse of women and children, or permit it if he had the power to interfere.

Tecumseh may have been with the intertribal Indian force which in 1790 defeated Josiah Harmar's* small army, the first sent out by the new government of the United States under the Constitution. There is no doubt he was present in the 1791 fighting, for Blue Jacket made him head of raiding and scouting parties which steadily harassed the advance of Arthur St. Clair's* column into the Ohio country. After the ambush of that column, a disaster for the United States, which seemed to demonstrate that there was still hope for the Indian cause, Tecumseh went southward at the invitation of his older brother, Cheesekau, to aid the Cherokees against the whites. In actions at this time he increasingly showed military leadership. Several times he demonstrated that he could hold together a war party that had been surprised and was verging on panic. In an attack on Buchanan's Station, near Nashville, Tennessee, on September 30, 1792, his beloved brother was killed. Tecumseh's bitterness increased, but so did his military knowledge. There he learned that it was generally bad tactics for Indians to attack a white fort.

By the time Major General Anthony Wayne* began his final march into the Ohio country in 1794, Tecumseh was back in the Old Northwest. Once again Blue Jacket made him chief scout to watch what turned out to be Wayne's inexorable advance. He was, of course, part of the intertribal body of warriors decisively defeated by Wayne at Fallen Timbers on August 20, 1794. He was not present, however, when Wayne met with intimidated chiefs the next year and got their agreement to the Treaty of Greenville which surrendered to the whites the southern half of Ohio. Tecumseh, denying the power of the chiefs to alienate that land, refused to honor the treaty. Afterwards, he drew apart from the tribal organization and began to gather his own band. His stature grew among the Indian tribes.

Up to this point Tecumseh had been little more than a raider and marauder who was playing out his own lust for revenge upon white civilization. All the while, of course, he had increased in skill as a war leader. But from this time on he began to become the dynamic agent who tried to unite the Indians against white encroachment. It was apparent to him, but to few other Indians, that only united military action could halt the juggernaut. Although he cannot have been aware of it, he was trying to draw together diverse peoples of the same race who were just emerging from the Stone Age to pit them against a society far more advanced in technology. At this point in history, technology notwithstanding, had the Indians listened to his message, they might have retained part of the nation for themselves.

The Battle of Fallen Timbers broke the fighting power of the tribes of the Old Northwest and brought relative peace to that frontier. But it did not lull Tecumseh into inaction. Instead he traveled thousands of miles, on foot and in canoes, with a small band of picked associates, to carry the message of Indian unity from tribe to tribe. He carried this message to Ottawa, Winnebago, Kickapoo, Wyandot, Delaware, Sauk and Fox, Chippewa, and Pottawatamie in the Old Northwest; to the Osage in the West; and to the Iroquois in the Northeast. Southward he reached Choctaw, Cherokee, Chickasaw, Creek, and Seminole. Unfortunately for the future of the Indians, he could not persuade the many tribes to act together.

During the first decade of the 1800s, Tecumseh's younger brother advanced to prominence as "The Prophet." He awakened in the Indians a religious revival similar to the one occurring among white folk, except he revived native practices. He and his brother favored repudiation of most of white culture, especially liquor. They advocated a return to the purer culture that had preceded the coming of the white man. All this suited Tecumseh, and he cooperated with his brother, but at no time was there any doubt among them as to who was the final authority. Tecumseh was, and his authority spread widely, at least as far as the Dakotas to the west.

In September 1809 William Henry Harrison* obtained from some chiefs the Treaty of Fort Wayne in which the whites bought 3 million acres in Indiana for

$10,500. This steal sent Tecumseh into a rage, and he vowed to kill any of the chiefs who signed the document if he encountered them. The signers, he said, had no right to alienate this land, and the white purchasers, therefore, no claim upon it.

In August 1811 Tecumseh once more journeyed southward to try again to convince the great southeastern tribes of the need for unity. His powers as an orator were at their height, and he brought the full force of them to aid this mission. His speeches were always given in Shawnee, but many of them are quoted extensively in English. One cannot know how well they were translated, but translation was not perfectly necessary to his listeners even if they did not understand the words. Note the testimony of Sam Dale, a frontiersman: "I have heard many great orators, but I never saw one with the vocal powers of Tecumseh, or the same command of the muscles of his face. Had I been deaf the play of his countenance would have told me what he said." To back up his oratory, Tecumseh had with him twenty-four braves who performed with precision an impressive ceremony, but none of this swayed the southern tribes to his cause. Unfortunately for him, at that time those tribes had a decent relationship with the United States and did not wish to upset it. They lacked the vision to look into the future as Tecumseh did, and so they did not see the Trail of Tears that would destroy them a few decades hence.

With Tecumseh out of the way, William Henry Harrison decided the time had come to eliminate the center from which Indian opposition radiated. This was Prophetstown on the Wabash River, the base for Tecumseh and his brother, the Prophet. Before he had gone south, Tecumseh had ordered his brother to avoid conflict until he returned, but as Harrison drew close to the Indian town, although he professed peace, the Prophet decided that his people must attack. He guaranteed them against harm from the white men's bullets. His assault began in the dark on November 7, 1811, and, after several hours, failed. Harrison, advancing from this action, known as the Battle of Tippecanoe, destroyed the Shawnee town and the crops. Thus, when Tecumseh returned, discouraged from his failure in the south, expecting to find warmth and comfort at home, instead he found the charred ruins of a deserted village. As soon as he had reestablished contact, he banished the Prophet, who from that time forward had no influence on events.

On June 18, 1812, the United States declared war on Great Britain. For years its government had believed that the British were behind Tecumseh's belligerence. In fact, the British had tried to restrain Indian aggression but had, of course, kept close touch with leaders like Tecumseh. By this time Tecumseh's hatred of the United States hardly had any bounds, and so he went over at once to the British side. He thought this was perhaps the last chance to work with an ally sufficiently powerful to face down the Americans. For an uneducated person, he knew a surprising amount of history and was, therefore, aware that the Indians had not profited from their connection with Britain in the American Revolution. Still, to ally with them once more seemed a gamble his people had to take.

Tecumseh successfully led the first actions after war was declared. Major

General Isaac Brock came to command in Upper Canada, and in him Tecumseh found a white man he could admire. The Indian cause seemed to be turning upward once more. Between them Brock and Tecumseh bluffed General William Hull* out of Canada and back into Detroit, a well-fortified community. Brock's staff counseled against assaulting the fort, but Tecumseh advised an attempt. This he did in spite of what he had learned about the danger of attacking forts. After all, he had also learned that whatever his people achieved had to be done by audacity. Brock agreed with Tecumseh, and the result was General Hull's surrender of the American position and force on August 15, 1812. Tecumsch and Brock had achieved the surrender of a superior to an inferior force, with the superior force established in a strong defensive position.

Brock left at once for the eastern theater, and his successor, Major General Henry Procter, would not follow up the stroke at Detroit. From the start Tecumseh felt only contempt for the British general. Contempt was intensified by the Battle of the River Raisin on January 22, 1813. Tecumseh was not present, and Proctor made no attempt to control the Indians with him. As a result, the Indians massacred the wounded and the prisoners. This gave the Americans a battle cry, "Remember the River Raisin." If Tecumseh had been present, he would at least have tried to stop the slaughter.

Victory in Upper Canada depended on control of Lake Erie, and the ground forces of both sides were held in place while a building race went on on the water. Lake control finally passed to the United States as a result of the Battle of Lake Erie fought on September 10, 1813, by squadrons of the two inland navies. General Proctor attempted to conceal the unfavorable outcome from Tecumseh, but at the same time he prepared hastily to retreat eastward. Tecumseh, dead set against this retreat, wanted to stand and fight it out, for by this time he realized that the British-Indian cause was losing, and he did not wish to survive its failure. The end came when the retreating force finally did make a stand beside the Thames River on October 5, 1813. Tecumseh controlled five hundred Indians who held the right of the British line. Early in the action it became known that Tecumseh had been killed, and that information caused the Indian resistance to decline. Afterwards, white men made political capital out of the claim that they had personally killed the Indian chief, but it was never established beyond doubt who had fired the bullets that brought him down.

During twenty-eight years of fighting white men, Tecumseh had never won a major victory for the Indians; nor is it likely that he made innovations that permanently altered the craft of combat. Has he a place, then, as a military leader? He did become a skilled leader of bands that carried out guerrilla-style operations. He had developed a fine sense for what his warriors could and could not do. He knew that they had to act audaciously. In most cases he would not throw them against a well-garrisoned white fort. He may have employed the ruse better than any other Indian leader. For example, at Detroit in August 1812, he sent his warriors in a continuous circle through an opening in the forest in view of the American garrison, until General Hull, at least, was convinced that an overwhelming body of Indians opposed his small army. He tried another type of ruse at Fort Meigs in the summer of 1813. He had little confidence in the siege which General Proctor was conducting of that American fort, but he did his best to abet it. With the garrison expecting reinforcements, Tecumseh caused his Indians to engage in a sham battle which he hoped the garrison would believe involved the relief column. If the garrison sallied out of the fort, it could be defeated. This ruse came close to success but failed in the end.

Tecumseh had charisma that made warriors willing to follow him. This came from a fine presence and great skill in sport and in warfare. The power of his speech added to it—and so did his unwillingness to torture and to slaughter women and children. All of his charismatic qualities were reinforced by his unswerving commitment to the great goal of Indian unity. It was the curse of the North American Indians that they could not see with his vision. Instead, they remained more loyal to individual tribes, even to the white man, than to Indianness. And so they lost their country.

Tecumseh, then, belongs in the roster of great American military leaders because he had the essential qualities of that leadership. He had courage, decisiveness, and a strong will. He had consideration for those who would follow him but restrained them when they slipped into savage practices. William Henry Harrison, who did more than any man among his contemporaries to frustrate Tecumseh's dream said: "If it had not been for the vicinity of the United States, he would perhaps be the founder of an Empire that would rival in glory that of Mexico or Peru." Tecumseh might have achieved a nobler goal than that. Instead of an empire, he might have founded a free place in which his people could have lived and followed their culture.

BIBLIOGRAPHY

Mahon, John K. *The War of 1812*. Gainesville: University of Florida Press, 1972.
Oskison, John M. *Tecumseh and His Times*. New York: G. P. Putnam's Sons, 1938.
Raymond, Ethel T. *Tecumseh*. Toronto: Broak and Company, 1915.
Tucker, Glenn. *Tecumseh: Vision of Glory*. Indianapolis, Ind.: Bobbs-Merrill Company, 1956.
Wilson, William E. *Shooting Star: The Story of Tecumseh*. New York: Farrar and Ringhart, 1942.

JOHN K. MAHON

TERRY, Alfred Howe (b. Hartford, CT, November 10, 1827; d. New Haven, Ct, December 16, 1890), professional soldier.

Born into a Connecticut family that could trace its New England lineage back to the middle of the seventeenth century, Alfred Terry was one of ten children of a prosperous merchant and book dealer. Moving with his parents from Hartford to New Haven in 1831, he considered the latter city to be his home for the remainder of his life. Educated in New Haven's public schools, he entered the law department of Yale in 1848. Unchallenged by the demands of the school's curriculum, Terry applied directly for admission to the state bar in 1849. Upon being accepted to practice, he left Yale without graduating, never to return. For the next twelve years he labored diligently but unsuccessfully to make a career as a trial lawyer. To occupy the time between cases he accepted positions in legal administration, becoming city clerk in 1850 and clerk of the county superior court in 1854. Still unfulfilled, Terry took up the study of military history and science as a hobby. Joining the New Haven Grays militia company in 1849, he rose to the rank of major by 1855.

Upon the outbreak of the Civil War in 1861, Terry was commissioned colonel of the Second Connecticut Volunteer Infantry, a militia regiment obligated to serve for ninety days. He led the regiment at First Bull Run, where it was part of E. D. Keyes's brigade. When the Second Connecticut mustered out of service in August, Terry recruited a three-year regiment, the Seventh Connecticut Infantry and became its colonel. In November 1861 the Seventh Connecticut became part of the Union expedition that seized Port Royal Sound and Hilton Head, South Carolina. Terry remained at Hilton Head until mid-December, using the time to train his unit to a high state of efficiency. At the end of the year he took his regiment south to Tybee Island, Georgia, to join the forces besieging Fort Pulaski. Upon the surrender of the fort in April 1862, Terry became its new commander. His promotion to brigadier general of volunteers followed before the end of the month.

By late summer of 1862 Terry had risen to command the several thousand Union troops at Hilton Head. During the year that he spent on Hilton Head administrative matters occupied most of his time, although he did lead a brigade during the abortive Federal raid on the Charleston and Savannah Railroad at Pocotaligo, South Carolina, in October 1862. Finally, in the summer of 1863 Terry's troops became involved in Major General Quincy Gillmore's campaign against Charleston, South Carolina. When Gillmore launched an expedition to seize Morris Island in July, Terry led a small force to nearby James Island to divert Confederate attention. The diversion was successful, with Federal forces gaining a permanent lodgment on Morris Island. Following two unsuccessful assaults on Confederate fortifications at the north end of the island, Gillmore reorganized his command and began siege operations. In the reorganization Terry became commander of the division of Federal troops on Morris Island. The Confederates abandoned Morris Island in September, but Gillmore and Terry were unable to make further inroads in Charleston's defenses.

Terry remained in the Department of the South as a district commander until April 1864, when he led the advance elements of Gillmore's troops to the Virginia theater of operations. There he assumed command of the First Division, X Corps, which he became part of Major General Benjamin Butler's* Army of the James. Terry led his division in Butler's Bermuda Hundred Campaign of May-June, 1864, taking part in minor actions at Chester Station and Wooldridge's Hill, and the major battle of Drewry's Bluff. At the conclusion of the latter battle on May

16, 1864, Terry played a conspicuous role in covering the retreat of the defeated
Army of the James to its Bermuda Hundred base. He continued to command his
division in operations around Bermuda Hundred, Petersburg, and Richmond
until October 1864, taking part in several sharp actions in front of the Richmond
defenses. He assumed command of the X Corps for several months late in the
year, and on one occasion briefly led the Army of the James during Butler's
absence. He had been promoted to major general of volunteers by brevet in
August, but administrative irregularities prevented the new rank from taking
effect until the end of the year.

In a reorganization of the Army of the James in December 1864 Terry's
command became the First Division of the XXIV Corps. Uninvolved in the
abortive first attempt to seize Fort Fisher, which protected the blockade-runner
haven of Wilmington, North Carolina, Terry commanded the second expedition
to Fort Fisher in January 1865. Working closely with the navy, he formulated
and successfully executed a model plan which resulted in the surrender of Fort
Fisher to his troops on January 15, 1865. For this service he received the thanks
of Congress and promotion to the rank of brigadier general in the regular army.
He finished the war by leading his troops inland from Wilmington in March,
ultimately uniting them with William Tecumseh Sherman's army in central North
Carolina.

Mustered out of the volunteer service in 1866 as a major general, Terry chose
to remain in the regular army. In the immediate postwar period, he briefly
commanded the Department of Virginia before going west to command the
Department of Dakota. In 1869 he was transferred to the Department of the
South, where he firmly but carefully used military force to eliminate domestic
turmoil and restore order in Georgia. After more than three years in Georgia he
again assumed command of the Department of Dakota. In the summer of 1876
he took the field in overall command of the expedition against the Sioux that
culminated in the loss of Lieutenant Colonel George Armstrong Custer* and five
companies of the Seventh Cavalry. Although controversy has swirled around
Terry's orders to Custer ever since, Terry refused to defend himself or castigate
Custer publicly. He remained in command of the Department of Dakota until
1886, when he was promoted to major general and given command of the
Division of the Missouri. By this time seriously ill, Terry spent most of the
following year on sick leave. Forced into retirement in 1888 by the state of his
health, he returned to New Haven, Connecticut, where he died of Bright's disease
on December 16, 1890.

Alfred Terry was one of the preeminent non-West Point officers in the American army of the nineteenth century. Trained in the legal profession, he gained
his military knowledge primarily by private study. This knowledge, coupled with
his innate intelligence, permitted him to perform creditably as a field officer
from the very beginning of the Civil War. His regimental commands, especially
the Seventh Connecticut Infantry, were models of efficiency. Many other vol-

unteer officers, however, could claim as much for themselves. As the war progressed, Terry began to rise from the crowd as he held successively more important commands. He proved as adept at administration of a district as he did in leading a division in the field. On several occasions he was given temporary command of an army corps, and at one point in the conflict he commanded an army. Recognition of his abilities by his superiors eventually led to his assignment to lead the second Fort Fisher expedition, an important independent command.

Terry's rise was due not to political favoritism but to pure ability and an exceptional personality. He proved able to work in harmony with such disparate superiors as West Point-trained Quincy Gillmore and political general Benjamin Butler. As his success against Fort Fisher showed, he was also able to develop a productive working relationship with the irascrible David Porter* of the navy. This ability to deal with others firmly and forthrightly but without rancor or partisanship was also displayed during his difficult tenure in Georgia in the Reconstruction period. His refusal to engage in public debate during the controversy over his orders to Custer provides further evidence of the strength of his character.

Alfred Terry's significance in American military history rests on two foundations. First, his activities as operational commander and military administrator in both war and peace and models of their kind. His campaign against Fort Fisher and his administration of Georgia during Reconstruction represent the twin highlights of his service to the nation. Second, and more important, Terry proved by the force of his own example that formal military education was not required for a successful military career in the nineteenth century. His career showed that a good mind, a strong character, and a willingness to learn from experience could overcome the lack of West Point training. He thus epitomized the ideal nineteenth century volunteer officer—a volunteer so competent in his adopted profession that he could make the transition to the regular army without visible difficulty or opposition.

BIBLIOGRAPHY

Hughes, Robert P. "The Campaign Against the Sioux in 1876," *Journal of the Military Service Institution of the United States*. Vol. 28, No. 79 (January 1896), 1-44.

Marino, C. W. *General Alfred Howe Terry: Soldier from Connecticut*. Ann Arbor: University Microfilms, 1970.

Walkley, Stephen. *History of the Seventh Connecticut Volunteer Infantry*. Hartford, 1905.

The War of the Rebellion: A Compilation of the Official Records of the Union and Confederate Armies. Washington, D.C.: Government Printing Office, 1880-1901.

Warner, Ezra J. *Generals in Blue: Lives of the Union Commanders*. Baton Rouge: Louisiana State University Press, 1964.

WILLIAM GLENN ROBERTSON

THAYER, Sylvanus (b. Braintree, Mass., June 9, 1785; d. South Braintree, Mass., September 7, 1872), military educator. Thayer is considered the father of West Point by modern authorities.

Sylvanus Thayer was born into an old Massachusetts family, his American ancestry dating from the first half of the seventeenth century. In 1803 he began a classical education at Dartmouth College, where he remained until 1807. That year he moved to the U.S. Military Academy at West Point, New York, which was then known chiefly as the only engineering school in the nation. Because there was no prescribed course of study, cadets passed examinations as quickly as the few professors allowed. Thayer graduated in 1808, receiving his commission in the Corps of Engineers. For the next few years, he was assigned to the construction of coastal fortifications in New York and the New England states.

On the eve of the War of 1812, Thayer was appointed a first lieutenant. He saw action in various quarters during the conflict, first as General Henry Dearborn's* chief engineer along the Niagara front, then with General Wade Hampton* on Lake Champlain, and finally with General Moses Porter in the defense of Norfolk, Virginia, in 1814. For distinguished service in Norfolk action, Thayer (then captain) was brevetted major. At the war's end, Major Thayer was sent to Europe to study the post-Napoleonic armies, fortifications, and military schools.

After touring various European countries for almost two years, Thayer was recalled to the United States early in 1817, and in July he was appointed superintendent of West Point to succeed Captain Alden Partridge. Partridge was loath to leave his post and protested mightily, but, for the most part, Thayer managed to remain above the imbroglio between the contentious Partridge and his superiors. Partridge ultimately resigned his commission, and Thayer won the post he would fill for the next sixteen years.

When Thayer came to the superintendency, West Point was much as he had left it some nine years before: a foundling government school attached to a river garrison, only casually committed to the notion of educating military officers for the nation. By the time Thayer resigned in 1833, West Point had been molded into an institution of military education (especially in engineering) commensurate with the demands of the United States for a professional officer corps.

During the egalitarian Andrew Jackson* administration, Thayer's West Point came under attack as an elitist institution. There was some justification in the charge, although Jackson's antagonism could also be traced to his own militia background. Thayer resigned the superintendency in protest and refused to return five years later when he was offered his old post again.

Nevertheless, Thayer's talents as an educator and engineer did not go unrewarded. On the strength of his performance as the superintendent of West Point, he advanced steadily in rank: in 1823 he was brevetted lieutenant colonel of engineers; in 1833 he was made a brevet colonel; and five years later he was made a lieutenant colonel of engineers—this at a time when promotions were notoriously slow in the United States' minuscule armed forces. Following his resignation from West Point, Thayer was named engineer in charge of the Boston Harbor defenses. He also served first as a member and then as president of the

Army's Board of Engineers until 1858, when he took a leave of absence from the Army because of failing health.

Thayer's interest in education continued throughout his life. Several years after his retirement from the Army (in 1863 as a brevet brigadier general), he busied himself with philanthropic endeavors, including the endowment of the Thayer School of Engineering at his old college, Dartmouth. He lived the remainder of his life at his birthplace, Braintree, Massachusetts.

Thayer's reputation properly depends upon his performance as superintendent of West Point. He was utterly devoted to the improvement of the Academy. When he arrived at West Point in 1817, the school had a deserved image as a national liability operating chiefly for the edification of military dilettantes. Discipline among the cadets was poor, and controversy stormed through the corps of cadets at the slighest provocation. Thayer quickly instituted a highly structured day of cadet instruction, buttressed by detailed regulations of conduct. Assessing the academic abilities of the corps of cadets shortly after his arrival, he found that one-fifth of the students had serious educational shortcomings and that fully half had accomplished only one year of study in as much as three years' residence. Drawing upon his observations in Europe, Thayer sought to model West Point upon France's *École Polytechnique*: small classes, daily recitations by each cadet, and regular postings of class standings to foster student competition. This body of regulations and method of instruction—though it evolved over the years—is still known as the Thayer System at West Point.

Under Thayer's strict management, West Point quickly took its place as one of the finest schools in the nation. Others interested in American higher education saw much that was admirable in Thayer's administration: as early as 1821, Thayer's old Dartmouth classmate, George Ticknor (now a young professor crusading for educational reform at Harvard), wrote in the Boston *Daily Advertiser* that the cadets of West Point "are constantly devoted to an intellectual discipline much more severe than their military discipline—who are much more thoroughly taught, what they pretend to learn, than any of the young men, who are sent to our colleges."

For the most part, such accolades were the result of Thayer's own hard work and devotion. He became so closely identified with the success of West Point that one contemporary is reputed to have said that "no man would be indiscreet enough to take the place after Thayer, it would be as bad as being President of the Royal Society after Newton." Yet Thayer was fortunate to have superintended the Academy under government administrations that approved of his mission and gave him the fullest possible support in his reforms at a time when the nation was retrenching militarily.

BIBLIOGRAPHY

Ambrose, Stephen A. *Duty, Honor, Country: A History of West Point*. Baltimore: Johns Hopkins University Press, 1967.
Cullum, George Washington, comp. *Biographical Register of Officers and Graduates of*

the United States Military Academy. 3d ed. Washington, D.C.: U.S. Government Printing Office, 1891.

Ellis, Joseph, and Robert Moore. *School for Soldiers: West Point and the Profession of Arms*. New York: Oxford University Press, 1974.

Tyack, David. *George Ticknor and the Boston Brahmins*. New York: Oxford University Press, 1967.

ROGER J. SPILLER

THOMAS, George Henry (b. Southampton County, Va., July 31, 1816; d. San Francisco, Calif., March 28, 1870), Army officer, Union Commander in the West during the Civil War.

George Henry Thomas, whose ancestors settled in America in the midseventeenth century, was of English, Welsh, and French Huguenot ancestry. Born in the midst of slave territory, at age fifteen he fled with his family from Nat Turner's Rebellion. After receiving a local education, he studied law and served as deputy to his uncle, clerk of the Southampton County court, who later helped secure his appointment to West Point. There Thomas showed an aptitude for many subjects, particularly artillery and cavalry tactics. He was graduated twelfth in the forty-two-man class of 1840 and was posted to the 3d Artillery Regiment.

For two decades he did garrison duty in the South and Northeast, finally attaining the lieutenant colonelcy of the 2d Cavalry (in place of Robert Edward Lee,* resigned) at the outbreak of the Civil War. During that period he also taught tactics at the Military Academy (1851–1854) and fought the Seminoles in Florida (1840–1842, 1849–1850) and other Indians in Texas (1856–1860). His most extensive combat service, however, was in the Mexican War, in which he won brevets for gallantry at Monterrey and Buena Vista.

When Texas seceded, the 2d Cavalry was sent to Carlisle Barracks, Pennsylvania, where Colonel Thomas reorganized and reequipped it. In June 1861 he joined an army that invaded his native state via the Shenandoah Valley. Leading a brigade of regulars and volunteers in the July 2 skirmish at Falling Waters, he precipitated the retreat of Confederates under Thomas Jonathan ("Stonewall") Jackson.*

When the Valley Campaign closed, Thomas went west as a brigadier of volunteers. He received a division in the Army of the Ohio under Brigadier General Don Carlos Buell.* In January 1862 Thomas led a dozen regiments against as many Rebels seeking to invade Bluegrass territory, routing them at Mill Springs.

Despite winning the Union's first decisive victory, Thomas was passed over for praise and promotion by the War Department, reportedly at the direction of Abraham Lincoln.* The government held him suspect because of his heritage, his pro-Southern views on politics and slavery, his efforts to become commandant of cadets at the Virginia Military Institute, and his slow, if steady, approach to warfare. In the months ahead he would receive tardy recognition for services rendered and would be overslaughed by several junior officers.

In February Thomas participated in a movement culminating in the occupation of Nashville. Two weeks later, leading Buell's reserves, he arrived too late to fight at Shiloh. On April 25, when transferred to command the right wing of Union forces under Major General Henry Wager Halleck* for the siege of Corinth, he received the major generalship of volunteers he had truly won at Mill Springs.

Reassigned to Buell's army in June, Thomas joined the withdrawal to Nashville, occasioned by another Confederate foray in Kentucky, this one by General Braxton Bragg* and Major General Edmund Kirby Smith.* Distressed by the retreat, the War Office ordered Thomas to supersede his superior. He refused, believing that Buell had been unfairly treated. In October at the Battle of Perryville, as Buell's second-in-command, Thomas helped stymie Bragg. Afterwards, however, Buell was compelled to step down, and Thomas accepted a division under Major General William Starke Rosecrans,* Thomas's former junior. Though stung by the affront, Thomas tenaciously held the center of the Army of the Cumberland's line at Stones River in December and January. By persuading Rosecrans to remain on the field despite initial setbacks, he ensured the withdrawal of Bragg's Army of the Tennessee.

During the next eight months, Thomas figured prominently in Rosecrans' successful campaign to maneuver Bragg into Georgia. On September 19, 1863, however, Bragg unexpectedly struck the Union Army along Chickamauga Creek. The next day, the Federal right and center broke and fled north to Chattanooga. Only Thomas's XIV Corps—twenty thousand men, later reinforced—held its position on the left. Having covered his comrades' retreat, Thomas withdrew in good order after midnight. By the time he rejoined Rosecrans, he had earned the rosbriquet ''Rock of Chickamauga.''

Rosecrans' defeat led to his relief and Thomas' elevation to command the Army of the Cumberland. Despite Bragg's heavy siege, which threatened the army with starvation, Thomas held Chattanooga until troops from Virginia under Joseph Hooker* and Vicksburg under Ulysses Simpson Grant* arrived to reopen its supply lines. With Grant as overall commander, the Union forces moved against Bragg late in November, and Thomas' army secured his advancement to brigadier general of regulars by an amazing feat of arms. On November 25 it attacked supposedly impregnable positions atop Missionary Ridge, southeast of Chattanooga, succeeding beyond Grant's expectations—and orders. Again Bragg was driven into Georgia and lost his command.

Due in part to Grant's coolness toward Thomas, another of Thomas' juniors, Major General William Tecumseh Sherman,* received command of the combined Federal forces in the West after Grant went to Virginia as general in chief in March 1864. During the Atlanta Campaign, Thomas led three infantry corps and three cavalry divisions, two-thirds of Sherman's army. His sixty-five thousand men were engaged at Dalton, Resaca, Cassville, Dallas, Pine and Kenesaw Mountains, Ruff's Station, Peach Tree Creek, and Jonesboro. At Jonesboro, August 31–September 1, they helped capture Atlanta's southern flank and the

"Gate City" itself. This revived sagging Union fortunes and helped ensure Lincoln's reelection.

In October, planning his March to the Sea, Sherman returned Thomas to Nashville to organize an army to resist a new advance by the Army of the Tennessee, which was now under Lieutenant General John Bell Hood.* Laboring under severe handicaps against a fast-approaching deadline, Thomas collected seventy thousand castoffs from Chattanooga, St. Louis, and elsewhere and formed them into a cohesive force. His advance units slowed Hood's northward march at Columbia and Franklin, November 26–30, until Nashville could be made impregnable.

Originally scheduled for early December, Thomas' movement against Hood's new position below Nashville was delayed several days by a snowstorm and eleventh-hour preparations. From Virginia, Grant demanded he attack at once, fearing Hood's ability to outflank him and push unopposed into Union territory. Finally, Grant prepared to go west and personally relieve Thomas. In the interim the weather cleared and the army advanced. On December 15 and 16 Thomas vindicated his thorough planning, inflicting on his enemy the most decisive defeat of the war. Utterly routed, Hood hastened into Alabama, pressed by a vicious pursuit. The triumph won Thomas the thanks of Congress and of the Tennessee Assembly and a major generalship in the Regular Army.

Still lacking Grant's complete faith, Thomas played no active role in the 1865 campaign, his army being fragmented and sent to other theaters. He held garrison and departmental command at Nashville and Louisville for four years, when transferred to California. He administered the Military Division of the Pacific until his death from a stroke at age fifty-three, leaving a widow but no children.

Thomas' painful decision to subordinate his state to his nation cost him the love of his sisters, who disowned and shunned him, while Virginia's secession left him stateless until Tennessee adopted him as a citizen in 1865. A formidable looking man, Thomas was characterized by one subordinate as "six feet tall, of Jove-like figure, impressive countenance, and lofty bearing." Due perhaps to his girth (he weighed over two hundred pounds), probably to a spinal injury suffered in an 1860 railroad mishap, and certainly to his natural inclination, he seemed always to move at a moderate pace. His troops affectionately called him "Old Slow Trot" and "Old Pap." Of the Union's many prudent, deliberate, conservative commanders, he was by far the most successful because, once resolved to act, he did so decisively, with great confidence and vigor. Moreover, he alone enjoyed experience in and mastery of the tactics of all three combat arms.

Because of his unyielding principles of warfare, his sometimes eccentric behavior, his plainspokenness, and his inability to conceal resentment over slights dealt him and his colleagues by civilian and military superiors, he alienated some who might have promoted his career. Early in the Chattanooga Campaign as well as at Nashville, he impressed Grant as dilatory and lacking in strategic perception. These facts, plus the circumstances that led officials in Washington to doubt his loyalty for so long, denied him timely promotions, the opportunity to command an army, and a place on center stage at war's finale.

BIBLIOGRAPHY

Cleaves, Freeman. *Rock of Chickamauga: The Life of General George H. Thomas.* Norman: University of Oklahoma Press, 1948.
Horn, Stanley F. *The Decisive Battle of Nashville.* Baton Rouge: Louisiana State University Press, 1956.
McKinney, Francis F. *Education in Violence: The Life of George H. Thomas and the History of the Army of the Cumberland.* Detroit, Mich.: Wayne State University Press, 1961.
O'Connor, Richard. *Thomas: Rock of Chickamauga.* New York: Prentice-Hall, 1948.
Tucker, Glenn. *Chickamauga: Bloody Battle in the West.* Indianapolis, Ind.: Bobbs-Merrill Company, 1961.
Van Horne, Thomas B. *The Life of Major-General George H. Thomas.* New York: Charles Scribner's Sons, 1882.

EDWARD G. LONGACRE

TRUSCOTT, Lucian King, Jr. (b. Chatfield, Tex., January 9, 1895; d. Washington, D.C., September 12, 1965), Army officer. Division, Corps, and Army commander in the Mediterranean during World War II.

Among the few chosen for top combat command in the U.S. Army in World War II was Lucian King Truscott, Jr., who rose in rank from colonel to general through successive battle commands of regiment, division, corps, and field army, a unique record. No other officer in the U.S. Army in World War II duplicated this feat.

Truscott was the son of Lucian King Truscott, a country doctor, and Maria Temple (Tully) Truscott. He was of Irish descent on his mother's side and English on his father's. When he was six his family moved to Oklahoma, where he attended grammar and normal schools in Norman, Oklahoma. For six years he taught school during the winters and studied at various teachers' institutes during the summers.

Truscott was attending the Cleveland Teachers' Institute when war broke out in 1917. He enlisted in the Army, was selected for officer training, and was assigned to the Officers Training Camp at Fort Logan H. Roots, Arkansas. On August 15, 1917, he was commissioned a second lieutenant of cavalry in the Officers Reserve Corps and was assigned to the 17th Cavalry at Douglas, Arizona. In December 1917 he became a first lieutenant.

In March 1919 Truscott accompanied the 17th Cavalry to Hawaii, where he spent the next two and a half years. In the summer of 1921 he was reassigned to the United States. His unit was transferred to Marfa, Texas, where he spent the next three years.

In October 1925 he was assigned to the Cavalry School at Fort Riley, Kansas, where he attended both the Troop Officers and the Advanced Equitation courses, and was retained as an instructor for four years. Truscott's next assignment was to the 3d Cavalry at Fort Myer, Virginia, where he commanded a troop for three years. In August 1934 he entered the Command and General Staff School at Fort Leavenworth, Kansas. Upon completing the course, he was retained as an instructor for four years. While at Leavenworth, Truscott was promoted to major, having served nineteen years as a company grade officer.

After duty at Fort Knox, Kentucky, and Fort Lewis, Washington, Truscott, then a colonel, was selected by General George Catlett Marshall* for assignment to Admiral Louis Mountbatten's Combined Operations Headquarters in London. Truscott's survey of the British Commandos led to the formation of American Ranger units, whose name he suggested to commemorate Robert Rogers'* Rangers.

Promoted to brigadier general in 1942, Truscott participated in the Dieppe raid. The following month he reported to General George Smith Patton, Jr.* to command sub-task force "Goal Post" of the Western Task Force in the landings on the West Coast of Africa. On November 8, 1942, his reinforced regiment secured Port Lyautey in Morocco. For his part in the North African landings, Truscott was awarded the Distinguished Service Medal and was promoted to major general. His citation mentioned both his planning and organizational skills, as well as his brilliant battlefield leadership.

In late 1942, General Dwight David Eisenhower* named Truscott his field deputy at his Advanced Command Post at Constantine, to provide timely information on the situation along the distant Tunisian front. As the Tunisian Campaign ended, Truscott assumed command of the 3d Infantry Division, where he instituted a rigorous training campaign in preparation for the invasion of Sicily. His "Truscott Trot," an accelerated pace over extended distances, paid off. The 3d Division spearheaded the Seventh Army landing, drove north to capture Palermo, and then east to Messina, covering some three hundred miles in thirty-eight days, over rugged, mountainous terrain against a determined enemy. *Life Magazine* referred to this operation as "a classic in military annals for speed and success." His battlefield leadership won him Patton's praise and the Distinguished Service Cross for gallantry in action. Among the many American division commanders in Sicily, Truscott was outstanding.

In September 1943 the 3d Division landed on the Salerno beachhead in Italy and continued up the peninsula with the Fifth Army forces to the Volturno River and the first winter line. In January the division was pulled out of the line to make an amphibious landing at Anzio, just south of Rome, as part of the VI Corps. In March Truscott was named VI Corps commander. General Mark Wayne Clark* said of Truscott, "I selected Truscott to become the new VI Corps commander because of all the division commanders...in the Anzio bridge-head...he was the most outstanding. He inspired confidence in all with whom he came in contact."

Truscott's VI Corps repulsed heavy enemy attacks and in May broke out of the beachhead to enter Rome on June 4. After the fall of Rome, the VI Corps was withdrawn from combat to plan and train for the invasion of southern France.

The VI Corps landing in southern France on August 15, 1944, was the culmination of Truscott's considerable experience in such matters and a masterpiece of execution. His subsequent pursuit and destruction of enemy forces up the Rhone Valley was noteworthy for speed and decisiveness. He considered the Battle of Montélimar his greatest tactical achievement. General Jean de Lattre, French Army "B," described the scene: "Over tens of kilometers there was nothing but an inextricable tangle of twisted steel frames and charred corpses— the apocalyptic cemetery of all the equipment of the Nineteenth (German) Army, through which only bulldozers would be able to make a way." In nineteen days the VI Corps captured Lyon and shortly thereafter linked up with elements of the XV Corps to the north, opening a badly needed line of communications for General Eisenhower's forces driving toward Germany.

Truscott's successful leadership of the VI Corps resulted in his promotion to lieutenant general and selection to command the Fifth Army in Italy, succeeding General Clark. There he confirmed the confidence in which he was held by his superiors. The Fifth Army burst out of its winter line in the spring of 1945, pushed across the Po Valley to the foothills of the Alps, and secured the first German surrender in Europe in May 1945.

In 1954 Truscott was promoted to the rank of general by special act of Congress. He died in Washington, D.C., on September 12, 1965, and was buried in Arlington National Cemetery.

Truscott's military success derived from two basic factors, his preparation for a military career and his ability to apply in war what he had learned in peacetime. He survived the rugged physical demands of his early service, where he learned the importance of mental and physical durability and where he developed a strong motivation for a military career. Another factor in Truscott's prewar formation was his intellectual capacity. Perceptual acuity, decisiveness, and self-confidence were founded on twelve years of military school experience.

Truscott's military ability was based more on personal character than on academic learning. Generals Marshall, Eisenhower, and Clark all observed in him the primary ingredients of a combat leader; that is, personal integrity, courage, and loyalty. Moreover, his leadership style was straightforward. He was open, direct, and forceful without guile or dissemblance. One of his close colleagues during World War II described him this way: "He had Patton's charisma, Bradley's soundness, and Eisenhower's diplomacy." Another said of him, "He was a tough, outspoken, aggressive soldier almost universally admired by his men and superiors." Another said, "His knowledge of men, skill in conditioning and training them and interest in their well-being brought high morale to his command. He was a great soldier who contributed measurably to the success of the Allied effort in World War II."

On the basis of his strong character and his unsurpassed combat record, Truscott deserves a firm place in history. In the opinion of many of those with whom he served, he was the outstanding combat commander of American Army forces in World War II.

BIBLIOGRAPHY

Blumenson, Martin. *Anzio: The Gamble That Failed.* Philadelphia and New York: J. B. Lippincott Company, 1963.

Clark, Mark W. *Calculated Risk.* New York: Harper and Brothers, 1950.

Truscott, L. K., Jr. *Command Missions: A Personal Story.* New York: E. P. Dutton and Company, 1954.

THEODORE J. CONWAY

TRUXTUN, Thomas (b. Long Island, N.Y., February 17, 1755; d. Philadelphia, Pa., May 5, 1822), naval officer. Truxtun was one of the first six captains appointed upon the establishment of the Navy in 1794.

Thomas Truxtun was the son of an English barrister practicing in New York. When his father died in 1765, the ten-year-old Truxtun came under the guardianship of John Troup of Jamaica, Long Island. Two years later, Truxtun embarked upon a seafaring career, sailing with Captains Joseph Holmes and James Chambers in the London trade. Taken off a merchant ship at the age of fifteen, Truxtun was pressed into service in the Royal Navy. On board the British warship *Prudent* (64–guns), he so impressed his British commanding officer with his natural abilities that the man offered Truxtun his aid in securing a midshipman's warrant in the Royal Navy. Truxtun, however, declined and gained his release from British service through the good offices of influential friends. He returned to merchant service and, by age twenty, rose to command of the *Andrew Caldwell.* By that time, 1775, relations between the colonies and Great Britain had begun to deteriorate, and Truxtun participated in the military preparations at Philadelphia by running huge quantities of gunpowder into the city. He continued those activities until later in the year when his ship was seized by the British warship *Argo* near St. Kitts in the Leeward Islands.

Truxtun managed to make it back to Philadelphia by the summer of 1776 when events in the colonies had reached the point of a complete rupture with Great Britain. There he signed on as a lieutenant in the *Congress*, the first privateer to be fitted out for service against the British. During the last part of the year, he took part in the capture of several prizes while cruising off the coast of Cuba. In 1777 Truxtun took command of and fitted out his first command, *Independence*, and sailed her to the Azores. After taking three prizes in the vicinity of the Azores, he returned home, fitted out *Mars*, and commanded her on a highly successful cruise of the English Channel. Following that, he commanded the *Independence* once more and then captained the privateers *Commerce* and *St. James.*

Truxton's activities during the Revolution went beyond privateering. His ships also carried precious cargoes of military stores into the beleaguered colonies. At the end of one voyage in the *St. James*, Truxtun landed the most valuable such cargo brought into Philadelphia during the conflict. It is said that in lauding him at a dinner in his honor, General George Washington* declared Truxtun's services to be worth that of a regiment. On another occasion, also during his command of the *St. James*, his ship carried the American consul-general to France. During the voyage, he encountered a 32–gun British ship and, after a sharp fight, managed to disable his opponent.

Truxtun returned to mercantile service after the successful conclusion of the Revolution and served as master for several East Indiamen in the late 1780s and early 1790s. In 1794 Congress established the Navy Department and authorized the construction of six new frigates. To command them, six captains were selected. Truxtun received his appointment as one of the six on June 4, 1798, and put to sea in his new command, the 36–gun frigate *Constellation*, later that month to prosecute the undeclared naval war between the United States and Revolutionary France. He returned to one of his old hunting grounds, the seas between St. Kitts and Puerto Rico, at the head of a squadron of smaller ships. On February 9, 1799, Captain Truxtun scored the first of his two most celebrated victories. After a fight of about an hour, the *Constellation* overwhelmed the French frigate *Insurgente*, killing twenty-nine and wounding forty-four of the Frenchmen's crew. He brought *Insurgente* into St. Kitts where she was refitted and commissioned in the U.S. Navy as the *Insurgent* under the command of Captain John Rodgers.*

Truxtun resumed his patrols of the West Indies and, almost a year after the *Insurgente* battle, joined his second, and most spectacular, scrape with a French man-of-war. On February 1, 1800, the 36–gun *Constellation* encountered the 50–gun frigate *La Vengeance* and gave chase. The pursuit lasted the entire day and into the evening. Finally, at around eight that evening, the *Constellation* ovehauled her adversary. For the next five hours, Truxtun used superior American gunnery and heavy seas to his advantage, overcoming the French ship's initial broadside advantage by 1:00 A.M. on February 2. Later reports indicate that the French warship had struck her colors several times during the engagement, but Truxtun could not see this because of darkness, weather, and the action itself. Consequently, the battle continued until every gun on board *La Vengeance* fell silent. At that point she sheered off to flee. Truxtun tried to follow; however, *Constellation* lost her main mast over the side as the result of the rigging being completely shot away. With the *Constellation* unable to follow, *La Vengeance* made good her escape. Truxtun refitted his ship at Jamaica and returned to Norfolk in March 1800.

Between the summer of 1800 and May of 1801, Truxtun cruised the West Indies once more, this time in the 44–gun frigate *President*. Upon his return home, he was appointed commodore of a squadron fitting out for an expedition against the Tripolitan pirates. Through a misunderstanding engendered by his request to have a captain appointed to command his flagship, the 38–gun frigate *Chesapeake*, Truxtun's unintended resignation was accepted by President Thomas Jefferson. He retired first to Perth Amboy, New Jersey, and thence to Philadelphia.

Throughout the remainder of his life, Thomas Truxtun participated actively in local politics in Philadelphia. In 1809 he led the agitation there against the Embargo and, the following year, made an unsuccessful bid for a seat in Congress as a member of the Federalist party. From 1816 to 1819 he served as the sheriff of Philadelphia. Commodore Truxtun died at Philadelphia on May 5, 1822, and was interred there at Christ Church.

Truxtun's place in the history of the U.S. Navy rests with his role in laying down the foundation of naval tradition by helping to win American independence as a privateer and in being one of the first six captains in the new Navy of 1794. While in command of the *Constellation*, he sought out the enemy actively and, even when confronted by the seemingly overwhelming odds presented by the 50–gun *La Vengeance*, charged to the attack with the 36–gun *Constellation* and emerged the victor. The dogged determination he exhibited has inspired Navy men to fight courageously against seemingly impossible odds. One needs only to look at the battle such as that fought off Samar in October 1944, when contemporary American sailors fought under Admiral Thomas Cassin Kinkaid* against similar odds and won a victory where defeat seemed more probable.

BIBLIOGRAPHY

Allen, Gardner W. *A Naval History of the American Revolution*. 2 vols. Boston: Houghton Mifflin Company, 1913.
————. *Our Naval War with France*. Boston: Houghton Mifflin Company, 1909.
Clark, William B. *Ben Franklin's Privateers: A Naval Epic of the American Revolution*. Baton Rouge: Louisiana State University Press, 1956.
Ferguson, Eugene S. *Truxtun of the Constellation: The Life of Commodore Thomas Truxtun, U.S. Navy, 1775–1822*. Baltimore: Johns Hopkins University Press, 1956.
Nash, Howard P. *The Forgotten Wars: The Role of the U.S. Navy in the Quasi War with France and the Barbary Wars, 1789–1805*. New York: A. S. Barnes and Company, 1968.

RAYMOND A. MANN

TURNER, Richmond Kelly (b. East Portland, Ore., May 27, 1885; d. Monterey, Calif., February 12, 1961), naval officer. Turner specialized in amphibious operations in the Pacific during World War II.

Richmond Kelly Turner, the seventh of eight children, was the son of Laura Frances Kelly and Enoch Turner, a school teacher, farmer, and printer. Kelly Turner entered the Naval Academy in 1904 and was graduated fifth in his class of 201.

Turner made his reputation in the Navy as a gunnery expert and war planning officer. After graduating from Annapolis, he served in various capacities in destroyers and cruisers, and then as gunnery officer in four battleships, including the *Pennsylvania*. Performing well in these positions, he then held the post of gunnery officer, staff, Scouting Fleet. Adding to his qualifications, Turner earned the pilot's wings of a naval aviator at age forty-two in 1927 and later assumed the position of commander, Air Squadron, Asiatic Fleet. In 1932 he became executive officer of the carrier *Saratoga*. Following three years at the Naval War

College (1935–1938), he was posted as commanding officer in the heavy cruiser *Astoria*.

In late 1940 Turner took charge of the War Planning Division in the Navy Department. Under the guidance of Admiral Harold Raynsford Stark,* chief of naval operations, Turner reoriented and developed the existing Navy war plans against Japan. Following the Japanese attack on Pearl Harbor, Admiral Ernest Joseph King* became commander in chief, U.S. Fleet, and he picked Turner as his war plans officer. Turner remained in that job after King relieved Stark as chief of naval operations. In 1942 Turner completed high-level plans for the Guadalcanal-Tulagi amphibious operation and was Admiral King's personal choice to conduct the amphibious assault on Guadalcanal.

Turner assumed command of Amphibious Force, South Pacific, on July 18, 1942, in Wellington, New Zealand. He sailed four days later to Koro Island in the Fijis, where his forces held a rehearsal for the Guadalcanal operation. Rough weather and poor beaches hampered the mock landings. Furthermore, missing from the rehearsal were four ships, a battalion of Marines, and four of Turner's eleven staff officers, including his chief of staff. Consequently, Turner himself handled a large share of the multitudinous details of amphibious staff work, honing the plans to a fine point.

The well-planned Guadalcanal-Tulagi landings on August 7, 1942, were successful but were followed the next night by the galling Savo Island defeat. In the early hours of August 9, a Japanese eight-ship task force, including destroyers and cruisers, completely defeated the ten-ship combined American-Australian Screening Group in Turner's command, sinking or severely damaging four Allied cruisers. Japanese losses were inconsequential. In the resulting investigations, Turner was saved by his having requested that Rear Admiral John S. McCain, commanding land and water-based aircraft in the area, search the vicinity where the Japanese task force must have been. McCain failed not only to have his planes make the search, but also to advise Turner that he had not done so.

Thenceforth, during the war in the Pacific, Admirals King and Chester William Nimitz* relied on Turner's planning sagacity and aggressive fighting spirit. For example, following the amphibious operation to seize the Russell Islands, Turner carefully and methodically overpowered the Japanese as he and his forces moved northward through the Solomons and on to New Georgia. In his campaigns, Turner integrated logistics into the planning and operations as never before in naval operations, and made excellent use of new landing craft that had been developed.

When the New Georgia Campaign was nearly finished, on July 15, 1943, Turner was promoted to lead all the amphibious forces in the Pacific. His new command, designated the 5th Amphibious Force, was expanded considerably and included many top-notch officers who helped to plan and later participated in the operations in the Gilbert Islands.

Tarawa Atoll in the Gilberts, perhaps the toughest amphibious assault of the Pacific war for the Marines, was taken in November 1943. The loss of Tarawa taught the Japanese that dying was not enough. The Japanese found themselves being outfought by equally good fighting men who desired to live and to fight again.

When the Gilberts had been secured, the Joint Chiefs of Staff directed Turner's amphibians to capture the Marshall Islands. The Gilberts served as a base for regular reconnaissance sorties and continuous bombing strikes against the Marshalls. Admiral Nimitz, commander in chief of U.S. naval forces in the Pacific, picked Kwajalein atoll as the key to the Marshalls.

Turner's primary subordinates for the Marshall's operation were two experienced amphibious commanders, Rear Admiral Richard L. Conolly, who had fought in the Sicilian and Salerno operations in the Mediterranean, and Rear Admiral Harry W. Hill, who had served as commander of the Southern Attack Force at Tarawa. The attack on the Marshalls commenced on January 31, 1944. Conolly's units hit Roi-Namur on the northern end of Kwajalein Atoll, while Turner directed the assault on the southern end of the atoll, at Kwajalein itself. Hill's forces attacked Eniwetok, 330 miles northwest of Kwajalein on February 17, 1944. The rest of the Japanese garrisons in the Marshalls were left to wither on the vine.

Plans to move on to the Marianas had been in the drafting stage for months. In April 1944 Admiral King approved expanding the 5th Amphibious Force from two to six amphibious groups. At about the same time, King approved Turner's plans for taking the islands of Saipan, Tinian, and Guam. Turner commanded the Saipan Attack Force, while Hill and Conolly commanded the Tinian and Guam Attack Forces, respectively. After tough fighting, the Marianas were captured, and the number of amphibious groups under Turner's command was increased from six to sixteen.

Admiral Turner's next objectives were Iwo Jima and Okinawa. D-Day for the attack on Iwo Jima, originally set for January 20, 1945, was pushed back to February 19. By then the Amphibious Attack Force numbered 495 vessels. Following a bloody landing and stiff resistance, Iwo Jima was secured by March 9, 1945, and Turner turned over operational command to Admiral Hill and departed for Okinawa.

Rehearsals for the Okinawa landings were held as far away as Guadalcanal and the Philippines. On April 1, 1945, twenty-seven hundred amphibious ships and craft took part in the assault on Okinawa.

The Japanese at Okinawa expanded and perfected their kamikaze operations, initiated at Iwo Jima. These deadly strikes, combined with submarine attacks, gave the amphibians a hot time during the long, drawn out land battle. Turner kept cool under fire, though the Japanese sank fifteen of his vessels and damaged 112 other craft. The carnage among sailors and officers was heavy; the Navy lost six hundred more men than the Army ashore and two thousand more than the Marines. With the Okinawa Campaign nearing its conclusion, Hill relieved Turner of command in mid-May 1945.

On May 24, Turner was promoted to four stars (admiral) and ordered to start planning for Operation OLYMPIC, the assault on the Japanese home islands, specifically on the southern island of Kyushu, scheduled for November 1, 1945. OLYMPIC became unnecessary when the Japanese surrendered, and Turner proceeded to Tokyo with Fleet Admiral Nimitz for the surrender ceremonies.

After the war, Turner served as naval representative on the United Nations Military Committee—crossing wits with the Soviets—until his retirement at age sixty-two on July 1, 1947.

Kelly Turner had an upright and spare physique, a severe countenance, and an ever-fruitful mind. He stood six feet tall and always impressed his subordinates with his drive, determination, and unselfishness. Turner regularly worked sixteen to eighteen hours a day, putting his staffs to shame. The Japanese admiringly called him an "alligator," meaning that he never let go when he bit into something. He unsparingly applied his high intelligence, fighting spirit, and masterful planning ability to the problems of the Pacific War. These attributes made him a highly successful naval war leader, and he was the first line officer in his Naval Academy class to be selected for the ranks of commander, captain, and rear admiral.

At age fifty-seven, the stresses and strains of command—including the success at Guadalcanal and the setback at Savo Island—led the long-time abstemious Kelly Turner to lean on the bottle. As the war continued, alcohol became more and more important to him, but barely failed to take charge, much to the relief of Turner's senior officers.

Afflicted by irascibility and the unnecessary habit of using vulgar language, Kelly Turner was a difficult shipmate in the last months of World War II. Because he had a life-long habit of reading widely and possessed a prodigious memory, he tended to disdain naval officers who had intellectual levels and capabilities below his own.

The tender love and patience of his wife, Harriet Sterling, whom he married in 1910, brought their marriage through fifty years. When she died on January 3, 1961, apparently the reason for living no longer existed. And so, thirty-seven days later, Turner died.

Turner had been given great responsibilities for planning, organizing, and leading complex amphibious operations during World War II. He upheld his responsibilities, leaving his mark on the U.S. Navy and the development of amphibious warfare.

BIBLIOGRAPHY

Dyer, George C. *The Amphibians Came to Conquer: The Story of Admiral Richmond Kelly Turner*. 2 vols. Washington, D.C.: U.S. Government Printing Office, 1972.

Forrestal, Emmet P. *Admiral Raymond A. Spruance*. Washington, D.C.: U.S. Government Printing Office, 1966.

King, Ernest, and Walter M. Whitehall. *Fleet Admiral King: A Naval Record*. New York: W. W. Norton and Company, 1952.

Morison, Samuel E. *History of United States Naval Operations in World War II*. 15 vols. Boston: Atlantic, Little, Brown and Company, 1947–1961.

Nimitz, Chester W., and E. B. Potter. *The Great Sea War*. Annapolis, Md.: Naval Institute Press, 1960.

GEORGE C. DYER

TWIGGS, David Emanuel (b. Richmond County, Ga., 1790; d. Augusta, Ga., July 15, 1862), senior U.S. and Confederate Army officer.

Twiggs was the son of Brigadier General John Twiggs, a Revolutionary War officer known as the "Savior of Georgia". He was educated in Georgia at Athens' Franklin College, after which he read law in Augusta. With the outbreak of the War of 1812, he entered the Army directly as a twenty-one-year-old captain in the 8th Infantry. His service on what was then the country's southeastern frontier was unspectacular but brought him a brevet as well as regular majority in the 28th Infantry in 1814. With the Army's postwar reduction, Twiggs was discharged in 1815, but later in the same year (not 1825 as some sources state) he was reinstated but this time as a captain in the 7th Infantry.

During the next several years he served under first Edmund Pendleton Gaines* and then Andrew Jackson* in the Indian campaigns and clashes with Spain in Florida, actions during which General Jackson reportedly developed an appreciation for Twiggs' vigor as a troop commander and disciplinarian. In 1821 Captain Twiggs transferred laterally to the 1st Infantry in which regiment he regained his majority in 1825.

By the turn of the decade Major Twiggs was on duty to the north in Wisconsin Territory where he commanded Fort Winnebago and became embroiled in a lengthy, extensive court case over his enforcement of locally unpopular Indian treaty obligations. In 1831 Twiggs was commissioned lieutenant colonel of the 4th Infantry, in which capacity he served during the Black Hawk War. Perhaps Twiggs' most well-known duty during that conflict was his command of cholera-infected Eastern reinforcements bound for Illinois via Great Lakes steamer, a nightmarish odyssey in which he lost about two-thirds of his troops to disease or desertion. Following the Black Hawk War, Twiggs was assigned—reportedly, by President Jackson himself—to command the federal arsenal at Augusta, Georgia, a sensitive duty near his home during the explosive Nullification Crisis. There followed an extensive tour of duty in New Orleans.

With the establishment of the 2d Regiment of Dragoons in 1836, Twiggs became its first colonel. He held this command during the subsequent ten years with the volatile William S. Harney as his lieutenant colonel. It was while commanding the 2d Dragoons that Twiggs returned to Florida to fight the Seminoles again under Gaines, following which he took an extended leave of absence—one of several such furloughs—to tend to family responsibilities.

Upon the outbreak of the Mexican War, Twiggs and his regiment were assigned to south Texas and General Zachary Taylor.* There, at Corpus Christi, he soon became embroiled in a petty but famous clash with Brigadier General William

J. Worth over which officer took precedence after Taylor, a dispute in which General Winfield Scott* eventually ruled in Twiggs' favor.

Once into northern Mexico, Twiggs acquitted himself well as a division commander during two of the war's initial clashes—Palo Alto and Resaca de la Palma—and served as military governor at Matamoros following its capture. With Congress' expansion of the Army, he was rewarded on June 30, 1846, with a regular brigadier's commission. Several months later, Twiggs' division joined in the successful but hotly contested assault on Monterrey, although it is not clear whether the general, suffering from a gastrointestinal illness, personally took the field. Twiggs' apparent absence during the siege makes it all the more "singular" that for the action at Monterrey he was brevetted a major general on September 23, 1846, and subsequently presented with ornate ceremonial swords by Congress, the Georgia legislature, and the city of Augusta.

During the balance of the Mexican War, Twiggs served as a division commander under Scott, first in the amphibious assault on Vera Cruz and then in the chain of engagements—especially Cerro Gordo, Cherubusco, and Chapultepec—leading to the fall of Mexico City. As at Matamoros and Monterrey earlier, Twiggs then acted as military governor of Vera Cruz from December 1847 to March 1848.

Following the war, Twiggs served in a number of senior assignments including command of the Department of the West and, beginning in 1857, command of the Department of Texas. The general became involved in an incident involving a flow of acerbic letters from Twiggs to Thomas S. Jesup, the quartermaster general, challenging the wisdom of his and Secretary of War John B. Floyd's decision to continue the experimental use of camels as military pack animals in Texas.

In March 1858 Twiggs, although second only to Scott in seniority, was ordered by Floyd and President James Buchanan to stand trial before a general court-martial on charges of insubordination. In addition, there are signs that Floyd intended the court-martial to serve as a highly visible example to the Army that breaches in discipline would not be tolerated, a signal transmitted just as Colonel E. V. Sumner, commander of the 1st Cavalry, was about to stand trial for the second time in six months.

Twiggs' trial took place at Newport Barracks, Kentucky, at the end of April 1858 and, because of his grade, required an unusual assembly there of the Army's most senior officers excluding General Scott. After three days the court convicted Twiggs, sentenced him to be reprimanded in orders by President Buchanan, and then recommended remission of the sentence in consideration of the general's "highly distinguished services," a recommendation that Secretary of War Floyd subsequently approved. Upon returning to Texas, the general continued his attack on the camel project while launching a new one on the Comanches. Later in the year he surfaced again in print—this time as "General Twigger," a buffoonish, rapacious character in *Mormoniad*, a lengthy anonymous poem published in Boston to satirize the Buchanan administration's military policies and leaders.

General Twiggs spent much of the balance of the antebellum period on medical leave in New Orleans, the home of his second wife, the former Mrs. Hunt. In December 1860, however, he returned to San Antonio and resumed command of the Department of Texas in the midst of the secession crisis. That month Twiggs wrote first to Scott and then to the Adjutant General's Office seeking instructions as to the disposition of Federal arms, ammunition, and property in the department. Scott responded on December 28 through his aide de camp who commented only in generalities. Not content, Twiggs wrote again to Scott on January 15, 1861, to note that he was a Southerner and that ''As soon as I know Georgia has separated from the Union I must, of course, follow her.'' Twiggs then went on to request that he be relieved of his command before March 4, the date of Abraham Lincoln's* inauguration. Two weeks later a Texas convention adopted an ordinance of secession, and on February 18, in order ''to avoid even the possibility of a collision between the Federal and State troops,'' Twiggs surrendered the department's posts and property to civilian commissioners of the Texas Committee of Public Safety with the understanding that the department's troops would be permitted to exit the state via the coast. The following day, with consummate poor timing, he was relieved of command upon the arrival of a federal colonel, and on March 1, 1861, as one of his last official acts, President Buchanan summarily dismissed Twiggs from the Army ''for his treachery to the flag of his country.''

Several months later, Twiggs surfaced as the major general commanding the Confederacy's Department No. 1 from New Orleans; as such, he was briefly the South's ranking military officer. From this vantage point, an embittered but ailing and inactive Twiggs twice wrote threatening letters to a retired Buchanan in 1861.

With the approach of General Benjamin Franklin Butler's* Federal troops, Twiggs hastily deposited his three ceremonial swords with a nineteen-year-old lady friend (from whom they were later seized by Butler), fled New Orleans, and retired to Augusta where he died of natural causes on July 15, 1862, at the age of seventy-two. It took until 1889 and a ruling by the U.S. Court of Claims before Twiggs' Monterrey swords were restored to his family. Major General Montgomery Meigs, the Union quartermaster general, commented upon his death that ''Twiggs has escaped the hangman; but will (he) escape that omniscient and omnipotent judge who, in the next world, makes even the false balances of this one?''

A balanced assessment of David E. Twiggs is difficult because he lacks a biographer, and no significant concentration of his personal papers has been located. In addition, the manner in which Twiggs left the U.S. Army marked him as one of those military and political figures on which the North's emotions and sense of betrayal focused. Since 1861 little has been written about his character or military performance that is dispassionate in tone.

Consequently, there is as yet no definitive examination of Twiggs' motives and actions in surrendering the Department of Texas. Left hanging in the balance, then, is a resolution of the question of whether or not Twiggs acted as part of a high-level secessionist conspiracy involved in the antebellum manipulation of money, troops, arms, ammunition and equipment to the South's advantage. The extent to which, if at all, bitterness over his 1858 court-martial affected Twiggs' loyalty to the Union three years later is a possibility that has never been explored, inasmuch as the trial itself has lapsed into obscurity. This writer's assessment is that Twiggs probably harbored little or no resentment over the incident, or at least nothing comparable to his reaction to his subsequent dismissal.

Likewise, there is little agreement on Twiggs' character, popularity, or command style. A biographical sketch published in 1850 commented that "He is a strict disciplinarian, but kind to his men. Perhaps no man in the army, after Taylor, is so popular with the soldiers." Yet other observers noticed traits running to the insensitive and even brutal. There is agreement, however, that, at least in terms of appearance, he was about six feet tall, somewhat beefy in build, and, by the Mexican War, was marked by a florid countenance fringed with white whiskers. While a courageous and competent officer, it does not appear that Twiggs was beset by flashes of brilliance in the tactical or strategic realm; his style was that of the frontal assault.

Perhaps it was Twiggs' fondness for the direct approach together with a streak of insensitivity that embroiled him in controversy during much of his career. If so, in this respect Twiggs was by no means atypical of the senior military and civilian commanders of the antebellum army. Congressional investigations, and even more petty disputes at times virtually paralyzed the antebellum army's command structure for weeks at a time. The question of the extent to which this apparent atmosphere of contention and litigiousness within the Army was the product of an impacted promotional system, the hypersensitivity of the chivalric code, sectional rivalries, frontier and cultural isolation, old age, personal medical histories, and other factors remains for another study. With it will come more insight into the performance of General David E. Twiggs, the U.S. Army's second most senior officer and briefly the Confederacy's ranking soldier.

BIBLIOGRAPHY

Bauer, K. Jack. *The Mexican War, 1846-1848*. New York: Macmillan Company, 1974.
Peterson, Charles J. *The Mexican War and Its Heroes*. Philadelphia: Lippincott, Grambo and Company, 1851.
———. *The Military Heroes of the War with Mexico: With a Narrative of the War*. Philadelphia: William A. Leary and Company, 1850.
Rodenbough, Theodore F. comp. *From Everglade to Canon with the Second Dragoons*. New York: D. Van Nostrand, 1875.
Warner, Ezra J. *Generals in Gray, Lives of Confederate Commanders*. Baton Rouge, La.: 1959.

WILLIAM P. MACKINNON

U

UPTON, Emory (b. near Batavia, N.Y., August 27, 1839; d. San Francisco, Calif., March 15, 1881), tactician, Army reformer. Upton's *Military Policy of the United States* was the first systematic, critical synthesis of American military history and has been the most influential statement of the case for a professional army as the cornerstone of national defense.

Upton grew up in the Burned-Over District of New York, the center of early nineteenth-century religious revivalism and related reform movements. His family was of New England Puritan background, turned Methodist, and was deeply involved in moral reform, especially temperance and abolitionism. His father, Daniel Upton, a farmer, was an acquaintance of the revivalist Charles G. Finney; from Finney, who became president of Oberlin College, Daniel secured scholarships to Oberlin for several of his sons. Emory matriculated there in 1854. Emory's ambition, however, was to attend the U.S. Military Academy, and he won an appointment in 1856. He graduated eighth in a class of forty-five on May 6, 1861. He retained his abolitionism, a rarity in the Army, and fought Cadet Wade Hampton Gibbes of South Carolina with swords over it. An intensity of moral commitment always marked everything Upton undertook.

Commissioned a second lieutenant in the 4th Artillery on graduation, Upton was promoted to first lieutenant in the 5th Artillery eight days later; the Civil War had begun. His entire class had already been ordered to Washington to help train volunteers. As aide de camp to Brigadier General Daniel Tyler, Upton aimed and fired the opening gun of First Bull Run. Soon wounded in the left side and arm, he nevertheless carried messages for Tyler throughout the day. He recovered to command Battery D, 2d Artillery in the Peninsula Campaign, distinguishing himself to earn command of the Artillery Brigade of the 1st Division, VI Corps, in time for the Maryland Campaign. Upton had found that he relished battle, and to avoid an assignment as instructor at West Point, he used his New York connections to be able to fill a vacancy as colonel of the 121st New York Infantry. His regiment was involved only in skirmishing at

Fredericksburg, but he led it in a costly and unsuccessful charge near Salem Church in the Chancellorsville Campaign. At Gettysburg, he led the 2d Brigade, 1st Division, VI Corps, which participated in the long march of the corps on July 2, 1863, to help pin down Little Round Top by nightfall. On November 7, Upton first won wide notice at the Battle of Rappahannock Station, where he wiped out a Confederate bridgehead, capturing sixteen hundred prisoners, eight colors, two thousand stand of arms, and the enemy pontoon bridge.

Upton's units were distinguished by their precise, careful training and discipline. From the attack near Salem Church onward, Upton felt deeply concerned that these qualities were not enough to carry positions against rifled firepower. Assigned on May 10, 1864, to lead an attack on the Mule Shoe—the later Bloody Angle—at Spotsylvania, Upton added to his command's assets meticulous preparation. Forming his task force in four lines of three regiments each, he conducted every regimental commander through a personal reconnaissance and explanation of what he intended. He personally placed the assault troops and the supporting artillery. The assault troops were not to pause to fire before they penetrated the enemy lines. Each of Upton's lines had a precise role to play. Upton broke the enemy defenses and captured over a thousand prisoners; but lack of followup by other troops finally compelled him to withdraw. This kind of experience left him critical of American officership as well as troubled over tactical problems. Cold Harbor did not improve his opinion of most of his seniors.

At the Battle of the Opequon on September 19, 1864, Upton succeeded David A. Russell in command of the 1st Division, VI Corps, and mounted a successful attack, only to have a femoral artery torn open by a shell fragment. Returning to active duty on December 13 as a major general of volunteers, he led the 4th Cavalry Division in the Selma Campaign of 1865. He emerged from the war a brevet major general of regulars.

His permanent rank was captain of the 5th Artillery (February 22, 1865), although he soon reached lieutenant colonel of the 25th Infantry (July 28, 1866; transferred to the 18th Infantry, March 15, 1869). He commanded cavalry of the District of East Tennessee from July to August 1865, and then the District of Colorado. By now he was laboring on an improved tactical system to try to cope with modern firepower. In January 1866 he requested permission to travel to Washington to submit his system to a board of general officers. On June 5 the War Department appointed a board to meet at West Point and study Upton's system, and Upton himself was ordered to West Point. For the next year, he met with the board and instructed cadets. In 1867, both the original board and the new one recommended adoption of Upton's tactics, which occurred August 1.

In November 1867 Upton took a year's leave, which he dedicated with his usual intensity to courtship and marriage of Emily Martin of Willowbrook, New York, and with a tour of Europe. Emily's health was precarious, and she died in Nassau, the Bahamas, in March 1870 while Upton was on duty at Atlanta. Thereafter Upton was yet more intense and humorless. From July 1870 to July 1875 he was a rigorous commandant of cadets at West Point. The commanding general of the Army, William Tecumseh Sherman,* sponsored a world tour for him in late 1875 and most of 1876, to observe foreign armies as a basis for still further American reforms. Out of the tour came *The Armies of Asia and Europe* (1878), which was largely devoted, implicitly where not explicitly, to Upton's ideas for reform not only in tactics now but also in organization and policy. Upton corresponded with other officers sympathetic to military reforms while he was superintendent of the Artillery School of Practice at Fortress Monroe beginning in March 1877, strongly influencing Sherman's and other senior officers' testimony before the Burnside Committee of Congress in 1878. Upton turned to the writing of another book, a critique of U.S. military policy presented through a study of American military history.

In July 1880 Upton received command of the 4th Artillery, with headquarters at the Presidio of San Francisco. The book was still incomplete, its narrative carried only to 1862, when increasingly frequent and extremely painful headaches grew so severe that Upton feared he no longer had the proper capacity to command. On March 15, 1881, he resigned his commission and shot himself through the head with his Colt .45.

Psychological depression was likely involved in the causes of his extreme physical pain and almost certainly contributed to Upton's suicide. Deeply dedicated to the improvement of the Army, he thought that the most fundamental reforms he advocated were unlikely to gain public and congressional acceptance. He had adapted tactics to rifled weapons, and his system of maneuvering by groups of four soldiers was to influence American tactics well into the next century. He advocated improved tactical organization, such as a three-battalion infantry regiment in place of the regiment of a single battalion; this kind of change might win approval in time, and did. But much more fundamental, and with much less chance to prevail, was Upton's prescripion for readying the Army for war in time of peace. This was the expansible Army plan, advocated earlier by Secretary of War John Caldwell Calhoun* among others, whereby the entire staff and the basic regimental organization of a war army would exist during peace. When war came, there would be, in words Upton borrowed from Calhoun, "nothing either to new model or to create."

No peacetime army that any Congress foreseeable in Upton's day would approve could be expansible enough to build a war army with nothing either to "new model or to create." Any peacetime army acceptable to Congress would be swamped as badly in war as the Regular Army of 1861 had been. This was one cause of Upton's depression. His tours had left him impressed above all with the German Army. His version of an American expansible army was an adaptation of the German system of cadres around which war formations were built by conscription. Conscription was implicit in his plan: the "truly democratic doctrine. . .that every American citizen owes his country military service." But Congress was even less likely to vote conscription than to build an adequately expansible army.

Upton admired German military organization in general. He also admired the

German system of an autonomous military, subject to minimal civilian control. "The disasters which ensued [in the Civil War]," he said, "...must...be credited to the defective laws which allowed the President to dispense with an actual General in Chief and substitute in his stead a civil officer." His opinion of close congressional scrutiny of military policy was no higher. Distrustful of civilian control, Upton was fundamentally distrustful of democracy itself. He doubted that American democracy could compete militarily with the great powers. "Whenever Congress has shown a disposition to adopt the principle of military organization observed in continental armies, it has been dissuaded from its purpose by the demagogic admonition that foreign organizations are dangerous to liberty."

The manucript of Upton's *Military Policy* circulated widely in the Army, and its ideas became well known in the officer corps before Secretary of War Elihu Root* arranged for its publication in 1904. Peter Smith Michie's biography also disseminated Upton's ideas. In the small army of the late nineteenth century, among officers frustrated by slow promotion, Upton's pessimistic attitudes found a receptive audience. Upton had set a model of excellence as a battle captain and a tactical reformer. His ability to combine an outstanding career as a practical soldier with the thought and writing of a military intellectual commands admiration. His deepest impact, however, was a tendency to alienate American soldiers from the democratic politics and society they served.

BIBLIOGRAPHY

Ambrose, Stephen E. *Upton and the Army*. Baton Rouge: Louisiana State University Press, 1964.
Brown, Richard C. "Emory Upton, The Army's Mahan." *Military Affairs* 17 (Summer 1953): 125–31.
Cooling, Benjamin Franklin. "The Missing Chapters of Emory Upton: A Note." *Military Affairs* 37 (February 1973): 13–15.
Michie, Peter Smith. *Life and Letters of General Emory Upton*. New York: Appleton, 1885.
Morris, Schaff. *The Spirit of Old West Point, 1858–1862*. Boston: Houghton Mifflin Company, 1909.
Weigley, Russell F. *Towards an American Army: Military Thought from Washington to Marshall*. New York: Columbia University Press, 1962.

RUSSELL F. WEIGLEY

V

VANDEGRIFT, Alexander Archer (b. Charlottesville, Va., March 13, 1887; d. Bethesda, Md., May 8, 1973), Marine Corps officer. Vandegrift successfully led the 1st Marine Division at Guadalcanal in World War II and was the eighteenth commandant of the Corps.

Archer Vandegrift, the son of a business contractor in Charlottesville, was descended from Dutch farmers who came to America in the eighteenth century and from a long line of Virginia magistrates and judges. He pursued a college education at the University of Virginia from 1905 to 1908. The legends of his grandfather's heroic service in the Civil War and the advice of his family's physician, Dr. Wilson Randolph, persuaded Vandegrift to embark upon a military career. He therefore left the university, attended Swaveley preparatory school in Washington, D.C., and passed the Marine Corps entrance examination.

On January 22, 1909, Vandegrift received his commission as a second lieutenant in the Marine Corps at the Washington Marine Barracks. After attending the Marine Officers' School at Fort Royal, South Carolina, Vandegrift was detailed to the Marine Barracks at Portsmouth, New Hampshire. From there he engaged in a number of combat roles in the Caribbean. Between 1909 and 1923, Vandegrift participated in Marine operations in Nicaragua, Panama, Mexico, and Haiti. His outstanding actions during the period included the Battle of Coyotepe in Nicaragua where Vandegrift served under both Colonel Smedley Darlington Butler* and Colonel Joseph Henry Pendleton.* While in Haiti in 1915, he became Butler's adjutant and helped train the Haitian gendarmerie to protect that nation from the depredations of the Caco bandits. On his second stint in Haiti in 1919, Vandegrift personally led a spirited pursuit that resulted in the capture and execution of the Caco chieftain Charlemagne M. Peralté.

Upon his return from Haiti in 1923, Vandegrift went to Quantico, Virginia, to become General Butler's aide and a battalion commander. In 1925 he served briefly as Butler's assistant chief of staff at the Marine Barracks in San Diego. Moving with Butler to San Francisco in 1926, Vandegrift helped organize the

Western Mail Guards to protect deliveries of the U.S. mails against armed robbery.

In 1927 Vandegrift again went overseas, this time to China, to defend the International Settlements at Shanghai from threats by Chiang Kai-Shek's Nationalist Army. He also assisted in the occupation of Tientsin under Smedley Butler as his operations officer.

At the end of 1928 Vandegrift returned to Washington to represent the Marine Corps in the Federal Co-ordinating Service whose job it was to prevent duplication of material requirements and procurement among the military services. He remained in that relatively quiet position for five years. In that time he managed to make some important contacts and made himself thoroughly familiar with the Washington scene. This experience would help him years later as commandant.

In 1933 Vandegrift returned to Marine duties as personnel officer for Brigadier General Charles Lyman, whose East Coast Expeditionary Force was stationed at Quantico, Virginia. Attached to the Marine Corps Schools at Quantico, Vandegrift ably assisted in the drawing up of the Marines' *Tentative Manual of Landing Operations*, the first formal expression of the amphibious doctrine that would guide marine operations in the Pacific during World War II. He also participated in the maneuvers at Culebra, Puerto Rico, which sought to put these new amphibious doctrines to the test.

For the next two years (1935 to 1937), Vandegrift served as executive officer and then commanding officer of the American Embassy Detachment at Peking. He had by then become a colonel. While in Peking, Vandegrift concentrated on drilling his men in marksmanship and equestrian training. He also learned a great deal about international diplomacy, associating daily with his British, French, and Japanese counterparts.

In early 1937 Vandegrift was recalled to Washington to serve as military secretary to the new commandant of the Marine Corps, Major General Thomas Holcomb. Later in 1940, as a sign of Holcomb's pleasure with his work, Vandegrift was elevated to assistant to the commandant. During this crucial transition period for both Vandegrift and the Marines, he was involved in such high-level staff duties as preparing budget presentations for Congress. He worked very closely with both Holcomb and the quartermaster, Seth Williams, to manage and control the Marine Corps' spiralling growth in the period 1937–1941.

In November 1941 Vandegrift joined the 1st Marine Division, which was then stationed at the New River, North Carolina, training center. He inherited command of the division in March 1942 upon the retirement of General Philip Torrey. This command took Vandegrift and his division to the forefront of the battle in the Pacific. In June 1942 Vandegrift received word that his division was to spearhead landing operations on Guadalcanal in the Solomon Islands in an attempt to stem the Japanese tide of victory. His main objective was to seize and hold the airfield on Guadalcanal which would enable American air power to punish Japanese bases and shipping. Vandegrift and his men succeeded in their mission despite heavy odds. Vandegrift was decorated with the Medal of Honor for his valor and courage in the four-month long seige against tenacious Japanese on-slaughts. In December 1942 Vandegrift and his bone-weary men were finally relieved by the Army under General Alexander McCarrell Patch* commanding the 25th Infantry Division and the 2d Marine Division.

From Guadalcanal, Vandegrift proceeded to the Southwest Pacific Area, under the command of General Douglas MacArthur.* Vandegrift and his men got much needed rest and rehabilitation in Melbourne, Australia. In the middle of 1943 Vandegrift was elevated to commanding general of the 1st Marine Amphibious Corps in the South Pacific Area. Although he was slated to go back to Washington to assume the post of commandant of the Marine Corps, the unexpected death of General Charles Barrett forced him to remain for the landing operations at Bougainville in November 1943.

After turning this command over to General Roy Stanley Geiger,* Vandegrift left for Washington where he spent the next four years as the eighteenth commandant. During four very eventful and tumultous years, he guided the Marines with a steady hand. The Corps increased in size (eventually containing more than five hundred thousand men) and conducted heroic actions at Okinawa and Iwo Jima, among others. In April 1945 Vandegrift became the first active duty Marine to attain the rank of four star general. Finally came the painful adjustments of postwar demobilization. In 1947 there was even an attempt to dismantle the Marine Corps which Vandegrift and his close aides were able to defuse. After leaving active service on December 31, 1947, he spent his retirement years in travel and charitable work.

Vandegrift's performance at Guadalcanal deserves greater attention from historians. On August 7, 1942, he landed his Marine forces on the northern coast of Guadalcanal in what became known as Operation SHOESTRING. His first tactic was to capture and hold the nearly completed Japanese airstrip, which the Marines dubbed Henderson Field (named after Major Lofton P. Henderson). Seizing and then fiercely defending the airfield in the months to come proved of immeasurable value to American operations in the area; for it was from Henderson Field that marine aviators were able to build up their so-called Cactus Air Force which provided crucial firepower to offset superior Japanese numbers. The main thrust of the campaign, however, was not just the holding of the airfield and its perimeter, but also the dogged determination which Vandegrift and his Marines showed in the face of mounting Japanese pressure and disease-ridden living conditions.

Command problems at the outset threatened to scuttle the entire Guadalcanal operation. Facing imminent Japanese attack, Vice Admiral Frank Jack Fletcher,* whose Task Force 62 brought the Marines to Guadalcanal, ordered his ships to sortie before the unloading of valuable supplies was complete. To make up for this loss, Vandegrift was constantly asking Washington for reinforcements and supplies. These requests largely went unheeded because the Battle of the Atlantic took precedence over campaigns in the Pacific. Finally, in November 1942 President Franklin D. Roosevelt broke the log jam and ordered the much needed supplies sent out quickly to Vandegrift. This relief enabled him to break out of his narrow perimeter around Henderson Field and defeat the very large concentrations of Japanese on the island. All told, Vandegrift, his talented staff, and his Marines conducted themselves with great perseverance in the Guadalcanal fight, making the first American offensive in the Pacific War a successful one.

BIBLIOGRAPHY

Asprey, Robert B., and Alexander Archer Vandegrift. *Once a Marine: The Memoirs of General A. A. Vandegrift, USMC.* New York: W. W. Norton, 1964.
Foster, John T. *Guadalcanal General: The Story of A. A. Vandegrift, U.S.M.C.* New York: William Morrow and Company, 1966.
Griffith, Samuel B. *The Battle for Guadalcanal.* Philadelphia: J. B. Lippincott, 1963.
Isley, Jeter A., and Philip A. Crowl. *The U.S. Marines and Amphibious War.* Princeton, N.J.: Princeton University Press, 1951.
Heinl, Robert D., Jr. *Soldiers of the Sea: The United States Marine Corps, 1775–1962.* Annapolis, Md.: Naval Institute Press, 1962.
Morison, Samuel E. *History of United States Naval Operations in World War II*: Vol. 5. *The Struggle for Guadalcanal, August 1942-February 1943.* Boston: Little, Brown and Company, 1949.

GIBSON BELL SMITH

VANDENBERG, Hoyt Sanford (b. Milwaukee, Wis., January 24, 1899; d. Washington, D.C., April 2, 1954), World War II air leader and second chief of staff of the U.S. Air Force.

Born in a prosperous section of Milwaukee, Wisconsin, Vandenberg spent his boyhood in Lowell, Massachusetts, where his interest in aviation and a military career took root after the United States entered World War I. Following his father's advice, he attended West Point to obtain a commission in the U.S. Army.

Vandenberg's record at West Point, where he graduated number 240 in a class of 262, gave little indication of the distinguished career that would follow. During pilot training at Brooks and Kelly Fields in Texas, however, his outstanding performance as a student pilot led to his assignment to the elite 3d Attack Group, a tenant unit at Kelly Field which later transferred to Fort Crockett, near Galveston, Texas. Within the 3d Attack Group, which was pioneering the development of attack aviation in the United States, he developed an excellent reputation as a pilot and as an officer. Manpower shortages resulting from budgetary cutbacks following World War I enabled young Vandenberg to gain experience in a variety of squadron duties prior to his first command, the 90th Attack Squadron. In October 1927 he began duty as a flight instructor in the newly reopened Air Corps Primary Flying School at March Field, California. He went to Schofield Barracks, Hawaii, in May 1929 and joined the 6th Pursuit Squadron at Wheeler Field, assuming command of that squadron in November 1929. Returning to the

United States in September 1931, he began a second tour as an instructor pilot, this time at the newly constructed Randolph Field in Texas.

Beginning in 1935, Vandenberg prepared himself for larger responsibilities. He attended first the Air Corps Tactical School at Maxwell Air Force Base, Alabama, and then, the following year, he completed the prestigious Army Command and General Staff School at Fort Leavenworth. An important aspect of his year at Leavenworth was the beginning of a life-long friendship with his senior and Leavenworth classmate, Carl Andrew Spaatz,* later commander of the U.S. Air Force in Europe and first chief of staff of the Air Force. Returning to the Air Corps Tactical School for two years as an instructor in the pursuit section, Vandenberg won recognition for his affable nature and ability to mollify dissident elements within the faculty of this crucible of Air Corps doctrine. In 1938 he was selected to attend the Army War College in the 1938–1939 class.

Upon graduation from the War College, and at the request of Major Carl Spaatz, Vandenberg was assigned to the Plans Section in Air Corps Headquarters. There he served in a key office during a critical period in Air Force history— the expansion of the air arm attendant to preparation for World War II. As a young staff officer, he was in a position to be observed by the Chief of the Air Corps, Major General Henry Harley Arnold,* on almost a daily basis. Arnold, on the lookout for bright, young officers who could meet the challenges imposed by the war, was impressed with Vandenberg. From this time on he rose in rank rapidly, assuming the rank of lieutenant colonel on November 15, 1941, and colonel on January 27, 1942.

In March 1942, upon reorganization of the Army Air Corps, Vandenberg became operations and training officer, A–3, of the new Air Staff. Although he was effective in this capacity, he was eager to join the conflict in Europe, and in June of 1942 he volunteered to participate in the planning and organization of the air effort for the North African invasion.

In August 1942 he went to England to serve as James Harold Doolittle's* chief of staff of the newly formed Twelfth Air Force. His performance in supporting the North African Campaign and, later, the invasions of Sicily and Italy, earned him the recognition and approval of Dwight David Eisenhower.* In December 1942 he was promoted to brigadier general.

Recalled from North Africa by Arnold in August 1943, Vandenberg assumed duties as deputy chief of the Army Air Force Headquarters Staff. In the fall of 1943, he joined Brigadier General John R. Deane as senior airman in the U.S. Military Mission to Russia. In this assignment he briefed senior Soviet officers on the potential of the combined bomber offensive and negotiated for bases used in "shuttle bombing" raids against targets in Eastern Europe. He returned to Air Corps Headquarters in December 1943 and helped in the early planning of the Allied invasion of Europe.

Promoted to major general in March 1944, Vandenberg rejoined Eisenhower's command, serving as deputy to the difficult Air Vice-Marshall Sir Trafford Leigh-Mallory, commander of the Allied Expeditionary Air Force, an organization formed to provide air support for the Normandy invasion. In July 1944 Vandenberg was selected by General George Catlett Marshall* to command the Ninth Air Force, ultimately the largest Air Force during World War II. In this position he directed the air support of General Omar Nelson Bradley's* 12th Army Group in its drive across Europe. His performance as commander of the Ninth Air Force won Eisenhower's recommendation for promotion to lieutenant general, the rank he held upon cessation of hostilities in Europe.

In July 1945 Vandenberg returned to Headquarters Army Air Forces as assistant chief of the air staff. In February 1946 he became assistant chief of staff, G–2, Intelligence, War Department General Staff, and in June 1946 he was named by President Harry S. Truman as the second director of the Central Intelligence Group, the forerunner of the present Central Intelligence Agency.

Vandenberg returned to Air Force duty in April 1947 and in June became deputy commander and chief of the air staff. Promoted to the rank of general, he became first vice chief of staff of the newly created U.S. Air Force in October 1947. General Carl Spaatz relinquished his position of chief of staff to Vandenberg in April 1948.

Vandenberg presided over the Air Force for more than five years. During his tenure the service carried the brunt of the Berlin Airlift, participated in the Korean War, and, with the combination of the long-range jet bomber and the atomic bomb, developed an impressive strategic air capability. Vandenberg was a determined and spirited advocate for air power throughout his tour as chief of staff. He retired from the Air Force in June 1953. His life was cut short by cancer, and he died in Walter Reed Hospital in April 1954 at only fifty-five years of age.

Vandenberg, who took over the Air force after Spaatz's brief tenure, was really the architect and builder of the new service. He devoted his efforts to creating an effective force in-being. The concept of deterrence was widely accepted within the Air Force hierarchy, and Vandenberg, realizing that budget constraints would make reliance on atomic-nuclear weapons all but inevitable, concentrated on enlarging the nation's strategic air capability. The building of such a force was not an easy task, but the articulate and determined Vandenberg led the struggle against a critical Congress and other services to build an air arm of such enormous striking power that no country would dare attack the United States.

BIBLIOGRAPHY

Arnold, Henry. *Global Mission*. New York: Harper and Row, 1967.
Craven, Wesley Frank, and James Lea Cate, eds. *The Army Air Forces in World War II*. 7 vols. Chicago: University of Chicago Press, 1948–1958.

Futrell, Frank B. *The United States Air Force in Korea, 1950–1953*. New York: Duell, Sloan, and Pearce, 1961.
Goldberg, Alfred, ed. *A History of the United States Air Force*. New York: Van Nostrand, 1957.

JON A. REYNOLDS

VAN FLEET, James Andrew (b. Coytesville, N.J., March 19, 1892) Army officer; Commander of the Eighth Army in Korea, 1951–1953.

Van Fleet was born in New Jersey, the son of William and Medora Scofield Van Fleet. The future general graduated from West Point as a second lieutenant of infantry, in the famed class of 1915, which included Dwight David Eisenhower* and Omar Nelson Bradley.* When the United States entered World War I in 1917, he was assigned to the 6th Infantry Division, which became part of the American Expeditionary Force sent to France. In July 1918 Van Fleet commanded the 17th Machine Gun Battalion and fought in the Gerardmer and Meuse-Argonne, where he was wounded in November. After the war, he served in the occupation forces until June 1919. In the early 1920s, he was an ROTC instructor at Kansas State, South Dakota State, and the University of Florida, where he also was head football coach. He commanded a battalion of the 42d Infantry in Panama in 1925. Van Fleet was an instructor at the Infantry School in Fort Benning, Georgia, both before and after graduating from the Advanced Infantry Course in 1929. He served in the 5th Infantry and as an Organized Reserve instructor in San Diego in the 1930s and was promoted to lieutenant colonel in 1936.

In September 1939 Van Fleet was a battalion commander in the 29th Infantry at Fort Benning. In 1941, after promotion to colonel, he assumed command of the 8th Infantry Regiment of the 4th Infantry Division. After the division trained in England, Van Fleet led its assault elements onto Utah Beach on D-Day, 1944. His courageous leadership in the battle for Cherbourg won him the Distinguished Service Cross and the Silver Star. He was also promoted to brigadier general and was made assistant commander of the 2d Infantry Division. For a short time, he was commanding general of the 4th Infantry Division before he assumed command of the troubled 90th Infantry Division in George Smith Patton, Jr.'s,* Third Army. Under Van Fleet in October-December 1944, the 90th made a spectacular but costly crossing of the Moselle River under heavy fire, helped capture the Metz fortress, and joined in the attack on the West Wall. Van Fleet was promoted to major general, but because of its heavy losses the 90th was withdrawn from the line until the last stages of the Ardennes fighting in January 1945, when it spearheaded Patton's counterattack. He received his third Distinguished Service Cross and the Distinguished Service Medal and briefly commanded the XXIII Corps in England. In March he led the III Corps of the First Army, which broke out of the Remagen bridgehead. After its transfer to the Third Army, Van Fleet's corps fought in the Ruhr pocket and was in Austria at war's end. In evaluating Van Fleet's rapid rise from regimental to corps commander, Eisenhower rated him competent to command an army.

Van Fleet continued to command the III Corps at Camp Polk, Louisiana, until early 1946. He served as commander, Second Service Command, and deputy commanding general, First Army, before his transfer to the European Command in Frankfurt in 1947. In early 1948 he was appointed director of the Joint U.S. Military Advisory and Planning Group in Athens and was assigned to assist the Greek government in its fight against Communist rebels. Shortly after, he was promoted to lieutenant general and appointed to the Greek National Defense Council. He directed the training, organization, and tactical employment of the national forces in Greece's civil war. In 1950 he was reassigned to the U.S. as Second Army commander.

Van Fleet assumed command of the Eighth Army in Korea on April 11, 1951, the same day that General Matthew Bunker Ridgway* relieved Douglas MacArthur* and that the Communist Chinese and North Korean armies launched a major offensive. He skillfully withdrew his frontline units and shifted parts of the IX and X Corps to reinforce positions in the west and to hold Seoul. After slowing the enemy offensive, Ridgway and Van Fleet attacked along the entire front. A short-lived Communist counterattack was stopped in May, and heavy casualties were inflicted by massed artillery fire. The Eighth Army then drove north of the 38th parallel and, by June, advanced to the Kumhwa-Chorwon base of the Iron Triangle. When the Truman administration initiated ceasefire talks, Van Fleet halted his army and constructed elaborate fortifications on the Kansas and Wyoming lines north of the 38th parallel. In August, after his promotion to general, he began limited objective attacks in eastern Korea because the truce talks had faltered. For the next two months, his troops fought bitterly for the Punchbowl and Bloody and Heartbreak ridges. In early October the Eighth Army attacked in west-central Korea but stopped when truce talks resumed at Panmunjom. On November 27 a ceasefire line similar to one Van Fleet had proposed was established. After being restricted to the maintenance of frontline defensive positions, Van Fleet announced that he had been given too little battlefield initiative. An embarrassed Truman administration authorized him to conduct limited attacks against Communist positions.

For the next year, the Eighth Army fought small-scale actions and artillery duels. Van Fleet started new training programs for the Republic of Korea Army and, without official sanction, expanded the South Korean forces and prepared them for offensive action. "Van Fleet's load" pinpointed the controversy over the massive expenditure of artillery rounds by the Eighth Army. In late 1951 operations, Van Fleet rationed rounds but was still criticized for excessive use of ammunition. Inadequate domestic production and resupply problems in 1952 forced him to ration ammunition again and to reorganize heavy artillery and mortar units. Even his counterbattery and flak suppression tactics were hampered by ammunition shortages. The same year, after prisoners of war were screened for repatriation, violent riots occurred in the Koje-do Island compounds. An

American general was seized, and Van Fleet had to use seasoned combat units to restore order but was criticized by Ridgway and his successor, General Mark Wayne Clark.* Both thought that Van Fleet identified too closely with Syngman Rhee's government, which opposed the truce and repatriation and wanted to unify Korea militarily. Van Fleet's outspoken insistence on a major offensive prompted Clark to reimpose restrictions on Van Fleet, but in summer-fall the Eighth Army was authorized to conduct limited attacks in the mountainous terrain overlooking the Iron Triangle. These costly and largely unsuccessful operations were terminated after President-elect Eisenhower announced his intention to reach a ceasefire. Embittered, Van Fleet decided to retire and in February 1953 turned over the Eighth Army to Maxwell Davenport Taylor.* On his return to the United States, Van Fleet claimed that he could have achieved total victory in Korea in 1951 but for pusillanimous military and political decisions. In April he retired as full general and the following year was sent by Eisenhower as special ambassador to the Far East.

Van Fleet ranks as an outstanding combat commander in World Wars I and II and an able leader of the Eighth Army in Korea. Although an aggressive and innovative tactician, he was not reckless in spite of the fact that his European and Korean commands suffered heavy casualties. He consistently demonstrated exceptional skill in battlefield manuever and in his use of artillery and tactical air support. He trained and revitalized the Greek and South Korean armies and made them formidable fighting forces. His attempts to interdict enemy supply lines and to isolate the battlefield with air power and long-range artillery in Korea were not successful, but these were largely due to his rejection of the strategy of limited war which led him into conflict with superiors and into disagreement with subordinates. His denunciation of static warfare and truce in Korea, his staunch defense of the authoritarian Rhee government, and his inconsistent statements about being denied decisive victory and having ammunition deliberately withheld interested anti-Communist politicians and congressional committees but brought criticism from Ridgway, Taylor, and Joseph Lawton Collins.* Van Fleet's conviction that communism must be militarily defeated contributed to the spirit of American intervention in Vietnam a decade later.

BIBLIOGRAPHY

Chandler, Alfred D., Jr.,and Stephen E. Ambrose, eds. *The Papers of Dwight D. Eisenhower: The War Years.* 5 vols. Baltimore: Johns Hopkins Press, 1970.

Cole, Hugh M. *The United States Army in World War II: The Lorraine Campaign.* Washington, D.C.: Government Printing Office, 1950.

Hermes, Walter G. *The United States Army in the Korean War: Truce Tent and Fighting Front.* Washington, D.C.: Government Printing Office, 1966.

MacDonald, Charles B. *The United States Army in World War II: The Last Offensive.* Washington, D.C.: Government Printing Office, 1973.

Rees, David. *Korea: The Limited War.* New York: St. Martin's Press, 1964.

Ridgway, Matthew B. *The Korean War*. New York: Doubleday and Company, 1967.
Schnabel, James P. *The United States Army in the Korean War: Policy and Direction,
    The First Year*. Washington, D.C.: Government Printing Office, 1972.

MARVIN CAIN

VAN RENSSELAER, Stephen (b. New York City, N.Y., November 1, 1764;
d. Albany, N.Y., January 26, 1839), philanthropist, politician, militia general.

In 1630 Kiliaen Van Rensselaer, an Amsterdam diamond merchant and member of the Dutch West India Company, secured a grant twenty-three miles long
which extended twenty-four miles on either side of the Hudson River near present-
day Albany. About 436,000 acres remained in the hands of his descendants in
1769 when a son, Stephen, was born to Stephen, the seventh patroon of the
Manor of Rensselaerwyck, and his wife the former Catherine Livingston. In
1769 the elder Stephen died, and his son became the ward of his maternal
grandfather, Philip Livingston. The young boy attended schools in Ablany,
Kingston, New York, and Elizabethtown, Pennsylvania, before entering Princeton in 1779. Three years later he transferred to Harvard where he graduated with
the class of 1782.

While still a minor Van Rensselaer, on June 6, 1783, eloped with Margaret
Schuyler, the daughter of Major General Philip Schuyler.* Two years later Van
Rensselaer assumed control of the manor which contained about three thousand
farms. He followed a policy of granting perpetual leases on moderate terms to
settlers on his land which hastened the settlement of the upper Hudson Valley.
As a landowner Van Rensselaer naturally entered politics as a Federalist. Although he lost an election to the state legislature in 1788, he won the following
year. In 1790 Van Rensselear moved to the State Senate where he served until
1795. In 1792 he ran for lieutenant governor on a ticket headed by John Jay but
lost in a hotly contested and probably fraudulent election. Three years later Jay
and Van Rensselaer won, as they did in 1798. In 1801 Van Rensselaer, as the
Federalist standardbearer, lost the election for governor. He temporarily retired
from politics, and on May 17, 1802, he married Cornelia Paterson of Baltimore,
his first wife having died.

Van Rensselaer joined the New York militia in 1786 as a major of infantry.
In 1801, following the creation of an independent cavalry division, he advanced
to major general as its commander. Except for muster days and ceremonial
duties, the patroon had no military experience. Despite his martial limitations,
his opposition to the War of 1812, and his probable role as Federalist nominee
for governor in 1813, Governor Daniel D. Tompkins appointed Van Rensselaer
to command of the militia defending the frontier along the St. Lawrence and the
Great Lakes. Tompkins chose the patroon because he was a moderate Federalist,
a senior militia officer, and a highly respected public figure.

Acutely aware of his own lack of field experience, Van Rensselaer chose his
cousin Colonel Solomon Van Rensselaer, a trained officer and former state
adjutant general, as military aide and advisor. Van Rensselaer arrived in Buffalo

in early August 1812. He secured the neutrality of the local Indians, but this proved to be about the only bright light in the situation. Only about one thousand men and a few light field guns defended the Niagara frontier. Van Rensselaer hastened additional militia to the area, taking advantage of Major General Henry Dearborn's* armistice along the northern frontier. Van Rensselaer's problems were compounded by the vacillating instructions he received from Dearborn and by the dispatch of a brigade of newly raised regular troops under Brigadier General Alexander Smyth. Smyth arrived in Buffalo on September 29 but showed his unwillingness to cooperate with the militia officer by reporting by letter, an unpardonable breach of military etiquette.

By mid-October Van Rensselaer commanded a respectable force of about six thousand men. The pressure to attack became overwhelming. His idle, ill-trained militia grew restless, and the general found his authority being undercut by political enemies in the Army. He also believed that his superiors expected an attack into Canada. His plan called for a two-pronged assault. Smyth's regulars would cross near the mouth of the Niagara River and seize Fort George, while the militia thrust across at Lewiston to seize the Queenston Heights. When Smyth refused to participate or to develop a plan more to his liking, Van Rensselaer decided to assail Queenston Heights with the militia and such regulars as he could secure.

The plan was ill-fated from the start. The assault, scheduled for October 11, had to be abandoned when the lieutenant responsible for delivering the thirteen boats to be used for the crossing decamped with their oars. The attack finally took place during the early hours of October 13. It involved an assault crossing by three hundred militia under Solomon Van Rensselaer and an equal number of regulars under Lieutenant Colonel John Chrystie of the 13th Infantry. The overly complicated plan miscarried. Van Rensselaer was severely wounded soon after landing, and Chrystie's boat was disabled during the crossing which left the tactical command to Captain John Ellis Wool.* He organized an attack that cleared the British from the battery at the top of the Heights. The Americans beat off a counterattack led by the British commander Major General Sir Isaac Brock, in which Brock was killed. By midafternoon the assault force had received seven hundred to eight hundred reinforcements, regular and militia. The remainder of the militia, however, refused to leave New York despite the pleading of Van Rensselaer and other officers. That permitted Brock's successor, Brigadier General Sir Roger Sharfe, to bring up enough reinforcements from Fort George to drive the Americans off the Heights onto the beaches below where they were forced to surrender. American casualties numbered about 60 killed, 170 wounded, and 764 prisoners, while the British lost 14 killed, 84 wounded, and 15 missing.

Little positive can be said of Van Rensselaer's attack beyond its proof of his willingness to carry out the directives of his superiors under extremely unfavorable conditions. The plan he devised involved a night river crossing which was too complicated for his unskilled troops and too limited in size. Nor was the objective of sufficient value to warrant the risks involved. But most of all

Van Rensselaer can be faulted for failing to determine that his militia would not cross. On October 16, in utter disgust, Van Rensselaer transferred command along the Niagara frontier to Smyth. Four days later he requested relief and on October 25 left for home. That completed his military service.

Despite the Queenston fiasco, Van Rensselaer was the Federalist candidate for governor in 1813. He lost handily to Tompkins and thereafter largely devoted his energies to less partisan public service. He had a longstanding interest in canals and had served before the war as a director of both the Western Inland Lock Navigation Company which built a waterway from the Mohawk River to Lake Ontario and its sister Northern Inland Lock Navigation Company which planned one to Lake Champlain. He served on the 1810 Canal Commission which studied the practicality of the Erie Canal as well as the group that directed its construction in 1817–1825. After 1825 he served as president of the Erie Canal Commission. He was an early supporter of railroad construction, acting as president of the Mohawk and Hudson at its formation in 1826. He was an initial investor in the Cohoes Company which developed the waterpower generated by the falls at the mouth of the Mohawk River and played a major role in attracting to the upper Hudson Valley skilled mechanics like Henry Burden who later developed the machine to mass-produce horseshoes.

Van Rensselaer actively supported both traditional and other education. He served as a trustee of Williams (1794–1819) and Union (1798–1800) colleges and twice sat on the Board of Regents of the University of the State of New York (1795–1801 and 1814–1839). More important was his interest in making broadly available the rapidly developing scientific knowledge of the age. In 1824 he founded the Rensselaer School (later Rensselaer Polytechnic Institute) to instruct "the sons and daughters of farmers and mechanics" in practical science. He was a devoted supporter of agricultural fairs as a means of spreading knowledge of improved farming methods and served as president of the State Board of Agriculture after 1820. He actively promoted the Lyceum movement. In 1820–1824 he financed geological surveys of Albany and Rensselaer counties and the lands along the Erie Canal.

Van Rensselaer returned to politics in 1821 with his election to the State Constitutional Convention. The following year he was elected to Congress and served until 1829. As congressman he cast the deciding vote in 1825 which elected John Quincy Adams as president. For the ten years following his retirement from the House of Representatives, Van Rensselaer continued to manage his estates and his philanthropies.

The patroon was an excellent example of the public-spirited early nineteenth-century monied gentleman. He contributed his name and financial support to the efforts to transmit the scientific knowledge of the day to the masses and to the industrial and transportation endeavors which contributed to the well-being of the upper Hudson Valley. His one excursion into military affairs, even though motivated by his strong sense of obligation, was the single great blot on his exemplary career of public service.

BIBLIOGRAPHY

Babcock, Louis L. *The War of 1812 on the Niagara Frontier*. Buffalo, N.Y.: Buffalo
    Historical Society, 1927.
Barnard, Daniel D. *A Discourse on the Life, Services and Character of Stephen Van
    Rensselaer*. Albany, N.Y.: Hoffman and White, 1839.
Fink, William Bertrand. *Stephen Van Rensselaer: The Last Patroon*. Ann Arbor, Mich.:
    University Microfilms, 1963.
Lossing, Benson J. *The Pictorial Field Book of the War of 1812*. New York: Harper and
    Brothers, 1868.
Van Rensselaer, Solomon. *A Narrative of the Affair at Queenstown in the War of 1812*.
    New York: Leavitt, Lord and Company, 1836.

                                                    K. JACK BAUER

VETCH, Samuel (b. Edinburgh, Scotland, December 9, 1668; d. London, England, April 30, 1732), governor of Nova Scotia, imperialist, entrepreneur, colonel, architect of the conquest of New France.

The son of a prominent Presbyterian churchman in Edinburgh, Vetch was sent to Holland at fifteen to be with his father, who was a fugitive from Charles II's justice. After study at the College of Utrecht, Samuel Vetch joined the army of William of Orange on its way to England in 1688. His regiment, the Royal Regiment of Dragoons of Scotland (Scots Greys), returned to the Continent the following year, and he spent the rest of King William's War on campaigns against the French in the Netherlands. By 1697 Captain Vetch was back in Dumfries, Scotland.

Within the next year he had sailed for Darien, Panama, in the service of the Company of Scotland Trading to Africa and the Indies. This promising Scots venture to establish an outpost on the Isthmus began well. One observer remarked: "They are healthy and in such a crabbed hold that it will be difficult to beat them out of it." Yet, in late summer of 1699 Vetch was in New York Harbor with the other tragic survivors of the collapsed colony. He would do much better in New York.

In 1700 he married Margaret Livingston, daughter of Robert, the colony's most prominent Scot. This immensely useful connection gave Vetch access to a thriving mercantile community and the great men of the Province. A man of abilities and ambition, he entered this world with ease. Several years later he relocated to Boston, with equal success. Between 1700 and 1706 Vetch was engaged in various commercial activities and on two occasions was charged with "trading with H.M. enemies." In a not unusual practice for the period, he left for England in 1706 to clear his name.

During the following two years he would pursue the "grand design," the "Glorious Enterprise," the plan for the conquest of Canada. The strategy Vetch presented to the Board of Trade in his "Canada Survey'd" (1708) had been the idea of "many intelligent persons." Vetch put together a remarkable synthesis, however, and delivered it with persuasive vigor. The Union of England and

Scotland the previous year and the dominance of the Whigs in English politics were auspicious factors in the consideration of the proposal by Queen Anne's Ministry. Vetch noted that the solution to the peace and stability of the Empire was the immediate elimination of the French from the North American continent. "Almost morally sure" that New France could be "easily taken by resolved men, well-equipped," he suggested that a massive strike would be the cheapest policy and could be accomplished through united action: a combined British-colonial force in two prongs, one via land through Albany and Montreal and the other by sea from New York and Boston via Port Royal to Quebec.

In February 1709 orders were given for the expedition, with Vetch commissioned as colonel and adjutant general of the sea arm of the colonial forces. He was promised the governorship of Canada if the project was successful. Vetch remarked that he would "rather have that of Canada with blood and blows" than any other with peace. Enthusiasm ran high. The prospect of inflicting a fatal blow on a common menace encouraged harmony between colonial and imperial interests and among the colonists themselves. Vetch was pleased that Colonel Francis Nicholson, a man of "known abilities" and "extraordinary zeal," would command the colonial-Indian forces for the inland thrust of the pincer projected to crush Canada.

Vetch, in charge of colonial preparations, visualized the expedition as "one of the greatest and most glorious enterprises Britain hath been concerned in for many years." It would be the American counterpart of Marlborough's campaigns in the European theater. Success in America might allow Britain to force peace and dominate Atlantic commerce. Britain was on the verge of peace and victory, and an imperial position rivaling that of Spain. The Empire would thus greatly benefit, and so would Vetch. This was the apex.

The supporting British fleet was expected to arrive in late spring 1709. Vetch was not informed until October that the Ministry had "laid aside" the project for that year. The anticipation of placing New France in Queen Anne's possession had become a "vast loss and disappointment." Colonial New England was left with bills and bitterness, and the continuing havoc of Indian marauders and French privateers. In an attempt to save what they could, the colonists pressed for an assault on Port Royal, "that nest of spoilers and robbers who are so great a plague to all Her Majesty's plantations." Once again lack of support from British naval units terminated the plan. Despite the discouragement, Vetch remained enamored with the larger project which he continued to recommend to the government "as one of the greatest pieces of service to the British Empire in general, as well as to the American parts in particular."

In 1710 an attack against Port Royal did materialize. As adjutant general to Colonel Nicholson, Vetch helped overwhelm the French garrison at the post, and, by orders of the queen, Vetch became governor of Nova Scotia. He was forty-one years old and had achieved his highest station. Indeed, he soon discovered that the capture of the now renamed "Annapolis Royal" was somewhat easier than the retaining of it. The fort was in a "ruined state," and he faced a host of problems concerning the garrison including much official neglect. His major difficulty was the "spirit of insurgency" among the "conquered residents," who complained that the governor treated them "like negroes." Vetch talked of deportation, forseeing no peace surrounded by subversive French Catholics and "savages yet more bigoted than they." Vetch later imported some Iroquois, a "terror" he found useful in encouraging more cooperative behavior among the inhabitants.

In 1711 Vetch was back in Boston to assume comand of some one thousand New England troops assembled for an assault on Quebec. He was a principal member of the powerful British force which entered the St. Lawrence in August, under Rear-Admiral Sir Hovenden Walker and Brigadier General John Hill, both of whom exhibited high standards of ineptitude. Vetch knew the troublesome waters and offered to assist as pilot, but Walker only curtly consulted him. After a large and tragic loss of men and vessels to the treacherous shoals, the expedition was aborted. By the fall, a disheartened Vetch was back in Boston. Things never got much better.

Returning to Annapolis Royal in 1712, Governor Vetch encountered the same old problem. The following year he was replaced as governor by Francis Nicholson, partially due to charges of maladministration leveled against him by the mercurial Nicholson. Vetch returned to England in 1714 to deal with them. The charges were unfounded, and he was reinstated as governor in 1715 (to 1717). During his confrontation with Nicholson, many individuals had testified on his behalf, before the Board of Trade. Said one London merchant, regarding Nicholson's "very violent and arbitrary" complaints: "Col. Vetch always had a very good character for integrity, sense, worth, honor, and military abilities," and very few men were more knowledgeable of American conditions than Samuel Vetch.

Vetch never returned to the New World after his departure in 1714. The remaining eighteen years were spent offering valuable counsel to the Board of Trade on colonial matters and seeking posts, including the governorship of Massachusetts in 1724. The governorship was an unsuccessful chase, despite the impressive list of supporters he put forth including prominent peers of the realm. Samuel Vetch's last years were a combination of frustration, disappointment, and despair. Always at the center of heady events as a young man, he died in 1732, a prisoner in King's Bench for debt. New France outlived him by approximately thirty years.

Samuel Vetch's place in American history is largely attributable to his *Canada Survey'd* of 1708, designed to make Great Britain the "sole empress of the vast North American continent." The grappling for empire could be brought to an immediate conclusion through a successful utilization of Britain's superior sea power, against a vulnerable French overseas empire. North America would thus be a major center for British military operations, a suggestion that foreshadowed the later and successful strategy of William Pitt in the Seven Years' War. Vetch, like the more cosmopolitan colonial figures, had not left the Old World for good. They visualized the emerging empire as a whole and thought in terms of a British "Atlantic" community. The mother country was a major component of the world they wished to build. Vetch did not foresee any serious difficulties surfacing between the British Isles and the British colonies should the French be eliminated from North America. Divergent colonial and imperial interests could be harmonized in an expanding commercial empire. An able and insightful individual, Vetch anticipated the dramatic expansion of the British Empire in 1713 and 1763, but not the equally dramatic subtraction of 1783.

BIBLIOGRAPHY

Brebner, John Bartlett. *New England's Outpost: Acadia Before the Conquest of Canada*. Hamden, Conn.: Archon Books, 1965.
Hayne, David M., ed. *Dictionary of Canadian Biography*. Vol. 2. Toronto: University of Toronto Press, 1969, pp. 650–52.
Leach, Douglas E. *Arms for Empire*. New York: Macmillan, 1973.
Parkman, Francis. *A Half Century of Conflict: France and England in North America*. Vol. 1. Boston: Little, Brown, 1903.
Peckham, Howard H. *The Colonial Wars, 1689–1782*. Chicago: University of Chicago Press, 1964.
Rawylk, George A. *Nova Scotia's Massachusetts: A Study of Massachusetts-Nova Scotia Relations, 1630 to 1784*. London: McGill-Queen's Press, 1973.
Waller, G. M. *Samuel Vetch: Colonial Enterpriser*. Chapel Hill: University of North Carolina Press, 1960.

JOHN C. KENDALL

W

WADSWORTH, Decius (b. Farmington, Conn., January 2, 1768; d. New Haven, Conn. November 8, 1821), first chief of ordnance, U.S. Army.

Born into a family that had lived in Connecticut for four generations, Decius Wadsworth grew up amid the turmoil of the American Revolution. Early displaying an intellectual bent, he completed his primary education rapidly and matriculated at Yale College at the age of fourteen. Graduating in 1785, he briefly considered a teaching offer in Virginia before returning to Yale for further study. These efforts culminated in a master's degree in 1788. Wadsworth next essayed to become a lawyer, but he soon discovered that the legal profession was not congenial to his temperament. In casting about for an alternative career, he chanced upon the U.S. Army, where Anthony Wayne* was drawing public attention with his preparations for a major campaign on the frontier.

When Congress created the Corps of Artillerists and Engineers in 1794, Wadsworth sought a commission in the new organization and was appointed captain in June of that year. Unfortunately, the glory and adventures he had anticipated were not immediately forthcoming. When the Army was reduced in size in 1796, Wadsworth's hopes of quick advancement dimmed, and he submitted his resignation in July 1796. His separation from the service lasted only until the crisis with France in 1798, when the Army once more expanded. Applying to President John Adams for a commission, he was again appointed a captain in the Corps of Artillerists and Engineers and assigned to the 2d Regiment in June 1798. For the next two years Wadsworth was caught up in the Army's preparations for war. By 1800 he had risen to the rank of major, which helped him to survive the Army reduction of 1802. Assigned to the artillery when a separate Corps of Engineers was established, Wadsworth ultimately persuaded Secretary of War Henry Dearborn* to approve his transfer to the new branch, and he reported to West Point for duty in July 1802.

Wadsworth's first assignment as an engineer was to supervise repairs at Fort Nelson, part of the defenses of Norfolk, Virginia. While he was so engaged, a controversy arose between Colonel Jonathan Williams, chief of the Corps of Engineers, and the War Department. Williams argued that whenever an engineer was the ranking officer of a garrison, he should command all the units present, including those of the line. Wadsworth and other engineer officers supported Williams, but Secretary Dearborn denied the validity of their contention. Unable to accept Dearborn's decision, Williams resigned his commission in June 1803. By virtue of seniority, Wadsworth became chief of the Corps of Engineers and superintendent of the U.S. Military Academy.

At work on the fortifications of Newport, Rhode Island, when notified of his elevation to command, Wadsworth was soon ordered to New Orleans to plan defenses for the newly acquired Louisiana Territory. A year later he reached West Point and assumed the superintendency. Rather than introduce major changes in the curriculum, he attempted only to enforce military discipline among both faculty and students. Discouraged by the resistance to his policies, Wadsworth consoled himself by taking up the fight formerly led by Williams. A plea signed by Wadsworth and other engineers seeking reversal of Dearborn's decision was dispatched to President Thomas Jefferson. When the president did not respond, Wadsworth resigned his commission in February 1805. Dearborn offered a compromise two months later, and Williams returned to the Corps of Engineers, but Wadsworth chose to seek his fortune outside the Army.

For the next seven years Wadsworth operated a successful mercantile business in Montreal, Canada. The outbreak of the War of 1812 found the United States in need of men with just such skills as he possessed, and he was invited by Secretary of War William Eustis to assume command of the newly created Ordnance Department. Accepting Eustis' offer with alacrity, Wadsworth closed his business in Montreal and returned to the United States. As commissary general of ordnance with the rank of colonel, he assumed control of the ordnance procurement and inspection process heretofore conducted by the secretary of war. He quickly established a small but efficient department organization in Washington and staffed it with bright young officers from the Corps of Engineers, the most notable being his deputy, George Bomford.*

In order to support American operations against Canada, Wadsworth created arsenals at Albany, New York, and Pittsburgh, Pennsylvania. He also attempted to standardize the Army's equipment and materiel, giving special attention to the artillery. In a war noted for its lack of organization and planing at the highest levels, Wadsworth's Ordnance Department performed brilliantly. In fact, the reorganization implemented by Secretary of War John Armstrong, Jr.,* in 1813, which divided the nation into nine military districts, generally reflected Wadsworth's existing ordnance supply system.

Several factors, notably the resignation of Chief Engineer Williams, Wadsworth's own engineering background, and British raids in the Chesapeake Bay area, led to Wadsworth's assignment in 1813 to improve the defenses of the Chesapeake tributaries. Most of his efforts went into adding armament to Fort Washington on the Potomac, all in vain as the post was destroyed and abandoned in August 1814. When the British routed American forces at Bladensburg, field works constructed at Wadsworth's direction were also abandoned. During the frantic evacuation of the capital, he became involved in a heated argument with Acting Secretary of War James Monroe over the placement of some guns. Shortly thereafter, Wadsworth submitted his resignation.

Although his resignation was not accepted, Wadsworth was allowed to return to Connecticut for a much-needed furlough. A sore that had developed on one of his fingers in 1806 had finally become cancerous and was seriously affecting his health. The consensus of medical opinion was that amputation was required, but Wadsworth refused to permit the operation. During his absence an Army reorganization permanently established the Ordnance Department and Corps, and delineated their functions. Offered the position of chief of ordnance, Wadsworth accepted the appointment but did not return to Washington until April 1815, after Monroe had left the War Department.

For the next six years, Wadsworth as chief of ordnance pursued his goals of "Uniformity, Simplicity, and Solidarity." The task of standardizing the Army's weapons and arranging for their manufacture were herculean, but Wadsworth's department vigorously assumed the responsibility. Several new arsenals were established, while the Springfield and Harper's Ferry Armories were brought under Ordnance supervision. Small arms types were standardized, and initial steps were taken to introduce the uniformity system into the manufacturing process. Similar efforts were made to standardize artillery weapons and materiel.

At Wadsworth's urging, the War Department in 1816 accepted the principle of a standardized system for American artillery, but left the details to be formulated by the chief of ordnance. Strongly influenced by British field carriages captured at Plattsburgh in 1814, Wadsworth devised a revolutionary system of field carriages for Army use. Previously, American gunners had used twin-trail designs dating back to the French Gribeauval system, but Wadsworth's design drew its inspiration from the British stock-trail carriage. When the new system was presented to Secretary of War John Caldwell Calhoun* in 1817, he refused to approve it without the concurrence of an ordnance board. Although personally selected by Wadsworth, the board unanimously recommended against the adoption of the new system. Following the board's recommendation, Calhoun approved a system based totally on the obsolete Gribeauval plan, much to Wadsworth's chagrin.

Badly bruised by the bureaucratic infighting over his artillery system, and failing in health, Wadsworth was unable to prevent Congress from abolishing the Ordnance Corps in the Army reorganization of 1821. Rather than continue the struggle, he retired in June to his home in New Haven, Connecticut. There he died of cancer five months later.

Decius Wadsworth's contribution to American military history is based solely on his service as commissary general of ordnance during the War of 1812 and chief of ordnance in the immediate postwar period. A man of strong organizational skills, Wadsworth deserves much of the credit for bringing order to the chaotic ordnance procurement process existing in 1812. Ordnance operations were among the few American successes emanating from the second war with Britain, a result for which Wadsworth and his assistants are responsible.

Wadsworth's strong support for the application of the uniformity system to small arms manufacture in the years 1815–1821 was crucial to the ultimate success of the interchangeability principle years later. Although not as visionary as Bomford, he nurtured most of the ideas championed by his able subordinate. As for artillery, Wadsworth's standardization plan of 1816 was a major achievement in itself, being considered the first complete system of artillery materiel in American military history. The War Department's failure to adopt his stock-trail field carriage meant that in carriage design American artillery would remain obsolete until 1836, when the stock-trail was finally adopted. Alone in the U.S. Army, Wadsworth had seen the utility of the British system of carriages. That the Army was eventually forced to recognize its mistake and adopt the stock-trail is the ultimate testimony to the strength of Wadsworth's vision.

BIBLIOGRAPHY

Ambrose, Stephen E. *Duty, Honor, Country: A History of West Point.* Baltimore: Johns Hopkins University Press, 1966.
Birkhimer, William E. *Historical Sketch of the Organization, Administration, Materiel and Tactics of the Artillery, United States Army.* Washington, D.C.: James J. Chapman, 1884.
Jacobs, James Ripley. *The Beginning of the U.S. Army, 1783–1812.* Princeton, N.J.: Princeton University Press, 1947.
Rodenbough, Theo F. and William L. Haskin, eds. *The Army of the United States.* Reprint edition, New York: Argonaut Press, 1966. [Originally published 1896.]
Smith, Merritt Roe. *Harpers Ferry Armory and the New Technology: The Challenge of Change.* Ithaca, N.Y.: Cornell University Press, 1977.

WILLIAM GLENN ROBERTSON

WAGNER, Arthur Lockwood (b. Ottawa, Ill., March 16, 1853; d. Ashville, N.C., June 17, 1905), military educator and writer. Wagner was a pioneer in the establishment of the U.S. Army's postgraduate school system.

Arthur L. Wagner, born and raised in Illinois of a modest family of German extraction, entered the U.S. Military Academy in 1870. His career at West Point was mediocre at best. One of the youngest in his class, Wagner ranked low in soldierly conduct as well as scholarship; his final standing in the class of 1875 was fortieth out of forty-three. Yet his outside interests as a cadet—military history and the cadet literary publications *Weekly Spy Glass* and *Howitzer*—served his subsequent military career well. It was as a writer and teacher of military history and tactics that Wagner made his reputation.

Following graduation from the Military Academy, however, he spent the next six years with his regiment, the 6th Infantry, on the frontier. As a young lieutenant he participated in the Sioux and Nez Perce campaigns of the late 1870s, helped construct telegraph lines in Dakota and Colorado, and in 1881 again engaged in active operations, this time against the Utes.

Wagner's role as a military educator began in 1881 when he served as professor of military science and tactics briefly at Louisiana State University and then for four years at East Florida Seminary. War Department inspectors consistently praised Wagner for his instruction while at the seminary. In 1884 he published an essay, "The Military Necessities of the United States, and the Best Method of Meeting Them," which won the gold medal of the Military Service Institution of the United States. According to a contemporary, Wagner's essay "was a powerful statement, was widely read and certainly exercised some influence." Certainly, publication of this essay and the award of the gold medal enhanced Wagner's reputation throughout the Army and marked him as a military thinker and writer.

Wagner rejoined the 6th Infantry in 1885 at Fort Douglas, Utah. One year later the War Department redeployed the regiment to Fort Leavenworth, Kansas—the site of the Infantry and Cavalry School. Because of Wagner's interest in military history, prior literary success, teaching experience, and expressed liking for the study of the art of war, the school commandant requested his services as an assistant instructor in tactics and military art. For the next eleven years Wagner remained at Leavenworth, eventually, in 1894, becoming head of the Military Art Department. With the support of reform-minded commandants and the assistance of able subordinates (especially Captain Eben Swift*), Wagner introduced the applicatory method of instruction, which encouraged learning by doing and generally invigorated the Leavenworth course.

While at the Infantry and Cavalry School, Wagner wrote several books which became standard texts of military history, doctrine, and tactics. He visited Europe to study Prussian military schools, the organization of the German Army, and the battlefields of the 1866 and 1870–1871 German wars. The information he compiled furnished material for his first book *The Campaign of Königgrätz*, published in 1889. Wagner's next two books, *The Service of Security and Information* (1893) and *Organization and Tactics* (1895), stemmed directly from his tactical instruction at Leavenworth. When he found no textbooks based on American experience and suitable for teaching tactics to American officers, he wrote his own.

In 1896 Wagner received a much sought after promotion to major and transferred from the school to the Adjutant General's Office at the War Department where he became head of the Military Information Division (MID). As head of the MID he helped gather intelligence and formulate plans for the 1898 campaign in Cuba. During that campaign he served on the staff of General William Rufus Shafter,* the expedition commander, and distinguished himself by making two important reconnaissances under enemy fire. Following the Santiago Campaign, Wagner served successively as a staff officer in Puerto Rico, the Department of Dakota, the Philippines, and the Department of the Lakes. Because of his knowledge and reputation as a tactician, the War Department selected Wagner as the chief umpire for the joint Army-militia maneuvers in 1902, 1903, and 1904. He returned to Fort Leavenworth in November 1903 as assistant commandant of the General Service and Staff College but remained only two months before the War Department reassigned him as a senior director of the newly established Army War College and chief of the 3d Division of the War Department General Staff. He held these positions from January 1904 until June 1905 when he died from the effects of acute tuberculosis at the age of fifty-two.

For over half of his thirty-year military career Wagner was involved in military education—he taught eleven years at Leavenworth where he tried to make the study of tactics more palatable, more interesting, and more realistic. Because he thought the purpose of the school was to improve an officer's efficiency as a leader, not merely to fill his head with facts, Wagner emphasized an analytical approach in studying tactics. Under his direction the Department of Military Art began using the applicatory method of instruction; this instructional technique was developed in the German Army, and refined and adapted to American needs by Wagner's assistant, Eben Swift.* Increasingly, the department used map problems, map maneuvers (also called wargames), and tactical rides (terrain exercises), and stressed the systematic issuance of orders.

In addition to improving instruction methods, Wagner served as a catalyst in changing the self-perception of the Infantry and Cavalry School. He focused attention on the more abstract, more theoretical aspects of the military profession and away from the school's prior concern as a school of application with drill, garrison duty, and company administration. The lieutenants who graduated during Wagner's tenure were competent company officers and tacticians. But the course of study followed by Wagner prepared them for duties throughout their military careers and allowed them to see and think of military problems beyond the dimensions of a late nineteenth-century garrison.

Wagner's influence on Leavenworth students was great. Through his writings he influenced the rest of the Army as well. By explaining recent European military experience and relating it to American experience and doctrine, Wagner's writing was an important part of the growing professionalization of the U.S. Army. For many he became the final American arbiter of military tactics and strategy.

Wagner believed that a critical analysis of recent military history was a good means of learning organization and tactics. A principal objective of the applicatory method of instruction was to immerse officers in the details of a variety of tactical situations from which they could draw their own conclusions as to the proper course to be followed. Because history offered an infinite variety of tactical situations to be analyzed, it became the basis of Wagner's three principal books.

A number of common themes emerge from these three works. An emphasis on the offensive as the strongest form of combat and on flexibility in determining offensive formations predominated. Yet Wagner recognized that by the end of the nineteenth century the improved range, rates of fire, and accuracy of infantry and artillery weapons had greatly strengthened the defensive. He believed that frontal assaults against an entrenched enemy could succeed only if undertaken by a force superior in numbers, morale, and leadership. Successful tactics, according to Wagner, depended on taking advantage of the terrain and the enemy's weakness; he stressed flexibility, not rigid doctrine. His books reiterated these lessons with examples from the mid-nineteenth-century German wars and especially from the American Civil War. Of Wagner's writings his friend and fellow Leavenworth instructor, Eben Swift, reported: "The army became students at once, and Wagner's books became as familiar as the drill books."

Contemporaries and historians alike have acknowledged Wagner's contribution to the service. General James Franklin Bell* spoke for many early twentieth-century Army progressives when he declared that more than any other officer of his era Wagner encouraged "acquirement of military knowledge." A former officer and Army historian, William A. Ganoe, praised Wagner for awakening the officer corps to the need for "endless study and practice" which contributed immeasurably to battlefield success in World War I. More recently, Russell F. Weigley credited him with cultivating "high standards of military scholarship and stimulting teaching" at Leavenworth. From 1890 until his death the name of Arthur L. Wagner was synonymous with tactical instruction in the U.S. Army and with the Leavenworth schools.

BIBLIOGRAPHY

Nenninger, Timothy K. *The Leavenworth Schools and the Old Army: Education, Professionalism, and the Officer Corps of the U.S. Army, 1881–1918*. Westport, Conn.: Greenwood Press, 1978.
Swift, Eben. "An American Pioneer in the Cause of Military Education." *Journal of the Military Service Institution* 44 (January-February 1909).
Wagner, Arthur L. *The Campaign of Königgrätz*. Leavenworth, Kans.: C. J. Smith and Company, 1889.
———. *Organization and Tactics*. Kansas City, Mo.: Hudson-Kimberly Company, 1895.
———. *The Service of Security and Information*. 4th ed. Kansas City, Mo.: Hudson-Kimberly Company, 1896.
Weigley, Russell F. *History of the United States Army*. New York: Macmillan Company, 1967.

TIMOTHY K. NENNINGER

WAINWRIGHT, Jonathan Mayhew (b. Walla Walla, Wash., August 23, 1881; d. San Antonio, Tex., September 2, 1953), Army officer. Wainwright conducted a delaying action against Japanese troops invading the Philippine Islands in 1941–1942.

Jonathan Mayhew Wainwright was born to the sound of trumpets, the heir of a proud military tradition. His grandfather, a Union naval officer, was killed in action at Galveston Harbor in 1863. An uncle was killed fighting Mexican pirates off the west coast of Mexico in 1870. Jonathan's father, Robert P.P. Wainwright, a cavalry officer, graduated from West Point in 1875, served on the Indian frontier, in the Spanish-American War, and died on active duty in Manila, Philippine Islands, in 1902.

That same year Jonathan reported to West Point. He distinguished himself academically, ranking twenty-fifth in a class of seventy-eight and also militarily, becoming first captain of the corps of cadets. Upon graduation in 1906, Wainwright opted for his late father's branch of service and learned his soldiering on the Texas plains as a second lieutenant with the 1st Cavalry Regiment. That regiment went to the Philippines in 1908 where he saw his first combat on Jolo Island against Moro rebels. Returning with the regiment to Idaho and Wyoming in 1910, Wainwright met and married Adele Howard Holley, the daughter of an Army colonel. He was promoted to first lieutenant in 1912.

Wainwright then alternated between the Mounted Service School and the border patrol in California. Promoted to captain in 1916, he commanded his own troop along the Texas-Mexican border where he earned his commander's commendation for leadership qualities he displayed during a pursuit of bandits through the arid Chiricahua Mountains. As the United States began to prepare for World War I, Wainwright found himself separated from his beloved cavalry.

He was promoted to temporary major of field artillery and assigned as adjutant of the first officers' training camp at Plattsburgh, New York, probably because his officer efficiency reports consistently recommended staff duty or assignment with militia units. He later joined the 76th Infantry Division, a unit broken up for use as replacements and cadres upon its arrival in France in July 1918. Wainwright went to the 27th Infantry Division then serving in the British sector southwest of Ypres and was awarded a Distinguished Service Medal while on this detached duty. He next moved to the 82d Infantry Division staff G–3, Operations, and he participated in the St. Mihiel and Meuse-Argonne offensives of 1918. When the 82d Division went into reserve on November 1, 1918, Wainwright, already promoted to temporary lieutenant colonel of cavalry, left the division for occupation duty in Germany with the Third Army staff following the Armistice.

Wainwright returned to the United States in 1920 and, after reverting to captain, received his majority that same year. He served as an instructor at the Cavalry School, Fort Riley, 1920–1921; as General Staff officer with the 3d Division and with the War Department, 1921–1923; and returned to his first love for troop duty with the 3d Cavalry at Fort Myer, 1923–1925. Another tour followed with the War Department General Staff from 1925 until 1928. Promoted the next year to lieutenant colonel, Wainwright entered the Command and General Staff School at Fort Leavenworth. He achieved a superior academic rating, graduating fourth in a class of 126. His instructors unanimously recommended him for advanced training in command positions. Wainwright did not hide behind books, however, as he was active in the Hunt Club and became master of the foxhounds. After graduation in 1931, he spent 1933–1934 at the Army War College, and the following year, as commandant of the Cavalry School, he received his colonelcy.

In 1936 Wainwright took command of the 3d Cavalry Regiment. His ability and effort resulted in his promotion to temporary brigadier general in 1938 and a new command, the 1st Cavalry Brigade at Fort Bliss. Already enjoying a career that most officers might have envied, his greatest challenges and rewards lay ahead.

Promoted to temporary major general, Wainwright arrived in Manila in 1940 to assume command of the Philippine Division, the largest single U.S. Army unit in the islands. From September 1941 he was the senior field commander under General Douglas MacArthur,* and both men worked together to prepare the islands' defense. Wainwright commanded the North Luzon Defense Force when troops of the Imperial Japanese Fourteenth Army forced their way ashore in December 1941. Lacking the highly trained troops and air power necessary to defend the landing beaches, Wainwright still conducted a complicated fighting withdrawal that transformed his green troops into the ''Battling Bastards of Bataan.'' He exhibited personal bravery and improved morale by visiting every line of the battlefield. These actions together with his leadership earned him the Distinguished Service Cross.

When President Franklin D. Roosevelt ordered MacArthur off Bataan in March 1942, MacArthur designated Wainwright the commander of the North Luzon Force, one of four new Philippine commands that MacArthur intended to control tactically from Australia as commander U.S. Army Forces Far East (USAFFE). Due to various misunderstandings, the War Department assumed that Wainwright, as senior commander, now commanded all U.S. forces in the Philippines, and it confirmed that position by announcing Wainwright's promotion to lieutenant general while naming him commander of the newly organized U.S. Forces in the Philippines (USFIP). Wainwright continued to delay the advancing Japanese forces for another month on Bataan. After the Bataan defenders surrendered on April 9, 1942, Wainwright carried on the struggle from the island fortress of Corregidor. Denied any reinforcements or substantial resupply, he surrendered Corregidor on May 6, 1942, primarily to avoid a massacre of his sick and wounded troops.

Wainwright entered captivity with no way of knowing how his conduct would be judged. His Japanese captors held Wainwright in prison camps in the Philippines, Taiwan, and finally Manchuria. Although his guards beat him and tried to humiliate him, Wainwright managed to maintain his dignity as a commander and as a man. Advancing Soviet troops liberated him in August 1945, and Wainwright was then flown to Tokyo to witness the Japanese surrender aboard the USS *Missouri* in Tokyo Bay.

In an emotional reunion with MacArthur, Wainwright, who believed himself in disgrace for surrendering, learned that the American public regarded him as a hero and that he would be reinstated in command. Even in his hour of vindication he retained his sense of perspective remarking, ''The last surrender I attended the shoe was on the other foot.'' He received a hero's welcome in the

United States, and President Harry S. Truman fastened the Medal of Honor around his neck. In January 1946 Wainwright took command of the Fourth Army at Fort Sam Houston, where he retired from active duty in August 1947.

Eight years to the day of the signing of the Japanese surrender, Wainwright died of a stroke. The nation showed it remembered his services by placing his body in state behind the Tomb of the Unknown Soldier, the first time since the interment of the unknowns that a soldier was so honored. He is buried in Arlington National Cemetery near his father, two Philippine soldiers reunited in death.

Wainwright's vigorous defense of the Bataan Peninsula against seemingly invincible Japanese hordes and his subsequent stand on Corregidor served as symbols of the American spirit at a time when the Allies had only a dismal record of consecutive defeats. Unknown to Wainwright, radio and press commentators in the United States lionized him as a fearless leader whose gallant stand against hopeless odds bought much needed time for the United States to prepare to meet the Japanese challenge in the Pacific.

In retrospect, it is doubtful that his delaying action accomplished very much militarily except to force his opponent, Lieutenant General Homma Masaharu, into premature retirement. The defense of Bataan did not disrupt the Japanese timetable for conquest in Southeast Asia. Indeed, Manila was the primary Japanese objective, and Japanese forces took Manila, as an open city, one month ahead of schedule.

Like MacArthur, Wainwright overestimated the strength and quality of his opposite number. The Fourteenth Army's best unit, the 48th Division, was diverted to Java, and Homma's spearhead unit, the 65th Brigade, was composed of recalled reservists, many of whom were over thirty and had been assigned in anticipation of garrison duty in the islands. General Homma himself was overly cautious, initially underestimating his opponent and then dispairing when his ill-planned attacks resulted in huge Japanese casualties. Nevertheless, given the uneven quality of his forces and lack of air cover, Wainwright led a complicated corps level retrograde movement in a textbook manner.

Wainwright was a loyal subordinate. He agreed with MacArthur, for example, that the beaches should have been defended at all costs. He accepted without question, however, MacArthur's decision to switch to War Plan Orange-Three. This plan, premised on the philosophy of a passive defense awaiting reinforcements, was contrary to Wainwright's cavalryman's instinct for the offensive. Yet he obeyed and conducted a difficult defensive maneuver. Wainwright also expected loyalty from his subordinates whose opinions he entertained but whose stragglers he could order summarily shot. As commander of U.S. Forces Philippines, his decision to retain the 2d Corps and create an Army headquarters meant that he had no direct contact with the forces in front of the enemy. The unified command also made it possible for Homma to demand that Wainwright surrender all U.S. forces in the Philippines.

Militarily, Wainwright is a forgotten man; his defense of Bataan is little remembered, studied, or criticized. He passed into history not as a battlefield commander but as a symbol of the price of unpreparedness.

BIBLIOGRAPHY

Beck, John J. *MacArthur and Wainwright: Sacrifice of the Philippines.* Albuquerque: University of New Mexico Press, 1974.
Kojima Noboru. *Taiheiyo senso* (1) (The Pacific War 1). Tokyo: Chuko shinsho, 1965.
Miller, Ernest B. *Bataan Uncensored.* Long Prairie, Minn.: Hart Publications, 1949.
Morton, Louis B. *The Fall of the Philippines.* Washington, D.C.: U.S. Department of the Army, 1953.
Wainwright, Jonathan Mayhew, and Robert Considine. *General Wainwright's Story.* Reprint edition, Westport, Conn.: Greenwood Press, 1973.

EDWARD J. DREA

WALKER, Walton Harris (b. Belton, Tex., December 3, 1889; d. Seoul, Korea, December 23, 1950), Army officer. Walker is renowned for his defense of the Pusan Perimeter in the Korean War.

Walton "Johnnie" Walker, the son of a drygoods merchant and the grandson of Confederate Army officers, was a product of the cotton-rich flatlands of Texas. He attended a local military academy and, in 1907, entered Virginia Military Institute, which he left the following year in order to matriculate at West Point. He was commissioned a second lieutenant upon his graduation in 1912. There followed a series of assignments to forts in Illinois, Oklahoma, and Texas. President Woodrow Wilson quarreled with the Mexican dictator, Victoriano Huerta, leading Wilson to order the seizure and occupation of the Mexican port city of Vera Cruz in 1914. Walker participated in this abortive seven-month expedition and then returned to routine stateside assignments.

The monotony of peacetime infantry life was broken by America's entry into World War I. Walker (by now a captain) was charged with organizing a company of the 13th Machine Gun Battalion. Walker and his machine-gunners engaged in some of the most bitter combat of the war, particularly in the campaigns of St. Mihiel and the Meuse-Argonne.

After a brief stint in the occupation forces, Walker returned to the United States, there to spend the decade of the 1920s involved in military education, both as student and teacher. He attended the Field Artillery School (1920); the Infantry School (1923); and the Command and General Staff School (1926). He taught at the Fort Benning Infantry School, and from 1923 until 1925 was an instructor of tactics at West Point. His final instructional post was at the Coast Artillery School, Fortress Monroe, Virginia.

During the early 1930s, Major Walker served in Tientsin, China, with the 15th Infantry on International Railroad Patrol duty. His tour was uneventful. In 1935 he was promoted to the rank of lieutenant colonel and entered the Army War College. In August 1937 Walker was sent to serve in the War Plans Division of the General Staff.

Walker's first important command responsibility came in the spring of 1941 when he was given the 36th Infantry Division, stationed at Camp Polk, Louisiana. A few months later he was transferred to command of the 3rd Armored Brigade at Camp Polk. When America entered World War II, Walker was given command of the IV Armored Corps, located at Camp Young, California.

General Walker was charged with responsibility for training armored units for combat in the forbidding terrain of North Africa. The Desert Training Center, which he established, provided trainees with a grueling regimen that slavishly duplicated the field conditions they would encounter. The success of the center marked Walker as a tough, talented officer.

Late in 1943 Walker's corps was redesignated the XX Corps and sent to England. This group became famous as the "Ghost Corps" in the Third Army of General George Smith Patton, Jr.* The XX Corps did not participate in the D-Day invasion of the Normandy beaches, but was instead held in reserve for forty-eight days. Once landed in France, Walker demonstrated that he was cast from the same mold as his superior, General Patton: he believed in hard, slashing onslaughts, not sophisticated envelopments. Walker plunged through France from the Loire to the Moselle, pausing before the great fortifications at Metz only because the XX Corps had—quite literally—run out of gas.

The most trying experience for the XX Corps came during the Battle of the Bulge. Almost all of the Third Army was pulled out of the line to force a corridor through to the besieged forces at Bastogne. Walker was given the task to hold with his corps the front previously held by an entire army. He triumphed, largely through vigorous patrolling and mining in depth.

After the Bulge, Walker drove the German forces from the Saar-Moselle triangle and participated in Patton's determined drive to the Rhine north of Coblenz. Using assault boats, the XX Corps crossed the Rhine at Mainz and pushed on through Kassel, Jena, Regensburg, and other German strongpoints. In the first week of May, as the war in Europe was ending, Walker reached Linz, Austria, which was the farthest point of advance achieved by any Third Army force.

In the interval between World War II and Korea, Walker was commanding general of the Fifth Army, a peacetime command based in Chicago (1946–1948). He was ordered to Japan in 1948 to assume leadership of the Eighth Army as a replacement for retiring General Robert Lawrence Eichelberger.* The Eighth Army was in a deteriorated condition; the four divisions of the Eighth had been weakened by the cuts in strength mandated by the military economy drive pursued by the Truman administration. Douglas MacArthur,* Walker's superior in the Far East, directed him to bring his command into a state of full combat readiness. Walker estimated he was twelve months from this goal when the fighting began in Korea; 90 percent of his forces lacked any combat experience.

Army units of Communist North Korea crossed the 38th parallel in an unanticipated invasion of the Republic of South Korea late in June 1950. With

President Harry S. Truman's consent, on July 5 MacArthur ordered Walker's ground forces into the fight to save South Korea. Hopelessly outnumbered by the well-equipped North Korean People's Army (NKPA), there was little Walker could do save to retreat southward down the peninsula. Under extreme enemy pressure, Walker established a thinly held defensive line stretching from Pusan on the Korean Straits northward some ninety miles along the Naktong and eastward to Pohang-dong on the Sea of Japan: this pocket became known as the Pusan Perimeter. Since there was nowhere left to go, except into the sea, the general told his troops: "There must be no further yielding under pressure of the enemy. From now on let every man stand or die."

The North Koreans maintained severe pressure against Walker's flanks, while constantly probing various points in the center for weakness. The perimeter was not a solid, continuous line, since there were not enough troops available. Instead, taking advantage of his interior lines, Walker shifted forces rapidly as enemy activity warranted. Walker succeeded in holding on for six harrowing weeks while MacArthur prepared a counterstroke to relieve the pressure on the Pusan Perimeter.

The Inchon invasion, begun on September 15, 150 miles north of Walker's position, by General Edward Mallory Almond's* X Corps, demonstrated the brilliance of MacArthur as a strategist. It also placed the North Koreans between a hammer and anvil, because Walker soon began to push north and westward out of his toehold. The North Korean forces disintegrated and began to flee, abandoning most of their heavy equipment. By the beginning of October, South Korea was virtually free of hostile forces.

Because the Truman administration agreed with MacArthur's suggested invasion of North Korea, Walker's Eighth Army was sent across the 38th parallel and up the western coast. At the same time, the X Corps was ordered to advance up the east coast in a sweeping envelopment. The terrain presented a serious difficulty; a desolate central massif separated the two forces, effectively precluding any efforts at coordination or mutual support. Thus, MacArthur (in Tokyo) assumed the task of tactical direction by long distance. (Some, such as Joseph Lawton Collins,* allege that it was a lack of confidence in Walker, not the terrain, that caused MacArthur to assume tactical direction of the Eighth Army from Tokyo.)

Walker had moved with great caution and concern for his flanks, not normal for an officer in the image of George Patton, but the cause for his trepidation was the threatened entry of the Chinese Communists into the conflict. On November 25 the very thing he dreaded most occurred as one hundred and eighty thousand Chinese troops (in eighteen divisions) struck at the Eighth Army. Walker fell back from this massive offensive as best he could, sustaining terrible losses. By December 5 the Eighth Army was again south of the 38th parallel, some 130 miles below the position held on November 24. As Walker regrouped, he tried to prepare his defenses for the anticipated Chinese invasion across the

38th parallel. But he did not live to fight that battle, which began on New Year's Day; General Walker died in an automobile accident in Seoul on December 23, 1950.

Walton Walker was not a great strategist or administrative genius. He was a military fundamentalist and a fine tactical officer. As a field commander he was highly visible to his troops, frequently appearing at the hottest spots on the front to reconnoiter the situation personally. He was thought of as a tough, hard, and direct leader. General Walker had a full measure of courage and gallantry and another quality which his successor, Matthew Bunker Ridgway,* described as "dogged tenacity."

Walker was an acknowledged expert in the tactical management of armor and of the integration of armored forces with infantry. In World War II he was Patton's most valued corps commander. His defense of the Pusan Perimeter is a classic manipulation of an inferior force, taking full advantage of interior lines. "All my life," Walker once said, "I've been a soldier and nothing else." His was a life lived to the fullest.

BIBLIOGRAPHY

Eisenhower, John. *The Bitter Woods.* New York: Putnam's, 1969.
Heller, Francis H., ed. *The Korean War: A 25-Year Perspective.* Lawrence: University Press of Kansas, 1977.
Manchester, William. *American Caesar: Douglas MacArthur, 1880–1964.* Boston: Little, Brown and Company, 1978.
Ridgway, Matthew B. *The Korean War.* Garden City, N.Y.: Doubleday, 1967.

RICHARD F. HAYNES

WALLACE, Lewis (b. Brookville, Ind., April 10, 1827; d. Crawfordsville, Ind., February 15, 1905), Army officer. Wallace held important commands in the Union Army during the Civil War.

Lewis (Lew) Wallace was born into a prominent Indiana family. Most of his education came from reading books in his father's library and the Indiana State Library. His primary interests were his father's gubernatorial career and militia activities. In 1846 he organized a militia company for the Mexican War and served as one of the unit's officers. He saw little action during the war, however. After the Mexican War, Wallace opened a law office in Crawfordsville and began his political career as a Democrat. In 1856 he organized a Zouave unit, the Crawfordsville Guards. Early in 1861 Wallace offered his services to Governor Oliver P. Morton, who appointed him adjutant general of Indiana. A few months later Wallace became colonel of the 11th Indiana Volunteer Infantry Regiment.

In the early months of the Civil War the 11th Indiana fought several battles in Virginia. Wallace's successes won him the rank of brigadier general of volunteers and a national reputation. After his transfer to the western theater in

September 1862, he won a second star for his service under Major General Ulysses Simpson Grant* at Forts Henry and Donelson. At the age of thirty-four Wallace became the first Indianan to attain the rank of major general.

The battle at Shiloh was the turning point in the military career and life of Lew Wallace. In the confusion of the battle, he and his division arrived on the field late the evening of the first day (April 6, 1862), much to the displeasure of Grant and his staff. Although Wallace distinguished himself the second day, in the battle's politically charged aftermath he fell into disfavor. He was placed on inactive duty and was rebuffed in his attempts to return to active command. He spent time on recruiting duty, served on the court of inquiry for General Don Carlos Buell,* and fended off the Confederate advance led by Edmund Kirby Smith* against Cincinnati.

In March 1864, thanks to pressure from political friends and relatives, Wallace was appointed to command the Middle Department and the VIII Army Corps in Baltimore. He won recognition in Baltimore's delicate political atmosphere, making friends for the administration of President Abraham Lincoln.* In July Wallace staged a holding action at Monocacy River, Maryland, which delayed General Jubal Anderson Early* long enought to permit Union reinforcements to reach Washington and save it from capture. This action restored Wallace to Grant's good graces and deepened his support in the Lincoln administration. Subsequently, the dependability Wallace had demonstrated brought him an appointment to the tribunal that tried Lincoln's assassins and led to his being named president of the military court that tried Captain Henry Wirz, commandant of the Confederate prison at Andersonville, Georgia.

After the Civil War, Wallace reentered the political arena. In 1870 he ran as a Republican candidate for Congress and was narrowly defeated. He served as one of the Republican "visiting statesmen" in Florida and Louisiana during the contested presidential election of 1876 (Republican Rutherford B. Hayes versus Democrat Samuel J. Tilden). In this role Wallace helped to hold these states for Hayes. In 1878 Hayes appointed Wallace governor of New Mexico Territory. He began his duties while the "Lincoln County War" raged, and he succeeded in bringing it to a conclusion. The settlement of the war involved him with a variety of outlaws including Billy the Kid. While serving as governor he completed his famous and popular novel, *Ben-Hur, A Tale of the Christ* (1880). Subsequently, President James A. Garfield appointed Wallace minister to Turkey (1881–1885). There he ingratiated himself with Sultan Abdul Hamid II and at the sultan's behest became involved in international power politics with the British over the control of Egypt and the Suez Canal.

Following his return to the United States, Wallace, then wealthy and internationally famous as a writer, operated behind the scenes in politics. He played an important role in the presidential nomination of his friend and fellow Indianan Benjamin Harrison. In 1898, at the age of seventy-one Wallace tried in vain to gain a general's commission during the Spanish-American War. The general lived out his remaining years in Crawfordsville.

Wallace's success in Virginia in 1861 earned him high general praise. But the praise, national attention, and rapid promotion went to his head. Wallace began to believe that his superiors did not appreciate him, and indeed actually discriminated against him. These beliefs grew after his transfer to the western theater where he became outspoken in his criticisms of General Henry Wager Halleck,* who was then overall commander of operations in the West.

Wallace played a pivotal role at Fort Donelson during General Grant's strange absence and soon thereafter was promoted to major general, developments that further inflated his ego. Nevertheless, until Shiloh, his rank, political connections, and military ability protected him from his antagonists. The reputation he received there for arriving late was undeserved, but was the excuse, not the reason, for his temporary removal from active command.

At Shiloh the Union Army and its field commanders were still learning. Security was inadequate, and maps were inaccurate. Wallace was stationed at Crump's Landing, five miles up the Tennessee River from the main Union force near Shiloh Church. Wallace's maps showed alternate routes, which appeared to be about equal in length, to Pittsburg Landing and the main force. In the battle, confusion, petulance, and indecision plagued the Union Army.

The morning of April 6, 1862, Wallace heard the gunfire and waited for Grant's orders. Grant only told him to be prepared to march in any direction. Wallace then placed himself in a position to move along either of the two routes. At about noon he received verbal orders from Grant to move to the right of the army, although Wallace had no fresh information as to where the right of the army was. Consequently, Wallace set out slowly, unsure as to where he would join the right of the army. At about 1:30 P.M. he received an order to hurry. At 2:00 P.M. he was finally informed that the army had been driven back to the river, placing him in what seemed to be the rear of the Confederate forces under Albert Sidney Johnston* and Pierre Gustauve Toutant Beauregard.* Wallace considered attacking, but countermarched to place his strongest elements in front and began marching toward the river road to Pittsburg Landing. At about 3:30 P.M. Colonel John A. Rawlins of Grant's staff rode up and proposed that Wallace abandon his artillery and hurry his forces piecemeal to the front. When Wallace refused, Rawlins considered arresting him. Henceforth, the two were bitter enemies. Wallace finally arrived on the field in early evening, too late to be of any help to Grant, but the next day helped lead the counterattack. Following the battle Grant and his staff came under heavy criticism from many quarters. Grant took note of any disagreement with his position and would not fully endorse Wallace's battle report. Moreover, Grant's staff began to criticize Wallace, calling him tardy and inefficient.

Had Wallace arrived on the battlefield earlier than he did, it would have made little difference on the first day. Indeed, if Rawlins' plan had been followed, his force would have been even less effective. Even so, Wallace's march of about fifteen miles took some six and one-half hours. However, after the war in his *Memoirs*, Grant exonerated Wallace of all fault at Shiloh, noting that based on

Wallace's information and the uncertainty of verbal orders it was understandable that he took the road he did.

The *Washington Post* called Wallace one of the scapegoats for the faults of his superiors, and to a degree he was. Wallace was the victim of the West Pointer's prejudices against political generals, the dislike of Grant's staff, and Halleck's animosity. But Wallace's own outspokenness and ego caused much of his trouble, and it was only months later that he realized he made many of his own problems.

Wallace was an able general who had proved that he could move men rapidly and maintain the enthusiasm of his troops. He proved this, as well as his tactical ability, at Romney, Forts Henry and Donelson, Cincinnati, and Monocacy. Monocacy in particular demonstrated this tactical ability in the face of a far larger and battle-seasoned foe. There is no question that he was a political general in the sense that he received consideration because of his connections and that he used these connections to further his career. Unfortunately, the label "political general" and the undeserved reputation earned at Shiloh have overshadowed his true ability and talent.

BIBLIOGRAPHY

McDonough, James L. *Shiloh: In Hell Before Night.* Knoxville: University of Tennessee Press, 1977.
Sword, Wiley. *Shiloh: Bloody April.* New York: Morrow, 1974.
Theisen, Lee Scott. "The Public Career of General Lew Wallace, 1845–1905." Ph.D. Dissertation, University of Arizona, 1973.
Vandiver, Frank E. *Jubal's Raid: General Early's Famous Attack on Washington in 1864.* New York: McGraw-Hill, 1960.
Wallace, Lewis. *An Autobiography.* 2 vols. New York: Harper and Brothers, 1906.

LEE SCOTT THEISEN

WASHINGTON, George (b. Westmoreland County, Va., February 22, 1732; d. Fairfax County, Va., December 14, 1799), first president of the United States.

Born into a family with seventeenth-century roots in Virginia, Washington had minimal education and suffered the loss of his father at age eleven. Although the Washingtons were only marginally members of the planter aristocracy, they had influential friends, and their status was enhanced by the marriage of George's half-brother Lawrence into the prestigious Fairfax clan. It was Lawrence, a veteran of the British Cartagena Expedition, who first aroused in Washington serious military ambition; and it was Washington who, through his brother's connections, succeeded Lawrence as an adjutant of militia in 1752.

Washington's intense desire for military recognition was evident in the French and Indian War, which had its immediate origins in his volunteering to carry a warning letter to French forces encroaching on English claims in the Ohio Valley in 1753. Soon after the French rejected Washington's message, he was commissioned a lieutenant colonel and sent back into the disputed area, where on May 27, 1754, he surprised and defeated a French party near Great Meadows,

Pennsylvania. Washington himself was compelled by a superior enemy force to surrender his own nearby post, Fort Necessity, on July 4.

Later, his "inclinations" still "strongly bent to arms," he served as a volunteer aide on the staff of British General Edward Braddock.* Although he failed to get the royal military commission he desperately wanted, he distinguished himself in Braddock's defeat on the Monongahela River. Now a seasoned veteran at age twenty-three, he accepted a militia colonel's commission and served as commander of Virginia's frontier defenses from 1755 to 1758. This was a difficult, often frustrating assignment which he carried out effectively, and it helped prepare him for his larger role in the American Revolution.

For seventeen years prior to 1775 Washington apparently never donned a military uniform, except when he posed for Charles Wilson Peale's portrait in 1772, a sign perhaps that he still fancied himself a military man, or at least an indication that he felt his greatest achievements were in soldiering. If those peacetime years were devoid of military activity, they still helped to prepare him for his role in the Revolution, for he gained valuable administrative experience as the master of Mount Vernon, where he took his new wife, Martha Custis, to live in 1759. He also added to his record of public service by occupying continuously, beginning that same year, a seat in the Virginia House of Burgesses.

Long critical of British commercial policies, a factor in his resolution to switch from growing tobacco to wheat, which did not have to be exported to the mother country, Washington vigorously opposed British efforts to tax the colonies after 1763. He took a more active political role than previously, especially in the nonimportation movement against English manufacturers. Chosen to command several independent militia companies, he was also a Virginia delegate to the First and Second Continental Congresses in 1774 and 1775. There he impressed colleagues with his knowledge of military affairs, and he served on important committees concerned with the defense of the colonies. Moreover, he hailed from an influential colony, crucial to the war effort. For all these reasons he was appointed commander in chief of the Continental armies on June 15, 1775.

Assuming direct command at Cambridge, Massachusetts, on July 3, 1775, Washington spent the next few months organizing the American forces and containing the British in Boston, which General William Howe evacuated on March 17, 1776. That year Washington subsequently moved to New York City and prepared it against Howe's anticipated invasion. Washington had doubts about the feasibility of defending the city, but from the beginning he steadfastly followed the orders of Congress, ever committed to the concept of civil control of the military. In a series of skirmishes and battles between August and November, Washington suffered defeat on Long Island, fell back north of Manhattan Island, and lost his forts on the lower Hudson River. Finally, with Howe in close pursuit, Washington withdrew his dwindling regiments across New Jersey and over the Delaware River into Pennsylvania in December. Howe settled his army into winter quarters in a series of posts through New Jersey and in New York City.

If Washington recognized the need to preserve his army at all costs, he was nonetheless an aggressive warrior by nature, willing to take risks when the stakes were high, when the cause needed a psychological uplift. So it was at the end of December 1776 when he suddenly swept back across the Delaware and in a lightning week of campaigning picked off the British garrisons at Trenton and Princeton—taking many prisoners and valuable supplies—before finding a sanctuary in the hills about Morristown for the winter.

The campaign of 1777, which opened in the summer, found Washington determined to stay close to Howe's army while the American Northern army, commanded by Philip Schuyler* and later Horatio Gates,* sought to block British General John Burgoyne's advance from Canada down the Lake Champlain-Hudson waterway. Howe found Washington to be a dogged, persistent adversary, perhaps so much a thorn in his side that he mainly ignored Burgoyne's army. Washington, aware of Howe's desire to take Philadelphia, prepared to harass Sir William's every step if the Briton moved overland toward the American capital. Instead, Howe traveled by sea, landing below the city only to find Washington sitting across his path. Although Washington experienced defeat at Brandywine Creek on September 11, 1777, and although Howe then occupied Philadelphia, Washington, as was his custom, lashed back, this time against Howe's major base at Germantown on October 3–4, 1777. After heavy losses on both sides, Washington withdrew to spend the now-famous winter of 1777–1778 at nearby Valley Forge.

Those were dark days for Washington, not only because of his failure to save Philadelphia and because of expiring enlistments—the severity of the winter weather itself has been exaggerated—but also owing to the so-called Conway Cabal to replace Washington as commander in chief. Washington's setbacks in Pennsylvania contrasted sharply with Gates' victory over Burgoyne at Saratoga, and Gates' admirers and Washington's critics were often one and the same. But contrary to the opinion of Washington's loyal followers, there appears to have been no well-organized effort to oust the commander in chief.

Spring of 1778 brought less talk of conspiracies and more optimism because of the new French alliance and the improved condition of the Continental Army, thanks in part to its drilling under Baron Frederic William von Steuben.* Proof of Washington's improving fortunes was seen in the British withdrawal across New Jersey and Washington's strong showing against the British at Monmouth, New Jersey, on June 28, 1778, when he took a heavy toll of the enemy before allowing Sir Henry Clinton's royal forces to continue on to New York City.

For the next three years Washington stayed encamped close by the enemy in New York City, but he lacked the forces and equipment to dislodge them. He did detach General John Sullivan* on a successful raiding expedition against the Iroquois tribes of western New York, and he tried to assist as best he could American forces in the South.

The arrival of French military and naval units led Washington to seize the initiative when the opportunity availed itself. Washington consulted with French

General Jean Baptiste de Rochambeau in Rhode Island, and the result was a plan to attack New York City, a plan that was soon changed in favor of cornering Lord Charles Cornwallis in Virginia. The Franco-American leaders had received word that French Admiral François de Grasse was sailing from the West Indies to Chesapeake Bay. With skill and boldness Washington raced to Virginia, where he besieged Cornwallis at Yorktown, while de Grasse's fleet cut off the British route of escape. Cornwallis' surrender on October 19, 1781, brought large-scale fighting in America to an end. Two years later, following the treaty of peace recognizing American independence, Washington resigned his commission after eight and a half years service as commander in chief.

During the postwar years Washington continued to express an interest in military affairs. In 1783 he had authored "Sentiments on the Peace Establishment," an essay urging that congressional jurisdiction be strengthened in the military sector, which included central government control over militia training. Likewise, as presiding officer at the Constitutional Convention of 1787, he supported those clauses of the new national charter that beefed up the federal government's authority to meet the nation's defensive needs. Even so, as the first president of the United States he found antimilitary sentiment still pervasive. His program to organize the militia according to federal standards met with only limited success, as did his desires to build a small but effective army and navy in response to Indian attacks and threats from the belligerents in Europe after the outbreak of war between England and France in the 1790s. Later, during President John Adams' administration Washington emerged from retirement to head a provisional army that was to be raised when the country seemed on the verge of war with France in 1798 following the XYZ Affair. But Adams managed to reduce Franco-American tensions, with the result that Washington never actually returned to the field as a military commander. He continued all the while to reside at Mount Vernon, where he died in 1799.

When one looks at Washington's military career in the American Revolution, the Virginian appears as a competent soldier but hardly exceptional as a tactician or strategist. But he showed the capacity for growth, and as one campaign followed another his mistakes became fewer and fewer. Fortunately for Washington, his military background of militia service was not the extreme limitation that it would have been in later wars. British officers in the eighteenth century were hardly specialists in the modern sense. Military schools were virtually nonexistent, and much military theory was romantic in nature, such as the idea of the "born general."

One of the greatest attributes of generaliship is that nebulous thing called character, and the Virginian had it in abundance. Persistent, dogged, determined, he never knew when he was beaten; he always bounced back when a lesser man might have become dispirited to the point of resignation. Recognizing the importance of holding his army together at all costs—it was the most tangible, meaningful symbol of the Revolution and emerging American nationalism—he nonetheless was hardly a Fabius, a commander who preferred to retire rather than fight. For it was Washington who sought battle at Long Island, Trenton, Princeton, Brandywine, Germantown, Monmouth, and Yorktown.

Deeply committed to the Revolutionary cause, Washington inspired confidence in civilians and soldiers alike. Hotheaded and inordinately ambitious in his youth, he learned the virtue of patience, and he was unfailingly deferential to Congress. He angrily denounced the so-called Newburgh conspirators in 1783, officers who wished to threaten Congress with fire and sword if the Army's grievances over pay and other benefits were not immediately remedied.

In fact, in a broad sense, Washington the statesman stood above Washington the narrow soldier. The Virginia planter, the former militia officer, and the ex-legislator understood the unique requirements of waging an American war, a conflict in which his diplomatic skills counted greatly with the Congress, the state governments, the Continental troops, the local militias, and the civilian population. Favoring the use of legal processes against the Loyalists, he wanted no hangman's harvest. He opposed a predominantly guerrilla war on the grounds that it might irreparably destroy the fabric of society. A respecter of private property, he took stern precautions against plundering, which might turn the American people against their own army. Truly a military statesman, he grasped the Revolution in its totality: the relationship between the homefront and the battlefront, and the relationship between the war years and the forthcoming years of peace.

BIBLIOGRAPHY

Cunliffe, Marcus. *George Washington: Man and Monument*. Boston: Little, Brown, 1958.

Flexner, James T. *George Washington*. 4 vols. Boston: Little, Brown, 1965–1972.

Freeman, Douglas S. *George Washington: A Biography*. 6 vols. New York: Charles Scribner's, 1948–1954.

Knollenberg, Bernard. *Washington and the Revolution*. New York: Macmillan Company, 1940.

———. *George Washington: The Virginia Period*. Durham, N.C.: Duke University Press, 1964.

Morris, Richard B. *Seven Who Shaped Our Destiny*. New York: Harper and Row, 1973.

Nettels, Curtis. *George Washington and American Independence*. Boston: Little, Brown, 1951.

Palmer, Dave. *The Way of the Fox: American Strategy in the War for America*. Westport, Conn.: Greenwood Press, 1975.

R. DON HIGGINBOTHAM

WATIE, Stand (b. Rome [Coosiewattie Stream], Ga., December 12, 1806; d. Deleware County, Indian Territory, September 9, 1871), Cherokee Indian leader. Stand Watie was the only Indian brigadier general in the Civil War.

Stand Watie was born three-fourths Cherokee Indian, receiving his white blood from his mother. Baptized Isaac Oowatie, his Indian name was Da-gata-ga, which in Cherokee meant to stand firm. In his early teens, while at the Moravian mission school in Brainard, Tennessee, the youth anglicized his Indian name and dropped the first two letters of his surname, thus becoming known as Stand Watie. Unlike his brother, Elias Boudinot, who adopted the name of his benefactor and became the very literate editor of the *Cherokee Phoenix* newspaper, Stand Watie cultivated the image of an action-oriented leader.

In the 1830s the unity of the Cherokee Nation was seriously split over the Indian Removal policy of President Andrew Jackson.* Watie became a leader of the "Treaty Party" of mixed-bloods that encouraged the move to Indian Territory. The competing John Ross faction of full-bloods resisted the move to lands west of the Mississippi River until forced to do so and, as a result, perpetuated the disharmony of the tribe for the next thirty years. This animosity came to a head in July 1861 when Ross, chief of the Cherokees, wanted to hold the tribe to an official neutrality in the Civil War, while Watie brought his followers into the conflict on the side of the South as the "Cherokee Mounted Rifles" with himself as colonel.

Watie's regiment of three hundred Indians was little more than an armed band linked to the Confederate States of America by an extralegal arrangement. Militarily, the unit's potential was great in that it could keep the northern border of Texas free from Union encroachment. In October 1861, partly in response to the Confederate victory at Wilson's Creek, Missouri, but more likely due to the political reality that if the South were triumphant Watie would be put in power and he in prison, John Ross signed the Cherokee Nation into an alliance with the Confederacy. The fact that Watie's regiment was separate from the full-blood force commanded by John Drew signaled that there was still no peace within the tribe.

The two Cherokee regiments left Indian Territory in March 1862 to attack the Union forces in Arkansas at Pea Ridge and Poison Springs, and both units acquitted themselves well. Beginning in June and extending through the end of the war with only a few notable exceptions, Watie's forces fought a familiar pattern of guerrilla-style engagements against superior Federal forces attempting to fight their way to the Red River. The Indian troops fought bravely, if in some disorder, until ammunition was exhausted, after which they retired. Generally, they were not pursued by the heavily damaged Union divisions. For Watie's Confederate Cherokees it was parry, thrust, and retreat, a war of attrition.

Nevertheless, by July 1862 Union forces reoccupied Fort Gibson, Indian Territory. Simultaneously, John Ross repudiated the Confederacy and John Drew's desertion-depleted regiment disbanded. It took another year before the Union domination of Indian Territory was confirmed. In July 1863, while Union and Rebel armies were battling at Gettysburg and Vicksburg, the Confederates of Indian Territory were defeated at Honey Springs, south of present Muskogee, Oklahoma. Watie was not present at this battle, nor could he prevent the retaking of Fort Smith on the Arkansas-Indian Territory border by the Federals, but for the remaining two years of the war only his frequent raids kept the Union troops close to their protective forts and away from the Red River.

In June 1864, a month after his commission to the rank of brigadier general, Watie captured a steamboat on the Arkansas River in a brilliant display of cavalrymanship. In September he led his troops in a singular rout of Union troops at Negro Creek near Fort Gibson, and a few days later he helped capture a supply train of three hundred loaded wagons with goods valued at $1.5 million, probably the largest supply capture anywhere during the war. But even those dramatic moves were not enough to forestall the inevitable. By the close of the year Watie, now known to his enemies as "The Indian Swamp Fox," sought only an honorable end to the struggle.

With the capitulation of Ross in 1862, the "Treaty Party" of Southern sympathizers named Watie chief of the tribe. Naturally, the Ross party failed to concur. The Cherokee became a nation of refugees as more than six thousand tribesmen fled from each other depending upon their allegiance to Ross or Watie, the Union or the Confederacy. All the old hatreds were rekindled, and Indian killed Indian sometimes more often than Indians killed either Johnny Reb or Billy Yank. Watie found no solution to this troubling situation during the war, but at least the close of the war was also the end of inter-tribal hostilities. At a Grand Council in May 1865, leaders representing several tribes in Indian Territory made a solemn covenant declaring, "An Indian shall not spill another Indian's blood."

By the time of the Grand Council the Civil War was effectively at an end. In February 1865 Watie had assumed command of all Confederate troops in Indian Territory, but there was little fighting yet to be done. Watie's main problem at this point was to halt thievery among his own troops as they sensed that the end of the war was also the end of opportunities for personal profit. General Robert Edward Lee* surrendered his troops on April 9, 1865, and on May 26 General Edmund Kirby Smith* gave up his command of the Trans-Mississippi Department. General Watie, however, held out until June 23 when he laid down his arms at Doaksville, Indian Territory, the last Confederate general to admit defeat.

In his remaining years Watie regathered his disrupted family and attempted to recover his lands and property. The untimely deaths of all three of his sons by 1867 was a particularly hard jolt to the old man. In an effort to bolster his declining health, Watie took frequent trips to drink the mineral waters at Sulphur Springs, Arkansas, and on one such trip, in 1871, he died unexpectedly at the home of a friend. His passing, coupled with Ross' death in 1866, at last accomplished the unity of the Cherokee Nation which he had sought so fruitlessly in life.

As a heroic public figure in the Cherokee tribe for more than three decades and the only Native American military leader of consequence in the Civil War, the life of Stand Watie has become mythologized by both whites and Indians. Watie is pictured by many as the classic red man warrior. Short, at about five and one-half feet tall, yet robust in appearance, Watie was dignified in manner. Taciturn, even introverted, he seldom made speeches, yet communicated a warmth and humanity to all who knew him. One biographer has written that "no man ever rose to such distinction among his people who had so little to say."

It was in his personal actions that Watie bound his followers to him. Almost fifty-five years old when the Civil War began, he led his poorly equipped regiment in raids, scouting forays, and battles, frequently riding a white horse but never receiving the slightest wound. Indeed, the Watie myth was fueled by the Cherokee superstition that "no weapon was ever made to kill Stand Watie," and it enhanced his leadership ability. It was said that the Confederate Cherokees followed no merc officer: they followed the man.

Detractors of Watie offer another image. Northern journalists during the Civil War, members of the Ross faction, and some Indian historians have regarded Stand Watie as a ruthless racist who supported slavery, the mixed-blood's interests, and his own political position with little interest for the Cherokee Nation as a whole. The most severe critics contended that Watie used his Civil War authority to mask his true intention of destroying the Ross partisans. Military historians, too, questioned Watie's worth, citing his failure to hold Indian Territory and the lack of discipline in his army.

The truth lies somewhere in the middle of these contrasting interpretations. Indian Territory was not held by the Confederates, but neither did the Union forces advance to the Red River. Watie was without mercy to his enemies, but there are those who consider this to be an attribute in wartime. Watie was, in summary, a courageous man of ability who accepted grave responsibility in a time of crisis. He fought valiantly enough to merit the praise of others, but not so gallantly as to turn the tide of the war or even merit national headlines. His unit probably made no difference in the Civil War, but his character has been a lasting heritage for the Cherokee people.

BIBLIOGRAPHY

Abel, Annie H. *The American Indian as a Participant in the Civil War*. Cleveland: Arthur H. Clark Company, 1919.

Cunningham, Frank. *General Stand Watie's Confederate Indians*. San Antonio: Naylor Company, 1959.

Franks, Kenny. "Stand Watie and the Agony of the Cherokee Nation." Ph.D. dissertation, Oklahoma State University, 1973.

Monaghan, Jay. *Civil War on the Western Border, 1854–1865*. Boston: Little, Brown, 1955.

Reed, Gerard A. "The Ross-Watie Conflict: Factionalism in the Cherokee Nation, 1839–1865." Ph.D. dissertation, University of Oklahoma, 1967.

ROBERT C. CARRIKER

WAYNE, Anthony (b. Waynesborough, Pa., January 1, 1745; d. Presque Isle, Pa., December 15, 1796), Revolutionary War general; commander in chief, U.S. Army, 1792–1796.

Anthony Wayne was born into a prominent family of some wealth in Chester County, Pennsylvania. He was the only son of Isaac Wayne, an assemblyman and militia officer who owned the largest tannery in the province. His grandfather was Anthony Wayne, an officer under William III and the Duke of Marlborough who emigrated to America and founded Waynesborough in 1724. Little is known of Wayne's early life; he attended the Academy in Philadelphia but did not graduate, instead becoming a surveyor. He attempted to establish a colony in Nova Scotia for a Philadelphia land syndicate, but the venture failed and Wayne returned to the family homestead to pursue a career in farming and the tanning business in partnership with his father. As a success in commerce and with many friends in Philadelphia society, Wayne gained local and then provincial recognition. By the eve of the War for Independence, he was a leader in the agitation against Britain, serving on various local and provincial committees for defense and nonimportation and sitting a term in the Pennsylvania Assembly. When fighting broke out, he recruited a regiment in Chester County. On January 3, 1776, he became colonel of the 4th Pennsylvania battalion in the new Continental Army authorized by Congress.

Wayne participated in most of the major campaigns of the Revolutionary War, achieving fame as a superior tactician and as perhaps the most aggressive battlefield commander in the Army. In 1776 he commanded troops sent to reinforce the effort to conquer Canada. His first major action was at Three Rivers, where he extricated his men from the swamp in which the American Army was caught, and then through his coolness and iron discipline helped in the withdrawal back into New York. After the winter in command at Fort Ticonderoga, Wayne joined the main army at Morristown, New Jersey, where as senior Pennsylvania brigadier he took command of his state's eight regiments.

During the campaigns of 1777, his division skirmished with British forces near New Brunswick and then moved with George Washington's* forces to defend Philadelphia. In September in the Battle of Brandywine, Wayne helped hold the center of the American line at Chad's Ford long enough for the rest of the army to escape the British envelopment. Ten days later, detached from the main army to attack the British baggage train, the brusque Pennsylvanian was surprised and nearly overwhelmed in a night raid by three British regiments. In this so-called Paoli Massacre, Wayne lost perhaps a quarter of his fifteen hundred men; a court of inquiry was held, and a subsequent court-martial exonerated him of any malfeasance. In October at Germantown he hurled his men at the center of the British line, but hearing firing to his rear and believing that the rest of John Sullivan's* division (to which he was attached) was in trouble, Wayne wheeled about and in the confusion of the morning fog fired on other American units.

In the next two years, however, Wayne finally established the reputation he always sought. At the Battle of Monmouth in June 1778, after General Charles Lee* ordered the American retreat, Wayne directed the makeshift force that held off the British while the rest of the army regrouped. Then, with five regiments at the orchard in front of the American line, he withstood three separate British assaults before a fourth forced his withdrawal. After being replaced in 1779 as head of the Pennsylvania line by Major General Arthur St. Clair,* the senior general from the state, Wayne formed a new corps of light infantry of units from different states. That July, in a night assault by bayonet alone, Wayne's men stormed the British garrison at Stony Point on the Hudson River, capturing over five hundred of the enemy and valuable ordnance and equipment. The victory was Wayne's own completely, a feat of extraordinary leadership and daring for which he gained great public acclaim.

The light infantry was soon disbanded, and for the rest of the war, Wayne fought in various theaters: with the main army around New York in 1780 (including a quick march at night to reinforce the troops at West Point in the wake of Benedict Arnold's* treason); with the Marquis de Lafayette's* forces in Virginia in 1781; and at Yorktown. In 1782, as part of Nathanael Greene's* Southern army, Wayne held an independent command in Georgia, battling the British, Indians, and Tories in an effort to return the state to American control.

What distinguished Wayne from his contemporaries in the winning of independence was his effectiveness as a commander: his ability to discipline a combat force and inspire them in battle, his continued advice in councils of war to take the offensive, and his dependable aggressiveness in pressing home the attack on the battlefield. Wayne was fearless, personally and as a leader. Wounded on several occasions, he always insisted on remaining on the field of battle. Twice he interposed himself physically before mutinying troops. He faced down at gunpoint a company at Ticonderoga in 1777; and when the Pennsylvania line revolted in January 1781, he tried initially to stop the men by himself, and then remained with them on the march to Philadelphia to prevent violence and to act as an intermediary. Wayne was not reckless or irresponsible, however. He always prepared himself and his men carefully for battle. The title ''Mad Anthony'' was apparently pinned on him in 1781 by a private, a Chester County neighbor, whom Wayne refused to free from arrest for desertion.

In many respects Wayne also typified the American generals in the Revolution. Egotistical and ambitious for fame and glory, he was extremely sensitive about his prerogatives and rank, and sulked at any slights to his dignity. (He carried on a running feud over rank with his senior, St. Clair, throughout the war.) Increasingly estranged from his wife after 1775, Wayne was a lonely man, mercurial, a martinet with a fiery temper, who alternated between gloom and enthusiasm and often acted in a testy and unreasonable manner. He could rage at the lack of civilian support for the war effort and at congressional tampering with the Army, voicing the same disgust for politicians that others at the head of the Continental Army often expressed.

Like many other general officers, Wayne was not particularly successful in business or politics after the war. Elected to the Pennsylvania Council of Censors in 1783 and the Pennsylvania Assembly in 1784 and 1785, he had always intended to work the Georgia land granted him by that legislature when the fighting ended. But mounting debts plagued his efforts, and the plantations never flourished. By the end of the 1780s, restless and bored, his property in Pennsylvania and Georgia in danger of confiscation, and he himself under threat of imprisonment for debt, Wayne sought federal office for the immunity it promised if for nothing else. Georgians sent him to the 2d Congress in 1791, and he finally cleared all his debts by abandoning almost all of his Georgia holdings, but within a few months the House unseated him for irregularities in his election.

At that low point, Wayne gained an opportunity for a second military career, and with it gained lasting historical recognition. Less than a month after Wayne's expulsion from Congress, President Washington named him to command the new five thousand man force authorized after two disastrous defeats by the Indians in the Ohio region annihilated the national army. Neither Washington nor the cabinet had great confidence in Wayne. "Open to flattery, vain," and perhaps "addicted to the bottle," noted Washington; "brave and nothing else," recorded Secretary of State Thomas Jefferson, a leader who might "run his head against a wall where success was both impossible and useless." But Wayne was the most experienced general officer from the Revolution available and physically able, and he wanted the position badly.

In two years, by his energy and the force of his personality, he transformed raw recruits into the first reliable national army after independence. He purged incompetent officers; he arranged for efficient logistical support; he instituted daily firing practice; he trained by means of full field maneuvers; he practiced savage, sometimes inconsistent, discipline. When the administration finally allowed him to attack in the fall of 1793, he moved slowly, using his espionage network and carefully fortifying his nightly encampments. The following year, when the Indians dissipated their strength in a futile attempt to overrun Fort Recovery, the most distant fort on the line of posts north from Cincinnati, Wayne moved decisively. His army stormed into the Maumee Valley, defeated the tribes at the Battle of Fallen Timbers (August 20, 1794), and burned Indian crops and towns. In a single campaign Wayne stifled British influence and broke the Indian domination of the Old Northwest. Equally important, he erased the strain of defeat on the Army, established pride and confidence in the officers and men, and gave the Army a cohesion and a tradition on which to build a permanent, peacetime frontier constabulary.

In the next two years, Wayne negotiated the Treaty of Greenville, which finally opened the Northwest Territory to peaceful white settlement. He also lobbied in Congress on behalf of the administration to keep the Army from being reduced in strength, now that the Indian War had ended, and tension with Great Britain had eased with the signing of Jay's Treaty. Less successfully, he fought off the effort of his subordinate, James Wilkinson,* to discredit Wayne's leadership, gain the fidelity of the officers corps, and replace Wayne in the command. On December 15, 1796, at Presque Isle near the end of an inspection trip to Detroit and other Northwest posts, the salty commander, age fifty-one, died of sickness—still battling his enemies and working to strengthen American military power.

BIBLIOGRAPHY

Knopf, Richard C. *Anthony Wayne, A Name in Arms, Soldier, Diplomat, Defender of Expansion Westward of a Nation: The Wayne-Knox-Pickering-McHenry Correspondence*. Pittsburgh, Pa.: University of Pittsburgh Press, 1960.

Kohn, Richard H. "American Generals of the Revolution: Subordination and Restraint." In *Reconsiderations on the Revolutionary War: Selected Essays*. Edited by Don Higginbotham. Westport, Conn.: Greenwood Press, 1978, pp. 104–23, 188–200.

———. *Eagle and Sword: The Federalists and the Creation of the Military Establishment in America, 1783–1802*. New York: Free Press, 1975.

Rankin, Hugh F. "Anthony Wayne: Military Romanticist." In *George Washington's Generals*. Edited by George Athan Billias. New York: William Morrow and Company, 1964, pp. 260–90.

Stille, Charles J. *Major General Anthony Wayne and the Pennsylvania Line in the Continental Army*. Philadelphia, 1893. Reprinted, Port Washington, N.Y.: Kennikat Press, 1968.

Wildes, Harry Emerson. *Anthony Wayne: Trouble Shooter of the American Revolution*. New York, 1941. Reprinted, Westport, Conn.: Greenwood Press, 1969.

RICHARD H. KOHN

WEATHERFORD, William (b. Coosada, Elmore County, Ala., ca. 1780; d. Baldwin County, Ala., March 9, 1824), Creek Indian leader and planter. Weatherford led the Creeks during the War of 1812 in their last major conflict in the Southeast against the United States.

William Weatherford (Red Eagle or Lamochatte) was born in about 1780 in the old town of Coosada on the Alabama River. His mother was Sehoy, a sister of General Alexander McGillivray, the "Emperor" of the Creeks to 1793. Charles Weatherford, a Scotch trader, was his father. Through his uncle, mother, and maternal grandmother, a member of the Wind Clan, Weatherford could claim a leadership role among the Muskhogean-speaking Creek Confederacy, which included at various times the Muscogees, Alabamas, Hitchitees, Euchees, and Seminoles.

Weatherford grew up in a lush country laced with streams around the Coosa, Tallapoosa, and Alabama rivers. As a young man, Weatherford earned a reputation as a warrior and leader. At maturity, he was handsome, physically strong, and known for his dignity, bearing, and truthfulness. Although Weatherford could not read or write, he spoke English fluently and some French and Spanish. His education came from travel, especially trips to Mobile and Pensacola. He gained linguistic and military ability from his uncle Le Clere Mitfort who, after twenty years among the Creeks, returned to France to serve Napoleon as a general officer. Weatherford loved racing and introduced blooded horses into the Indian country. By 1810 Weatherford lived on a comfortable plantation worked by slaves on the first high ground below the confluence of the Tallapoosa and Coosa rivers.

Following the death of Alexander McGillivray, the Creeks came under increased pressure from the United States, Georgia, and Mississippi settlers for land cessions and roads. The issue of building a road across Creek lands to white settlements on the Tombigbee River divided the Confederacy, and Weatherford regarded the chiefs who agreed to the road as having betrayed the interests of the nation. At the same time, both the Spanish in Florida and British agents fanned the fire of Indian resistance to the United States.

In the midst of internal turmoil, Tecumseh,* a mixed-blood Shawnee and Creek from north of the Ohio River, visited the Creeks. Tecumseh hoped to organize an intertribal alliance to halt American expansion and preached nativism to all Indians. After Tecumseh's council in October 1811 with the Creeks, Weatherford hoped his people would unite as one with the northern Indians to preserve their lands, even if he did not embrace nativism. The breach between Creek factions was so great, however, that Big Warrior, a pro-United States Creek leader, opposed the intertribal confederacy. Weatherford, under pressure and after some reflection, joined, aided by the Creek prophets Josiah Francis, Sinquista, and High Head Jim. Weatherford hesitated because a war would likely pit Indian against Indian rather than Indian against white.

Weatherford's fear of civil war was realized after an incident in Chickasaw Country. A party of Creeks killed a number of white men. The Chickasaws feared they might be blamed and demanded the offenders be put to death. They were executed by the pro-United States group, setting off fighting between Creek factions. This civil war then merged with the War of 1812 between the United States and Great Britain. Creeks joined both sides, and Weatherford's faction, the "Red Sticks" (so-called because they painted their war clubs red), took the offensive against the United States.

A clash between whites and Indians on July 27, 1813, at Burnt Corn Creek, eighty miles north of Mobile, opened the Creek War. Settlers in this region took refuge in palisaded defensive forts, and Weatherford led a major attack force against Fort Mims on the lower Alabama River. The fighting began at noon on August 30, 1813, when the Indians caught Major Daniel Beasly unprepared and the gates of the fort open. The reduction of the fort took six hours of hand-to-hand fighting. Fires broke out, and Weatherford tried to restrain his warriors from massacring the survivors, including women and children. Opposed by his own warriors, when he saw that he could not prevent the killing, Weatherford rode away on his black horse. Weatherford had lost control, and over five hundred people died at Fort Mims. He knew such pitiless warfare could bring only retribution and the destruction of the Indians.

Weatherford withdrew to the upper Creek towns where he planned to concentrate his forces at Emuckfau, Tohopeka, and the Holy Ground, a new town on the east bank of the Alabama River. If he could organize for conventional warfare, the chief hoped to hold off the enemy coming from Tennessee commanded by Major General Andrew Jackson* and Georgia under Brigadier General John Floyd. A raiding party led by the Prophet Francis struck at Ransom Kimball's house near the fork of the Alabama and Tombigbee rivers to keep Americans in the Southwest off balance. The Spanish ordered Weatherford away from Mobile in the South, even though the town had fallen into American hands. Hence, he sent two columns of warriors north and east to meet Jackson and Floyd.

In November 1813 John Coffee, Jackson's lieutenant, destroyed the Indian town of Tallushatchee while Jackson attacked Talladega where Tennesseans killed more than five hundred warriors. The following month, Brigadier General Ferdinand C. Claiborne and his Mississippi riflemen advanced from the Southwest on the Holy Ground which Weatherford had fortified. Weatherford led an attack on Claiborne's right wing but was pushed back. Many Indians fled across the river which had been left unguarded. Weatherford tried in vain to rally his warriors, and, pressed to the river's edge, he leapt on his horse into the water from a fifteen-foot high bluff and escaped.

Weatherford moved against the Georgians in January 1814 and turned them at Calibee Creek, forcing Floyd back into Georgia. Jackson attacked the "Red Sticks" at Emuckfau and was repulsed on January 22. Two days later, a second battle took place at Enotachopco, and Jackson fell back on Fort Strother to reorganize for a final push to Tohopeka nestled in the Horseshoe Bend of the Tallapoosa River.

When Jackson's two to three thousand Tennesseans and Creek allies attacked Tohopeka, Weatherford was absent. The tribesmen from the Oakfusky, Newyorka, Hillabees, Fish ponds, and Eufaula towns had gathered one thousand warriors and five hundred women in the fortress town. A five- to eight-foot high breastwork protected the position, and it was almost surrounded by the river. To prevent escape, Coffee and his cavalry joined by Cherokees took position on the opposite side of the river from the "Red Sticks." Jackson first used artillery without effect, and then ordered a diversion from the rear while he stormed the breastworks. The fighting became savage, and the "Red Sticks" refused to surrender. The battle closed with nine hundred Indians killed.

The Battle of Horseshoe Bend broke the Creek's will to carry on the war despite the impending arrival of British troops on the Gulf coast. After a bloody war which may have cost as many as four thousand Creek lives, Jackson ordered the chiefs of the Confederacy to deliver Weatherford to him tied as a prisoner. To save his chiefs this last embarrassment, William Weatherford rode unarmed into Jackson's camp at old Fort Toulouse (Fort Jackson). Weatherford asked for protection while informing the victorious general that he would still be fighting if he had an army. Impressed by Weatherford's speech and demeanor, Jackson sheltered him at the "Hermitage" against the wrath of whites who had suffered at the hands of the "Red Sticks."

Weatherford's role as a leader ended, although he helped to pacify the country by persuading the last of the belligerents to surrender. Jackson imposed the Treaty of Fort Jackson on the Creeks in August 1814 and stripped the Indians of most of their Alabama lands. The United States accepted the treaty, even though it was void under Article IX of the Treaty of Ghent with Great Britain. Creek independence in the Southeast ended. Weatherford did not live to see the removal of his people, but he accepted the inevitable by gathering up his personal property and continuing to live as a planter until his death on March 9, 1824, from fatigue following a bear hunt.

William Weatherford represents the mixed-blood leadership among the southern tribes at the opening of the nineteenth century. Personally interested in the preservation of Indian lands for his own and his tribe's use, Weatherford attempted, first, to prevent the Creeks from weakening the tribe's position and, second, to bar the United States from absorbing Indian lands. Confronted with a civil war, Weatherford hesitated, but finally led the resistance to save Creek lands. He proved unable to control his own people, to change traditional Creek ways of fighting, and to muster large forces for conventional engagements to halt the White advance. Given the relative strength of the United States and the Creeks and the lack of Indian unity, effective resistance was probably impossible.

BIBLIOGRAPHY

Cotterill, R. S. *The Southern Indians: The Story of the Five Civilized Tribes Before Removal*. Norman: University of Oklahoma Press, 1954.
Eggleston, George C. *Red Eagle and the Creek Indians of Alabama*. New York: Dodd, Mead and Company, 1878.
Hodge, Frederick W. *Handbook of American Indians North of Mexico*. 2 Parts. New York: Pageant Books, 1960. Part II.
Pickett, Albert J. *History of Alabama and Incidentally of Georgia and Mississippi, From the Earliest Period*. Birmingham, Ala.: Webb Book Company, Publishers, 1900.
Prucha, Francis P. *The Sword of the Republic: The United States Army of the Frontier 1783–1846*. Toronto: Macmillan Company, 1969.
Owen, Thomas M. *History of Alabama and Dictionary of Alabama Biography*. 4 vols. Chicago: S. J. Clarke Publishing Company, 1921, Vol. 4.
Remini, Robert V. *Andrew Jackson and the Course of American Empire, 1767–1821*. New York: Harper and Row, Publishers, 1977.

PETER M. WRIGHT

WEDEMEYER, Albert Coady (b. Omaha, Nebr., July 9, 1897), World War II Army commander and strategist.

Upon graduation from the U.S. Military Academy in 1919, Albert Wedemeyer toured European battlefields that summer and resumed his military education in the autumn at the Infantry School. In 1920 he was promoted to first lieutenant, graduated from the Infantry School, and began a two-year assignment with the 29th Infantry at Fort Benning. During the period 1922–1935 he served with infantry regiments in the Philippines and in China, while spending nearly seven years as aide de camp to generals in Washington, D.C., and the Philippines. Promoted to captain in 1935, he graduated from the Command and General Staff School the next year. He attended the *Kriegsakademie*, the German War College, in 1936–1938 and then returned to troop assignments at Fort Benning the following two years. Elevated to the rank of major in mid-1940, he was shortly transferred to the Training Section of the Office of the Chief of Infantry.

A rapid rise in rank and influence began for Wedemeyer when he was assigned to work under Brigadier General Dwight David Eisenhower* in the War Plans Division of the War Department General Staff in the spring of 1941. That fall he was promoted to lieutenant colonel, five months later to colonel, and in July 1942 to brigadier general. He gained distinction in September 1941 as the principal author of the Victory Program, a carefully prepared, comprehensive study of manpower and materiel resources likely to be needed to defeat the Axis, which proved amazingly accurate in the ensuing war years. He based his program calculations on, and became a persistent advocate of, a strategy of direct confrontation with the German armies in Western Europe as quickly and decisively as possible after America's entry into the war. He frequently accompanied Chief of Staff George Catlett Marshall* on trips abroad, including the Casablanca and Quebec conferences of 1943. He served as chief of the Strategy Section of the War Plans Division and later became chief of the Strategy and Policy Group of the Operations Division, as well as the War Department's representative on the Joint and Combined Staff Planners. In September 1943 he was advanced to the rank of major general.

When the Southeast Asia Command was established in October 1943, with headquarters at New Delhi, India, Wedemeyer was appointed deputy commander under Admiral Lord Louis Mountbatten. For the next year he wrestled with various problems of that low-priority theatre, endeavoring to accelerate the buildup for offensives in Burma and China, planning (in vain) for future operations in Sumatra and Malaya, and traveling with Mountbatten to a number of Allied strategy sessions, including the Cairo and Teheran conferences. Some of his time was also expended in reconciling clashes between British, Chinese, and American commanders, especially General Joseph Warren Stilwell,* who headed the American Army forces in the China-Burma-India Theatre and was chief of staff to Generalissimo Chiang Kai-shek.

With Stilwell's sudden relief from all his commands in October 1944, Wedemeyer was appointed chief of staff to Chiang and commander of American forces in China (the theater's reorganization excluded Burma and India from his jurisdiction). Inheriting the tangle of problems that had contributed to Stilwell's undoing, he worked zealously to improve the flow of supplies to China, the training of Chiang's troops, and the coordination of Nationalist and Communist operations. In early 1945 he was promoted to lieutenant general. His wartime services in Washington and Asia brought him the Distinguished Service Medal with two Oak Leaf Clusters as well as other American and Allied decorations. He held his position in China until April 1946, his postwar responsibilities primarily involving the demobilization and repatriation of over 1.5 million Japanese troops in China besides a considerable number of Japanese civilians.

In July 1947 Marshall, then secretary of state, sent Wedemeyer on a two-month "fact-finding mission" to appraise the political, military, and economic conditions in China and Korea. The report on his mission, which he submitted that September, warned of an imminent Communist triumph in China unless greater American support of the Nationalists was forthcoming. The State Department suppressed it for two years as allegedly too sensitive for publication.

Besides his Asian mission in 1947, Wedemeyer's positions after World War II included tours of duty as commanding general of the Second Army, 1946–1947; director of the Plans and Operations Division of the War Department General Staff, 1947–1949; and commanding general of the Sixth Army, 1949–1951. He retired in 1951 and was promoted to the permanent rank of general three years later. He served as board director with several firms in the 1950s and 1960s, such as Avco Manufacturing Corporation, Rheem Manufacturing Company, and National Airlines. He was a key member of Senator Robert A. Taft's campaign staff in his bid for the Republican presidential nomination in 1952 and was often consulted thereafter by the conservative Republican wing as a knowledgeable advisor on military affairs and foreign policy. His memoirs, entitled *Wedemeyer Reports!* (1958), mainly covers 1941–1947, the most significant period of his career.

In physical appearance, during the 1940s Wedemeyer was strikingly handsome, lean, and over six feet tall. An admiring correspondent in 1945 characterized him as "quiet, yet friendly; frank, yet modest and unself-seeking; honest, but shrewd; clever, aggressive, and full of typical American energy." On the other hand, a hostile Foreign Service officer who served with the American Embassy in wartime Chungking described him as possessing "lofty intellectual pretensions and few fixed convictions" while also "pretending to be humble and uninformed." The truth about his personal traits, which, indeed, were sometimes contradictory, probably lies somewhere between these differing views, but he surely possessed more tact, finesse, and patience in dealing with Mountbatten, Chiang, and their staffs than did his predecessor in China, Stilwell.

It would be difficult to exaggerate Wedemeyer's impact as a strategic planner during 1941–1943. The citation for the Distinguished Service Medal which he received in 1943 indicates the War Department's evaluation of his role: "By his outstanding ability, resourcefulness, tact, initiative, and profound strategical judgment, he contributed in large measure to the adoption by the United States and by the United Nations of sound strategical plans which have formed the basis for the successful prosecution of the war on all fronts."

His command in China, 1944–1946, coincided with the termination of the war against Japan and the escalation of the Chinese civil conflict. Regarding his part in wartime China, Wedemeyer said that his "main aim was simply to see to it that, in spite of her exhaustion and the terrible sacrifices and privations of her people, she [China] should play an active role in this war." Most authorities agree that, although he came to China during the ebb of that nation's will to fight, he did a creditable job of trying to improve Chinese morale and military effectiveness for the duration of the war with Japan.

Unlike Stilwell and Marshall, and despite the wake of public controversy in America that followed the belated release of his 1947 mission report, Wedemeyer did not participate significantly in the American efforts to mediate between the Chinese Communists and Nationalists in the aftermath of the war against Japan. He was strongly pro-Nationalist, however, and as Chinese forces of opposing sides raced each other to disarm Japanese units and seize strategic points in North China in the fall of 1945, he employed American forces and transportation to assist Chiang's forces. But, particularly in view of the utter chaos prevailing in China at that time, it is to his credit that he did not use American troops and resources to suppress civil strife, and he carefully avoided clashes with Communist forces. If later he would regret that the United States had not done more to assist the Nationalists, Wedemeyer exerted responsible leadership after World War II and did not allow his units to become inextricably entangled in the tragedy of the growing civil war. That feat, albeit passive in essence, required a leadership of unprecedented political, social, military, and psychological circumstances that few military commanders in history have had to demonstrate.

BIBLIOGRAPHY

Cline, Ray S. *Washington Command Post: The Operations Division: U.S. Army in World War II: The War Department*. Washington, D.C.: Office of the Chief of Military History, U.S. Department of the Army, 1951.
Leighton, Richard M. and Robert W. Coakley. *Global Logistics and Strategy, 1940–1943. U.S. Army in World War II: The War Department*. Washington, D.C.: Office of the Chief of Military History, U.S. Department of the Army, 1955.
Matloff, Maurice. *Strategic Planning for Coalition Warfare, 1943–1944. U.S. Army in World War II: The War Department*. Washington, D.C.: Office of the Chief of Military History: U.S. Department of the Army, 1959.
———, and Edwin M. Snell. *Strategic Planning for Coalition Warfare, 1941–1942. U.S. Army in World War II: The War Department*. Washington, D.C.: Office of the Chief of Military History, Department of the Army, 1953.
Romanus, Charles F. and Riley Sunderland. *Time Runs Out in CBI. U.S. Army in World War II: The China-Burma-India Theater*. Washington, D.C.: Office of the Chief of Military History, U.S. Department of the Army, 1959.
U.S. Department of State. *United States Relations with China, with Special Reference to the Period 1944–1949*. Washington, D.C.: U.S. Government Printing Office, 1949.
Wedemeyer, Albert C. *Wedemeyer Reports!* New York: Henry Holt, 1958.

D. CLAYTON JAMES

WELLES, Gideon (b. Glastonbury, Conn., July 1, 1802; d. Hartford, Conn., February 11, 1878), Secretary of the Navy. Welles revitalized the Navy Department as Lincoln's Secretary of the Navy during the Civil War.

Gideon Welles was born of hard-working, civic-minded, and fairly prosperous Yankee stock. Welles' ancestors had been integrally involved in the political growth and development of Connecticut, and their example of public service strongly influenced his ideas and ambitions as he grew to manhood. Welles received a good education at the Episcopal Academy at Cheshire, Connecticut, and later attended the fine academy at Norwich, Vermont, which later became Norwich University. There he obtained a solid grounding in the humanities and in law, but did not graduate. Instead, the young man was caught up in state politics and began a career in journalism.

In the 1820s Welles wrote for the New York *Mirror* and later, back in Connecticut, for the Hartford *Times*. The *Times* had been founded in 1817 by John Niles. Welles based his beliefs on the premise that states' rights, not federal power, represented the main bulwarks of a democracy. He and his mentor, Niles, however, regarded sectionalism—or a combination of states against the nation—as pure treason.

Welles was a leader in organizing the Democratic party in Connecticut and vigorously supported Andrew Jackson* in his bid for the presidency in the election of 1828. After Jackson's victory, Welles acted as his confidential advisor on matters relating to the employment of political patronage within Connecticut.

In 1835 Welles married Mary Jane Hale, an eighteen-year-old cousin. During that same year, he served as comptroller of Connecticut, and he again held that office in the 1840s. In 1836 he was appointed postmaster of Hartford and turned over the editorial direction of the *Times* to a competent staff member. The following year, he was elected to a seat in the Connecticut legislature.

The year 1846 was a turning point for Welles as he then first emerged upon the national political scene. President James K. Polk appointed him chief of the Naval Bureau of Provisions and Clothing, which he headed for the next three years. This position gave Welles invaluable experience and laid the groundwork for his later work as Secretary of the Navy for Abraham Lincoln.* In 1849 the new president, Zachary Taylor,* a Whig, removed Welles from office, and he returned to Connecticut.

Four years later, Welles was dismayed when Franklin Pierce, a fellow Democrat whose stand on slavery had been ambiguous and uncertain, was elected president. Welles had strongly opposed the extension of slavery into the Western territories. When the Republican party with its antislavery platform was formed in 1855, Welles became its candidate for governor of Connecticut. Although he was unsuccessful in this venture, in 1860 Welles headed the Connecticut delegation to the national convention that nominated Lincoln for the presidency.

Probably Welles headed Lincoln's list of desirable choices for his cabinet; soon after the election, the Republican victor appointed Welles Secretary of the Navy. When Welles took over the Navy Department in March 1861, it was in a state of complete disarray and disintegration. Many naval officers from the seceded states had resigned, and morale was at a low ebb throughout the naval service. At the beginning of the Civil War, the small U.S. Navy was dispersed in distant waters around the world. There were only twelve ships at home, and eight of these were in Southern ports. Only a man of great administrative genius could have pulled together the weak and fragmented parts of the scattered United

WELLES, GIDEON

States Navy and welded them into a strong and unified instrument capable of winning and profitably employing control of the sea.

The first problem to which Welles addressed himself was that of acquiring, arming, outfitting, and manning many merchant vessels and readying them for action. He then stationed these improvised men-of-war along the Confederate coast to blockade Southern ports. All the shipyards in the North were put to work building true warships—many of them ironclads—for sea or river service. During the first year of the Civil War, the *Monitor*—a newly constructed, revolutionary, turreted, armored warship designed and built by John Ericsson* under Welles' auspices—engaged and checked the dreaded CSS *Virginia* (ex-USS *Merrimac*). In doing so, the *Monitor* revolutionized naval warfare.

The Union Navy faced the monumental task of trying to blockade more than three thousand miles of Southern coastline, thereby isolating the Confederacy from the rest of the world. The old Navy was comprised of only seventy-six ships which carried 1,783 guns. At the outset of the war, the Navy was divided into two squadrons—one for the Atlantic coast and one for the Gulf of Mexico. This organization proved to be unwieldy, and the Atlantic jurisdiction was given to two squadrons—north and south—in 1861; the Gulf forces were similarly split—east and west—in 1862. Subsequently, a Potomac Flotilla was organized, and another flotilla was established on the Mississippi River to help bisect the Confederacy and open the western waters for Union navigation.

During the Civil War, Welles successfully increased the size of the Navy in number of ships, guns, and seamen. Furthermore, Welles utilized former slaves for service in behalf of the Union as he saw the importance of increasing and consolidating the North's power and strength in every possible way. Welles' contribution to the war effort was far-reaching and significant. Under his admininistration, the keels of 208 ships were laid down, and most of them were completed. Welles supervised the purchase of more than four hundred additional ships. The number of men in the Navy increased from 7,600 to 51,500, and the number of workers in the shipyard grew from approximately 3,800 to 16,880. These figures demonstrate graphically the rapid growth of the Navy under Welles' guiding hands.

Welles served Lincoln as secretary of the Navy until his administration came to a violent end with the president's assassination. He stayed on in the cabinet under Andrew Johnson and brought the Navy back to a peacetime level after the Civil War ended. Welles, who looked upon thrift in government and a balanced budget as sacred trusts, reduced the Navy to a planned quota of one hundred ships, which was one-sixth of its wartime strength. He worked with great dedication to serve President Johnson and stood loyally by him through four difficult years of Reconstruction. On March 4, 1869, Gideon Welles retired when Ulysses Simpson Grant* assumed office as the new president. Welles' diary was published posthumously.

Gideon Welles' contribution to the nation during the Civil War sprang from his remarkable ability to pull together the many weak and diffuse elements in the American Navy and blend them into a viable and powerful force. During his time in office, there was no naval general staff or chief of naval operations. Therefore, besides overseeing the administration of the Navy, he was responsible for determining naval strategy and directing operations suitable to achieve the goals established by that strategy.

Welles commanded respect from politicians and sailors, and he inspired confidence in those around him. He was able to initiate change and progress in the Navy despite the crisis the Civil War presented to the institution. He had an innovative and creative mind and was daring enough to try new things in hope of improving the Union's chances of winning. Only a man of creative imagination and great courage could have lifted the pre-Civil War Navy out of the doldrums and set in firmly on the course to victory. Welles occasionally was short on tact, but his honesty and directness were largely responsible for his getting things done effectively.

Welles stands high on the list of U.S. secretaries of the Navy, if not at its very top. He never faltered in his duty; never wavered in his resolution; and always put the welfare of his country ahead of any personal ambition.

BIBLIOGRAPHY

Beale, Howard K., ed. *The Diary of Gideon Welles*. 3 vols. New York: W. W. Norton and Company, 1960.
Niven, John. *Gideon Welles: Lincoln's Secretary of the Navy*. New York: Oxford University Press, 1973.
West, Richard S., Jr. *Gideon Welles, Lincoln's Navy Department*. Indianapolis, Ind.: Bobbs-Merrill Company, 1943.
———. *Mr. Lincoln's Navy*. New York: Longmans, Green and Company, 1957.

JAMES L. MOONEY

WESTMORELAND, William Childs (b. Spartanburg County, S.C., March 26, 1914), Army officer; commander, U.S. Forces in Vietnam, 1964–1968; chairman, Joint Chiefs of Staff, 1968–1972.

The son of a textile plant manager, William C. Westmoreland attended public schools in Spartanburg, South Carolina, and after a year at The Citadel secured an appointment to West Point. While at the Academy, he displayed signs of the ambition and drive that would characterize his career. He was active in athletics, won the coveted Pershing Award for military proficiency and leadership, and during his final year was first captain of cadets. Unable to pass the rigorous eyesight tests required for flight training, he entered the artillery and held prewar assignments at Fort Sill, Oklahoma, in Hawaii, and at Fort Bragg, North Carolina.

Westmoreland served with distinction in the North African and European campaigns of World War II, establishing a reputation for combat leadership that would mark him for future top positions in the Army. A lieutenant colonel at the age of twenty-eight, he commanded the 34th Field Artillery, 9th Infantry Division, in North Africa, getting his artillery into position in time to prevent a German breakthrough at the Kasserine Pass. Following combat in Sicily, he served as executive officer of the 9th Infantry and participated in the landing on Utah Beach. Promoted to colonel, he became chief of staff of the 9th Infantry in July 1944. His combat record from France to the Elbe won plaudits from such future luminaries as James Maurice Gavin* and Maxwell Davenport Taylor.*

Remaining with the occupation forces in Germany after V-E Day, Westmoreland returned to the United States in 1946, took paratroop training, and was given command of the 504th Paratroop Infantry Regiment. He subsequently became chief of staff of the 82d Airborne Division at Fort Bragg. During the interval between World War II and Korea, he also taught at the Command and General Staff College at Fort Leavenworth and at the Army War College in Carlisle, Pennsylvania. He commanded the 187th Airborne Regimental Combat Team in Korea, the only paratroop unit to see action in the war.

Intense, ambitious, and hardworking, Westmoreland advanced rapidly in the years after Korea. He returned to the United States in 1953 to become deputy assistant chief of staff for manpower control. After attending the advanced management program in the Harvard Graduate School of Business Administration, he was appointed secretary to the General Staff, serving under Army Chief of Staff Maxwell Taylor. The youngest major general in the Army, he assumed command of the 101st Airborne Division, the famous "Screaming Eagles," in 1958, where he achieved public notice by jumping with his men in training exercises, sometimes jumping ahead of them to test wind conditions. Superintendent of West Point from 1960 to 1963, he fought vigorously for and eventually won presidential commitment to double the size of the corps. He returned to Fort Bragg in 1963 to command the XVIII Airborne Corps.

Westmoreland was an obvious choice to succeed General Paul Donal Harkins* in Vietnam in 1964. Considered one of the top three generals in the Army, he had a deserved reputation for efficiency and excellence in command. Strikingly handsome, hard working, and supremely confident, he seemed the ideal person for a most difficult position. He was close to Taylor, then chairman of the Joint Chiefs of Staff and soon to become ambassador to South Vietnam. Appointed deputy to Harkins in January 1964, he succeeded to the command in June.

Almost from his arrival in Saigon, Westmoreland urged an increased American military commitment. Supported by North Vietnamese regulars, the Vietcong had exploited the political chaos that followed the overthrow of Ngo Dinh Diem by drastically stepping up military operations. Westmoreland was certain by early 1965 that the embattled South Vietnamese Army could not stand up to the Vietcong by itself. Warning Washington that there was no solution but to "put our own finger in the dike," he pressed vigorously for the bombing of North Vietnam and subsequently for the deployment of American combat forces. In

July 1965 President Lyndon B. Johnson gave him one hundred thousand ground troops and a free hand in their use.

Given three hundred thousand additional men between 1965 and 1967, Westmoreland waged a devastating war of attrition against the enemy. Relying on superior air power, firepower, and mobility, he dispatched American units across South Vietnam on large-scale operations to search out and destroy Vietcong and North Vietnamese regulars. The infusion of American military power and West moreland's aggressive strategy staved off what had appeared near certain defeat in 1965 and resulted in huge enemy losses.

In 1967 Westmoreland engaged Washington in a strategic debate that would last for over a year and would eventually lead to his recall. Persuaded that he was making steady progress, he requested an additional two hundred thousand troops and authority to pursue the enemy into his sanctuaries in Laos and Cambodia and across the demilitarized zone in order to speed up the timetable of victory. Johnson rejected his requests. Many of the president's civilian advisors had concluded that the search and destroy strategy could produce no better than a bloody stalemate. Johnson himself feared that expansion of the war might provoke Chinese or Soviet intervention. By 1967 the war had aroused widespread protest at home, and the president was unwilling to risk the political consequences of a major escalation.

The debate over strategy erupted anew after the Tet Offensive of 1968. Although caught off guard by the all-out Vietcong assault on South Vietnam's cities, U.S. forces quickly recovered, recouping early losses and inflicting devastating casualties on the attackers. Interpreting Tet as a major U.S. victory, Westmoreland urged that the advantage be exploited, and he reopened his request for additional troops and expansion of the war. The early enemy successes had produced profound shock in the United States, however, and after weeks of deliberation, Johnson decided upon a basic change of policy. He not only turned down Westmoreland's proposals but also withdrew from the presidential race and sought a negotiated settlement of the war. Westmoreland was called home to become chairman of the Joint Chiefs of Staff, a position he retained until 1972.

Upon retirement, Westmoreland returned to his native South Carolina and ran unsuccessfully for the Republican gubernatorial nomination of 1974. In his memoirs, *A Soldier Reports*, and in numerous speeches, he actively involved himself in the postwar debate on Vietnam.

Westmoreland has been sharply criticized for his conduct of the war; he has even been held responsible for the disaster that befell the United States in Vietnam. The search and destroy strategy, it has been argued, represented a futile attempt to apply traditional U.S. Army concepts of warfare in a situation where they could not work. The strategy was enormously destructive, moreover, doing permanent ecological damage to the landscape of South Vietnam and producing huge numbers of civilian casualties and refugees. By disrupting the already

tattered social fabric of South Vietnam and turning the people against a government already lacking in support, U.S. military operations, in the eyes of many
critics, were counterproductive. Westmoreland has also been criticized for his
reports of progress, which, if not deliberately deceptive, reflected a poor understanding of the war he was fighting; for his failure to anticipate the devastating
attacks of Tet; and for his alleged attempt to cover the failure by expanding the
war.

The general has responded vigorously to his critics. Given the political decay
in South Vietnam and the number and strength of enemy forces, he argued,
had no choice but to seek out and destroy the adversary. There could be no
political stability until the military threat had been removed. While carefully
avoiding a direct attack on President Johnson, Westmoreland has placed responsibility for the American failure on the civilians in Washington, particularly
Secretary of Defense Robert Strange McNamara* and his civilian advisors. The
civilians' insistence on a graduated bombing campaign against North Vietnam
nullified the effectiveness of American air power. The search and destroy strategy
would have brought victory if he had been given the troops and the authority to
pursue the enemy into the sanctuaries. Westmoreland conceded that his command
misread the intelligence before Tet, but, he argued, the United States rebounded
to inflict a decisive defeat on the Vietcong. Had the media and the civilians in
Washington not been consumed by defeatism, the war could have been won.
The principal lesson of Vietnam, Westmoreland has concluded, is that gradualism
and partial measures do not work. Once engaged in war, the United States must
employ its military power decisively.

It remains difficult to arrive at a balanced assessment of Westmoreland's
generalship. He handled superbly the massive logistical buildup of 1965–1966.
Despite the wretched conditions under which the war was fought and the ambiguity of American objectives, U.S. troops fought well under his command and
morale remained high. American military power saved South Vietnam from
certain collapse in 1965 and at least held the line in the face of the furious enemy
offensive of 1968. As a strategist, on the other hand, Westmoreland is vulnerable
to criticism. He may be correct in arguing that the situation he faced in 1965
left him few choices. It is difficult to see, for example, how the so-called enclave
strategy advocated by James Gavin could have produced better results. Ultimate
responsibility for the strategic failure in Vietnam rests with the leadership in
Washington, which never gave Westmoreland strategic guidance or devised a
viable grand strategy. Nevertheless, it is still clear that the strategy of attrition
could not have worked in Vietnam. North Vietnam had an inexhaustible reservoir
of manpower and the determination to prevail at any cost. The sanctuaries
permitted them to control their losses and to retain the strategic initiative. Whether
the United States could have achieved its goals in Vietnam under any circumstances will long be debated. If this was to be done, it would have required an
ingenious politico-military strategy adapted to the peculiar nature of the war and
the restrictions imposed by Washington. Westmoreland was not the man to

perform such feats. Methodical rather than imaginative, an organizer rather than
a creative genius, he applied with relentless precision the accumulated experience
of thirty years in an army geared for conventional warfare. Formal and courtly,
as "cleancut as Tom Mix," he struck observers as out of place in Vietnam, and
in many ways he was. His failure as a strategist reflects in the broadest sense
the inapplicability of traditional American methods of warfare in the alien and
inhospitable environment of Vietnam.

BIBLIOGRAPHY

Furguson, E. B. *Westmoreland: The Inevitable General.* Boston: Little, Brown and
    Company, 1968.
Halberstam, David. *The Best and the Brightest.* New York: Random House, 1972.
Lewy, Guenter. *America in Vietnam.* New York: Oxford University Press, 1978.
Palmer, Dave Richard. *Summons of the Trumpet: U.S.-Vietnam in Perspective.* San
    Rafael, Calif.: Presidio Press, 1978.
The Senator Gravel Edition: The Pentagon Papers. Boston: Beacon Press, 1971. Vols.
    3, 4.
Westmoreland, William C. *A Soldier Reports.* New York: Doubleday and Company,
    1976.

GEORGE C. HERRING

WHEELER, Joseph (b. Augusta, Ga., September 10, 1836; d. Brooklyn,
N.Y., January 25, 1906), Army officer. Wheeler was the principal Southern
cavalry commander in the western theater during the Civil War.

Joseph Wheeler was born to New England parents who had migrated to Geor-
gia. His maternal grandfather was General William Hull,* a veteran of the
American Revolution and War of 1812. After Wheeler's mother died in 1842,
he went to Connecticut to live with her sisters and attend Cheshire Academy.
In 1854, at age seventeen, he secured an appointment to the U.S. Military
Academy at West Point, which at that time required five years for graduation.
Wheeler finished fourth from the bottom in a class of twenty-two. Although he
received his poorest grades in cavalry tactics, in 1859 he was brevetted a second
lieutenant and sent to cavalry school at Carlisle Barracks, Pennsylvania, for
special training.

In 1860 the War Department raised Wheeler to full rank and assigned him to
duty with the Regiment of Mounted Riflemen at Fort Craig, New Mexico Territory. While en route to the Southwest with a wagon train, Wheeler earned the
nickname "Fightin' Joe" in a skirmish with hostile Indians. Except for isolated
incidents, however, Indians caused the Army relatively little concern in New
Mexico during Wheeler's brief stint there, and he and the numerous other Southerners stationed at Fort Craig had ample time to ponder the threat of war and
secession which loomed over the nation.

When Georgia left the Union in January 1861, Wheeler resigned his commission in the U.S. Army and accepted an appointment as lieutenant in the forces
of his native state. Assigned to Fort Barrancas, Florida, he expertly supervised

the remounting of spiked Union guns and won the admiration of influential Alabama officers who persuaded the Confederate War Department to promote him. Thus at age twenty-four, Wheeler, who stood only five feet-five inches tall and weighed about 120 pounds, became a full colonel and commander of the 19th Alabama Infantry, part of the Gulf Coast defense force under General Braxton Bragg.*

In February 1862 Wheeler's regiment was among the Confederate units that concentrated near Corinth, Mississippi, to stop the advance of Federal forces up the Tennessee River toward the Mobile and Ohio railroads. In April Wheeler saw his first action, at Shiloh, and won considerable praise for successfully covering the Confederate withdrawal, a task he performed time and again during the next three years. Wheeler succeeded quickly to command of an infantry brigade, and in July 1862 Bragg put him in charge of the cavalry of the Army of the Mississippi.

In August and September 1862, Wheeler accompanied Bragg and General Edmund Kirby Smith* on the ill-fated campaigns through middle Tennessee into Kentucky. Federal troops under Don Carlos Buell* repulsed the Confederates at Perryville, and both Bragg and Smith placed all their cavalry under Wheeler and instructed him to protect their retreat. Wheeler and his men felled trees to obstruct roads and fought on horseback and on foot for a week, while the two Confederate armies escaped without losing a single wagon or gun to the Federals. For these efforts Wheeler was commissioned a brigadier general and made chief of cavalry in the newly formed Army of the Tennessee.

Eventually, Wheeler rose to lieutenant general, but except for occasionally harassing communications behind Union lines, he spent the rest of the war fighting rearguard actions. After brilliantly circling the Federal Army of the Cumberland led by General William Starke Rosencrans* south of La Vergne, Tennessee, and destroying hundreds of Federal supply wagons, Wheeler covered Bragg's withdrawal from Murfreesboro, Tennessee, in January 1863. In September of that same year Wheeler carried out mop-up operations after Bragg won a tactical victory at Chickamauga, Georgia, below Chattanooga. Between early May and late July 1864, the gritty little Georgian covered the retreat of General Joseph Eggleston Johnston* from Chattanooga to Atlanta, and between November 1864 and April 1865 Wheeler provided almost the only significant resistance to General William Tecumseh Sherman* on his famous march through Georgia and the Carolinas. Federal troops finally captured Wheeler in May 1865, while he was trying to prevent the capture of Confederate President Jefferson Davis* in Georgia.

Wheeler spent two months in a Federal prison before being paroled. Afterward, he lingered a short time in his native Augusta and then entered the hardware business in New Orleans. In 1866 Wheeler married a wealthy young widow he had met during the war. Four years later they moved near her home in Lawrence County, Alabama, where he became a successful planter. During his spare time Wheeler studied law and passed the bar, and in 1880 leading northern Alabama

Democrats persuaded him to run for Congress. After an abortive first attempt, in 1883 Wheeler won a seat in the 47th Congress, where he pursued a middle course between Bourbonism and Populism. The voters of his district returned him to Congress seven times.

Through membership on the House Military Affairs Committee, Wheeler maintained his interest in the Army. When hostilities with Spain seemed imminent in 1898, he offered his services to the War Department. Following the American declaration of war on April 25, 1898, President William McKinley commissioned Wheeler a major general of volunteers, and the War Department gave him command of the cavalry forces in the invasion of Cuba. On June 24, 1898, he launched an unauthorized but successful attack against the Spanish at Guásimas and removed the first obstacle to the American advance on Santiago. Illness kept Wheeler from taking part in the Battle of San Juan Hill, but afterward he was active until the end of the Cuban Campaign.

Following an unsuccessful effort to resume his seat in Congress, Wheeler wrangled an assignment as brigadier general of volunteers in the Philippines in June 1899. He saw only limited action in the insurrection there and returned to the United States in January 1900. A short time later McKinley commissioned him a brigadier general in the Regular Army and made him commander of the Department of the Lakes. Wheeler retired in September 1900 and spent much of the rest of his life traveling. He died in Brooklyn, New York, while visiting his sister.

Wheeler is remembered primarily as the principal Confederate cavalry officer in the western theater during the Civil War. As chief of cavalry first in the Army of the Mississippi and later in the Army of the Tennessee, Wheeler carried out every major rearguard operation from Shiloh to Perryville to Atlanta. He lacked the flare of his somewhat more famous contemporaries, John Hunt Morgan and Nathan Bedford Forrest,* but he equaled them in aggressiveness and exceeded them in reliability and devotion to discipline and training. Much of Wheeler's personal success, as well as that of his commands, resulted from his patience, persistence, and ability to carry out orders. He was most effective when performing routine duties, such as covering Bragg's or Johnson's front or flanks and disrupting communications behind Union lines; he was least effective when attempting large-scale independent missions, such as trying to take Kingston, Tennessee, during the campaign against Knoxville in December 1863 and sweeping through middle Tennessee in September 1864.

In keeping with his reputation for discipline and training, during the spring of 1863 Wheeler wrote a Confederate cavalry manual. It was one of the first that unhesitatingly favored mounted infantry over heavy cavalry. Entitled *A Revised System of Cavalry Tactics for the Use of the Cavalry and Mounted Infantry, C.S.A.*, the manual reflected Wheeler's experience with the Regiment of Mounted Riflemen in New Mexico and his success in covering Bragg's and

Smith's withdrawal from Kentucky in 1862. Wheeler contended that mounted infantry performed especially well in broken and wooded terrain.

After the war Wheeler came to symbolize the restoration of traditional white rule in the Southern states and political reconciliation between the South and the North. Elected to Congress by Bourbon Democrats, he maintained a paternal attitude toward blacks, opposed civil rights legislation, and called upon Southerners to forget the Civil War and devote their energies to industrialization. In 1898 President William McKinley decided to commission several ex-Confederates, including Fitzhugh Lee* and Wheeler, to help heal sectional differences, make the Spanish-American War a national effort, and provide additional support for his administration.

BIBLIOGRAPHY

Cosmas, Graham A. *An Army for Empire: The United States Army in the Spanish-American War*. Columbia: University of Missouri Press, 1971.
Dubose, John W. *General Joseph Wheeler and the Army of Tennessee*. New York: Neale Publishing Company, 1912.
Dyer, John P. *"Fightin' Joe" Wheeler*. Baton Rouge: Louisiana State University Press, 1941.
Horn, Stanley F. *The Army of Tennessee: A Military History*. Indianapolis, Ind.: Bobbs-Merrill Company, 1941.
Lee, Fitzhugh, and Joseph Wheeler. *Cuba's Struggle Against Spain*. New York: American Historical Press, 1899.

GEORGE R. ADAMS

WILKES, Charles (b. New York City, N.Y., April 3, 1798; d. Washington, D.C., February 8, 1877), naval officer, explorer, scientist. Wilkes led a nineteenth-century expedition to the South Seas and Antarctica.

Charles Wilkes' great-grandfather was a prosperous London brewer, and his great uncle was the celebrated and flamboyant eighteenth-century British politician, John Wilkes. Charles' father was the first family member to emigrate to America. Young Charles attended various schools and passed from tutor to tutor. He had no taste for business, and "hankering after naval life and roving life," he entered the merchant service at the age of seventeen.

Wilkes sailed in merchant ships until 1818, when, with the sponsorship of Mr. Hyde de Neuville, the French ambassador in Washington and a friend of his father, he was appointed a midshipman in the U.S. Navy. The new midshipman's first principal assignment was in the 44-gun frigate *Guerriere*, captained by Thomas Macdonough.* Cruising for three years in Mediterranean and European waters on board the *Guerriere*, Wilkes learned the trade of a naval officer and became interested in coastal surveying.

Following a cruise off South America, Wilkes returned to Washington and was promoted to lieutenant several days after his marriage to Jane Renwick in 1826. He applied for coast survey duty in keeping with his scientific interests.

Wilkes had earlier studied under Ferdinand Hassler, founder of the U.S. Coast Survey.

In 1830, Wilkes was assigned as chief of the Depot of Charts and Instruments—a dream assignment for an officer of scientific talents. At his own expense he built an astronomical observatory which marked the beginning of the world-renowned U.S. Naval Observatory. In 1837 congressmen were holding discussions in Washington regarding a major exploring venture to the South Seas. For one reason or another, several senior officers refused command of such an expedition. Finally, it was offered to Charles Wilkes, a relatively junior lieutenant. He accepted, and this generated no little rancor in naval ranks.

A group of selected officers and an elite corps of civilian scientists assembled with their instruments and boarded the ships of the South Seas Surveying and Exploring Expedition—the sloop *Vincennes* (the flagship), the sloop *Peacock*, the brigantine *Porpoise*, the schooner *Sea Gull*, the schooner *Flying Fish*, and the storeship *Relief*. The expedition departed Norfolk, Virginia, on August 18, 1838, for an adventure that lasted almost four years. Before sailing, Wilkes had pressed without success for a presidential promotion to captain, believing he was entitled to this rank by virtue of his important command. Disappointed but undaunted, Wilkes unofficially promoted himself, put on a captain's uniform, and broke out a squadron commodore's broad pendant.

Wilkes' ships weathered Cape Horn to begin exploring, surveying, and performing all manner of scientific studies in the Pacific and Antarctic regions. In the coming years, the scientists and sailors collected a treasure trove of plant, animal, and sea specimens. The *Sea Gull* was lost at sea with all hands while on detached duty before the squadron reached Australia. As the *Vicennes* inched along the Antarctic ice barrier in early 1840, Wilkes took sightings that identified Antarctica as a continental land mass for the first time, a point raising some scientific controversy when the expedition returned.

Subsequently, the expedition surveyed the Fiji Islands and the Hawaiian Islands. Two young officers, including Wilkes' nephew, were murdered by natives on Malolo Island in the Fijis. Wilkes retaliated immediately with a landing force, putting the entire island to the torch. The squadron arrived in the Hawaiian Islands in September 1840. There Wilkes undertook extensive scientific observations, including those made from the summit of Mauna Loa and the rim of Kilauea's vast volcanic crater.

Departing Hawaii in the spring of 1841, the expedition surveyed Puget Sound and the northwest coast of America. The sloop *Peacock* grounded in the mouth of the Columbia River and was abandoned. The remaining ships headed into the western Pacific for the last long homeward-bound leg via the Philippines, Singapore, and Cape Town before arriving in New York Harbor on June 10, 1842.

Charles Wilkes, a quarrelsome martinet, had had serious disagreements with many of the expedition's officers and civilians. Within a month after reaching New York, he was ordered to stand trial before a court-martial. The court found him guilty of improperly punishing some sailors in the expedition and sentenced him to a public reprimand by the Secretary of the Navy.

The years between the return of the expedition and the Civil War found Wilkes devoting much of his time to editing the expedition's narrative volumes. He was promoted to commander in 1843 and captain in 1855.

Captain Wilkes' most important duty during the Civil War took place while he commanded the screw frigate *San Jacinto*. At Havana, Cuba, Wilkes learned that the Confederate Commissioners James Mason and John Slidell would take passage in the British mail steamer *Trent*; he decided to wait in the Old Bahama channel and waylay her. The *Trent* hove into sight on November 8, 1861, and Wilkes ordered a shot fired across her bow, inducing her captain to stop. A *San Jacinto* boarding party took off the Southern diplomats, and then Wilkes allowed the *Trent* to go on her way. Wilkes carried his prisoners to Boston where he was lionized by the citizenry. It was soon apparent, however, that the *"Trent* Affair'' had caused big waves on both sides of the Atlantic. Incensed by the boarding of a neutral British flag vessel and the seizure of Mason and Slidell, the British Foreign Office roared out its protest against Wilkes' action and talked of war. Lord John Russell, the British foreign secretary, demanded that President Abraham Lincoln* order the release of the Confederates. The storm subsided when Mason and Slidell were quietly set free and allowed to continue to Europe. Wilkes saw this as a personal rebuff, bitterly blasted the capitulation of the American government as "cowardly," and roundly condemned British officials and U.S. Secretary of State William Seward.

Nevertheless, during the next three years Wilkes commanded in turn the James River Flotilla, the Potomac Flotilla, and the West India Squadron. Wilkes criticized Secretary of the Navy Gideon Welles,* however, styling him "a third or fifth rate politician" who was "completely incompetent" to administer the Navy. Wilkes' indiscretion led to another court-martial. He was found guilty on April 26, 1864, of disobedience of orders and insubordination. The court ordered a public reprimand and three years' suspension. The president reduced the suspension to one year, but Wilkes' active service with the Navy was effectively ended.

After the Civil War, Wilkes resumed work on the Exploring Expedition's publications. In 1871, at age seventy-three, he began writing his autobiography.

Charles Wilkes' distinguished naval service started shortly after the War of 1812 and spanned much of the nineteenth century. The *"Trent* Affair'' probably brought Wilkes into more prominence than the South Seas Exploring Expedition. Yet, Wilkes' command of that expedition was the crowning point of his career. The achievements of the expedition were momentous and contributed significantly to man's store of knowledge.

Wilkes was a keen observer. Through his *Autobiography* readers can meet leading personalities and relive the tumultuous life at sea in the early Navy, as well as glimpse bygone aspects of American culture, politics, and society of the nineteenth century, all as viewed by Wilkes, of course. His persistent and aggravating self-righteousness, and his disdain for the views of others were characteristics not calculated to endear him to fellow officers and civilian officials. Nevertheless, Wilkes was a man of imagination and action, a highly talented and bold naval officer who was devoted to the service of his country.

BIBLIOGRAPHY

Ferris, Norman B. *The* Trent *Affair: A Diplomatic Crisis.* Knoxville: University of Tennessee Press, 1977.

Morgan, William James, et al., eds. *Autobiography of Rear Admiral Charles Wilkes, U.S. Navy, 1798–1877.* Washington, D.C.: U.S. Government Printing Office, 1978.

Stanton, William. *The Great United States Exploring Expedition of 1838–1842.* Berkeley: University of California Press, 1975.

Tyler, David B. *The Wilkes Expedition.* Philadelphia: American Philosophical Society, 1968.

WILLIAM JAMES MORGAN

WILKINSON, James (b. Benedict, Md., 1757; d. Mexico City, December 28, 1825), Army officer; general of the Army, 1796–1815. Wilkinson is best known for his intrigues with Vice President Aaron Burr and Spanish officials in the West while serving as the highest ranking general in the American Army.

James Wilkinson's early years were spent on a Maryland plantation operated by his father Joseph. The family had hopes of rearing their son to be a doctor, and James received an education in medicine. Initially, he studied with a local physician, John Bond, but in his seventeenth year, his parents sent him to Philadelphia for further training. Landing in this metropolis in the fall of 1773, Wilkinson soon became actively engaged in the revolutionary movement, subsequently joining the Army as a private.

Possessing a fair education and charm, he soon impressed superiors with his ability to lead men and advanced in rank to major. In January 1777 he gained the notice of General Horatio Gates,* assuming a position on his staff at the rank of lieutenant colonel. After Gates saved New England at the decisive victory near Saratoga, Wilkinson, just in his twentieth year, was made a brigadier general. Unfortunately, he possessed a penchant for becoming involved in controversy and he soon quarreled with Gates, fought a duel with his benefactor, and lost favor with many of the field officers serving in the Revolutionary Army. During this diffucult period, Wilkinson married Anne Biddle, the beautiful daughter of a wealthy Quaker merchant, whom he had met prior to the war. Using connections offered by her family, he joined the army commanded by George Washington* as its clothier general, a post he held until the conclusion of the war.

Being furloughed in 1783, Wilkinson sought wealth and prominence in Kentucky where his wife's family had begun to speculate in land. With financing furnished by his wife's family and land warrants that they had purchased from discharged soldiers, Wilkinson laid claim to several large land tracts near the frontier towns of Louisville and Lexington. He soon merged his speculative venture with a mercantile business, established in Lexington, and became heavily involved in opening the Mississippi River to commerce.

The Spanish at New Orleans had withheld rights of deposit to Americans until Wilkinson personally undertook an effort in 1787 to export produce. In the process, he courted the Spanish governor Rodríguez Esteban Miró, telling him in several letters of his willingness to help Spain defend its possessions in North America and even separate Kentucky from the Republic. Meanwhile, his success in gaining a more favorable trading climate in New Orleans quickly garnered for Wilkinson the support of many of his fellow frontiersmen back in Lexington. Moreover, his success brought alarm in Washington, where government officials worked to keep the frontier attached to the Union and solve the problems created by Spanish intransigence.

Perhaps for this reason, as well as because of growing troubles with Indians in Ohio, President Washington offered Wilkinson a commission in the U.S. Army in 1791 as a lieutenant colonel. Pressed by debts from his numerous speculative ventures, Wilkinson accepted. He took command of Fort Washington near Cincinnati and became actively involved in the campaigns headed by General Anthony Wayne* against the Ohio Indian confederacy. Wilkinson fought bravely at Fallen Timbers, spiriting one of the major assaults on the strongholds held by the men of Little Turtle* and Red Jacket. During these years, he was advanced to brigadier general, the second highest ranking soldier in the American Army. In 1796, after Wayne's death, Wilkinson assumed the position as general of the Army.

Even though he advanced in the ranks, Wilkinson continued to maintain contacts with Spanish officials. In exchange for gold, he fed them information, often of little value, through a chain of co-conspirators. Although his intrigues subsided briefly in the late 1790s, after the general realized that American officials were becoming suspicious, he renewed them in 1804, when he moved to New Orleans to establish U.S. authority after the Louisiana Purchase. On one occasion, Spanish officials sent him $12,000 in gold for "opinions" and assistance, although the fees were usually somewhat smaller.

The general's growing reputation for intrigue soon put him in contact with Vice President Aaron Burr, an ambitious politician who had been spurned by the Jefferson administration. Although the extent of Wilkinson's role in Burr's conspiracy will never be known, it appears that he was aware that the New York politician intended to separate the Mississippi Valley from the Union well before he exposed the plot. The two men became partisans in late 1804 and passed coded letters back and forth during the next two years. Meanwhile, the general became governor of upper Louisiana and sent young Zebulon Montgomery Pike* on two exploring expeditions, the second of which included a survey of Spanish strength in the Southwest. Although Pike probably was not a party to the Wilkinson-Burr conspiracy, his second expedition created suspicions. It is likely that

Burr and Wilkinson thought seriously of including the Spanish domain in their grandiose schemes of empire.

During the summer of 1806, all the scheming came to a head, as Burr informed Wilkinson that he intended to attack New Orleans. The general, aware that rumors of Burr's movements and plans had leaked to the country at large. quickly extricated himself from the conspiracy. He wrote President Thomas Jefferson warning of a "powerful association, extending from New York through the Western states to the territories bordering on the Mississippi" that planned to split the country. At the same time, he exposed his compatriot Burr to the viceroy in Mexico and signed the famous neutral-ground treaty with him, securing a western boundary on the Sabine River. Ironically, Wilkinson then asked the viceroy for a sum of money for defending Spanish sovereignty. Burr was soon arrested and brought to trial for treason. But since neither he nor Wilkinson dared testify against each other, both men escaped without conviction. With Jefferson's support, Wilkinson went back on active duty as general of the Army.

By this time, Wilkinson had become so infamous and detested by a segment of Washington politicians, that tracts were being published about his activities. The most damning came out in 1809, entitled *Proofs of the Corruption of General James Wilkinson*. It was filled with innuendoes regarding his intrigues with the Spanish and Burr, as well as charges that he constantly padded his expense accounts. Wilkinson had always lived extravagantly. The book soon brought calls for another investigation; a committee convened and eventually exonerated him in 1810.

As war with England broke out two years later, the general, now in his mid-fifties, took command of the second invasion of Canada. Ill conceived and poorly supported, the campaigns finally got underway in November 1813. Although designed to take Montreal, the assaults failed and Wilkinson was for the third and final time brought before the public's notice and tried. Charged with drunkenness and neglect of duty, he again escaped punishment, but his military career was now at an end. In 1815, he returned to Philadelphia to write his memoirs, a rambling diatribe that justified his many controversial acts.

Wilkinson spent his final years in the South and Mexico. Just prior to the war, he had taken a second wife. Anne had died during his years in the West. His new in-laws were Louisiana merchants, and Wilkinson settled on a sugar plantation near New Orleans in 1816. His one goal in life—wealth—had still escaped him. For this reason, he went to Mexico City in 1822 to obtain a colonization grant for Texas lands. There he died in December 1825, alone and miserable, after several months of sickness.

General Wilkinson lived an exciting life, albeit a controversial one. His greatest fault was a lack of dedication to his country. Yet as a soldier, he never ran from battle and led men successfully in numerous campaigns. Furthermore, his intrigues never severely damaged the country. Burr's fiasco probably would have failed even with the general's help, and the Spanish threat to America was minimal at best. Finally, an objective view of Wilkinson must include a sound understanding of the age in which he lived. The West was unsettled and American institutions, both political and social, were still in an infant stage. No one knew what course the development of the continent would take. This uncertainty provided fertile ground for the likes of James Wilkinson, soldier, speculator, and intriguer.

BIBLIOGRAPHY

Abernethy, Thomas Perkins. *The Burr Conspiracy*. New York: Oxford University Press, 1954.
Hay, Thomas Robson, and M. R. Werner. *The Admirable Trumpeter: A Biography of General James Wilkinson*. Garden City, N.Y.: Doubleday and Company, 1941.
Jacobs, James Ripley. *Tarnished Warrior: Major-General James Wilkinson*. New York: Macmillan Company, 1938.
Shreve, Royal O. *The Finished Scoundrel: General James Wilkinson*. Indianapolis, Ind.: Bobbs-Merrill Company, 1933.

GARY CLAYTON ANDERSON

WILSON, JAMES HARRISON (b. near Shawneetown, Illinois, September 2, 1837; d. Wilmington, Delaware, February 23, 1925), Army Officer; during the Civil War, Wilson perfected the practice of speeding cavalry to a battlefield, then having them dismount and fight on foot, in the manner of mechanized infantry of the 20th century.

"Harry" Wilson was born near Shawneetown, Illinois, and matriculated at local schools. At age seventeen he attended McKendree College in Lebanon, Illinois. The next year (1855) he obtained an appointment to the U.S. Military Academy, which was then instituting a five-year course, and was graduated with the Class of 1860, standing sixth out of forty-one. Wilson took a commission in the topographical engineers and was posted to Fort Vancouver on the northwest coast.

Wilson's advancement in rank from lieutenant to major general of volunteers during the Civil War naturally led to his being touted as one of the Union's "boy generals"—along with George Armstrong Custer,* Nelson Appleton Miles,* and Wesley Merritt.* Wilson spent much of the war as a staff officer, serving as engineer for expeditions against Port Royal, South Carolina (1861) and Fort Pulaski, Georgia (1862). Wilson gained a spot on the staff of Major General George Brinton McClellan* during the Antietam campaign (September 1862). Promoted to lieutenant colonel of volunteers, Wilson went west to become inspector general of the Army of the Tennessee under Major General Ulysses Simpson Grant.* Favorably impressing Grant on numerous occasions, Wilson participated in the maneuvers and battles in Mississippi that led to the surrender of Vicksburg (July 4, 1863). Remaining with Grant, Wilson witnessed the fighting around Chattanooga (October-November). Achieving flag rank, Brigadier General Wilson used his engineering expertise to help Major General William

Tecumseh Sherman* effect the relief of the Union garrison at Knoxville, Tennessee (December).

Despite the fact that Wilson had never served with the cavalry, on the recommendation of an influential friend, Assistant Secretary of War Charles A. Dana, he was made Chief of the Cavalry Bureau in Washington, D.C. Demonstrating his organizational abilities in a few months (February-April 1864), Wilson corrected major deficiencies in the Bureau. Especially noteworthy was his adoption of the Spencer repeating carbine as the general issue cavalry carbine.

Then Wilson got his chance for field leadership. Grant assigned him to command the 3rd Division of the Cavalry Corps of the Army of the Potomac, under Major General Philip H. Sheridan.* Wilson developed the tactic of riding to the point of attack, then dismounting and carrying the assault on foot, using the firepower provided by the Spencer carbine. Confederates handled Wilson roughly several times (Catharpin Road and Orange Turnpike in the Wilderness, for example), and in one battle after a successful raid (Ream's Station) he lost his artillery and wagons, narrowly escaping with his life. Sheridan did not like Wilson personally, but respected his aggressiveness. Wilson fought hard at Spotsylvania and during Sheridan's Raid on Richmond, including Yellow Tavern where Jeb Stuart* was killed (May 1864). Again under Sheridan, Wilson led his division in the Union victory over Jubal Early* at Winchester (September 19). A few days later Sheridan approved Wilson's transfer to the West to become chief of cavalry in Sherman's Military Division of the Mississippi.

Wilson drew in units that were scattered across the Western Theater, reorganized them, and considered a scheme for cavalry employment. Meanwhile, Wilson had to lead his troops against Confederate General Nathan Bedford Forrest* at Franklin, Tennessee (November 1864), and fought under Major General George Thomas* to defeat a Confederate army led by John B. Hood* at Nashville (December 15-16).

In winter quarters, Wilson trained his men in dismounted tactics and got Grant's permission for what looked like a raid through Alabama and Georgia. Actually, Wilson's mounted expedition of more than 14,000 soldiers conducted a major campaign, destroying supplies, railroads, and factories and defeating Forrest at Selma, Alabama (April 2, 1865). This campaign, overshadowed by the surrender of the army of Robert Edward Lee* in Virginia, guaranteed that President Jefferson Davis* and other Confederate leaders had no redoubt for a last stand in the Deep South.

After martial success during the Civil War, the postwar routine dissatisfied Wilson. Appointed lieutenant colonel of the 35th Infantry Regiment in the reduced peacetime Army, Wilson got himself reassigned as an Army engineer, improving the navigability of the Mississippi River. He resigned from the Army on December 31, 1870. Turning to building railroads, he worked in the Mississippi Valley, relocated to New England, and finally moved to Wilmington, Delaware in 1883. Wilson devoted considerable time to writing, including biographies of Grant and other Civil War figures, as well as numerous magazine articles.

In 1898, upon the outbreak of war with Spain, Wilson, an avowed expansionist, applied for active service. He was appointed major general of volunteers and given command of the VI Corps, but the corps was never activated. While the war's main campaign was winding down in Cuba, Wilson took command of the 1st Division of the I Corps in Puerto Rico under the direction of Major General Nelson Miles, senior officer in the Army. Only a sideshow, the Puerto Rican campaign was progressing smoothly against light opposition when an armistice ended all hostilities (August 12, 1898). Wilson sought the position of military governor of Cuba, but had to take the Department of Matanzas, one of the island's three subdivisions. Trying unsuccessfully to use his political contacts to obtain appointment as either governor-general of the Philippines or governor-general of Puerto Rico, Wilson wrangled the assignment as second-in-command to Major General Adna Romanza Chaffee, leader of the China Relief Expedition against the "Boxer Rebellion" in China (July-November, 1900).

Wilson left active service in March, 1901, with the rank of brigadier general, Regular Army. He was granted the rank of major general on the retired list in 1915. Wilson wrote an extensive and flavorful autobiography (*Under the Old Flag*, 2 vols., 1912). He died on February 23, 1925, in Wilmington.

Throughout his life James H. Wilson had no doubt that he was the best at what he did and, to the dismay of many of his contemporaries, often he was right. Wilson was the most sophisticated and professionally accomplished of the Union's "boy generals." As Edward Longacre, Wilson's biographer, concluded, he was "a general whose contributions to military science were not restricted to application during his own era but which have significant application for modern warfare."

Wilson had an exceptional outlook for a cavalryman of the 19th century. He believed that the days of flashing sabers and Light Brigade charges were passed. Instead he envisioned that cavalry would be most effective as mounted infantry, soldiers who used their horses as transportation to the battle, and who would be expected to fight on foot over any terrain, attack fortified positions, destroy the enemy's economic resources, disrupt enemy communications. Then they would remount and ride to the next battle, to or across enemy lines, striking deep into enemy territory, like the panzer grenadiers or mechanized (motorized) infantry of the 20th century. Wilson thought that a rapid-fire rifle should become the trooper's main weapon. His vision is particularly striking when one realizes that most cavalry commanders (even up to and during the Great War) continued to think that the top priorities of the *arm blanche* were hell-for-leather charges with the saber or opportunistic pursuits of routed enemies with the lance.

At the Cavalry Bureau, Wilson worked wonders. Although Stephen Z. Starr discounts some of Wilson's accomplishments, it is certain that the two nonentities who preceded him had been unproductive as bureau chiefs. However, in a short time Wilson quickly established a system permitting the Army to acquire sound horses where inadequate ones had been accepted before, strictly enforced War Department regulations (heretofore disregarded) for penalizing fraudulent horse contractors, and astutely adopted the Spencer carbine. Older officers opposed adopting the Spencer, arguing that the troopers would freely use the seven-shot repeater, thus wasting ammunition. Instead, cavalrymen who had the Spencer (not all units could be supplied with it before the war ended) greatly increased their firepower and hence increased their impact on the enemy.

How would Wilson demonstrate that cavalry had been misused throughout most of the Civil War? Some other commanders, notably Sheridan in the Shenandoah, coordinated the cavalry with infantry and artillery. Wilson fought under Sheridan, but it was not until he got to the Western Theater that he really could use his scheme to the fullest, and even there he had to wait until the war was nearly over. Actually, Wilson began using his ideas almost immediately—and effectively—at Nashville. His dismounted cavalry played a principal role in administering the defeat to Hood, then pursued him unmercifully. Nashville was one of the most decisive victories by any army during the war.

The showcase of Wilson's tactics was his three-division drive through Alabama and Georgia, spearheaded by the division of his close friend, Emory Upton.* Traveling lightly with few wagons, some pontoons, and some artillery, Wilson scorched a destructive swath through Dixie's heart. True enough, Wilson's veteran troops fought against hastily gathered Confederates. Their leader, the undaunted N. B. Forrest, had pulled miracles from his hat before. But not this time. In two months Wilson's divisions campaigned 525 miles, inflicted nearly 8,000 casualties on the Confederates (6,800 of them prisoners) while only suffering 700, captured 288 cannon and nearly 100,000 small arms, destroyed various factories, foundries, arsenals, shops, and mills as well as 35 locomotives, more than 500 railroad cars, and many miles of track; bridges, trestles, depots, warehouses, and cotton (perhaps 100,000 bales) were torched. Wilson in his memoirs described the campaign as one of " 'breaking things' along the main line of Confederate communications.'' The great destruction and the great success went almost unreported to the public because Wilson had not permitted journalists to accompany him, and at about the same time Lee surrendered. Wilson drove out any lingering thoughts about last ditch Confederate resistance. And one of his detachments captured Jefferson Davis at Irwinsville, Georgia. There would be no government in exile.

Five years after the war, Wilson decided to resign from the Army, and encouraged his friend Upton to do the same. Upton demurred, believing that he could still contribute to the service. Wilson's postwar years were lucrative: railroad construction, books contracted for and written, presidencies of railroads. But it must have been frustrating for Wilson to go on active service again in 1898, even with high rank. Wilson had a political appointment, the kind that he and Upton had disparaged in their younger years. The promise of corps command went unfulfilled. The infantry campaign in Puerto Rico was disappointing. The occupation of Cuba was one continuous round of political infighting among Wilson, Leonard Wood,* Fitzhugh Lee,* and Major General John R. Brooke, military governor of the island. During the occupation a fire destroyed Wilson's house and killed his wife. His position in the China Relief Expedition brought him to a skirmish with the Boxers at the Eight Temples. He went home to retirement.

It is speculative to consider what, if any, influence Wilson would have had on the conservative Indian-fighting army in the Trans-Mississippi—its organization, its equipment (the Army dropped the Spencer for the single-shot Springfield carbine), its training and doctrine. Would he have led units in the field, and to what result? Those fights went to Sheridan, Miles, Custer, Merritt, and Ranald MacKenzie.*

BIBLIOGRAPHY

Ambrose, Stephen E. *Upton and the Army*. Baton Rouge: Louisiana State University Press, 1964.
Healy, David F. *The United States in Cuba, 1898-1902: Generals, Politicians, and the Search for Policy*. Madison: University of Wisconsin Press, 1963.
Jones, James P. *Yankee Blitzkrieg: Wilson's Raid through Alabama and Georgia*. Athens: University of Georgia Press, 1976.
Longacre, Edward G. *From Union Stars to Top Hat: A Biography of the Extraordinary General James Harrison Wilson*. Harrisburg, Pa.: Stackpole, 1972.
Starr, Stephen Z. *The Union Cavalry in the Civil War*. 2 vols. Baton Rouge: Louisiana State University Press, 1979-1981.
Trask, David F. *The War with Spain in 1898*. New York: Macmillan, 1981.

                                                                                    JOSEPH G. DAWSON III

WINDER, William Henry (b. Somerset County, Md., February 18, 1775; d. Baltimore, Md., May 24, 1824), Army officer during the War of 1812. Winder commanded the American forces at the Battle of Bladensburg.

William H. Winder was born into one of the oldest families in Maryland, and among his ancestors were some of the earliest and most influential members of the state's legislature and judiciary. He was educated at Washington Academy in Somerset County and the University of Pennsylvania. After graduating from the University of Pennsylvania, he studied law, first with his uncle John Henry, a Maryland delegate to the Continental Congress throughout most of the Revolutionary War, and then in the Annapolis office of Judge Gabriel Duval. He traveled to Nashville upon gaining admission to the bar, expecting excellent opportunities for a young lawyer in Tennessee. His expectations were unfulfilled, however, and he soon returned to Somerset County. At the age of twenty-three, he was elected to the state legislature; a year later he married his cousin Gertrude Polk. He moved to Baltimore in 1802, where he quickly established a flourishing legal practice, and within ten years he was one of the leading attorneys in the state.

Early in 1812 Winder realized that it was highly likely that the United States and Great Britain would soon be at war, and although he was a staunch Federalist, he immediately offered his services to the Madison administration. He was appointed lieutenant colonel in the newly created 14th U.S. Infantry Regiment on March 12 and was assigned the task of recruiting troops from Baltimore and Montgomery County. On July 7 he was promoted to full colonel and given command of the regiment. The next month he was ordered to report as quickly as possible to Major General Henry Dearborn's* army on the Niagara frontier, where on November 28 his command had the distinction of being the only American force to cross the Canadian shore during Brigadier General Alexander Smyth's abortive attack on the British forces in the vicinity of Fort Erie.

On March 12, 1813, at the suggestion of Secretary of State James Monroe, Winder was made a brigadier general, and on May 27, his brigade supported the successful American assault on Fort George. On June 5 he and Brigadier General John Chandler were attacked at Stoney Creek by about seven hundred British regulars; in the ensuing confusion both he and Chandler were taken prisoner. While in captivity, Winder embarked on negotiations with the commander of the British forces in Canada which ultimately resulted in an agreement for the repatriation of the prisoners held by both sides.

Winder was given his freedom in April 1814, and a month later Secretary of War John Armstrong, Jr.,* proposed to assign him to a position on the staff of Major General George Izard,* who commanded the American forces around Plattsburgh, New York. Izard objected, however, and Winder was ordered to report to Baltimore. He arrived at that city in early June and was given a tumultuous welcome by its citizens.

On July 2 Winder was named commander of the newly created Tenth Military District, which included Maryland, the District of Columbia, and that part of Virginia between the Rappahannock and Potomac rivers, and was assigned the task of defending Washington and Baltimore. On August 19 over four thousand British regulars under the command of Major General Robert Ross landed at Benedict, Maryland, on the Patuxent River, and Winder responded by marching his small army of two thousand men to the Woodyard, approximately ten miles southeast of Washington. Concluding that the oncoming enemy column was too large to attack successfully, he fell back, first to Old Fields and, when the British Army appeared to be heading there, to Washington itself. By July 24 it was apparent that Ross was in fact advancing on Bladensburg, and as the last-minute arrival of militia units from Maryland and Virginia had increased the size of the American Army to nearly 6,000 men, Winder hurried to confront them there. He reached the town moments before the British general, but when Ross's veteran troops began their attack, his mostly ill-trained and undisciplined troops gave way after offering brief but determined resistance.

By nightfall, Winder was back in Washington, but as the bulk of his army had scattered during the retreat, he continued to retire until he reached Montgomery Court House. He learned the next day that the British, having briefly occupied the capital, were now moving against Baltimore, and he hastened to that city to assume command of the defenses. Arriving on July 27, he found Major General Samuel Smith in command, and as a result, he was relegated to playing a relatively minor role in repelling the British assault.

Late in September he was ordered to report to Izard's army, and, although a congressional committee was investigating the American defeat at Bladensburg, he went willingly. When the committee issued its report, however, he considered it to be extremely unfair, and he asked for a court of inquiry. His request was granted, and, meeting on January 26, 1815, the members of the court ruled that his conduct during the battle deserved considerable commendation. When the war ended, he was again given command of the Tenth Military District, but a month later, he indicated that he wished to resign from the Army in order to make room for the advancement of younger officers with more fortunate records. He then returned to Baltimore, reestablished his law practice, and was elected twice to the State Senate.

Winder was a better lawyer than he was a soldier. As the commander of first a regiment and then a brigade on the Niagara frontier, he displayed only modest abilities, and his services were lost to the United States for nearly a year, when he was taken prisoner during the Battle at Stoney Creek. In fact, his most notable accomplishment during this period was his success in negotiating the exchange of prisoners between his government and the British in Canada, an achievement that depended far more on his talents as a lawyer than as a general.

When President James Madison decided to appoint Winder commander of the Tenth Military District, he overlooked his slender military record in favor of what he believed to be more important considerations—that Winder was in Baltimore and immediately available and that his uncle Levin Winder was the governor of Maryland and might now be expected to be less critical of the administration's war effort. From the beginning, however, Winder's actions revealed that he lacked the experience and judgment necessary to carry out the task assigned to him. Although he took up his command more than six weeks before Ross's regulars set foot on American soil, he neglected both to formulate a plan for the defense of Washington and to begin the construction of fortifications at important points such as Bladensburg.

When Winder received word of the British landing at Benedict, he failed to send out parties to harass the advancing regulars, and, what was worse, he made only one meager attempt to fell trees and tear up bridges in order to obstruct their passage. Instead, he exhausted his army and himself by advancing hurriedly to the Woodyard and then falling back precipitously to Washington. Then, when he realized that the British were marching toward Bladensburg, which was defended only by Brigadier General Tobias Stansbury's Maryland militia, he foolishly divided his army, leaving Captain Joshua Barney's command to protect the navy yard, while he advanced with the rest of his force to engage the enemy.

When Winder reached Bladensburg, he found that Stansbury's regiments were already firing on the fast-approaching enemy, but, for reasons known only to himself, he failed to position the rest of his army within supporting distance of Stansbury's men. As a result, Ross's troops were free to attack each American line in turn. When Winder saw what was happening, he ordered an immediate retreat, despite the fact that Barney, who had appealed to Madison to be allowed to participate in the battle, was standing fast against the British onslaught. Unfortunately, Winder's withdrawal, which had begun in good order, turned into a rout, and Ross was able to occupy the capital without further resistance.

In fairness to Winder, it must be said that Secretary of War Armstrong also did much to make the unfortunate outcome of the battle at Bladensburg inevitable. Armstrong was certain that it was inconceivable that the British would bother to attempt an attack on Washington. Not only did he refuse to do anything to strengthen the city's pathetically few defenses, but when Winder asked for immediate authority to call out the militia units that were to make up the bulk of his army, he denied his request, replying offhandedly that militia fought best when called to the field just before an engagement. As a result of this fallacious reasoning, Winder had fewer than eleven hundred men under his command only eleven days before the battle. The secretary of war was also perversely reluctant to help the American commander assemble a competent staff; for this reason, Winder was compelled to perform personally as routine a task as scouting the Maryland countryside. It is at least conceivable that had Armstrong been less an obstructionist, Winder's performance at Bladensburg would have been more effective.

BIBLIOGRAPHY

Coles, Harry L. *The War of 1812*. Chicago: University of Chicago Press, 1968.
Cruikshank, Ernest, ed. *The Documentary History of the Campaign on the Niagara Frontier, 1812–1814*. New York: Arno Press and The New York Times, 1971.
Ingraham, Edward Duncan. *A Sketch of the Events Which Preceded the Capture of Washington by the British*. Philadelphia: Carey and Hart, 1849.
Mahon, John K. *The War of 1812*. Gainesville: University of Florida Press, 1972.
Swanson, Neil H. *The Perilous Fight*. New York: Farrar and Rinehart, 1945.
Williams, John S. *History of the Invasion and Capture of Washington*. New York: Harper and Brothers, Publishers, 1857.

BARRY SUDE

WINSLOW, John (b. Marshfield, Mass., May 10, 1703; d. Hingham, Mass., April 17, 1774), provincial officer and commander in British service during the French and Indian War.

Winslow could boast "that the command in the Military and Civil way in New England has often been in our Family from 1620." A great-grandfather (Edward Winslow) and a grandfather (Josiah Winslow) were governors of Plymouth; his father and a brother were distinguished militia officers.

Winslow's first important military service came in 1740 when the Duke of Newcastle asked colonies from New England to North Carolina for soldiers to attack the Spanish Caribbean. He was then a major in the Massachusetts militia.

With the help of William Shirley,* a protegé of Newcastle who was to replace Jonathan Belcher as Massachusetts governor in 1741, Winslow quickly persuaded a hundred men, thirty of them Indians, to join his company. For West Indian adventure and an army commission, Winslow spent his own money recruiting and left his wife, farm, and a job as register of probate and county recorder that paid, he said, £200 sterling annually. Not receiving his valued captaincy until arrival in the West Indies did not daunt him. Winslow joined thirty-six hundred Americans, fifty-six hundred British soldiers, and sixty warships in a fruitless attack on Cartagena in April 1741. He survived a climate that killed 90 percent of his comrades. When the remants of the expedition transferred to Guantanamo Bay for an ill-conceived and never-to-be-completed march on Santiago, the Army's commander, Major General Thomas Wentworth, sent Captain Winslow home to recruit reinforcements. In October and November of 1741 the popular Winslow did persuade one hunded and fifty gullible enlistees to accept his version of the possibilities in Cuba, but in 1742 Wentworth and Vice-Admiral Edward Vernon ended the expedition and discharged Winslow's regiment. Winslow and other surviving American officers desired promotions and permanent rank. Armed with a recommendation from Shirley, he sailed to London and besieged Newcastle with pleas that they were related (because Winslow was a great-grandson of Herbert Pelham) and complaints that Wentworth had been prejudiced against promoting Americans. The American officers were not promoted, but they all were granted at least half-pay status, and Winslow received active duty as a captain in another regiment. He served in Nova Scotia at that rank until 1751 and then retired on half-pay.

The coming of the French and Indian War began Winslow's second phase of military activity. In 1754 Governor Shirley was alarmed by reports that French troops had ascended the Chaudière River from Quebec and built a fort at the carrying place between the Chaudière and Kennebec where they were inciting Penobscot and Norridgewock Indians against English settlers. Shirley asked the Massachusetts General Court for troops to oust the French. The legislature quickly authorized eight hundred men, and Shirley appointed Winslow to lead them. Winslow was one of the Kennebec Proprietors, a company whose claims to land along the river dated from the seventeenth century; the Proprietors were most enthusiastic about the expedition. In July and August 1754 Winslow and his men advanced up the Kennebec and built two forts: Fort Western, at Koussinoc, now Augusta, where Winslow's great-grandfather had traded in the 1620s; and Fort Halifax, below the Ticonic Falls, where the Kennebec and Sebasticook rivers join. They found no Frenchmen and no hostile Indians, but the expedition confirmed English claims to the area, and, Shirley believed, anticipating Benedict Arnold's* 1775 campaign, demonstrated that Quebec could be approached via the Kennebec and the Chaudière. Winslow's interest in the Kennebec persisted later: in 1761 he surveyed territory around Fort Western that became Augusta, and in 1766 the Kennebec Proprietors assigned him a share in land at Fort Halifax that became the towns of Winslow and Waterville.

In 1755 the British planned attacks against four French strongholds: Fort Duquesne, Crown Point, Niagara, and Fort Beauséjour, which Franch had established in Nova Scotia on the Chignecto Isthmus on the western side of the Missaquash River. Only the Nova Scotian Campaign was successful, and Winslow played a major role in it. Shirley and Governor Charles Lawrence of Nova Scotia considered the province the key to Canada and New England, and they resolved to capture Fort Beauséjour. With Governor Lawrence paying all expenses, Massachusetts created a regiment of two thousand, divided into two battalions, to serve one year. Winslow directed recruiting and was commissioned lieutenant colonel of the first battalion with actual command of the entire regiment since Shirley, the nominal colonel, went to Virginia to meet Edward Braddock.* The commander in chief of the expedition was Lieutenant Colonel Robert Monckton, a regular officer. Winslow, his reputation enhanced by the Kennebec Expedition, easily recruited the regiment. The New Englanders left Boston on May 26, 1755, and joined 250 regulars at Fort Lawrence, on the east side of the Missaquash, on June 22. On June 4 the troops crossed the Missaquash, brushing back French resistance, and camped near Beauséjour. Winslow's men seized a hill overlooking the French fort and, on June 14, began a bombardment. On June 16 Fort Beauséjour surrendered. The French were given honors of war, and the British promised not to punish Acadians in the garrison. But despite the surrender terms, Governor Lawrence and the Nova Scotia Council ordered all Acadians exiled, for they had refused an oath of allegiance to King George II; their culture, religion, and past behavior made them unreliable subjects. Winslow's regiment bore the brunt of the distasteful task of removing the Acadians. On September 5, 1755, Winslow announced their fate to 418 Acadian men in the church at Grand Pré. Eventually nearly seven thousand Acadians were torn from their homes.

Throughout the Nova Scotian Campaign there was conflict between Winslow and Monckton. Monckton accused New Englanders of stealing sheep, wasting ammunition, and drinking excessively. Winslow complained that Monckton denied the provincials food and rum, and that he had reneged on promised of extra wages for heavy labor. On several occasions Winslow thought Monckton treated him in an "Ungentel Ilnatined" way. Monckton and Lawrence's dispatches to England gave no credit to Winslow and the New Englanders, a grievous hurt to Winslow who craved a regular regiment. Most resented was Monckton's forcing New England men to enlist in the regulars.

In 1756, after Braddock's defeat and Sir William Johnson's* clash with Baron de Dieskau at Lake George, Shirley, now commander in chief of the British Army in America, selected Winslow (to the chagrin of Sir William Pepperrell* who wanted the assignment) to lead an assault on Ticonderoga and Crown Point. Winslow was recalled from Nova Scotia to command seven thousand New Englanders and New Yorkers with the Provincial rank of major general. In July 1756, as Winslow struggled with supply shortages near Lake George, his patron Shirley was superseded by John Campbell,* the earl of Loudoun. Loudoun and his deputy, Major General James Abercromby, distrusted Winslow's provincials and were horrified by the juxtaposition of latrines, kitchens, graves, slaughter houses, and tents. Loudon and Abercromby favored leavening the provincials with regulars, which provoked a crisis. If regulars had operated with provincials, British captains would have been senior to provincial general and field grade officers, and men would have been subject to martial law. American officers opposed any merger of regulars and provincials, and Loudoun thought them mutinous. In a compromise, Winslow and his officers acknowledged Loudoun's authority but won the favor of operating separately unless aid from regulars became essential. Upon the fall of Oswego (August 14, 1756), Loudoun canceled Winslow's advance upon Ticonderoga and Crown Point and ordered him to defend Albany. When winter ended the 1756 campaign, most of the provincials returned home, and Winslow's active military career ended.

Later in the 1750s and in the 1760s Winslow served in the Massachusetts legislature. His name remained on the half-pay list as a regular captain until thirteen years after his death. In 1725 he married Mary Little; she died in 1744. He remarried, and his second wife, Bethiah Barker Johnson, survived him. Several of his relatives became Loyalists, including a brother, a nephew, and one of the two sons he had by his first wife.

Winslow's career was inspired by family tradition, desire for military prestige and emoluments, and land hunger. He may have sought land in the Caribbean; his land speculations certainly motivated him to lead the Kennebec Expedition. Winslow appraised the farmland when he served in Nova Scotia, but he removed the Acadians because he was ordered to do so, not because he coveted their land. The removals pained him; he carried out his assignment as humanely as possible. His great abilities as a recruiter, which British officials fully appreciated, testify to his popularity with his troops. Despite ignorance of camp hygiene, he cared deeply about their welfare. He was incensed when Monckton abused them, and he resisted Loudoun's upsetting proposals. Winslow understood the patronage system. He maintained his friendship with Shirley and cultivated Newcastle and the earl of Halifax. Although not a policymaker, Winslow was a trustworthy, well-liked, efficient officer.

BIBLIOGRAPHY

Gipson, Lawrence Henry. *The British Empire Before the American Revolution*. Vol. 6. New York: Alfred A. Knopf, 1946.
Pargellis, Stanley M. *Lord Loudoun in North America*. New Haven, Conn.: Yale University Press, 1933.
———. *Military Affairs in North America: 1748–1765*. New York: Appleton-Century, 1936.
Parkman, Francis. *Montcalm and Wolfe*. 2 vols. Boston: Little, Brown, 1925.

Schutz, John A. *William Shirley*. Chapel Hill: University of North Carolina Press, 1961.
Shirley, William. *Correspondence of William Shirley*. Edited by Charles H. Lincoln. 2
    vols. New York: Macmillan, 1912.

JOSEPH A. DEVINE, JR.

WINTHROP, Fitz-John   (b. Ipswich, Mass., March 14, 1638; d. Boston,
Mass., November 27, 1707), military and political leader.

John Winthrop III, known during his youth and by posterity as "Fitz" or
"Fitz-John," was named after his father and his illustrious grandfather. Born
in Massachusetts, he moved with his family to Pequot—the future town of New
London—Connecticut in 1646. Despite his father's best efforts, Winthrop showed
little promise as a scholar. In 1654 his academic preparation was deemed inadequate, denying him entrance into Harvard College with the class of 1658. In
a vain attempt to rectify this deficiency, he remained in Cambridge under the
tutelage of a cousin. Frustrated by a lack of success, Winthrop abandoned his
formal education and returned to New London the following year.

During the succeeding two years Winthrop became increasingly restless because of his inability to find a satisfying career. In the fall of 1657, he set sail
for England, seeking adventure and advancement in the Commonwealth of Oliver
Cromwell. Winthrop arrived in London by January 1658 where influential family
members, such as Hugh Peter and Colonel Stephen Winthrop, were able to place
their young kinsman in a Gloucester regiment. Several months later, following
the death of Colonel Winthrop, Fitz-John journeyed to central Scotland where
another relative, Colonel Thomas Reade, procured him a lieutenant's commission
in his own regiment of foot soldiers. During the winter of 1659–1660, this
regiment marched south to London with General George Monck, preparing the
groundwork for the eventual restoration of Charles II. Continually aided by family
connections, Winthrop received two promotions, attaining the rank of full captain
before he was mustered out of the Army in October 1660. He returned to
Connecticut in early 1663 with a solid reputation as a soldier.

During the two decades following his return to New England, Winthrop was
seemingly reluctant to shoulder the public responsibilities expected of one born
to a lofty social position. He was more concerned with the family estate, land
speculation, his personal status, and the latest English fashions than in standing
for political office. He did, however, respond to the call of military service by
his fellow townsmen and the leaders of Connecticut who percieved him, on the
basis of his experience in the English Civil War, as accomplished in that area.
Winthrop was appointed commander of the New London County militia in 1672
and sergeant major of the colonial forces on Long Island during the Anglo-Dutch
War (1672–1674). In February 1674 his judicious placement of troops repulsed
a larger Dutch force which had assaulted the town of Southold. Although illness
prevented Winthrop from assuming his rightful place on the battlefield during
King Philip's War (1675–1676), he did perform valuable service behind the
lines.

The attempt by Whitehall to restructure the administration of overseas colonies resulted in the annulment of the Massachusetts charter in late 1684. In May 1686 Joseph Dudley was installed as head of a provisional government for the Bay Colony which also had jurisdiction over the Narragansett Country, a land tract of disputed ownership located between Connecticut and Rhode Island. Because of Winthrop's substantial proprietary interests in this area, he was appointed as its representative on the council of the Dudley government. When Sir Edmund Andros assumed control of the Dominion of New England in December 1686, he retained Winthrop's place on the council. The friendship between these two men, which had developed during the late 1670s, proved advantageous to Winthrop throughout the brief tenure of the Dominion. In 1687 he was appointed commander of the militia for Rhode Island, the Narragansett Country, and Connecticut and was promoted to the rank of major general, the second highest military position in New England. Despite these honors, Winthrop—pleading illness—not only declined to lead a military expedition against the Indians of Maine in 1688, but he also remained neutral during the overthrow of Andros and the Dominion in April 1689. His old aversion to political office reappeared in May 1689 when he refused election as magistrate in the restored government of Connecticut.

The outbreak of hostilities between England and France in 1689 drew the North American colonies of each country into open conflict. In retaliation for the sacking of Schenectady by the French, the northern English colonies planned a three-pronged assault on Canada during the summer of 1690. Following an initial disagreement among the participants, Winthrop was selected to lead the proposed overland attack on Montreal. Although the plan was workable and the commander well chosen, this phase of the operation was continually plagued by misfortune. The failure of New York and the Indian allies to supply their respective quotas of men combined with rancid meat, an insufficient number of canoes, and an attack of smallpox to doom the expedition. Winthrop was forced to turn back two hundred miles shy of Montreal. To compound this fiasco Governor Jacob Leisler* of New York accused Winthrop of "treachery and cowardice" and had him arrested. After a contingent of Indians rescued Winthrop from Leisler's grasp, he vigorously defended his actions. The colony of Connecticut not only supported Winthrop's conduct, but it also voted him £40 for his efforts.

Three years of inactivity followed Winthrop's participation in the ill-fated Canadian venture. In 1693 he finally began to assume the burdens of public office which were his birthright. Between 1693 and 1707 the "ancient liberties" granted by the charter of Connecticut and the charter itself were besieged by opponents who lived not only within the colony but also beyond its boundaries in such diverse places as New York, Massachusetts, and England. In the face of these repeated internal and external assaults, Winthrop strenuously defended the integrity of the charter: first as the colony's agent in England (1693–1697) and then as its governor (1698–1707). During his ten years as governor, he pursued a moderate course, repulsing attempts to reinstitute royal government and to initiate wide-ranging democratic reforms.

Advancing age, poor health, and the weight of public responsibility exacted their toll in November 1707. While visiting relatives in Boston, Winthrop was stricken with a fatal illness. After a lavish funeral he was interred in the same tomb as his father and grandfather in the churchyard of King's Chapel.

Although Winthrop cannot be considered a great military leader in his own right, his career is representative of an important element in the military experience of seventeenth-century America: the role of the gentleman-soldier. In a traditional society the advantages of membership in the upper class are accompanied by the obligation to serve the common good. Born to one of the first families in New England, Winthrop was expected by contemporaries to assume a leadership role in society. Despite his reluctance to hold a political position, he readily accepted—and consistently held—military office, the form of service most compatible with his inclination and experience. For example, Winthrop served as commander of the New London County militia for over eighteen years and as major general of the New England militia under Governor Andros. In time of war, he put aside personal affairs to assume military command. Winthrop led several forays across Long Island Sound during the Anglo-Dutch War; performed rearguard service—despite ill-health—during King Philip's War; and commanded the overland assault on Montreal during King William's War.

Social rank alone does not explain Winthrop's repeated selection as a military leader. Equally important is the perception of contemporaries that he was an accomplished soldier. Winthrop's military reputation began to develop as a result of his experience in the English Civil War. It was enhanced by virtue of his stature as one of the few professionally trained soldiers in early New England and by his successful defense of the town of Southold. This combination of social standing and military reputation made Winthrop an appropriate choice for military command in seventeenth-century New England. By accepting his social responsibilities as a leader, Winthrop epitomizes a significant element in the military heritage of colonial America: the gentleman-soldier.

BIBLIOGRAPHY

Black, Robert C., III. *The Younger John Winthrop*. New York: Columbia University Press, 1966.

Bushman, Richard L. *From Puritan to Yankee: Character and the Social Order in Connecticut, 1690–1765*. Cambridge, Mass.: Harvard University Press, 1967.

Caulkins, Frances Manwaring. *History of New London, Connecticut, From the First Survey of the Coast in 1612 to 1860*. New London, Conn.: H. D. Utley, 1895.

Craven, Wesley Frank. *The Colonies in Transition, 1660–1713*. New York: Harper and Row, 1968.

Dunn, Richard S. *Puritans and Yankees: The Winthrop Dynasty of New England, 1630–1717*. Princeton, N.J.: Princeton University Press, 1962.

Leder, Lawrence H. *Robert Livingston, 1654–1728, and the Politics of Colonial New York*. Chapel Hill: University of North Carolina Press for the Institute of Early American History and Culture at Williamsburg, Va., 1961.

ROBERT C. LEMIRE, JR.

WOLFE, James (b. Westerham, Kent, England, January 2, 1727 [December 22, 1726, OS]; d. Quebec, Canada, September 13, 1759), British general. Wolfe served at Louisbourg in 1758 and commanded the army that captured Quebec in 1759.

James Wolfe's career in the British Army was founded on a combination of opportunity, ambition, and talent. He was born into an army family: his great-grandfather and grandfather had served under Charles I and William of Orange; his father, a veteran of Marlborough's campaigns in Flanders, was a lieutenant colonel of infantry who would one day become a lieutenant general. As a child, Wolfe played at being a soldier, attended school with other sons of officers, and dreamed of military glory. In 1741, when he was fourteen and Britain was entering a period of prolonged warfare, Wolfe received a commission in his father's regiment of marines. Soon thereafter he transferred to another, more prestigious regiment and began to establish himself as an unusually zealous and competent young officer. He served as an adjutant at the Battle of Dettingen in 1743, as a captain with the Fourth Foot in 1744, and as a brigade major during both the Scottish Rebellion of 1745–1746 and the campaign of 1747 in Flanders. He repeatedly distinguished himself in combat—at Dettingen, Falkirk, and Laffeldt—and, at the end of the War of the Austrian Succession, was permitted to buy a majority in the 20th Regiment of Foot. Wolfe was then twenty-two, a tall, thin, and awkward young man with a good mind and an extraordinary appetite for combat, command, and fame.

Because of his age and ambition, he found the ensuing years of peace (1749–1756) more frustrating than rewarding. He did succeed to the lieutenant colonelcy of his regiment and, in the absence of successive colonels, commanded the regiment for nearly eight years. He also found time for his own education and amusement—for studying algebra, geometry, and Latin; for reading extensively in military history and theory; and for going abroad to improve his French as well as his riding, dancing, and fencing. But for most of the years between the wars, he complained bitterly of being kept in rustic seclusion, building roads and preserving the peace in the Highlands of Scotland, or garrisoning remote towns in the South of England. Short of money, frustrated in his efforts to get leave to observe the armies of Europe, and denied further promotion, he became preoccupied with his health, moods, and motives: he bathed in self-pity and looked forward to war as a panacea.

But war was slow to solve Wolfe's problems—to give him the opportunities he sought. The resumption of fighting between British and French forces in North

America during the summer of 1755 shook Wolfe from his dark, introspective musings: he began enthusiastically preparing himself and his regiment for action. Yet for the next two years, while his regiment was posted in the south of England guarding against invasion and maintaining order, he failed repeatedly—for want of seniority and influence—to gain promotion or reassignment. Finally, in the summer of 1757 he was appointed quartermaster general and chief of staff to Sir John Mordaunt who was being sent to carry out a diversionary raid on the French coast at Rochefort. Although the raid was a failure, Wolfe managed both by his performance and by his subsequent testimony against his friend Mordaunt to establish himself as an aggressive officer, an officer well suited to carry out the new, offensive strategies of William Pitt, the king's principal minister.

In January 1758 Pitt did, in fact, choose Wolfe to serve as a brigadier general under Major General Jeffery Amherst* in the primary offensive planned for 1758—an amphibious campaign against Canada that was to begin with an attack on the French fortress at Louisbourg on Cape Breton Island and end with the reduction of Quebec. Pitt's choice proved remarkably sound: Wolfe supplied much of the energy and aggressive leadership needed to carry out Amherst's plans. In early June Wolfe directed the initial landing on Cape Breton, exploiting the chance of discovery of a lightly defended cove to secure a beachhead close to Louisbourg. Subsequently, he erected batteries to destroy the French warships defending the harbor and one flank of the fortifications about the town, repelled a succession of raiding parties, and pushed forward the British lines until the garrison surrendered at last on July 26. By then it was too late to go on to Quebec, but Wolfe did conduct a raid in the Gulf of St. Lawrence before returning home for the winter.

Although the campaign of 1758 had not accomplished all the British expected, it enhanced Wolfe's reputation and brought him an independent command. In December Pitt chose Wolfe to lead an army of eighty-five hundred regulars (supported by forty-nine warships and nearly two hundred auxiliary vessels) to capture Quebec and join other British forces in completing the conquest of Canada. Wolfe left England in February, assembled his army at Halifax and Louisbourg, and arrived off Quebec in late June 1759.

He soon discovered that taking Quebec would be more difficult than he anticipated. The French had chosen to defend the lightly fortified town by defending the adjacent north bank of the St. Lawrence River. Most of their fifteen thousand regular and provincial troops were entrenched below Quebec to oppose any landing between the town and the Montmorency River, more than six miles to the east. The remainder were in and above Quebec posted atop cliffs that bound the St. Lawrence for nearly four miles and made a most forbidding natural palisade. Here then was a position too extensive to be invested, too well secured by forests and difficult terrain to be easily turned, and too strong to be assaulted with impunity.

Although Wolfe was confident in the superiority of his troops, he was reluctant to risk them in attacking or turning the French lines. He decided, therefore, to try to draw the French from their works and into a general engagement on his terms. He began by bombarding Quebec and establishing an unfortified camp east of the Montmorency in hopes that the French would be tempted to attack in force. When they were not, Wolfe decided to attack their lines on the Montmorency. His ill-conceived and poorly-executed attempt of July 31 cost 440 killed and wounded (the French lost sixty) and gained nothing. Even then, Wolfe persisted in his tactics. He continued to bait the French, sending one detachment to destroy shipping above Quebec and others to burn farmhouses in the surrounding countryside; and he planned, alternatively, another attack on the French at Montmorency.

Finally, ill and desperate, he sought and took his brigadiers' advice, withdrew from Montmorency, and transported nearly five thousand troops up the St. Lawrence in order to land above Quebec and force a general action. But instead of landing at least ten miles from Quebec as his brigadiers proposed—instead of giving the French time to choose where and how to engage—he decided to gamble on landing within two miles of the town. He would risk scaling the cliffs at the Anse au Foulon to surprise the French and force them to fight before they were fully prepared. On September 13—and with as much luck as planning—he succeeded, winning a brief, decisive battle that cost him his life and gained Quebec.

It is ironic that Wolfe's fame should rest mainly upon the campaign of 1759 and the dramatic events of September 13. To be sure, he managed on September 13 to solve a very difficult tactical problem and to demonstrate that he was a gifted battlefield commander. Yet his success in bringing the French to action and in gaining a decisive victory owed as much to his brigadiers' advice and to good luck as to his own leadership; and prior to September 13, he had persisted in tactics that were at best unsuccessful and at worst nearly disastrous. So jealous was Wolfe of the glory that was to be his in taking Quebec that for more than two months he refused not only to consult his principal officers—most of whom he had chosen—but even to let them know what he planned. While relying on his own judgment, he could find no better way to bring the French to action than to attack their works at Montmorency. Had the French been as fortunate as he on September 13, Wolfe might be remembered as an officer who sacrificed his army in pursuit of glory.

But even if there were no monuments to Wolfe, he would deserve to be remembered as an extraordinary regimental officer. Perhaps more than any officer of his generation he combined a genuine enthusiasm for training with a passion for leading men in combat. He was widely regarded as an authority on military literature and a person who applied what he had read. Moreover, he insisted that those under his command be competent and obedient, that his officers be able not just to fight bravely but also to ensure that their men were properly cared for and trained. He sought a regiment that would march with precision, fire with accuracy, and obey without hesitation—a regiment that would prove absolutely reliable in combat. In short, Wolfe took extraordinary trouble in preparing for war because he found victory supremely satisfying, "the highest joy mankind is capable of receiving, to him who commands."

BIBLIOGRAPHY

Leach, Douglas E. *Arms of Empire*. New York: Macmillan Company, 1973.

Stacey, C. P. *Quebec, 1759: The Siege and the Battle*. New York: St. Martin's Press, 1959.

Waugh, W. T. *James Wolfe: Man and Soldier*. Montreal: L. Carrier and Company, 1928.

Whitworth, R. H. "Some Unpublished Wolfe Letters 1755–58." *Journal of the Society for Army Historical Research* 53, No. 214 (Summer 1975): 65–86.

Willson, Beckles. *The Life and Letters of James Wolfe*. London: William Heinemann, 1909.

[Wolfe, James,] *General Wolfe's Instructions to Young Officers: Also His Orders for a Battalion and an Army*. 2d ed. London: J. Millan, 1780. [Ottawa: Museum Restoration Service, 1967.]

Wright, Robert. *The Life of Major-General James Wolfe Founded on Original Documents and Illustrated by His Correspondence....* London: Chapman and Hall, 1864.

IRA D. GRUBER

WOOD, Leonard (b. Winchester, N.H., October 9, 1860; d. New York City, New York, August 7, 1927), Army officer. Wood was chief of staff of the Army, 1910–1914.

Leonard Wood was the son of a moderately successful doctor, and, desiring to emulate his father's career, young Leonard entered Harvard Medical School in 1880. He finished training three years later, but he found standard medical practice much too constricting. On an impulse he accepted a commission in the U.S. Army, and in June 1885 he entered military service as a medical officer.

He was assigned to Fort Huachuca, Arizona, where he served on several expeditions against the Apache Indians. In May 1886 he joined the famous Henry Lawton* Expedition formed to chase down the Apache chieftain Geronimo.* The capture of Geronimo and his band in September 1886 brought the participants immediate public fame, and Wood's star rose with the others. In 1898, in a decision that aroused much controversy throughout the Army, the government awarded Wood the Congressional Medal of Honor for his courageous service during the Geronimo campaign.

Despite the honors, Wood's career languished in the aftermath of the Geronimo Campaign, threatening to plunge him into the anonymous obscurity of most peacetime Army officers. Two developments saved him from this fate: one was his friendship with a young assistant Secretary of the Navy named Theodore Roosevelt,* and the other was the outbreak of war with Spain. Using Roosevelt's political connections, they were able to gain command of one of the recently created volunteer regiments, the 1st Volunteer Cavalry, popularly known as the "Rough Riders."

With Wood's administrative ability and Roosevelt's enthusiasm, the two young

commanders pulled together a melange of Eastern socialites and Western frontiersmen into a respectable military force. The regiment served well in Cuba,
taking part in Roosevelt's famous charge up San Juan Hill. Before the final
battle, Wood had already been promoted to commander of the 2d Cavalry Brigade
and, on the basis of his performance during the campaign, General William
Rufus Shafter,* commander of the V Corps, appointed him governor of Santiago
de Cuba. Thus, Wood began a career in colonial administration that would
establish him as America's leading proconsul.

Between 1900 and 1902 Wood served as military Governor of Cuba. Seeing
himself as a Progressive reformer in the midst of Old World decadence and
corruption, he enthusiastically embarked on a political, social, and economic
reform program aimed at transforming Cuba into a progressive society on the
American model. He sought to bring American-style local government to Cuba
and helped create a central government modeled on America's. Wood fostered
medical, judicial, sanitary, and educational reforms and improvements. Economically, he encouraged American investments in Cuba and pushed hard for
a reciprocal trade treaty with the United States. Throughout his governorship,
Wood was an outspoken annexationist who frankly admitted that all his reform
efforts were aimed at tying the Cubans closer to the United States.

Before leaving Cuba in 1902, Wood was promoted to brigadier general in the
Regular Army. By this time his Rough Rider comrade was president of the
United States, brightening considerably Wood's prospects for career advance-
ment. In 1904 Roosevelt appointed Wood as governor of Moro Province in the
Philippines. For the next two years he gained combat experience fighting the
Moros. Within four years, in a move that brought a storm of criticism from
within and without the Army, Roosevelt promoted Wood to major general and
appointed him commander of the Philippine Division. The promotion made Wood
very nearly the top-ranking Army officer, and in 1910, at Roosevelt's insistence,
President William Howard Taft named Wood chief of staff of the Army. In a
little more than a decade, Wood had advanced from a captain in the Medical
Department to the highest post in the U.S. Army.

When Wood arrived in Washington in 1910, the General Staff system was
less than ten years old, but it had already failed to live up to its potential. The
main reason for this failure was the persistent power of the War Department
bureaus, particularly the Adjutant General's Office. Wood was determined to
make the chief of staff the supreme military head of the Army, setting the stage
for a dramatic bureaucratic struggle with the sitting adjutant general, Fred Clayton
Ainsworth.* With the aid of Secretary of War Henry Lewis Stimson,* Wood
brought Ainsworth down by forcing the old bureaucrat into an insubordinate act
and then persuading him to resign rather than face a court-martial. Wood's victory
laid the foundation for the future strengthening of the staff system, a feat that
along with his and Stimson's administrative reforms made Wood's tenure as
chief of staff one of the most significant in the Army's history. Wood left the
General Staff in 1914 somewhat dissatisfied with his efforts. He had achieved

some successes, but to his mind they fell far short of his expectation of creating a modern American Army.

Believing that shortsighted politicians were primarily responsible for this failure, he decided to take the military issue to the America people. With the outbreak of war in Europe providing him with a sense of urgency, Wood became a leading advocate of peacetime preparedness. He purposefully chose the Department of the East (with headquarters in New York) for his next assignment because he wanted to exploit the mass media of the populous Northeast. Between 1914 and 1917 he supported preparedness organizations such as the National Security League, made countless speeches, and wrote articles and letters spreading the preparedness message. Moreover, he persuaded the War Department to sponsor summer officer training camps—the most famous at Plattsburgh Barracks—which he used to make civilian converts to the preparedness cause.

In this frenetic effort, Wood collided head-on with President Woodrow Wilson and his administration, which had set itself squarely against preparedness. When several Republican leaders seized the issue as a means of opposing Wilson, Wood found himself in a political struggle with his commander in chief. Public clashes between an obstinate president and an equally stubborn subordinate led Wood to the brink of insubordination and a civil-military crisis. The administration, in turn, found Wood a difficult problem because he was too politically powerful to be disciplined and not insubordinate enough to be court-martialed. It finally settled on keeping him out of the war in Europe.

Wood's preparedness campaign provided him with an immense public following, and after the war he set his sights on the Republican nomination for the presidency. Publicly declaring himself a candidate in January 1920, Wood immediately surged to the front of the other candidates, but he arrived at the convention without a majority of the delegates in his camp. The stalemate at the convention was finally broken on the tenth ballot when the convention nominated Warren G. Harding.

Although embittered by his defeat, Wood supported Harding in his successful campaign in 1920, hoping a victorious Harding would appoint him secretary of war. The new president instead offered Wood the governorship of the Philippines. At first, Wood rather indignantly turned down the offer, but Harding persuaded him to head an investigation of American rule in the islands, and after spending several weeks in the Philippines, the old general accepted Harding's offer for the position of governor general.

Wood died in office in 1927. A head injury incurred while he was governor of Santiago had caused a tumor growth, and two operations had failed to remove it. A third operation in August 1927 proved fatal. Wood lost consciousness on the operating table, hemorrhaged, and died.

In two important ways Leonard Wood was a pivotal figure in American military history. First, he played a critical role in the development of America's modern professional army. He was greatly influenced by the Progressives' search for an

1212   WOOL, JOHN ELLIS

orderly, efficient, rational society. With this background and with a personal will to action, Wood came to the office of the chief of staff just as an earlier promising professional development—the General Staff reform of 1903—was languishing. His victory in the struggle for supremacy of the chief of staff over the War Department bureaus may well have saved the General Staff system for the role it was to play in directing two world wars.

Second, Wood saved the military establishment from suffocating in "Uptonian pessimism." Influenced by the writings of General Emory Upton,* most Regular Army officers had come to distrust America's citizen-army tradition and yet were convinced (correctly) that the nation would not support a large peacetime army. Wood rejected this dilemma and, instead, attempted to revive the democratic theory of military service. Through the "Plattsburgh Idea," and through an extraordinary proselytizing effort just prior to American intervention in World War I, Wood sought to convert the American people to the idea that, along with rights, citizens had military obligations. The success of his efforts can be measured by the nation's peaceful acquiescence to military conscription during World War I and by the fact that it successfully fought the war as Wood had said it would: with a speedily trained citizen-army.

These achievements were somewhat overshadowed by Wood's aggressive manner, his excessive ambition, and a self-righteousness that made him intolerant of opposing opinions. These personality flaws probably prevented Wood from achieving true greatness.

BIBLIOGRAPHY

Hagedorn, Hermann. *Leonard Wood: A Biography*. 2 vols. New York: Harper, 1931.
Lane, Jack C. *Armed Progressive: Leonard Wood*. San Rafael, Calif.: Presidio Press, 1978.
Millis, Walter. *Arms and Men: A Study in American Military History*. New York: Putnam, 1956.
Weigley, Russell. *History of the United States Army*. New York: Macmillan Company, 1967.
———. *Towards an American Army: Military Thought from Washington to Marshall*. New York: Columbia University Press, 1962.

JACK C. LANE

WOOL, John Ellis (b. Newburgh, N.Y., February 29, 1784; d. Troy, N.Y., November 10, 1869), inspector general; veteran of War of 1812, Mexican War, and Civil War.

John E. Wool was born in Newburgh, New York, shortly after George Washington's* army disbanded there. The son of a heelmaker, he spent his early childhood in New York City, and at his father's death went to live on his grandfather's farm near Troy. Apprenticed to a Troy innkeeper, Wool constantly sought to advance in the world. He opened a store, studied law briefly, ran for public office, and joined the local militia in 1807, serving as adjutant and quartermaster.

At the outbreak of war in 1812, Wool was commissioned a captain (April 14) in the new 13th Infantry Regiment. He raised a company in the Troy-Albany area, joined the American forces on the Niagara frontier, and won laurels in the Battle of Queenstown. There on September 13 he crossed the river with Colonel Solomon Van Rensselaer's forces, and although wounded led the assault that drove the British from Queenstown Heights. Promoted to major, Wool served as a staff officer at Fort George and then was transferred to the 29th Infantry at Plattsburgh, New York. He accompanied Wade Hampton's* army on its march west along the Chateaugay River to join General James Wilkinson's* expedition descending the St. Lawrence to capture Montreal. After this movement proved a fiasco, Wool spent January-February of 1814 at Plattsburgh as an aide to Wilkinson, and participated in the general's abortive thrust at La Colle's Mill in March. When a large British army marched on Plattsburgh in August, Wool with a small force of regulars, an artillery piece, and several hundred militia momentarily stalled the British advance, giving Alexander Macomb* time to complete his fortifications. The small American army held off the enemy until an American victory on neighboring Lake Champlain prompted British withdrawal. For his bravery Wool was brevetted a lieutenant colonel.

In 1815 Wool was retained in the peacetime army as a major in the 6th Infantry. The following year, however, he secured the position of inspector general (with colonel's pay and privileges) in General Jacob Jennings Brown's* newly created Northern Division, an area extending from Maine west to Wisconsin Territory and north of the Ohio. During 1816–1821 Wool regularly inspected the five departments within the division. Upon the reorganization of the Army in 1821, he became one of two inspectors general of the Army. Five years later (April 29, 1826) he was awarded the brevet of brigadier general for ten years in grade (as acting colonel).

As an inspector general Wool focused his attention on a variety of military problems. Greatly concerned over antiquated weaponry, he promoted the creation of an ordnance department and urged the acquisition of modern artillery. In 1832, Wool was sent to Europe to purchase cannon and carriages. While there he watched French artillery maneuvers on the Rhine, observed the siege of Antwerp, and visited the British artillery school at Woolwich. He failed, however, to acquire models of new weapons.

Wool frequently received special assignments. He mediated a strike at the government arsenal at Springfield in 1833, directed operations in Tennessee and Georgia in 1836–1837 to round up the Cherokees for removal west, and in 1837–1838 blocked gun running to Canadian patriots from the New York-Vermont .ontier. He then headed a team that reconnoitered the disputed Maine boundary and selected sites for military installations there. In 1841 Wool was promoted to regular brigadier general (June 25) and succeded Winfield Scott* as commander of the Eastern Department.

With the declaration of war on Mexico in May 1846, the War Department dispatched Wool to the Ohio Valley to muster, equip, and forward ten thousand volunteers to Zachary Taylor's* army in Texas. In September he marched from San Antonio with an expedition of regulars and volunteers, bound for Chihuahua, eventually joining Taylor at Saltillo in January 1847. Wool selected the battlefield at nearby Buena Vista for Taylor's five thousand men to face Santa Anna's twenty thousand. Through Wool's energetic maneuvering of regiments and artillery pieces on February 22–23, Taylor repulsed repeated Mexican assaults. At Taylor's departure for the states, Wool commanded the occupation forces in northern Mexico from 1847 to 1848. For his wartime services, he was brevetted a major general and received swords from Congress, the state of New York, and the city of Troy. He resumed command of the Eastern Department in 1848.

In 1854 Wool was sent to California to upgrade the garrisons there, halt filibustering activities, and quell Indian hostilities within the Division of the Pacific. He battled with Secretary of War Jefferson Davis* over military policies, blocked William Walker's attempt to recruit troops to invade Sonora, and shuttled troops to Oregon and Washington to neutralize irresponsible volunteer campaigns against local Indian tribes. His order closing eastern Washington to settlement created an uproar. Early in 1857 he was transferred back to his old command in the East.

Although seventy-seven years old in 1861, Wool played a critical role in the early days of the Civil War. When communications with Washington, D.C., were disrupted in April, he authorized state governors from Maine to Illinois to seize government arsenals, and he chartered vessels to ship troops from New York City to the national capital. Demanding an active command, Wool was sent in August to Fortress Monroe, Virginia, a strategic installation on the Confederate frontier. There he supervised a staff that handled mail and interrogated persons passing through the lines. Wool also endeavored to create jobs for black refugees and, early in 1862, clashed with George Brinton McClellan* over troop assignments. With naval support he captured Confederate Norfolk in May and recieved a promotion to regular major general (May 15). Imposing harsh policies on Norfolk, Wool was quickly transferred to Baltimore to head the Middle Department. There he tried to stamp out secessionism and at Robert Edward Lee's* invasion of Maryland in the fall, feverishly shuttled regiments by rail to intercept the Rebel Army. Assigned to the newly created Department of New York and New England in December, Wool's last duty involved suppressing the New York draft riots in July 1863.

Retired from service on August 1, he returned to his home in Troy. His last major public appearance was as speaker at the Soldiers and Sailors' Convention at Cleveland in September 1866.

John E. Wool played a distinguished role in three major wars. At Queenstown and Plattsburgh, at Buena Vista, and at Norfolk, he commanded troops that brought valor to American arms. He demanded much from his men, but no more than he demanded of himself. In army circles Wool was regarded as a good organizer, an effective disciplinarian, and a resolute commander. Mexican War

volunteers labeled him a sour-faced little martinet—inflexible and nitpicking—
and unfortunately, this image has survived in the works of many military historians.

Wool's long career clearly mirrored the development of the Army. As an
inspector general, he took an active interest in promoting improvements in both
the personnel and materiel branches of the military. His work in reforming and
modernizing the artillery arm was particularly valuable. Wool also was outspoken
on staff changes, frontier policies, and treatment of the Indian.

Wool ranked second to Winfield Scott in performing delicate assignments. As
an inspector he early learned the value of tact in dealing with departmental and
garrison commanders, and he applied this lesson when called on to round up
the Cherokees for removal, to restrain New Yorkers from aiding Canadian patriots, to curb filibustering in California, and to command Fortress Monroe.

Wool's career also reflected the role of politics in the Army—and of the Army
in politics. As a young officer he cultivated ties with state and national politicians,
ties that later proved critical in promotions, assignments, and courts of inquiry.
Wool's name also was prominently mentioned for the governorship of New York
in 1850 and for a favorite son nomination for president at the Democratic National
Convention in 1852. Perhaps his most active political role was in helping swing
New York for Andrew Jackson* in 1832. Even in retirement he regularly commented on political issues in newspaper articles.

An able commander, a dedicated patriot, and a public-spirited citizen, John
E. Wool by word and deed left an indelible mark in the military annals of the
early republic.

BIBLIOGRAPHY

Bauer, K. Jack. *The Mexican War, 1846-1848*. New York: Macmillan Company, 1974.
Harper's Encyclopedia of United States History. Vol. 10. New York: Harper and Brothers,
     Publishers, 1901.
Hinton, Harwood P. "The Military Career of John Ellis Wool, 1812–1863." Unpublished
     Ph.D. dissertation, University of Wisconsin, 1960.

                                                              HARWOOD P. HINTON

WORDEN, John Lorimer (b. Westchester County, N.Y., March 12, 1818;
d. Washington, D.C., October 18, 1897), naval officer. Worden commanded
the USS *Monitor* during her engagement with the CSS *Virginia* (ex-USS
Merrimac).

On January 10, 1834, Worden—at the age of fifteen—was appointed a mid-
shipman and served in the 18-gun sloop-of-war *Erie* for three years off the
Atlantic coast of South America with the Brazil Squadron. Then, following a
cruise to the Mediterranean in the 18-gun sloop *Cyane*, Worden studied in the
Philadelphia Naval School and became a passed midshipman on July 16, 1840.
The next years were spent first in the Pacific Squadron and then in Washington,
D.C., serving at the Naval Observatory from 1844 to 1846. During the Mexican
War, Worden served on the storeship *Southampton* which supplied the warships

on the West Coast. After that conflict ended, he returned to the East in the 74-gun ship-of-the-line *Ohio*. During 1846 Worden was promoted to master and later advanced to lieutenant. During the 1850s the youthful naval officer served in the Mediterranean again on board the frigate *Cumberland*, completed a second two-year tour at the Naval Observatory, and finally took the position of first lieutenant at the New York Navy Yard. He was stationed in Washington just before the outbreak of the Civil War.

On April 7, 1861, Lieutenant Worden was sent to Pensacola, Florida, with secret orders—memorized and then destroyed—to the squadron there for reinforcement and defense of Fort Pickens. Worden was not to find the results of his courageous trip very satisfying. While returning north, he was arrested near Montgomery, Alabama, and was held prisoner there until exchanged some seven months later.

When Worden was released, he was in poor health, and a few months of recuperation were necessary. In January 1862, Worden was ordered to Greenspoint, Long Island, for duty as the prospective commanding officer of the innovative turreted ironclad, *Monitor*, which was under construction there. In the following weeks he supervised the completion of the unique vessel—which was ridiculed by wags as looking like "a tin can on a shingle"—and placed her in commission on February 25, 1862.

Early in March 1862 Worden began the ship's maiden voyage down the coast toward Hampton Roads, Virginia. This passage was fraught with near disasters caused by leaks, foul air, faulty steering gear, and other defects always found in experimental vessels. Worden later commented that this treacherous trip was as dangerous as the subsequent battle.

Upon arriving at Hampton Roads on the night of March 8, 1862, the crew of the *Monitor* prepared to do battle with the CSS *Virginia*, the former USS *Merrimack*. The *Virginia* had been constructed out of the *Merrimack*'s scuttled hull and machinery, and had been sheathed with iron casemate armor between bow and stern. Its deck was only slightly above the waterline; as a result, to onlookers the *Virginia* resembled "a half-submerged crocodile." The previous day, this Confederate ironclad had successfully rammed and sunk the U.S. frigate *Cumberland* and then, with furnace-heated shot, had set the frigate *Congress* ablaze in an attempt to break the Union naval blockade of Hampton Roads. Approaching darkness, however, prompted the *Virginia*'s wounded commanding officer, Flag Officer Franklin Buchanan,* to withdraw to safety for the night and then return to Hampton Roads the next day to complete the task.

At dawn the following morning, March 9, 1862, the Confederates caught their first glimpse of the *Monitor*. Several hours later the battle began, and, for the next two hours, the *Monitor* outmaneuvered her opponent. Neither ship, however, inflicted any significant damage on the other. The *Monitor* withdrew to restock her ammunition, and, when the fighting resumed, the *Virginia* employed a new tactic. She concentrated her fire on the pilothouse, and a shot struck the sighthole of the *Monitor* and injured Worden. He presented a ghastly sight as the blood gushed from his face, and he was temporarily blinded by powder and chips of iron that had been driven into his eyes. Worden turned over command of the ship to his executive officer, Lieutenant Dana Greene, who ably guided the vessel through the rest of the battle, which ended in a standoff. Worden had to be taken to Washington to recover from his wounds.

Although the naval encounter between the two ironclads ended in a draw, the North did not have to worry anymore about the *Virginia*'s threat. On May 1, 1862, after Norfolk had been evacuated, the Confederates were forced to destroy the *Virginia*—which could not retire up the shallow James River to safety at Richmond—lest she fall into enemy hands. The *Monitor*, too, came to an untimely demise when she was lost in a storm off Cape Hatteras on December 31, 1862. The naval battle between the ironclads initiated a new era of maritime warfare. The *Monitor* introduced a novel concept to the art of ship design with her revolving turret, an idea that dominated naval combat until superseded by naval airplanes during World War II and rockets in its aftermath.

Worden's courageous and resolute conduct won him national recognition. Congress gave him a special vote of thanks and he was promoted to commander on July 16, 1862, and to captain on February 3, 1863. The esteem felt for Worden reached even to the White House. On March 10, 1862, President Abraham Lincoln* was informed that Lieutenant John Worden had just arrived in Washington by ship, was badly wounded and resting at a friend's home. Lincoln hurried to the house and found the naval officer with his face and eyes swathed in bandages. Worden said: "Mr. President, you do me great honor by this visit." Lincoln was silent for a moment and then replied: "Sir, I am the one who is honored."

After Worden had recovered sufficiently from his wounds, he received orders to command the new *Passaic*-class monitor, *Montawk*. Early in 1863 he led his ship in the bombardment of Fort McAllister, Georgia, and, under the guns of this fort, destroyed with five accurate shots the blockade runner *Rattlesnake*, the former Confederate cruiser *Nashville*. For the rest of the war, Captain Worden was stationed in New York assisting in the construction of ironclads.

Worden was promoted to commodore on May 26, 1868, and the following year he became the superintendent of the Naval Academy. He succeeded the dynamic Admiral David Dixon Porter* in this position. During his tenure of five years, Worden continued the reforms at the Academy which Porter had begun, but otherwise conducted a conservative administration. While serving as superintendent, he attained his final rank of rear admiral on November 20, 1872. One of Worden's noteworthy and lasting contributions during his years at Annapolis was the creation of the U.S. Naval Institute—of which he was president in 1874—which ever since has served the naval community in the United States as a clearinghouse of professional information and a protector of American naval tradition.

From 1875 to 1877 Worden commanded the European Squadron. He then served as a member and later as president on both the Examining and Retiring Boards until his voluntary retirement on December 23, 1886.

Besides his role as the commanding officer of the *Monitor* during her historic action with the *Virginia*, Worden's greatest contribution to the Navy was his steadfast devotion to duty and his Christian sense of justice and mercy. He disciplined transgressors when necessary but always tempered his rule with compassion. Worden epitomized the U.S. naval officer at the highest level of leadership and also evoked feelings of affection and obedience from the men who served under him. This fortunate combination of attributes places Worden in a select group of military leaders who were able to command both respect and affection from their subordinates.

Worden was not an innovator. During his time as superintendent of the Naval Academy, he continued Porter's efforts to reinvigorate the school but initiated no new programs of his own. During these years, however, the hazing problem became acute, and, at the end of his term of office, an antihazing bill was enacted in June 1874. This law made every form and degree of hazing a court-martial offense.

Throughout his career John Worden embodied the attributes of the "Old Navy." He was perfectly contented to perform his duty and to carry out his orders to the best of his ability, never questioning procedure or seeking new roads of glory.

BIBLIOGRAPHY

Davis, William C. *Duel Between the First Ironclads*. Garden City, N.Y.: Doubleday and Company, 1975.

Greene, S. Dana. "In the *Monitor* Turret." In *Battles and Leaders of the Civil War*. Edited by Roy P. Nichols. 4 vols. (Vol. 1, pp. 719–29). New York: Thomas Yoseloff, 1956.

Jones, Virgil C. *The Civil War at Sea*. Vols. 1 and 2. New York: Holt, Rinehart and Winston, 1960, 1961.

Worden, John L. *The Monitor and the Merrimack*. New York: Harper and Brothers, 1912.

JAMES L. MOONEY

Y

YORK, Alvin Cullum (b. Pall Mall, Tenn., December 13, 1887; d. Nashville, Tenn., September 2, 1964), combat infantryman. York performed a spectacular feat of individual heroism during World War I.

Alvin C. York was born in the Cumberland Mountains of Tennessee not far from the Kentucky line. His parents had little money but eleven children, so the boy began working on the family farm before he was six. Schools in the region were poor, and with the demands of providing for such a large household, York received only about three years of formal education. Instead, he learned farming and blacksmithing from his father and, since hunting was still important for supplying food, became an excellent shot with rifle and pistol.

As a young man, York was caught up in the usual vices of his isolated homeland—drinking, gambling, and brawling—but a religious experience in 1915 changed the course of his life and made him a devout fundamentalist Christian. He became an elder in the Church of Christ in Christian Union, a small sect that imposed strict discipline on its members. Because the church was opposed to violence, when the United States entered World War I in 1917 York requested deferment as a conscientious objector. His numerous appeals were denied, however, and he was drafted in November 1917.

Throughout his training period, York was torn between his sincere religious convictions and the call of patriotism. Unable to reconcile the two, he finally took his dilemma to his commanding officer who tried to use the Bible to show York that Christianity approved the use of force in a just cause. After a short leave to think things over, York returned to camp convinced that America was fighting God's battle in the Great War and that his Christian duty demanded he take up arms. York's faith and his patriotism now became mutually reinforcing drives that transformed him into a soldier of the Lord.

York sailed for France with the 82d Division on May 1918. His outfit was given frontline experience during the summer of that year and in the fall played a small part in the American reduction of the St. Mihiel salient. He became a corporal on the eve of the push into the Argonne Forest where his shootout with a German machine gun battalion won him nationwide acclaim. During operations on October 8, York's unit was pinned down by hostile fire. York and sixteen other men crept off to get behind the machine guns hitting them from the left. Moving cautiously, the small party surprised a German battalion headquarters at breakfast and captured it, but almost immediately the Americans found themselves under fire from machine gun emplacements on a hill some twenty-five yards ahead. Nine Americans were killed or wounded in the initial burst, and all the others took cover except York who was positioned close to the prisoners. Because of his proximity to their comrades, the German gunners had to raise their heads to aim at him; thus, the Tennessee mountaineer sat in the mud and picked them off. When the Germans at last realized they were fighting only one man, they decided to rush him. Reasoning that York was firing from a five-round clip, six Germans charged down the hill, but York had kept his .45 pistol dangling from one finger and shot all six of them starting with the man furthest away, a trick he said he learned hunting wild turkeys in Tennessee. With over twenty of his men dead and his pistol empty from his own attempts to kill York, the battalion commander then offered to surrender the gunners. As they returned to American lines, York forced the major to order other machine gunners they passed to surrender also. In the end he was credited with killing twenty-five Germans, capturing 132, and silencing thirty-five machine guns. York himself was unscratched. For the feat that Allied Commander Marshal Ferdinand Foch called "the greatest thing accomplished by any private soldier of all the armies of Europe," York was promoted to sergeant and given the Congressional Medal of Honor and the *Croix de Guerre*.

An article in the *Saturday Evening Post* made York a national figure, and he returned home to a tremendous welcome in New York City as well as in Tennessee. He was offered between a quarter and a half a million dollars in show business contracts and product endorsements, but he refused everything saying, "Uncle Sam's uniform" was not for sale. Instead, York returned to his native Fentress County to resume the life the war had interrupted, although Rotary Clubs of Tennessee did raise the money to buy him four hundred acres of farmland.

After the war, York gave much of his time to community service. His concern for education, especially vocational education, prompted him to undertake repeated lecture tours to raise money to build what became the York Institute, a large modern high school that still serves the people of Fentress County. York also worked to bring better roads to the area and, in the 1940s, became involved in oil drilling in the Cumberland Mountains. On the eve of World War II he finally capitulated to persistent requests that he permit a motion picture to be made of his life when friends convinced him that his story would inspire patriotism in those difficult days. York also wanted to build an interdenominational Bible school for the mountains and realized the income from the film would make its construction possible. *Sergeant York* was a great success and won an Academy Award for its star, Gary Cooper.

York's last years were difficult ones. A 1954 stroke left the old hunter bed-ridden, while the $150,000 he made from the film got him into trouble with the Internal Revenue Service. Inexperienced in handling such sums and plagued by bad advice, York ended up with a tax bill plus interest of $172,423.10 before the IRS agreed to settle for $25,000 in 1961. Speaker of the House Sam Rayburn led a drive to raise the money by popular subscription, and industrialist S. Halleck du Pont created a trust fund to give York an income for the rest of his life. He died in Veterans Hospital in Nashville in 1964.

The real importance of Sergeant York lies in his role as a symbol. In the context of 1919 when he first became prominent, he was a reassuring figure. To a nation returning from a frightening war fought with mass armies and destructive machinery, his achievement reaffirmed the value of the individual in the industrial age. This perception was enhanced by the fact that York was a "citizen-soldier" rather than a professional soldier who literally returned to the plow when the fight ended. At a time when many Americans feared foreigners and radical ideas, York seemed a genuine pioneer restored to life to uphold the virtues of home, patriotism, and piety. In a broader sense, York represented a set of values and a life-style that Americans continued to honor even as they rejected them. He was a farmer at a time when a majority of Americans lived in urban areas. While American society generally was becoming more materialistic, York showed his indifference to material concerns by rejecting several hundred thousand dollars in commercial offers. Briefly, York represented not what Americans were, but what they wanted to think they were. As a result, he won a special place in the American imagination that lingered long after "the war to end all wars" had become an empty phrase.

BIBLIOGRAPHY

Cowan, Sam. *Sergeant York and His People*. New York: Funk and Wagnalls, 1922.

Skeyhill, Thomas. *Sergeant York: Last of the Long Hunters*. Chicago, Philadelphia, and Toronto: John C. Winston Company, 1930.

Stallings, Laurence. *The Doughboys: The Story of the AEF, 1917–1918*. New York, Evanston, and London: Harper and Row, 1963.

York, Alvin. *Sergeant York: His Own Story*. Edited by Thomas Skeyhill. New York: Doubleday, 1928.

DAVID LEE

YOUNG, Samuel Baldwin Marks (b. Forest Grove, Pa., January 9, 1840; d. Helena, Mont., September 1, 1924), combat soldier and military administrator. Young was the last commanding general and the first chief of staff of the U.S. Army.

Young enlisted as a private in Company K, 12th Pennsylvania Infantry, a ninety-day regiment, on April 25, 1861, and served until the regiment was mustered out of service. He raised a company of what became the 4th Pennsylvania Cavalry and received a commission as captain to date from September 6, 1861. After service in the fortifications of Washington, the regiment joined the division of Brigadier General George A. McCall and served through the Peninsula Campaign in the V Army Corps. At Antietam Young distinguished himself in command of a squadron and was promoted to major on September 20, 1862.

Courageous, possessed of good judgment, and aggressive, he had all the attributes required of a young cavalry officer. Forty years later another member of the regiment still remembered Young "swinging a sabre at Brandy Station, his other arm in a sling." At Sulphur Springs, Virginia, in the fall of 1863 he was wounded again; a shattered right arm kept him convalescing in Pittsburgh for several months. He received promotions to lieutenant colonel and colonel in May and June 1864. Returning to duty at the time Lieutenant General Jubal Anderson Early* menaced Washington, he took command of a provisional brigade of dismounted cavalry and one-hundred-day infantry regiments attached to Major General George Crook's* VIII Army Corps. Young commanded his brigade in the Union defeat at Kernstown where he was wounded seriously once again.

He eventually rejoined his regiment and at Hatcher's Run, during the battles around Petersburg, led the 4th Pennsylvania in an unsupported charge on the infantry division of Brigadier General John Pegram. The attack routed the Confederates and killed Pegram. At Farmville, Virginia, two days before Robert Edward Lee's* surrender, a Confederate counterattack stampeded the cavalry brigade of Brigadier General J. Irving Gregg of which the 4th Pennsylvania formed a part. Gregg was captured, but Young's gallant efforts to rally the panicked troopers attracted the attention of his division commander, George Crook, who gave Young command of the brigade. In the cavalry action at Appomattox Court House, Young captured the last battle flags lost by the Army of Northern Virginia prior to its surrender. He continued in command of the brigade until mustered out of service on July 1, 1865.

The war had taken Young out of civil life and given him the opportunity to successfully command successively larger units. After a short time he decided he liked soldiering. As early as 1863 he attempted to secure a commission in the Regular Army. He tried once again at the end of the war, and by then he enjoyed the patronage of Crook and Gregg as well as the congressmen from western Pennsylvania. Appointed a second lieutenant in the 12th Infantry on May 11, 1866, Young took up station with his company on Reconstruction duty at Fredericksburg, Virginia. Gregg helped Young obtain promotion to captain on July 28, 1866, in the 8th Cavalry, a new regiment which Gregg was organizing. He also recommended Young for brevets of major, lieutenant colonel, and colonel in the Regular Army and brigadier general in the volunteers, which the War Department awarded on the basis of Young's distinguished Civil War record.

During the next fifteen years, Young fought Indians in the West. He joined his troop at Fort Mohave, Arizona Territory, shortly before the outbreak of the Walapais War (1867–1868), an affair of ambushes and lightning raids characteristic of warfare in the Southwest. He achieved the Army's most notable success of the campaign when he surprised the rancheria of Scherum, one of the head men of the Walapais, in February 1868. Young did not have enough men to destroy the camp, but he administered a defeat that led to the surrender of the Indians to Colonel W. R. Price and Young the following fall.

In 1870 Young went to Chicago on recruiting duty for his regiment. The Great Fire of 1871 destroyed all his personal property. In its aftermath he served with federal forces under Lieutenant General Philip Henry Sheridan* policing the city. Rejoining his regiment, he participated in the Red River War of 1874. Three years later he commanded the cavalry, some eight troops, in Colonel Ranald Slidell Mackenzie's* campaign into Mexico. Young recalled with pride that he had ferried his entire command with pack and train across the Rio Grande without the loss of a horse or a mule. The comment typified the kind of reputation which service in the West had gained for Young—that of a good practical soldier. As Lieutenant Colonel Elwell S. Otis expressed it: ''I do not know of any officer in the army who can handle a battalion of cavalry with more skill.''

As the Army turned from the Indian Wars, Young's career reflected both the professional and social concerns of the era. In 1881 he became an instructor at the Infantry and Cavalry School, which opened that yeat at Fort Leavenworth, Kansas, under Colonel Otis. Young wrote a textbook on the care of the horse. Promoted to major in the 3d Cavalry in 1892, he commanded a squadron of cavalry in Sacramento, California, during labor disturbances in 1894. Two years later Brigadier General James W. Forsyth appointed Young to command the cavalry sent to protect Yosemite National Park from sheep herders. Young served as acting superintendent during the summer of 1896. The following year he became acting superintendent of Yellowstone National Park, where he became acquainted with Theodore Roosevelt.*

Promoted colonel of the 3d Cavalry in 1897, Young spent the winter of 1897–1898 in Washington, D.C. He concluded that war with Spain was inevitable and agreed that Theodore Roosevelt and Captain Leonard Wood,* a young medical officer who had seen service in the Apache campaigns, should raise a volunteer regiment and serve in his command. ''How particularly gratifying,'' Young later told Roosevelt, ''that it all came out even rosier than our enthusiasms had pictured it.''

Young's Civil War and frontier service and good connections with the Pennsylvania congressional delegation earned him the grade of brigadier general in the volunteers and command of the 1st Brigade of Major General Joseph Wheeler's* Cavalry Division of the V Army Corps mobilized at Tampa, Florida. In the ensuing Santiago Campaign Young was even more of a fire-eater than his division commander. Although the corps commander, Major General William Rufus Shafter,* intended to build up his logistic base before advancing inland,

Wheeler placed his division in the van contrary to instructions, and Young precipitated the first American combat of the expedition, the skirmish at Las Guasimas. His dispositions raise serious questions about his tactical skill, but the Spanish retreated. A bad case of malaria, however, prevented his active participation in the remainder of the campaign.

Promoted major general of volunteers, he commanded the reception camp for the V Corps at Montauk Point, Long Island, and then the II Army Corps. The partial demobilization of the volunteer army resulted in a reduction in rank to brigadier general. In June 1899 he sailed for the Philippines where he commanded successively the 3d and Provisional Brigades of the 1st Division, VIII Army Corps. Young thought that the corps commander, his old friend Otis, was too hesitant and urged that his division commander, Major General Henry Ware Lawton,* be given control of all tactical operations in the islands. The main Philippine army and the insurgent government headed by Emilio Aguinaldo occupied a position midway up the Lingayen Valley. Young, with Lawton's enthusiastic support, proposed to turn the Filipino left flank and cut them off from the sanctuary of the mountains of northern Luzon. Otis accepted the plan in part, and, although he did not make all the logistic arrangements which Young and Lawton deemed necessary, he combined it with an amphibious assault in Lingayen Gulf in the insurgent rear.

On October 12, 1899, the Provisional Brigade began its advance. Lawton devoted all his energies to keeping Young's command supplied, but miserable weather and rugged terrain defeated his efforts. On November 6, in the midst of monsoon rains, Young abandoned his supply lines. The gamble succeeded; only bad luck prevented him from intercepting the fleeing Aguinaldo. Young pursued with a small column, bringing northwestern Luzon under nominal American control. The successful conclusion of this, the most impressive feat of arms of the Insurrection, brought Young only bitterness and frustration. Otis believed that Young had exceeded his instructions, and, when Lawton was killed at San Mateo in November 1899, Otis gave command of the division to Brigadier General R. P. Hughes, Young's junior. Young also disagreed vehemently with the policy of conciliation toward the Filipinos followed by Otis and his successor, Major General Arthur MacArthur.* In his private correspondence Young referred to the natives as "child devils" and officially recommended draconian measures against the population. Very shortly thereafter, the War Department assigned him to command jointly the Departments of California and Columbia.

Beginning with Colonel Emory Upton* in 1878, professional American soldiers had periodically called for the creation of a general staff modeled after the Prussian Great General Staff. When Elihu Root* became secretary of war in 1899, he assumed the burden of correcting the deficiencies revealed by the Spanish war and accepted the need for a general staff. His proposals met vehement opposition from the commanding general, Lieutenant General Nelson Appleton Miles,* a man with political ambitions and connections. Root needed a soldier who was loyal to the Roosevelt administration and who possessed sufficient prestige to offset Miles before Congress. Young, promoted to brigadier general in the Regular Army in January 1900 and major general in 1901, satisfied the requirements.

Root appointed Young president of the War College Board, a post he held from 1902 to 1903. On August 9, 1903, he was promoted to lieutenant general and succeeded Miles to become the last commanding general of the U.S. Army. Six days later Young became the Army's first chief of staff. He reached the age for mandatory retirement in January 1904. He subsequently served once again as superintendent of Yellowstone National Park from 1907 to 1908, as president from 1909 to 1910 of a board of inquiry which confirmed President Roosevelt's dismissal from the service of 159 black enlisted men of the 24th Infantry for their alleged participation in the 1906 riot at Brownsville, Texas, and as president of the Soldier's Home, 1910 to 1920.

Young's career exemplifies that of a whole generation of Army officers. Entering the regulars as a junior officer after serving as a colonel in the volunteers during the Civil War, he spent almost seventeen years as a captain. Only at the end of his career could he reach grades that carried important responsibilities. He served less than seven years at the rank of colonel or above in the regulars.

Young had real if limited abilities as a combat soldier. He was an excellent cavalry squadron and troop commander. Most regiments on the frontier developed one or two officers upon whom the regimental commander could depend; Young filled this role in the 8th Cavalry. As a large unit commander Young exhibited excessive aggressiveness, which made him excellent in pursuit but raised questions about his ability to cope with other kinds of situations. Although in his thirties when he met Ranald S. Mackenzie, Young appears to have adopted Mackenzie as his model. Gracious and charming in the drawing rooms of the East Coast, Young was a brutally efficient suppressor of native uprisings on the colonial periphery.

Aside from his initial appointment in the regulars and the transfer to the 8th Cavalry, Young did not attempt to use political connections to advance his career. The possibilities for promotion created by the war with Spain destroyed his restraint. Then his every disappointment produced another batch of letters to the War Department from Pennsylvania politicians. His service in Cuba created a powerful patron in Roosevelt, who thought Young a "cracker jack officer." A combination of powerful friends and the fact that he was younger than Miles created the opportunity for his advancement to chief of staff, an attainment which his abilities as a combat leader, if not his achievements, made possible.

His years in Washington proved strangely anticlimactic. The War College Board which he headed did not deal with questions about the philosophy of military administration or the alternatives to existing American practices. These had been the subjects addressed by an earlier board presided over by Brigadier General William Ludlow. During Young's tenure, the War College Board considered the internal organization of the General Staff and the best method of selecting officers to serve on it. Young was an avid but narrow professional reader, restricting himself to cavalry topics. He did not bring an independent judgment to his position and appears to have leaned heavily on Brigadier General William H. Carter, the author of the General Staff legislation. Young must assume the blame, however, for allowing the board to take responsibility for a mass of minor administrative details which, bequeathed to the War Department General Staff, would hamper the function of that organization down to World War I. He served too briefly as chief of staff to make much of an impression on the institution. In fact, Young's major contribution to American history came when he fell ill after Las Guasimas. It gave Roosevelt the opportunity to lead the Rough Riders up Kettle Hill, a necessary if not sufficient condition for Roosevelt's subsequent elevation to the presidency.

BIBLIOGRAPHY

Crook, George. *General George Cook: His Autobiography*. Edited by Martin F. Schmitt. Norman: University of Oklahoma Press, 1960.

Gates, John M. *Schoolbooks and Krags: The United States Army in the Philippines, 1898–1902*. Westport, Conn.: Greenwood Press, 1973.

Sexton, William Thaddeus. *Soldiers in the Sun*. Harrisburg, Pa.: Military Service Publishing Company, 1939.

Thrapp, Dan L. *The Conquest of Apacheria*. Norman: University of Oklahoma Press, 1967.

EDGAR F. RAINES

Z

ZUMWALT, Elmo Russell, Jr. (b. San Francisco, Calif., November 29, 1920), naval officer. Zumwalt served a controversial tenure as chief of naval operations, 1970–1974.

Elmo R. Zumwalt, Jr., the son of Elmo R. Zumwalt and Frances Zumwalt, was born on November 29, 1920, in San Francisco. Both of his parents were medical doctors. The Zumwalts were of Swiss ancestry, but three generations of the family had lived in the United States when the future admiral was born. Elmo, Jr., graduated as valedictorian of the Tulare, California, High School in 1938. In anticipation of applying for one of the service academies, he attended Rutherford Preparatory School in Long Beach, California. Zumwalt was appointed to the U.S. Naval Academy in 1939, and, due to the acceleration of Academy classes to meet the needs of World War II, graduated three years later. At Annapolis, Zumwalt stood academically in the top 5 percent of his class and distinguished himself as a public speaker.

As a junior officer, Zumwalt served in Pacific Fleet destroyers and participated in several major actions, including the Battle of Surigao Straits for which he was decorated for heroism. At the end of the war, he became the prize crew commander of a captured Japanese gunboat, HIJMS *Ataka*. That ship was the first unit flying the American flag to enter Shanghai, China, since December 1941. While in that port, Zumwalt met Mouza Coutelais-du-Roche, the offspring of a White Russian mother and a French father. They were married at Shanghai in October 1945. Two sons and two daughters were born of the marriage.

In the immediate postwar years, Zumwalt served as executive officer in two destroyers, had a tour with the Naval Reserve Officers Training Corps of the University of North Carolina, and in June 1950 received his first command, the destroyer escort *Tills*. During the spring of 1951, he reported as navigator for the battleship *Wisconsin*. He later received a letter of commendation for his contributions to that ship's operations in the Korean conflict. Over the following seven years, Zumwalt attended the Naval War College, had two tours with the

Bureau of Naval Personnel, was a special assistant to the assistant secretary of the Navy for personnel and reserve forces, and commanded a destroyer.

Zumwalt's increased prominence was reflected in his selection in 1959 as the initial commandiing officer of the new frigate *Dewey*, the first vessel built in the United States from the keel up as a guided missile ship. Two years later, now in the rank of captain, he attended the National War College. There he met Paul H. Nitze, thereby beginning a long professional and personal association with this prominent leader in national security affairs. In 1962 Zumwalt served under Nitze in the Office of the Assistant Secretary of Defense for International Security Affairs. When Nitze became Secretary of the Navy in 1963, Zumwalt became his executive assistant and senior aide. At the conclusion of that tour, Zumwalt received an early promotion to flag rank.

Continuing his association with the surface navy, the new admiral's first tour was as the commander of a cruiser-destroyer flotilla. In 1966 he returned to Washington to direct the Systems Analysis Division of the Office of the Chief of Naval Operations. In that billet, Zumwalt directed broad assessments of naval weapons systems and tactics. Two years later, he became commander of the U.S. naval forces in Vietnam, with the rank of vice admiral. While in Vietnam, Zumwalt oversaw the turnover to Vietnamese forces of many functions and operations handled previously by the U.S. Navy. This "Vietnamization" coincided with the policy of the Nixon administration to encourage America's allies to assume greater responsibility for their own defense.

In the spring of 1970 Zumwalt was nominated by President Richard M. Nixon to serve as chief of naval operations. Upon assuming that post on July 1, 1970, the admiral became the youngest officer in the Navy's history to serve in that capacity.

Over the next four years, Zumwalt achieved national prominence, especially due to a series of more than 120 personal directives (known as "Z-grams") ordering many structural changes in the service's personnel system. Among these were the elimination of regulations considered to be demeaning to naval personnel, measures to demonstrate the Navy's commitment to equal opportunity for minority and female members, and the establishment of grievance procedures. A number of these departures became highly controversial due to their alleged effect on naval discipline and the integrity of the Navy's chain of command. This was especially the case following a series of racial disturbances on board naval ships in 1972 that resulted in a congressional investigation. The admiral, however, defended these measures in terms of their social equity, as well as their influence in attracting and retaining talented naval personnel during a period in which all of the military services were under popular suspicion.

Another major effort of Zumwalt as the new chief of naval operations was the modernization of a fleet that in 1970 still depended heavily upon ships built in World War II. Behind this program was the admiral's conviction that the growing Soviet Navy posed an ominous challenge to the security of the United States. In order to free funds for the building of a sufficient number of modern units to counter the Russian threat, the admiral expedited the decommissioning of older ships, a policy that combined with the post-Vietnam demobilization to reduce the number of major warships from 769 to 512 during his tenure. He also argued for a new construction policy calling for the building of numerous, relatively low-cost ships with specialized capabilities, as well as the continued production of sophisticated, nuclear-propelled, multipurpose vessels. By the end of his term, however, Zumwalt concluded that there was a continuing erosion of American naval power in relation to the capabilities of the Soviet Union. In part, this trend arose from disagreement within naval and nonnaval circles over the wisdom of building large numbers of less capable, if relatively inexpensive, ships. More important, in Zumwalt's opinion, was the failure of the Nixon administration to support increased naval expenditures.

Two years after Zumwalt retired in 1974, he published a memoir entitled *On Watch*. In this outspoken volume, the admiral vigorously defended his social program. Furthermore, he used *On Watch* to attack officials within and without the Navy who, in the admiral's estimation, had impeded the development of a fleet capable of countering the Soviet Union in a sea war.

Also in 1976, Zumwalt made an unsuccessful attempt to win a seat in the U.S. Senate from the state of Virginia as a candidate of the Democratic party. As was true of his naval leadership, Zumwalt's political platform was liberal in a social sense, while at the same time urging stronger national defense. Following the admiral's defeat at the polls, he moved to Milwaukee, Wisconsin, where he became president and chief executive officer of American Medical Buildings, Incorporated.

Elmo Zumwalt continues to be a controversial figure, and his service is too recent to allow a rounded evaluation. To his critics, he was responsible for undermining naval discipline, especially by diminishing the authority of commanding officers. On the other hand, Zumwalt's admirers view him as a bold leader who modernized naval personnel practices at a time of great social change, hence assuring that the service would attract competent officers and enlisted personnel. They point to his vigorous efforts to improve the naval balance between the United States and the Soviet Union as an example of his courage and vision.

The problems addressed by Admiral Zumwalt continue to be of great concern to the Navy. Their resolution in future years will largely determine the admiral's historical reputation.

BIBLIOGRAPHY

Korb, Lawrence J. "The Erosion of American Naval Preeminence, 1962–1978." In, *In Peace and War: Interpretations of American Naval History, 1775–1978.* Edited by Kenneth J. Hagan. Westport, Conn.: Greenwood Press, 1978.

Moritz, Charles, ed. *Current Biography Yearbook, 1971.* New York: H. W. Wilson Company, 1971.
Zumwalt, Elmo R., Jr. *On Watch: A Memoir.* New York: Quadrangle, 1976.

DEAN C. ALLARD

Chronology of American Military Developments

This chronology is intended to assist the general reader and by no means pretends to comprehensiveness. For a fuller accounting of the developments listed here, the reader's attention is invited to R. Ernest and Trevor Dupuy, *The Encyclopedia of Military History from 3500 B. C. to the Present* (New York: Harper and Row, 1970); Richard B. Morris, editor, *The Encyclopedia of American History* (New York: Harper and Row, 1971); Charles Van Doren and Robert McHenry, editors, *Webster's Guide to American History* (Springfield, Mass.: G. & C. Merriam Company, Publishers, 1971); and Bernard and Fawn Brodie, *From Crossbow to H-Bomb* (Bloomington, Ind.: Indiana University Press, 1973), works from which this chronology has been drawn. Finally, because the course of American military history has often been influenced by developments abroad, some of these are noted here in order to provide a modicum of perspective.

AMERICAN MILITARY DEVELOPMENTS	DEVELOPMENTS ABROAD
1607 Jamestown established.	
1609–14 First Powhatan uprising in Virginia.	
1613 Virginians raid Mount Desert Island, Maine, a rival French settlement.	
1614 Virginians raid Port Royal, Nova Scotia, a rival French settlement.	
	1615 Le Bourgeoys, French gun-smith, invents flintlock musket.
	1616 Thirty Years War begins in Europe.
1620–21 Founding of Plymouth colony. Peace agreed between	

AMERICAN MILITARY DEVELOPMENTS	DEVELOPMENTS ABROAD
	Governor William Bradford and Massasoit, Narragansett headman.	
1622–32	Second Powhatan uprising in Virginia.	
1635	English establish Fort Saybrook on Connecticut River.	
1637	The Pequot War in Connecticut.	
1638	First American military unit formally established in Boston: the Ancient and Honorable Artillery Company.	
1641–45	Algonquin War against Dutch and English settlements in New York.	
		1642	English Civil War begins.
1643	New England Confederation formed for common defense against Dutch, French, and Indians.	
1644–46	Third Powhatan uprising in Virginia.	
		1648	Treaty of Westphalia concludes Thirty Years War.
		1649	Execution of King Charles I of England.
		1649–60	Protectorate of Oliver Cromwell in England.
		1650s	British naval officers argue use of formal, line-of-battle tactics versus melee tactics.
		1652–54	First Anglo-Dutch War.
		1660	Restoration of King Charles II of England.
		1662–64	Second Anglo-Dutch War.
1664	English forces capture New Amsterdam (New York).	
		1672–74	Third Anglo-Dutch War.
1676	King Philip's War in New England.	
	Bacon's rebellion in Virginia.	
1687	Revolt of the Yamassee Indians in Georgia and Florida.	

AMERICAN MILITARY DEVELOPMENTS		DEVELOPMENTS ABROAD
	1688	War of the League of Augsburg begins in Europe.
1689	King William's War (War of the League of Augsburg) begins in America. French and Indian allies attack English settlements in New England. Iroquois alliance with English colonists. Leisler's Rebellion in New York.	
1690	French and Indian allies attack Schenectady, New York. English seize Port Royal, Nova Scotia, from the French.	
1691	Jacob Leisler executed in New York.	1691	British Navy adopts ''Fighting Instructions'' in order to encourage cohesive combat doctrine throughout the Fleet.
1696	English and Indian allies attack French Quebec. Treaty of Ryswick concludes King William's War in America and the War of the League of Augsburg in Europe.	
	1701	The War of Spanish Succession begins in Europe.
1702	Queen Anne's War (War of Spanish Succession) begins in America. English attack Saint Augustine, Spanish Florida.	
1704	French and Indian allies attack Deerfield, Massachusetts. English attack Port Royal.	
1706	Franco-Spanish fleet unsuccessfully attacks Charleston in the Carolinas.	
1707	English colonists attempt expedition against French Acadia.	
1708	French and Indian allies raid Haverhill, Massachusetts.	
1710	British naval force and Eng-	

AMERICAN MILITARY DEVELOPMENTS	DEVELOPMENTS ABROAD
	lish colonists attack and seize Port Royal.	
1711	Failure of English colonial campaign against Montreal.	
	Tuscarora War begins in Carolina with massacre of 150 settlers.	
1712	Carolina militia retaliates against Tuscaroras at Neuse River.	
1713	Tuscarora War ends.	
	Queen Anne's War (and War of Spanish Succession in Europe) ends with Treaty of Utrecht.	
		1739–43 War of Jenkins' Ear.
		1740s–50s Frederick the Great, King of Prussia, improves field (light) artillery.
1740	James Oglethorpe leads unsuccessful expedition against Saint Augustine.	1740 War of Austrian Succession begins in Europe.
	Combined British-colonial expedition against Cartagena, the West Indies, and Santiago, Cuba.	
1741	British attack on Santiago.	
1742	Battle of Bloody Marsh (Saint Simon's Island, Georgia) between Spanish and Oglethorpe's militia.	
1743	Oglethorpe invades Spanish Florida once more.	
1744	King George's War (War of the Austrian Succession) begins in America.	
	French attack Annapolis Royal (formerly Port Royal).	
1745	New Englanders seize the fortress at Louisbourg.	
	French and Indian allies invade New York.	
1746	French expedition against Cape Breton and Nova Scotia fails.	

AMERICAN MILITARY DEVELOPMENTS	DEVELOPMENTS ABROAD

AMERICAN MILITARY DEVELOPMENTS

1748   Treaty of Aix-la-Chapelle ends King George's War (and the War of the Austrian Succession in Europe).

1754   July. Battle of Great Meadow between Virginia militia and French Canadian militia begins the French and Indian War.

1755   June. British colonial expedition against French outposts on the Bay of Fundy, Canada.

July. General Braddock's army of British regulars and colonial militia routed by French at the Battle of the Wilderness.

August-September. British colonial expedition seizes Crown Point at Lake George, New York. British colonial expedition seizes Fort Niagara.

September. Battle of Lake George.

British War Office authorizes raising the first British regiments in America, the Royal Americans, now the King's Royal Rifle Corps.

DEVELOPMENTS ABROAD

1756–60s   Several European armies experiment with "light" infantry for skirmishing in advance of their main body of troops.

1756   August. Marquis de Montcalm begins French offensive against Forts Oswego and Ticonderoga in New York.

1757   June-September. British expedition against the Fortress of Louisbourg fails.

1756   Britain formally enters the Seven Years' War.

AMERICAN MILITARY DEVELOPMENTS	DEVELOPMENTS ABROAD

August. French and Indians besiege and massacre British garrison at Fort William Henry.

1758   May-July. French surrender Louisbourg to British under Amherst and Wolfe.

July. Battle of Ticonderoga.

July-November. British expedition against Fort Duquesne.

August. British take Fort Frontenac, Lake Ontario.

1759   June-July. British campaigns along the Mohawk River to Niagara and against Ticonderoga. General Wolfe's campaign against Quebec begins in June.

September. Battle of the Plains of Abraham outside Quebec.

1760   April. French counterattack against Quebec fails.

September. British campaign against Montreal. French surrender Canada to the British.

1763   February. Treaty of Paris concludes French and Indian War (and in Europe, the Seven Years' War).

May-November. Revolt of Pontiac against British western outposts.

August. Battle of Bloody Ridge breaks Pontiac's uprising. Fort Pitt, besieged by Indians, is relieved.

1765   June (?). Formation of the Sons of Liberty in British colonies to combat British enforcement of the Stamp Act.

1759   In France Duke de Broglie combines infantry and artillery regiments into divisions.

1765   Jean Baptiste de Gribeauval, French officer, experiments with field artillery, improving upon Frederick the Great's innovations.

AMERICAN MILITARY DEVELOPMENTS	DEVELOPMENTS ABROAD

AMERICAN MILITARY DEVELOPMENTS

1768   October. Two regiments of
British troops posted to
Boston to enforce public
order.

1770   January. Battle of Golden Hill
in New York between
Sons of Liberty and Brit-
ish regulars.
Boston Massacre.

1771   January-June. War of the
Regulators in North
Carolina.
May. Battle of Alamance,
North Carolina.

1773   December. Boston Tea Party.

1774   September-October. Ist Conti-
nental Congress calls for
formation of American
militia units.
October. "Minute Men"
formed in Massachusetts.
Battle of Point Pleasant,
Virginia.
September-October. Lord
Dunmore's War (Shaw-
nee uprising in western
Virginia).

1775   April. Battles of Lexington
and Concord begin
American Revolution.
April. Siege of Boston by colonial militia begins.
May. Americans seize Fort
Ticonderoga.
June. 2d Continental Congress
appoints George Wash-
ington commander of the
Continental Army. Battle
of Bunker Hill.
July. Washington assumes
command of the Conti-
nental Army.
August-November. American
expedition against Mon-
treal fails.

AMERICAN MILITARY DEVELOPMENTS	DEVELOPMENTS ABROAD
November 10. Congress authorizes formation of the Continental Marines (forerunners of the U.S. Marine Corps).	
December. Benedict Arnold's expedition against Quebec fails.	
1776 February. American Commodore Esek Hopkins' raid on the Bahamas. Battle of Moores Creek Bridge, North Carolina.	
March. Congress authorizes naval privateering. British troops evacuate Boston.	
June. Battle of Trois Rivieres, Canada.	
June-July. Americans retreat from Canada.	
July. American Declaration of Independence. France and Spain pledge assistance to Americans.	
August. Battle of Long Island.	
September. Americans use first submarine, "The American Turtle," in warfare. Americans retreat from New York. Battle of Harlem Heights.	
October. Battle of White Plains. Battle of Valcour Island on Lake Champlain, New York.	
November. British capture Forts Washington and Lee.	
November-December. Americans retreat through New Jersey.	
December. Battle of Morristown. Battle of Trenton.	
1777 January. Battle of Princeton.	

AMERICAN MILITARY DEVELOPMENTS   **DEVELOPMENTS ABROAD**

July. British seize Fort
Ticonderoga.

August. Battle of Oriskany,
New York. Battle of
Bennington, Vermont.

September. Battle of Freeman's Farm, New York.
Battle of the Brandywine,
Pennsylvania. British
take Philadelphia.

October. Battle of Bemis
Heights. British force un-
der General Burgoyne
surrenders at Saratoga,
New York. Battle of
Germantown,
Pennsylvania.

Winter of 1777–78. Continental Army bivouacs at
Valley Forge.

1778   February. Franco-American
Alliance. Baron von
Steuben begins Prussian-
style training in the Continental Army.

April-May. John Paul Jones
raids British waters in
Ranger.

June. France and England declare war. British troops
evacuate Philadelphia for
New York. Battle of
Monmouth, New Jersey.

July. French fleet under
Comte d'Estaing arrives
in American waters.

August. Franco-American expedition against Newport,
Rhode Island, fails.

December. British forces capture Savannah, Georgia.

1779   January. British forces seize
Augusta, Georgia.

February. Battle of Port
Royal, South Carolina.

AMERICAN MILITARY DEVELOPMENTS	DEVELOPMENTS ABROAD

Battle of Kettle Creek,
South Carolina.

March. Battle of Briar Creek,
Georgia.

June. Battle of Stono Ferry,
Georgia.

September. John Paul Jones'
Bonhomme Richard de-
feats Britain's HMS
Serapis.

September-October. Franco-
American siege of
Savannah.

December. British force under
General Clinton leaves
New York for Southern
Campaign.

1780   Treason of General Benedict
Arnold.

February-May. British successfully besiege
Charleston.

May-August. Guerrilla warfare in South Carolina.

July. French forces under
General Rochambeau ar-
rive at Newport, Rhode
Island.

August. Battle of Camden,
South Carolina.

October. Battle of King's
Mountain, South
Carolina.

1781   January. Battle of the Cow-
pens, South Carolina.

January-February. American
retreat northward to the
Dan River, North
Carolina.

March. Battle of Guilford
Courthouse, North Caro-
lina. First Battle of the
Virginia Capes between
French and British fleets.

May. Captain John Barry's
Alliance raiding in the

AMERICAN MILITARY DEVELOPMENTS		DEVELOPMENTS ABROAD
	North Atlantic. British General Cornwallis arrives in Virginia.	
	May-June. Americans besiege Fort Ninety-Six in South Carolina.	
	August. French Admiral de Grasse sails from the West Indies for American waters. Washington begins to move the Continental Army toward Virginia.	
	September. Second Battle of the Virginia Capes. Battle of Eutaw Springs, South Carolina.	
	September-October. Franco-American army besieges British at Yorktown, Virginia.	
	October. General Cornwallis surrenders the British forces at Yorktown.	
1782		February-September. Anglo-French naval actions off the coast of India.
		April. Naval battle of Saints, West Indies.
1783	April 15. Treaty of Paris ratified by Congress, concluding the American Revolution.	
	November. British forces under Clinton evacuate New York City.	
1784		British Army Lieutenant Henry Shrapnel invents the exploding artillery shell.
1786	August-February. Shays' Rebellion in Massachusetts.	
1789	August. Congress creates the War Department.	
1789		French Revolution begins with the storming of the Bastille in Paris.

AMERICAN MILITARY DEVELOPMENTS	DEVELOPMENTS ABROAD
September. Henry Knox named first secretary of war.	
1790 Maumee Indian uprising in the American Northwest Territories.	
October. Indians defeat General Harmar's expeditionary column in the Northwest Territory.	
	1790s British Admiral Horatio Nelson adopts "melee" naval tactics.
1791 November. Indians defeat General St. Clair's expeditionary column in the Northwest Territory.	
1792 Congress passes the Militia Act.	1792 War of the First Coalition against Revolutionary France.
Congress creates the Legion of the United States with General Anthony Wayne as commander.	
1794 May. Congress passes the Navy Act.	1794 French Minister of War Lazare Carnot adds cavalry to French Army divisional organizations.
July-November. Whiskey Rebellion in Pennsylvania.	
August. Battle of Fallen Timbers breaks Indian uprising in the Northwest Territory.	
1795 Treaty of Greenville concludes hostilities in the Northwest Territory.	1795 Napoleon Bonaparte takes command of French Army in Italy.
1797 First of the "Humphreys Frigates" launched.	
1798 "Quasi-War" with France.	1798–1800 War of the Second Coalition against Revolutionary France.
Eli Whitney begins manufacturing muskets using interchangeable parts at his works in New Haven, Connecticut.	
May. Congress establishes Navy Department.	

AMERICAN MILITARY DEVELOPMENTS	DEVELOPMENTS ABROAD

1799	American naval actions against French fleet in the western Atlantic and the West Indies.		
		1800	Napoleon becomes first consul of France. Napoleonic armies develop the infantry "attack column," stress use of massed artillery, and depot logistics. General Jean Moreau, commander of the French Army of the Rhine, first organizes corps.
		1800–15	Napoleonic Wars. British Colonel Sir William Congreve experiments with military rockets.
1801–5	Tripolitan War.		
1801	July. U.S. naval expedition sent to western Mediterranean to combat piracy.	1801	April. British fleet under Horatio Nelson victorious over Danes at Copenhagen.
1802	July. U.S. Military Academy opens at West Point, New York.	1802	British Royal Military College established at Sandhurst.
1803–6	Lewis and Clark explorations in the Trans-Mississippi West.		
1803	August. Commodore Edward Preble polices western Mediterranean against Barbary pirates. October. USS *Philadelphia* captured by the Tripolitans.		
1804	February. USS *Philadelphia* scuttled at Tripoli by U.S. naval raiders.	1804	Baron Antoine Henri Jomini publishes *Treatise on Great Military Operations.*
1805	Zebulon Pike's explorations of the West. April. U.S. naval force captures Derna in Tripolitania. August. U.S. Navy forces peace with Tunisian pirates.	1805	October. Naval Battle of Trafalgar, off Spain. December. Battle of Austerlitz.

AMERICAN MILITARY DEVELOPMENTS	DEVELOPMENTS ABROAD
	1806 October. Battle of Jena.
1807 June. Naval action between HMS *Leopard* and USS *Chesapeake*.	1807 British Army makes first use of division organization.
	1808 French School of War opens at St. Cyr.
	1809–14 British Army under Wellington campaigns in the Peninsula (Spain and Portugal).
	1810 Prussian War Academy opens in Berlin.
1811 Shawnee uprising in the Northwest under Tecumseh.	
May. Naval action between HMS *Little Belt* and USS *President*.	
November. Battle of Tippecanoe, Indiana.	
1812 June. Congress declares war on Great Britain, beginning the War of 1812.	1812 June. Napoleon invades Russia.
July. British forces capture Fort Mackinac.	
August. British forces capture Fort Dearborn (Chicago). Naval action between USS *Constitution* and HMS *Guerriere*.	
	September. Battle of Borodino.
October. Battle of Queenston, Canada. Naval action between USS *Wasp* and HMS *Frolic*. Naval action between USS *United States* and HMS *Macedonian*.	
November. American campaign on Lake Champlain.	
December. Naval action between USS *Constitution* and HMS *Java*.	December. Napoleon's Russian Campaign ends with French Army retreat.

AMERICAN MILITARY DEVELOPMENTS	DEVELOPMENTS ABROAD

1813 January. Battle of the Raisin 1813
     River (Frenchtown),
     Michigan.
    February. Naval action be-
     tween USS *Hornet* and
     HMS *Peacock*.
    April. American forces attack
     and burn York (Toronto).
    May. Battles of Fort George
     and Stoney Creek near
     Niagara. Battle of Sack-
     ets Harbor, New York.
    June. Naval action between
     HMS *Shannon* and USS
     Chesapeake.
    July. Creek Indians ally with
     British.
    August. Naval action between
     HMS *Pelican* and USS
     Argus.
    September. Naval action be-
     tween USS *Enterprise*
     and HMS *Boxer*. Ameri-
     can naval forces win con-
     trol of Lake Erie.
     American naval and land
     forces expel British from
     Detroit.
    September-November. Ameri-
     can campaign against
     Montreal fails.
    October. Battle of the Thames October. Battle of Leipzig.
     River, Canada. Battle of
     Chateaugay River,
     Canada.
    November. Battle of Chrys-
     ler's Farm, Canada. Bat-
     tle of Talladega,
     Alabama.
1814 February-March. Americans 1814
     resume Canadian
     offensive.
    March. British defeat Ameri-
     cans at Battle of La Colle
     Mill, Canada. Battle of

AMERICAN MILITARY DEVELOPMENTS	DEVELOPMENTS ABROAD
Horseshoe Bend, Alabama. USS *Essex* taken by British warships in Pacific after commerce raiding cruise around the Horn begun in October 1812.	
April. Naval action between USS *Peacock* and HMS *Epervier*. General Jacob Brown takes command on the Niagara Front.	April. Napoleon abdicates.
June. Commerce raiding by USS *Wasp* in the English Channel.	
July. American offensive on the Niagara Front. Battle of Chippewa, Canada. Battle of Lundy's Lane, Canada.	
August. British invasion of New York begins. Treaty of Fort Jackson ends Creek involvement in the war. British land raiding force near Washington, D.C. Battle of Bladensburg, Maryland. Washington, D.C., sacked and burned by British troops.	
September. British attack on Baltimore repulsed. Battle of Plattsburgh, New York. Battle of Lake Champlain.	
November. U.S. forces under General Andrew Jackson invade Florida and take Pensacola. Jackson's forces march to defend New Orleans against British. British fleet departs Jamaica for invasion at New Orleans.	
1815 January. American forces un-	

AMERICAN MILITARY DEVELOPMENTS   **DEVELOPMENTS ABROAD**

der Jackson defeat British
at the Battle of New Or-
leans. USS *President*
taken by British
warships.

February. Congress ratifies the
Treaty of Ghent, con-
cluding the War of 1812.
Naval action between
USS *Constitution*, HMS
Cyane, and HMS *Levant*.
Congress orders demobi-
lization of U.S. Army to
10,000 men.

March. Naval action between
USS *Hornet* and HMS
Penguin.

March-June. U.S. naval expedition against Algerian
pirates in the
Mediterranean.

June. Battle of Waterloo

1818   April-May. First Seminole
War. Punitive expedition
by U.S. forces takes
Pensacola.

1820s   French artillery officer Henri-
Joseph Paixhans develops
light, shell-firing cannon
for naval use.

1831   Prussian War Academy posthumously publishes Karl
von Clausewitz's *On
War*.

1832   April-August. Black Hawk
War, Illinois frontier.
August. Battle of Bad Axe,
Wisconsin.

1835-37.   Second Seminole War.

1835   December. Dade Massacre by
Seminoles in Wahoo
Swamp, Florida.

1836   January-May. Texas   1836   Antoine Henry Jomini pub-
Revolution.   lishes his *Summary of the
Art of War*.

AMERICAN MILITARY DEVELOPMENTS	DEVELOPMENTS ABROAD

1837   December. Seminoles defeated
        at the Battle of Lake
        Okeechobee, Florida.

1842   May. Dorr Rebellion in Rhode   1840s   Working independently, Jo-
        Island.   seph Whitworth of Eng-
                                                     land and Giovanni
                                                     Cavalli of Italy develop
                                                     accurate, breech-loading,
                                                     rifled cannons.

1844   America launches USS
        Princeton, first screw-
        type naval steamer.

1844–45 Lieutenant Thomas J. Rodman
        develops a method of
        cooling cast iron cannon
        barrels from the inside
        out, thus strengthening
        barrels.

1845   March. Mexico threatens war
        as U.S. annexes Texas.
        July. U.S. forces under Gen-
        eral Zachary Taylor or-
        dered to Corpus Christi,
        Texas.
        October. Secretary of the
        Navy George Bancroft
        establishes the Naval
        School at Annapolis,
        forerunner of the U.S.
        Naval Academy (1850).

1846   March. U.S. forces under
        Taylor take positions
        along the Rio Grande
        River in disputed
        territory.
        April. Mexican and U.S. cav-
        alry clash along the Rio
        Grande.
        May. Battle of Palo Alto.
        Battle of Resaca de la
        Palma. U.S. declares war
        on Mexico. U.S. forces
        invade Mexico.
        June. Commodore John Sloat
        occupies Monterey,
        California.

AMERICAN MILITARY DEVELOPMENTS   **DEVELOPMENTS ABROAD**

	June-December. U.S. forces march from New Mexico to occupy California.
	September. Battle of Monterrey, Mexico.
	November. U.S. forces under General John Wool take Saltillo, Mexico.
	December. Battle of San Pascual, California.
1847	January. Battle of San Gabriel, California.
	February. Battle of Buena Vista, Mexico. Battle of the Sacramento River, Mexico.
	March. U.S. forces under General Winfield Scott make amphibious landings near Vera Cruz, Mexico. U.S. forces occupy Vera Cruz.
	April. Battle of Cerro Gordo, Mexico.
	April-September. U.S. forces march on Mexico City.
	August. Battle of Contreras, Mexico. Battle of Churubusco, Mexico.
	August-September. Armistice.
	September. Battle of Molino del Rey, Mexico. Battle of Chapultepec, Mexico City. Mexico City surrenders to Scott's forces.
	September-October. Mexican forces besiege Puebla.
1847	Dennis Hart Mahan publishes *Outpost*.
1848	Treaty of Guadalupe Hidalgo concludes Mexican War.

1849–50s Navy Lieutenant John Dahlgren engineers a new basic heavy cannon which the Navy adopts— the "Dahlgren gun."

1849 French Captain E. E. Minie adapts a cylindro-conoidal bullet tested by the British in the 1820s, eventually called the "Minie ball."

AMERICAN MILITARY DEVELOPMENTS   **DEVELOPMENTS ABROAD**

1850   U.S. Navy outlaws flogging.
        U.S. Naval Academy opens
            at Annapolis, Maryland.

1850s   Inventor Samuel Colt experi-   1850s   French Army tests a machine
            ments with rapid-fire   gun, the Mitraillouse,
            weapons.   and a 12-pounder,
1850–65 Irregular warfare on the West-   smoothbore field gun,
            ern frontier. More than   dubbed "the Napoleon"
            thirty significant armed   after Emperor Napoleon
            conflicts between the   III.
            Army and Indian tribes.
                                           1853–56 The Crimean War.

1856   "Bleeding Kansas." Depreda-
            tions along the Kansas-
            Missouri border by pro-
            and antislavery gangs.
1857-58 Mormon expedition under   1858   British Army adopts breech-
            A. S. Johnston and Jo-   loading, rifled field gun
            seph E. Johnston.   introduced by English en-
                                                       gineer William
                                                       Armstrong.
1859   October. John Brown's raid   1859   British Navy Captain Cowper
            on Harper's Ferry.   Coles devises ship's re-
                                                       volving gun turret.
                                                   French launch the armored
                                                       warship *Gloire*.
1860   After several experiments,   1860   British launch the armored
            Robert Parrott manufac-   warship *Warrior*.
            tures a small rifled can-
            non—the "Parrott Gun."
1861   Inventor John Ericcson de-
            signs revolving gun turret
            for USS *Monitor*.
        January-April. Prelude to
            Civil War. Southern
            States secede from the
            Union.
        February 8. Confederate
            States of America provi-
            sionally formed.
        April 12–14. Confederate
            forces under General

AMERICAN MILITARY DEVELOPMENTS   **DEVELOPMENTS ABROAD**

P.G.T. Beauregard bombard Fort Sumter, South Carolina.

April 23. Confederate naval officer Matthew F. Maury begins experiments with "torpedoes" (underwater mines).

May. Union naval blockade of the South begins.

July 21. Confederates defeat Federals at the first Battle of Bull Run. Confederate reinforcements arrive on battlefield by railroad.

August 10. Battle of Wilson's Creek, Missouri.

August 27. Naval action at Hatteras Inlet, North Carolina.

October 21. Battle of Ball's Bluff, Virginia.

November 7. Union forces seize Port Royal, South Carolina.

1862   Dr. Richard Gatling carries out test on a machine gun, the "Gatling Gun."

February. General U. S. Grant begins Union campaign against Forts Henry and Donelson, Tennessee. Union offensive against New Madrid and Island Number 10 begins the Mississippi River Campaign.

February 7. Union naval expedition captures Roanoke Island, Virginia.

March 7–8. Battle of Pea Ridge, Arkansas.

March 8–9. Naval action between armored ships *Monitor* and *Merrimac* at Hampton Roads, Virginia.

AMERICAN MILITARY DEVELOPMENTS	DEVELOPMENTS ABROAD

March 23. Battle of Kernstown, Virginia.

April 5. General George B.
McClellan begins siege
of Yorktown, Virginia.

April 6–7. Battle of Shiloh,
Tennessee.

April 11. Union takes Fort
Pulaski, Georgia, im-
proving blockade.

April 16. Confederacy institutes first conscription
act.

April 24. Union naval squad-
ron forces passage by
Confederate forts below
New Orleans.

April 28. CSS *Florida* arrives
in Bahamas and prepares
to raid Northern
shipping.

May. Confederate campaign
begins in the Shenandoah
Valley under "Stone-
wall" Jackson.

May 1. Union forces take
New Orleans.

May 5. Battle of Williamsburg, Virginia.

May 8. Battle of McDowell,
Virginia.

May 9. Confederates evacuate
naval base at Norfolk.

May 25. First Battle of Winchester, Virginia.

May 31-June 1. Battle of
Seven Pines.

June 1. General Robert E. Lee
assumes command of the
Army of Northern
Virginia.

June 6. Battle of Memphis,
Tennessee.

June 8. Battle of Cross Keys,
Virginia.

June 9. Battle of Port Republic, Virginia.

AMERICAN MILITARY DEVELOPMENTS   **DEVELOPMENTS ABROAD**

June 12-15. General J.E.B. Stuart's raid around the Army of the Potomac.

June 17. Federal Congress authorizes the enlistment of black troops.

June 25-July 1. In Virginia, the Seven Days' Battles: Mechanicsville (June 25); Gaines' Mill (June 27); and Malvern Hill (July 1).

July 29. CSS *Alabama* leaves England to raid on Union shipping.

August 5. Battle of Baton Rouge, Louisiana.

August 9. Battle of Cedar Mountain, Virginia.

August 29-30. Second Battle of Bull Run, Virginia.

September 4. Army of Northern Virginia crosses the Potomac River to campaign in Maryland.

September 14. Battle of South Mountain, Maryland.

September 17. Battle of Antietam, Maryland.

September 18. Army of Northern Virginia retreats across the Potomac to Virginia.

September 22. President Lincoln issues Preliminary Emancipation Proclamation.

October 3-4. Battle of Corinth, Mississippi.

October 8. Battle of Perryville, Kentucky.

November. Beginning of the Fredericksburg Campaign. Beginning of the Vicksburg Campaign.

December 13. Battle of Fredericksburg.

AMERICAN MILITARY DEVELOPMENTS	DEVELOPMENTS ABROAD

December 29. Battle of
   Chickasaw Bluffs,
   Mississippi.

December 31. Battle of Murfreesboro, Tennessee.

1863   March 3. Union institutes
   conscription.

April. Chancellorsville Campaign begins.

April 7. Union naval expedi-
   tion under Admiral S. F.
   DuPont repulsed at
   Charleston.

April 17. Colonel B. F. Grierson begins raid through
   Mississippi.

May 1–4. Battle of Chancellorsville, Virginia.

May 7–19. Big Black River
   Campaign in Mississippi.

May 16. Battle of Champion's
   Hill, Mississippi.

May 19-July 4. Siege of
   Vicksburg, Mississippi.

May 22. Federal War Department establishes Bureau
   of Colored Troops.

June-July. Gettysburg
   Campaign.

June 9. Largest cavalry battle
   of the war at Brandy Station, Virginia.

June 13–14. Second Battle of
   Winchester.

June 23-July 2. Tullahoma
   Campaign in Tennessee.

July-December. Siege of
   Charleston.

July 1-3. Battle of Gettysburg.

July 4. Surrender of
   Vicksburg.

July 8. Port Hudson, Louisiana, surrenders, giving
   control of Mississippi
   River to the Union.

September 19–20. Battle of
   Chickamauga, Georgia.

AMERICAN MILITARY DEVELOPMENTS   **DEVELOPMENTS ABROAD**

September-October. Siege of
Chattanooga, Tennessee.

October 5. Confederate torpe-
doboat, *David*, attacks
Union ship in Charleston
Harbor.

November-December. Siege
of Knoxville, Tennessee.

November 24–25. Battle of
Chattanooga.

1864   March-May. Red River Campaign, Louisiana.

March 9. General U. S. Grant
takes command of Union
Army.

May 4, Opening of the Wilderness Campaign.

May 5. Atlanta Campaign
opens.

May 5–6. Battle of the Wilderness, Virginia.

May 5–16. Bermuda Hundred
Campaign, Virginia.

May 8–18. Battle of Spotsylvania, Virginia.

May 11. Battle of Yellow
Tavern, Virginia.

May 15. Battle of New Market, Virginia.

May 16. Battle of Drewry's
Bluff, Virginia.

June. Siege of Petersburg
begins.

June 3–12. Battle of Cold
Harbor, Virginia.

June 10. Battle of Brice's
Cross Roads, Mississippi.

June 15–18. Battle of Petersburg, Virginia.

June 19. Naval action between
USS *Kearsarge* and Con-
federate raider *Alabama*.

June 27. Battle of Kennesaw
Mountain, Georgia.

July 9. Battle of the Monocacy, Maryland.

July 14–15. Battle of Tupelo,
    Mississippi.
July 20. Battle of Peachtree
    Creek, Georgia.
July 22. Battle of Atlanta.
August 5. Naval battle of Mo-
    bile Bay.
August-October. General Phil
    Sheridan's Shenandoah
    Valley Campaign.
September 19. Third Battle of
    Winchester.
September 22. Battle of
    Fischer's Hill, Virginia.
October 19. Battle of Cedar
    Creek, Virginia.
November 16. Sherman and
    Union Army begin
    "March to the Sea."
November 30. Battle of
    Franklin, Tennessee.
December 9–21. Union in-
    vestment of Savannah,
    Georgia.
December 15–16. Battle of
    Nashville, Tennessee.

1865   January 19. Sherman and
    Union Army begin march
    from Savannah, Georgia,
    through South Carolina.
February 7. Confederates
    evacuate Charleston.
February 22. Main port of
    Confederacy at Wilming-
    ton, North Carolina, falls
    to Union forces.
March 19–20. Battle of Ben-
    tonville, North Carolina.
March 25. Battle of Fort Sted-
    man, Petersburg,
    Virginia.
March 29–31. Battle of Din-
    widdie Courthouse,
    Virginia.
April 1. Battle of Five Forks,
    Virginia.

AMERICAN MILITARY DEVELOPMENTS		DEVELOPMENTS ABROAD	
	April 2. Battle of Selma, Alabama. Confederates evacuate Petersburg.		
	April 6–7. Battle of Sayler's Creek, Virginia.		
	April 9. Battle of Appomattox, Virginia. General Lee surrenders Confederate forces at Appomattox Court House.		
	April 12. Confederates surrender at Mobile, Alabama.		
	April 14. President Lincoln is assassinated.		
	April 26. General Joseph E. Johnston surrenders to General Sherman at Durham Station, North Carolina.		
	May 26. Confederates in Trans-Mississippi Department surrender at New Orleans.		
	May 29. Formal conclusion of Civil War; President Andrew Johnson grants amnesty.		
	November 6. Commerce raider CSS *Shenandoah* surrenders flag in Great Britain.		
1865–68	Intermittent campaigning by U.S. Army against Indians in Far West and Northwest.		
1866	December. Fetterman massacre in Wyoming.	1866	June-August. Austro-Prussian War.
1867–75	Intermittent campaigning by U.S. Army against Indians in the Central Plains and Southwest.		
		1870–71	Franco-Prussian War.
1872–73	The Modoc War, California.		
1873	Army campaigns against the Apaches in the Southwest.		

AMERICAN MILITARY DEVELOPMENTS	DEVELOPMENTS ABROAD

AMERICAN MILITARY DEVELOPMENTS

1876   February-June. Big Horn
        Campaign in Montana
        and Wyoming.
        March. Battle of Slim Buttes.
        June 17. Battle of the
        Rosebud.
        June 25. Battle of the Little
        Big Horn.
        November. Battle of Crazy
        Woman Fork.
1877   January. Battle of the Wolf
        Mountains.
        June. Nez Perce War begins.
        Battle of White Bird
        Canyon.
        July-August. Battles of the
        Clearwater and Big Hole
        Basin.
        October. Battle of Eagle
        Creek.
1878   Bannock War, Northwest
        Territories.
1878–79 Army campaigns against
        Northern Cheyennes.
1881   Army establishes School of
        Application for Infantry
        and Cavalry at Fort
        Leavenworth, Kansas.
1882   March. Navy establishes Of-
        fice of Naval
        Intelligence.
1885–86. Army campaigns against Ger-
        onimo's Apaches.
1886   U.S. Naval War College
        opens at Newport, Rhode
        Island.
1890   May. A. T. Mahan publishes
        *The Influence of Sea
        Power upon History.*
1895   Inventor John M. Browning
        develops an air-cooled
        machine gun that utilizes
        gas pressure for its
        operation.

DEVELOPMENTS ABROAD

1885   Sir Hiram Maxim develops a
        machine gun that loads,
        fires, and ejects shells us-
        ing its own recoil.

AMERICAN MILITARY DEVELOPMENTS	DEVELOPMENTS ABROAD

1898 February 15. USS *Maine* explodes in Havana Harbor.

April 25. U.S. declares war on Spain.

May 1. Admiral George Dewey's fleet defeats Spanish at Manila Bay, Philippines.

May-July. U.S. naval blockade of Santiago Bay, Cuba.

June. U.S. forces land at Santiago.

July 3. Battle of Santiago Bay.

July 17. U.S. forces capture Santiago.

July 25. U.S. forces land in Puerto Rico.

August. U.S. forces capture Manila.

December. Treaty of Paris concludes Spanish-American War.

1899 January. Filipino insurgents declare independence of the Philippines.

February. Filipino insurgency against U.S. occupation begins.

1902–5 U.S. forces campaign against insurgents on Luzon and Moros on Mindinao.

1903 Secretary of War Elihu Root sponsors reform of U.S. Army, creating a General Staff and a War College.

1904–5 Russo-Japanese War.

1906 First modern battleship, HMS *Dreadnought*, constructed in Great Britain.

1907–9 Voyage of U.S. Navy's "Great White Fleet."

1910 U.S. Marine Corps establishes the Advanced Base School for amphibious assault training.

AMERICAN MILITARY DEVELOPMENTS

DEVELOPMENTS ABROAD

1911   Chinese Revolution begins.

1912   U.S. intervention in Honduras
        and Nicaragua.
        Admiral Bradley Fiske devel-
        ops techniques for aerial
        torpedo launching.

1914   U.S. expedition occupies Vera   1914   August. World War I begins
        Cruz, Mexico.   in Europe.
                                            1915   May. German submarine sinks
                                                    British liner *Lusitania*.

1916   U.S. sends Punitive Expedi-   1916   January-December. German
        tion against Villistas in   Zeppelin raids on
        northern Mexico.   London.
                                                    February-December. Battle of
                                                    Verdun.
                                                    May-June. Naval battle of
                                                    Jutland.

1917   January. Germany declares   1917   March. Russian Revolution
        unrestricted submarine   begins as Czar Nicholas
        warfare.   II abdicates.
        March. German submarines   April-May. Mutinies in the
        sink four American mer-   French Army.
        chant ships.   November. Petrograd revolt
        April 6. U.S. declares war on   begins Bolshevik Revolu-
        Germany.   tion. British use first ma-
        May 19. Congress passes Se-   jor tank formations in
        lective Service Act.   Battle of Cambrai.
        June. General John J. Persh-
        ing becomes commander,
        American Expeditionary
        Force. U.S. 1st Infantry
        Division arrives in
        France.

                                            1917–18 German aircraft attacks on
                                                     England.
                                            1917–22 Russian Civil War.
1918   May. Battle of Cantigny (first   1918
        U.S. action on the West-
        ern Front).
        May-June. Battles of Chateau
        Thierry and Belleau
        Wood.
        July-August. Second Battle of
        the Marne.
        September. U.S. forces lead
                                                     September. British put the air-

AMERICAN MILITARY DEVELOPMENTS

offensive against the
Saint-Mihiel salient.
September-November. Meuse-
Argonne Offensive.
November 11. Armistice.

1918–19 Allied forces (including U.S.)
intervene in Russia.
1919 Reserve Officers Training
Corps (ROTC) estab-
lished in National De-
fense Act of 1919.
1920 Congress passes National Defense Act of 1920, re-
flecting ideas of General
J. M. Palmer.

1920–21 Washington Naval
Conference.
1922–27 U.S. Navy experiments with
the aircraft carrier *Langley*, a converted collier.
1925 December. Court-martial of
Colonel William
Mitchell.
1928 U.S. Navy puts aircraft carriers *Lexington* and *Saratoga* into service.

1931 U.S. Naval Research Laboratory begins studies of
"radar" (radio detection
and ranging) device.
1933–35 U.S. Army participates in Civilian Conservation Corps
activities.

1936 April. Rudimentary radar developed by U.S. Naval
Research Laboratory.

1937 U.S. Navy commissions aircraft carrier *Yorktown*.

DEVELOPMENTS ABROAD

craft carrier *Argus* to sea,
the first of its kind with a
full-length flight deck.
October. British researchers
develop "asdic" sound-
ing device to locate
submarines.

1919 Treaty of Versailles ends
World War I.

1920s-30s British military theorists
J.F.C. Fuller and B. H.
Liddell Hart develop and
proselytize views on
combined arms warfare
later called *blitzkrieg*.

1928 Many nations of the world
sign Kellogg-Briand Pact
to outlaw offensive war.
1929 Allied forces evacuate the
Rhineland.
1931 Mukden incident begins Japanese seizure of
Manchuria.
1933 Establishment of Nazi dicta-
torship in Germany.

1935–36 Italo-Ethiopian War.
1936 Germany reoccupies the
Rhineland.

1936–39 Spanish Civil War.
1937 Sino-Japanese War begins.

AMERICAN MILITARY DEVELOPMENTS	DEVELOPMENTS ABROAD
1938 U.S. Navy commissions carrier *Enterprise*.	1938 Germany annexes Austria.
	1938–39 Russo-Japanese hostilities in Manchuria.
1939 Radars installed on U.S. ships. September. United States declares neutrality.	1939 Germany invades Poland. World War II begins.
	1939–40 Russo-Finnish War.
	1940 April-June. German conquest of Norway and Denmark. May-June. German conquest of the Low Countries and France. British share knowledge of radar with United States. August-November. Battle of Britain.
1940 September. Anglo-American "destroyers for bases" agreement is made. Selective Service Act passed by Congress.	
	September. Italians invade Egypt. October. Italians invade Greece.
1941	1941 January. British offensive in North Africa begins.
March. U.S. Lend Lease aid begins. April. United States stations forces in Greenland.	March. German offensive in North Africa begins. April. Germans invade Greece. German Army besieges Tobruk in North Africa. May. The battle for Crete. June. British offensive in North Africa. German invasion of Russia.
July. United States stations forces in Iceland.	July. Japanese Navy approves plans and training for attack on Pearl Harbor.
August. Atlantic Conference. September. Selective Service Act extended. U.S. con-	November-December. British Army launches offensive in North Africa. Defense

AMERICAN MILITARY DEVELOPMENTS

DEVELOPMENTS ABROAD

voy escorts begin in
North Atlantic.

September-December. American Volunteer Group
("The Flying Tigers") is
formed in China.

December 7. Japanese launch
surprise attack against
American Pacific Fleet at
Pearl Harbor, Hawaii.

December 8. Japanese launch
surprise attack on Americans at Clark Field, the
Philippines.

December 10. Japanese attack
American base on Guam.

December 22. Japanese launch
invasion of Luzon, the
Philippines.

December 22–January 14. Arcadia Conference.

1942 January. Battle of the Atlantic
begins against German
submarine "wolfpacks."

January 7–26. Defense of Bataan, the Philippines.

January 23. Naval battle of
the Macassar Strait, off
Borneo.

February-August. Battle for
Guadalcanal.

February 1. U.S. naval attack
on Gilbert and Marshall
Islands.

February 4. Naval battle of
the Madoera Strait,
Dutch East Indies.

February 27. Naval battle of
the Java Sea.

April 18. First American air
raid on Tokyo (The
Doolittle Raid).

of Moscow and Russian
counteroffensive.

December 10–31. Japanese
launch offensive in
Malaya.

December 25. Japanese capture Hong Kong.

1942 January-February. Japanese
invade Netherlands East
Indies. Air battles for
Rangoon, Burma.

January 12–29. Japanese invade Burma.

February 8–15. Singapore
Campaign.

February 19. Japanese launch
air raids on Darwin,
Australia.

February 29–March 9. Battle
for Java.

April 10–19. Battle of Yenangyaung, China.

April-May. Japanese invest
and finally take U.S.
forces on Corregidor.

AMERICAN MILITARY DEVELOPMENTS	DEVELOPMENTS ABROAD
May 7–8. Battle of the Coral Sea (first naval engagement fought entirely by aircraft of opposing carriers).	May. Allied retreat from Burma. May 30–31. RAF Bomber Command's first thousand-plane raid against Germany launched from England. May-June. Battle of Gazala in North Africa.
June 3–7. Japanese Aleutian Offensive. June 4–6. Naval Battle of Midway.	June 28–July 7. German summer offensive in Russia. June-September. Japanese offensive against Port Moresby, New Guinea. August 24-December 31. Battles for Stalingrad. August 31. Battle of Alam Halfa, North Africa.
September-November. Allied campaigns against Buna and New Guinea. October 11–13. Battle of Cape Esperance, off Guadalcanal. November 12–15. Naval battle for Guadalcanal.	October 23-November 4. Battle of El Alamein, North Africa. November. Allies land on Moroccan coast (Operation TORCH).
1943 January-December. The Solomons Campaign. January 14-23. Casablanca Conference. February 7. Japanese forces evacuate Guadalcanal. February 14. Battle of Kasserine Pass, Tunisia.	1943 February-April. Allies launch first Chindit Raid into Burma. February 3. German Army surrenders at Stalingrad. February-March. German counteroffensive begins at Kharkov, Russia.
March 2–4. Battle of the Bismarck Sea. May 3–13. Battle of Tunisia. July 2–August 25. Allied landing on New Georgia, Solomon Islands.	July. Russian Army goes on the offensive. July 5–16. Battle of Kursk,

AMERICAN MILITARY DEVELOPMENTS	DEVELOPMENTS ABROAD
July 9–10. Allied landings on Sicily.	Russia. Largest tank battle of the war.
	July 24. Mussolini deposed in Italy.
	July 26–29. Air Battle of Hamburg, Germany.
August 1. Allied air forces raid oilfields at Ploesti, Rumania.	
September 3. Armistice in Italy. Allied landings at Salerno, Italy.	
October 12-November 14. The Volturno River Campaign, Italy.	
October 14. Allied air raid on Schweinfurt, Germany.	
October 19 30. Allied leaders meet for Moscow conference.	
October-December. Battle for Bougainville, Solomon Islands.	
November. General Dwight D. Eisenhower named supreme commander, Allied Expeditionary Force, Europe. Battle of Tarawa, Gilbert Islands.	November-December. Air Battle of Berlin.
	December-February 1944. Arakan Campaign in Burma.
December. Allied forces under General Joseph Stilwell launch offensive into Burma.	

	AMERICAN MILITARY DEVELOPMENTS		DEVELOPMENTS ABROAD
1944	January-March. The New Britain Campaign.	1944	January 15–19. Liberation of Leningrad.
	January-May. Allied bomber offensive against Germany.		January-February. Russian winter offensive continues.
	January 15-25. The Rapido-Cassino battles in Italy.		
	January 22. Allies make landings at Anzio, Italy.		
	January 29-February 1. Battle of Kwajalein, Marshall Islands.		

AMERICAN MILITARY DEVELOPMENTS

April. Battles of Aitape and
Hollandia, New Guinea.
May 17–18. Allies launch as-
sault and siege of Myit-
kyina, Burma.
June. Rome taken by Allied
forces.
June-August. The Marianas
Campaign.
June 6. D-Day. Allies land in
Normandy.
June 15. First strike of Allied
strategic bombing offen-
sive against Japanese
mainland.
June 15-July 13. Battle of
Saipan, Marianas Islands.
June 19–21. Battle of the
Philippine Sea.
July 21. Battle of Guam
begins.
July 25-31. Allies begin
breakout from Normandy
beachhead. Operation
COBRA.
August 13–19. Battle of the
Falaise-Argentan gap,
France.
August 15. Allied landings in
Southern France (Opera-
tion ANVIL-DRAGOON).
August-September. Vosges
Mountain Campaign,
France.
September 17–26. Allied in-
vasion of Belgium (Oper-
ation MARKET-GARDEN).
September-December. Stil-
well's offensive in China.
October. General Stilwell is
relieved of command.

DEVELOPMENTS ABROAD

March-July. Allies launch second Chindit raid into
Burma.
March-September. Imphal-Ko-
hima Campaign, India.
June. Russian summer offensive begins.

July. Russian Army drives
into Poland.

AMERICAN MILITARY DEVELOPMENTS **DEVELOPMENTS ABROAD**

October 20–22. Allies invade
 Leyte Island, the
 Philippines.
October 23–25. Naval Battle
 of Leyte Gulf.
October-November. Battle for
 the Scheldt Estuary,
 Holland.
November-December. Battles
 of the Huertgen Forest,
 Germany.
November 16-December 15.
 The Lorraine Campaign.
 The Alsace Campaign.
December-January 1945. Ger-
 man counteroffensive in
 the Ardennes.
December 26-January 2,
 1945. The defense of
 Bastogne.

1945 January-February. Reduction   1945
 of the Colmar Pocket by
 Allied forces, Alsace.
January-August. The Luzon
 Campaign, Philippines.
January 9. Allies land at Lin-
 gayen Gulf, Luzon,
 Philippines.
January 27. Allies reopen the
 Burma Road.
February-March. The Rhine-
 land Campaign. Allies
 liberate Manila.
February-August. Allies cam-
 paign in Mindinao, the
 Philippines.
February 13–14. Allied air
 forces firebomb Dresden,
 Germany.
February 19-March 24. Battle
 of Iwo Jima.
March 7. Allied forces seize
 the Remagen Bridgehead
 across the Rhine River.
March 9–21. Battle of Manda-
 lay, Burma.

AMERICAN MILITARY DEVELOPMENTS

DEVELOPMENTS ABROAD

March 9–10. Allied Air Forces firebomb Tokyo.

March 14-June 22. Battle of Okinawa.

March 15-August 15. Philippine Mountain Campaign.

April. Po Valley Campaign, Italy.

May 2. Allied forces liberate Rangoon, Burma.

May 7-8. Germany surrenders.

July 16. First explosions of the atomic bomb at Alamagordo, New Mexico.

August 6. First atomic bomb used in warfare dropped on Hiroshima, Japan.

August 9. Second atomic bomb used in warfare dropped on Nagasaki, Japan.

August 9. Russia enters war against Japan with an invasion of Manchuria.

August 10. Japanese cabinet tenders offer to surrender.

August 15. Warring powers agree to a ceasefire in Asia.

August 28. American occupation forces arrive in Japan.

September 2. Japan formally surrenders, concluding World War II.

1946   March 5. Prime Minister Winston Churchill makes his "Iron Curtain" speech in Fulton, Missouri, warning of Soviet expansionist policies.

November 20, 1945-October 1, 1946. Nuremberg War Crimes Trials.

June 3, 1946-November 12, 1948. Tokyo War Crimes Trials.

AMERICAN MILITARY DEVELOPMENTS

DEVELOPMENTS ABROAD

1947 March 12. President Truman enunciates his "containment doctrine" against communism and Soviet expansion.

June 5. Truman approves Marshall Plan for the economic reconstruction of Europe.

July. "The Sources of Soviet Conduct" by "Mr. X" (George Kennan) is published in the journal *Foreign Affairs*.

July 26. National Security Act creates National Military Establishment, a secretary of defense, and the U.S. Air Force as a separate military service.

October 3–27. The "Revolt of the Admirals."

1948 March. Key West Conference between military service chiefs determines postwar military roles and missions.

June 21. Congress passes new Selective Service Act.

June 24-May 12, 1949. Berlin Blockade and Airlift.

1949 April 4. Establishment of North Atlantic Treaty Organization (NATO).

August 10. Congress passes National Security Act, creating Department of Defense.

1950 April 7. NSC–68 promulgated, articulating national military policy of deterrence.

May. President Truman orders desegregation of armed forces.

June 25. North Korean troops begin invasion of South Korea.

1948 Israeli War of Independence.

AMERICAN MILITARY DEVELOPMENTS

DEVELOPMENTS ABROAD

June 27. U.N. member states begin to send armed forces to the aid of South Korea. Korean War effectively begins.

July 20. United States partially mobilizes for the Korean War.

August 6-September 15. Battle of the Pusan Beachhead.

September 15. U.N. troops land at Inchon.

September 26. U.N. troops take Seoul.

October 20. U.N. troops take Pyongyang.

October 26. China intervenes in the Korean War. Chinese troops cross the Yalu River.

November 25-26. Communist forces launch counteroffensive against U.S. Eighth Army.

November 27-December 9. U.S. X Corps withdraws to Hungnam perimeter.

December 5-December 15. X Corps evacuates to Pusan.

1951   January 4. U.N. troops evacuate Seoul.

March. U.N. counteroffensive retakes Seoul.

April 11. President Truman relieves General Douglas MacArthur of U.N. command.

April-May. General Communist offensive in Korea.

May. U.N. forces launch counteroffensive and retake line north of 38th parallel.

AMERICAN MILITARY DEVELOPMENTS

DEVELOPMENTS ABROAD

July. Negotiations begin for Korean armistice.

November 12. Peace talks open at Panmunjom, Korea.

1952 Military stalemate continues on 38th parallel while peace talks are held. Active raiding and counter-raiding by combatants.

November. U.S. tests first hydrogen bomb at Eniwetok Island in the Pacific Ocean. Warring powers sign armistice in Korea.

1953 July 27. Korean Armistice formally signed.

August. The Sequoia Conference: U.S. service chiefs agree upon the politico-military doctrine of "massive retaliation."

United States begins military aid to France in Indochina.

1954 January 22. President Eisenhower announces a "new look" in American military policy.

January 25. Secretary of State Dulles articulates policy of "massive retaliation."

September 8. Southeast Asia Treaty Organization (SEATO) is formed.

September 30. U.S. Navy launches the first nuclear-powered submarine, USS *Nautilus*.

1954 August. Soviet Union tests its first hydrogen bomb.

May 7. French stronghold of Dienbienphu falls to Vietminh forces.

AMERICAN MILITARY DEVELOPMENTS	DEVELOPMENTS ABROAD

1954–55   Tension between United States and China over Nationalist Chinese occupation of Quemoy, Matsu, and other offshore islands.

1955   January 20. United States begins direct military aid to South Vietnam.

June. U.S. Air Force Academy opens at Colorado Springs, Colorado.

1956   May. "The Colonels' Revolt." Public dispute between Army and Air Force staff officers over primacy of air power in national security policy.

                                                          1956

                                                          October. Hungarians revolt against Russian occupation.

October-November. Suez Crisis. Second Arab-Israeli War.

1957   January 5. The Eisenhower Doctrine: United States will aid Middle East countries threatened by Communist subversion or invasion.

1958   May. President Eisenhower proposes reorganization of U.S. military command structures.

July-October. America intervenes in Lebanon.

August 6. Congress passes Defense Reorganization Act.

1960   Presidential candidate Kennedy proposes that "flexible response" replace "massive retaliation" as cornerstone of national security policy.

December 15. United States announces aid to Laos.

AMERICAN MILITARY DEVELOPMENTS	DEVELOPMENTS ABROAD

1961　February. United States tests first intercontinental ballistic missile (ICBM).

April 15-20. U.S.-sponsored army of Cuban exiles attempts invasion of Cuba at the Bay of Pigs.

August 13. East Germans begin construction of the Berlin Wall. U.S. forces put on alert.

1962　February 8. U.S. Military Assistance Command, Vietnam (MACV) is established in Saigon.

September-November. Cuban Missile Crisis.

October 5. U.S. military advisors withdrawn from Laos.

1963　January. In the Battle of Ap Bac, Vietcong defeat several regiments of the South Vietnamese Army.

November 1. South Vietnam government of Ngo Dinh Diem overthrown by military coup. Diem is assassinated.

1964　January 29. Young South Vietnamese officers led by General Nguyen Khanh take control of government.

August 1. North Vietnamese patrol boats reportedly attack USS *Maddox* in the Gulf of Tonkin.

August 4. USS *Maddox* and USS *C. Turner Joy* reportedly attacked by North Vietnamese patrol boats in the Gulf of Tonkin.

August 7. Congress passes the Gulf of Tonkin Resolu-

AMERICAN MILITARY DEVELOPMENTS	DEVELOPMENTS ABROAD

tion, authorizing the use
of force for the protection
of U.S. units. (In the absence of a formal decla-
ration of war, this
resolution is generally regarded as marking the
beginning of the war in
Vietnam.)

December 24. Vietcong sap-
pers bomb U.S. officers'
billet in Saigon.

1965 January. First North Vietnamese Army regiment re-
portedly enters South
Vietnam.

February 6. Vietcong attack
on U.S. base at Pleiku.

February 7. President Johnson
orders commencement of
air operations against
North Vietnam. Opera-
tion ROLLING THUNDER
begins on March 2.

March 6. President Johnson
orders two battalions of
Marines to South
Vietnam.

April 28-June28. United
States intervenes in the
Dominican Republic.

June 9. United States begins
construction of port at
Cam Ranh Bay.

June 18. United States begins
B–52 strikes against sus-
pected Vietcong en-
claves, known as ARC
LIGHT.

June 27. U.S. troops initiate
first major offensive in
War Zone D, South
Vietnam.

July 28. President Johnson announces reinforcement of
U.S. forces in Vietnam
to 125,000.

AMERICAN MILITARY DEVELOPMENTS	DEVELOPMENTS ABROAD

October-November. Battle of
the Ia Drang Valley.

1966 February 6–8. Honolulu Con-   1966
ference: President John-
son and Premier Ky of
South Vietnam confer on
conduct of the war.

March 31. France withdraws
from NATO.

May 1. First targets hit in
Vietcong sanctuaries in
Cambodia.

June 11. United States announces increase in troop
strength in Vietnam to
285,000.

June 29. United States makes
first air attacks on oil installations at Hanoi and
Haiphong, North
. Vietnam.

November 24. Operation AT-
TLEBORO: 22,000 U.S.
and South Vietnamese
troops sweep War Zone
C (Tay Ninh Province).

1967 January 6. U.S. and South   1967
Vietnamese armies
launch offensive in the
Mekong Delta.

January 8. Operation CEDAR
FALLS, a combined offen-
sive in the "Iron Trian-
gle" northwest of
Saigon.

February 23-May 15. Operation JUNCTION CITY: larg-
est allied operation of the
year.

June. Fourth Arab-Israeli
War.

July 15. Massive Vietcong
mortar attack on U.S.
base at Da Nang.

September 27. Battle of Con
Thien begins, lasting
more than a month and a
half.

AMERICAN MILITARY DEVELOPMENTS	DEVELOPMENTS ABROAD

November 23. Battle for Dak Tho.

1968 January 21-April 5. The siege of Khe Sanh. Operation PEGASUS relieves Khe Sanh on April 8.

January 23. Seizure of USS *Pueblo* off North Korean coast.

January 30. The Tet Offensive

March 11. U.S. counteroffensive in the "Iron Triangle."

March 31. United States announces temporary cessation of air war against North Vietnam.

April 21. Operation DELAWARE in the A Shau Valley.

May 13. Peace talks begin in Paris.

June 19. General Westmoreland leaves Vietnam to be Army chief of staff. General Abrams takes command of U.S. Military Assistance Command, Vietnam on July 3.

June 27. U.S. forces abandon base at Khe Sanh.

December-May 1969. In the Mekong Delta's dry season, Operation SPEEDY EXPRESS begins.

1969 May 10–28. Battle of the A Shau Valley.

July 8. First U.S. troops depart Vietnam as part of withdrawal schedule.

September 3. Ho Chi Minh dies in Hanoi.

October 4. In the United States, a Gallup Poll shows 58 percent of Americans think involvement in Vietnam is a mistake.

AMERICAN MILITARY DEVELOPMENTS   **DEVELOPMENTS ABROAD**

October 9. Secretary of Defense Melvin Laird confirms American policy to "Vietnamize" the war.

November 12. Army announces investigation of the My Lai massacre.

1970   April 29-June 30. U.S. and South Vietnamese forces invade Cambodia.

May 4. National Guard troops kill four students during antiwar protest at Kent State University, Ohio.

1971   January 30-April 3. Operation LAM SON 719 (NVA) drives into Laos to interdict North Vietnamese Army supply routes into South Vietnam.

June 13. *The New York Times* begins to publish the "Pentagon Papers."

1972   April 1. Last units of U.S. Navy depart South Vietnam.

April 15. Americans turn over Da Nang to South Vietnam.

May 9. Cam Ranh Bay Air Base turned over to South Vietnam.

August 11. The last U.S. ground combat units in South Vietnam, the 3d battalion, 21st Infantry, is ordered to stand down.

1973   January 23. The United States and North Vietnam agree on ceasefire in South Vietnam. Accord is formally signed on January 27.

March 29. U.S. Army, Vietnam, is formally disestablished.

	1974	December-April 1975. Fall of South Vietnam.
		December. North Vietnamese begin offensive against South Vietnam by attacking Phuoc Long.
1975	1975	January 7. NVA takes Phuoc Binh.
		March 10. Ban Me Thuot falls to NVA.
		March 19. Quang Tri falls to NVA.
		March 20. An Loc falls to NVA.
		March 24. Tan Ky falls to NVA.
		March 25. Quang Ngai falls to NVA.
		March 29. Da Nang falls to NVA.
		April 1. Qui Nhon falls to NVA.
		April 3. Nha Trang falls to NVA.
		April 4. Dalat falls to NVA.
		April 20. Xuan Loc falls to NVA.
April 29. Americans remaining in Saigon are evacuated.		April 30. Saigon falls to NVA.

American Military Ranks

After 1806, Army officers were awarded honorary increases in rank, called "brevets." A practice taken from the British, brevetting temporarily conferred a higher rank upon an officer either for exceptional service or to provide for command over several formations headed by officers of the same rank (as in the case of the Navy's commodore). Brevetting was troublesome, to say the least, to the nineteenth-century army. Although many deplored its confusing effects upon the command structure, the practice survived until the latter part of the century, when medals became the vogue. Today there is a practice known as "frocking," which also advances an officer to a higher rank, but it is strictly limited to very special circumstances.

Customarily, wartime occasions quick promotions for military officers. Modern armies tend to retain larger numbers of officers during peacetime than they actually need. Even so, mobilization for war expands armies with so many recruits that even more officers than are on hand are required. Career officers tend to benefit from such developments. Of course, wartime casualties increase the pace of advancement as well. Among America's professional officers, careers that in peacetime seemed completely stagnated were rejuvenated by the onset of war. Dwight D. Eisenhower, a lieutenant colonel at the beginning of World War II, could four years later wear the four stars of a full general, a feat of advancement that would have been impossible during peacetime, no matter what his talents.

World War II was the first American war whose end did not signal massive reversions to prewar rank. After the Civil War, the Spanish American War, and World War I, it was not at all unusual for an officer who had held an exalted wartime rank to revert to a company or field-grade position. Thus, officers who held the temporary rank of major general during the Civil War could easily become captains again with the surrender at Appomattox, perhaps never to reclaim their once-high status.

Eighteenth Century

ARMY	NAVY	MARINES
Ensign (to 1813)	Midshipman	———
Lieutenant	Sailing Master	Lieutenant
Captain	Lieutenant	Captain
Major	"Lieutenant Commanding"	Major
Lieutenant Colonel	Master Commandant	———
Colonel	Captain	———
Brigadier General	Commodore*	———
Major General	Rear Admiral	———
Lieutenant General	Vice Admiral	———

*Senior captain commanding two or more ships.

Early Nineteenth Century

ARMY	NAVY	MARINES
Coronet (officer aspirant)	Midshipman	———
Second Lieutenant	———	Second Lieutenant
First Lieutenant	Master (Lieutenant, junior grade, after 1883)	First Lieutenant
Captain	Lieutenant	Captain
Major	Lieutenant Commanding (Lieutenant Commander after 1883)	Major
Lieutenant Colonel	Master Commandant (Commander after 1883)	Lieutenant Colonel
Colonel	Captain	Colonel
Brigadier General	Commodore	———
Major General	Rear Admiral	———
Lieutenant General	Vice Admiral	———

Late Nineteenth Century

ARMY	NAVY	MARINES
Second Lieutenant	Ensign	Second Lieutenant
First Lieutenant	Lieutenant, junior grade	First Lieutenant
Captain	Lieutenant	Captain
Major	Lieutenant Commander	Major
Lieutenant Colonel	Commander	Lieutenant Colonel
Colonel	Captain	Colonel
Brigadier General	Rear Admiral, lower half	Brigadier General
Major General	Rear Admiral, upper half	Major General
Lieutenant General	Vice Admiral	———
General	Admiral	———

Late Twentieth Century

ARMY	NAVY	AIR FORCE	MARINES
Second Lieutenant	Ensign	Second Lieutenant	Second Lieutenant
First Lieutenant	Lieutenant, junior grade	First Lieutenant	First Lieutenant
Captain	Lieutenant	Captain	Captain
Major	Lieutenant Commander	Major	Major
Lieutenant Colonel	Commander	Lieutenant Colonel	Lieutenant Colonel
Colonel	Captain	Colonel	Colonel
Brigadier General	Commodore	Brigadier General	Brigadier General
Major General	Rear Admiral	Major General	Major General
Lieutenant General	Vice Admiral	Lieutenant General	Lieutenant General
General	Admiral	General	General
General of the Army	Fleet Admiral	General of the Air Force	———

Military Units

Military units obey only the most general standards of measurement. Even now, the actual dimensions of military units are so variable as to confound discussing them with precision. Historically, units have been formed to counteract the tendency of formations to disorganize under the stresses of campaigning. Technically, units are built to divide armies and navies into controllable pieces; to facilitate their training, provisioning, and movement; and to orchestrate their mixtures of weapons so as to be most effective against the enemy. This is particularly true of armies. Naval and air services, shaped as they are around "capital" weapons such as the warship and the airplane, have had the luxury of simpler organizations.

Military organizations, carefully crafted in times of peace, often are overturned by the demands of actual warfare. Dissimilar units may be collected together temporarily to achieve a particular objective. Units designed, trained, and equipped for one purpose may be used for an entirely different mission. Often, units are misnamed and their real functions obscured by that old talent for euphemism which seems congenital in all military organizations. The Airborne Divisions of World War II were in fact light infantry units whose only distinction was the way in which they arrived on the battlefield. After their arrival, they were an extremely light force and so fought. Armored divisions were not divisions full of tanks, but carried significant complements of "mechanized infantry."

Among those historians who study the armies of the Middle Ages, numbers and dimensions of any sort, from the size of a force to distances marched in a day, are regarded with great suspicion. The great German military historian of the last century, Hans Delbrück, virtually made his reputation challenging figures from military antiquity. Yet even in later centuries, precise strengths of military formations are often difficult to accept with confidence. In peacetime, a military unit is rarely kept at full strength. After the War of 1812, for instance, companies commonly were held at about fifty men, or roughly half their technical size. And although a unit may go to war at something like full strength (but just as often not), it is not long before war's price is exacted. During the Civil War, some regiments were so depleted they were mistaken for companies.

Various armies have had different policies (and at different times, other policies) about how to contend with a unit that has been "fought down." Sometimes a unit simply disappears, its survivors being amalgamated into other units; at other times, the unit retrieves its strength through reinforcement. Each technique has its benefits, but for the student of military history both mean that while numbers imply precision they rarely deliver precision.

Perhaps, then, military units are best thought of in terms of their characteristics. Companies, regiments, divisions, and so on are generally considered capable of carrying out certain missions. Professional soldiers develop a sense of what a squad can and cannot do, of what can and cannot be accomplished with a battery of artillery. The wise military historian and student of military history will attempt to develop that same sense.

The brief glossary of military units that follows does not include naval formations, and that is because naval formations are especially suited to what strategists call "force tailoring." Although today's navy is organized (in descending order) into fleets, forces, groups, elements, and units, the number and type of vessels composing each formation is highly variable, determined in the main by the mission being undertaken. And while admirals typically command fleets (the largest possible fighting naval organization), echelons below fleet may have been commanded by commodores or captains and even lower ranks. Thus, what follows is a list of army units and air force units, given roughly in ascending order.

Squad—the smallest military formation. Major General Emory Upton recommended what he called a "system of fours" after the Civil War in an attempt to control the advance of a company against enemy fire. In World War I, the infantry squad contained eight men as a rule, but in this as in all other cases the squad's strength depended upon the strength of its parent unit, the platoon.

Platoon—derived from the French *peloton*; originally a "group" of soldiers who, during the sixteenth century, were gathered to deliver fire simultaneously against their enemies. Platoon strength is ordinarily around seventy soldiers. In modern armies, the platoon may sometimes undertake independent action, but only for the lightest of missions. In the Air Force, platoons are called "flights," a term that is also employed to describe a flying formation of four aircraft or more.

Company—in modern terms, a collection of several platoons comprising one to two hundred men. As military formations, companies have a venerable tradition, being raised frequently from the same community or general area and so in previous centuries often akin to fraternal organizations as well. The company is capable of independent but not sustained action; however, on the American frontier during the late nineteenth century, companies manned forts and garrisons for years on end without rejoining their parent units. That the company became the organizational backbone of the Army during these years indicates the small size to which it had fallen after the Civil War. In the cavalry and artillery, company-size formations are called, respectively, troops and batteries.

Battalion—a fighting unit of several companies combined. A formation whose invention is attributed to Maurice of Nassau (who is said to have modeled it upon the old Roman *cohort*), the battalion became the vogue in Western armies in the late eighteenth and nineteenth centuries and is used extensively today. The equivalent echelon in the Air Force is the squadron, composed of three or four flights.

Regiment—often confused and used interchangeably with battalion; may be at once an administrative formation that oversees several battalions or companies, or a tactical unit. The customs of national armies vary widely with regard to this formation. During World

War I, for instance, the British Army raised quite a few battalions under one regimental banner, while the Americans preferred to keep regiments at only a few battalions each. In the modern army, the use of regiments is nearly extinct.

Brigade—a tactical organization of two or more battalions (or regiments). In older usage, regiments or battalions brought together temporarily were "brigaded," and the senior colonel from among these formations was made the "brigadier" in an arrangement similar to that of the Navy's "commodore" (a senior captain given command of several ships for a particular mission). Formerly, brigadiers were not considered general officers. Today modern brigades are typically commanded by senior colonels. In the Air Force, the wing (composed of several squadrons) is roughly equivalent.

Group—a relatively modern formation, roughly equivalent to a brigade. The group is formed by several battalions of the same type and function and is usually confined to a specialized support mission such as transport, supply, engineers, or military police. A collection of squadrons can also form a group in the Air Force.

Division—a French invention of the late eighteenth century; intended to operate as a relatively small, maneuverable, and powerful combat force of infantry and artillery. Under Napoleon, divisions of one fighting arm, such as cavalry, were created as well. In the United States, divisions were used extensively during the Civil War, and then not again until the turn of the century. A combination of more than one wing may also make an Air Force division.

Corps—also a French invention, created during the Napoleonic period to ease the difficulties of commanding armies of nearly a quarter of a million men. A collection of divisions (usually three) make up a corps, which in essence is a small field army, encompassing all combat arms and support capable of sustained and independent action. At this echelon in the Air Force is the so-called numbered Air Force (for example, Ninth Air Force).

Army—a collection of several corps under one commander's control; before World War I, the largest possible military formation, sometimes equivalent to an entire national army. A general or field marshal commands.

Army Group—literally, a group of armies; at least two armies along with several lesser formations such as corps or divisions, acting in concert to achieve a theater-level objective. Both world wars saw the extensive use of army groups on virtually every front. Some army groups could number more than a million men.

Persons by Birthplace

American Born

Alabama

Bullard, Robert Lee
Gorgas, William Crawford
Smith, Holland McTyeire
Weatherford, William

Arizona

Geronimo
Patch, Alexander McCarrell

Arkansas

MacArthur, Douglas
Somervell, Brehon Burke

California

Doolittle, James Harold
McNamara, Robert Strange
Oldendorf, Jesse Barrett
Patton, George Smith, Jr.
Zumwalt, Elmo Russell, Jr.

Colorado

Burke, Arleigh Albert
Lea, Homer

Connecticut

Allen, Ethan
Arnold, Benedict

Beaumont, William
Chauncey, Isaac
Foote, Andrew Hull
Foulois, Benjamin Delahauf
Hull, Isaac
Hull, William
Leavenworth, Henry
Terry, Alfred Howe
Wadsworth, Decius
Welles, Gideon

Delaware

Macdonough, Thomas

Florida

Smith, Edmund Kirby
Stilwell, Joseph Warren
Summerall, Charles Pelot

Georgia

Clay, Lucius DuBignon
Flipper, Henry Ossian
Frémont, John Charles
Gordon, John Brown
Hardee, William Joseph
Hodges, Courtney Hicks
Meigs, Montgomery Cunningham
Osceola
Tattnall, Josiah

Twiggs, David Emanuel
Watie, Stand
Wheeler, Joseph

Illinois

Black Hawk
Dean, William Frishe
Harbord, James Guthrie
Palmer, John McAuley
Radford, Arthur William
Short, Walter Campbell
Wagner, Arthur Lockwood
Wilson, James Harrison

Indiana

Billings, John Shaw
Burnside, Ambrose Everett
Dodge, Henry
Eads, James Buchanan
Hershey, Lewis Blain
Little Turtle
Smith, Walter Bedell
Wallace, Lewis

Iowa

Fletcher, Frank Jack
Leahy, William Daniel
Parker, George Marshall

Kansas

Chaffee, Adna Romanza, Jr.
Ellis, Earl Hancock
Johnson, Hugh Samuel

Kentucky

Allen, Henry Tureman
Bell, James Franklin
Canby, Edward Richard Sprigg
Davis, Jefferson
Doniphan, Alexander William
Hood, John Bell
Johnson, Richard Mentor
Johnston, Albert Sidney
Kimmel, Husband Edward
Lincoln, Abraham
McClernand, John Alexander
Pope, John
Scott, Hugh Lenox

Louisiana

Beauregard, Pierre Gustauve Toutant
Collins, Joseph Lawton
Lejeune, John Archer

Maine

Howard, Oliver Otis
Preble, Edward

Maryland

Barney, Joshua
Buchanan, Franklin
Decatur, Stephen
Hammond, William Alexander
Rodgers, John
Rodgers, John, Jr.
Schley, Winfield Scott
Semmes, Raphael
Shelby, Isaac
Spruance, Raymond Ames
Stoddert, Benjamin
Wilkinson, James
Winder, William Henry

Massachusetts

Abrams, Creighton Williams
Bancroft, George
Barton, Clara
Church, Benjamin
Fox, Gustavus Vasa
Greely, Adolphus Washington
Harkins, Paul Donal
Hooker, Joseph
Knox, Henry
Lincoln, Benjamin
Lovell, Joseph
MacArthur, Arthur
Marcy, Randolph Barnes
Marcy, William Learned
Miles, Nelson Appleton
Morison, Samuel Eliot
Pepperrell, Sir William
Phips, Sir William
Porter, David
Putnam, Israel
Rogers, Robert
Shays, Daniel
Swift, Joseph Gardner

Thayer, Sylvanus
Winslow, John
Winthrop, Fitz-John

Michigan

Drum, Hugh Aloysius
Hart, Thomas Charles
Macomb, Alexander
Pontiac
Shafter, William Rufus
Squier, George Owen

Minnesota

McNair, Leslie James

Mississippi

Conner, Fox
Middleton, Troy Houston
Sultan, Daniel Isom

Missouri

Bradley, Omar Nelson
Craig, Malin
Pershing, John Joseph
Taylor, Maxwell Davenport

Montana

Crazy Horse
Looking Glass

Nebraska

Red Cloud
Wedemeyer, Albert Coady

New Hampshire

Butler, Benjamin Franklin
Dearborn, Henry
Kinkaid, Thomas Cassin
Long, Stephen Harriman
Porter, Fitz-John
Ripley, Eleazar Wheelock
Sullivan, John
Wood, Leonard

New Jersey

Bainbridge, William
Du Pont, Samuel Francis

Halsey, William Frederick, Jr.
Hewitt, Henry Kent
Kearny, Stephen Watts
Lawrence, James
Morgan, Daniel
Pike, Zebulon Montgomery
Stockton, Robert Field
Van Fleet, James Alward

New York

Bomford, George
Brant, Joseph
Carlson, Evans Fordyce
Clark, Mark Wayne
Cullum, George Washington
Donovan, William Joseph
Duane, William
Fiske, Bradley Allen
Forrestal, James Vincent
Gavin, James Maurice
Goethals, George Washington
Groves, Leslie Richard
Halleck, Henry Wager
Isherwood, Benjamin Franklin
Luce, Stephen Bleeker
Mackenzie, Ranald Slidell
Mahan, Alfred Thayer
Mahan, Dennis Hart
Marshall, Samuel Lyman Atwood
Melville, George Wallace
Merritt, Wesley
Quitman, John Anthony
Roosevelt, Theodore
Root, Elihu
Sampson, William Thomas
Schofield, John McAllister
Schuyler, Peter
Schuyler, Philip
Sharpe, Henry Granville
Sheridan, Philip Henry
Sternberg, George Miller
Stimson, Henry Lewis
Truxton, Thomas
Upton, Emory
Van Rensselaer, Stephen
Wilkes, Charles
Wool, John Ellis
Worden, John Lorimer

North Carolina

Atkinson, Henry
Bragg, Braxton
Clinch, Duncan Lamont
Daniels, Josephus
Moore, James
Mordecai, Alfred
Polk, Leonidas

Ohio

Alger, Russell Alexander
Buell, Don Carlos
Corbin, Henry Clark
Crook, George
Custer, George Armstrong
Dickman, Joseph Theodore
Eichelberger, Robert Laurence
Funston, Frederick
Grant, Ulysses Simpson
King, Ernest Joseph
Lawton, Henry Ware
LeMay, Curtis Emerson
McDowell, Irvin
McPherson, James Birdseye
Rosecrans, William Starke
Sherman, William Tecumseh
Stanton, Edwin McMasters
Tecumseh

Oregon

Joseph, Chief
Turner, Richmond Kelly

Pennsylvania

Armstrong, John, Jr.
Arnold, Henry Harley
Biddle, James
Bliss, Tasker Howard
Brereton, Lewis Hyde
Brown, Jacob Jennings
Butler, Smedley Darlington
Conner, David
Dahlgren, John Adolphus Bernard
Devers, Jacob Loucks
Gibbon, John
Gorgas, Josiah
Grierson, Benjamin Henry
Hancock, Winfield Scott

Harmar, Josiah
Haupt, Herman
Humphreys, Joshua
Kent, Jacob Ford
Letterman, Jonathan
Liggett, Hunter
McClellan, George Brinton
McNarney, Joseph Taggart
March, Peyton Conway
Marshall, George Catlett
Menoher, Charles Thomas
Pendleton, Joseph Henry
Pickens, Andrew
Porter, David Dixon
Spaatz, Carl Andrew
Stark, Harold Raynsford
Wayne, Anthony
Young, Samuel Baldwin Marks

Rhode Island

Casey, Silas
Greene, Nathanael
Hopkins, Esek
Metacomet
Perry, Matthew Calbraith
Perry, Oliver Hazard

South Carolina

Calhoun, John Caldwell
Jackson, Andrew
Lee, Stephen Dill
Longstreet, James
Marion, Francis
Westmoreland, William Childs

South Dakota

Sitting Bull

Tennessee

Andrews, Frank Maxwell
Farragut, David Glasgow
Forrest, Nathan Bedford
Pillow, Gideon Johnson
York, Alvin Cullum

Texas

Chennault, Claire Lee
Eaker, Ira Clarence

Eisenhower, Dwight David
Graves, William Sidney
Hobby, Oveta Culp
Murphy, Audie
Nimitz, Chester William
Parker, Quanah
Smith, Oliver Prince
Swift, Eben
Truscott, Lucian King, Jr.
Walker, Walton Harris

Utah

Allen, Terry de la Mesa

Vermont

Ainsworth, Fred Clayton
Dewey, George
Hitchcock, Ethan Allen

Virginia

Almond, Edward Mallory
Anderson, Joseph Reid
Byrd, Richard Evelyn
Clark, George Rogers
Clark, William
Cooke, Philip St. George
Early, Jubal Anderson
Evans, Robley Dunglison
Gaines, Edmund Pendleton
Hampton, Wade
Harrison, William Henry
Henderson, Archibald
Hill, Ambrose Powell
Jackson, Thomas Jonathan
Johnston, Joseph Eggleston
Lee, Fitzhugh
Lee, Henry
Lee, Robert Edward
Lee, Samuel Phillips
Lewis, Meriwether
Maury, Matthew Fontaine
Opechancanough
Pickett, George Edward
Puller, Lewis Burwell
Reed, Walter
Ridgway, Matthew Bunker
Rockenbach, Samuel Dickerson
Scott, Winfield

Stuart, James Ewell Brown
Taylor, Zachary
Thomas, George Henry
Vandegrift, Alexander Archer
Washington, George

Washington

Wainwright, Jonathan Mayhew

Washington, D.C.

Davis, Benjamin Oliver, Sr.
Davis, Benjamin Oliver, Jr.
Ewell, Richard Stoddert
Ingersoll, Royal Eason
Ringgold, Samuel

West Virginia

Baker, Newton Diehl
Hines, John Leonard
Lucas, John Porter
Patrick, Mason Matthews

Wisconsin

Barnett, George
Dawley, Ernest Joseph
Mitscher, Marc Andrew
Vandenberg, Hoyt Sanford

Wyoming

Fredendall, Lloyd Ralston

Foreign Born

Canada

Kenney, George Churchill
Sims, William Sowden

England

Amherst, Jeffery
Bacon, Nathaniel, Jr.
Berkeley, Sir William
Braddock, Edward
Campbell, John (Fourth Earl of Loudoun)
Forbes, John
Gates, Horatio
Izard, George
Lee, Charles
Oglethorpe, James Edward

Shirley, William
Smith, John
Standish, Miles
Wolfe, James

France

Lafayette, Marquis de
Mitchell, William

Germany

Krueger, Walter
Leisler, Jacob
Schriever, Bernard Adolph
Steuben, Frederick William, Baron von

Ireland

Barnwell, John
Conway, Thomas
Johnson, Sir William
Montgomery, Richard
Patterson, Robert

Poland

Kósciuszko, Tadeusz Andrzej Bonaventura

Russia

Rickover, Hyman George

Scotland

Jones, John Paul
McDougall, Alexander
St. Clair, Arthur
Vetch, Samuel

Spain

Meade, George Gordon

Sweden

Ericsson, John

Switzerland

Bouquet, Henry

Trinidad

Mallory, Stephen Russell

Entries by Conflict

French and Indian War to the Vietnam War

The names in the appendix are arranged alphabetically, by conflict. Naturally, some names appear more than once, while other entries found in the dictionary are not accounted for here. For ease of reference, some conflicts (such as the numerous Indian campaigns following the Civil War) have been combined into one category.

French and Indian War

Amherst, Jeffery
Bouquet, Henry
Braddock, Edward
Campbell, John (Fourth Earl of Loudoun)
Forbes, John
Gates, Horatio
Hopkins, Esek
Johnson, Sir William
Lee, Charles
Marion, Francis
Montgomery, Richard
Pontiac
Rogers, Robert
St. Clair, Arthur
Schuyler, Peter
Schuyler, Philip
Washington, George
Winslow, John
Wolfe, James

American Revolution

Allen, Ethan
Armstrong, John, Jr.
Arnold, Benedict
Barney, Joshua
Brant, Joseph
Clark, George Rogers
Conway, Thomas
Dearborn, Henry
Gates, Horatio
Greene, Nathanael
Hampton, Wade
Harmar, Josiah
Hopkins, Esek
Hull, William
Humphreys, Joshua
Jones, John Paul
Knox, Henry
Kósciuszko, Tadeusz Andrzej Bonaventura
Lafayette, Marquis de

Lee, Charles
Lee, Henry
Lincoln, Benjamin
McDougall, Alexander
Marion, Francis
Montgomery, Richard
Morgan, Daniel
Pickens, Andrew
Preble, Edward
Putnam, Israel
Rogers, Robert
St. Clair, Arthur
Schuyler, Philip
Shays, Daniel
Shelby, Isaac
Steuben, Frederic William (Baron von)
Stoddert, Benjamin
Sullivan, John
Truxton, Thomas
Washington, George
Wayne, Anthony
Wilkinson, James

Frontier and Naval Expeditions, 1783–1812

Bainbridge, William
Biddle, James
Chauncey, Isaac
Clark, William
Dearborn, Henry
Decatur, Stephen
Gaines, Edmund Pendleton
Harmar, Josiah
Harrison, William Henry
Hull, Isaac
Lawrence, James
Lewis, Meriwether
Little Turtle
Macdonough, Thomas
Morgan, Daniel
Perry, Oliver Hazard
Pike, Zebulon Montgomery
Porter, David
Preble, Edward
Rodgers, John
Stoddert, Benjamin
Tecumseh
Truxton, Thomas
Wilkinson, James

War of 1812

Armstrong, John, Jr.
Atkinson, Henry
Bainbridge, William
Barney, Joshua
Beaumont, William
Biddle, James
Black Hawk
Brown, Jacob Jennings
Chauncey, Isaac
Clinch, Duncan Lamont
Conner, David
Dearborn, Henry
Decatur, Stephen
Dodge, Henry
Farragut, David Glasgow
Gaines, Edmund Pendleton
Hampton, Wade
Harrison, William Henry
Henderson, Archibald
Hull, Isaac
Izard, George
Jackson, Andrew
Johnson, Richard Mentor
Kearny, Stephen Watts
Lawrence, James
Leavenworth, Henry
Lovell, Joseph
Macdonough, Thomas
Macomb, Alexander
Marcy, William Learned
Patterson, Robert
Perry, Matthew Calbraith
Perry, Oliver Hazard
Pike, Zebulon Montgomery
Porter, David
Ripley, Eleazar Wheelock
Rodgers, John
Scott, Winfield
Shelby, Isaac
Stockton, Robert Field
Swift, Joseph Gardner
Tattnall, Josiah
Taylor, Zachary
Tecumseh
Twiggs, David Emanuel
Van Renssalaer, Stephen
Wadsworth, Decius

Wool, John Ellis
Worden, John Lorimer

Civil War

Alger, Russell Alexander
Anderson, Joseph Reid
Barton, Clara
Beauregard, Pierre Gustauve Toutant
Billings, John Shaw
Bragg, Braxton
Buchanan, Franklin
Buell, Don Carlos
Burnside, Ambrose Everett
Butler, Benjamin Franklin
Canby, Edward Richard Sprigg
Casey, Silas
Cooke, Philip St. George
Corbin, Henry Clark
Crook, George
Cullum, George Washington
Custer, George Armstrong
Dahlgren, John Adolphus Bernard
Davis, Jefferson
Dewey, George
Du Pont, Samuel Francis
Eads, James Buchanan
Early, Jubal Anderson
Ericsson, John
Evans, Robley Dunglison
Ewell, Richard Stoddert
Farragut, David Glasgow
Foote, Andrew Hull
Forrest, Nathan Bedford
Fox, Gustavus Vasa
Frémont, John Charles
Gibbon, John
Gordon, John Brown
Gorgas, Josiah
Grant, Ulysses Simpson
Greely, Adolphus Washington
Grierson, Benjamin Henry
Isherwood, Benjamin Franklin
Halleck, Henry Wager
Hammond, William Alexander
Hancock, Winfield Scott
Hardee, William Joseph
Haupt, Herman
Hill, Ambrose Powell

Hitchcock, Ethan Allen
Hood, John Bell
Hooker, Joseph
Howard, Oliver Otis
Jackson, Thomas Jonathan
Johnston, Albert Sidney
Johnston, Joseph Eggleston
Kent, Jacob Ford
Lawton, Henry Ware
Lee, Fitzhugh
Lee, Robert Edward
Lee, Samuel Phillips
Lee, Stephen Dill
Letterman, Jonathan
Lincoln, Abraham
Longstreet, James
Luce, Stephen Bleeker
MacArthur, Arthur
McClellan, George Brinton
McClernand, John Alexander
McDowell, Irvin
MacKenzie, Ranald Slidell
McPherson, James Birdseye
Mahan, Alfred Thayer
Mallory, Stephen Russell
Marcy, Randolph Barnes
Maury, Matthew Fontaine
Meade, George Gordon
Meigs, Montgomery Cunningham
Melville, George Wallace
Merritt, Wesley
Miles, Nelson Appleton
Mordecai, Alfred
Patterson, Robert
Pickett, George Edward
Pillow, Gideon Joseph
Polk, Leonidas
Pope, John
Porter, David Dixon
Porter, Fitz-John
Rodgers, John, Jr.
Rosecrans, William Starke
Sampson, William Thomas
Schley, Winfield Scott
Schofield, John McAllister
Scott, Winfield
Semmes, Raphael
Shafter, William Rufus

Pershing, John Joseph
Rockenbach, Samuel Dickerson
Roosevelt, Theodore
Root, Elihu
Sampson, William Thomas
Schley, Winfield Scott
Shafter, William Rufus
Sharpe, Henry Granville
Sims, William Sowden
Summerall, Charles Pelot
Wilson, James Harrison
Wood, Leonard
Young, Samuel Baldwin Marks

World War I

Allen, Henry Tureman
Allen, Terry de la Mesa
Almond, Edward Mallory
Arnold, Henry Harley
Baker, Newton Diehl
Barnett, George
Brereton, Lewis Hyde
Bullard, Robert Lee
Butler, Smedley Darlington
Chaffee, Adna Romanza, Jr.
Clark, Mark Wayne
Clay, Lucius Du Bignon
Collins, Joseph Lawton
Craig, Malin
Daniels, Josephus
Dawley, Ernest Joseph
Devers, Jacob Loucks
Dickman, Joseph Theodore
Donovan, William Joseph
Drum, Hugh Aloysius
Eichelberger, Robert Lawrence
Ellis, Earl Hancock
Fletcher, Frank Jack
Foulois, Benjamin Delahauf
Fredendall, Lloyd Ralston
Geiger, Roy Stanley
Gorgas, William Crawford
Graves, William Sidney
Halsey, William Frederick, Jr.
Harbord, James Guthrie
Hart, Thomas Charles
Hershey, Lewis Blain

Hewitt, Henry Kent
Hines, John Leonard
Hodges, Courtney Hicks
Johnson, Hugh Samuel
Kenney, George Churchill
Kimmel, Husband Edward
King, Ernest Joseph
Kinkaid, Thomas Cassin
Knox, William Franklin
Krueger, Walter
Leahy, William Daniel
Lejeune, John Archer
Liggett, Hunter
Lucas, John Porter
MacArthur, Douglas
McNair, Leslie James
McNarney, Joseph Taggart
March, Peyton Conway
Marshall, George Catlett
Marshall, Samuel Lyman Attwood
Menoher, Charles Thomas
Middleton, Troy Houston
Mitchell, William
Nimitz, Chester William
Oldendorf, Jesse Barrett
Palmer, John McAuley
Patch, Alexander McCarrell
Patrick, Mason Matthews
Patton, George Smith, Jr.
Pershing, John Joseph
Radford, Arthur William
Rockenbach, Samuel Dickerson
Sharpe, Henry Granville
Short, Walter Campbell
Smith, Holland McTyeire
Smith, Walter Bedell
Somervell, Brehon Burke
Spaatz, Carl Andrew
Squier, George Owen
Stark, Harold Raynsford
Stilwell, Joseph Warren
Stimson, Henry Lewis
Sultan, Daniel Isom
Summerall, Charles Pelot
Swift, Eben
Truscott, Lucien King, Jr.
Van Fleet, James Alward

Hershey, Lewis Blain
LeMay, Curtis Emerson
MacArthur, Douglas
Marshall, George Catlett
Puller, Lewis Burwell
Radford, Arthur William
Ridgway, Matthew Bunker
Smith, Oliver Prince
Taylor, Maxwell Davenport
Van Fleet, James Alward
Walker, Walton Harris
Westmoreland, William Childs

Zumwalt, Elmo Russell, Jr.

Vietnam War

Abrams, Creighton Williams
Davis, Benjamin Oliver, Jr.
Harkins, Paul Donal
Hershey, Lewis Blain
McNamara, Robert Strange
Taylor, Maxwell Davenport
Westmoreland, William Childs
Zumwalt, Elmo Russell, Jr.

Entries by Service

The divisions made in this appendix—Army, Navy, Marines, Air Force, Native Americans, Militia, and Civilians—refer to the sort of activity in which the subjects engaged; other notations are made only when a subject belongs to a foreign establishment. No distinctions are made between Continental, American, or Confederate armies in the "Army" section. Similarly, the "Air Force" section lists those who served in either the early Air Service, Army Air Corps, or U.S. Air Force. Of course, some subjects served in more than one category (Militia and Continental Army, for instance); in such cases, the listing is made on the basis of highest service performed. Under the heading of "Civilians," some subjects also served in one branch or another, but their contributions hinged less upon that service than upon their work elsewhere. Although several men who became presidents are listed here, only one, Abraham Lincoln, is listed for his service as president per se. Of course, such divisions are always subjective and therefore problematical. Within each category, listings are alphabetical.

Army

Abrams, Creighton Williams
Ainsworth, Fred Clayton
Allen, Henry Tureman
Allen, Terry de la Mesa
Almond, Edward Mallory
Amherst, Jeffery (British Army)
Anderson, Joseph Reid
Armstrong, John, Jr.
Arnold, Benedict (American and British Armies)
Atkinson, Henry
Beaumont, William
Beauregard, Pierre Gustauve Toutant
Bell, James Franklin
Billings, John Shaw

Bliss, Tasker Howard
Bomford, George
Bouquet, Henry (British Army)
Braddock, Edward (British Army)
Bradley, Omar Nelson
Bragg, Braxton
Brown, Jacob Jennings
Buell, Don Carlos
Bullard, Robert Lee
Burnside, Ambrose Everett
Butler, Benjamin Franklin
Campbell, John, (Fourth Earl of Loudoun) (British Army)
Canby, Edward Richard Sprigg
Casey, Silas

Chaffee, Adna Romanza, Jr.
Clark, George Rogers
Clark, Mark Wayne
Clark, William
Clay, Lucius Du Bignon
Clinch, Duncan Lamont
Collins, Joseph Lawton
Conway, Thomas
Cooke, Philip St. George
Corbin, Henry Clark
Craig, Malin
Crook, George
Cullum, George Washington
Custer, George Armstrong
Davis, Benjamin Oliver, Sr.
Davis, Jefferson
Dawley, Ernest Joseph
Dean, William Frishe
Dearborn, Henry
Devers, Jacob Loucks
Dickman, Joseph Theodore
Doniphan, Alexander William
Donovan, William Joseph
Drum, Hugh Aloysius
Duane, William
Early, Jubal Anderson
Eichelberger, Robert Lawrence
Eisenhower, Dwight David
Ewell, Richard Stoddert
Flipper, Henry Ossian
Forbes, John
Forrest, Nathan Bedford
Fredendall, Lloyd Ralston
Frémont, John Charles
Funston, Frederick
Gaines, Edmund Pendleton
Gates, Horatio
Gavin, James Maurice
Gibbon, John
Goethals, George Washington
Gordon, John Brown
Gorgas, Josiah
Gorgas, William Crawford
Grant, Ulysses Simpson
Graves, William Sidney
Greely, Adolphus Washington
Greene, Nathanael
Grierson, Benjamin Henry

Groves, Leslie Richard
Halleck, Henry Wager
Hammond, William Alexander
Hampton, Wade
Hancock, Winfield Scott
Harbord, James Guthrie
Hardee, William Joseph
Harkins, Paul Donal
Harmar, Josiah
Harrison, William Henry
Haupt, Herman
Hershey, Lewis Blain
Hill, Ambrose Powell
Hines, John Leonard
Hitchcock, Ethan Allen
Hobby, Oveta Culp
Hodges, Courtney Hicks
Hood, John Bell
Hooker, Joseph
Howard, Oliver Otis
Hull, William
Izard, George
Jackson, Andrew
Jackson, Thomas Jonathan
Johnson, Hugh Samuel
Johnston, Albert Sidney
Johnston, Joseph Eggleston
Kearny, Stephen Watts
Kent, Jacob Ford
Knox, Henry
Kósciuszko, Tadeusz Andrzej Bonaventura
Krueger, Walter
Lafayette, Marquis de
Lawton, Henry Ware
Lea, Homer (Chinese Army)
Leavenworth, Henry
Lee, Charles
Lee, Fitzhugh
Lee, Henry
Lee, Robert Edward
Lee, Stephen Dill
Letterman, Jonathan
Lewis, Meriwether
Liggett, Hunter
Lincoln, Benjamin
Long, Stephen Harriman
Longstreet, James
Lovell, Joseph

Lucas, John Porter
MacArthur, Arthur
MacArthur, Douglas
McClellan, George Brinton
McClernand, John Alexander
McDougall, Alexander
McDowell, Irvin
Mackenzie, Ranald Slidell
McNair, Lesley James
McNarney, Joseph Taggart
Macomb, Alexander
McPherson, James Birdseye
Mahan, Dennis Hart
March, Peyton Conway
Marcy, Randolph Barnes
Marshall, George Catlett
Marshall, Samuel Lyman Atwood
Meade, George Gordon
Meigs, Montgomery Cunningham
Merritt, Wesley
Middleton, Troy Houston
Miles, Nelson Appleton
Montgomery, Richard
Mordecai, Alfred
Palmer, John McAuley
Parker, George Marshall, Jr.
Patch, Alexander McCarrell
Patterson, Robert
Patton, George Smith, Jr.
Pershing, John Joseph
Pickett, George Edward
Pike, Zebulon Montgomery
Pillow, Gideon Joseph
Polk, Leonidas
Pope, John
Porter, Fitz-John
Putnam, Israel
Quitman, John Anthony
Reed, Walter
Ridgway, Matthew Bunker
Ringgold, Samuel
Ripley, Eleazar Wheelock
Rockenbach, Samuel Dickerson
Rosecrans, William Starke
St. Clair, Arthur
Schofield, John McAllister
Schuyler, Philip
Scott, Hugh Lenox

Scott, Winfield
Shafter, William Rufus
Sharpe, Henry Granville
Sheridan, Philip Henry
Sherman, William Tecumseh
Short, Walter Campbell
Smith, Edmund Kirby
Smith, Walter Bedell
Somervell, Brehon Burke
Squier, George Owen
Sternberg, George Miller
Steuben, Frederic William
Stilwell, Joseph Warren
Stimson, Henry Lewis
Stuart, James Ewell Brown
Sullivan, John
Sultan, Daniel Isom
Summerall, Charles Pelot
Swift, Eben
Swift, Joseph Gardner
Taylor, Maxwell Davenport
Taylor, Zachary
Terry, Alfred Howe
Thayer, Sylvanus
Thomas, George Henry
Truscott, Lucian King, Jr.
Twiggs, David Emanuel
Upton, Emory
Van Fleet, James Alward
Wadsworth, Decius
Wagner, Arthur Lockwood
Wainwright, Jonathan Mayhew
Walker, Walton Harris
Wallace, Lewis
Washington, George
Watie, Stand
Wayne, Anthony
Wedemeyer, Albert Coady
Westmoreland, William Childs
Wheeler, Joseph
Wilkinson, James
Wilson, James Harrison
Winder, William Henry
Wolfe, James (British Army)
Wood, Leonard
Wool, John Ellis
York, Alvin Cullum
Young, Samuel Baldwin Marks

Navy

Bainbridge, William
Barney, Joshua
Biddle, James
Buchanan, Franklin
Burke, Arleigh Albert
Byrd, Richard Evelyn
Chauncey, Isaac
Conner, David
Dahlgren, John Adolphus Bernard
Decatur, Stephen
Dewey, George
Du Pont, Samuel Francis
Evans, Robley Dunglison
Farragut, David Glasgow
Fiske, Bradley
Fletcher, Frank Jack
Foote, Andrew
Fox, Gustavus Vasa
Halsey, William Frederick, Jr.
Hart, Thomas Charles
Hewitt, Henry Kent
Hopkins, Esek
Hull, Isaac
Ingersoll, Royal Eason
Isherwood, Benjamin Franklin
Jones, John Paul
Kimmel, Husband Edward
King, Ernest Joseph
Kinkaid, Thomas Cassin
Lawrence, James
Leahy, William Daniel
Lee, Samuel Phillips
Luce, Stephan Bleeker
Macdonough, Thomas
Mahan, Alfred Thayer
Maury, Matthew Fontaine
Melville, George Wallace
Mitscher, Marc Andrew
Morison, Samuel Eliot
Nimitz, Chester William
Oldendorf, Jesse Barrett
Perry, Matthew Calbraith
Perry, Oliver Hazard
Porter, David
Porter, David Dixon
Preble, Edward
Radford, Arthur William

Rickover, Hyman George
Rodgers, John
Rodgers, John, Jr.
Sampson, William Thomas
Schley, Winfield Scott
Semmes, Raphael
Sims, William Sowden
Spruance, Raymond Ames
Stark, Harold Raynsford
Stockton, Robert Field
Tattnall, Josiah
Truxton, Thomas
Turner, Richmond Kelly
Wilkes, Charles
Worden, John Lorimer
Zumwalt, Elmo Russell, Jr.

Air Force

Andrews, Frank Maxwell
Arnold, Henry Harley
Brereton, Lewis Hyde
Chennault, Claire Lee
Davis, Benjamin Oliver, Jr.
Doolittle, James Harold
Eaker, Ira Clarence
Foulois, Benjamin Delahauf
Kenney, George Churchill
LeMay, Curtis Emerson
Menoher, Charles Thomas
Mitchell, William
Patrick, Mason Matthew
Schriever, Bernard
Spaatz, Carl Andrew
Vandenberg, Hoyt Sanford

Marines

Barnett, George
Butler, Smedley Darlington
Carlson, Evans Fordyce
Ellis, Earl Hancock
Geiger, Roy Stanley
Henderson, Archibald
Lejeune, John Archer
Pendleton, Joseph Henry
Puller, Lewis Burwell
Smith, Holland McTyeire
Smith, Oliver Prince
Vandegrift, Alexander Archer

Native Americans

Black Hawk
Black Kettle
Brant, Joseph
Crazy Horse
Geronimo
Joseph, Chief
Little Turtle
Looking Glass
Metacomet
Opechancanough
Osceola
Parker, Quanah
Pontiac
Red Cloud
Sitting Bull
Tecumseh
Weatherford, William

Militia

Allen, Ethan
Bacon, Nathaniel, Jr.
Barnwell, John
Berkeley, Sir William
Church, Benjamin
Dodge, Henry
Johnson, Richard Mentor
Leisler, Jacob
Marcy, William Learned
Marion, Francis
Morgan, Daniel
Oglethorpe, James
Pepperrell, Sir William
Phips, Sir William

Pickens, Andrew
Rogers, Robert
Roosevelt, Theodore
Schuyler, Peter
Shays, Daniel
Shelby, Isaac
Shirley, Sir William
Van Rensselaer, Stephen
Vetch, Samuel
Winslow, John
Winthrop, Fitz-John

Civilians

Alger, Russell Alexander
Anderson, Joseph Reid
Baker, Newton Diehl
Bancroft, George
Barton, Clara
Calhoun, John Caldwell
Daniels, Josephus
Eads, James Buchanan
Ericsson, John
Forrestal, James
Humphreys, Joshua
Lincoln, Abraham
McNamara, Robert Strange
Mallory, Stephen Russell
Moore, James
Root, Elihu
Smith, John
Standish, Miles
Stanton, Edwin McMasters
Stoddert, Benjamin
Welles, Gideon

Index

ABC–1 agreement, 1046
Abercromby, James, 28, 334, 531
Abrams, Creighton William, Jr., 5–8; at West Point, 5; 1st Cav. Division, 5; as COMUSMACV, 6; and Tet Offensive, 6; Oxford Riots, 6; as Chief of Staff, 6–7
Adams, John, 492, 571, 651
Adams, John Quincy, 475, 477, 616, 811
Adams, Samuel, 368
Admirals' Revolt, 131
Adobe Walls, battle of, 821
Advance Base Force, 140, 305, 627
Aguinaldo, Emilio, 358, 591
Ainsworth, Fred Clayton, 8–12; at Dartmouth, 8; at West Point, 8; in Bannock War, 8; Record and Pension Division, 9; Ford Theater disaster, 9; National Defense Act of 1916, 11; 1210
Air Corps Act of 1926, 828
Aisne-Marne Offensive, 129, 848
Alabama, 720, 975
Albany Congress, 530–31
Alencaster, Joaquin del Real, 861
Alexander, Harold, 245
Alexander, R.L.G., 667
Alger, Russell Alexander, 12–15; in 2d Michigan Volunteers, 12; as entrepreneur, 13; as GAR commander, 13; as Secretary of War, 13–14; 211, 759, 769

Allen, Ethan, 15–19; and Green Mountain Boys, 15; capture of Fort Ticonderoga, 16; attack on Montreal, 16–17; as POW, 17; and Arlington Junta, 17; and Washington, 18; 39
Allen, Henry Tureman, 19–22; Santiago Campaign, 19; attaché in Russia, 19; aide to Miles, 19; commands US forces in Germany, 20–21; explorations, 21; as presidential candidate, 21; and League of Nations, 21; 97
Allen, Terry de la Mesa, 22–24; at West Point, 23; in World War I, 23; commands 1st Infantry Division, 23; commands 104th Infantry Division, 23; in North Africa Campaign, 24; 352, 1021
Allied Kommandatura, 186
Almond, Edward Mallory, 25–27; in World War I, 25; in World War II, 25, in Korean War, 25–26; as X Corps Commander, 25; as commander of 92d Infantry Division, 26, 1155
Amelia Island, 189
Americal Division, 824, 826
American Colonization Society, 841, 1062
American Expeditionary Force, 438
American Historical Association, 934
American Liberty League, 141
American Military Library, 283, 284

American Public Health Association, 87–88

American Red Cross, 69

Amherst, Jeffery, First Baron, 27–31; at Battle of Dettingen, 27; at Battle of Fontenoy, 27; aide to Duke of Cumberland, 27; plan to take New France, 28; captures Louisbourg, 28; captures Fort Ticonderoga, 29; conquest of Canada, 29; 103, 532, 871, 892, 966

Anaconda Plan, 644, 974

Anderson, Joseph Reid, 31–33; at West Point, 31; and Tredegar Iron Works, 31; and City of Richmond, 32; 390

Andrews, Frank Maxwell, 33–36; and H. T. Allen, 33; at West Point, 33; 258

Andre, John, and Benedict Arnold, 41

Anglo-Powhatan Wars, 808, 809

Annapolis. See U. S. Naval Academy

Annapolis Royal, 1140

Antietam, battle of, 69, 134, 218, 434, 471, 485, 488, 494, 555, 657, 1068

ANVIL-DRAGOON, 468, 794

Anzio, battle of, 118, 667, 1111

Appomattox, 224, 382

Arapaho Indians, 92–93

Argonne Forest, 641

Arikara War, 45

Armed Forces Special Weapons Project, 417

Armies of Asia and Europe (Upton), 1125

Armstrong, John, Jr., 36–38; as Secretary of War, 37; 252; Montreal Campaign, 433; 452, 516, 533, 578, 1084; reorganization of War Department, 1144

Army Air Forces, 697

Army and Navy Journal. 11, 163

Army and Navy Register, 11

Army Ground Forces, 180, 697

Army Medical Department, 72

Army Medical Museum, 88, 429

Army Medical School, 905

Army Officers' Guide, 445

Army of the James, 76

Army of the Ohio, 125

Army of the Potomac, 133, 138

Army of the Tennessee, 113

Army of the West, 271

Army Service Forces, 697, 1029

Army War College, 942

Army War College Board, 96, 97

Arnold, Benedict, at Fort Ticonderoga, 16; 38–42; march to Quebec, 39; Danbury raid, 40; as British officer, 41; 250, 366, 448, 584, 779; treason, 948

Arnold, Henry Harley, 42–45; MacKay Trophy, 42; and George C. Marshall, 42; aviation pioneer, 43; motion picture industry, 43; second MacKay Trophy, 43; and scientific community, 43; and World War II, 44; 118, 218, 293, 774, 1032, 1131

Arthur, Chester A., 70, 643

Artillery School of Practice, 148

Asi-Yahola (*see also* Osceola), 811

Astor Battery, 722

Astor, John Jacob, 168, 705

Atkinson, Henry, 45–48; and Wade Hampton, 45; and James Wilkinson, 45; Missouri Expedition, 45; 90, 267, 549

Atlanta campaign, 443, 1108

Atlantic, battle of, 574

Atlantic Charter Conference, 563

Atomic Energy Commission, 417

AVALANCHE, 245, 246

B–17, 346

Bache, Benjamin Franklin, 282

Bacon, Nathaniel, Jr., 49–52; early life, 49; emigration to America, 49–50; declared a rebel, 50; "Declaration of the People," 50–51; 82; rebellion, 82

Bad Axe, battle of, 91, 269

Bad Hand, 693

Bainbridge, Joseph, 254

Bainbridge, William, 52–54, 196, 319, 497, 498, 588, 841, 886

Baker, Newton Diehl, 54–57; and ROTC, 54; Council of National Defense, 54–55; conscription, 55; 401, 722, 755, 848, 934, 982

Baker Board, 35, 56, 277, 280, 345

Baldwin, Roger, 142

Ball's Bluff, battle of, 403

Bancroft, George, 57–60; Secretary of the Navy, 58; naval reform, 58; and Mexican

and service integration, 236; and Sky Marshal program, 236

Davis, Benjamin Oliver, Sr., 235, 237–40; at Tuskegee Institute, 238; 10th Cavalry, 238; in Spanish-American War, 238; commands 2d Cavalry Division, 238; Inspector General's Dept., 239; and World War II service integration, 239; 1020

Davis, Jefferson, 76, 78, 112, 137, 205, 240–44; at West Point, 240; and "Mississippi Rifles," 241; as congressman, 241; at Battle of Buena Vista, 241; as Senator, 241; as Secretary of War, 241; as President of the Confederacy, 241–42; postwar image, 243; 338, 390, 441, 475, 476, 536, 539, 613, 749, 784, 863, 866

Dawley, Ernest Joseph (Mike), 244–47; in World War I, 244; at Paris Peace Conference, 244; commands VI Corps, 245; relieved of command, 245

Dean, William Frishe, 247–50; in World War II, 247; military governor of South Korea, 247; commands 24th Infantry Division, 247; defense of Taejon, 248; Chinese prisoner of war, 248–49

Deane, Silas, 202

Dearborn, Henry, 250–54; as physician, 250; at Breed's Hill, 250; captured at Quebec, 250; at Yorktown, 250; appointed major general, 251; as Secretary of War, 251; attack on York, 252; and army reform, 252; establishment of West Point, 253; 283, 503, 861

Decatur, Stephen, 52, 84, 169, 196, 254–57; early duels, 254; raid on *Philadelphia*, 254; acclaimed as naval hero, 254; captures *Macedonian*, 255; expedition against Barbary Pirates, 256; surrenders *President*, 255; duel with James Barron, 256; 587, 841, 886

DEEPFREEZE, 144

Dempsey, Miles C., 372

Department of the Gulf, 137

Department of the Ohio, 136

Dern, George, 214

Desert Training Center, 1154

DeSmet, Pierre-Jeane, 1007

Detroit, surrender of, 1100

Devers, Jacob Loucks, 257–60; at West Point, 257; and bases-for-destroyers agreement, 258; 6th Army Group, 258; as combat developer, 259

Dewey, George, 79–80; 260–63; at Naval Academy, 260; service with Farragut, 260; and naval reforms, 261; on Asiatic station, 261; and Battle of Manila Bay, 261–62; as President of Navy General Board, 262; and Naval War Plans, 263; and battleship development, 263; 455, 759, 933, 954, 955

Dewey, Thomas E., 281

Dickman, Joseph Theodore, 263–66; at West Point, 264; duty in Asia, 264; Leavenworth instructor, 264; and *Field Service Regulations*, 264; commands 3d Division, 264; commands IV Corps, 264; stand on the Marne, 265; 641

Diem, Ngo Dinh, 445, 1180

Dix, Dorothea, 69

Dodge, Henry, 267–69; as militiaman, 267; as frontiersman, 267; Black Hawk War, 267; as Dragoon commander, 268; as Territorial Governor, 268; as Senator, 268

Dodge Commission, and Russell Alger, 15

Dominion of New England, 851

Doniphan, Alexander William, 269–73; as frontier lawyer, 270; in Mormon War, 270; commands Army of the West, 271; captures Santa Fe, 271; Battle of Chihuahua, 272; Battle of El Paso, 272

Donovan, William Joseph ("Wild Bill"), 273–76; in World War I, 273; as politician, 273–74; Assistant Attorney General, 274; and Office of Strategic Services, 274; 281

Doolittle, James Harold, 276–79; wins Schneider Cup, 277; at MIT, 277; as pioneer aviator, 277; commands Twelfth Air Force, 277; Tokyo Raid, 277; and Baker Board, 277; commands Eighth Air Force, 278; postwar career, 278; 425, 775, 1131

Doolittle Board, 278, 767

Dorchester Heights, 570

Dorn, Earl Van, 412

Douglas, Stephen A., 682
Draft Act of 1917, 816
DRAGOON, 825
Dreadnought, 936
Drewry's Bluff, battle of, 76
Drum, Hugh Aloysius, 279–82; aide to Frederick Funston, 279; in World War I, 280; and separate air force, 280; offered China command, 281
Drum Board, 280–81
Duane, William, 282–84; edits *Aurora,* 282; as journalist in England, 282; career in India, 282; military writings, 283; translates Jomini, 284
Dulles, Allen, 275
Dulles, John Foster, 194, 1026
Du Pont, Francis, 927
Du Pont, Samuel Francis, 230, 284–87; naval appointment, 285; and Naval Academy, 285; and Mexican War, 285; Superintendent of Naval Academy, 285; expedition to China, 285; Port Royal expedition, 286; attack on Charleston, 286; relieved, 333; 349
Du Pont de Nemours, Pierre Samuel, 285

Eads, James Buchanan, 289–92; as salvor, 289; and armored gunboat development, 289–90; 332; designs Brooklyn Bridge, 291
Eads Gunboats, 290, 291, 332
Eaker, Ira Clarence, 292–95; enters Air Service, 292; as aviation pioneer, 292; studies in journalism, 293; aviation writing with H. H. Arnold, 293; in World War II, 293; postwar career, 293; advocates daylight bombing, 294; in Mediterranean campaigns, 294; commands Eighth Air Force, 294; 704, 1031
Early, Jubal Anderson, 218–19, 224, 295–98; at West Point, 295; in Mexican War, 295; as Virginia politician, 295; at First Manassas, 296; at Gettysburg, 296; at Fredericksburg, 296; in the Shenandoah Valley, 296; opposes Philip Sheridan, 296; postwar career, 297; relieved of command, 296–97; as combat com-

mander, 297–98; 316, 387, 489, 607, 615, 659, 991
Eastern Solomons, battle of, 326, 567
Eaton, William, 497
École Polytechnique, 914, 1106
Eichelberger, Robert Lawrence, 298–301; at West Point, 299; as Leavenworth instructor, 299; in military intelligence, 299; and Siberian expedition, 299; and New Guinea campaign, 300; and Hollandia, 300; commands 6th Army, 300; Philippine campaign, 300; commands I Corps, 300; as Superintendent of West Point, 300; 580, 1154
Eighth Route Army (Chinese), 158–59
82d Airborne Division, 370
Eisenhower, Dwight David, 24, 108, 118, 131, 181, 186, 194; as Fox Conner's pupil, 200; 245, 258, 277, 281, 301–4; early life, 301; at West Point, 301; interwar career, 302; in Operations Division, 302; and World War II strategy, 302; TORCH, 302; commands OVERLORD, 302; as President of Columbia, 303; as U.S. President, 303; the "New Look," 303; as NATO commander, 303; and civil rights, 303; 351, 468–69, 483, 666, 700, 703, 724, 766, 825, 833, 848, 911, 1174
El Caney, battle of, 557, 590
Elliot, Jesse D., 256
Ellis, Earl, 304–8; commissioned in Marines, 305; advance base theory, 305; expansion of USMC, 306; aide to George Barnett, 306; Guam defenses, 306; physical and mental collapses, 306; Operations Plan 712, 306; secret mission to Mexico, 306; secret mission to Western Pacific, 307; suspicious death, 307; and Micronesia Plan, 308; 374, 628
Emancipation Proclamation, 645–46
Embalmed Beef scandal, 14, 770
Embargo Act, 844
Emerson, Ralph Waldo, 477
Empress Augusta Bay, battle of, 130
Endicott Board, 959
English Civil War, 81–82
Ericsson, John, 290, 308–10; patents screw propeller, 308; builds *Monitor,* 309; sup-

port by Robert Stockton, 309; builds
Princeton, 309; 1062
European Recovery Act, 736
Eustis, William, 37, 251, 1084
Eutaw Springs, battle of, 410, 431, 432,
610, 732, 854
Evans, Robley Dunglison, 310–13; as na-
val academy instructor, 311; in Civil War,
311; and Chilean crisis, 311–12; com-
mands *Iowa,* 312; in Spanish-American
War, 312; Battle of Santiago, 312; and
Great White Fleet, 312; 467, 566
Ewell, Richard Stoddert, 313–17; at West
Point, 314; frontier duty, 314; in Mex-
ican War, 314; joins Confederacy, 314;
at Seven Days' Battle, 315; commands
II Corps, 315; at Gettysburg, 315; at
Spotsylvania, 316; Battle of the Wilder-
ness, 316; 527, 607, 614
Explorer's Club, 406

Fair Oaks, battle of, 494, 539, 680
Fall, Albert, 329
Fallen Timbers, battle of, 115, 182, 1098,
1169, 1190
Farnsworth, Elon, 224
Farragut, David Glasgow, 123, 137, 156,
157, 260, 291, 319–22; as ward of David
Porter, 319; in War of 1812, 319; in South
America, 319; in Mexican War, 320; on
the Brazilian station, 320; observes
French action in Mexico, 320; com-
mands European Squadron, 320; on
Lower Mississippi, 320; attack on New
Orleans, 320–21; Vicksburg blockade,
321; Red River blockade, 321; on Gulf
blockade, 321; Battle of Mobile Bay,
321–22; 349, 454, 618, 876, 877, 881,
954
Fechet, Edmund, 1009
Fechet, James, 344
"Fencibles," 896
Fernandina Island, 189
Fetterman, William J., 216
Fetterman Massacre, 902
Field, Marshall, and Russell Alger, 13
Field Service Regulations of 1910, 90
5th Cavalry Regiment, 1081

Fillmore, Millard, 842
1st Dragoons, 206
1st Marine Aviation Force, 373
1st Marine Raider Regiment, 158
1st U. S. Volunteer Cavalry Regiment, 933
Fisher's Hill, battle of, 298
Fiske, Bradley Allen, 232, 261, 263, 322–
25; and naval technology, 323; President
of U.S. Naval Institute, 323; on Naval
General Board, 323; and naval radios,
323; at Battle of Mobile Bay, 323; dispute with Josephus Daniels, 323; advocates National Security Council, 324;
advocates Naval General Staff, 324; innovations in naval technology, 324; creation of Chief of Naval Operations, 324;
670
V Amphibious Corps, 159
Five Forks, battle of, 398, 857–58, 991
505th Parachute Infantry Regiment, 370
503d Parachute Infantry Battalion, 370
Five-Paragraph Field Order, 1082
Fletcher, Frank Jack, 325–28; wins
Congressional Medal of Honor, 325; at
Naval Academy, 325; commands TF 14,
325; commands TF 17, 326; defense of
Aleutians, 326; at Battle of the Coral
Sea, 326; at Marshall and Gilbert Islands, 326; at Battle of Midway, 326
Flexible Response, 372, 700, 1092–93
Flipper, Henry Ossian, 328–31; as first black
graduate of West Point, 328; writes *The
Colored Cadet at West Point,* 328;
"Flipper's Ditch," 328; service on the
frontier, 328; court martial, 328; confi-
dential observer of Mexican Revolution,
329; as mining engineer, 329; Special
Agent for Department of Justice, 329;
with Sierra Mining Company, 329; as
assistant to Secretary of the Interior, 329;
in Venezuela, 329; ostracism at West
Point, 329; as translator, 330
Florida, 720
Florida Campaign of 1778, 853
Floyd, John B., 749, 862
Flying Tigers (American Volunteer Group),
171
Foote, Andrew Hull, 230, 291, 331–34; at

French and Indian War, 491
Frolic, 84
Front Royal, battle of, 315, 525
Fuller, John Frederick Charles, 615, 738
Funston, Frederick, 279, 357–61; as botanical expeditionary, 357; Yukon expedition, 357; in Spanish-American War, 358; and Cuban independence, 358; in Philippine Insurrection, 358; captures Emilo Aguinaldo, 358; wins Congressional Medal of Honor, 358; and San Francisco earthquake relief, 359; commands Punitive Expedition in Mexico, 359; commands Vera Cruz expedition, 359; as possible AEF commander, 360
Furse, Armand, 984

Gage, Thomas, 39, 892
Gaines, Edmund Pendleton, 38, 189, 191, 363–66; arrests Aaron Burr, 363; as military surveyor, 363; on Florida frontier, 363; defense of Fort Erie, 364; First Seminole War, 364; commands Western Department, 364; 475, 517, 706, 811, 813, 918
Gaines' Mill, battle of, 485
Gale, Anthony, 461
Gall, 217
Garand Rifle, adoption by the Army, 215
Gardiner, Lion, 1018
Gardiner, Thomas, 50
Garfield, James A., 209, 398, 436, 643
Garrison, Lindley M., 54
Gates, Horatio, 36, 40, 202, 366–69; French and Indian War, 366; at siege of Boston, 366; dispute with Schuyler, 366–67; duel with James Wilkinson, 367; in Southern Campaigns, 367; at Newburgh, 367; at Saratoga, 368; at Camden, 369; 409, 576, 967
Gavin, James Maurice, 369–72; early life, 370; at West Point, 370; as West Point instructor, 370; as pioneer paratrooper, 370; Mediterranean campaigns, 370; assault on Normandy, 370–71; commands 82d Airborne Division, 371; Battle of the Bulge, 371; and "New Look" policies, 371; commands VII Corps, 371; Weapon

Systems Evaluation Group, 371; 911, 1093
Geiger, Roy Stanley, 372–77; as lawyer, 373; in Nicaraguan constabulary, 373; as naval aviator, 373; on Guadalcanal, 373; professional education, 373; commands Tenth Army, 374; Battle of Okinawa, 374; Battle of Guam, 374; assault on Peleliu, 375
Gendarmerie d'Haiti, 140
General Headquarters (GHQ) Air Force, 280, 345
General Monk, 63
General Orders Number 40, 436
General Staff, 150
General Staff Act of 1903, 940
General Staff Corps, 97
General Staff reforms, 770
Germantown, battle of, 448, 572, 688, 1072
Geronimo, 219, 377–80; capture at San Carlos, 377; border raids, 377–78; surrender to George Crook, 378; pursuit by Nelson A. Miles, 378; surrender to Miles, 378; at Fort Pickens, 379; at Fort Sill, 379; as guerrilla, 379; 590, 672, 822
Gettysburg, battle of, 86, 224, 296, 381, 387, 459, 460, 471, 472, 485, 490, 607, 857, 1069
Ghent, treaty of, 521
Ghost Corps, 1154
Ghost Dance, 903, 1009
Gibbon, John, 225, 380–83; at West Point, 380; as West Point instructor, 380; and Seminole removals, 380; charged with disloyalty, 381; as artillery chief, 381; commands Iron Brigade, 381; at Fredericksburg, 381; at Gettysburg, 381; at Petersburg, 382; at Appomattox, 382; in Sioux campaigns, 382; pursuit of Nez Perce, 382; martial law in Seattle, 382; 435, 661
Gillem Board, 236, 239
Gillmore, Quincy, and Charleston campaign, 1102
Gladwin, Henry, 869
Glorieta, battle of, 155
Glorious Revolution, 622
Goethals, George Washington, 383–87; in

sion, 412; and William T. Sherman and
U. S. Grant, 412; at Battle of Holly
Springs, 412; and Mississippi Raid, 412–
13; operations against Nathan Bedford
Forrest, 413; and Hood's Retreat, 413;
at Brice's Crossroads, 413; relieved of
command, 413; in Mississippi and Alabama, 413; on Reconstruction duty, 413;
organizes Cavalry for Wesley Merritt,
413; commands 10th Cavalry, 413; fron-
tier duty, 414; in Apache Wars, 414;
"Grierson's Raid," 414; views toward
Indians, 415
Groves, Leslie Richard, 415–19, at MIT,
415; at West Point, 415; early career,
416; Manhattan Project, 416; and atomic
policy, 417
Guadalcanal, battle of, 158, 193, 426, 567,
575, 775, 889, 1128
Guam, battle of, 375
Guardia Nacional, 158
Guayacanas, 836–37
Guilford Court House, battle of, 410, 610
Gung Ho, 159

Haiti, 140
Haldimand, General Sir Frederick, 17
Hall, Charles P., 79, 99, 101
Halleck, Henry Wager, 77, 125, 221, 396,
421–25; and coastal fortifications, 421;
as student of Denis Hart Mahan, 421;
Elements of Military Art and Science,
421; resigns commission, 422; legal career, 422; and California constitution,
422; translates works of Henri Jomini,
422; commands Division of the Pacific,
423; commands Department of the Missouri, 422; as Chief of Staff, 423; as
General in Chief, 423; the Henry-
Donelson campaign, 423; as field commander, 424; style of command, 427–
28; 488, 644, 680, 708, 745
Halsey, William Frederick, Jr., 326, 375,
425–28; at Naval Academy, 425; in
World War I, 425; as naval aviator, 425;
at Pearl Harbor, 425; and Doolittle Raid,
425; attack on Marshall Islands, 425;
Solomon Islands campaign, 426; Rabaul

campaign, 426; invasion of Philippines,
426; Battle of Leyte Gulf, 426–27; advocate of naval air power, 427; made
Fleet Admiral, 427; 467, 509, 1033
Hamilton, Alexander, 119, 203, 411, 422,
516, 570, 893
Hammond, William Alexander, 428–31;
medical training, 428; as Army surgeon,
428; at University of Maryland, 429; in
Civil War, 429; as Surgeon General, 429;
establishes Army Medical Museum, 429;
improvements in military medicine, 429;
and Jonathan Letterman, 429; as naturalist, 430; as novelist, 430; as neurol-
ogist, 430; relieved, 430; 633
Hampton, Wade, 431–34; in Sumter's Cavalry, 431; as frontier entrepreneur, 431;
political career, 431; succeeds James
Wilkinson, 432; at Lake Champlain, 432;
relations with Wilkinson, 432; Montreal
campaign, 432; at Chateaugay, 432; basis of generalship, 432–33; 516, 607,
1213
Hancock, Winfield Scott, 224, 382, 414,
434–37; early career, 434; rise to Corps
command, 434; Battle of Williamsburg,
434; at Gettysburg, 434; Battle of the
Wilderness, 435; postwar service, 435;
Reconstruction duty, 435–36; professional reputation, 436; skill as combat
commander, 436; as presidential candidate, 436; 768
Handy, Thomas T., 704
Harbord, James Guthrie, 437–41; early life,
437; enlisted service, 437; as cavalryman, 437; friendship with John J. Pershing, 437–38; in Philippine Constabulary,
438; as Chief of Staff, AEF, 438; service
in World War I, 438; commands Marine
Brigade, 438; commands Services of
Supply, AEF, 438; professional strengths,
439–40; as Deputy Chief of Staff, 439;
mission to Armenia, 439; President of
RCA, 439; as combat commander, 440;
as military administrator, 440; and "scientific management," 440
Hardee, William Joseph, 161–62, 441–44;
as cavalryman, 441; in Mexican War,

nole War, 521; as war hero, 521; Governor of Florida, 521; presidency, 521; as amateur soldier, 521–22; personality, 522; attitudes toward militia, 522; style of command, 523; 534, 811, 830, 849, 878, 973, 1171

Jackson, Thomas Jonathan ("Stonewall"), 296, 314, 436, 471, 473, 494, 523–27; at West Point, 523; in Mexican War, 524; as Virginia Military Institute instructor, 524; joins Confederacy, 524; at First Battle of Bull Run, 524; Shenandoah Valley campaigns, 525; at Winchester, 525; at Front Royal, 525; at Cross Keys, 525; in Seven Days' campaign, 525; at Second Battle of Bull Run, 525; at Antietam, 525; at Fredericksburg, 525; killed at Chancellorsville, 526; habit of command, 526; 607, 613, 992

Java, 52

Java Sea, battle of the, 457

Jay, John, 688

Jefferson, Thomas, 36, 63, 178, 282, 285, 501, 544, 569, 577, 578, 635, 651, 855, 1191

Jefferson Barracks, 46–47, 73

Jellicoe, Sir John, 327

Jenkins' Ear, War of, 802

Jesup, Thomas, 150, 191, 813

Joffre, Joseph, 200

John Adams, 168

Johns Hopkins Hospital, 88

Johnson, Andrew, 32, 398, 435, 618

Johnson, Guy, 114

Johnson, Hugh Samuel, 385, 527–30; legal training, 527; writings, 527; at West Point, 527; frontier duty, 527; and World War I mobilization, 527; and Punitive Expedition, 527; business career, 528; and Bernard Baruch, 528; and Franklin D. Roosevelt, 528; and wartime supply system, 528; supports Wendell Wilkie, 528; heads NRA, 528; and wartime conscription, 529

Johnson, Louis, 215, 343

Johnson, Lyndon, 303, 445, 1181

Johnson, Richard Mentor, 530–33: political career, 530; as War Hawk, 530; in War of 1812, 530; aide to William Henry Harrison, 530; and Kentucky volunteers, 530; pursuit of Tecumseh, 531; postwar political career, 531; as vice president, 531; leadership style, 532

Johnson, Sir William, 114, 533–36; in Mohawk Valley, 533; relations with Iroquois, 533; at Albany Congress, 533; as Indian Superintendent, 534; dispute with William Shirley, 534; at Battle of Lake George, 534; in French and Indian War, 534; baronetcy, 534; Niagara campaign, 535; expedition against Montreal, 535; as frontier diplomat, 535; Treaty of Fort Stanwix, 532; 871, 929, 966, 1201

Johnston, Albert Sidney, 76, 112, 125, 155, 205, 240, 337, 396, 485, 536–38; at West Point, 536; in Black Hawk War, 536; Texas Secretary of War, 536; in Mexican War, 536; commands 2d Cavalry, 536; and Mormon Rebellion, 536; joins Confederacy, 536; commands Western Theater, 536; at Shiloh, 537; Henry and Donelson campaign, 537; as commander, 538; 606, 613, 725, 866, 882

Johnston, Joseph Eggleston, 76, 205, 240, 316, 391, 397, 423, 442, 475, 486, 524, 538–41; at West Point, 538; frontier duty, 538; in Mexican War, 538; joins Confederacy, 538; at Battle of Bull Run, 538; at Battle of Fair Oaks, 539; and Vicksburg Campaign, 540; with Army of the Tennessee, 540; friendship with W. T. Sherman, 540; defense of Atlanta, 540; relieved of command, 540; tactical ability, 541; 607, 613, 621, 657, 681, 692, 709, 831, 977, 994

Joint Chiefs of Staff, 564

Jomini, Baron Antoine Henri, 37, 77, 284, 422, 670, 713, 716, 974

Jones, John Paul, 541–45: early seafaring, 541–42; in Continental Navy, 542; commands *Ranger*, 542; commerce raiding, 542; commands *Bonhomme Richard*, 542; English coastal raids, 542; at Flamborough Head, 543; as French Hero, 543; as Chevalier de France, 543; postwar career, 543–44; in Russian Navy, 544; de-

1326

INDEX

tive reforms, 574; relations with FDR, 575

Knoxville, battle of, 135

Korean War, 110, 676

Kościuszko, Tadeusz Andrzej Bonaventura, 575–79; in Polish Army, 576; as military engineer, 576; emigrates to America, 576; studies abroad, 576; designs West Point fortress, 576; at Saratoga, 576; with Horatio Gates, 576; in Southern campaigns, 576; and Society of the Cincinnati, 576; recalled to Polish service, 576; and Russian invasion, 577; leads Polish Revolution, 577; defense of Warsaw, 577; imprisoned, 577; in exile, 577; return to America, 577; friendship with Thomas Jefferson, 578; criticisms of, 578; Nathanael Greene's opinion of, 578

Kriegsakademie, 1082

Kriegspiel, 1082

Krueger, Walter, 579–82; enlists for Spanish-American War, 579; early scholarship, 579; commands AEF Tank Corps, 579; Japanese invasion of Philippines, 580; commands Sixth Army, 580; Southwest Pacific campaign, 580; Battle of Manila, 580; prepares for invasion of Japan, 580; as military educator, 581; command abilities, 581; opinions of, 581

Kurita, Takeo, 567

Lady Franklin Bay expedition, 404

Lafayette, Marquis de, 203, 204, 501, 583–86; early life, 583; service in America, 583; at Battle of Brandywine, 583; at the Battle of Monmouth, 583; furlough in France, 583; as American hero, 583; and Arnold conspiracy, 584; and Yorktown campaign, 584; career in France, 584; military skills, 584–85; contribution to patriot cause, 584; devotion to Washington, 585; defense of Richmond, 585; as combat leader, 585; at Battle of Yorktown, 586; 689

Lake Champlain, battle of, 706

Lake Erie, battle of, 843, 845

Lake George, battle of, 114, 531

Las Trencheras, battle of, 836, 837

Laurens, Henry, 202, 853

Lawrence, James, 196, 586–89; early life, 586; enters naval service, 587; and Barbary Pirates, 587; in the *Philadelphia* raid, 587; attacks on Tripoli, 587; and Barron court-martial, 587; commerce raiding, 588; in War of 1812, 588; as naval hero, 588; and *Chesapeake-Shannon* combat, 588

Lawson, Thomas, 74

Lawton, Henry Ware, 557, 589–92; enlists in Union Army, 589–90; at Harvard, 590; frontier service, 590; pursuit of Geronimo, 590; Congressional Medal of Honor, 590; Cuban campaigns, 590; Battle of El Caney, 590–91; Santiago campaign, 591; in Luzon, 591; Cavite campaign, 591; death in battle, 591; views on colonial people, 592; 1209, 1224

Lazear, Jesse W., 88

Lea, Homer, 592–95; early military interests, 592–93; affection for Chinese culture, 593; at Stanford, 593; Chinese reform movement, 593; in Chinese Revolution, 593; military advisor to Sun Yatsen, 593–94; return to U. S., 593; military prophecies, 595; compared with A. T. Mahan, 595

League of Nations, 98

Leahy, William Daniel, 511, 563, 595–99; at Naval Academy, 595–96; at Santiago Bay, 596; Nicaraguan expedition, 596; as Naval Academy instructor, 596; as gunboat captain in China, 596; friendship with FDR, 596; service in World War I, 597; as Chief of Bureau of Ordnance, 597; as gunnery officer, 597; Ambassador to Vichy France, 597; Governor of Puerto Rico, 597; as Chief of Naval Operations, 597; as Chief of Staff to FDR, 597–98

Leavenworth, Henry, 550, 599–602; in War of 1812, 599; at Chippewa, 599; at Lundy's Lane, 599; in New York Legislature, 599; establishes Fort Snelling, 599; frontier expeditions, 599; and Ashley expedition, 600; and Arikara expedition,

657–58; at Chickamauga, 657; postwar career, 658; postwar criticisms, 658; generalship, 658; temperament, 658; friendship with Lee, 659; 746, 857, 873, 882, 944

Looking Glass, 659–62; parleys with Howard, 660; as fugitive, 660; march of the Nez Perce, 660; as tribal leader, 660; Battle of Camas Meadows, 661; Battle of Big Hole, 661; Battle of Bear Paws, 661; killed in battle, 661; 769

Lord Dunmore's War, 532, 987

Lord Haldane, on Root Reforms, 941

Louisbourg Expedition, 837, 838

Louisiana Lottery Company, 77

Louisiana Maneuvers, 580

Lovell, Joseph, 72, 74, 87, 150, 662–65; studies at Harvard, 662; as regimental surgeon, 662; in War of 1812, 662; as first Surgeon General, 662; reforms, 662–63; recruitment, 663; surgeon's examinations, 663; and William Beaumont's experiments, 663; preventive medicine, 663; and National Library of Medicine, 663; hospital construction, 664; accomplishments, 664; collections of scientific data, 664–65

Lucas, John Porter, 665–68; as cavalryman, 665; early duty, 665; and Villa's raid on Columbus, 665; border duty, 665; amphibious warfare training, 666; as artillery commander, 666; interwar education, 666; North African and Sicilian campaigns, 666; at Anzio, 666; relieved, 667; Volturno River crossing, 667; reasons for relief, 667; mission to China, 667

Luce, Stephen Bleeker, 261, 668–70; at Naval Academy, 668; appointed midshipman, 668; early sea duty, 668; as Naval Academy instructor, 668; Civil War service, 668–69; blockade duty, 669; observes Franco-Prussian naval actions, 669; as first President of Naval War College, 669; naval writings, 669; association with Emory Upton, 669; at Naval War College, 670; and naval professionalism, 670; as intellectual, 670; 711, 951

Lundy's Lane, battle of, 120, 284, 599, 917

Luzon, invasion of, 676

MacArthur, Arthur, 79, 358, 591, 671–75; ancestry, 671; Civil War service, 671; Congressional Medal of Honor, 671; commands 24th Wisconsin, 671; commissioned in Regular Army, 672; Reconstruction duty, 672; frontier service, 672; Geronimo campaign, 672; as Leavenworth instructor, 672; Philippine service, 673; as Military Governor, 673; disagreements with William Howard Taft, 673; disappointments over career, 674; and Army professionalism, 674; as combat commander, 674; 675, 722, 759

MacArthur, Douglas, 25, 110, 165, 185, 194, 213, 280, 299, 302, 375, 426, 455, 456, 474, 482, 553, 567, 580, 672, 675–78; at West Point, 675; early career, 675; World War I service, 675; Superintendent of West Point, 675; as Chief of Staff, 675; Philippine duty and retirement, 675–76; recalled for World War II, 676; counteroffensive in New Guinea, 676; invasion of Luzon, 676; as SCAP, 676; postwar Japanese reforms, 676; Korean War, 676; as CINC, UN Command, 676; relieved by President Truman, 677; memoirs, 677; personality, 677; strategic skills, 677; West Point reforms, 677; occupation of Japan, 678; 736, 798, 818, 900, 911, 1022

McCallum, Daniel C., 459

McCarthy, Joseph R., 160, 912

McClellan, George Brinton, 124, 133, 134, 155, 162, 207, 223, 424, 434, 476, 524, 525, 539, 615, 633, 645, 678–81; at West Point, 678; in Mexican War, 678; observes Crimean War, 679; invents "McClellan Saddle," 679; resigns commission, 679; return to service, 679; Western Virginia campaigns, 679; Army of the Potomac, 679; as General in Chief, 679; Peninsula Campaign, 679–80; siege of Yorktown, 680; Battle of the Seven Days, 680; Antietam campaign, 680; re-

and National Defense Act of 1920, 734; at U. S. Army Infantry School, 735; protégés at Fort Benning, 735; and Civilian Conservation Corps, 735; as Chief of Staff, 735; and World War II, 735; wartime conferences, 736; mission to postwar China, 736; as Secretary of Defense, 736; Marshall Plan, 736; heads American Red Cross, 736; as Secretary of State, 736; wins Nobel Peace Prize, 737; 766, 817, 848, 890, 1021, 1025, 1059

Marshall, Samuel Lyman Atwood, 737–42; early life, 737; World War I service, 738; journalistic career, 738; military studies, 738; recruited by Henry Stimson, 738; writes *Blitzkrieg*, 738; in Pacific campaign, 739; and combat history, 739; in European campaigns, 739; writes *Men Against Fire*, 739; Korean War duty, 739–40; support for Israel, 740; work in Vietnam War, 740; techniques, 741

Marshall Islands campaign, 159, 1117

Mather, Increase, 851

Maumee Villages, 450

Maury, Matthew Fontaine, 32, 718, 742–44; early sea duty, 742; pioneer in oceanography, 742; writes text on navigation, 742; as navy critic, 742; oceanographic writings, 742–43; at Virginia Military Institute, 743; joins Confederate Navy, 743; wartime mission to England, 743; service with Emperor Maximillian, 743; and Amazon expedition, 743; and Trans-Atlantic cable, 743; astronomical observations, 743; and Panama Canal, 743; scientific contributions, 744

Mayflower, 1038

Mayo, Henry T., 562

Meade, George Gordon, 134; as commander of Army of the Potomac, 397; 434, 691, 744–48; at West Point, 744; as civil engineer, 745; in Mexican War, 745; early Civil War campaigns, 745; succeeds Joseph Hooker, 745; and Gettysburg campaign, 745; generalship, 745; casualties at Gettysburg, 746; Pickett's Charge, 746; relations with U. S. Grant, 747; Virginia campaign, 747; Recon-

struction duty, 747; leadership at Gettysburg, 747; Lee's opinion of, 747

Medicine Lodge, treaty of, 94, 821

Meigs, Montgomery Cunningham, 418, 748–51; at West Point, 748; as engineer, 748; with Robert E. Lee, 748; and Washington Aqueduct, 748–49; relief of Fort Pickens, 749; Quartermaster General, 749; dispute with Secretary of War, 749; accomplishments, 749–50; and Field Supply techniques, 750; departmental reforms, 750

Melville, George Wallace, 751–54; engineering studies, 751; joins Union Navy, 751; early naval service, 751; capture of *Florida*, 751; capture of Fort Fisher, 751; postwar expedition, 751–52; Arctic disaster, 752; rescue of Adolphus Greely, 752; Engineer in Chief of Navy, 752; scientific honors, 752; and naval construction techniques, 752–53; and technological innovations, 753

Menoher, Charles Thomas, 754–58; at West Point, 754; artillery innovations, 754; interest in aeronautics, 754; and J. Franklin Bell, 754; regimental organization of artillery, 754–55; Air Service disputes, 755; commands VI Corps, 755; Director of Air Service, 755; commands Rainbow Division, 755; and Billy Mitchell controversy, 756; and Air power, 756

Merrimac (CSS *Virginia*), 32, 1087

Merritt, Wesley, 78, 224, 413, 758–61; at West Point, 758; as cavalryman, 758; aide to Philip St. George Cooke, 758; Civil War service, 758; service with George A. Custer, 758; frontier service, 758–59; commands 5th Cavalry, 759; in Nez Perce campaign, 759; commands Philippine Army of Occupation, 759; as Superintendent of West Point, 759; as reluctant imperialist, 760; sympathy for Indians, 760; predicts Philippine insurrection, 760; supports General Staff reforms, 760–61; 980, 1080

Mescalero Indians, 414

Metacomet, 761–65; early life, 761; English name, 761; in King Philip's War,

Northern Department, 966–67; siege of St. Johns, 967; negotiations with Iroquois, 967; rescue at Three Rivers, 967; service with Horatio Gates, 967; evacuation of Ticonderoga, 967–68; and Burgoyne's invasion, 968; relieved, 968
Scientific Expedition of 1819, 653
Scott, Hugh Lenox, 96, 969–72; at West Point, 970; Indian affairs, 970; and Ghost Dancers, 970; Cuban occupation, 970; and Leonard Wood, 970; as Chief of Staff, 970; and Mexican diplomacy, 970; and Pancho Villa, 970; diplomatic skills, 971; as student of Indian culture, 971; with Elihu Root to Russia, 971; and universal military service, 971
Scott, Winfield, 38, 46, 75, 120, 137, 150, 155, 161, 191, 197, 222, 272, 284, 364, 390, 395, 434, 441, 476, 487, 517, 551, 599, 644, 657, 706, 728, 813, 830, 841, 856, 862, 882, 896, 914, 972–75; ancestry, 972; early education, 972; as cavalryman, 972; dispute with James Wilkinson, 972; military studies, 973; at Battle of Queenston Heights, 973; at Battles of Chippewa and Lundy's Lane, 973; writes *Infantry Tactics,* 973; in Black Hawk War, 973; and Mexican War, 973; reforms as Commanding General, 973; political machinations, 973; dispute with Andrew Jackson, 973; Mexico City campaign, 973–74; as presidential candidate, 974; and Anaconda Plan, 974; as military savant, 974; 976
2d Cavalry Regiment, 536
2d Marine Raider Battalion, 158
2d Michigan Volunteer Cavalry, 12
2d Regiment of Dragoons, 1119
Sedan Incident, 266
Sedgwick, John, 489, 494, 555
Selective Service Acts, 735, 464, 817
Selma campaign, 1195
Seminoles, 111, 632, 811–12; wars, 364, 522, 538, 664, 811
Semmes, Raphael, 721, 881, 975–78; as midshipman, 975; in Mexican War, 975; service under Conner, 975; commands *Aurora,* 976; world cruise, 976; resig-

nation, 976; joins Confederate Navy, 976; as commerce raider, 976; commands naval brigade, 977; commands James River Squadron, 977; action against *Kearsarge,* 977
"Sentiments on the Peace Establishment," 1162
Sergeant York, 1221
Seven Days, battle of, 32, 162, 471, 488, 525, 613, 680–81, 1068
Seven Pines, battle of, 162, 768
Seven Years' War, 29
7th Cavalry, 78, 94, 216–17, 224
Seward, William H., 347, 644
Shafter, William Rufus, 328, 556, 590, 674, 693, 769, 920, 935, 952, 955, 978–81; Civil War service, 978; wins Congressional Medal of Honor, 978; commands black troops, 978; at Battle of Nashville, 978; commands 24th Infantry, 978; on Texas frontier, 979; Staked Plains expedition, 979; commands 1st Infantry, 979; commands Cuban expedition, 979; Santiago campaign, 979; relations with press, 979; negotiates Spanish surrender, 980
Sharpe, Henry Granville, 385, 981–85; at West Point, 981; in Philippines, 981; in Puerto Rican campaign, 981; as commissary officer, 981; as Quartermaster General, 982; and Supply Department, 982; and logistics, 982; and General Staff, 982; removed from office, 982; writes memoirs, 983; as scapegoat, 983; and COM-Z concept, 984; writes logistics text, 984; wins Gold Medal Prize, 984; and modern logistics, 984
Sharpsburg, battle of (*see also* Antietam, battle of), 296–97, 607
Shawnee Prophet, 89
Shays, Daniel, 985–86; service in Revolution, 985; at Bunker Hill, 985; march on Springfield, 985; Lafayette's gift, 985; postwar politics, 985; Battle of Petersham, 986; attack on arsenal, 986; pardoned, 986
Shays Rebellion, 501, 570, 571, 648
Shelby, Isaac, 533, 986–89; as commis-

tary aviation, 1037; technological achievements, 1038

Standish, Miles, 173, 1018, 1038–41; joins Pilgrims, 1038–39; founding of Plymouth, 1039; and colonial defense, 1039; Treaty with Wampanoags, 1039; raid on Massachusetts Indians, 1040; arrest of Thomas Morton, 1040; and civic duties, 1040; founds Duxbury, 1040; style of leadership, 1040

Stanton, Edwin McMasters, 69, 155, 162, 423, 429, 459, 489, 645, 679, 682, 1041–44: early life, 1041; legal career, 1041; appointed Secretary of War, 1042; removed from office, 1042; appointed to Supreme Court, 1042; relations with Army, 1043; aversion to West Pointers, 1043; suspension of recruiting, 1043; and Lincoln assassination, 1043; contributions to Union victory, 1044

Stanwix, John, 103

Stark, Harold Raynesford, 510, 561, 563, 1044–47; at Naval Academy, 1045; nickname, 1045; early sea duty, 1045; and Great White Fleet, 1045; friendship with FDR, 1045; World War I service, 1045; service with William Sims, 1045; interwar career, 1046; as Chief of Naval Operations, 1046; as CINCUSNAVEUR, 1046; contributions, 1046; "Plan Dog Memorandum," 1046; and Pacific War, 1047; and Combined Chiefs of Staff, 1047

Stephens, Alexander, 242

Sternberg, George Miller, 88, 905, 1047–50; early medical studies, 1048; Civil War service, 1048; interest in Yellow Fever, 1048; research in Havana, 1048; studies in Bacteriology, 1048–49; and Army Medical School, 1049; and Reed Board, 1049; appointed Surgeon General, 1049; medical writings, 1049

Steuben, Frederic William, "Baron von," 409, 421, 500, 586, 1050–53; early service in Prussia, 1050; studies under Frederick the Great, 1050–51; joins Patriots, 1051; as drillmaster, 1051; as Inspector General, 1051; Southern campaigns, 1051; at Valley Forge, 1051; writes The

Blue Book, 1051; postwar career, 1052; and questionable nobility, 1052; accomplishments, 1052

Stewart, Charles, 53

Stillman's Run, battle of, 91

Stilwell, Joseph Warren, 117, 172, 245, 281, 376, 735, 1053–57; at West Point, 1053; in Philippines, 1053; World War I service, 1053; as intelligence officer, 1053; early duties in Far East, 1053–54; interwar career, 1054; nickname, 1054; commands III Corps, 1054; as Chief of Staff to Chiang Kai-shek, 1054; retreat from Burma, 1054; commands Tenth Army, 1055; command controversies, 1055; recalled, 1055; scope of command, 1055–56; temperament, 1056; Stilwell Road, 1075, 1076; 1174

Stimson, Henry Lewis, 10–11, 54, 281, 416, 738, 816, 1057–61; early life and education, 1057–58; early legal and political career, 1058; and World War I service, 1058; association with Theodore Roosevelt, 1058; as Secretary of War, 1058; and General Staff controversy, 1058; interwar diplomatic career, 1058–59; World War II service, 1059; and George C. Marshall, 1059; as Secretary of War in World War II, 1059; and Japanese internment, 1060; and atomic bomb, 1060–61; 1210

Stockton, Robert Field, 285, 309, 355, 551, 1061–64; early sea duty, 1061; defense of Fort McHenry, 1061; studies abroad, 1062; as Jacksonian, 1062; and John Ericsson, 1062; as Whig politico, 1062; and Liberian settlement, 1062; and American Colonization Society, 1062; commands Princeton, 1062; in Mexican War, 1062–63; commands Pacific Squadron, 1063; alliance with John C. Frémont, 1063; and Bear Flag Rebellion, 1063; as war hero, 1063; as senator, 1063

Stoddert, Benjamin, 314, 506, 1064–67; in Revolution, 1064; as businessman, 1064; as Secretary of the Navy, 1064; and leading naval captains, 1065; organizing the Navy, 1065; duties, 1065; opposes de-

Contributors

GEORGE R. ADAMS is Director of the Education Division of the American Association for State and Local History.

LARRY H. ADDINGTON is Professor of History at The Citadel.

JAMES B. AGNEW (1930–1980), Colonel, U.S. Army, was Director, U.S. Army Military History Institute.

DEAN C. ALLARD is Historian and Archivist with the U.S. Naval Historical Center.

STEPHEN E. AMBROSE is Professor of History at the University of New Orleans.

GARY CLAYTON ANDERSON is Assistant Professor of History at Texas A&M University.

WAYNE AUSTERMAN is a Historian with the U.S. Air Force, Colorado Springs, Colorado.

MERRILL L. BARTLETT, Lieutenant Colonel, U.S. Marine Corps, is on the history faculty at the U.S. Naval Academy.

DONALD L. BAUCOM, a Lieutenant Colonel, U.S. Air Force, is Editor of *The Air University Review*.

K. JACK BAUER is Professor of History at Rennselaer Polytechnic Institute.

EDWIN C. BEARSS is a Historian with the U.S. National Park Service.

ROGER BEAUMONT is Professor of History at Texas A & M University.

DANIEL R. BEAVER is Professor of History at the University of Cincinnati.

ARTHUR W. BERGERON, JR., is Curator, Port Hudson State Military Park, Louisiana.

RICHARD BLANCO is Professor of History, State University of New York, College at Brockport.

HARRY R. BOROWSKI, Lieutenant Colonel, U.S. Air Force, is on the faculty of history at the U.S. Air Force Academy.

LARRY G. BOWMAN is Professor of History at North Texas State University.

CARL BOYD is Associate Professor of History at Old Dominion University.

JAMES C. BRADFORD is Assistant Professor of History at Texas A&M University.

WILLIAM R. BRAISTED is Professor of History at the University of Texas.

RALPH ADAMS BROWN is Emeritus Professor of History, State University of New York, College at Cortland.

THOMAS B. BUELL, Commander, U.S. Navy, retired, formerly was on the history faculty at the U.S. Military Academy, West Point.

JOHN L. BULLION is Associate Professor of History at the University of Missouri.

MARVIN CAIN is Professor of History at the University of Missouri-Rolla.

JACK J. CARDOSO is Professor of History, State University of New York, College at Buffalo.

DAVID CARRAWAY is a Major, U.S. Army, on active service.

ROBERT C. CARRIKER is Professor of History at Gonzaga University.

PHILANDER D. CHASE is Assistant Editor of *The Papers of George Washington*.

DAVID CHILDRESS is Associate Professor of History at Jacksonville (Alabama) State University.

PAUL W. CLARK, Lieutenant Colonel, U.S. Air Force, retired, is now with the Transglobe Expedition.

EDWARD M. COFFMAN is Professor of History at the University of Wisconsin.

PAOLO E. COLETTA is Professor of History at the U.S. Naval Academy.

MARY E. CONDON is a Historian with the U.S. Army Center of Military History.

JANE D. CONNELLY is working toward a doctorate in history at George Washington University.

THEODORE J. CONWAY, General, U.S. Army, retired, is completing his doctorate in history at Duke University.

BENJAMIN FRANKLIN COOLING is a Historian with the Office of the Chief of Air Force History.

NORMAN V. COOPER is Adjunct Professor of History at the University of Alabama-Birmingham.

DUDLEY T. CORNISH is Professor of History at Pittsburg State University, Kansas.

GRAHAM A. COSMAS is a Historian with the U.S. Army Center of Military History.

ALBERT E. COWDREY is a Historian with the U.S. Army Center of Military History.

THEODORE J. CRACKEL, Lieutenant Colonel, U.S. Army, retired, is a military affairs specialist with the Heritage Foundation.

ROBERT J. CRESSMAN is a Historian with the U.S. Marine Corps Historical Center.

J. THOMAS CROUCH holds a doctorate in history and is now a free-lance writer.

RICHARD N. CURRENT is Professor of History at the University of North Carolina-Greensboro.

BRUCE DANIELS is Professor of History at the University of Winnipeg, Canada.

VAN M. DAVIDSON, JR., former Major, U.S. Army, is associated with the law firm of Camp, Carmouch, Palmer, Barsh and Hunter in Lake Charles, Louisiana.

WILLIAM C. DAVIS is Senior Editor of *Civil War Times Illustrated*.

JOSEPH G. DAWSON III is Assistant Professor of History at Texas A&M University-Galveston.

JOSEPH A. DEVINE, JR., is Associate Professor of History at Stephen F. Austin State University.

BRUCE J. DINGES is Assistant Editor of *Arizona and the West*.

RALPH W. DONNELLY, formerly Reference Historian with the U.S. Marine Corps Historical Division, is now retired.

JEFFERY M. DORWART is Professor of History at Rutgers University-Camden.

EDWARD J. DREA is Assistant Director for Historical Services, U.S. Army Military History Institute.

WILLIAM S. DUDLEY is the Senior Historian at the U.S. Naval Historical Center.

GEORGE C. DYER, Vice Admiral, U.S. Navy, retired, is a naval historian.

EDWARD K. ECKERT is Associate Professor of History at Saint Bonaventure University.

RALPH L. ECKERT is Assistant Professor of History at Pennsylvania State University-Erie.

R. DAVID EDMUNDS is Professor of History at Texas Christian University.

THOMAS R. ENGLISH is Professor of History at Delaware County Community College, Media, Pennsylvania.

UZAL W. ENT, Colonel, U.S. Army, retired, is the Historian of the 28th Infantry Division.

STANLEY L. FALK, formerly Head of the Southeast Asia Branch, U.S. Army Center of Military History, is now retired.

J. FREDERICK FAUSZ is Professor of History at St. Mary's College of Maryland.

CLYDE R. FERGUSON is Professor of History at Kansas State University.

JOHN FERLING is Associate Professor of History at West Georgia College.

MARVIN E. FLETCHER is Professor of History at Ohio University.

GEORGE Q. FLYNN is Professor of History at Texas Tech University.

ROGER B. FOSDICK, Major, U.S. Air Force, is on the history faculty of the U.S. Air Force Academy.

WILLIAM M. FOWLER, JR., is Professor of History at Northeastern University.

ROBERT FRANK is a Lieutenant Colonel, U.S. Army, on active service.

PATRICK J. FURLONG is Associate Professor of History at Indiana University.

GEORGE W. GEIB is an Associate Professor of History at Butler University.

MARY GILLETT is a Historian in the U.S. Army Center of Military History.

RICHARD D. GLASOW, formerly at the Applied Research Laboratory, Pennsylvania State University, is Education Director of the National Right to Life Committee.

CHARLES LEON GORDON is completing graduate work at the State University of New York, College at Albany.

MARTIN K. GORDON is a Historian with the U.S. Army Office of the Chief of Engineers.

LLOYD J. GRAYBAR is Professor of History at Eastern Kentucky University.

IRA D. GRUBER is Professor of History at Rice University.

RICHARD L. HAHN is Professor of History at Hartwick College.

DENNIS G. HALL, Major, U.S. Air Force, is on the history faculty of the U.S. Air Force Academy.

HOLMAN HAMILTON (1910–1980) was Emeritus Professor of History at the University of Kentucky.

JACK L. HAMMERSMITH is Professor of History at the University of West Virginia.

JOSEPH P. HARAHAN is a Historian in the Office of the Chief of Air Force History.

RICHARD J. HARGROVE, JR., is Associate Professor of History at Western Illinois University.

JAMES W. HARPER is Associate Professor of History at Texas Tech University.

COLLIER C. HARRIS, JR., is a Historian on the staff at Colonial Williamsburg.

WARREN W. HASSLER, JR., is Professor of History at Pennsylvania State University.

HERMAN HATTAWAY is Professor of History at the University of Missouri-Kansas City.

JOHN B. HATTENDORF is Associate Professor of Strategy at the Naval War College.

RICHARD F. HAYNES is Professor of History at Northeast Louisiana University.

GEORGE C. HERRING is Professor of History at the University of Kentucky.

R. DON HIGGINBOTHAM is Professor of History at the University of North Carolina.

HARWOOD P. HINTON is Editor of *Arizona and the West* and Professor of History at the University of Arizona.

JOSEPH P. HOBBS is Professor of History at North Carolina State University.

I. B. HOLLEY, JR., is Professor of History at Duke University.

HERBERT T. HOOVER is Professor of History at the University of South Dakota.

DONALD E. HOUSTON is Historian of the 2d Armored Division.

JOHN T. HUBBELL is Editor of *Civil War History* and Professor of History at Kent State University.

ALFRED F. HURLEY, Brigadier General, U.S. Air Force, retired, is President of North Texas State University.

JOHN W. HUSTON is Professor of History at the U.S. Naval Academy.

PAUL A. HUTTON is Associate Editor of the *Western Historical Quarterly* and Assistant Professor of History at Utah State University.

D. CLAYTON JAMES is Professor of History at Mississippi State University.

PERRY JAMIESON is a Historian with the U.S. Air Force Space Command.

PAUL V. JOLIET is Associate Professor of History at Saint Bonaventure University.

PHILIP D. JONES is Associate Professor of History at Bradley University.

VINCENT C. JONES is a Historian with the U.S. Army Center of Military History.

DANIEL P. JORDAN is Professor of History at Virginia Commonwealth University.

THOMAS L. KARNES is Professor of History at Arizona State University.

JOHN C. KENDALL is Professor of History at California State University-Fresno.

BROOKS E. KLEBER is Assistant Chief of Military History of the U.S. Army.

RICHARD H. KOHN is Chief Historian of the U.S. Air Force.

JACK C. LANE is Professor of History at Rollins College.

HAROLD D. LANGLEY is a Curator and Supervisor at the Smithsonian Institution.

KARL G. LAREW is Professor of History at Towson State University.

DENNIS S. LAVERY is Production Editor for the West Publishing Company.

ELLEN L. LAWSON is a Historian with the Women's History Project at Oberlin College.

DOUGLAS EDWARD LEACH is Professor of History at Vanderbilt University.

WILLIAM M. LEARY, JR., is Associate Professor of History at the University of Georgia.

WILLIAM H. LECKIE is Vice-President for Academic Affairs and Professor of History at the University of Toledo.

DAVID LEE is Associate Professor of History at Western Kentucky University.

ROBERT C. LEMIRE, JR., is a Department Chairman at the Collegiate Schools of Richmond, Virginia.

JOHN M. LINDLEY is a student of American military history.

GEORGE H. LOBDELL is Professor of History at Ohio University.

DAVID F. LONG is Professor of History at the University of New Hampshire.

E. B. LONG (1919–1981) was Professor of American Studies at the University of Wyoming.

EDWARD G. LONGACRE is a Historian with the U.S. Air Force Strategic Air Command.

JOHN L. LOOS is Professor of History at Louisiana State University.

MARK M. LOWENTHAL is an Analyst in National Defense, Congressional Research Service, at the Library of Congress.

MARION LUCAS is Professor of History at Western Kentucky University.

JOHN B. LUNDSTROM is a Historian at the Milwaukee Public Museum, Milwaukee, Wisconsin.

JAY LUVAAS is Harold K. Johnson Professor of Military History at the U.S. Army War College.

ARCHIE P. McDONALD is Professor of History at Stephen F. Austin State University.

JAMES LEE McDONOUGH is Professor of History at David Lipscomb College.

KEITH D. McFARLAND is Professor of History at East Texas State University.

CHRISTOPHER McKEE is Professor of History at Grinnell College.

WILLIAM P. MacKINNON is Vice-President for Personnel of the General Motors Corporation.

JOHN K. MAHON is Professor Emeritus of History at the University of Florida.

LINDA M. MALONEY is Associate Professor of History at the University of South Carolina.

RAYMOND A. MANN is a Historian at the U.S. Naval Historical Center.

EDWARD J. MAROLDA is a Historian at the U.S. Naval Historical Center.

JAMES KIRBY MARTIN is Professor of History at the University of Houston.

JAMES M. MERRILL is Professor of History at the University of Delaware.

FRANK C. MEVERS is State Archivist at the Division of Archives, Concord, New Hampshire.

JOHN R. MILLER is a Major, U.S. Army, on active service.

ALLAN R. MILLETT is Professor of History at Ohio State University and Director of the Mershon Institute.

JAMES L. MOONEY is a Historian at the U.S. Naval Historical Center.

PEGGY HAMILTON MOONEY is a student of naval history.

WILLIAM JAMES MORGAN, formerly Senior Historian of the U.S. Naval Historical Center, is now retired.

PAUL D. NELSON is Professor of History at Berea College.

TIMOTHY K. NENNINGER is a Historian with the National Archives.

JOHN D. NEVILLE is a Historian with the General Records Office, Virginia State Library.

ROGER L. NICHOLS is Professor of History at the University of Arizona.

PHILIP Y. NICHOLSON is Professor of History at Nassau Community College.

JOHN NORVELL, Major, U.S. Air Force, is on the history faculty of the U.S. Air Force Academy.

JOHN KENNEDY OHL is Professor of History at Mesa Community College.

DWIGHT OLAND is a Historian at the U.S. Army Center of Military History.

WILLIAM E. PARRISH is Professor of History at Mississippi State University.

LOUIS PEAKE is a student of military history.

HOWARD PECKHAM, formerly Professor of History and Director of the Clements Library at the University of Michigan, is now retired.

ROBERT F. PIERCE is a graduate student in American Civilization at Brandeis University.

WALTER E. PITTMAN is Professor of History at the Mississippi University for Women.

FORREST C. POGUE is Director of the Dwight D. Eisenhower Institute for Historical Research at the Smithsonian Institution.

JAMES W. POHL is Professor of History at Southwest Texas State University.

JOSEPH C. PORTER holds a doctorate in American History from the University of Texas and is a museum curator in Omaha, Nebraska.

E. B. POTTER is Emeritus Professor of History at the U.S. Naval Academy.

JAMES PULA is Associate Dean and Director of Continuing Education at St. John Fisher College.

J. MICHAEL QUILL is Assistant Professor of History at the University of Wisconsin-Lacrosse.

GEORGE C. RABLE is Assistant Professor of History and Director of American Studies at Anderson College.

EDGAR F. RAINES is a Historian at the U.S. Army Center of Military History.

EDWARD RANSON is associated with the faculty of Kings College, University of Aberdeen, Scotland.

EDWARD A. RAYMOND is Professor of History at the University of Connecticut.

MARTIN REUSS is a Historian with the U.S. Army Office of the Chief of Engineers.

CLARK G. REYNOLDS is Curator and Museum Director of the Patriots Point Naval and Maritime Museum, Mount Pleasant, South Carolina.

JON A. REYNOLDS, Colonel, U.S. Air Force, formerly on the history faculty of the U.S. Air Force Academy, is now on active service.

RONALD RIDGLEY is Professor of History at Brunswick Junior College.

DAVID F. RIGGS is a Historian with the U.S. National Park Service.

WILLIAM GLENN ROBERTSON is a Historian at the U.S. Army Command and General Staff College.

CHARLES P. ROLAND is Professor of History at the University of Kentucky.

DAVID ALAN ROSENBERG is Assistant Professor of History at the University of Houston.

T. MICHAEL RUDDY is Associate Professor of History at Saint Louis University.

JOHN J. SBREGA is Chairman of the Department of Social Sciences at Tidewater Community College.

HANS SCHMIDT is Senior Lecturer at the University of Zambia, Africa.

DALE J. SCHMITT is Professor of History at East Tennessee State University.

THOMAS E. SCHOTT is a Historian with the U.S. Air Force Engineering Installation Center, Oklahoma City, Oklahoma.

JOHN A. SCHUTZ is Professor of History at the University of Southern California.

ROBERT SEAGER II is Professor of History at the University of Kentucky.

JAMES E. SEFTON is Professor of History at California State University-Northridge.

WILLIAM L. SHEA is Associate Professor of History at the University of Arkansas.

JOHN F. SHINER is a Lieutenant Colonel, U.S. Air Force, on active service.

RICHARD SHOWMAN is Editor of the *Nathanael Greene Papers*.

CHARLES R. SHRADER, Lieutenant Colonel, U.S. Army, is on the faculty of the NATO Defense College, Rome.

JACK SHULIMSON is a Historian at the U.S. Marine Corps Historical Center.

B. MITCHELL SIMPSON III, Lieutenant Commander, U.S. Navy, retired, is associated with the law firm of Callahan and Sayer, Newport, Rhode Island.

LYNN L. SIMS is Command Historian of the U.S. Army Logistics Center.

DAVID CURTIS SKAGGS is Professor of History at Bowling Green State University.

C. EDWARD SKEEN is Associate Professor of History at Memphis State University.

DWIGHT L. SMITH is Professor of History at Miami University, Ohio.

GIBSON BELL SMITH is an Archivist at the National Archives.

MYRON SMITH is Professor of History at Salem College.

DONALD SMYTHE, S.J., is Professor of History at John Carroll University.

PHINIZY SPALDING is Professor of History at the University of Georgia.

VERNON GLADDEN SPENCE is Professor of History at George Mason University.

ROGER J. SPILLER, was an Associate Professor of Military History at the U.S. Army Command and General Staff College.

STEPHEN Z. STARR, formerly Director of the Cincinnati Historical Society, is the author of four books on the Civil War.

WILLIAM N. STILL, is Professor of History at East Carolina State University.

RICHARD G. STONE, JR., is Professor of History at Western Kentucky University.

JOSEPH A. STOUT, JR., is Professor of History at Oklahoma State University.

BARRY SUDE is enrolled in graduate studies at Temple University.

ROY TALBERT is Associate Vice Chancellor at Carolina Coastal College.

MICHAEL L. TATE is Associate Professor of History at the University of Nebraska-Omaha.

WILLIAM TEAGUE is Professor of History at Texas College.

JACK W. THACKER is Professor of History at Western Kentucky University.

LEE SCOTT THEISEN is Adjunct Professor of History at Arizona State University.

CLIFFORD EARL TRAFZER is Associate Professor of History at Washington State University.

DAVID F. TRASK is Chief Historian of the U.S. Army.

HEATH TWICHELL, Colonel, U.S. Army, now retired, was formerly on the faculty at the U.S. Naval War College.

BETTY MILLER UNTERBERGER is Professor of History at Texas A&M University.

ALDEN T. VAUGHAN is Professor of History at Columbia University.

JOHN C. WALTER is Professor of History at Bowdoin College.

HARRY M. WARD is Professor of History at the University of Richmond.

JAMES A. WARD is Professor of History at the University of Tennessee-Chattanooga.

JAMES WARE is Assistant Professor of History at Louisiana State University-Eunice.

BERNARD C. WEBER is Professor of History at the University of Alabama.

DANA M. WEGNER is an Archivist at the National Archives.

RUSSELL F. WEIGLEY is Professor of History at Temple University.

JOHN M. WERNER is Professor of History at Western Illinois University.

FRANK J. WETTA is Professor of History at Galveston College.

MICHAEL WHALON is Associate Professor of History at the University of Tulsa.

GERALD E. WHEELER is Professor of History at San Jose State University.

T. HARRY WILLIAMS (1909–1979) was Boyd Professor of History at Louisiana State University.

DAVID L. WILSON is Associate Editor of the U.S. Grant Association and Assistant Professor of History at Southern Illinois University.

TERRY P. WILSON is Professor of History at the University of California, Berkeley.

ALAN WILT is Professor of History at Iowa State University.

ROBERT E. WOLFF is a student of American military history.

PETER M. WRIGHT is Associate Professor of History at the University of Alabama-Birmingham.

CHESTER RAYMOND YOUNG, is Professor of History at Cumberland College.

PHYLLIS ZIMMERMAN is Assistant Professor of History at Ball State University.

About the Editors

ROGER J. SPILLER was Associate Professor of Military History at the U.S. Army Command and General Staff College and is Special Assistant to the Commander-in-Chief, United States Readiness Command. He is the author of *Not War, But Like War*, a study of American intervention in Lebanon in 1958, and articles in *Military Review, Military Affairs,* and *The South Atlantic Quarterly*.

JOSEPH G. DAWSON III is Assistant Professor of History at Texas A&M University at Galveston. He is the author of *Army Generals and Reconstruction: Louisiana, 1862-1877*. His articles have appeared in *Civil War History, Southern Studies, Louisiana History, Red River Valley Historical Review*, and the *Dictionary of Literary Biography*.